RESEARCH IN PERSONALITY

RESEARCH IN PERSONALITY

EDITED BY

MARTHA T. MEDNICK
SARNOFF A. MEDNICK
University of Michigan

Holt, Rinehart and Winston, Inc.

NEW YORK   CHICAGO
SAN FRANCISCO   TORONTO
LONDON

April, 1964

Preface

THE AREA OF PERSONALITY has been the most imperialistic of all areas of research in psychology. Its methods and concepts have been borrowed from fields as widely divergent as cultural anthropology and the psychophysics of sensation. Perhaps as a consequence of this, the many subareas of the field bear almost no relationship to one another, and what is included under the heading of "Personality" is often more a matter of sentiment than of logic. However, when one is teaching a course in this field, its boundaries must be arbitrarily defined if only for reasons of time. The definition proposed by the papers in this book is based on a course in Personality as taught by the second author. In this course the emphasis is placed on recent experimental research and current theoretical viewpoints. Such a combination is a very effective vehicle for transmitting to the student some of the vitality and excitement to be found in the area as it develops in the journals.

This book consists of groups of research papers that have been found to be of value in communicating the contents and methodologies of particular areas of research in Personality. Some of the grand old names in the field of Personality are conspicuously absent. This is because *no* space has been allotted to theories that are not generating new research. Where such theories form the historical background for current research, the original writings are probably the best source of materials.

As a background for the research papers, the student is provided with a frame of reference and an acquaintance with basic concepts through a series of presentations of dominant theoretical viewpoints and issues. Following this section are groups of research papers centered on particular problems. Within each group there is generally an intensive presentation of the theories that guide and motivate the research. In certain areas that contain an unusual wealth of background research, reviews of the literature are included to provide a setting for the experimental reports.

In several cases, an article is presented together with critiques and countercritiques. We have observed that tracing the logic of these controversies holds more than a passing interest for students. In addition to this motivational function these materials also serve to sharpen the student's grasp of the points under debate as well as to encourage him to direct his thoughts along more critical paths.

We wish to thank Theodore M. Newcomb and Theodore R. Sarbin for their critical review of our selections. There has been a group of people who have helped with the clerical and secretarial work necessary to the completion of this volume:

v

Miss Bonnie Cross, Miss Elizabeth Lutz, Mrs. A. Rosenberg-Nielsen, Mrs. David Silber, and Miss Karin Winther Pedersen. At the beginning of each article acknowledgment is made to the authors and publishers of the individual papers. We are conscious of our debt both to the generosity of these individuals and to the field of psychology as a whole for making this volume possible.

Martha T. Mednick
Sarnoff A. Mednick

Psychological Institute
Kommunehospitalet
Copenhagen
March 1963

Contents

Chapter 3 · ANXIETY AND STRESS   **203**

Chapter 4 · EXPRESSION OF CONFLICT THROUGH FANTASY   **315**

PART I

Background Papers

THE TWO DISCIPLINES OF SCIENTIFIC PSYCHOLOGY

Lee J. Cronbach

No man can be acquainted with all of psychology today, as our convention program proves. The scene resembles that of a circus, but a circus grander and more bustling than any Barnum ever envisioned—a veritable week-long diet of excitement and pink lemonade. Three days of smartly paced performance are required just to display the new tricks the animal trainers have taught their charges. We admire the agile paper-readers swinging high above us in the theoretical blue, saved from disaster by only a few gossamer threads of fact, and we gasp as one symposiast thrusts his head bravely between another's sharp toothed jaws. This 18-ring display of energies and talents gives plentiful evidence that psychology is going places. But whither?

In the simpler days of psychology, the presidential address provided a summing-up and a statement of destination. The President called the roll of the branches of psychology—praising the growth of some youngsters, tut-tutting patriarchally over the delinquent tendencies of others —and showed each to his proper place at the family table. My own title is reminiscent of those grand surveys, but the

Reprinted by permission of the American Psychological Association and the author from the *American Psychologist,* Vol. 12, 1957.

last speaker who could securely bring the whole of psychology within one perspective was Dashiell, with his 1938 address on "Rapprochements in Contemporary Psychology" (15). My scope must be far more restricted.

I shall discuss the past and future place within psychology of two historic streams of method, thought, and affiliation which run through the last century of our science. One stream is *experimental psychology;* the other, *correlational psychology*. Dashiell optimistically forecast a confluence of these two streams, but that confluence is still in the making. Psychology continues to this day to be limited by the dedication of its investigators to one or the other method of inquiry rather than to scientific psychology as a whole.

A stream of thought is identified by many features: philosophical underpinnings, methods of inquiry, topical interests, and loci of application. The experimental and correlational streams have all these aspects, but I am concerned with them as disciplines within scientific psychology. The job of science is to ask questions of Nature. A discipline is a method of asking questions and of testing answers to determine whether they are sound. Scientific psychology is still young, and there is rapid turnover in our interests, our experimental apparatus and our tests, and our theoretical concepts. But our methods of inquiry have become increasingly stable, and it is these methods which qualify us as scientists rather than philosophers or artists.

The Separation of the Disciplines

The experimental method—where the scientist changes conditions in order to observe their consequences—is much the more coherent of our two disciplines. Everyone knows what experimental psychology is and who the experimental psychologists are. Correlational psychology, though fully as old as experimentation, was slower to mature. It qualifies equally as a discipline, however, because it asks a distinctive type of question and has technical methods of examining whether the question has been properly put and the data properly interpreted.

In contrast to the Tight Little Island of the experimental discipline, correlational psychology is a sort of Holy Roman Empire whose citizens identify mainly with their own principalities. The discipline, the common service in which the principalities are united, is the study of correlations presented by Nature. While the experimenter is interested only in the variation he himself creates, the correlator finds his interest in the already existing variation between individuals, social groups, and species. By "correlational psychology" I do not refer to studies which rely on one statistical procedure. Factor analysis is correlational, to be sure, but so is the study of Ford and Beach (23) relating sexual behavior to differences along the phylogenetic scale and across the cultural spectrum.

The well-known virtue of the experimental method is that it brings situational variables under tight control. It thus permits rigorous tests of hypotheses and confident statements about causation. The correlational method, for its part, can study what man has not learned to control or can never hope to control. Nature has been experimenting since the beginning of time, with a boldness and complexity far beyond the resources of science. The correlator's mission is to observe and organize the data from Nature's experiments. As a minimum outcome, such correlations improve immediate decisions and guide experimentation. At the best, a Newton, a Lyell, or a Darwin can align the correlations into a substantial theory.

During our century of scientific psychology, the correlators have marched under many flags. In perhaps the first modern discussion of scientific method in psychology (1874), Wundt (54) showed how "experimental psychology" and "ethnic psychology" (i.e., cross-cultural correlations) supplement each other. In one of the most recent (1953), Bindra and Scheier (4) speak of the interplay of "experimental" and "psychometric" method. At the turn of the century, the brand names were "experimental" and "genetic" psychology, although experimenters were also beginning to contrast their "general psychology" with the "individual psychology" of Stern and Binet.

In 1913, Yerkes made the fundamental point that all the correlational psychologies are one. His name for this branch was "comparative psychology."

Although comparative psychology in its completeness necessarily deals with the materials of the psychology of infant, child, adult, whether the being be human or infra-human; of animal or plant [!]—of normal and abnormal individuals; of social groups and of civilizations, there is no reason why specialists in the use of the comparative method should not be so distinguished, and, if it seems necessary, labelled (55).

Even in advocating research on animals (56), Yerkes is emphatic in defining the goal as correlation across species. In France, *la psychologie comparée* continues to include all of differential psychology; but in America, as Beach (2) has lamented, comparative psychology degenerated into the experimental psychology of the white rat and thereby lost the power of the correlational discipline.

Except for the defection of animal psychologists, the correlational psychologists have remained loosely federated. Developmental psychologists, personality psychologists, and differential psychologists have been well acquainted both personally and intellectually. They study the same courses, they draw on the same literature, they join the same divisions of APA.

Experimental and correlational psychologists, however, grew far apart in their training and interests. It is now commonplace for a student to get his PhD in experimental psychology without graduate training in test theory or developmental psychology, and the student of correlational branches can avoid experimental psychology only a little less completely. The journals of one discipline have small influence on the journals of the other (14). Boring even dares to say (5, p. 578) that there is a personality difference between the fields: the distinction being that correlational psychologists like people!

Certainly the scientific values of psychologists are sharply divided. Thorndike (9, 44) recently asked American psychologists to rate various historic personages by indicating, on a forced-choice questionnaire, which have made the greatest contributions to psychology. A factor analysis of the ratings shows two distinct factors (Figure 1). One bipolar factor (irrelevant to our present discussion) ranges from verbal to quantitative psychologists. The other factor has at one pole the laboratory experimenters like Stevens, Dodge, and Ebbinghaus, and at the opposite pole those like Binet, May, and Goodenough who collect and correlate field data. A psychologist's esteem for the experimenters is correlated —.80 (—1.00, corrected for attenuation) with his esteem for scientists who use correlational methods.

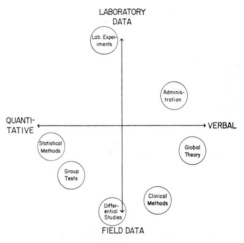

Fig. 1. Factors accounting for esteem of leaders in psychology by American psychologists (based on correlations presented by Thorndike (44), corrected for attenuation and refactored).

There was no such schism in 1913 when Yerkes stated the program of correlational psychology. Genetic psychology and experimental psychology were hard at work on the same problems. Terman demonstrated in his 1923 presidential address (43) that the mental test was within the tradition of experimental, fundamental research in psychology, and had quotations to show that the contemporary experimentalists agreed with him. Wells and Goddard, in 1913, had been asked to lecture on mental tests within the Holy Temple itself, the Society of Experimental Psychologists. And, in 1910, the High Priest Titchener had said:

Individual psychology is one of the chief witnesses to the value of experiment. It furnishes the key to many, otherwise inexplicable differences of result, and it promises to allay many of the outstanding controversies. . . . There can be no doubt that it will play a part of steadily increasing importance (46).

But when Terman spoke in 1923, the common front had already been fatally breached. Watson had announced that experimental treatment could make and unmake individual differences at will, thus stripping them of scientific importance. Thurstone had taken the first firm stride in the opposite direction:

I suggest that we dethrone the stimulus. He is only nominally the ruler of psychology. The real ruler of the domain which psychology studies is the individual and his motives, desires, wants, ambitions, cravings, aspirations. The stimulus is merely the more or less accidental fact . . . (45, p. 364).

The personality, social, and child psychologists went one way; the perception and learning psychologists went the other; and the country between turned into desert.

During the estrangement of correlational and experimental psychology, antagonism has been notably absent. Disparagement has been pretty well confined to playful remarks like Cattell's accusation that the experimental psychologist's "regard for the body of nature becomes that of the anatomist rather than that of the lover" (7, p. 152), or the experimentalist Bartlett's (1, p. 210) satire on the testers emerging from World War I, "chanting in unaccustomed harmony the words of the old jingle

'God has a plan for every man
And He has one for you.' "

Most correlationists have done a little experimenting in the narrow sense, and experimenters have contributed proudly to testing work under wartime necessity. But these are temporary sojourns in a foreign land. (For clear expressions of this attitude, see 5, pp. 570–578 and 52, p. 24.)

A true federation of the disciplines is required. Kept independent, they can give only wrong answers or no answers at all regarding certain important problems. It is shortsighted to argue for one science to discover the general laws of mind or behavior and for a separate enterprise concerned with individual minds, or for a one-way dependence of personality theory upon learning theory. Consider the physical sciences as a parallel. Physics for centuries was the study of general laws applying to all solids or all gases, whereas alchemy and chemistry studied the properties and reactions of individual substances. Chemistry was once only a descriptive catalogue of substances and analytic techniques. It became a systematic science when organized quantitative studies yielded principles to explain differences between substances and to predict the outcomes of reactions. In consequence, Mendeleev the chemist paved the way for Bohr the physicist, and Fermi's physics contributes to Lawrence's chemistry; the boundary between chemistry and physics has become almost invisible.

The tide of separation in psychology has already turned. The perceiver has reappeared in perceptual psychology. Tested intelligence and anxiety appear as independent variables in many of the current learning experiments. Factor analytic studies have gained a fresh vitality from crossbreeding with classical learning experiments (e.g., 18, 22). Harlow, Hebb, Hess, and others are creating a truly experimental psychology of development. And students of personality have been designing subtle combinations of experimental and correlational method (see, for example, 29) which may ultimately prove to be our parallel to the emergence of physical chemistry.

Characterization of the Disciplines

In the beginning, experimental psychology was a substitute for purely naturalistic observation of man-in-habitat. The experimenter placed man in an artificial, simplified environment and made quantitative observations of his performance. The initial problem was one of describing accurately what man felt, thought, or did in a defined situation. Standardization of tasks and conditions was required to get reproducible descriptions. All experimental procedures were tests, all tests were experiments. Kraepelin's continuous-work procedure served equally the general study of fatigue and the diagnosis of individuals. Reaction time was important equally to Wundt and to Cattell.

The distinctive characteristic of modern experimentation, the statistical comparison of treatments, appeared only around 1900 in such studies as that of Thorndike and Woodworth on transfer. The experimenter, following the path of Ebbinghaus, shifted from measurement of the average mind to measuring the effect of environmental change upon success in a task (51). Inference replaced estimation: the mean and its probable error gave way to the critical ratio. The standardized conditions and the standardized instruments remained, but the focus shifted to the single manipulated variable, and later, following Fisher, to multivariate manipulation. The experiment thus came to be concerned with between-treatments variance. I use the word "treatment" in a general sense; educational and therapeutic treatments are but one type. Treatment differences are equally involved in comparing rats given different schedules of reinforcement, chicks who have worn different distorting lenses, or social groups arranged with different communication networks.

The second great development in American experimental psychology has been its concern with formal theory. At the turn of the century, theory ranged far ahead of experiment and made no demand that propositions be testable. Experiment, for its part, was willing to observe any phenomenon, whether or not the data bore on theoretical issues. Today, the majority of experimenters derive their hypotheses explicitly from theoretical premises and try to nail their results into a theoretical structure. This deductive style has its undeniable defects, but one can not question the net gains from the accompanying theoretical sophistication. Discussions of the logic of operationism, intervening variables, and mathematical models have sharpened both the formulation of hypotheses and the interpretation of results.

Individual differences have been an annoyance rather than a challenge to the experimenter. His goal is to control behavior, and variation within treatments is proof that he has not succeeded. Individual variation is cast into that outer darkness known as "error variance." For reasons both statistical and philosophical, error variance is to be reduced by any possible device. You turn to animals of a cheap and short-lived species, so that you can use subjects with controlled heredity and controlled experience. You select human subjects from a narrow subculture. You decorticate your subject by cutting neurons or by giving him an environment so meaningless that his unique responses disappear (cf. 25). You increase the number of cases to obtain stable averages, or you reduce N to 1, as Skinner does. But whatever your device, your goal in the experimental tradition is to get those embarrassing differential variables out of sight.

The correlational psychologist is in love with just those variables the experimenter left home to forget. He regards individual and group variations as important effects of biological and social causes. All organisms adapt to their environments, but not equally well. His question is: what present characteristics of the organism determine its mode and degree of adaptation?

Just as individual variation is a source of embarrassment to the experimenter, so treatment variation attenuates the results of the correlator. His goal is to predict variation within a treatment. His experimental designs demand uniform treatment for every case contributing to a correlation, and treatment variance means only error variance to him.

Differential psychology, like experimental, began with a purely descriptive phase. Cattell at Hopkins, Galton at South Kensington, were simply asking how much people varied. They were, we might say, estimating the standard deviation while the general psychologists were estimating the central tendency.

The correlation coefficient, invented for the study of hereditary resemblance, transformed descriptive differential research into the study of mental organization. What began as a mere summary statistic quickly became the center of a whole theory of data analysis. Murphy's words, written in 1928, recall the excitement that attended this development:

The relation between two variables has actually been found to be statable in other terms than those of experiment . . . [Moreover,] Yule's method of "partial correlation" has made possible the mathematical "isolation" of variables which cannot be isolated experimentally. . . . [Despite the limitations of correlational methods,] what they have already yielded to psychology . . . is nevertheless of such major importance as to lead the writer to the opinion that the only twentieth-century discovery comparable in importance to the conditioned-response method is the method of partial correlations (35, p. 410).

Today's students who meet partial correlation only as a momentary digression from their main work in statistics may find this excitement hard to comprehend. But partial correlation is the starting place for all of factor analysis.

Factor analysis is rapidly being perfected into a rigorous method of clarifying multivariate relationships. Fisher made the experimentalist an expert puppeteer, able to keep untangled the strands to half-a-dozen independent variables. The correlational psychologist is a mere observer of a play where Nature pulls a thousand strings; but his multivariate methods make him equally an expert, an expert in figuring out where to look for the hidden strings.

His sophistication in data analysis has not been matched by sophistication in theory. The correlational psychologist was led into temptation by his own success, losing himself first in practical prediction, then in a narcissistic program of studying his tests as an end in themselves. A naive operationism enthroned theory of test performance in the place of theory of mental processes. And premature enthusiasm [1] exalted a few measurements chosen almost by accident from the tester's stock as the ruling forces of the mental universe.

In former days, it was the experimentalist who wrote essay after anxious essay defining his discipline and differentiating it from competing ways of studying mind. No doubts plagued correlationists like Hall, Galton, and Cattell. They came in on the wave of evolutionary thought and were buoyed up by every successive crest of social progress or crisis. The demand for universal education, the development of a technical society, the appeals from the distraught twentieth-century parent, and finally the clinical movement assured the correlational psychologist of his great destiny. Contemporary experimentalists, however, voice with ever-increasing assurance their program and social function; and the fact that tonight you have a correlational psychologist discussing disciplinary identities implies than anxiety is now perched on *his* windowledge.

Indeed, I do speak out of concern for correlational psychology. Aptitude tests deserve their fine reputation; but, if practical, validated procedures are to be our point of pride, we must be dissatisfied with our progress since 1920. As the Executive Committee of Division 5 itself declared this year, none of our latter-day refinements or innovations has improved practical predictions by a notice-

---

[1] This judgment is not mine alone; it is the clear consensus of the factor analysts themselves (see 28, pp. 321–325).

able amount. Correlational psychologists who found their self-esteem upon contributions to theory can point to monumental investigations such as the *Studies of Character* and *The Authoritarian Personality*. Such work does throw strong light upon the human scene and brings important facts clearly into view. But theories to organize these facts are rarely offered and even more rarely solidified (30; 31, p. 55).

Potential Contributions of the Disciplines to One Another

Perhaps it is inevitable that a powerful new method will become totally absorbing and crowd other thoughts from the minds of its followers. It took a generation of concentrated effort to move from Spearman's tetrad equation and Army Alpha to our present view of the ability domain. It took the full energies of other psychologists to move from S-R bonds to modern behavior theory. No doubt the tendency of correlationists to ignore experimental developments is explained by their absorption in the wonders and complexities of the phenomena their own work was revealing. And if experimentalists were to be accused of narrow-minded concentration on one particular style and topic of research, the same comment would apply.

The spell these particular theories and methods cast upon us appears to have passed. We are free at last to look up from our own bedazzling treasure, to cast properly covetous glances upon the scientific wealth of our neighbor discipline. Trading has already been resumed, with benefit to both parties.

The introduction of construct validation into test theory (12) is a prime example. The history of this development, you may recall, was that the APA's Committee on Psychological Tests dis-

covered that available test theory recognized no way of determining whether
a proposed psychological interpretation
of a test was sound. The only existing
theory dealt with criterion validation and
could not evaluate claims that a test
measured certain psychological traits or
states. Meehl, capitalizing on the methodological and philosophical progress of
the experimenters, met the testers' need
by suggesting the idea of construct validity. A proposed test interpretation, he
showed, is a claim that a test measures a
construct, i.e., a claim that the test score
can be linked to a theoretical network.
This network, together with the claim,
generates predictions about observations.
The test interpretation is justified only
if the observations come out as predicted. To decide how well a purported
test of anxiety measures anxiety, construct validation is necessary; i.e., we
must find out whether scores on the test
behave in accordance with the theory
that defines anxiety. This theory predicts
differences in anxiety between certain
groups, and traditional correlational
methods can test those predictions. But
the theory also predicts variation in anxiety, hence in the test score, as a function
of experience or situations, and only an
experimental approach can test those
predictions.

This new theory of validity has several very broad consequences. It gives
the tester a start toward the philosophical
sophistication the experimenter has
found so illuminating. It establishes the
experimental method as a proper and
necessary means of validating tests. And
it re-establishes research on tests as a
valuable and even indispensable way of
extending psychological theory.

We may expect the test literature of
the future to be far less saturated with
correlations of tests with psychologically

enigmatic criteria, and far richer in
studies which define test variables by
their responsiveness to practice at different ages, to drugs, to altered instructions, and to other experimentally manipulated variables. A pioneering venture
in this direction is Fleishman's revealing
work (21, 22) on changes in the factorial content of motor skills as a function of practice. These studies go far
beyond a mere exploration of certain
tests; as Ferguson has shown (19, 20),
they force upon us a theory which treats
abilities as a product of learning, and a
theory of learning in which previously
acquired abilities play a major role.

Perhaps the most valuable trading
goods the correlator can offer in return
is his multivariate conception of the
world.

No experimenter would deny that situations and responses are multifaceted,
but rarely are his procedures designed
for a systematic multivariate analysis.
The typical experimental design and the
typical experimental law employ a single
dependent variable. Even when more
than one outcome is measured, the outcomes are analyzed and interpreted separately. No response measure, however,
is an adequate measure of a psychological construct. Every score mixes general
construct-relevant variance with variance
specific to the particular measuring operation. It is all right for the agriculturist
to consider size of crop as the fundamental variable being observed: that is
the payoff for him. Our task, however,
is to study changes in fundamental aspects of behavior, and these are evidenced only indirectly in any one measure of outcome.

The correlational psychologist discovered long ago that no observed criterion
is truly valid and that simultaneous consideration of many criteria is needed for

a satisfactory evaluation of performance. This same principle applies in experimentation. As Neal Miller says in a recent paper on experiments with drugs:

Where there are relatively few facts it seems easy to account for them by a few simple generalizations. . . . As we begin to study the effects of a variety of drugs on a number of different behavioral measures, exceptions and complexities emerge. We are forced to reexamine and perhaps abandon common-sense categories of generalization according to convenient words existing in the English language. As new and more comprehensive patterns of results become available, however, new and more precise generalizations may emerge. We may be able to "carve nature better to the joint" and achieve the simplicity of a much more exact and powerful science (32, pp. 326–327).

Theoretical progress is obstructed when one restricts himself to a single measure of response (34). Where there is only one dependent variable, it is pointless to introduce intervening variables or constructs. When there are many response variables, however, it is mandatory to subsume them under constructs, since otherwise we must have a separate set of laws for every measure of outcome. Dealing with multiple response variables is, as Miller says (33), precisely the problem with which the factor analysts have been concerned. Factor analysis, by substituting formal for intuitive methods, has been of great help in locating constructs with which to summarize observations about abilities. It is reasonable to expect that multivariate treatment of response measures would have comparable value in experimental psychology.

Experimenters very probably have even more to gain from treating *independent* variables as a continuous multivariate system. The manifold treatment categories in a Fisherian design are established a priori. In agriculture, the treatment dimensions the farmer can manipulate are obvious: fertilizer, water, species of seed, and so on. In a more basic science, we require genotypic constructs to describe situations, constructs like the physical scientist's temperature and pressure. The conditions the psychologist most easily manipulates—stimulus form, injunction to the subject, strength of electric shock—are not chosen because we intend to apply these specific conditions when we get around to "controlling behavior." They are used because these conditions, we hope, embody scientifically useful constructs.

The experimenter has no systematic way to classify and integrate results from different tasks or different reinforcers. As Ferguson remarks (20, p. 130; see also 19, p. 100): "No satisfactory methodology has emerged for describing particular learning tasks, or indicating how one task differs from another, other than by a process of simple inspection." We depend wholly on the creative flair of the theorist to collate the experiments and to invent constructs which might describe particular situations, reinforcements, or injunctions in terms of more fundamental variables. The multivariate techniques of psychometrics are suited for precisely this task of grouping complex events into homogeneous classes or organizing them along major dimensions. These methods are frankly heuristic, but they are systematically heuristic. They select variables with minimal redundancy, and they permit us to obtain maximum information from a minimum of experimental investment.

In suggesting that examining treatment conditions as a statistical universe is a possible way to advance experimental thinking, I am of course echoing the recommendations of Egon Brunswik (6, esp. pp. 39–58). Brunswik criticized the Fisherian experimenter for his ad

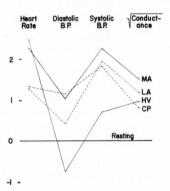

FIG. 2. Mean response to four stressors expressed in terms of resting standard scores (data from [50]).

hoc selection of treatments and recommended that he apply the sampling principles of differential psychology in choosing stimuli and conditions. A sampling procedure such as Brunswik suggests will often be a forward step, but the important matter is not to establish laws which apply loosely to a random, unorganized collection of situations. The important matter is to discover the organization among the situations, so that we can describe situational differences as systematically as we do individual differences.

Research on stress presents a typical problem of organization. Multivariate psychophysiological data indicate that different taxing situations have different effects. At present, stressors can be described and classified only superficially, by inspection. A correlational or distance analysis of the data groups treatments which have similar effects and ultimately permits us to locate each treatment within a continuous multidimensional structure having constructs as

reference axes. Data from a recent study by Wenger, Clemens, and Engel (50) may be used as an illustration. Figure 2 shows the means of standardized physiological scores under four different stress conditions: mental arithmetic, a letter association test, hyperventilation, and a cold pressor. The "profiles" for the four conditions are very significantly different. I have made a distance analysis to examine the similarity between conditions, with the results diagrammed in Figure 3. There is a general factor among all the treatments, which distinguishes them from the resting state, and a notable group factor among three of them. According to these data, a mental test seems to induce the same physiological state as plunging one's foot into ice water!

Much larger bodies of data are of course needed to map the treatment space properly. But the aptness of an attempt in this direction will be apparent to all who heard Selye's address to the APA last year. His argument (40) that all stressful situations lead to a similar

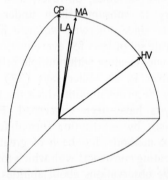

FIG. 3. Multivariate diagram showing similarity between four stressors.

syndrome of physiological changes is strongly reminiscent of Spearman's argument regarding a general factor linking intellectual responses. The disagreement between Selye and other students of stress clearly reduces to a quantitative question of the relative size of specific and nonspecific or general factors in the effects of typical stressors.

Applied Psychology Divided against Itself

Let us leave for the moment questions of academic psychology and consider the schism as it appears in applied psychology. In applied psychology, the two disciplines are in active conflict; and unless they bring their efforts into harmony, they can hold each other to a standstill. The conflict is especially obvious at this moment in the challenge the young engineering psychology offers to traditional personnel psychology.

The program of applied experimental psychology is to modify treatments so as to obtain the highest average performance when all persons are treated alike —a search, that is, for "the one best way." The program of applied correlational psychology is to raise average performance by treating persons differently —different job assignments, different therapies, different disciplinary methods. The correlationist is utterly antagonistic to a doctrine of "the one best way," whether it be the heartless robot-making of Frederick Taylor or a doctrinaire permissiveness which tries to give identical encouragement to every individual. The ideal of the engineering psychologist, I am told, is to simplify jobs so that every individual in the working population will be able to perform them satisfactorily, i.e., so that differentiation of treatment will be unnecessary. This goal guides activities ranging from the sober to the bizarre: from E. L. Thorndike and Skinner, hunting the one best sequence of problems for teaching arithmetic, to Rudolf Flesch and his admirers, reducing

Paradise Lost to a comic book. If the engineering psychologist succeeds: information rates will be so reduced that the most laggard of us can keep up, visual displays will be so enlarged that the most myopic can see them, automatic feedback will prevent the most accident-prone from spoiling the work or his fingers.

Obviously, with every inch of success the engineer has, the tester must retreat a mile. A slight reduction in information rate, accomplished once, reduces forever the validity and utility of a test of ability to process data. If, once the job is modified, the myopic worker can perform as well as the man with 20/20 vision, Snellen charts and orthoraters are out of business. Nor is the threat confined to the industrial scene. If tranquilizers make everybody happy, why bother to diagnose patients to determine which treatments they should have? And if televised lessons can simplify things so that every freshman will enjoy and understand quantum mechanics, we will need neither college aptitude tests nor final examinations.

It is not my intention to warn testers about looming unemployment. If test technology is not greatly improved, long before the applied experimentalists near their goals, testing deserves to disappear. My message is my belief that the conflicting principles of the tester and the experimenter can be fused into a new and integrated applied psychology.

To understand the present conflict in purposes, we must look again at historical antecedents. Pastore (36) argues with much justice that the testers and classifiers have been political conservatives, while those who try to find the best common treatment for all—particularly in education—have been the liberals. This essential conservatism of personnel psychology traces back to the days of Darwin and Spencer.

The theory of evolution inspired two antagonistic movements in social thought (10, 42). Darwin and Herbert Spencer were real determinists. The survival of the fittest, as a law of Nature, guaranteed man's superiority and the ultimate triumph of the natural aristocrats among men. As Dewey put it, Spencer saw "a rapid transit system of evolution . . . carrying us automatically to the goal of perfect man in perfect society" (17, p. 66). Men vary in their power of adaptation, and institutions, by demanding adaptation, serve as instruments of natural selection among men. The essence of freedom is seen as the freedom to compete for survival. To Spencer, to Galton, and to their successors down to the present day, the successful are those who have the greatest adjustive capacity. The psychologist's job, in this tradition, is to facilitate or anticipate natural selection. He seeks only to reduce its cruelty and wastage by predicting who will survive in schools and other institutions as they are. He takes the system for granted and tries to identify who will fit into it. His devices have a conservative influence because they identify persons who will succeed in the existing institution. By reducing failures, they remove a challenge which might otherwise force the institution to change (49).

The experimental scientist inherits an interpretation of evolution associated with the names of Ward, James, and Dewey. For them, man's progress rests on his intelligence; the great struggle for survival is a struggle against environment, not against competitors. Intelligent man must reshape his environment, not merely conform to it. This spirit, the very antithesis of Spencerian laissez-faire,

bred today's experimental social science which accepts no institution and no tradition as sacred. The individual is seen as inherently self-directing and creative. One can not hope to predict how he will meet his problems, and applied differential psychology is therefore pointless (39, p. 37).

Thus we come to have one psychology which accepts the institution, its treatment, and its criterion and finds men to fit the institution's needs. The other psychology takes man—generalized man—as given and challenges any institution which does not conform to the measure of this standard man.

A clearer view of evolution removes the paradox:

The entire significance of the evolutionary method in biology and social history is that every distinct organ, structure, or formation, every grouping of cells or elements, has to be treated as an instrument of adjustment or adaptation to a particular environing situation. Its meaning, its character, its value, is known when, and only when, it is considered as an arrangement for meeting the conditions involved in some specific situation (16, p. 15).

We are not on the right track when we conceive of adjustment or adjustive capacity in the abstract. It is always a capacity to respond to a particular treatment. The organism which adapts well under one condition would not survive under another. If for each environment there is a best organism, for every organism there is a best environment. The job of applied psychology is to improve decisions about people. The greatest social benefit will come from applied psychology if we can find for each individual the treatment to which he can most easily adapt. This calls for the joint application of experimental and correlational methods.

Interaction of Treatment and Individual in Practical Decisions

Goldine Gleser and the writer have recently published a theoretical analysis (11) which shows that neither the traditional predictive model of the correlator nor the traditional experimental comparison of mean differences is an adequate formulation of the decisions confronting the applied psychologist. Let me attempt to give a telescoped version of the central argument.

The decision maker has to determine what treatment shall be used for each individual or each group of individuals. Psychological data help a college, for example, select students to be trained as scientists. The aim of any decision maker is to maximize expected payoff. There is a payoff function relating outcome (e.g., achievement in science) to aptitude dimensions for any particular treatment. Figure 4 shows such a function for a

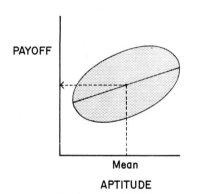

PAYOFF

Mean

APTITUDE

FIG. 4. Scatter diagram and payoff function showing outcome as a function of individual differences.

single aptitude. Average payoff—if everyone receives the treatment—is indicated by the arrow. The experimentalist assumes a fixed population and hunts for the treatment with the highest average and the least variability. The correlationist assumes a fixed treatment and hunts for aptitudes which maximize the slope of the payoff function. In academic selection, he advises admission of students with high scores on a relevant aptitude and thus raises payoff for the institution (Figure 5).

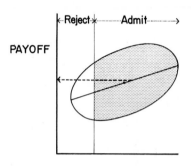

←Reject→ ←------Admit------→

PAYOFF

APTITUDE

FIG. 5. Increase in payoff as a result of selection.

Pure selection, however, almost never occurs. The college aptitude test may seem to be intended for a selection decision; and, insofar as the individual college is concerned only with those it accepts, the conventional validity coefficient does indicate the best test. But from a societal point of view, the rejects will also go on into other social institutions, and their profit from this treatment must be weighed in the balance along with the profit or social contribution from the ones who enter college. Every decision is really a choice between treatments. Predicting outcome has no social value unless the psychologist or the subject himself can use the information to make better choices of treatment. The prediction must help to determine a treatment for every individual.

Even when there are just two treatments, the payoff functions have many possible relationships. In Figure 6 we have a mean difference between treat-

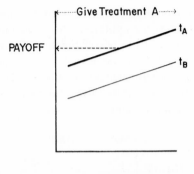

FIG. 6. Payoff functions for two treatments.

ments, and a valid predictor. The predictor—though valid—is useless. We should give everyone Treatment A. In Figure 7, on the other hand, we should divide the group and give different treatments. This gives greater payoff than either treatment used uniformly will give.

Assigning everyone to the treatment with the highest average, as the experimentalist tends to recommend, is rarely the best decision. In Figure 8, Treatment C has the best average, and we might assign everyone to it. The outcome is greater, however, if we assign some persons to each treatment. The psychologist making an experimental comparison arrives at the wrong conclusion if he ignores the aptitude variable and recommends C as a standard treatment.

Applied psychologists should deal with treatments and persons simultaneously. Treatments are characterized by many dimensions; so are persons. The two sets of dimensions together determine a payoff surface. For any practical problem, there is some best group of treatments to use and some best allocation of persons to treatments. We can expect some attributes of persons to have strong interactions with treatment variables. These attributes have far greater practical importance than the attributes

which have little or no interaction. In dividing pupils between college preparatory and noncollege studies, for example, a general intelligence test is probably the wrong thing to use. This test, being general, predicts success in all subjects, therefore tends to have little interaction with treatment and if so is not the best guide to differential treatment. We require a measure of aptitude which predicts who will learn better from one curriculum than from the other; but this aptitude remains to be discovered. Ultimately we should *design* treatments, not to fit the average person, but to fit groups of students with particular aptitude patterns. Conversely, we should seek out the aptitudes which correspond to (interact with) modifiable aspects of the treatment.

My argument rests on the assumption that such aptitude-treatment interactions exist. There is, scattered in the literature, a remarkable amount of evidence of significant, predictable differences in the way people learn. We have only limited success in predicting which of two *tasks* a person can perform better, when we allow enough training to compensate for differences in past attainment. But we do find that a person learns more easily from one *method* than another, that this

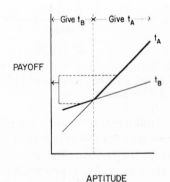

FIG. 7. Payoff functions for two treatments.

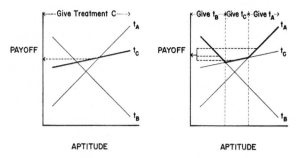

FIG. 8. Payoff functions for three treatments.

best method differs from person to person, and that such between-treatments differences are correlated with tests of ability and personality. The studies showing interaction between personality and conditions of learning have burgeoned in the past few years, and the literature is much too voluminous to review in passing. Just one recent finding will serve in the way of specific illustration, a study done by Wolfgang Böhm at Vienna (38, pp. 58–59). He showed his experimental groups a sound film about the adventures of a small boy and his toy elephant at the zoo. At each age level, a matched control group read a verbatim text of the sound track. The differences in average comprehension between the audiovisual and the text presentations were trivial. There was, however, a marked interaction. For some reason yet unexplained, a general mental test correlated only .30 with text learning, but it predicted film learning with an average correlation of .77.[2] The difference was consistent at all ages.

Such findings as this, when replicated and explained, will carry us into an educational psychology which measures readiness for different types of teaching and which invents teaching methods to fit different types of readiness. In gen-

eral, unless one treatment is clearly best for everyone, treatments should be differentiated in such a way as to maximize their interaction with aptitude variables. Conversely, persons should be allocated on the basis of those aptitudes which have the greatest interaction with treatment variables. I believe we will find these aptitudes to be quite unlike our present aptitude measures chosen to predict differences *within* highly correlated treatments.

The Shape of a United Discipline

It is not enough for each discipline to borrow from the other. Correlational psychology studies only variance among organisms; experimental psychology studies only variance among treatments. A united discipline will study both of these, but it will also be concerned with the otherwise neglected interactions between organismic and treatment variables (41). Our job is to invent constructs and to form a network of laws which permits prediction. From observations we must infer a psychological description of the situation and of the present state of the organism. Our laws should permit us to predict, from this description, the behavior of organism-in-situation.

There was a time when experimental psychologists concerned themselves

---

[2] Personal communication.

wholly with general, nonindividual constructs, and correlational psychologists sought laws wholly within developmental variables. More and more, nowadays, their investigations are coming to bear on the same targets. One psychologist measures ego involvement by a personality test and compares the behavior of high- and low-scoring subjects. Another psychologist heightens ego involvement experimentally in one of two equated groups and studies the consequent differences in behavior. Both investigators can test the same theoretical propositions, and to the extent that their results agree they may regard both procedures as embodiments of the same construct.

Constructs originating in differential psychology are now being tied to experimental variables. As a result, the whole theoretical picture in such an area as human abilities is changing. Piaget (37) correlates reasoning processes with age and discovers a developmental sequence of schemata whose emergence permits operational thought; Harlow (24) begins actually to create similar schemata in monkeys by means of suitable training. It now becomes possible to pursue in the controllable monkey environment the questions raised by Piaget's unique combination of behavioral testing and interviewing, and ultimately to unite the psychology of intelligence with the psychology of learning.

Methodologies for a joint discipline have already been proposed. R. B. Cattell (8) has offered the most thorough discussion of how a correlationist might organize data about treatment and organism simultaneously. His factor analytic procedures are only one of many choices, however, which modern statistics offers. The experimenters, some of

them, have likewise seen the necessity for a united discipline. In the very issue of *Psychological Review* where the much-too-famous distinction between *S-R* and *R-R* laws was introduced, Bergmann and Spence (3) declared that (at the present stage of psychological knowledge) the equation $R = f (S)$ must be expanded into

$$R = f (S, T, D, I)$$

The added variables are innate differences, motivation, and past experience—differential variables all. Hull (26, 27) sought general laws just as did Wundt, but he added that organismic factors can and must be accounted for. He proposed to do this by changing the constants of his equations with each individual. This is a bold plan, but one which has not yet been implemented in even a limited way. It is of interest that both Hull (27, p. 116) and Tolman (47, p. 26) have stated specifically that for their purposes factor analytic methods seem to have little promise. Tucker, though, has at least drawn blueprints of a method for deriving Hull's own individual parameters by factor analysis (48). Clearly, we have much to learn about the most suitable way to develop a united theory, but we have no lack of exciting possibilities.

The experimenter tends to keep his eye on *ultimate* theory. Woodworth once described psychological laws in terms of the *S-O-R* formula which specifically recognizes the individual. The revised version of his *Experimental Psychology* (53, p. 3), however, advocates an *S-A-R* formula, where *A* stands for "antecedent conditions." This formulation, which is generally congenial to experimenters, reduces the present state of the organism to an intervening variable

(Figure 9). A theory of this type is in principle entirely adequate to explain, predict, and control the behavior of or-

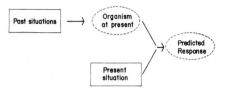

FIG. 9. Theoretical model for prediction from historic data.

ganisms; but, oddly enough, it is a theory which can account only for the behavior of organisms of the next generation, who have not yet been conceived. The psychologist turns to a different type of law (Figure 10) whenever he deals with a

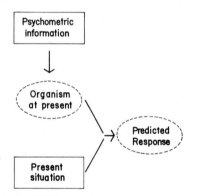

FIG. 10. Theoretical model for prediction from ahistoric data.

subject whose life history he has not controlled or observed in every detail. A theory which involves only laws of this type, while suitable for prediction, has very limited explanatory value. The theory psychology really requires is a redundant network like Figure 11. This network permits us to predict from the past experience or present characteristics of the organism, or a combination of the two, depending on what is known. Filling in such a network is clearly a task

for the joint efforts of experimental and correlational psychology.

In both applied work and general scientific work, psychology requires combined, not parallel, labors from our two historic disciplines. In this common labor, they will almost certainly become one, with a common theory, a common method, and common recommendations for social betterment. In the search for interactions we will invent new treatment dimensions and discover new dimensions of the organism. We will come to realize that organism and treatment are an inseparable pair and that no psychologist can dismiss one or the other as error variance.

Despite our specializations, every scientific psychologist must take the same scene into his field of vision. Clark Hull, three sentences before the end of his *Essentials of Behavior* (27, p. 116), voiced just this need. Because of delay in developing methodology, he said, individual differences have played little part in behavior theory, and "a sizeable segment of behavioral science remains practically untouched." This untouched segment contains the question we really want to put to Nature, and she will never answer until our two disciplines ask it in a single voice.

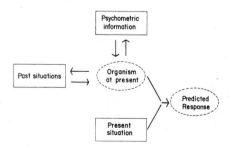

FIG. 11. Theoretical network to be developed by a united discipline.

References

1. BARTLETT, F. C. Fifty years of psychology. *Occup. Psychol.*, 1955, **29**, 203–216.

2. BEACH, F. A. The snark was a boojum. *Amer. Psychologist,* 1950, **5**, 115–124.

3. BERGMANN, G., & SPENCE, K. W. The logic of psychophysical measurement. *Psychol. Rev.*, 1944, **51**, 1–24.

4. BINDRA, D., & SCHEIER, I. H. The relation between psychometric and experimental research in psychology. *Amer. Psychologist,* 1954, **9**, 69–71.

5. BORING, E. G. *History of experimental psychology.* (2nd ed.) New York: Appleton-Century-Crofts, 1950.

6. BRUNSWIK, E. *Perception and the representative design of psychological experiments.* Berkeley: Univer. California Press, 1956.

7. CATTELL, J. McK. The biological problems of today: Psychology. *Science,* 1898, **7**, 152–154.

8. CATTELL, R. B. *Factor analysis.* New York: Harper, 1952.

9. CLARK, K. E. *America's psychologists.* Washington, D.C.: APA, 1957.

10. CORWIN, E. S. The impact of the idea of evolution on the American political and constitutional tradition. In S. PERSONS (Ed.), *Evolutionary thought in America.* New Haven: Yale Univer. Press, 1950. Pp. 182–201.

11. CRONBACH, L. J., & GLESER, GOLDINE C. *Psychological tests and personnel decisions.* Urbana: Univer. Illinois Press, 1957.

12. CRONBACH, L. J., & MEEHL, P. E. Construct validity in psychological tests. *Psychol. Bull.,* 1955, **52**, 281–302.

13. CRONBACH, L. J. & NEFF, W. D. Selection and training. In Com. on Undersea Warfare Panel on Psychology and Physiology, *Human Factors in Undersea Warfare.* Washington, D.C.: Nat. Res. Coun., 1949. Pp. 491–516.

14. DANIEL, R. S., & LOUTTIT, C. M. *Professional problems in psychology.* New York: Prentice-Hall, 1953.

15. DASHIELL, J. F. Some rapprochements in contemporary psychology. *Psychol. Bull.,* 1939, **36**, 1–24.

16. DEWEY, J. *Studies in logical theory.* Chicago: Univer. Chicago Press, 1903.

17. ———. *The influence of Darwin on philosophy and other essays.* New York: Holt, 1910.

18. EYSENCK, H. J. Reminiscence, drive, and personality theory. *J. abnorm. soc. Psychol.,* 1956, **53**, 328–333.

19. FERGUSON, G. A. On learning and human ability. *Canad. J. Psychol.,* 1954, **8**, 95–112.

20. ———. On transfer and human ability. *Canad. J. Psychol.,* 1956, **10**, 121–131.

21. FLEISHMAN, E. A. Predicting advanced levels of proficiency in psychomotor skills. In *Proc. Sympos. on Human Engng.* Washington, D.C.: Nat. Acad. Sci., 1956. Pp. 142–151.

22. FLEISHMAN, E. A., & HEMPEL, W. E., JR. Changes in factor structure of a complex psychomotor test as a function of practice. *Psychometrika,* 1954, **19**, 239–252.

23. FORD, C. S., & BEACH, F. A. *Patterns of sexual behavior.* New York: Harper, 1952.

24. HARLOW, H. F. The formation of learning sets. *Psychol. Rev.,* 1949, **56**, 51–65.

25. ———. Mice, men, monkeys, and motives. *Psychol. Rev.,* 1953, **60**, 23–32.

26. HULL, C. L. The place of innate individual and species differences in a natural-science theory of behavior. *Psychol. Rev.,* 1945, **52**, 55–60.

27. ———. *Essentials of behavior.* New Haven: Yale Univer. Press, 1951.

labels. But whether the terms are adequate or not, I hope at least to be able to tell you what I mean by them.

Partly what led me to a reorganization of my ideas about individuality around these concepts was a sort of inherent reasonableness about them. With the swift passage of the years one becomes acutely aware that human life is finite. It lasts only a limited time, and each person has only a limited number of hours each day at his disposal. Only a small fraction of the potentialities with which his life begins can ever become realities. By the time his infancy is over, a considerable number of them have already been ruled out by the fact that he has spent his most formative years in one particular kind of home rather than another. But the person is still confronted at each step of his life with an incredibly complex assortment of stimulating conditions and behavior possibilities. In order to function at all, each of us must choose from this plethora of possibilities and organize what he has chosen.

Consider, for example, Barker's report on the Midwest study (Barker & Wright, 1955). If even in one little town there are 585 distinguishable behavior settings, 60 to 79% of them open to children, and if during the course of a single day one child engages in almost 2,500 behavior transactions with 749 different behavior objects, the *possibilities* for influence that might help to determine individuality are absolutely staggering. It seems plausible to me to assume that one of the main things that happens as the boy or girl interacts with this complex milieu is that he develops patterns of choices that serve to let some things in and to keep others out. If to this screening function we add some sort of organizational process acting upon the

experience choice has admitted, we begin to come close to the meaning of individuality. In counseling and therapy we are actually using this sort of conceptualization in our attempts to understand clients, although it is not always expressed very clearly, and, as we shall see, some research workers have been developing methods of assessment that can be considered pilot projects on the way to a new technology.

Let us then take a look at choice and organization separately, realizing as we do so that they are not independent and do not actually occur separately. I have mentioned that I do not think choice is a very good word for the phenomenon, but I have not been able to think of a better one. Perhaps some other figurative statements can serve to make its meaning clearer, however. I have compared it a moment ago to a screen. This is really too fixed and static a picture. We might see life instead as a restaurant with a large number of items on the menu from which two or three are to be selected. Or we might take our cue from the poets who have seen life as a road, which forks every now and then requiring that the traveler go in one direction or the other.

All these analogies have the merit of reminding us that a person's life is always bounded by limits of one kind or another. He is not free to do anything he wants to or to go in any direction. I do not think it is necessary to get into the old controversy over determinism versus free will at all. Certainly at any one time a large number of behavior possibilities are ruled out by external circumstances, by personal inadequacies, and by previous commitments. But within these analyzable limits there is a larger or smaller space in which movement of different sorts is possible. It is this movement in one direction rather than another, within defining limits, that I am calling choice.

It seems clear to me also that a large part of the choice process is unconscious. The individual's choice of the aspects of a complex stimulating situation to which he will respond is a universal process, constantly going on. It is only the small part of it of which we are aware that we call freedom. In a very real sense it *is* freedom, because in human choices, awareness makes a difference. It changes the nature of the total situation and thus leads to choices that may be different from those that would have been made unconsciously. And in this small margin of difference that awareness makes lies out best hope for progress in living our own lives wisely and helping those it is our responsibility to help.

A workable psychology of individuality would provide us with ways of recognizing significant patterns of choices that have been made at previous stages of life, consciously or unconsciously, and of widening the margin of awareness in any individual's present experience. To accomplish this we need a different approach, a different kind of assessment from the customary measurements of traits or dimensions. Let us go back for a moment to our restaurant analogy. Two men are having dinner together. One orders jambalaya, artichokes, and crepe suzette. The other orders fried chicken, corn on the cob, and apple pie. Conceivably we could scale the degree of liking for each of these foods and compare the two men on these several scales. But if we did just this, we would miss the main distinction here. It is the choice of the particular *combination* of foods, jambalaya *and* artichokes *and* crepe suzette, or chicken *and* corn *and* apple pie that reveals something about each

person. Measuring the strength of these preferences is unnecessary and irrelevant.

It is here, in connection with the assessment of the meaning of combinations of choices, that the research activity on which I have been principally engaged enters the picture. In one way or another I have been dealing for some 20 years with the responses men and women, boys and girls make to Like and Dislike items on the blanks we have been calling interest tests. But it was not until a couple of months ago that it suddenly dawned on me that the major significance of all of this work is that it points the way to a kind of assessment quite different from trait measurement, namely, the direct assessment of choice patterns. True, we have been expressing what we found in terms of traits or dimensions that we labeled "interest in science," "masculinity-femininity," or "occupational level." But when we did this, the findings never fit the labels very well. On the Strong test, for example, the correlations of the numerical scores people make on the various scales with criteria purporting to represent degrees of success and satisfaction have almost always turned out to be rather low. The really impressive relationships Strong (1955) has obtained in his 20-year follow-up of Stanford students have been based on *letter grades* as predictors of a special kind of criterion—that of remaining in the original occupation vs. shifting to another.

The letter grades on the Strong are derived from the scores but carry a different meaning from customary trait measurements. An "A" means "Yes" with regard to the question of whether a certain person belongs in a certain occupation, a "C" means "No," and a "B" means "We cannot be sure." We can relate these grades to the concept of choice we have been considering by putting it this way: An A signifies that the person's characteristic pattern of acceptance and rejection of life's varied possibilities is like the choice pattern characteristic of persons in a certain occupation. What we should expect then to be able to predict from such a score is not how well the person will do the work of his chosen occupation, or how much satisfaction he will express with his job, but simply the way he will make his choices at later junctures of his life. This makes sense of the high degree of validity Strong's recent studies have shown for the test. What they are telling us is that an indicator of the nature of an individual's complex pattern of choices in the occupational area predicts well later complex choices in the same area.

My own special research activities have focused on an attempt to trace such choice patterns backward into childhood rather than forward into maturity. In 1946 I entered upon a longitudinal study of about 200 children, beginning at the time they entered school. The first half of this group is graduating from high school this year. They have taken the Strong test each year during the high school period, so that I have a clear picture of what their interests are like now at the end of adolescence. I am attempting to relate these interest patterns (or choice patterns, as I should now prefer to call them) to various personality characteristics, background factors, and special abilities, measured now and at earlier periods of the subjects' lives.

At the outset I was thinking of each of the variables as a trait and planning to correlate them with one another. The shift to this concept of choice patterns has changed my plans for analyzing the data. The appropriate type of measurement for these problems is *nominal,* not ordinal or interval—that is, simple categorization rather than continuous distribution. And to relate one of these choice categories to another, the appropriate statistic is not correlation, but some nonparametric significance test leading to a statement of probabilities. What this means concretely so far as my particular body of data is concerned is that I will classify my subjects in various ways, based on their final Strong scores, and then ask specific questions of the data from earlier stages. For example, I shall place all boys whose scores point to the choice of some science career in one group, those who definitely are not in the science group in another. I will then tabulate other test results and biographical data for these groups, using total scores, subscores, and in some cases separate items, and look for patterns or combinations of characteristics related to this particular choice pattern. (Such findings will of course need to be cross-validated. For some of the relationships, supplementary data on other groups not in the main study will serve this purpose; in other cases extra studies will need to be run.)

The main point I am trying to make here is that to work out a technology of choice measurement we must use classifications with regard to choices rather than continua, validate our assessments using choice criteria rather than measures of degrees of happiness or success, and state the relationships as probabilities that one thing will lead to another rather than as correlation coefficients. The work with the Strong Vocational Interest Blank is important to all of us who are concerned about personality assessment not just because it has a great deal of demonstrated practical value, but because it demonstrates that this kind of assessment, of choice patterns rather than traits, does work. Eventually we may have many such assessment devices, covering a much wider variety of patterned choices. Measures of preferences, values, and attitudes would seem to be clearly in this area, but as yet we are still trying to score and interpret them as traits or dimensions.

The work with the Strong test demonstrates that we need not abandon the concept of predictive validity when we shift from traits to discontinuous patterns of choices. The only difference is that we need to find criteria that represent choices rather than distances along some scale. There are many of these. My impression is that criteria are far less of a problem here than in customary validation studies. In the academic area they would include things like staying in school vs. dropping out, selecting one major rather than another, choosing "easy" or "hard" electives, going in for social success or for academic success. In a broader social framework, choice criteria would include such things as suing for divorce vs. attempting to work out marital problems, or parole keeping vs. violation. Choice criteria in the clinical area would include such things as the development of one kind of symptom rather than another, or the decision to seek psychotherapy vs. reliance on tranquilizers. These have all been used in research but not for the purpose for which they would seem to be particularly appropriate—research on the relationship of choice patterns to one another.

It is quite feasible, then, for us to carry on research that will enable us eventually to make much sounder inferences about individuals by observing what they choose. But this is only part of the story. I have been convinced, primarily as a result of my counseling activities, that the *how* is as important as the *what*. There are several aspects of choice we must consider. I have already touched briefly on the matter of differences in *awareness*. To understand an individual we must know how conscious he is of the choices he is making. Another aspect probably related to this is the age or developmental stage at which the first step in this direction was taken. It seems probable that some of the most important choices of all are made in the earliest years, long before the child is clearly aware of the direction he is taking. Whether to be active or passive in one's encounters with life, whether to seek security through dependence or independence, whether to relate oneself to persons or nonpersons (to use Anne Roe's terms), these are the kinds of fundamental early choices I have in mind. Research on concepts of sex role seems to show that a basic decision to accept one's own sex and to live by the code that goes with it is often made by the age of three. The Freudian concept of cathexis is clearly relevant here. Existentialist writers like Sartre have also emphasized unconscious choices and their significance in personality.

Another aspect of choice, perhaps somewhat easier to study, is the question of whether it has been made positively or negatively. It may make a considerable difference in the quality of an individual's life whether the choices that constitute its basic structure have been made by grasping what one wants or by rejecting what one does not want. I ran into this problem years ago when I first began to work with blanks calling for Like and Dislike responses. I became convinced that this negative choice process is far more significant in human life than we are assuming it to be. If we examine the scoring weights for most scales of the Strong test we find that so-called interest scores are based more on what we reject or rule out than on what we wish to do. Dislikes influence scores more than Likes do. My work with children in grade school suggests that interest development is primarily a matter of learning to rule out clusters of things and activities one once liked.

There are probably clear-cut individual differences in this area of positive vs. negative choices, and they would be well worth some special study. In our own profession, for example, it is conceivable that some of us are here because no other direction for our efforts was open to us. We needed to avoid, say, low prestige, low pay, mathematics, routine activities, and religious dogma. When we got through ruling out the occupations that would not do for one or another of these reasons, we found ourselves in a graduate psychology program. Others of us may be here because of an intense curiosity about human behavior and motivation, a strong urge to try out different experimental procedures and see what happens. Probably most of us have some of both kinds of motivation. Probably most of us score A on the Strong key for Psychologist, but that in itself does not show whether positive or negative choices predominate, since there are different combinations of items that will produce such a score.

Another of these "How" questions in which I am interested has to do with the *basis* upon which choices have been made. Do they grow out of identification with a parent or some other significant person? Do they reflect the point of view of some group to which the person belongs? Have they been influenced by particular experiences or by specific kinds of information? How much thoughtful consideration of possible alternatives has gone into them?

There is one more aspect of choice as a clue to individuality which is in some ways the most important of all, though it is the hardest to investigate. I mean the question as to how *central* or deeply rooted any given pattern of choice is for an individual. It is these basic *unalterable* choices that give a person a firm sense of self. Just making choices with regard to separate objects and actions is not enough. It is necessary that a person in some way *choose to be himself*. The idea is beautifully expressed in the words Yourcenar attributes to Hadrian in the novel *Hadrian's Memoirs:*

Whatever I had I chose to have, obliging myself only to possess it totally, and to taste the experience to the full. . . . And it is in such a way, with a mixture of reserve and of daring, of submission and revolt carefully concerted, of extreme demand and prudent concession, that I have finally learned to accept myself.

There is no dearth of discussion of self concepts, self-acceptance, and identity in psychology today. What I have been thinking about a great deal is how to make these ideas more "workable." Here too I think we can use interest tests as tools for work on the larger problem.

To sum up, the thing that distinguishes the kinds of research studies I have been using as examples from much of the previous work on individual differences in personality is a design based on classification rather than measurement (or on nominal rather than interval measures, if we wish to use Stevens' terminology). We select a group that appears to be homogeneous with regard to one particular aspect of their choices. By contrasting them with another group, we can obtain evidence about what this aspect of choice means—the kind of previous experience that is associated with it, the kind of subsequent choice behavior to which it leads. But because we are interested in the choices made by *individuals,* we will not stop with the statement that a relationship is significant at a given probability level but will attempt also to explore the differences between the persons who do and those who do not follow the prevailing trend.

I hope that nothing I have said will be taken to mean that I think we should discard the measuring techniques we now have for appraising the individual, or the knowledge that has accumulated from their use. Certainly the differences in physical and biochemical characteristics, that can be measured with considerable accuracy and expressed as continuous variables, are very significant. The research that has been going on for many years at the California Institute for Child Welfare has shown us how meaningful such a variable as age of reaching sexual maturity can be when we try to understand individual growth patterns. Certainly the differences in mental abilities and achievements that we pick up by means of our standardized tests represent important components of individuality. What I am trying to suggest is that, when we have recognized that there are choice patterns that are *not* continuous variables, we will be able to *utilize* more effectively all the resources we now have. We can still use our measures of physical characteristics, intelligence, special abilities, and personality traits to give us an approximate picture of an individual. The information about his distinctive patterns of choices will enable us to sketch in the finer lines of his portrait—to make it definitive.

As I stated in the beginning, individ-ual uniqueness for me is described primarily in terms of *choice* and *organization,* and I consider it the task of psychologists to make those concepts workable—to bring them into the general stream of thinking in research, assessment, and practical activities. I have used up about nine-tenths of my time talking about choice. This is not because I consider it the more important of the two, but simply because my own research activity has been in that area and I have done more thinking about it. Fortunately, an increasing number of psychologists have been presenting interesting new methods of assessing the ways individuals organize their experience. Perhaps the best known of these methods is Stevenson's Q sort. Other sorting techniques, originally developed as research tools in the study of concepts, now are being applied to the study of individuals. George Kelly's Role Construct Repertory Test is an ingenious way of finding out something about the organization of the persons's relationships to other people who are significant in his life. Osgood's semantic differential represents still another approach to the assessment of individual patterns of organization. While a number of other things could be mentioned, perhaps these examples are sufficient to indicate directions I should like to have us move in our attempts to understand individuality.

There are many related areas we might consider if time permitted. We might turn to the experimental work on choice and decision in general psychology. We might look at the flourishing new mathematics of decision processes. We might attempt to relate some philosophical systems to these ideas. We might take up the implications of these ideas for psychotherapy and education.

What interests me most right now,

however, is the significance of concepts of choice and organization in an inclusive psychology of the *development* of the human individual. We are coming to see development as a lifelong process in which choice and organization play a crucial part. In a certain sense each per- son *is* a "self-made man." At each stage of our lives, we impose limits on the next stage, by the choices we make and the ways in which we organize what we have experienced. There is an important some- thing that each individual must do for himself.

References

1. BARKER, R. G., & WRIGHT, H. F. *Midwest and its children.* Evanston, Ill.: Row, Peterson, 1955.

2. STRONG, E. K., JR. *Vocational interests 18 years after college.* Minneapolis: Univer. Minnesota Press, 1955.

BASIC CONCEPTS OF PSYCHOANALYSIS   Ruth L. Munroe

The chapter is addressed primarily to the reader who knows very little about psychoanalysis, or whose knowledge has been mainly theoretical. It falls into two parts: the first deals with Freud's *under- lying premises* as currently used by all analytic schools; the second, much long- er, deals with the major concern of psychoanalysis—*unconscious processes.*

It has seemed to me, however, that many arid disputes about the status of psychoanalysis as a science, and much incomprehension and bewilderment about the strange "evidence" adduced by psychoanalysts, might be avoided if outside critics had more understanding of how this "evidence" is obtained and used. Because of its complex nature, it is not easily controllable by the method- ologies developed in "psychology." Since it deals with nonrational materials, it often sounds fanciful and random until one begins, with Freud, to see the con- sistencies in the language of the uncon- scious, until one sees how these slippery data are carefully checked and rechecked in the course of analytic work. I shall not deal in this book with the problem of methodology as such, but the lengthy discussion of the unconscious is intended as an explanation of the psychoanalytic method and is implicitly a defense of the right of psychoanalysts to call their meth- od scientific.

Underlying Premises

PSYCHOLOGICAL DETERMINISM

In a sense, the concept of determinism is as old as human thought, and as broad in scope. It ranges from very complex philosophical theories to the fatalism of the soldier who believes that he will be

Reprinted by permission of the author and the publisher from Ruth L. Munroe, *Schools of Psychoanalytic Thought,* New York: Holt, Rinehart and Winston, Inc., 1955. The ma- terial presented here is excerpted from Chap- ter 2 and the reader is referred to the text for the complete work.

killed only by the bullet with his name on it. Determinism *vs.* free will, mechanism *vs.* vitalism, science *vs.* religion —these are the hoary controversies usually implied.

But this is not the sense in which the term is used in psychoanalysis. As a philosopher, Freud was primarily a scientist who believed fervently in the power of rational understanding, rooted in empirical observation. He was no more "deterministic" than any scientist. His primary motivation was to obtain deeper insight into "what makes people tick." His ultimate achievement was to bring new areas of the human psyche into the field of scientific investigation and to reorient such investigation toward the study of dynamic trends *within* the individual instead of universal laws applied *to* the individual.

A major aspect of Freud's approach was the tenet that none of human behavior is "accidental"; * hence the emphasis on the word *determinism*. Earlier scientific psychologists were prepared to maintain, usually on the analogy of nineteenth-century physics, that our slightest action is determined by ultimate universal laws. But they attributed our actions to rational motives or instincts quite narrowly defined to mechanical linkages by contiguity or similarity, or to chance —that is, to a multitude of "causes" acting independently. The small mistakes of everyday life, our reveries and dreams, the queer symptoms of the mentally diseased, were, to be sure, determined, but only as the flight of a feathered seed is determined by wind, gravity, its minute peculiarities in structure, and a host of other factors too transient for fruitful in-

vestigation. Over-all laws of association could be established; mental disorders could be usefully classified; dreaming could be explained as the reappearance of the past under certain physiological conditions with characteristic distortions of logical thinking. Unfortunately, the more carefully such laws and classifications were worked out, the further psychology traveled from common-sense usefulness.

Freud began his investigations as a doctor attempting to treat the bizarre symptoms of a mental disorder: hysteria. With Breuer (*Studies in Hysteria,* 1896), he observed that the peculiar behavior of a patient *made sense* in terms of an important episode in her past which she had forgotten. Of course, the patient was ill, but her illness appeared to consist precisely in re-enacting a fragment of the past (recoverable under hypnosis). Her specific symptom was not "accidental." In 1896 hysteria was a well-known phenomenon. Many efforts had been made to explain it and to trace its course. The old idea of the patient's being "possessed" had long been abandoned. The supreme importance of the new Breuer-Freud formulation lay in its insight into the meaningful *continuity of events* in the mental life of the individual. Hysteria was no longer considered as a strange pathological incursion but as the *exaggerated expression of psychological processes common to mankind*. Choice of symptom, which had previously seemed arbitrary, became a revelation of the specific psychic stresses of the patient.

With the observed "logic" of the hysterical symptom as his point of departure, Freud rapidly went on to show a similar "logic" in the unconsidered fragments of normal life: dreams and small mistakes (1). Freud's psychological determinism very markedly reduced the

---

* *None* is too strong a word for most psychoanalysts, and Freud himself was not puristic in his attempts to interpret every fragment of behavior as unconsciously determined.

areas that earlier psychologists considered unexplorable because they thought them to be ruled by chance—that is, by the independent action of so many transiently operating causes that the scientist cannot hope to measure and predict the outcome. Freud showed that the queernesses of mental life not only have meaning but provide especially useful clues to underlying continuities in the personality which profoundly affect even the rational goals of the normal person. Such continuities help to explain the development of mankind's conscience, ideals, and thoughtfulness, as well as of the bizarre hysterical symptom.

THE ROLE OF THE UNCONSCIOUS

For Freud, the initial observations on hysteria raised fundamental questions. *How* were these continuities determined? Clearly the new psychological determinism operated outside of full consciousness. *The role of the unconscious* may be called the second basic concept in psychoanalysis. Obviously, the hysterical patient was not aware of the meaning of her behavior prior to therapeutic intervention. Yet she acted in many ways *as if* she remembered. The memory was not conscious, but it was certainly not dead. On the contrary, it played a very active role in determining her actions. Freud went on to a very careful study of the unconscious as such.

MOTIVATION AND DYNAMICS

With only a promissory note about the unconscious, I come to a third basic concept, which can be labeled *motivation,* or, simply, *dynamics.* The concept is given heavy emphasis in most of modern psychology. Indeed, modern psychological determinism may be thought of as the organizing of behavior by the needs and aims—that is, the motivation

—of the person. It was Freud among the analysts who took the all-important first step toward appreciation of the essentially *goal-directed* quality of human behavior as a matter of necessary and feasible inquiry. And it was psychoanalysis, broadly speaking, that contributed most largely (though not exclusively) toward making this formulation a commonplace in contemporary psychological science.

In describing Freudian doctrine, I shall begin from a contemporary point of view, with the clear purpose of presenting understandably ideas which Freudians *now* consider basic. Here I offer an oversimplified account of Freud's very first position. He corrected and elaborated it himself, but it shows with peculiar sharpness the leap Freud made toward effective grasp of the function of *goals* in human behavior. (The contrast is obvious both with the atomistic brass-instrument psychological science of his time and with the speculative approach of philosophers who emphasized "the will.")

Freud perceived not only that the strange symptoms of the hysteric were comprehensible as partial reinstatements of forgotten episodes but that they seemed to have a *purposiveness* of their own. He saw that the episodes had been forgotten for good reason: they were painful or dangerous to the conscious self. In one patient after another, the forgotten memories recovered during hypnosis or later through the technique of free association seemed to concern sexual events in early childhood. It seemed to Freud at first that the unconscious phenomena he was learning to see had as their purpose the fulfillment of a *wish,* apparently a sexual wish dating from infancy, which was intolerable to the adult personality. The wish was therefore *censored* and could strive for expression only in the disguised form of the symptom.

This statement is full of exaggerations, crudities, and errors of omission, even beyond those of Freud's first formulation. But it contains the nuclear principles of virtually the whole of modern dynamic psychology.

Let us first consider the *wish*. For a time Freud was as sophistical about discovering the underlying "wish" element as ever La Rochefoucauld or the hedonists were in identifying their special talismans, but Freud's "wish" very readily gave way to libidinal needs and instinctual needs, and, with little strain, to the abstract concept of goal-directedness—whatever one's definition of goal. The modern idea of goal-striving had other origins too, of course, but the orientation of looking for the underlying goal in any item of human behavior undeniably took on enormous impetus from the psychoanalyst's practical habit of looking for the aim of the item rather than for the "laws" governing its appearance. Breuer did not see the unconscious as *purposive;* rather he saw in unconscious processes a falling apart of purposiveness under conditions of stress or psychic weakness. The goal-directed quality of the unconscious was a Freudian concept.

From the outset Freud saw that the nature of the unconscious purpose could be subjected to investigation. His emphasis on sexuality arose very clearly from observation of his patients, and his observations have been confirmed thousands of times. No psychoanalyst today doubts the importance of sexuality, especially infantile sexuality, in psychic life. Freud's destruction of the mythological age of innocence has been generally accepted. What is *not* accepted by non-Freudian psychoanalysts, and still more heatedly denied by nonpsychoanalytic

psychological schools, is Freud's idea of *the preponderant role played by infantile sexuality* in the development of human goals. The point here is that Freud, perhaps even more clearly than his divergent followers, *tried* to find the basis of his theories about goals in the actual productions of his patients and to base his theories on observation. Perhaps he did not wholly succeed—certainly he did not succeed completely, since no investigator can wholly escape the ingrained preconceptions of his own period. At the very least, however, Freud opened up for investigation a new range of human motives with the paradigm that one may try to discover underlying trends by looking at the data with as little bias as possible.

Freud saw from the outset that "the unconscious," with its sexual wish, was only part of the personality. Here again we encounter crossroads of development. Some investigators, notably Adler, leaped at once to the idea that the whole of the personality is directly determined by unrecognized wishes, not necessarily sexual. Adler saw in Freud's early formulations implications for the understanding of character as well as of the neurotic symptom, for the determination of the psychology as well as the psychopathology of everyday life. He extended the concept of purposiveness to the total adjustive process of living and tried to show how every act directly reflects the central goal of the human personality: the goal of superiority. Adler thus arrived at a radically holistic view of human nature whereby all behavior falls into place in the wake of its goal as water takes a predictable form in the wake of a ship. Any fragment of behavior could be interpreted by insight into the specific goal of the individual (his path to superiority) and could be changed automatically by persuading the person to change his goal. The later non-libido psychoanalysts also emphasize the *immediate* structuring power of an underlying need. For them also, the neurotic symptom or character trend must be understood *directly* as the expression of the person's current need for security, for significance, or whatever.

Freud himself took a longer way around to an understanding of the goal-directed quality of the total personality. The sexual wish, he observed, appeared to press for immediate gratification, regardless of consequences, and was regularly opposed by *something,* which he at first called the *censor,* lumping together all the social, moral, and rational forces behind the opposition. From the outset he assumed that these forces were also "instinctual," and later on he searched energetically to discover exactly where they came from, and how. During the 1920's he developed what he called the structural approach—an analysis of the process whereby the ego (mainly rational) and the superego (mainly moral) are crystallized out of the id (primitive instinctual). *Once crystallized out,* these provinces of the mind tend, according to Freud, to function to a large extent independently and act readily in complex opposition to the id, from which they came.

Freud—in his structuring of the id, ego, and superego—erected quite specific *categories of human function,* a framework which Adler vehemently repudiated and which the other non-libido analysts tend to view with suspicion. The slavish devotion to these categories among some lesser Freudians today readily promotes sympathy with Adler's vehemence. Doubtless any rigid categorization of creatively interacting systems holds dangers for essentially pedantic minds.

It is no part of the purpose of this chapter to defend Freud's structural approach in its specificity. In a discussion of basic concepts, however, it is important to underline how Freud arrived at his "provinces of the mind" (institutions, spheres—various terms are used) in contrast to the older "faculties of the mind," so long the bulwark of psychological thought. It is not enough to say that Freud was more empirical. On the contrary, the older categories are much more obvious. We remember, we imagine, we feel, we will. The armchair psychologists concocted these faculties because they fitted quite well with experience thought of from a chair. Even today it is easier to get beginning psychology students to understand this kind of categorization from their own experience as they sit in class before the professor than to put them through the task of understanding the Freudian id, ego, and superego. Freud was more empirical—but with patients rather than with normal adults, and with a more penetrating empiricism. His was a sort of *laboratory* empiricism, dealing with active trends in the relative isolation dictated by their pathological exaggeration.

THE GENETIC APPROACH

Freud's categorization was genetic—a product of the experience of the growing child. *We may call the genetic approach the fourth basic concept accepted by all psychoanalytic schools.* The old "faculties" were just there, somehow or other, as attributes of the human mind. They were either purely descriptive or dragged into an evolutionary scheme by speculative analogy. Freud dismissed them cheerfully—the more so because in his medical training he, unlike the professional psychologists of his time, had probably never encountered them vividly as a coordinated science. Freud set himself the task of explaining *how* and *why* people come to have moral and rational judgments, and *why* they care about their fellows. When he got around to it, Freud naturally approached his study of the forces *opposing* expression of the sexual wish in the same empirical *developmental* fashion as his study of the sexual drives themselves. Freud's provinces of the mind grow out of the experience of the human organism in its milieu. The complex attributes of the adult are built out of his living; they are not simply *there* for identification.

Again there was a bifurcation or multifurcation in the later development of psychoanalytic theory. Psychoanalysts differ as to just *how* early experiences structure later personality trends and as to the specific role of the infantile unconscious. Adler and Horney tend to think of the problem mainly through a more careful interpretation of the old saw: as the twig is bent so the branch inclines. In their view, early experience sets the pattern for later expectations and later techniques of adaptation. Freudians, however, tend to think of a relatively separate history for the various aspects of development, of the actual freezing of some aims at the infantile level by the mechanism of repression, while other aims develop more or less in accordance with the requirements of the social milieu and are only *influenced by* the persistence of the repressed aims.

Only the basic concept is highlighted here: whatever psychological patterns one considers significant in the adult personality are the product of the *adaptive experience of the person*. The longitudinal patterning of human systems must be considered as well as, or even more carefully than, their cross-sectional structure. Prediction depends upon history, the line of new development being subtended from the past—obviously in creative interaction with the present.

Early childhood is the time when the malleable, adaptable, flexible human psyche takes on the essential directions it will pursue. Because the human infant is so unformed by nature, because these experiences are the first, the events of infancy have a psychological importance very naturally overlooked by the adult philosopher in his study or the adult scientist among his instruments. More than any other single discipline, psychoanalysis drew attention to the overwhelming importance of this early period of life and offered new indications of what to look for in studying children.

In partial summary of the dynamic aspects of Freud's contribution as followed up by every psychoanalytic school (and most of the other contemporary schools), we may note first a thoroughgoing concept of psychological determinism, valuable because it showed a way of interpreting both the queernesses and the sublimities of the human psyche by the scientific method of empirical examination and investigation. The goal-directed quality of human activity attained scientific status as a premise and as a focus of investigation—with recognition of hidden (unconscious) goals as a necessary part of any psychology, and with emphasis on early childhood as the period when the major directions of the personality are set.

The Unconscious Processes

The promissory note mentioned earlier is honored at this point. The following discussion is drawn mainly from Freud, but all psychoanalytic schools make constant use of the principles and procedures here presented. I will, so far as possible, arbitrarily eliminate considerations of deep psychological dynamics and confine discussion to the technical problem of *how* the operations of the unconscious can be observed and interpreted.

By definition the operations of the unconscious cannot be directly discovered by introspection. The person is not aware of his unconscious drives—a tautology of some value in view of the scientist's very frequent repudiation of psychoanalytic interpretations of motivation on the grounds of his inability, expressed sincerely and in all good will, to remember or feel any of the things attributed to him by psychoanalytic theory. This repudiation is profoundly true whether he is asked to remember his Oedipal attachments *à la* Freud or to feel the violent hostility which makes him extra tender *à la* Horney. The more deeply unconscious the motivation, psychoanalytically speaking, the more obvious it is that the person will *not* be aware of it. In fact—just to prevent such awareness, which would be experienced as threatening—defenses are often built up in the form of militantly *opposite* conscious attitudes.

Freud early distinguished between a *primary process,* whereby the instinctual drives manifest themselves psychologically and a *secondary process,* whereby these drives are ordered and controlled by rational thought and voluntary action.

So far as we know [Freud writes], a psychic apparatus possessing only the primary process does not exist, and is to that extent a theoretical fiction; but this at least is a fact: that the primary processes are present in the apparatus from the beginning, while the secondary processes only take shape gradually, during the course of life, inhibiting and overlaying the primary. . . . (2)

Freud does *not* conceive of an "unconscious mind" as a separate, unchangeable entity somehow inhabiting our mortal flesh. The non-libido analysts would also find such a notion wholly unacceptable. It is mentioned here as a common misinterpretation of psychoanalytic doctrine, understandable because in all psychoanalytic literature conscious and unconscious processes are informally contrasted and goal-directedness is ascribed to each with some separateness —in fact, often with complete antagonism. The popular dichotomy, however, is far too simple.

Freud approaches the concept of *a* timeless unconscious most closely in his emphasis upon relatively focused infantile wishes which become *repressed* and continue in their initial direction the more insistently because they are cut off from normal integration with the emerging secondary processes. They may become elaborated as they attach to themselves the new materials and even the new partial integrations of ongoing experience. Thus, intricate patterns may be formed at the unconscious level which function to some extent as a dynamic unit and which combine in a variety of ways with the secondary processes as they take shape during the course of life.

Adler, and in less measure the other non-libido analysts, prefer to envisage the operations of the unconscious in a much more immediate relationship to problems which begin at birth and are continuously determining throughout life. Modes of coping with them initiated in infancy tend to persist as a life style or safety device in adult situations, where they are no longer appropriate. The underlying problems and the essential nature of the devices employed in attempts at solution are, of course, largely unconscious. The major difference from Freud's view of the unconscious lies in repudiation of the idea that the infantile problems are in any sense split off from the functioning personality as a whole, so as to function in any sense as partially separable dynamic units in the unconscious.

We have noted that for all schools the unconscious is a process—or better, processes—conceived within a dynamic (motivational) theory of human behavior. It is *never* thought of as an isolated entity which can be studied independently of the total personality, according to its own peculiar laws. I insist upon the point with fervor, because the rest of this chapter will be devoted to just such study, *artificially* dissected from its proper context. My reason for the dissection seems sound: every psychoanalytic school today, and many nonpsychoanalytic psychological approaches, constantly use within the constellation of their various dynamic theories the techniques and observations herewith presented. But people who have little direct acquaintance with psychoanalytic procedures often do not understand how the analyst arrives at his conclusions. On the contrary, people unfamiliar with analytic *techniques* tend to evaluate psychoanalytic theories on the basis of their own conscious experience, or to apply scientific checks inappropriately—just as people at one time repudiated theories of radioactivity and electromagnetism because they did not conform to the scientific tenets of the times. Science expands *partly* through the development of new techniques designed to explore new areas. Understanding critique of the new area (here the unconscious processes) depends *partly* on understanding the avenues of information available and something of the nature of the new area.

The purpose of this section is, therefore, mainly to *describe* (1) how information about unconscious processes may be obtained and (2) the characteristics of unconscious processes. Variants in phraseology are used without precision simply in the interest of avoiding stylistic monotony. "The unconscious" must not be considered to imply a distinctly separable entity. The phrase "thought processes" does not imply "thought" rigorously divorced from impulse or emotion. In a section aimed at description of processes which are essentially dynamic, it is not possible to eliminate dynamic concepts altogether, but the dynamic concepts have deliberately been kept vague and secondary. Interpretation has been offered only on terms acceptable to almost everyone, or has been only implied, with the recommendation that the reader carry it further himself with whatever dynamic insights he may have. The point here is merely to suggest *how* psychoanalytic interpretation is reached.

AVENUES OF INFORMATION

Freud grasped early the general principle that the unconscious reveals itself most readily when the rational goal-directedness of our usual activities is abated, either temporarily, as in the small errors and slips of everyday life and in sleep, or in major derangements. Inaccessible to direct observation, the unconscious can be studied through those fragments of behavior which the conscious mind dismisses as silly mistakes and accidents or rationalizes as having a different intent from the one actually operating. Of somewhat late development in Freudian theory, although emphasized from the outset by Adler, is the analysis of extensive systems of behavior (character trends, ostensible vocational goals, deeply held "rational" convictions and aspirations) for their unconscious directives. Thus, the *pattern of behavior* over large sectors of the life span as well as the out-of-key fragments reveals unconscious purpose.

Because inquiry into the unconscious came into scientific prominence via pathology, most of us fail to realize that perfectly normal goals are in large part unconsciously determined. No healthy person lives by a minute-to-minute ordering of his activities and feelings according to a conscious plan rationally determined and executed at all points. His life is mainly ordered unconsciously, as the poets have always known. So long as his unconscious goals are in harmonious relationship with his conscious aims and are pursued according to the canons of reasonableness approved by his society, they are very difficult to discern. Being out of key with consciousness is not a necessary attribute of the unconscious but merely isolates it for study—much as a single voice in a good chorus is hardly perceptible as such unless it is off pitch.

The following pages describe the various ways by which the analyst gains information about the unconscious. Discussion is focused on rather well-codified approaches available to the analyst in his office. They were developed and are still mainly used in therapy. I have, however, suggested extensions currently in use beyond the intimate doctor-patient contact, notably in psychoanalytically oriented study of the life history and in that branch of psychological testing currently known as the projective method.

Free association. Freud's early grasp of the general principle of studying the unconscious under conditions of relaxation of conscious control led to the development of a technique basic to psychoanalysis as a therapeutic method: *free association.* The patient is asked to try deliberately to relax his normal directedness of thinking and speak out everything that comes into his mind— good, bad, or utter twaddle. This request is not an invitation to the subject to confide his innermost thoughts, as many outsiders seem to believe. On the contrary, the analyst usually listens patiently to a confidential outpouring of unseemly thoughts and actions considered top secret, and then begins the real work of psychoanalysis. The patient finally just talks with no idea of revealing or concealing. (Some types of patient find this "fundamental rule of psychoanalysis" extremely difficult.) Occasionally this technique leads to a concrete memory hitherto forgotten, the reinstatement of which has the dramatic consequences cited in the very early cases of cure through recovery of memories in hypnosis. Much more often the free associations cover mere fragments of past events from childhood or more recent years, bits of things read or heard, casual judgments, hopes, feelings, none of which is important in itself. Curiously enough, these unrelated bits and pieces which merely pop into the mind tend to show a theme of their own. They are not truly random but are guided by unconscious preoccupations.

Illustration is difficult because the free associations of any person are highly idiosyncratic, involving happenings and ideas peculiar to his own life, fleetingly alluded to in circumstances which reduce the task of ordered social communication to a minimum. The analyst, if he is to understand the allusions without constant interruption, must eventually become familiar with his patient's acquaintanceship back to the nursery, his literary, musical, and artistic affiliations, his ordinary quirks of phrase and thought. In view of the fact that the average analysis requires five hour-long sessions per week for one to three years, such familiarity with the details of the patient's life is not beyond the compass of the doctor's mind. It is difficult, however, to reproduce a convincing five minutes of free association in illustration without ten pages of annotation. The following is a telescoped reconstruction of a sequence described by an unusually cultured patient (a friend of the author). It is a useful example provided that the reader realizes that the usual analytic free associations contain a much higher proportion of inert ingredients.

The patient begins with a brief report of the previous day—a sort of routine in his analytic sessions. Nothing special: he had a conference with his boss about a going project. He didn't quite like the boss's policy, but it was not too bad and who was he, in the hierarchy of his institution, to contradict the boss? By now this was an old issue in the analysis: did he habitually give in too easily, or did he evaluate correctly the major contours of his job? In any event, the conference was just a conference like any other. He'd had a dream—something about an ironing board, but that was as far as he could go. Associations to ironing board? Well, we have one. "Matter of fact, my wife said our maid irons badly. She could iron my shirts better herself, but I don't think she could and I'm sure she wouldn't. Anyhow, my shirts look all right to me. I wish she wouldn't worry so much. I hope she doesn't fire that maid." The patient suddenly hums a bit from *Lohengrin* and has to hunt for the words on the request of the analyst. It is the passage where Lohengrin reveals his glorious origin. ("My father, Parsifal, wears his crown and I am his knight, Lohengrin.") Patient: "Now I think of that last report X [his boss] turned in. That was *my* work—only I can't say so. That ironing board—my mother was ironing. I jumped off the cupboard, wonderful jump, but I sort of used her behind as support—she was leaning over.

She told father I had been disrespectful and he gave me a licking. I was awfully hurt. I hadn't even thought about her old behind—it was just a wonderful jump. Father would never let me explain. My sister says he was proud of me. He never acted that way. He was awfully strict. I wish he hadn't died when I was so young—we might have worked things out."

It is the task of the analyst to select from this material the themes most worthwhile to pursue at any given period. For us it is enough to observe that the *non sequiturs* of the patient's own job situation (where he did not *consciously* feel threatened), the ironing board, with his wife's attitude toward the maid's job, the enormous self-reassurance of the *Lohengrin* passage, and finally the resurgence of a childhood memory are all closely related.

The process is quite different from the rational consideration: "I am worried about my job, the boss is not such a hotshot as he thinks, and I am sorry for the maid because she seems to be in the same situation." Or perhaps, "My wife is as censorious and unjust as my mother," etc. (The reader will doubtless identify other themes of deeper importance.) On the contrary, the patient would honestly deny any such concerns, at least on the occasion of an ordinary job conference. Indeed, at the time the wife-maid sequence appears, the patient has not remembered the childhood episode and is not aware that he is making more than a passing comment on a trifling domestic incident consciously considered as being outside his own sphere of interest. Far from seeking consolation in the *Lohengrin* saga consciously, he does not even realize what he is humming until the analyst asks him.

This kind of thematically oriented *non*

sequitur occurs daily, five times a week, in any successfully moving analysis. The orderliness of such random thought serves as evidence for the existence of a structuring power in the mind beyond the consciously directed mental process. For more than fifty years analysts have used the technique of free association as a very important avenue of information toward the unconscious problems of the patient—information rather easily shared with the patient himself as he too comes to recognize the underlying themes.

Resistance. Thus far the impression may have been created that such free flow of unconscious material is of perfectly regular occurrence. One may even wonder why analysis takes so long when an intelligent patient could surely see from a dozen sessions the major contours of his unconscious life. The dynamic—and hence therapeutic—aspects of the problem will be considered later. At this point, we shall consider only the fact of *resistance*.

Consciously or unconsciously, the patient often does not see the underlying theme, apparently does not *want* to see it. He may *consciously,* without quite meaning to frustrate his expensive treatment, break off the train of associations when it approaches uncomfortable territory. For example, the patient just cited might so love his wife as to wish to keep their relationship free from the possible misunderstandings of the analyst, himself prejudging the relationship as essentially good and too sacred for prying inquiry. Thoughts concerning his wife may therefore not be reported, with good conscience. Or some ideas may be so offensive to his self-esteem that he does not speak them out. Or he may feel sure that the analyst will misconstrue their meaning. Or he himself may be convinced that they are entirely trivial.

Sometimes the patient's judgment is correct, but at all points he *quite consciously* breaks the fundamental rule of psychoanalysis—to report everything. Such conscious resistance is of no theoretical interest for this chapter—except as special areas of conscious resistance may become indexes of an unconscious *pattern*. The psychoanalyst's task in dealing with it is hardly different from that of the medical doctor whose patient deliberately conceals his symptoms or misrepresents his adherence to the doctor's prescription.

Freud early noted, and all psychoanalysts have confirmed, the fact of *unconscious resistance*. A highly intelligent patient may honestly fail to see connections obvious to a child. For example, our patient may stoutly maintain that the *Lohengrin* passage is a favorite of his because of the lovely music, and that his sudden humming had nothing to do with the words. The patient is sometimes correct in rejecting a particular tie-up suggested by the analyst (analysts are fallible like anyone else), but more often he is wrong, no matter how ingenious his "reasons" for criticism. The patient quoted has engaged in a successful professional life for years, on the basis of a carefully modulated evaluation of himself and his superiors. The sudden incursion of "my father Parsifal" and "I his knight" strikes him quite legitimately as absurd—and in so far as he has been unconsciously toning down his own demands for prestige out of unconscious fear, the interpretation is positively frightening. The *analyst* may see that the patient is actually demanding, unconsciously, an infantile absolute acceptance of his powers with fears which belong to his early relationship with his parents. It is in the highest degree unlikely that in the early stages of analysis the *patient* could effectively recognize as part of his own psyche attitudes at such variance with his whole attitude toward himself and his relations with other people. At any point at which the evidence is overwhelming, he may offer an intellectual acquiescence, but he will remain at first unconvinced as to the general operation in his own life of the trends so acknowledged. Thus, for a long time, the interpretation of every new instance is again resisted in the same manner.

This quasi-reasonable repudiation of the analyst's interpretation is only one of the manifestations of unconscious resistance—actually one of the most subtle and most difficult to disentangle from genuinely reasonable criticism.* Much more obvious is the sudden failure of the free-association sequence. The invitation to talk about anything at all sounds easy. Doubtless there is always something or other in our minds which should be reportable if we do not have to care what it is. Yet every analytic patient reports at times that his mind becomes a complete blank, or that it jumps about like a spoonful of water in hot grease, with so many burning droplets of ideas that any selection feels like a matter of arbitrary, *conscious* choice. The *Lohengrin* tune imposed itself, as it were, when the mind was left relaxed. But how to choose among a dozen pressing ideas which seem somehow simultaneously present when one tries to relax?

Psychoanalysts have observed over and over that such blockage of the asso-

ciational stream typically occurs when topics are approached which the patient unconsciously does not want to have clarified. Each school has its own theories as to *why* such unconscious protectiveness sets in and as to what to do about it, but they all recognize its occurrence. In a way, this readily observable *stoppage* of the associational process is as convincing evidence for the unconscious as the phenomena (described above) that occur when it is moving freely. Provided that blockage does not continue too long, it can be as useful an avenue of information toward specific unconscious content as is free association. If one traces carefully where the breaks occur, one can discern quite clearly the items within the unconscious processes about which the patient is most anxious—that is, most coy, reserved, and protective.

A great many other techniques may be employed by the patient's unconscious in resistance. We shall see later that some patients report the events of the day, dreams, childhood memories, in such a manner as to make them genuinely trifling—that is, with semiconscious control. The associations come freely enough, but only along a familiar track thoroughly sanctioned by the "censor" and hence dynamically insignificant. We may extend the concept of resistance in psychoanalysis somewhat beyond the handling of free association as an isolated technique. The patient may suddenly come late to appointments, forget appointments, make mistakes about payment or protest the amount he has to pay, criticize the analyst's office furnishings, quote derogatory remarks about him sometimes heard months earlier, and so forth. These small unpleasantnesses occur so regularly in any analysis as to be an expected part of the treatment and should be seen in broader context than

---

* Analysts generally handle this problem in practice by a very sparing use of complex interpretations. Usually the analyst *leads the patient to formulate his own interpretations*—by interjecting a question, by suggesting a new juxtaposition of materials presented by the patient, often simply by repeating the patient's own words with slightly different emphasis.

resistance to a specific line of interpretation. They tend to occur specifically, however, when the analysis threatens to uncover unconscious processes that the person cannot tolerate.

We have noted that things become unconscious for a reason important to the personality and are kept unconscious for a reason, and not through inadvertence or ignorance. Resistance, therefore, is an *active* process which serves to maintain the repression in opposition to the new forces, leading toward insight and release, brought into play by the analysis. It is especially important in revealing the nature of the opposing forces. Many analysts nowadays feel that analyzing with the patient the precise nature of his resistances is quite as fruitful as overcoming them in the sense of allowing the repressed materials to appear.

The dream. Next to free association and the related problem of resistance, the avenue of information about the unconscious most generally used in psychoanalysis is the *dream.* Analysts vary widely, even within their school affiliations and from patient to patient, in the amount of attention devoted to the dream in the therapeutic session. Interpretation varies somewhat with the theoretical orientation of the analyst, and there is some difference of opinion as to the role of the dream in the total psychic economy. But these variations within psychoanalysis are trivial in comparison with the overwhelming judgment of all analysts that the dream "has meaning" and is a very important source of information. The variations among analysts will be mentioned where they become appropriate. No further discussion of the dream is offered here because it will be used as a point of departure for our discussion of the characteristics of unconscious thought processes.

The life pattern. Study of the *life pattern* as a source of information about the unconscious was of comparatively late development in psychoanalysis except for the Adlerian school. At the outset Freud was primarily interested in the neurotic symptom as a more or less isolated phenomenon. He observed in some patients an amazing recurrence of the same kind of disastrous "accidents" over an extended sector of the life span—a pattern which he called the *Schicksal,* or "fate," neurosis. These patients seemed pursued by a malign fate. Far from profiting by sad experience, Freud noted, they seemed compelled somehow to repeat the same mistake and unconsciously to call down the same misfortune upon their heads time after time. We shall see that this "repetition compulsion" was one of the observations which led Freud to the formulation of a *death instinct,* essentially destructive in its aim.

Many Freudians and all of the non-libido analysts prefer a different explanation of the same phenomenon, which seems actually more common than Freud at first suggested—indeed, in some measure, it appears to be a general characteristic of neurosis. The explanation preferred by the non-libido analysts (notably Horney) is that so long as the same unconscious problems persist, the neurotic naturally persists in trying to solve them in the neurotic manner characteristic for him. He is not aiming for repetitious disaster, even unconsciously (except as an unconscious need for punishment may be one of his problems). Repetitious disaster is merely an incidental consequence of his continued pursuit of unconscious aims which inevitably get him into trouble. An example familiar to the tabloids is that of the rich man who falls in love with one bleached blonde after another, with mounting alimony expenses. Most of us have had the experience of helping a friend through marital or job difficulties only to find that, through no apparent fault of his own, he encountered similar misfortune in the new situation, although it looked more promising and so different.

Adler pointed out long ago that careful consideration of the life story of an individual could show a kind of coherence attributable to the structuring power of his unconscious goals. Indeed, Adler relied more upon such analysis of the "life style" than upon the specialized techniques thus far described for information about the underlying trends of the patient. At the present time it is probably correct to say that every psychoanalyst of whatever school uses the *pattern* of the patient's behavior over his whole life span to understand and to demonstrate to the patient the nonrational directives of his personality.

The projective method. Akin to the study of the pattern of the patient's life story and everyday behavior is the *projective method of psychological testing,* * which has come into prominence in America within the last ten to twenty years. (It was accepted much earlier in Europe.) It is interesting to note that the two major tests of this nature, the Rorschach and the Thematic Apperception Test, were developed by psychoanalytically oriented psychiatrists (Rorschach and Murray). Psychologists trained in carefully objective, standardized techniques of test construction initially viewed the new method with great suspicion; psychiatrists were unwilling to entrust it to psychologists who lacked training and experience with the kind of judgment required for insight into unconscious trends. Indeed, the tests can be used only by psychologists who understand the special principle on which they are based and who have sufficient background to apply it wisely.

Successful interpretation depends upon appreciation of the *pattern* of the subject's reaction to the test stimuli in infinite variety. No two subjects are exactly the same, as no two daisies are alike; no single test element carries a specific meaning. Rather crude (standardizable) indexes may be used for the identification of gross differences in personality, as a daisy may be readily distinguished from a rhododendron. Such differences are usually so apparent that special testing is unnecessary. The projective method becomes indispensable when a significant differentiation can be made only by examination of *patterns* too intricate for the objective measurement of single trends as prefigured in the well-constructed standardized test.† No one would confuse an elm leaf with a holly leaf, but we may well reflect upon the difficulties of differentiation by separate, isolated measures of length, breadth, serration, etc. Like judgment in the analytic hour, accurate interpretation of these complex, spontaneous test mate-

---

* The test stimulus is made as unstructured, loose, ambiguous, "meaningless" as possible (ink-blots, vague pictures, half-heard sounds, drawings made with minimal directives, etc.), and the subject is asked to tell what it might mean or somehow to take focused action. The meaning and focus are thus introduced by the subject. His unguided choice provides the material used by the examiner in interpretation.

† These abbreviated statements about test construction are, I think, comprehensible to most of the "psychologists" who read this book. The point is dear to my heart because much of my own work in research, teaching, and private practice concerns the projective methods. It is not a *necessary* part of this book, however, and I suggest that any reader who does not understand the terms used here cheerfully disregard all my comments on psychological testing!

rials often depends upon appreciation of the direction and interaction of many small items, any one of which might be interpreted differently in a different context. Like the psychoanalyst, the examining psychologist must learn the language of the unconscious, but he applies it with special reference to the test stimuli.

It is the latter point which differentiates the test from the analytic situation. The analyst offers the patient virtually no specific reality problem and carefully adapts his provocative comment to the current needs of the patient. The test stimuli, however vaguely structured, have more definition—as established by the many subjects who have reacted to them. The essential test criterion of comparing an individual's performance with that of his peers is preserved. Thus, the subject who calls a certain ambiguous figure (Card 3 of the T.A.T.) a *woman* is objectively just as "correct" as the one who sees it as a *man,* but if the examiner knows that the majority of subjects unhesitatingly see this figure as masculine, he is alerted to something special about the subject who calls it a woman or remarks that its sex is not clear. Homosexual trends are one *possibility,* but the examiner will not proffer this explanation unless he finds that the subject deviates at other points as well in a manner characteristic for homosexual identifications. Perhaps the subject is generally a doubting Thomas; perhaps he has special reasons to think of women in shorts.

A doubting Thomas doubts almost all his test judgments. The doubting, overcritical attitude of some persons stands out against the more casual approach of the vast majority of subjects. Furthermore, since any construction the subject may make from the formless test mate-

rials involves tolerance of some inaccuracies, examination of the *pattern of criticism* becomes revealing. Again the tester has the advantage of knowing which inaccuracies are usually tolerated and is impressed when the subject strains at an inaccuracy most people consider a gnat and swallows a number of camels, sometimes of his own invention.

The response determined by an idiosyncratic experience of the subject usually sticks out *as such.* It may be dismissed as an incidental, unusable item. Occasionally it is so distinctive that the examiner can make a very sharp guess about the nature of the experience, especially if he knows the language of unconscious symbols. Such guesses may seem like black magic, and they are relatively rare in test interpretation. They are more than guesses only when the tester is so well acquainted with the test situation and with psychodynamics that he can appreciate the significance of the response which is idiosyncratic in the test setting.

Summary. In partial summary we may say that free association, resistance, dreams, and the life pattern are used routinely by all psychoanalysts (with some variation) in their effort to understand the unconscious processes operating in their patients. The projective method of psychological testing was a relatively late development based on the same principles, with the added feature of enabling the interpreter to compare the "unconscious" response of one person with the "unconscious" response of his peers in the test situation.

A number of other avenues of information are also available: memories recaptured under hypnosis or drugs; the influence of traumatic states, accidental or induced, on the emotionality of the patient and hence, often, on his accessibility to therapeutic intervention; his bodily reactions (motility, including but going beyond facial expression, vasomotor changes seen grossly as flushing or blanching, variations in timbre of voice or tempo of speech beyond what the words communicate). There are in addition a host of cues which psychiatrists are only beginning to order scientifically, although such cues may doubtless be perceived in any sensitive interpersonal contacts. These avenues of information are omitted from discussion here because at present they are merely lanes used by relatively few psychoanalysts. Probably they will never be accepted at the same level as the current verbalistic modes of expression for the excellent reason that the language of the body is less differentiated than speech. As the *adjunctive* value of these subsidiary avenues becomes clarified, one may prophesy developments far beyond their current status. For patients (or cultures) whose difficulties in verbal exchange are almost insuperable, they may become the main avenue of information. Their neglect here should be seen in historical perspective, and in the perspective of the major therapeutic aims of psychoanalysis.

CHARACTERISTICS OF UNCONSCIOUS THOUGHT PROCESSES

Critics of psychoanalysis often complain not only that they cannot observe in themselves the motivations and feelings ascribed to the unconscious but that psychoanalysts resort to fantastically farfetched arguments in support of their position. The rational man is not easily impressed by a pun offered in sober scientific proof or by the solemn statement that a particular item must be true because it is so vehemently denied. Yet if the reader has been able to follow with any sympathy the foregoing discussion of avenues of information about the unconscious, he has already demonstrated a measure of understanding of peculiar ("unconscious") modes of thought and behavior which nevertheless have a kind of coherence in their very peculiarity.

Freud was deeply interested in this peculiar coherence from the outset of his work with the unconscious. He describes himself with some justice as a man concentrated rather narrowly on scientific matters. He approached the scientific problem as a doctor concerned with finding a cure for hysteria, as a reflective man (he has been called the last of the great philosophers) concerned with universal meanings. Nevertheless, he found time during the early years to write four long books and numerous papers on trivial and peripheral matters: *The Interpretation of Dreams, The Psychopathology of Everyday Life, Wit and Its Relation to the Unconscious, Totem and Taboo.* During this same period he was writing *Three Contributions to a Theory of Sex* and other papers of definitely clinical or metapsychological nature. Why did a "narrowly scientific" man trouble himself with the small mishaps of trivial social situations, with jokes, with remote savages, at a time when interest in these matters among psychologists was far less common than it is today?

Freud's major purpose in these books was to clarify how the unconscious operates, not only in disease, but also in many aspects of normal living. His important dynamic concepts concerning the nature of instincts and the complex adjustive mechanisms of the personality as a whole are brought into the discussion only toward the end of each of these works. Through hundreds of pages Freud merely traces the regularities observable in the primary process, the techniques of expression characteristic of the unconscious. His observations have long been freely used by everyone who works with unconscious materials, no matter how divergent the motivational theory finally used in interpretation.

The Interpretation of Dreams (1900) is by far the most useful book in this series—and the most systematic. Chapter 7, "The Psychology of the Dream Processes," remains the most inclusive statement of the dynamics of thinking in Freud's work. Freud himself said of this book that it represented a discovery so great as to be given to a man to make only once in a lifetime. The discovery was not merely of the importance of the dream process, but actually of the orderliness and significance of all the irrational aspects of psychic life. It was the gift of a new language—the paving of a highroad into a wilderness whose very existence had been unknown to science.

I have chosen the dream as the point of departure for my exposition of the techniques of the unconscious partly because it was the focus of Freud's most systematic analysis but also because the reasons behind Freud's choice are still cogent. All analysts use the dream in therapy. We all dream, and the conditions of our dreaming are roughly similar throughout the world—*i.e.,* we are asleep, and for the nonce relieved of responsibility for direct action in a social world. Therefore, it is comparatively easy to understand the peculiarities of the dream as contrasted with consciously directed thought, regardless of special background and knowledge on the part of either the dreamer or the interpreter. Our special background always plays a role in our dreaming, as we shall see, but the essential language of the dream seems to be much more universally human than the language of our waking hours,

which is always carefully adapted to the small daily requirements of our quite special role in our quite special social group.

The role of dreaming. *The Interpretation of Dreams* will be used, then, to present in some detail a description of the language of the unconscious, with the understanding that the dream is only one instance of processes readily observable elsewhere. At the risk of tedious protraction, I would like to preserve Freud's essential comments on the place of the dream in the total economy of mental life as a vivid illustration of the caution required in *any* interpretation of the unconscious. The primary process never appears as an isolated phenomenon. Indeed, we can see it only through characteristic distortions of the secondary process under certain conditions. There are always, of course, varying admixtures of stimuli and judgments proper to "rational" thought. When one is thirsty, it is not entirely rational to dream of a bubbling brook instead of getting up for a glass of water, but all the ingredients of common-sense response to a strong stimulus are present, and not even Freud finds this kind of dream very useful as an expression of perduring unconscious trends. In 1900 Freud was more concerned than need be reported here with theories of the dream proposed prior to his own discovery. He stated that he found little to *reject* in these theories beyond a dogmatic claim to all-sufficient explanation. What will be reported here (unfortunately too briefly for historical acknowledgment) are the outlines of Freud's placement of dream processes *of all sorts* within a dynamic psychology which relates primary and secondary modes of thought.

In sleep the conscious mind is *relatively* inactive, mainly because it is released from its reality-testing functions and from immediate responsibility for the execution of its decisions. The motorium is almost entirely excluded from participation in the psychic life, the sensorium drastically limited. Thus, the inward intellective and affective processes continuously operative have relatively free play without the usual corrective controls of immediate physical and social contacts. Consequently, as in free association, structuring by unconscious "wishes" is much more obvious, once one learns to understand the curious language in which they find expression.

It should not be thought that the unconscious expresses its wishes or goals openly, even in sleep. Very few dreams show their meaning directly. Children's dreams may show such directedness before the psyche has become intricately organized. What Freud called "dreams of convenience"—as when we dream of a stream of refreshing water after a midnight snack of salty food, or when the intern awake most of the night on an emergency case reacts to the morning alarm clock with the dream that he has gone to the hospital on schedule, while still remaining cozily in bed—may also require no great subtlety of interpretation.

Somewhat akin to this very direct representation of a current reality need which penetrates sleep is the continuation or repetition of a waking process in sleep or near-sleep. Poincaré, for example, reports the correct solution of an abstruse mathematical problem during the night. The victim of traumatic neurosis often relives quite literally in his dreams the original shocking experience. But more often the dream process translates the cogent activity of the day into concrete "symbols" and provides only an illusory solution, if any. Mental labor may appear as the sawing of endless blocks of wood, and the dream solution of a fantastic gadget for getting through with the task more quickly does not prove practical when applied to the real, mental task.

From these "easy" symbolizations one may learn one of the important tricks of the dream process cited by many students of the dream even outside the psychoanalytic camp: the concretization of an abstract problem, usually in visual terms.

An experience of my own in a hypnogogic state close to full dreaming may clarify this point. In bed, I was still planning a lecture on Freud to be delivered the next day; specifically, I was planning how to introduce the superego as the product of the child's relationship with the parents and the hostility of this differentiated part of the id to other infantile id demands. Suddenly I realized that I was no longer thinking abstractly. I was simply watching a well-groomed little boy walk upstairs between a nice-looking couple, while another little boy, of the gamin type, dodged about from room to room bent on mischief and occasionally making provocative gestures toward the child walking so decorously with his parents. The analogy to Freud's theory is not good enough to serve in a lecture and was by no means planned as such, but it is clear enough. The little scene is a pretty fair concretization of the abstract ideas with which my conscious mind was concerned at the moment of falling asleep.

Such dreams are comparatively rare in adults and perhaps occur mainly in the half-dream state, in which conscious preoccupations still dictate the contour of the dream. Much more typically, the dream is a highly complex amalgam of unconscious wishes and fears, goals and needs, repressed or carefully controlled during waking life, which find expression *along with* an even more primitive type of resistance than we have thus far discussed. Freud points out that *even in sleep direct expression of wishes is censored* because of the concomitant danger which such expression entails in the infantile unconscious.

Censorship, rooted in fear, is as sleepless as the wish. The rules of censorship change somewhat in sleep, but they are followed rigidly. In fact, if the patient dreams too nakedly, he scares himself into waking up. I remember a horror story on the radio in which a woman who had committed a secret crime could not sleep because a recurrent dream constantly took her to the brink of destruction and she awakened just in time. Her affectionate husband, on medical advice, slipped a soporific into her coffee, and at the appropriate point in her dream she died. This was horror fiction. So far as we know, people do not actually die in their sleep for any such reason—but unconscious fear, according to Freud, operates in a similar manner to waken the sleeper from what he conceives as mortal danger.

Most wishes are repressed (*i.e.,* become unconscious) originally because their fulfillment is considered dangerous by the same childish aspect of the mind which formulated them. The psychic processes continue by night as by day, and one function of the dream is to prevent "mental" excitation from building up to the point at which the only defense is to wake up. Thus, Freud considers a major biological function of the dream to be that of preserving sleep.

Dream materials and the meaning of dreams. However bizarre at first glance, the dream *materials,* its sensorimotor ingredients and memories, are similar to those of waking life. This fact was recognized by scientific students of the dream long before Freud. Current bodily sensations and external stimuli undoubtedly contribute to its formation.

The often-cited "guillotine" dream of Maury is too long to repeat here, but the reader may remember that a coherent drama almost as complex as *A Tale of Two Cities* was precipitated by a slight blow on the neck from which the dreamer awakened almost immediately. The reader is probably familiar with the involuntary muscle jerks which often follow unwonted strenuous physical exercise. For years my dream state produced a rationalization of this jerk as jouncing down a curb in a small wagon —an absurd bit which, under the proper physical conditions, would inject itself without adequate setting into almost any dream. Presumably this dream rationalization harks back to some real experience of affective importance which I have never been able to recover. Together with the long Maury dream, this item shows how the dream work may use *in quite different ways* a sensorimotor stimulus which breaks through the threshold of all-obliterating sleep.

For Freud (and most previous investigators), much more important than such stimuli was the residue of the day's activities. What one has just been doing or thinking tends to crop up in the dream, and many people still seem to feel that a dream has been *explained* when the elements have been identified as somehow present in recent recollection. Freud observed that the dream materials were very likely to come from *childhood* as well as from the quite recent past, with relatively sparse representation of conscious memories in between.

What impressed Freud was that the

dream residue of events current in the life of the patient was so often apparently trivial. After a day filled with important happenings and thoughts, the dream often perversely selects some tiny observation, a phrase from someone's conversation, any trifling bit of nonsense. Freud points out that these fragments seem to gain access to the association process by virtue of their ability to evoke the energy belonging to childhood events, as the current mention of the ironing board in the dream described derived its strength from the early incident.

Even important current attitudes seemed to Freud capable of appearing in the dream only as they related to infantile attitudes (with the possible exception of the repetitive dreams following severe shock). He substantiated his case by the analysis of hundreds of dreams in which a preliminary analysis of some subtlety, revealing current worries or semiconscious conflicts—such as, let us say, our patient's worry about his job and resentment toward his wife in the first aspect of the ironing-board dream—ultimately leads back to the infantile unconscious. Freud felt that the infantile unconscious provided the major dynamics of the dream, could be considered almost as its "cause." The non-libido analysts believe that the childhood material is brought in because it is part of the same unconscious attitude, and that it is *the deeply ingrained attitude* which structures the dream.

Usually the meaning of the dream emerges through the free associations of the patient to its elements. The analyst is often familiar enough with the patient's life to seize upon relationships among events not fully apparent to the patient. (Note the importance of the concept of *pattern.*) Connections may be plain to the analyst which are quite obscure to the patient. A brilliant *tour de force* of this nature is reported by Monroe Meyer. The patient could recall from his dream only the word "Lindbergh" and could produce no associations. He had come for treatment because of a depression. His attitude toward the analyst was challenging; his productions were extremely meager and flat. Although the patient was married, strong homosexual trends were apparent. He had mentioned with his customary detachment that his son had announced his engagement the previous day. The kidnapping of the Lindbergh baby happened to be front-page news at the moment. The analyst quietly asked: "Is your son's fiancée older than he?" The patient confirmed this fact with popeyed astonishment and was probably somewhat more amenable to psychoanalytic treatment thereafter. The analyst, of course, promptly explained his "magical" inference. How was the first news of the kidnapping likely to affect this patient unconsciously to the point of dreaming "Lindbergh"? The *analyst* here made the association between "cradle snatcher," as a term for an older woman marrying a younger man, and the front-page kidnapping; the *analyst* realized that the marriage of the son was likely to affect the patient profoundly.

The illustration is by no means typical of everyday practice, and it should be noted that the analyst introduced his interpretation with an innocent factual question easily dropped if the highly inferential guess had proved wrong. (With a challenging, detached patient a small, concrete demonstration of almost magical insight may be a useful device if employed very sparingly.) In the present context the "Lindbergh" dream is used to illustrate how a single word, clearly a residue from the day's newspaper, represents a highly complex and important psychological configuration, even when the connections are entirely obscure to the patient.

This point brings us now to a formal distinction accepted by all analysts: that between the *manifest dream content*—its actual materials as reported by the dreamer, whatever their origin—and the *latent dream thoughts* which reveal its unconscious meaning. Tracing the origin of the manifest dream materials no more explains the dream for the psychoanalyst than identifying the sounds of speech in the babbling infant explains language. Interpretation depends upon perception of the purposive process underlying the selection of materials. Why, out of all the day's residue was the trivial episode about the ironing board selected? Surely not on grounds of recency, frequency, or vividness, but intelligibly enough in terms of the unconscious themes of the patient's life as suggested also by his free associations. The dream is not thought of as a mysteriously inspired psychic event. What happens is merely that deep-lying goals continuously operative are *differently* and *less drastically* modified by the secondary process during sleep, for the reasons mentioned at the outset of this discussion. Any of the examples used in this chapter show that the *latent dream thought* has a compelling organization beyond the bizarre manifest content of the dream. This organization usually follows unconscious themes. The skeptical reader may be referred to *The Interpretation of Dreams,* which presents a far more careful analysis of many more dreams.

Discerning the *latent* meaning of the dream requires special familiarity with the language of the unconscious and, almost always, supplementary materials, such as the patient's associations, or an intimate knowledge of the patient's experience and way of reacting. It requires a dynamic theoretical orientation—that is, a capacity to perceive patterns from a few disjointed fragments.

Overdetermination. One more general principle must be presented before we can come to the long-promised discussion of interpretation: *the principle of overdetermination.* Perhaps *multiple determination* would be a more descriptive term, but overdetermination is the one commonly used by Freudians.

Several different trends, conscious and unconscious, typically operate *simultaneously* to determine a given psychic event. The infantile unconscious, for example, could not gain access to the motorium or any kind of conscious expression unless it could seize upon some currently activated pathway. On the other hand, the current activation might not be sufficient for overt expression even in the dream without reinforcement from the persisting infantile layers. The principle need not be limited to current and infantile materials. Psychoanalysts generally accept the idea that the same event is determined in multiple ways at different levels of psychic function and that it can be interpreted with some coherence at any level.

The example of free association given earlier can serve to illustrate how a number of different themes appear together in the same time span. The principle of overdetermination is important enough to warrant a further example from everyday experience. Why does a boy enlist in the army? (1) His country has a cause to defend. (2) His friends are enlisting. (3) He does not know what else to do vocationally. (4) He is in difficulties with his girl or his parents. (5) He has glamorous illusions about the army. (6)

He responded to the personal appeal of a recruiting officer, or maybe he got drunk, or both. One could continue to list at least a dozen familiar reasons, and it will surprise no one to hear that in a specific case they were *all* operating. We become uneasy only when someone maintains that men enlist *only* for the glory of their country, *only* on the rebound from a love affair, etc. Thus, there is no reason why a limited item should not participate in many systems of psychic events simultaneously and have a different underlying meaning as one looks successively to one system or another for its explanation. A hidebound analyst who insisted that a dream element means one thing and nothing else would be not unlike a recruiting officer who maintained that men enlist for one reason only—and as rare.

The unconscious processes in operation.

Alogic. We may now begin the description of the characteristics of unconscious processes. One characteristic of the unconscious which Freud noted especially was that *diametrically opposite meanings frequently stand side by side. Consciously,* our enlister may join the army to escape paternal authority and then find that the sergeant is even more authoritarian. *Consciously,* he feels he made a sad mistake, although his friends point out that the army is noted for its discipline. Very frequently the fact is that *unconsciously* he wanted *both* freedom and authority and that his enlistment was determined by both wishes simultaneously. The unconscious is not troubled by contradictions. It is completely *non*logical (as logic is considered in the secondary process), every aspect of the unconscious system demanding full and immediate gratification, regard-

less of the rest. Indeed, in the later discussion of dynamics we shall see that, regardless of whether one adopts Freud's concept of reaction formation or Horney's concept of the vicious circle or any of the other dynamic concepts, one comes to the conclusion that opposites are especially likely to appear together in the unconscious processes. The important characterization here, however, is the lack of consideration in the unconscious for those rules of thinking which the conscious mind takes for granted.

An important subdivision of this nonlogical quality of the primary process is its disregard for time. Freud emphasized the timeless quality of the affects and judgments attached to infantile events, which undergo repression and emerge again with pristine freshness, undulled by time, unstaled by custom. The nonlibido analysts protest this concept of the freezing of infantile experience with later "return of the repressed." For them there is a much more constant restructuring of the attitudes proceeding from infantile events in the course of later experience. But for them, too, the unconscious is, in a sense, timeless. Grief over the death of one's child may appear in the same dream sequence as the destruction of one's doll at the age of five, and the childhood event helps to explain the special flavor of the present event. By no analytic theory is mature grief to be simply equated with a broken doll, but in every analytic study of the unconscious, as in poetry, time as such plays a very small role—time as rationally demarcated, that is. Old events, old attitudes are as immediately present in the dream as things that happened yesterday. The time sequence of the dream (or of any other unconscious expression) does not follow a calendar. When the creative artist interweaves present and

past in building up the mood or message of his creation, he uses a technique present in the unconscious processes of all of us, but he selects from the array of items those that are relevant to a particular mood and are more generally evocative.

The unconscious also disregards the exigencies of space. The dream transfers us from Europe to America without so much as a by-your-leave. Two objects may occupy the same space at the same time, or, rather, the same object often somehow *is* two things simultaneously, without even the brief temporal transformation of baby into pig as observed by Alice. Size relationships and plausibilities of locale are often neglected. A patient who had just undergone an abdominal operation fell into a morphine-induced sleep after reading a novel in which two young people were searching desperately for the tombstone of their mother. She awoke with the conviction that they would not find it because it was in her own stomach, and that she should get out of bed and let them know. Amusingly enough, she finally rationalized staying in bed on the ground that the tombstone in her stomach could not be the proper one because her operation had taken place after the publication of the book. The patent absurdity of the space relationship, not to mention the more complex incongruities, did not occur to her until the following day.

An early reader of this manuscript suggests the following example of such absurdities in waking life. "I have caught myself thinking somewhat similar nonsense on occasion, for a fraction of a second, before having time to discard it. Most recent: We sit in a diner, our baby on my lap. I hear a dish breaking behind the counter and wonder for a moment how our baby managed to break something that far away. Then I tell my wife the silly idea that had just occurred to me and we both laugh."

Spatial distortion is a common effect of some drugs and of some organic conditions (*e.g.,* encephalitis). Children—even though they are able to match shapes and sizes very competently on an intelligence test—not infrequently fear that they will slip down the drain when the water is going out of the bathtub, or that a huge animal will spring out of the toilet bowl. Such basic misconceptions are very common also in the thinking of adult psychotics—indeed, they may be used in the differential diagnosis between psychosis and severe neurosis. An extreme example is the woman who screamed with pain when she saw a trolley car a block away because it was "running over [her] stomach." Radical indifference to ordinary evaluations of time and space is by no means peculiar to the dream, nor is it of any great importance in dream interpretation. It is characteristic of any condition where conscious control is in abeyance. It belongs to the primary process.

Since many of the illustrations of unconscious processes given in this book will seem very close to ordinary ways of thought, it is well to recognize clearly the fundamental alogic of the unconscious connections as such and the absence of the most primitive attention to the requirements of external reality. Such recognition will prevent many unjustified criticisms of psychoanalytic interpretations as "far-fetched" or "impossible." The unconscious recognizes no impossibles. In so far as its associations are not guided by the *learned* processes of adaptation to everyday reality and the rules of thinking more or less elaborately developed in any culture (the secondary process), its conclusions can be more

fantastic than any the adult mind can imagine. Only with a full understanding of this principle can we begin to read the cryptography of those partially rationalized fragments made available to us in dreams and other avenues of information.

Dramatization; imagery; use of words. Ideals and affects are very often *dramatized*—that is, cast in loose narrative form with mainly *visual* imagery. The semi-dream cited earlier, in which two little boys represented the dynamics of the id and the superego, can serve again as illustration of a process so general that most of us think of a dream as a story. Such dramatization, however, is not *necessary* to the dream, as in the very succinct dream statement quoted: "Lindbergh." Freud observed that a phrase remembered on waking as having been spoken (*i.e.,* definitely *heard* as such rather than loosely imagined in the dialogue of the story) very often carries special unconscious significance. The same is true of odd proper names, numbers—probably any vivid peculiarity in the typical dream process. I remember a long dream of my own in which my analyst took me on a yacht—a dream crowded with the problems and trends we had been discussing, expressed with very patent symbolism. The analyst put it through the usual paces with no great enthusiasm—whereas *I* thought it was a remarkably useful dream. Finally he asked: "What was the name of that yacht, again?" I repeated the name—*Newland,* which I accented like the word *England.* It was not until he remarked that this was the part of the dream he liked best that the obvious words *new land* struck me, and that it even occurred to me that the name of the yacht was unusual. Actually, it looked as though the dream story as a whole was merely a rehash in dream language of points already discussed in analysis and intellectually accepted, whereas the important item was the obviously unconscious shift away from a pessimistic absorption in the past to an incipient hopefulness.

The illustration points to another characteristic of most dreams: their *verbalistic* quality, with ambiguous use of word meanings. The dream is an arrant punster. The primary process has no such settled notions as the conscious mind about the proper realm of discourse of any word, or any great respect for its format. Reik (6) reports a dream in which the recurrent and apparently irrelevant auditory phrase "I am afraid of the dog" resisted all efforts at analysis along lines of canine associations but yielded at once to the transposition of dog into God. Although brought up in a strongly religious family, and himself strongly religious in early adolescence, the patient had later adopted a contemptuous atheism. The dream phrase made very good sense wherever it occurred once it was seen as a continuing fear of the Lord with deep unconscious roots, plus the later contempt.

Condensation. Dreams very often have a knack of *condensing* or telescoping complex ideas into a word, a phrase, a brief scene or story which would do credit to the greatest wit. Freud discusses this characteristic at length in *Wit and Its Relation to the Unconscious.* These attributes of the dream work (the unconscious) are just as strange to waking experience as the juxtapositions in space and time, which find their analogue in poetry. Indeed, poetry also constantly uses words in contexts that would be absurd or repellent if given full literal meaning. A teetotaller relishes Homer's phrase "the wine-dark sea," and no one is so besotted as to wish that the sea

were actually made of wine. To be thoroughly literal, wine comes in a variety of colors, so one may well argue that the phrase has no sensible meaning at all. "Wine-dark" is more poetic than "purple" or "reddish" because of the inspiriting connotations of wine in human history, which go far beyond the dictionary definitions or even our personal experience with the drink. The adjective brings the ocean into the sphere of human feeling as vividly as Proteus rising from the sea or Triton blowing his wreathed horn in Wordsworth's sonnet.

The phrase "I am afraid of the dog" is not likely to strike the rest of us as either wit or poetry. But as an expression of three separate important trends in the patient's personality it is a marvel of condensation and telescoping. He is afraid of God; he conceals his fear; he is contemptuous. The setting of the phrase in the dream yields still further information about the origin and role of "God" in the patient's psyche.

Displacement, devaluation, substitution. Other very common mechanisms in the dream, and in other manifestations of the primary process, are the phenomena of *displacement, devaluation,* and *substitution.* Very often—indeed, typically—the real focus of the dream appears as a quite incidental element, and the apparent psychic intensity falls elsewhere. The major purpose of this lack of proper proportion, this *displacement* of affect, seems to be the familiar one of avoiding censorship. Appropriate feeling directly expressed would excite the dreamer to the waking point. The same intensity expressed about some sanctioned or trivial matter can be tolerated.

My dream about the yacht *Newland* is as good an illustration as I can think of for relatively pure displacement (usu-

ally some *substitution* is intrinsic to the process) and offers a good review of the process of censorship and resistance. The analyst fastened on this quite incidental item, and I failed to notice anything odd about the name at first, even when he singled it out for attention. A little more background is necessary to understand why a dream thought so agreeable should undergo censorship and arouse resistance. I had entered treatment in a state of mild depression following the death of a dearly loved person. Anyone will recognize the formulation of the bereaved: life is empty; I can never be happy again; I cannot form new attachments; I cannot really care about anything. Mourning quite generally involves impulses of clamping down on renewed expansiveness—sporadic and transitory in most cases, very troublesome to many of us. Thus it had actually been easier for me, as patient, to recognize a number of trends ordinarily censorable than to accept a growing optimistic, outgoing, energetic outlook. In the dream this feature was well concealed by its *triviality,* and the sense of well being was ascribed to trends which, to be sure, are generally considered censorable, but which had been given sanction during the treatment.

Akin to displacement in the pure sense is the technique of *devaluation:* the censorable situation is presented more or less directly, but the dreamer is quite casual about it. A rather prudish woman, for example, commented that her unconscious must be unusually free because she often dreamed of finding herself in her chemise, barefoot, or even naked on public occasions with no more than a feeling that her habiliments were in poor taste—whereas many people report feelings of severe shock in dreams involving nudity. A surgeon somewhat inclined to

worry told of similar "casual" dreams in which, although the patient died under his knife, he was distressed only by some minor point of operating-room etiquette. He even came to worry about whether his dreams represented a genuine lack of human concern. He wondered whether his conscious worries about his patients were a mere disguise for neurotic compulsiveness.

The actual dynamics behind such dreams are too complex to discuss here, but it is safe to say that the woman is not "free" and the surgeon is not indifferent to the fate of his patients. Such dreams can occur only when the obvious meaning has been somehow devalued for the time being. It is as if the dreamer said to himself, "Look here, these things are not really so dangerous; they don't matter to me a whit," and could thus allow quite open expression.

It is difficult to find illustrations for displacement and devaluation in pure form, because typically they appear through the further mechanism of *substitution*. The displacement is accomplished by substituting a different person or thing for the censorable object. An important dream thought is devalued by translating it into some trivial circumstance, representing it by its opposite, and so on. A death wish toward the father may be represented by dreaming of his going on a journey; the analyst may be portrayed as a strange man whose only similarity to the analyst is a pointed beard; the envied scientific work of a colleague may appear as a pamphlet criticized by the father in the dreamer's childhood. A patient, after a bitter quarrel with his father about his future career, dreamed of visiting some queer, gigantic ruins. A mole scuttled out of the ground and laughed at him. (Like Hamlet's query to his father's ghost: "Dost work

i' the ground so fast, old mole?") Almost any dream contains such substitutions and is subject to analysis only as the true object and attitude are clarified.

The substitution apparently takes place along the lines familiar to the old associationist psychology—by contiguity or similarity, provided these principles are broadly construed. Any aspect of an object or event can stand for the whole thing; any similarity will serve; any chance simultaneity of events, even in the remote past; even any opposite. The line of association may be concrete, highly abstract, or purely verbal. A neat illustration is given by Freud from one of his own dreams (though in a different connection). He had reacted resentfully to the criticism of an eminent scientific friend by a younger man; the same night he dreamed that Goethe attacked another young man of his acquaintance. Here there is an analogy with the eminence of Goethe, the substitution of another young man, and a reversal of the real situation which obviously supplied the material for the manifest dream content.

Such displacements and substitutions occur constantly in waking life as well. Probably many of our feelings of attraction or repulsion for new acquaintances are due to some quite incidental similarity to significant persons of our past whom we loved or hated, often a similarity of which we are quite unaware. We take an instant dislike to Mr. Smith because his hearty manner *unconsciously* reminds us of Uncle Henry, who so often embarrassed and disappointed us in our childhood. A friend who had almost consciously selected as husband a man who was temperamentally the exact opposite of a "hated" father came to realize in analysis that she was *also* powerfully drawn to him because he was in some

ways physically *like* her father. She came to remember the exciting awareness of her father's unusually hairy arms when he fondled her as a child, and to recognize some of the excitement and terror of her relations with her husband as connected by displacement with this childhood experience—via the fact that her husband too is unusually hirsute. It would be a mistake to suggest that this woman's marital choice was dictated entirely or even primarily by this small physical likeness of husband and father. But one can understand how she might be powerfully attracted to her husband beyond the many aspects of congeniality with him and rebelliousness toward the father operating concurrently, and how difficulties in sexual relations might arise as the hairy husband reminded her *unconsciously* of the hairy father of her childhood.

Symbolization. One further characteristic of the primary unconscious processes must be mentioned: *the use of symbols.* In a broad sense, any *pars pro toto* may be considered a symbol, any item which *stands for* something else. The mole in the dream reported above is a symbol for the father. As a matter of fact, any word or gesture is a symbol. Exact sciences abound in symbols very carefully developed to stand for extremely complex experience and concepts. *In psychoanalytic parlance,* however, the word *symbol* usually refers to a representation of greater durability than the temporary substitution in a dream, more widely shared with other individuals, but without such rationally delimited universality as the scientific symbol. The word *dawn* for *beginning* is almost as universally understood as *x* for the unknown, but on a rough experiential basis. It does not belong to a codified notational system which can be law-

fully manipulated as such. It derives from an experiential observation common to the entire race. However unprecise, its meaning is clear and can be applied "symbolically" in many situations in which the literal shift from night to day is irrelevant.

Psychoanalytic parlance *usually* requires a further consideration—that the quasi-universal meaning be *repressed.* Thus, "dawn" as a symbol has little interest for the psychoanalyst because its meaning is almost as overt and conventionalized as "beginning." The term *symbol* is reserved for the use of this mechanism in the primary process rather than in the conscious or preconscious. The symbols of everyday life and of science are often called *signs.*

Freud observed that symbols of a more or less universal nature are employed by the dream or other unconscious manifestations, and that they must be interpreted as such apart from the particular associations and experiences of the individual. In *The Interpretation of Dreams,* he comments, with somewhat reluctant appreciation, on Stekel's elaborated development of this idea. Freud cites a number of dreams which can be interpreted adequately only by recognizing the symbolic meaning of many elements. Freud lists Stekel's observations with some emendations of his own. He points out that *sexual* symbols, as uncovered by the psychoanalyst, typically have primitive or censorable implications and are, therefore, not consciously recognized, as is our introductory example of the dawn. It is the *sexual* symbols and a few others related to universal interpersonal experience (mother, father, siblings, etc.) that are usually meant when the Freudian psychoanalyst speaks of *symbolism.*

Freud's uneasiness in the matter lay

in the temptation to *mis*apply symbol interpretation as a sort of sophisticated dream-book approach. In any given dream, an element *may* have this universal significance, or it may have the more idiosyncratic background already described. Or, by the principle of over-determination, it may have *both* implications. In either case, the symbol would be used by the dreamer along the purposive lines which Freud considered basic to sound psychological interpretation. Any routinized application of universal symbolic meanings would tend to destroy the dynamic approach to the understanding of the dream process which Freud correctly viewed as his major discovery.

Jung is the analyst who has carried the idea of universal symbols furthest. At the present time, all analysts work with it to some extent, and so do "psychologists" in their interpretation of projective test materials. Most "psychologists" are hesitant in its application, for the very good reasons suggested by Freud himself (and emphasized by Jung as well). Any sticklike object *may* be a symbolic phallus—or it may be a sticklike object of some quite special concern to the patient in a transitory manner or with particular nonphallic associations of long standing, or it may be something else. It seems overly cautious to blind oneself altogether to symbolic interpretations which enrich the reading of almost any product through which unconscious manifestations reveal themselves. In handling relatively brief samples of such manifestations, however, a high degree of caution is essential for discriminating use of this valuable avenue of information.

The problem of interpreting the unconscious. In somewhat spotty and incomplete fashion, we have reviewed the techniques of the unconscious thought processes (the primary process) in contrast to the more ordered procedures of rational thinking (the secondary process). The reader who has never worked with this kind of material may well wonder how interpretations of these processes can be made with anything like scientific accuracy when every element *may* mean exactly what it seems to mean, or its opposite, or something quite different, by virtue of highly idiosyncratic associations and quasi-universal symbols; when the sequential meaning may be reversed, condensed, telescoped, displaced, devalued; when the material means several different things at once; and when interpretation admittedly requires—and varies with—an underlying theoretical approach on the part of the interpreter. Skeptics have often said that sequential interpretation reflects *merely* the wildcat theoretical bias of the interpreter, and that a child, if asked for his untutored judgments, would chance upon the crazy notions of the analyst.

The latter half of this criticism tends to backfire. Actually, children and the insane very often *do* interpret unconscious materials very much along the lines suggested by the analysts, clearly without sophisticated theoretical bias. Since children and psychotics are much closer to the primary process in their natural living than the careful scientist, the observed truth in the skeptical wisecrack becomes an important independent confirmation. Young children and the insane are too biased by their own limited experience to serve as reliable interpreters for the whole range of unconscious phenomena that comes to the attention of the mature scientist. Nevertheless, their objective judgment of materials within their range, as well as their own spontaneous productions, tend to support Freud's conclusions from dreams, jokes, and the small mistakes of everyday life. "Savages" seem equally clever in "inventing" the ways of thought described by Freud. Dreams of hypnotic subjects who are given the suggestion to dream about a topic unacceptable or disturbing to them in their waking state show distortion along the lines described by Freud.(7)

It should be noted that the psychoanalyst—or the psychologist interpreting materials from projective tests—gradually acquires from the actual experience of interpretation a *sense* for the unconscious processes that cannot be gained from merely reading about them. Reik, in *Listening with the Third Ear,* has described the semi-intuitive approach of the analyst. Not all analysts would agree entirely with so forthright a statement of the doctor's participation, but most of them recognize a measure of identification with the patient—a slipping into his unconscious patterns for the moment—as a valid part of sound interpretation. The analyst is, of course, in a position almost simultaneously to step outside the patient's pattern for purposes of rational review and understanding.

The danger that too personal a relationship with the patient may lead to uncritical distortion by the analyst's own (unconscious) attitudes is recognized by Freudians and is termed "countertransference." The problems of countertransference and of limitations in theoretical insight undoubtedly affect any interpretation. It would be a mistake to claim complete objectivity for work with such fluid data. Yet such "intuitiveness," controlled by careful training and experience with many kinds of patients, allows for a much sounder grasp of the unconscious process than rigid application of rules. The skilled analyst is rarely guilty of de-

ductions from fragmentary data—unlike the amateur who recalls some of Freud's principles and catchy examples and then applies them rigorously.

Accuracy in the interpretation of elements with such slippery meanings is achieved mainly through the context or pattern within which they appear. Four kinds of check in common use may be mentioned:

(1) *The underlying trend is discernible through many types of material, derived from different sources.* It is impossible to illustrate this point by a brief example, because it requires complex analysis of independent sequences, each too involved for compact presentation. Any of Freud's longer analyses of dreams in *The Interpretation of Dreams* will show the curious reader how successive attention to the sources of different elements reveals a constant theme despite the diversity of the background.*

(2) *The latent dream thought or underlying unconscious trend observed in other materials has internal consistency, both as regards content and type of "thinking."*

(3) *It is consistent with what is already known about the patient in analysis.*

(4) *It leads readily to fruitful elabora-*

---

* The psychological tester may regard some aspects of his interpretation of a patient's Rorschach responses as intuitive to the point of fancifulness, but if the same trends appear in the patient's performance on the Thematic Apperception Test or other projective methods, the tester offers a much bolder statement than would be justified by the data available from any one of the tests. Within a single test, as within a single dream, the same trend may reveal itself in different ways which *for the subject* are independent of one another. Slight variations in the use of shading in the Rorschach, in the way movement is projected, in content, etc., often yield quite convincing evidence of a trend *when taken together,* although separately the variations are too slight to carry interpretive weight.

*tion along lines consonant with the grad-
ually emerging understanding of the patient.*

Clearly, all these points are concrete
variations on the theme of interpretation
via the *pattern* of the patient's productions. And in practice they are not easily
separable. As a rule, the pattern is so
plainly visible to the analyst that the introduction of any element atypical for
the patient stands out prominently. It
may be the harbinger of a much desired
and carefully prepared change—like the
yacht *Newland*. It may indicate retro-
gression, or it may merely suggest that
the pattern envisaged at first was oversimplified, if not incorrect.

In the analytic situation, interpretation regularly includes modification and
correction in the light of the total picture presented by the patient, past, present, and *future,* in the sense that a tentative hunch from any small bit of evidence may later be fully confirmed—or
discarded. Thus, although the analyst is
aided by training in such "principles"
as have been briefly described here, his
sense of confidence comes from his grasp
of the on-going dynamics of the patient's
psychic life, where information from different modalities and temporal sequences
together form a reasonably reliable pattern.

In illustration, the dream about the
mole laughing in the ruins may be reviewed from the angle of consistency in
itself and in a wider view of the patient.
The young man himself promptly gave
the association to *Hamlet,* but the point
of interest here is that the analyst would
expect this association from an intellectual urbanite. By itself the mole might
have other meanings, of course, referable either to the habits of the animal or
to specific experiences with it. By the
principle of overdetermination, it is even

likely that several meanings are operating at once. But since the associations
brought to light no special memories
about moles for this patient, the *Hamlet*
reference appeared to be the major determinant. One may fruitfully ask, however, why Hamlet addressed his revered
father as an old mole, and why the line is
so familiar to people of the patient's cultural background. There is more than a
hint of universal symbolism here.

The mole laughs at the dreamer—distinctly un-mole-like behavior, distinctly
appropriate to the father who had ridi-
culed the patient's cherished aspirations.
Furthermore, moles are not usually associated with gigantic ruins. Yet how
poetically consonant this metaphor for
fallen ambitions is with the flavor of the
Hamlet reference. The dream is no random linkage of chance experiences and
ideas. One may note also the emphasis
on *size*—the gigantic ruins; the tiny, sub-
terranean mole. To the simple formulation "My father laughed at me and
ruined my hopes" one may add the vast-
ness of the hopes and the contempt for
the father, with the curious backtwist
that the mole is, after all, triumphant.
The analyst may wonder whether the
problem does not go deeper than a quarrel about work. The dream suggests also
an evaluation of the self of quite heroic
proportions, with an extreme sense of
vulnerability; also, very ambivalent attitudes toward the father. The introduction of *Hamlet* into the structure of the
dream work on the reality problem of
the previous day suggests a possible
identification with the melancholy Dane
beyond this single reference, which might
further clarify the deeper intention of the
dream.

None of these elaborations would be a
thoroughly defensible conclusion from
the short dream taken by itself. When

they fit the pattern of the patient's attitudes as earlier observed from other dreams and materials, the analyst feels increasingly sure of his interpretation. Many straws determine the direction of the wind with a good deal of certainty.

The reaction of the patient to the analyst's interpretative comment also helps to confirm or correct it. Mere acquiescence in its general plausibility, such as I hopefully expect from the reader, is of no great value in treatment. Of greater therapeutic importance is the patient's sense of revelation, accompanied by release of further confirmatory material, usually emotionally toned, when the interpretation hits home sharply. Or there may be unduly sharp resistance on some points, quite different in tone from the relatively neutral pros and cons the reader may adduce in intellectual consideration of somebody else's dream. This, too, may offer confirmation— where it fits a pattern. For example, the patient may bitterly protest the attitude of contempt for the father suggested by the mole. The *bitterness* of the protest— or it may be the amount of time devoted to it—will paradoxically confirm the truth of the interpretation—especially if the patient has repeatedly overreacted to interpretation along these lines.

No analyst would doubt that this dream refers, at least in part, to the father and to the vocational aspirations of the son. Every analyst would be impressed by the difference in size, by the reference to Hamlet, etc. The Adlerian would probably concentrate on the inflated goals of the son; the Freudian would probably want, eventually, to concentrate on the relationship of son to father in its Oedipal origins and meanings; and so through the other schools. It is at this point that the bias of the analyst's theoretical approach enters the picture. Very probably, a dozen analysts would give a dozen different interpretations, *if they could be persuaded to undertake interpretation of an isolated dream at all*—which is very unlikely in view of their insistence on the importance of seeing the dream and associations to it within the ongoing pattern of the patient's reactions in analysis as viewed from many angles. (Parenthetically, I remind the reader again that I have written at length about the dream only because it offers a relatively clear example of the characteristics of the unconscious processes, not because it is in any sense unique in this respect.)

Very likely, variations in interpretation would occur *mainly* along lines of the theories espoused by the different psychoanalytic schools, but undoubtedly some "Freudians" would be closer to some "non-libido" analysts, as here differentiated, than to what I may call *orthodox* Freud—that is, to points of view which Freud himself modified but which are sacrosanct to some of his early disciples and to some people trained under them. (I have used the adjective "classical" for Freudians who keep to Freud's major emphases in a more flexible manner.) There would be intraschool variation, due either to subdivisions within schools or to the special proclivities of the analyst as a person.

So far as the *patient* is concerned, the variations from school to school are more a matter of emphasis than of sharp contrast. In all schools, the analyst makes every effort *not* to impose a theoretical interpretation. In fact, overintellectualization is generally recognized as a hindrance in therapy. The problem is to help the patient become aware of aspects of attitudes and feelings that he has in one way or another shut off from the major flexibly integrative powers of his personality (very roughly, from "consciousness"). In their books and papers, psychoanalysts of different schools offer elaborate and contradictory interpretations. But in treating the patient, "interpretation" usually consists of no more than a pointed question (*e.g.,* my own analyst: "What was the name of that yacht?"), a pregnant silence, a striking parallel from the patient's own account of his action in other situations, etc., etc., with *occasionally* a brief, trenchant comment of a summarizing nature. Thus, in treatment it is mainly the *patient* who does the "theorizing," if he is so inclined, on the basis of quite fragmentary remarks from the analyst. He develops "insight" in his own way, not by applying textbook "rules."

The more I have studied carefully the theories of the various psychoanalytic schools, and the more I have inquired about what analysts really do in practice (listening to many sources, and at times myself offering the pointed questions, etc., like the properly trained interviewer, although much more informally), the more I have felt I understood why *all* psychoanalytic schools have so many successes—and all of them some failures. They all deal with *essentially* the same basic trends and patterns, regardless of their specific theoretical systematization, and they all *essentially* see their job as helping the patient to understand himself through the peculiar resources of the analytic session. The theoretical aura attached to a specific unconscious manifestation does not greatly affect the quality of the *patient's* insight, in a treatment designed to help the patient help himself. *Occasionally* the major problems of a patient are strongly focused about a point a special analytic school is not well equipped to understand. Such cases offer the spectacular examples of cure by one school after failure by another that are so often quoted in every camp. In my observation there is not so great a preponderance of spectacular cures by any one school as to constitute proof of the superiority of its special theory.

Summary

Four basic concepts are accepted by all schools of psychoanalysis: psychological determinism, "the unconscious," goal-directedness, a genetic approach. By his observation of the structuring power of unconscious motives, Freud extended scientific ordering of data to aspects of human function that had previously been considered "accidental" or that had been wrongly attributed to limited rational or instinctual forces. By emphasis on the importance of early experience, he suggested a dynamic origin for attributes of the human psyche that had previously been considered descriptively and statically as faculties prefigured in the species.

The bulk of this chapter was devoted to a description of the avenues of information toward "the unconscious" available to the psychoanalyst, and to a discussion of its outstanding characteristics.

References

1. S. FREUD, *The Interpretation of Dreams* and *Psychopathology of Everyday Life,* both in *The Basic Writings of Sigmund Freud,* Random House, Modern Library, 1938.

2. ——, *The Interpretation of Dreams,* p. 536.

3. P. BLOS, *The Adolescent Personality,* Appleton-Century, 1941. L. B. Murphy and H. Ladd, *Emotional Factors in Learning,* Columbia University Press, 1944. I. E. Bender

et al., Motivation and Visual Factors, Dartmouth College Publications, 1942. R. L. Munroe, *Teaching the Individual,* Columbia University Press, 1942.

4. H. SILBERER, "Report on a Method of Eliciting Certain Symbolic Hallucination-Phenomena," in D. Rapaport (ed.), *Organization and Pathology of Thought,* Columbia University Press, 1951, pp. 195–207; "On Symbol-formation," *loc. cit.,* pp. 208–233.

5. S. FREUD, *The Interpretation of Dreams,* in *The Complete Psychological Works of Sigmund Freud,* London: Hogarth Press, 1953, IV, Chap. 1.

6. T. REIK, *Listening with the Third Ear,* Farrar, Straus & Co., 1948, p. 338.

7. M. NACHMANSOHN, "Concerning Experimentally Produced Dreams," in D. Rapaport, *loc. cit.,* pp. 257–287. G. Roffenstein, "Experiments on Symbolization in Dreams," *loc. cit.,* pp. 249–256. K. Schroetter, "Experimental Dreams," *loc. cit.,* pp. 234–248.

THE TREND IN MOTIVATIONAL THEORY

Gordon W. Allport

Motivational theory today seems to be turning a corner in the road of scientific progress. In attempting to characterize this change in direction I wish to pay special attention to the problem of psychodiagnostic methods. For the successes and failures of these methods can teach us much about psychodynamic theory.

Let us start by asking why projective methods are so popular in both diagnostic practice and research. The answer, I think, is to be found in the history of motivational theory during the past century. All of the major influences have pressed in a single direction. Schopenhauer, with his doctrine of the primacy of the blind will, had little respect for the rationalizations invented by the individual's intellect to account for his conduct. Motives, he was sure, could not be taken at their face value. Darwin followed with his similar anti-intellectual emphasis on primordial struggle. McDougall refined the Darwinian stress on instinct, retaining in his horme the flavor

Reprinted by permission of the journal and author from *The American Journal of Ortho-psychiatry,* Vol. 23, 1953.

of Schopenhauer's will, Darwin's struggle for survival, Bergson's *élan,* and Freud's libido. All these writers were irrationalists—confident that underlying genotypes in motivation should be sought rather than the surface phenotypes. All of them were reacting against the naïve intellectualism of their predecessors and against the rationalizations offered by self-justifying mortals when called on to account for their conduct. Among these irrationalists who have dominated western psychology for the past century Freud, of course, has been the leading figure. He, like the others, correctly perceived that the mainsprings of conduct may be hidden from the searchlight of consciousness.

In addition to irrationalism modern dynamic psychology has developed another earmark: geneticism. The original instincts laid down in our nature are regarded as decisive, or if not, then the experiences of early childhood are held to be crucial. At this point, the leading nondynamic school of thought, stimulus-response psychology, joins forces with geneticism. Stimulus-response theorists agree with instinct psychologists and psychoanalysts in viewing adult motives as conditioned, reinforced, sublimated, or otherwise elaborated editions of instincts, drives, or of an id whose structure, Freud said, "never changes."

Not one of these dominating theories of motivation allows for an essential transformation of motives in the course of life. McDougall explicitly denied the possibility; for our motivational structure is laid down once and for all in our equipment of instincts. New objects may become attached to an instinct through learning, but the motive power is always the same. Freud's position was essentially identical. The concept of "sublimation" and of shifting object "cathexis" chiefly accounted for whatever apparent alterations occur. Stimulus-response psychology is likewise geared to the assumption of remote control operating out of the past. We respond only to objects that have been associated with primary drives in the past, and we do so only in proportion to the degree that our responses have been rewarded or gratified in the past. From the stimulus-response point of view the individual can hardly be said to be *trying* to do anything at all. He is simply *responding* with a complex array of habits that somehow were rewarded year before last. The prevailing dictum that motivation is always a matter of "tension reduction" or of "seeking equilibrium" is consistent with this point of view, but scarcely consistent, I think, with all the known facts.

This prevailing atmosphere of theory has engendered a kind of contempt for the "psychic surface" of life. The individual's conscious report is rejected as untrustworthy, and the contemporary thrust of his motives is disregarded in favor of a backward tracing of his conduct to earlier formative stages. The individual loses his right to be believed. And while he is busy leading his life in the present with a forward thrust into the future, most psychologists have become busy tracing it backward into the past.

It is now easy to understand why the special methods invented by Jung (forty years ago), Rorschach (thirty years ago) and Murray (twenty years ago) were seized upon with enthusiasm by psychodiagnosticians. At no point do these methods ask the subject what his interests are, what he wants to do, or what he is trying to do. Nor do the methods ask directly concerning the subject's relation to his parents or to authority figures. They infer this relationship entirely by assumed identifications. So popular is this indirect, undercover approach to motivation that many clinicians and many university centers spend far more time on this type of diagnostic method than on any other.

Occasionally, however, a client may cause the projective tester consternation by intruding his unwanted conscious report. The story is told of a patient who remarked that a Rorschach card made him think of sexual relations. The clinician, thinking to tap a buried complex, asked him why. "Oh, because," said the patient, "I think of sexual relations all the time anyway." The clinician scarcely needed a Rorschach card to find out this motivational fact.

Still it is probably true that most psychologists prefer to assess a person's needs and conflicts by going the long way around. The argument, of course, is that everyone, even a neurotic, will accommodate himself fairly well to the demands placed upon him by reality. Only in an unstructured projection situation will he reveal his anxieties and unmasked needs. "Projective tests," writes Stagner, "are more useful than reality situations for diagnostic purposes" (16). To my mind this uncompromising statement seems to mark the culmination of a century-long era of irrationalism, and therefore of distrust. Has the subject no right to be believed?

Fortunately, the extensive use of projective methods at the present time is yielding results that enable us to place this technique in proper perspective, and to correct the one-sided theory of motivation upon which their popularity rests.

Let us consider first the wartime research conducted with 36 conscientious objectors who lived for six months on a semistarvation diet (5). Their diet was so rigorously meager that on the average they lost one quarter of their initial body weight in the course of the six months. The food need was agonizingly great; their incessant hunger most poignant. Unless occupied with laboratory or other tasks they found themselves thinking of food almost constantly. Typical daydreaming is reported by one subject as follows: "Today we'll have Menu No. 1. Gee, that's the smallest menu, it seems. How shall I fix the potatoes? If I use my spoon to eat them I'll be able to add more water. . . . If I eat a little faster the food would stay warm longer —and I like it warm. But then it's gone so quickly." Now the curious thing is that while these men were clearly obsessed by their food drive, and all their energy seemed directed toward its fulfillment, yet on projective tests the need failed to appear. The investigators report that among the tests used (free word association, first letters test, analysis of dreams, Rorschach, and Rosenzweig's P-F Study) only one gave a limited evidence of the preoccupation with food, viz., the free association test.

Here is a finding of grave significance. *The most urgent, the most absorbing motive in life failed completely to reveal itself by indirect methods.* It was, however, entirely accessible to conscious report. Part of the explanation may be that the subjects turned in relief to laboratory tasks to forget for a while their obsessive motive. They responded to the projective tests with heaven knows what available, habitual associational material. The failure of night dreams to reveal a significant amount of wish fulfillment is somewhat more perplexing. It can scarcely be ascribed to a defensive mental set. But both types of result suggest a possible law: Unless a motive is repressed it is unlikely to affect distinctively the perception of, and responses to, a projective test. It is too early to tell whether this is a valid generalization, but it is a hypothesis well worth testing.

Other studies on hunger seem to yield supporting evidence (11, 15). Their trend suggests that on projective tests the number of explicit food associations actually declines in longer periods of fasting, apparently because the motive itself gradually becomes completely conscious and is not repressed. It is true that instrumental associations (ways of obtaining food) continue to appear in the subject's word-responses as the state of hunger grows. This finding, however, is quite consistent with the hypothesis, since while hunger is fully conscious, the subject in the experimental situation is prevented from seeking satisfaction, and thus is still repressing his instrumental action-tendencies.

Another revealing line of evidence comes from the research of J. W. Getzels

(6). This investigator utilized two forms of a sentence completion test—one couched in the first person and one in the third. His pairs are of the following type:

When they asked Frank to be in charge he. . . .
When they asked me to be in charge I. . . .

When Joe meets a person for the first time he usually. . . .
When I meet a person for the first time I usually. . . .

In this experiment, of course, the items were randomized. In all there were 20 diagnostic items of each type. The subjects were 65 veterans, 25 diagnosed as well adjusted; 40 were psychoneurotic cases discharged from service with disability involving personality disorder.

It turned out that to a highly significant degree the well-adjusted men gave *identical* responses to the first and to the third person completions. If we assume that the third-person sentence is a "projective method" then the results obtained by this method for well adjusted subjects squared almost perfectly with the results obtained from the direct, first-person questioning. The psychoneurotics, on the other hand, to a highly significant degree varied their responses. They said one thing when queried directly (e.g., "When they asked me to be in charge I agreed") and another on the projective item (e.g., "When they asked John to be in charge he was afraid"). The first-person completion is so direct that in the psychoneurotic it invokes the mask of defense and elicits a merely conventionally correct response.

Thus the direct responses of the psychoneurotic cannot be taken at their face value. The defenses are high, the true motives are hidden and are betrayed only by a projective technique. The normal subjects, on the other hand, tell you by the direct method precisely what they tell you by the projective method. They are all of a piece. You may therefore take their motivational statements at their face value, for even if you probe you will not find anything substantially different.

This research adds weight to the tentative judgment we formed in the case of the starving subjects. It is not the well-integrated subject, aware of his motivations, who reveals himself in projective testing. It is rather the neurotic personality, whose façade belies the repressed fears and hostilities within. Such a subject is caught off guard by projective devices; but the well-adjusted subject gives no significantly different response.

There is, however, one difference between the two researches. The starving subjects actually *avoided* any betrayal of their dominant motive in the projective tests. The well-adjusted veterans, on the other hand, gave essentially the *same* type of response in both direct and in projective testing. It may be that the dissimilar nature of the tests used in the two situations accounts for this difference in results. But this detailed difference need not detain us here. What seems to be important is the implication of these researches that *a psychodiagnostician should never employ projective methods in the study of motivation without at the same time employing direct methods*. If he does not do so he will never be able to distinguish a well-integrated personality from one that is not. Nor will he be able to tell whether there are strong conscious streams of motivation that are entirely evading the projective situation (as in the case of the starving subjects).

The trend of evidence that I have presented seems to indicate that a normal, well-adjusted individual with strong goal-directedness may on projective tests do one of two things: 1) either give material identical with that of conscious report—in which case the projective method is not needed; or 2) give no evidence whatever of his dominant motives. It is only when emotionally laden material comes forth in projective responses that is contradictory to conscious report, or to other results of direct assessment, that we find special value in projective testing. And we shall never know whether or not a neurotic situation prevails unless we use both diagnostic approaches and compare the yield.

Consider for a moment the diagnosis of anxiety. Using various responses on the Rorschach and TAT cards the clinician might infer a high level of anxiety. Now this finding taken by itself tells us little. The subject may be the sort of person who is enormously effective in life because he harnesses his anxiety to performance. He may know perfectly well that he is a harried, worried, bedeviled overachiever. Anxiety is an asset in his life, and he has enough insight to know the fact. In this case the yield by projective methods is matched by the yield from direct methods. The projective technique was not really needed, but it does no harm to use it. Or, as in our starvation cases, we might find that projective protocols reveal no anxiety while in actuality we are dealing with a person who is as harried, worried and bedeviled as our first subject, but who effectively controls his jitters. In this case we assume that his large measure of control enables him to tackle the projective tests with some mental set unrelated to his anxious nature. But we may also find— and here is where projective methods have their uses—that an apparently bland and calm individual, denying all anxiety, reveals profound disturbance and fear in projective performances. It is this type of dissociated nature that projective tests help to diagnose. Yet they cannot do so unless direct methods also are employed.

In speaking so frequently of "direct" methods I have referred chiefly to "conscious report." To ask a man his motives, however, is not the only type of "direct" method that we may employ. It is, however, a good one—especially to start with.

When we set out to study a person's motives we are seeking to find out what that person is trying to do in this life, including of course what he is trying to avoid, and what he is trying to be. I see no reason why we should not start our investigation by asking him to tell us the answers as he sees them. If the questions in this form seem too abstract they can be recast. Particularly revealing are people's answers to the question, "What do you want to be doing five years from now?" Similar direct questions can be framed to elicit anxieties, loyalties and hostilities. Most people, I suspect, can tell what they are trying to do in this life with a high degree of validity, certainly not less on the average than the prevailing validity of projective instruments. Yet some clinicians disdain to ask direct questions.

But by "direct methods" I mean also to include standard pencil-and-paper measures, such as the Strong Interest Inventory and the recently revised Allport-Vernon-Lindzey Study of Values. Now it often happens that the yield on such instruments is not what would come from the subject's conscious report. The subject may not have known, for example, that compared with most people his pattern of values is, say, markedly theoretical and aesthetic, or far below average in economic and religious interest. Yet the final score on the Study of Values is itself merely a summation of a series of separate conscious choices that he has made in 45 hypothetical situations. While his verbal report on the pattern as a whole may be faulty, yet this pattern not only squares with all his separate choices, but is known on the average to have good external validity. People with certain patterns of interests as measured by the test do in fact make characteristic vocational choices and do in their daily behavior act in ways that are demonstrably consistent with the test results.

To sum up: direct methods include the kind of report that is elicited in careful interviewing, whether it be of the simple psychiatric variety, the sort employed in vocational or personal counseling, or in nondirective interviewing. Autobiographic methods when employed at their face value are likewise direct. So too are the results of any kind of testing where the final scores represent a sum or pattern of a series of conscious choices on the part of the subject.[1]

The currently fashionable term *psychodynamics* is often equated explicitly with psychoanalytic theory. Projective techniques are considered psychody-

namic because they are thought to tap deepest layers of structure and functioning. We have already indicated reasons for doubting the sufficiency of this assumption. Many of the most dynamic of motives are more accurately tapped by direct methods. At the very least the discoveries by projective techniques cannot be properly interpreted unless they are compared with discoveries yielded by direct methods.

Devotees of psychodynamics often say that no discoveries are of value unless the unconscious is explored. This dictum we find in the valuable book by Kardiner and Ovesey, *The Mark of Oppression* (9), dealing with the seriously disordered and conflictful motivational systems of Negroes in a northern city. Unless I am greatly mistaken, however, the authors discover little or nothing about their cases through psychoanalytic probes that is not evident in the manifest situation. The conscious handicaps of a Negro in our society, the economic misery, the deteriorated family situations, the bitterness and despair, constitute a painful psychodynamic situation in individual lives that in most instances receives no further illumination when depth analysis is employed.

Most of the psychodynamic evidence given by Kardiner and Ovesey concern-

[1] For the purposes of the present argument this simplified discussion of "direct" and "indirect" techniques is adequate. Psychodiagnosis requires, however, a much more discriminating classification of the methods currently employed, and of the "levels" of organization that each normally taps. An excellent beginning is Rosenzweig's proposal that three classes of methods be distinguished, each adapted in principle to tapping three levels of behavior (14). What he calls *subjective* methods require the subject to take himself as a direct object of observation (questionnaires, autobiographies). *Objective* methods

require the observer to report on overt conduct. *Projective* methods require both subject and observer to "look the other way" and to base the diagnosis on the subject's reaction to apparently "ego-neutral" material. Broadly speaking, Rosenzweig's subjective and objective procedures correspond to what I here call "direct" methods, and projective procedures to "indirect" methods.

Especially noteworthy is the author's statement that the significance of projective methods (e.g., his own P-F Study) cannot be determined unless the subject's projective responses are examined in the light of his subjective and objective responses.

ing their cases is, in fact, drawn from straightforward autobiographical report. Their use of this method is acceptable and their findings highly instructive. But their theory seems to me out of line with both the method actually used and the findings obtained. Psychodynamics is not necessarily a hidden dynamics.

This point is well made by the psychiatrist J. C. Whitehorn (17), who correctly holds that psychodynamics is a general science of motivation. Into its broad principles one may fit the specific contributions and insights of psychoanalysis. But psychoanalysis itself is by no means the sum and substance of psychodynamics. Whitehorn insists that the proper approach to psychotic patients, especially to those suffering from schizophrenic or depressive disorder, is through such channels of their normal interest systems as remain open. It is not the region of their disorder that requires primary attention, but those psychodynamic systems that still represent sturdy and healthy adaptations to reality. In Whitehorn's words, the therapist should seek "to activate and utilize the resources of the patient and to help him thereby to work out a more satisfying way of life with a less circumscribed emphasis upon these special issues" (p. 40).

Sometimes we hear it said that psychoanalytic theory does not do justice to psychoanalytic practice. What is meant is that in the course of therapy an analyst will devote much of his time to a direct discussion with his patient of his manifest interests and values. The analyst will listen respectfully, accept, counsel and advise concerning these important, and *not* buried, psychodynamic systems. In many instances, as in the cases presented by Kardiner and Ovesey, the motives and conflicts are taken at their face value. Thus the method of psychoanalysis as employed is not fully sustained by the theory that is affirmed.

Nothing that I have said denies the existence of infantile systems, troublesome repressions, or neurotic formations. Nor does it deny the possibility of self-deception, rationalization and ego defense. My point is merely that methods and theories dealing with these aberrant conditions should be set in a broad conception of psychodynamics. The patient should be assumed insightful until he is proved otherwise. If you asked a hundred people who go to the icebox for a snack why they did so, probably all would answer, "Because I was hungry." In ninety-nine of these cases we may—no matter how deeply we explore—discover that this simple, conscious report is the whole truth. It can be taken at its face value. In the hundredth case, however, our probing shows that we are dealing with a compulsive overeater, with an obese seeker after infantile security who, unlike the majority of cases, does not know what he is trying to do. It is peace and comfort he is seeking—perhaps his mother's bosom—and not the leftover roast. In this case—and in a minority of all cases—I grant we cannot take the evidence of his overt behavior, nor his account of it, at their face value.

Freud was a specialist in precisely those motives that cannot be taken at their face value. To him motivation resided in the id. The conscious, accessible region of personality that carries on direct transactions with the world, namely the ego, he regarded as devoid of dynamic power.

It is a misfortune that Freud died before he had remedied this one-sidedness in his theory. Even his most faithful followers tell us now that he left his ego psychology incomplete. In recent years many of them have labored to redress the balance. Without doubt the principal current in psychoanalytic theory today is moving in the direction of a more dynamic ego. This trend in theory is apparent in the work of Anna Freud, Hartmann, French, Horney, Fromm, Kris, and many others. In a communication to the American Psychoanalytic Association, Kris points out that the attempt to restrict interpretations of motivation to the id aspect only "represents the older procedure." Modern concern with the ego does not confine itself to an analysis of defense mechanisms alone. Rather it gives more respect to what he calls the "psychic surface." Present psychoanalytic techniques, he tells us, tend to link "surface" with "depth" (10). In a similar vein Rapaport (13) has argued that a measure of true autonomy must now be ascribed to the ego.

To illustrate the point at issue, we might take any psychogenic interest of maturity, for example, the religious sentiment. Freud's handling of the matter is well known. To him religion is essentially a neurosis in the individual, a formula for personal escape. The father image lies at the root of the matter. One cannot therefore take the religious sentiment, when it exists in a personality, at its face value. A more balanced view of the matter would seem to be this: *sometimes* one cannot take this sentiment at its face value, and *sometimes* one can. Only a careful study of the individual will tell. In a person in whom the religious factor serves an obviously egocentric purpose— talismanic, bigoted, self-justificatory— we can infer that it is a neurotic, or at least immature, formation in the personality. Its infantile and escapist character is not recognized by the subject. On the other hand, in a person who has gradually evolved a guiding philosophy of life where the religious sentiment

exerts a generally normative force upon behavior and confers intelligibility to life as a whole, we infer that this particular ego formation is not only a dominant motive, but that it must be accepted at its face value. It is a master motive and an ego ideal whose shape and substance are essentially what appear in consciousness (1).

Let us consider a final example. It is well known that most boys around the age of four to seven identify with their fathers. They imitate them in many ways. Among other things they may express vocational aspirations for daddy's job. Many boys when grown do in fact follow their fathers' footsteps.

Take politics. Father and son have been politicians in many families: the Tafts, Lodges, Kennedys, La Follettes, Roosevelts, to mention only a few. When the son is at a mature age, say 50 or 60, what is his motivation? Is he working through his early father identification or is he not? Taken at its face value the interest of the son in politics now seems to be absorbing, self-contained, a prominent factor in his own ego structure. In short, it seems to be a mature and normal motive. But the strict geneticist would say: "No, he is now a politician because of a father fixation." Does the geneticist mean that an early father identification started him in a political direction of interest? If so, the answer is yes, of course. All motives have their origin somewhere. Or does he mean, "This early fixation now, today, sustains the son's political conduct?" If so, the answer is normally, no. The political interest is now a prominent part of the ego structure, and the ego is the healthy man's source of energy. To be sure, there may be cases where a person mature in years is still trying to curry father's favor, to step into his shoes, to displace him with the mother.

A clinical study of a second-generation politician may conceivably show that his behavior is compulsively father-identified. In such a case his daily conduct is in all probability so compulsive, so ungeared to realistic situational needs, so excessive, that the diagnosis can be suspected by any skilled clinical observer. But such instances are relatively rare.

To sum up: we need in our motivational theory to make a sharper distinction between infantilisms and motivation that is strictly contemporary and at age.

I am fully aware of my heterodoxy in suggesting that there is in a restricted sense a discontinuity between normal and abnormal motivation, and that we need a theory that will recognize this fact. Discontinuities are distinctly unpopular in psychological science. One theory of abnormality tells us that we are merely pleased to regard the extremes on our linear continuum as abnormal. Further, some culture theorists insist that abnormality is a relative concept, shifting from culture to culture, and from one historical period to another. Likewise, there are many borderline cases which even the most experienced clinician could not with confidence classify as normal or as abnormal. Finally, and most important, is the fact that in many normal people one can by scratching deeply enough find *some* infantilism in their motivation.

Granted all these familiar arguments, there is still a world of difference—if not between normal and abnormal people —then between the healthy and unhealthy mechanisms involved in the development of motivation. What we call integrative action of the nervous system is basically a wholesome mechanism that keeps motivation up to date. It tends to bring about both an internal consistency and a reality testing among the elements entering into motivational patterning. Effective suppression is another healthy mechanism, not only harmless to the individual, but making possible the arrangement of motives in an orderly hierarchy (4, 12). With the aid of effective suppression the individual ceases to act out infantile dramas. Insight, a clear self-image, and the little understood factor of homeostasis may be mentioned among the balancing mechanisms.

As Getzels' experiment shows, direct and projective performances in healthy people are all of a piece. A further test of normality—unfortunately one psychologists have not yet developed—may lie in the harmony of expressive behavior (facial expression, gestures, handwriting) with the individual's fundamental motivational structure. There is evidence that discoordination between conscious motives and expressive movement is an ominous sign (3). This lead for research should be followed through.

In unhealthy motivation, unbalancing mechanisms have the upper hand. There is always some species of dissociation at work. The individual represses ineffectively; repressed motives erupt in autistic gestures, in tantrums, in nightmares, in compulsions, perhaps in paranoid thinking. Above all, self-knowledge is lacking in large regions of the life.

My point is that normally the balancing mechanisms have the upper hand. Sometimes, in certain badly disordered lives, the unbalancing mechanisms take over. Occasionally too, we find them operating in a segmental way in lives that are otherwise healthy. When the clash in mechanisms is marked, diagnosis is then aided by the use of projective techniques. But when there is essential harmony within the personality system projective methods will teach us little or nothing about the course of motivation.

From what has been said it is clear that a satisfactory conception of psychodynamics will have the following characteristics. 1) It will never employ projective methods nor depth analysis without allowing for a full diagnosis of motives by direct methods as well. 2) It will assume that in a healthy personality the great bulk of motivation can be taken at its face value. 3) It will assume that normal motivation of this order has a present and future significance for the individual that is by no means adequately represented by a study of his past life. In other words, it will allow that the present psychodynamics of a life may in large part be functionally autonomous, even though continuous with early motivational formations (2, esp. pp. 76–113). 4) It will at the same time retain the epochal insights of Freud and others to the effect that infantile fixations frequently occur, and that we do well to check on conscious report and to supplement direct methods by indirect.

Before such an adequate conceptualization can be achieved there is one current dogma in motivational theory that demands re-examination. I refer to the oft-encountered statement that all motives aim at "the reduction of tensions." This doctrine—found in instinctivism, psychoanalysis, and in stimulus-response psychology—operates to keep us on a primitive level of theorizing.

We cannot, of course, deny that basic drives seem to seek "reduction of tension." Oxygen need, hunger, thirst, elimination are examples. But these drives are not a trustworthy model for all normal adult motivation. Goldstein remarks that patients who seek only tension reduction are clearly pathological. They are preoccupied with segmental irritations from which they seek relief.

There is nothing creative about their interests. They cannot take suffering, or delay, or frustration as a mere incident in their pursuit of values. Normal people, by contrast, are dominated by their "preferred patterns" of self-actualization. Their psychogenic interests are modes of sustaining and directing tension rather than escaping it (7).

We should, I think, agree with Goldstein that tension reduction is not an adequate statement of the functioning of mature psychogenic motives. At the time of his inauguration as president of Harvard, James Bryant Conant remarked that he was undertaking his duties "with a heavy heart but gladly." He knew he would reduce no tensions by committing himself to the new job. Tensions would mount and mount, and at many times become almost unbearable. While he would in the course of his daily work dispatch many tasks and feel relief, still the over-all commitment—his total investment of energy—would never result in any equilibrium. Psychogenic interests are of this order: they lead us to complicate and strain our lives indefinitely. "Striving for equilibrium," "tension reduction," "death wish" seem trivial and erroneous representations of normal adult motivation.

Recent years, as I have said, have brought a wholesome turn in theorizing. Few authorities on war neuroses, for example, wrote in terms of tension reduction. They spoke rather of "firm ego structure" or "weak ego structure." Grinker and Spiegel say, "As the ego becomes stronger the therapist demands increasing independence and activity from the patient" (8, p. 94).

After successful therapy these and other writers sometimes remark, "The ego now seems in full control." In such expressions as these—and one encounters them with increasing frequency— we meet post-Freudian ego psychology again. True, the flavor of these theoretical statements varies. Sometimes they still seem close to the conception of the ego as rationalizer, rider and steersman. But often, as in the statements just quoted, they go far beyond. They imply that the ego is not only normally able to avoid malignant repression, chronicity and rigidity, but that it is also a differentiated dynamism—a fusion of healthy psychogenic motives that can be taken at their face value.

There is no need to take fright at the conception of an "active ego." As I see the matter, the term "ego" does not refer to a homunculus, but is merely a short-hand expression for what Goldstein calls "preferred patterns." The term means that normally healthy personalities have various systems of psychogenic motives. They are not limitless in number. Indeed in a well-integrated adult they may be adequately indicated on the fingers of two hands, perhaps one. What a person is trying to do persistently, recurrently, as a function of his own internal nature, is often surprisingly well focused and well patterned. Whether these leading motives are called desires, interests, values, traits or sentiments does not greatly matter. What is important is that motivational theory—in guiding diagnosis, therapy and research—should take these structures fully into account.

References

1. ALLPORT, G. W. *The Individual and His Religion,* Macmillan, New York, 1950.

2. ———. *The Nature of Personality: Selected Papers.* Addison-Wesley, Cambridge, 1950.

3. ALLPORT, G. W., and P. E. VERNON. *Studies in Expressive Movement.* Macmillan, New York, 1933.

4. BELMONT, L., and H. G. BIRCH. *Re-Individualizing the Repression Hypothesis.* J. Abnorm. Soc. Psychol., 46: 226–235, 1951.

5. BROZEK, J., H. GUETZKOW, M. V. BALDWIN, R. CRANSTON. *A Quantitative Study of Perception and Association in Experimental Semi-Starvation.* J. Personal., 19: 245–264, 1951.

6. GETZELS, J. W. *The Assessment of Personality and Prejudice by the Methods of Paired Direct and Projective Questionnaires.* Unpublished thesis. Harvard Coll. Lib., Cambridge, 1951.

7. GOLDSTEIN, K. *Human Nature in the Light of Psychopathology.* Harvard Univ. Press, Cambridge, 1940.

8. GRINKER, R. R., and J. P. SPIEGEL. *War Neuroses.* Blakiston, Philadelphia, 1945.

9. KARDINER, A., and L. OVESEY. *The Mark of Oppression.* Norton, New York, 1951.

10. KRIS, E. *Ego Psychology and Interpretation in Psychoanalytic Therapy.* Psa. Quart., 20: 15–30, 1951.

11. LEVINE, R., I. CHEIN, and G. MURPHY. *The Relation of the Intensity of a Need to the Amount of Perceptual Distortion: A Preliminary Report.* J. Psychol., 13: 283–293, 1942.

12. McGRANAHAN, D. V. *A Critical and Experimental Study of Repression.* J. Abnorm. Soc. Psychol., 35: 212–225, 1940.

13. RAPAPORT, D. *The Autonomy of the Ego.* Bull. Menninger Clin., 15: 113–123, 1951.

14. ROSENZWEIG, S. *Levels of Behavior in Psychodiagnosis with Special Reference to the Picture-Frustration Study*. Am. J. Orthopsychiatry, 20: 63–72, 1950.

15. SANFORD, R. N. *The Effect of Abstinence from Food upon Imaginal Processes*. J. Psychol., 2: 129–136, 1936.

16. STAGNER, R. *Homeostasis as a Unifying Concept in Personality Theory*. Psychol. Rev., 58: 5–17, 1951.

17. WHITEHORN, J. C. *Psychodynamic Considerations in the Treatment of Psychotic Patients*. Univ. West. Ontario Med. J., 20: 27–41, 1950.

PRINCIPLES OF INTRAPERSONAL CONFLICT

Judson S. Brown

It is difficult to escape the conclusion that, from the very dawn of life, living organisms have been constantly subjected to the disrupting effects of conflicting tendencies to action. Whenever and wherever they have moved, the forces inciting them to action have been opposed by other agencies demanding either alternate responses or the cessation of action; for even the simplest movement cannot be executed unless the friction and inertia of bodily members are overcome; and no movement can long continue if the chemical products of fatigue are allowed to accumulate or if competing muscular contractions are not inhibited. For the individual organism, then, conflict is an inevitable consequence of an inherent capacity to act in any manner and especially of the ability to perform a multiplicity of acts.

It is with these intrapersonal conflicts, arising from competitions among incompatible tendencies to act, that the present paper is concerned. Its specific aim is to review in brief, and in some cases to enlarge upon, a selected group of explana-

Reprinted by permission of the journal and the author from *Conflict Resolution*, Vol. 1, 1957.

tory principles that have proved valuable in the analysis of intraindividual conflict behavior.

Unfortunately, progress toward a scientific understanding of either individual or group conflicts has been relatively meager and has been limited to a trivial period of time. What Ebbinghaus said of psychology can, with equal cogency, be said of conflict: it has had a long past but a short history. As ancient as man is the knowledge that individuals are continuously racked by antagonistic tendencies to action, and students of literature and history would have little difficulty in finding innumerable early references to the phenomenon. But prior to the twentieth century they would find neither significant theoretical analyses of the problem nor relevant experimental data. During the first three decades of this century, however, remarkable strides were taken, those by Freud (7) and by Pavlov (27) looming large above others. It was Freud, of course, who so clearly perceived the extensive and insidious effects of severe emotional conflicts upon personality and behavior. His principle, that such conflicts, especially at the unconscious level, are the primary factors underlying neurotic behavior, has become the working assumption of nearly all therapists. Pavlov, during his extensive studies of salivary conditioning, discovered that dogs, if repeatedly presented with tasks involving extremely difficult discriminations, would develop persisting neurotic-like syndromes of behavior. His investigations of this phenomenon of "experimental neurosis" not only contributed to our fund of empirical knowledge but, more importantly, paved the way for the admission of such seemingly pure clinical problems into the traditionally aloof stronghold of experimental psychology. Freud and Pavlov were indeed the giants, but important clinical and experimental contributions were made by many others. It is not our purpose here to summarize the work of these men, but a history of intrapersonal conflict would be incomplete without the mention of Janet (14), McDougall (19), Rivers (30), Prince (28), and Liddell and Bayne (17). And since about 1930 the names of Lewin (16), Gantt (8), Guthrie (10), Hull (13), Miller (21), Hovland and Sears (12), and Masserman (18) have become prominent in this field, and their respective contributions will be familiar to many readers.

In the first flush of enthusiasm following Pavlov's dramatic demonstrations of experimental neuroses, research studies were directed primarily toward the problem of whether animals other than dogs could be driven to similar neurotic extremes. Considerable success was attained with pigs, sheep, and goats, and useful procedural information was amassed. Generally speaking, however, the experiments were not sufficiently systematic to yield sound empirical laws and were seldom guided by adequate theoretical models.

By way of contrast, current psycho-logical research on conflict seldom deals with behavior having the manifest characteristics of extreme neuroticism. Instead, emphasis is placed on the study of reactions in situations where incompatible tendencies of diverse kinds and strengths are aroused and on the problems of formulating stable functional relationships among relevant variables. But this shift in emphasis has made it difficult, in many so-called studies of conflict, to discern any relationships or behavior which identify them unambiguously as experiments on conflict. Thus we are faced with the problem of trying to discuss research on conflict when we are no longer certain which experiments deal with conflict and which do not.

One solution to this problem may lie in restructuring our thinking about conflict. In essence, this reorganization stresses the principle *that the important determinants of behavior in conflict-producing situations are indistinguishable from those in ordinary unambivalent situations and that no sharp dividing line can be drawn between the two kinds of behavior.* The acceptance of this view means that the usual definition of conflict, as the simultaneous arousal of incompatible tendencies to action, applies without exception to any and all behavior. Consequently, the term "conflict" will be retained solely for convenience to denote one end of a continuum, the other end of which might be labeled "non-conflictive" or "unambivalent." If one chooses to study behavior attributable primarily to the presence of a single, strongly dominant tendency, one is choosing the "unambivalent" end of the continuum. But if one selects instances in which two incompatible tendencies are relatively equal, one is concerning one's self with "conflict." On this view, then, the conclusion is reached that *an*

*experiment deals with conflict if it is a
study of behavior in situations where one
reactive tendency is opposed by at least
one other of sufficient strength to make
a discernible difference in behavior.*

This notion that ambivalent and unambivalent behavior are not essentially
different in kind but fall at different
points on the same continuum is not, of
course, novel. Arguments for the essential continuity of these two supposedly
diverse forms of action have been presented by students of normal behavior
as well as by clinically oriented workers.
Melton (20), for example, has insisted
that frustration, conflict, and thwarting
are inevitable accompaniments of all
learning and problem-solving situations.
And Miller and Dollard (23), among
others, have maintained that conventional learning principles govern the acquisition and interplay of the competitive
tendencies underlying most neuroses.
The potential utility of this conception,
however, has not always been clearly
recognized. In an effort to expand and
clarify it, I shall turn now to a discussion
of what seems to be the basic conflict
paradigm as it relates to theory and experiment in this area.

A Basic Paradigm for
Intrapersonal Conflict

A fundamental paradigm to which all
intrapersonal conflicts can perhaps be
reduced is shown in Figure 1. Here *S*
designates a stimulus complex or pattern
of cues having a high probability, when
presented to an organism, of evoking
two different and incompatible responses,
R1 and *R2*. In any specific situation, the
tendency *(T1)* for *S* to elicit *R1* may be
stronger than the tendency *(T2)* to
evoke *R2,* or the reverse may be true, or
the two may be equal; and, when equal,
they may be strong or weak. When one

of the antagonistic tendencies becomes
strong enough to modify the behavior-
determining action of the other, the paradigm illustrates conflict, as it has been
described above. But if one of the tendencies is too weak to modify the action
of its competitor, the paradigm is descriptive of commonplace, unambivalent
behavior. Here and in what follows, unambivalent behavior refers to actions
that can be satisfactorily explained by
the invocation of a single dominant tendency, with minor disrupting effects of
weakly antagonistic tendencies being ignored.

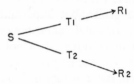

FIG. 1. Basic conflict paradigm. *S* is a
stimulus complex capable of arousing two
tendencies (*T*1, and *T*2) to perform antagonistic responses (*R*1, and *R*2). For
simplicity, it has been assumed that only
two antagonistic reactions are involved.

The simple paradigm of Figure 1 is
also co-ordinate with a number of important problems investigated by students of conflict. Here are some examples. If *T1* is initially dominant, what
are the effects upon *R1,* say, of a gradual
increase in the strength of *T2?* At what
point during the course of this increase
will the effects on *R1* be most marked?
How are the results of the competition
between *R1* and *R2* affected by modifications in the degree of physical incompatibility between *R1* and *R2?* What are
the results of changes in the characteristics of *S;* of changes in the conditions
under which *R1* and *R2* are learned; of
shifts in the general motivational level;
or of prolonged exposure to *S?*

To put more flesh on the bare bones

of this paradigm, let us assume that S denotes the configuration of cues at a given location in space and that a hungry organism has approached that region and has been fed. Such reinforcement is expected to lead to the growth of a tendency $(T1)$ to make an approach response $(R1)$ to that region. Now if, on one or more occasion, the organism is severely punished for approaching the food, an antagonistic tendency $(T2)$ to make an avoidance response $(R2)$ will be established. Since the approach and avoidance responses are physically incompatible, conflict is the result. This is an example of what is currently called an *approach-avoidance* conflict.

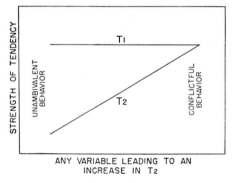

FIG. 2. Diagrammatic representation of relationships characterizing the continuum between unambivalent behavior and conflictful behavior.

An attempt has been made, by means of the diagram in Figure 2 to summarize the critical elements in this and in other examples of conflict and to expand the fundamental paradigm for conflict. In this diagram the base line represents any variable, such as frequency or intensity of punishment, that might lead to an increase in the strength of $T2$. For simplicity, the strength of $T1$ is assumed to remain constant. Now if, as the diagram shows, $T2$ increases from a very low value at the left up to equality with $T1$

at the right, the difference between the strengths of the two tendencies is reduced, and the effects of competition should become greater. In the present view, a marked inequality in the strengths of the tendencies is characteristic of unambivalent behavior, and equality is typical of conflictful behavior. The left- and right-hand ends of the diagram have been labeled *unambivalent* and *conflictful,* respectively, to indicate these assumptions. If $T1$ is taken as the approach tendency and $T2$ as the avoidance tendency in an approach-avoidance conflict and if the variable leading to an increase in $T2$ is nearness to the goal, it is evident that behavior will change from unambivalent to conflictful as the ambivalent goal is approached.

The basic paradigm and its extension in Figure 2 also suggest the kinds of therapeutic methods or individual adjustive reactions that will reduce or resolve conflicts. Since conflict is characterized by the arousal of strong interfering tendencies, it must continue as long as the appropriate cues are present and as long as the strengths of the tendencies are maintained. Conversely, conflict must decline if the strengths of both tendencies can be reduced to an ineffective level or if the difference between them can be markedly increased. A simultaneous reduction in the values of the tendencies can be accomplished by removing or weakening the stimulus complex or by various methods of re-education or extinction. The alcoholic seeking a cure can avoid his conflicts, to a degree, by staying away from the stimuli provided by bars, and the neurotic may reduce conflict by the development of hysterical blindness. In both cases, cues tending to evoke antagonistic responses are rendered impotent, at least temporarily. More permanent and satisfactory solutions will be achieved, however, if, through re-learning, both tendencies can be reduced to a sub-threshold level or if the difference between them can be markedly increased. As may be seen from Figure 2, increasing the difference between the tendencies by a marked weakening of one must, in view of the assumed relations, resolve the conflict, since unambivalence is the necessary result of such weakening.

Predicting Behavior in Conflict Situations

Turning now to the problem of forecasting the kinds of behavior that should occur in conflict situations, we shall review three major suggestions advanced by students of conflict. Consider again the diagram in Figure 2, where the tendency for S to evoke $R1$ is initially very strong and where there is a progressively increasing tendency to execute $R2$. One assumption from which predictions can be made for these conditions is that *the two tendencies summate algebraically.* Thus, as $T2$ gains in strength, it simply detracts increasingly from the strength of $T1$. This assumption has been made by Hull (13), Miller (21), and Brown (3) in their discussions of both spatial and discriminatory conflicts. It leads to the prediction that $R1$ should show increases in latency, decreases in amplitude, and the like, as the tendency to perform $R2$ increases. Available experimental data (6, 3, 15) support this suggestion, though they are not unequivocal.

· A second possibility would be to postulate that $T2$ *does not weaken $T1$ or $R1$, but functions instead to reduce the probability that $R1$ will be elicited by S.* On this hypothesis, conflict would be revealed by a tendency for $R2$ to appear occasionally, at full strength, in place of $R1$, the likelihood of such alternation in-

creasing as $T2$ approaches equality with $T1$. This conception has apparently never been explicitly formulated or its implications carefully studied, but qualitative observations of both humans and animals in conflict-producing environments suggest that it may have merit.

At this point, a parenthetical remark may be in order. Neither of these two views as to the probable consequences of competition appeals to any concepts or variables not commonly used in theories of "normal" behavior. Neither view makes any reference to an emotional state such as conflict, anger, or frustration. The predicted behavior is a function solely of the strengths of the individual tendencies and of special hypotheses as to the manner in which such tendencies interact. Thus one can have a theory of conflict behavior that is essentially indistinguishable from a theory of unambivalent behavior in respect of the number and kind of assumptions involved. The initial successes achieved by theorists like Miller, who have followed this course, argue strongly for its utility and for the present view, which stresses the essential continuity of ordinary and conflictful behavior.

Returning to the problem of prediction, a third possibility is that behavior in a conflict situation will be determined by new variables in addition to those of conventional behavior theory. The most popular idea of this sort is that *two tendencies, in competing with each other, generate an emotional state or condition having certain of the functional properties of drives.* In particular, responses elicited at the time of conflict, or shortly thereafter, should be intensified by the dynamogenic properties of the conflict-produced drive, and new responses should be learned if they are followed by an escape from conflict and the attendant decrease in drive. Variously structured formulations of this notion have been presented by Lewin (16), Miller and Stevenson (24), Sheffield (32), Brown and Farber (5), and Amsel and Roussel (1). At first sight, it might seem as if the postulation of a unique emotional state due to conflict constitutes a special theory applicable only to conflictive behavior. If so, it might provide grounds for rejecting the view that unambivalent and conflictful behavior are essentially continuous. In all the versions we have mentioned, however, competition in any amount is assumed to lead to some degree of emotionality and to the production of some increment in drive. And in none of the theories is the suggestion made that sharp discontinuities exist between weakly emotional non-conflictful behavior and strongly emotional conflictful behavior.

Variables Affecting the Strengths of Competitory Tendencies

Regardless of whether one deals with conflict in terms of the algebraic summation of tendencies, in terms of alternations between tendencies, or in terms of competition-produced drive increments, all predictive statements must hinge upon estimates of the relative or absolute strengths of the competing tendencies. This means that much of conflict research must be given over to the consideration of variables affecting the strengths of competitory tendencies. Since this is also a major task for the student of ordinary behavior, the continuity between the two areas is further emphasized. In their details, assertions about factors determining reactive tendencies differ according to the nature of one's general behavior theory. But in their broader aspects, nearly all theories concur in the belief that such variables as

magnitude of reward, drive strength, number of trials, number of non-reinforcements, distribution of acquisition and extinction trials, and frequency and intensity of punishment are important determinants of tendencies to act. By manipulating one or more of these variables, both the relative and the absolute strengths of competitory tendencies can be altered over a wide range. Such variations may either increase or decrease the disparity between incompatible tendencies and hence will shift the behavior either toward or away from the unambivalent end of the continuum.

After the tendencies have reached relatively stable levels, further extensive changes may be achieved by altering the stimulus complex. For instance, reducing the physical intensity of S or eliminating a large number of its component elements may weaken both $T1$ and $T2$ to subthreshold levels, where neither $R1$ nor $R2$ will occur. Changes in S may also affect $T1$ and $T2$ differentially, changing one at a different rate from that at which the other is modified. This may make $T1$ and $T2$ either more or less equal and lead to either more or less conflict.

Varieties of Conflicts

Of recent years, psychologists have rather commonly classified conflicts into three major groups: (1) spatial conflicts, (2) discrimination-induced conflicts, and (3) temporal conflicts. If tendencies are present both to approach and to retreat from a given point in space, the conflict is identified as *spatial*. Conflicts arising from pressures to avoid objects on the left as well as on the right or from tendencies to approach two spatially separated goals would also be described by the adjective "spatial." *Discrimination-induced* conflicts are marked by the requirement that a difficult discrimination must be made between quite similar cues. As we have seen, this was the method used by Pavlov to produce experimental neuroses in his dogs. The third group, the *temporal* conflicts, includes those in which the degree of equality of competitory tendencies varies as a function of nearness in time to a particular event. These temporal conflicts have never been critically analyzed, and a preliminary attempt will be made to alleviate this deficiency in a later section of this paper. The central point to be stressed, however, in connection with these varieties of conflict is that, *in essence, they are simply three different techniques for manipulating the stimulus complex of our simple paradigm.* Shifting an organism's position in space cannot possibly affect its tendencies to action unless that shift produces a change in stimuli. Space, as such, can have no causal efficacy with respect to behavior. Nor, for that matter, can the passage of time. If the proverbial tendency of the male to avoid marriage increases with temporal proximity to that event, it must be a consequence not of the flow of time, qua time, but of the changing stimulus patterns correlated with that flow. In the case of conflicts arising where difficult discriminations are required, it is evident that the relative strengths of the competing tendencies are changed through the experimenter's manipulations of the positive and negative stimuli.

SPATIAL CONFLICTS

Up to this point, as a consequence of an attempt to reduce the problem of conflict to its barest essentials, the discussion has been couched in extremely general terms. To increase the intelligibility of a subsequent treatment of temporal conflicts and to illustrate concretely the type of analysis that currently seems most

fruitful, we turn now to a brief review of some typical spatial conflicts. The type of analysis to be followed is essentially identical with that of Miller (21), whose treatment rested on a foundation laid down by Lewin (16) and Hull (13).

In a *spatial approach-avoidance conflict,* as we have already seen, the organism is both attracted to and repelled from a specific region in his environment, and conflict increases as the antagonistic tendencies approach equality. For any practical analysis of such conflicts,

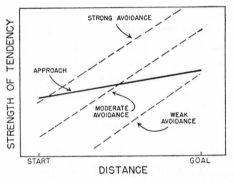

FIG. 3. Schematic diagram representing a single approach gradient (*solid line*) and three avoidance gradients (*dashed lines*) of differing over-all strengths. The gradients have been drawn as straight lines merely to simplify exposition.

however, information as to the manner in which the tendencies might normally be expected to vary with distance from the point of reward and punishment is an important prerequisite. Previous research and theory (21, 4) provide strong support for the idea that in a wide variety of situations the numerical values of both approach and avoidance tendencies increase as the organism moves nearer to the goal, with the avoidance tendency rising more rapidly than the approach. Figure 3 represents these assumptions in a purposely oversimplified form. Here the solid line denotes the approach tendency, and the dashed lines are weak, moderate, and strong avoidance tendencies. If, for the moment, we consider only the approach and the moderate avoidance tendencies, it will be apparent that their intersection near the center marks the region of maximum conflict. With departures from equality in either direction, the situation tends, increasingly, to evoke unambivalent behavior. If the individual is placed at the starting position, he should approach in an unambivalent manner toward the goal, since the avoidance tendency is relatively weak at the starting point. Or, if placed in the situation near the goal, where the tendencies are also unequal, the subject should exhibit unambivalent avoidance. Let us assume, for the moment, however, that the avoidance subtracts from the approach at the left and the approach subtracts from the avoidance on the right. On this assumption, both approach and avoidance reactions would become weaker as the center is neared, and the subject should remain at the point of intersection of the gradients so long as their values remain unchanged. Reasoning in this manner, one arrives at an acceptable account of such conflict-situation behavior as going partway forward toward an ambivalent goal object or retreating partway and then pausing.

If the height of the avoidance gradient is reduced (*lower dashed line*) through the extinction of fear or if the positive gradient is elevated, the locus of conflict will be shifted toward the goal. This will produce an expansion in a goalward direction of the region of unambivalent approach in which the positive tendency is dominant. Throughout a greater proportion of the distance from the start, therefore, the behavior will be free of competition, and the goal may actually be reached without excessive slowing down or hesitation. Conversely, either an increase in the negative gradient (*upper dashed line*) through intensified punishment or a decrease in the positive tendency following satiation will shift the intersection toward the left. This will expand the region throughout which unimpeded avoidance should occur and will lessen the likelihood of the organism's ever reaching the goal.

As to the resolution of this type of conflict, under the restriction that the intersection of the gradients occurs between the starting point and the goal, the following may be said. Whenever the individual behaves by avoiding when the negative tendency is clearly dominant or by approaching when the positive is preeminent, he is inevitably sucked into the maelstrom of conflict. Behavior is self-regulating in this situation, but, since the position of equilibrium is conflictful, it can best be described as a kind of *pernicious homeostasis*. Because of this self-balancing aspect, an approach-avoidance conflict can never be resolved unless the values of the tendencies are markedly altered. Perhaps this self-regulatory feature of behavior in ambivalent situations accounts for the relative inescapability of such conflicts and for their stubborn resistance to therapeutic amelioration.

In a *spatial avoidance-avoidance conflict,* an individual, in attempting to avoid one threatening object, must move toward another that is equally threatening. On the assumption that the strength of the tendency to avoid each object decreases with distance, the situation would be marked by relationships like those of Figure 4. Here again, for purposes of simplification, the avoidance gradients have been drawn as straight lines of essentially equal slopes, with their intersection falling halfway between the two fear-arousing regions. Subtracting one tendency from the other yields the dashed-line gradients to the right and left on the upper surfaces of the cross-hatched areas. The left-hand one of these is the net tendency to avoid the region at the left, and the right-hand one is the net tendency to escape from the right.

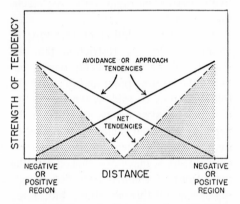

FIG. 4. Schematic diagram of gradients in the strength of tendencies either to avoid or to approach two spatially separated goals. The dashed-line gradients denote the net tendencies obtainable by algebraically summating the overlapping gradients.

From our preceding analysis it should now be obvious that, at the extreme ends of this spatial array, behavior will be unambivalent, and unimpeded avoiding reactions will take place. But the occurrence of such avoidance drives the organism into the central region, where the tendencies are equal, and conflict results. If barriers are present to prevent the individual from leaving the situation, conflict must continue. Again, the regulatory mechanism is pernicious, since behavior consistent with the dictates of the tendencies always leads back to a region of conflict. Under these conditions, conflict can be alleviated by drastically reducing the strength of one or both tendencies. If the object at the right, for

example, is no longer feared, the corresponding gradient would be eliminated, and behavior throughout the entire space between the two negative regions would qualify as unimpeded avoidance behavior with respect to the left-hand object. In the absence of restrictive barriers, of course, an individual can resolve or reduce the conflict by moving away from both feared objects at the same time. By moving far enough, the tendencies, though still theoretically equal, would be too weak to operate effectively in the production of any behavior.

The diagram of Figure 4 may also be used to illustrate the relevant variables in an *approach-approach conflict*. Here the two points of reinforcement are equally desirable objects, and the solid-line gradients represent increasing positive tendencies to approach each. The dashed-line gradients now denote the net tendencies to approach either side. In an environment where these relations hold, the organism can never undergo prolonged conflict. In contrast with the approach-avoidance and avoidance-avoidance kinds of conflict, the behavioral homeostatic mechanism in this case has benign rather than pernicious consequences. Regardless of the individual's position, if he responds in accordance with the demands of the tendencies, he will always progress from a region of relative equality and conflict to a region of conflictless inequality. Even if he were placed precisely at the point where the tendencies are equal, any slight change in the stimulus conditions would upset the momentary balance, and he would tend to move toward one or the other goal. The approach-approach conflict is thus self-resolving, whereas the others are self-perpetuating. Presumably, such self-resolving conditions would never lead to neurotic tendencies, and clinical experience probably bears this out.

Under the circumstances of everyday living, however, it is doubtful whether pure approach-approach conditions such as these ever exist. In nearly every case, the choice of one goal generates an avoidance tendency due to the fact that the other goal may have to be relinquished. As Godbeer (9) and Miller (21) have shown, such double approach-avoidance conflicts are not readily resolved. By and large, these double approach-avoidance conflicts reduce to a kind of avoidance-avoidance paradigm, and they need not, therefore, be considered further here.

DISCRIMINATION CONFLICT

Conflict arising when an individual is required to perform difficult discriminations are amenable to theoretical analyses (3) that parallel, in many respects, those we have discussed in connection with spatial conflicts. Suppose, for example, that a subject has been trained to push a lever forward when a high-frequency tone is sounded and to refrain from responding when a low-frequency tone is sounded. Now, if on successive trials, the pitch of the high tone is progressively reduced and the pitch of the low one is raised, the accuracy of the subject's performance will decline, and, as the two tones approach equality, he may exhibit symptoms of indecision and conflict. Clearly, this discrimination situation differs from those we have already described as spatial, since the subject neither approaches nor avoids a spatial region and since the conflict-inducing stimuli, being under the experimenter's control, are not altered appreciably by the subject's behavior.

In interpreting discrimination-induced conflicts such as these, it is convenient to invoke the *principle of stimulus generalization*. According to this principle, after a response has been associated with one stimulus, other stimuli similar to the first will also elicit the same response without further training. Moreover, the greater the similarity between the old and the new cues, the higher the probability that the new ones will elicit the same response as the old.

The application of this concept of stimulus generalization to our hypothetical discrimination problem with the high and low tones is illustrated in Figure 5. Here the abscissa represents the tonal continuum ranging from the low to the high tone used in the problem. And the ordinate, as before, represents the strengths of the reaction tendencies. The solid-line gradient on the right indicates, in accord with stimulus generalization, that the tendency to respond by pushing the lever is strongest at the point where training has been conducted (high tone) but is present in appreciable degree at all other points on the dimension. Similarly, the dashed line depicts the generalized tendency to refrain from responding to the low tone.

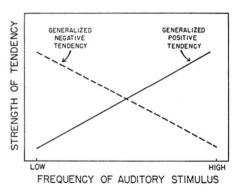

FIG. 5. Generalized tendencies to respond and to refrain from responding as a function of distance on a frequency dimension.

If the actual relationships were as shown in this figure, it would follow that if either the high tone or the low tone were presented, no conflict would result, since the generalized tendencies to make the incompatible responses are minimal at those (unambivalent) points. But tones near the middle of the dimension would tend to elicit both positive and negative generalized responses. And the closer the stimuli approached the middle of the dimension, the more equal would the competing tendencies become and the stronger the conflict.

With respect to the resolution of discrimination-induced conflicts, it is clear from Figure 5 that an increase or decrease in the height of either gradient will increase the disparity between the strengths of the two tendencies at certain points on the dimension and thus reduce conflict at those points. This can be accomplished by retraining, by extinction procedures, by changing the nature of the stimuli, or by alterations in the individual's motivational level.

It is impossible here to present all the theoretical ramifications or implications of a theory such as this, but its possible application to a specific practical situation is perhaps worth noting. Suppose, for instance, that a child reacts in a strongly ambivalent manner to, say, a male teacher *upon first meeting him.* Such behavior might be explained as a discrimination conflict if it can be shown that the child hates his father and loves his uncle and that the teacher resembles both father and uncle. It is even possible that the principle of stimulus generalization as used in the interpretation of discrimination-induced conflict could be applied with profit to the analysis of social prejudices, role conflicts, and the like.

With these brief reviews of spatial and discrimination conflicts to provide a background we turn now to a consideration of temporal conflicts.

TEMPORAL CONFLICTS

As has been indicated, conflicts may arise from changes in an organism's temporal nearness to any event that elicits competing tendencies to action. There are almost no experimental studies of temporal conflicts in the psychological literature, however, and even in Miller's (21) extensive review only a sentence or two is devoted to them. In view of this relative neglect of what may be an important area, it is interesting to see whether a meaningful analysis of temporal conflicts can be achieved within the general conceptual framework employed here.

To extend the principles of conflict from the spatial and similarity dimensions to the dimension of time we must begin by asking whether it is realistic to suppose that both positive and negative tendencies change systematically as a consequence of stimulus variations attending the passing of time. That is, are there positive and negative gradients in time?

Positive temporal gradients. The presence of a positive temporal gradient would be implied by the observation that the tendency to perform a periodically evoked response increases with nearness to the moment at which the response has usually been elicited and rewarded. Such observations have indeed been made in the case of both classically conditioned (27) and instrumentally conditioned responses (31). Moreover, human subjects, when required to make simple manual movements to a regularly recurring signal, exhibit progressively shorter reaction times as the customary time for the appearance of the signal is approached (25). These data are paralleled by such common place observations as that of the mounting excitement shown by children with the approach of Christmas. There appear to be adequate grounds, therefore, for supposing that after a response has been reinforced at regular intervals the strength of the tendency to make that response will increase as the usual time of its elicitation approaches. This is clearly analogous to the approach gradient described previously for spatial conflict situations.

Negative temporal gradients. It is also reasonable to believe that the strengths of tendencies to avoid or to fear an expected noxious or painful event increase with nearness to that event. If one arranges to have a wisdom tooth extracted at some time in the future, the dread of pain is relatively mild when the appointment is made. But, as the fateful hour draws close, fear mounts increasingly. Everyday observations of this kind are supported by experimental data from studies by Brown (2) and by Rigby (29). These investigators have shown that rats' fears of a painful shock become intensified as the customary time for being shocked grows near.

Incidentally, much of the process of socialization in children seems to be directed toward extending their gradients of fear in time. If the child's fear is not aroused until the actual moment of punishment, the fear cannot function as a deterrent to the performance of socially tabooed acts. One must learn to fear parental displeasure long before the strap descends if disapproved actions are to be inhibited. To achieve a disciplined society, anxieties concerning the punishments to be expected for robbery, arson, rape, and the like must be aroused long before the penitentiary doors swing open.

Having decided, then, that both positive and negative temporal gradients may reasonably be assumed to exist under specific conditions of learning and reinforcement, the next question is how conflicts, if any, develop or decline through time. A number of different possibilities suggest themselves here, and we shall consider each of them briefly.

Thwarted-avoidance conflict. One variety of temporal conflict, which might be called *thwarted-avoidance conflict,* is characterized by the fact that, as time passes, a noxious state of affairs comes nearer and nearer, but escape is prevented by physical barriers. The convicted murderer awaiting certain death in the electric chair provides a grim but realistic example. For such an unfortunate individual, dread of the coming traumatic episode increases with time, but all avoidance responses are thwarted by strong barriers.

A comparable situation, more directly analogous to the kinds of conflicts we have already considered, exists where the restraints against escape are social or cultural rather than physical. Thus the tradition that one's honor must be maintained at any cost might force one to engage in a duel having a high probability of leading to death. Such conditions existed for Gary Cooper in the movie *High Noon,* as you may recall. The time-induced conflict here involves an increasing fear of death as the dueling hour approaches and a competitive fear of social disgrace or ostracism. Assuming the fear of dishonor to remain constant, the conflicting tendencies may be represented by the solid-line gradient and either of the dashed-line gradients in the sketch of Figure 6. If the fear of dishonor is greater than the weak fear of death, the duel will actually be carried out. But if the over-all strength of the tendency to fear death is increased, the gradients will cross at an earlier point in time. The period of maximum conflict will then occur sooner, and the individual may well escape entirely from the situation. There are also, of course, various factors that would operate to increase the strength of the tendency to carry out the feared act and to decrease the anticipation of trauma. Primitive tribesmen, when going to war, commonly fortify themselves by specialized rituals involving singing, dancing, and appeals to the gods for supernatural aid. Even civilized man knows that alcohol may sometimes function to alleviate or obliterate fears of impending pain. The relationships diagramed in Figure 6, though superficially different from some we have considered, are comparable in many respects to those of spatial avoidance-avoidance conflicts. Time moves in only one direction, however, and hence the difference between the competitive tendencies must always decrease (up to the point of equality), and conflict or frustration must always increase.

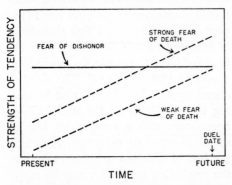

FIG. 6. Competing tendencies involved in thwarted-avoidance temporal conflict.

Thwarted-approach conflict. Conflictful situations also exist in which, for assorted reasons, *one simply cannot perform a given response until a certain period of time has elapsed.* In some localities, eager young couples cannot become legally united until a "cooling-off" period of several days has elapsed following the purchase of the marriage license. And many of us often find that we must wait until the arrival of a salary check at the end of the month to buy a much wanted, but expensive, article. In these and in similar instances the tendency to perform the thwarted act increases with time. But time cannot be hurried, and its very stodginess is often frustrating and irritating. Social rules and taboos, of course, are the primary factors providing the restraints, but the restraints are inextricably geared to the flow of time.

A diagrammatic representation of the reactive and restraining tendencies in a conflict of this type would be essentially identical with the previous sketch. For example, let the line labeled "fear of dishonor" in Figure 6 represent the strength of the restriction against marrying, and let the temporal base line represent the "cooling-off" period. If the lower of the two dashed-line gradients is taken to indicate the strength of the young couple's tendency to get married, it follows that conflict should increase with nearness to the deadline. And, so long as the restriction or fear of punishment is stronger than the positive desire, the couple will wait until the approved time. But if, as a consequence of biological or social incentives or goads, the tendency to consummate the marriage becomes excessively strong, the period of maximal conflict will occur during the waiting period, and the lovers may rush off to a Gretna Green to get married more quickly.

This situation also resembles, to a degree, the spatial approach-avoidance conflict. In the thwarted-approach paradigm the strength of the inhibiting tendency is greater than the positive tendency up to the point of equality, and hence the response is prevented from occurring until that point is reached or passed. In the spatial approach-avoidance, however, the positive tendency exceeds the negative at the more remote distances from the goal, and the response will tend to occur up to the point of equality, but not beyond.

Temporal approach-avoidance conflicts. An attractive possibility in considering temporal conflicts is that there might exist situations which could best be described by appeal to positive and negative gradients of the sort already utilized in spatial approach- avoidance behavior. For example, when the amorous swain, under the influence of a full moon and other stimulants, proposes marriage, the positive aspects of an imagined life with his inamorata are doubtless preeminent. As the succeeding days of the engagement period pass, however, the potentially negative aspects of marriage—loss of freedom, family responsibilities, and financial burdens—may loom larger and larger. The result may be—and often is, apparently—that the period just before the wedding becomes especially conflictful. And in extreme cases, when the avoidance becomes stronger than the approach, the bride may be left standing at the altar.

To explain such behavior it might be assumed that the strength of the tendency to avoid marriage increases at a more rapid rate with nearness to the event than do the more positive aspects. Assuming, further, that the positive and negative tendencies summate algebraically, it follows that the likelihood of getting married decreases, but conflict increases, with nearness to the nuptial day. Perhaps this is co-ordinate with the common notion that long engagements are less likely to lead to marriage than short ones.

Apparently, the only published experimental study of a temporal approach-avoidance conflict is that by Rigby (29). As has already been observed, he obtained gradients in the amplitudes of both approach and avoidance responses as a function of nearness to an event that was both rewarding and punishing. He was unable, however, to support the suggestion that the avoidance gradient might be steeper than that for approach. Such experimental verification will be needed if further attempts to extend the theory into temporal dimensions are to prove fruitful.

It is also possible to describe, within the general outline of the temporal conflict paradigm, situations analogous to the approach-approach and avoidance-avoidance schema we have already considered. Since these have not been previously described, a brief analysis of them appears justified.

Conflict as a function of temporal nearness to an approach-approach situation. In this type of conflict the passage of time brings an organism increasingly close to a situation in which strong incompatible approaching responses will be simultaneously evoked. Suppose, for example, that equally attractive movies are announced a week in advance at two different theaters. On the day when these productions are actually being shown, the situation is identical with the simple approach-approach type of conflict. But when the "coming attractions" are announced, the tendencies to approach both theaters, though equal, should be extremely weak or non-existent. As the days go by, the two tendencies should increase in strength and reach their maximum at the instant of final decision when the moviegoer is standing between the two theaters with his money in his hand. In these circumstances the moviegoer is, in a manner of speaking, drawn into the presence of cues to competing actions by the passage of time. Ordinarily, there is nothing he can do either to hasten or to delay the appearance of the movies. Time flows past the motionless individual, and in so doing brings to him events capable of arousing incompatible proclivities to respond.

An attempt to diagram these relations is reproduced in Figure 7. Here the back wall of a three-dimensional structure represents, in its left-right dimension, the spatial separation of the two positive goals, i.e., the movie theaters. The height of any point on that wall indicates the strength of the tendency to approach, and the lines *ABC* and *DBE* represent

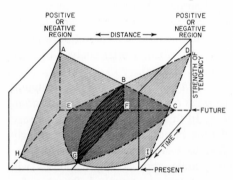

FIG. 7. A tridimensional space-time structure designed to represent changes in the strengths of competing tendencies as a function of temporal nearness to either an approach-approach or an avoidance-avoidance conflict situation.

identical intersecting approach gradients. To this spatial wall there is added another dimension, that of time. This is shown as extending outward from the wall toward the viewer. Finally, it is assumed that the approach tendencies spread out into this new dimension in such a way as to form two conical surfaces. The plane of intersection of these cones is indicated by the letters *BFG* and the dotted shading. Our attention centers

on this plane. If, when the movies are announced, the movie fan is at the space-time point *G,* the strength of the tendencies to approach either theater are equal but negligible. As the days go by, the back surface of the figure may be thought of as moving forward toward the moviegoer. Consequently, the strengths of the two competitive tendencies increase simultaneously in a manner indicated by the changing height of the curved line *GB* above the floor of the structure. At the final instant of decision, the subject is at point *F,* and both tendencies are maximally strong, having a value corresponding to the length of line *BF*.

The behavioral consequences to be predicted from this analysis depend on one's theory of whether variations in the absolute strengths of two equal positive tendencies do, indeed, lead to modified actions. Approach-approach conflicts are presumably always self-resolving unless covert avoidance tendencies are also present. Ease of conflict resolution may not, therefore, be affected by variations in the absolute strengths of two competing positive tendencies. But it is quite possible that degree of emotional arousal and hence drive level would increase as the time for decision approaches. It is also clear that if the slopes of the gradients varied with changes in their absolute heights at the point of intersection, differences in the speed of conflict resolution might be predicted. Thus, if the gradients were very flat at the crossing point, we would expect a definite reaction toward one of the two alternatives to have a longer latency than if the gradients rose steeply on each side of the junction.

Conflict as a function of temporal nearness to an avoidance-avoidance situation. Consider now the case of an infantryman who is told that in exactly one hour he must charge forward from his relatively safe dugout into the face of strong enemy fire or remain and struggle with enemy forces advancing from the rear. Both these alternatives are undesirable, and at the zero hour he will be enmeshed in a strong avoidance-avoidance situation. But until that hour arrives he is temporally remote from both these fear-producing possibilities. When the gravity of the situation first becomes clear, his fears may be aroused, but, since he is still somewhat remote from the crucial moment, the conflict should not be exceptionally strong. As time passes, however, he finds himself in the presence of cues which, to an ever increasing degree, elicit incompatible avoidance reactions and stronger and stronger fears.

The principal variables in this type of spatiotemporal conflict may be represented by a geometrical figure like the one we have just seen. Thus in Figure 7 the lines ABC and DBE may be taken to represent the strengths of the tendencies to avoid the two enemy forces situated at the two negative regions on either side. When the dilemma is presented, the soldier may be thought of as located somewhere near G on the line GF. With each tick of the clock, however, point F comes closer, and the absolute strengths of the (equal) negative tendencies increase along the line GB.

Since the flow of time is unidirectional, the soldier in this example cannot back up along the line FG toward G and thereby effect a simultaneous reduction in the strengths of both negative tendencies. By and large, escape is impossible, and one might predict that the degree of emotional arousal would become magnified with nearness to the "moment critique," that the level of motivation should increase, and that the

frequency and magnitude of oscillations might change. Precisely which of these alternatives would be predicted would depend upon the specific assumptions one makes as to the shapes of the avoidance gradients. Curvilinear gradients would lead to different predictions than linear gradients.

It would also be possible to describe conflicts which are a function of temporal nearness to double approach-avoidance situations. As we have previously noted, however, such types of competition reduce essentially to the avoidance-avoidance type, and a separate analysis of them seems unnecessary.

Applications of the Theory to Social Behavior

Before concluding our analysis of conflict principles, it should be noted that a number of attempts have been made to extend this type of theory to the behavior of individuals in social situations. These attempts have not been widespread, however, and they are too recent to justify estimates of their probable success.

In perhaps the most obvious extension of the theory, the impersonal goal objects of which we have typically spoken would be replaced by living organisms. Thus, for example, conflict would be engendered in a child having tendencies both to approach and to avoid its father, and the strengths of these tendencies might be a function of many of the same variables that operate in impersonal situations. In cases such as this, the ambivalence-generating goal object is capable of speaking, of gesticulating, and of moving toward or away from the individual in conflict. Hence any attempts to evaluate the antagonistic tendencies precisely would doubtless involve these activities as additional significant variables. There seems to be no reason, however, why the behavior of the conflictful person would not, in principle, be interpretable by reference to the same basic relationships as those we have already considered. The substitution of a living goal object for an inanimate one permits us to classify the conflict behavior as essentially social. But it does nothing to destroy the intrapersonal nature of the conflict.

Miller (22), in seeking to relate the psychoanalytic concept of displacement to the stimulus-response concept of stimulus generalization, has made effective use of the kinds of theoretical mechanisms we have been discussing. To take but a single example from his paper, con-

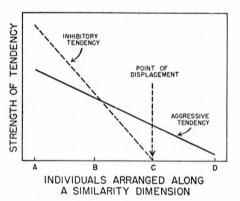

FIG. 8. Strengths of tendencies to be aggressive (*solid line*) and to inhibit aggression (*dashed line*) against individual *A*. Displacement should occur to individual *C*, since the net tendency to aggress is greatest at that point. Adapted from Miller (22).

sider the case of the businessman who dares not attack his intensely frustrating boss and who therefore displaces his aggressive actions to someone else, such as the office boy. Miller accounts for such actions by assuming (1) that tendencies to be aggressive toward the boss and tendencies to inhibit such behavior are simultaneously present; (2) that, as a re-

sult of stimulus generalization, these tendencies will be evoked by other similar individuals; and (3) that the tendency to inhibit aggression decreases more rapidly along a dimension of stimulus similarity than does the tendency to perform the inhibited act. These relationships are represented schematically in Figure 8, which has been adapted from a similar diagram from Miller. On the assumption that the boss is located at point *A* and the office boy at point *C* on the similarity dimension, it follows that the aggressive act should be directed toward the office boy, since the net tendency to be aggressive is maximally strong at point *C*. It is also apparent that individual *B* should arouse the greatest degree of conflict in the businessman, since *B* elicits aggressive and inhibitory tendencies of equal strength. Reference to our earlier discussion of discrimination-induced conflicts will reveal the several ways in which it parallels this displacement theory. In Miller's more detailed exposition of the theory, a number of additional deductions are presented which outline the expected consequences of changes in the relative strengths of the tendencies, of changes in the assumed shapes of the gradients, and the like.

A further extension and application of Miller's displacement paradigm has been presented recently by the anthropologist-psychologist team of Whiting and Child (33). In studying the origins of the fears of others, they advance the hypothesis that such fears may arise in part out of the displacement of aggression. Moreover, by assuming that conflict leads to an increment in drive, they have arrived at testable predictions concerning the relative strengths of fears of animal spirits and ghosts in primitive tribes. These predictions are supported by data drawn from cross-cultural analyses.

In closing, it is of interest to note that both Murdock (26) in his analysis of social structure and Horton (11) in his study of the social aspects of alcohol have found the conception of intersecting gradients to be useful. According to Murdock, the selection of sexual and marriage partners in human societies can be understood in terms of a series of interacting gradients of attraction and repulsion, where the degree of attraction or repulsion is assumed to vary in pro-portion to social distance. Horton's principal notion is that the anxiety levels of individuals—and hence their conflicts—can be reduced through the consumption of alcohol. From the assumption that such reductions in anxiety are rewarding, he predicts—and confirms his predictions by means of cross-cultural data —a number of interesting relationships between variables such as food scarcity and alcohol consumption.

References

1. AMSEL, A., and ROUSSEL, J. "Motivational Properties of Frustration. I. Effect on a Running Response of the Addition of Frustration to the Motivational Complex," *Journal of Experimental Psychology*, XLIII (1952), 363–68.

2. BROWN, J. S. "A Note on a Temporal Gradient of Reinforcement," *Journal of Experimental Psychology*, XXV (1939), 221–27.

3. ———. "Factors Determining Conflict Reactions in Difficult Discriminations," *ibid.*, XXXI (1942), 272–92.

4. ———. "Gradients of Approach and Avoidance Responses and Their Relation to Level of Motivation," *Journal of Comparative and Physiological Psychology*, XLI (1948), 450–65.

5. BROWN, J. S., and FARBER, I. E. "Emotions Conceptualized as Intervening Variables—with Suggestions toward a Theory of Frustration," *Psychological Bulletin*, XLVIII (1951), 465–95.

6. FINGER, F. W. "Quantitative Studies of 'Conflict.' I. Variations in Latency and Strength of the Rat's Response in a Discrimination-jumping Situation," *Journal of Comparative Psychology*, XXXI (1941), 97–127.

7. FREUD, S. *A General Introduction to Psychoanalysis*. New York: Boni & Liveright, 1920.

8. GANTT, W. H. "An Experimental Approach to Psychiatry," *American Journal of Psychiatry*, XCII (1936), 1007–21.

9. GODBEER, E. "Factors Inducing Conflict in the Choice Behavior of Children." Unpublished Master's thesis, Yale University, 1940.

10. GUTHRIE, E. R. *The Psychology of Human Conflict*. New York: Harper & Bros., 1938.

11. HORTON, D. "The Functions of Alcohol in Primitive Societies: A Cross-cultural Study," *Quarterly Journal of Studies on Alcohol*, IV (1943), 199–320.

12. HOVLAND, C. I., and SEARS, R. R. "Experiments on Motor Conflict. I. Types of Conflict and Their Modes of Resolution," *Journal of Experimental Psychology*, XXIII (1938), 477–93.

13. HULL, C. L. "The Goal-Gradient Hypothesis Applied to Some 'Field-Force' Problems in the Behavior of Young Children," *Psychological Review*, XLV (1938), 271–99.

14. JANET, P. *Psychological Healing*. Translated by EDEN and CEDAR PAUL. 2 vols. New York: Macmillan Co., 1925.

15. KAUFMAN, E. L., and MILLER, N. E. "Effect of Number of Reinforcements on

Strength of Approach in an Approach-Avoidance Conflict," *Journal of Comparative and Physiological Psychology*, XLII (1949), 65–74.

16. LEWIN, K. "Environmental Forces in Child Behavior and Development." In MURCHISON, C. (ed.), *A Handbook of Child Psychology*. Worcester, Mass.: Clark University Press, 1931.

17. LIDDELL, H. S., and BAYNE, T. L. "The Development of 'Experimental Neuroasthenia' in the Sheep during the Formation of Difficult Conditioned Reflexes," *American Journal of Physiology*, LXXXI (1927), 494.

18. MASSERMAN, J. H. *Behavior and Neurosis*. Chicago: University of Chicago Press, 1943.

19. McDOUGALL, W. *Outline of Abnormal Psychology*. New York: Charles Scribner's Sons, 1926.

20. MELTON, A. W. "Learning." In MONROE, W. S. (ed.), *Encyclopedia of Educational Research*. New York: Macmillan Co., 1941.

21. MILLER, N. E. "Experimental Studies of Conflict." In HUNT, J. McV. (ed.), *Personality and the Behavior Disorders*. New York: Ronald Press Co., 1944.

22. ———. "Theory and Experiment Relating Psychoanalytic Displacement to Stimulus-Response Generalization," *Journal of Abnormal and Social Psychology*, XLIII (1948), 155–78.

23. MILLER, N. E., and DOLLARD, J. *Social Learning and Imitation*. New Haven: Yale University Press, 1941.

24. MILLER, N. E., and STEVENSON, S. S. "Agitated Behavior of Rats during Experimental Extinction and a Curve of Spontaneous Recovery," *Journal of Comparative Psychology*, XXI (1936), 205–31.

25. MOWRER, O. H. "Preparatory Set (Expectancy): Some Methods of Measurement," *Psychological Monographs*, Vol. LII, No. 2 (1940) (whole No. 233).

26. MURDOCK, G. P. *Social Structure*. New York: Macmillan Co., 1949.

27. PAVLOV, I. P. *Conditioned Reflexes*. Translated by G. V. ANREP. London: Oxford University Press, 1927.

28. PRINCE, M. *The Unconscious, the Fundamentals of Human Personality, Normal and Abnormal*. New York: Macmillan Co., 1921. 2d ed. rev., 1924.

29. RIGBY, W. K. "Approach and Avoidance Gradients and Conflict Behavior in a Predominantly Temporal Situation," *Journal of Comparative and Physiological Psychology*, XLVII (1954), 83–89.

30. RIVERS, W. H. R. *Conflict and Dream*. London: Kegan Paul, 1923.

31. ROSENBAUM, G. "Temporal Gradients of Response Strength with Two Levels of Motivation," *Journal of Experimental Psychology*, XLI (1951), 261–67.

32. SHEFFIELD, V. F. "Resistance to Extinction as a Function of the Distribution of Extinction Trials," *Journal of Experimental Psychology*, XL (1950), 305–13.

33. WHITING, J. W. M., and CHILD, I. L. *Child Training and Personality: A Cross-cultural Study*. New Haven: Yale University Press, 1953.

PART II

Selected Research Areas

CHAPTER 1

Experimental Studies of Development

THE NATURE OF LOVE   Harry F. Harlow

Love is a wondrous state, deep, tender, and rewarding. Because of its intimate and personal nature it is regarded by some as an improper topic for experimental research. But, whatever our personal feelings may be, our assigned mission as psychologists is to analyze all facets of human and animal behavior into their component variables. So far as love or affection is concerned, psychologists have failed in this mission. The little we know about love does not transcend simple observation, and the little we write about it has been written better by poets and novelists. But of greater concern is the fact that psychologists tend to give progressively less attention to a motive which pervades our entire lives. Psychologists, at least psychologists who write textbooks, not only show no interest in the origin and development of love or affection, but they seem to be unaware of its very existence.

The apparent repression of love by modern psychologists stands in sharp contrast with the attitude taken by many famous and normal people. The word

Reprinted by permission of the American Psychological Association and the author from the *American Psychologist,* Vol. 13, 1958.

Address of the President at the 1958 meeting of the American Psychological Association [Ed.].

"love" has the highest reference frequency of any word cited in Bartlett's book of *Familiar Quotations.* It would appear that this emotion has long had a vast interest and fascination for human beings, regardless of the attitude taken by psychologists; but the quotations cited, even by famous and normal people, have a mundane redundancy. These authors and authorities have stolen love from the child and infant and made it the exclusive property of the adolescent and adult.

Thoughtful men, and probably all women, have speculated on the nature of love. From the developmental point of view, the general plan is quite clear: The initial love responses of the human being are those made by the infant to the mother or some mother surrogate. From this intimate attachment of the child to the mother, multiple learned and generalized affectional responses are formed.

Unfortunately, beyond these simple facts we know little about the fundamental variables underlying the formation of affectional responses and little about the mechanisms through which the love of the infant for the mother develops into the multifaceted response patterns characterizing love or affection in the adult. Because of the dearth of experimentation, theories about the fundamental nature of affection have evolved at the level of observation, intuition, and discerning guesswork, whether these have been proposed by psychologists, sociologists, anthropologists, physicians, or psychoanalysts.

The position commonly held by psychologists and sociologists is quite clear: The basic motives are, for the most part, the primary drives—particularly hunger, thirst, elimination, pain, and sex—and all other motives, including love or affection, are derived or secondary drives. The mother is associated with the reduction of the primary drives—particularly hunger, thirst, and pain—and through learning, affection or love is derived.

It is entirely reasonable to believe that the mother through association with food may become a secondary-reinforcing agent, but this is an inadequate mechanism to account for the persistence of the infant-maternal ties. There is a spate of researches on the formation of secondary reinforcers to hunger and thirst reduction. There can be no question that almost any external stimulus can become a secondary reinforcer if properly associated with tissue-need reduction, but the fact remains that this redundant literature demonstrates unequivocally that such derived drives suffer relatively rapid experimental extinction. Contrariwise, human affection does not extinguish when the mother ceases to have intimate association with the drives in question. Instead, the affectional ties to the mother show a lifelong, unrelenting persistence and, even more surprising, widely expanding generality.

Oddly enough, one of the few psychologists who took a position counter to modern psychological dogma was John B. Watson, who believed that love was an innate emotion elicited by cutaneous stimulation of the erogenous zones. But experimental psychologists, with their peculiar propensity to discover facts that are not true, brushed this theory aside by demonstrating that the human neonate had no differentiable emotions, and they established a fundamental psychological law that prophets are without honor in their own profession.

The psychoanalysts have concerned themselves with the problem of the nature of the development of love in the neonate and infant, using ill and aging human beings as subjects. They have discovered the overwhelming importance of the breast and related this to the oral erotic tendencies developed at an age preceding their subjects' memories. Their theories range from a belief that the infant has an innate need to achieve and suckle at the breast to beliefs not unlike commonly accepted psychological theories. There are exceptions, as seen in the recent writings of John Bowlby, who attributes importance not only to food and thirst satisfaction, but also to "primary object-clinging," a need for intimate physical contact, which is initially associated with the mother.

As far as I know, there exists no direct experimental analysis of the relative importance of the stimulus variables determining the affectional or love responses in the neonatal and infant primate. Unfortunately, the human neonate is a limited experimental subject for such researches because of his inadequate motor capabilities. By the time the human infant's motor responses can be precisely measured, the antecedent determining conditions cannot be defined, having been lost in a jumble and jungle of confounded variables.

Many of these difficulties can be resolved by the use of the neonatal and infant macaque monkey as the subject for the analysis of basic affectional variables. It is possible to make precise measurements in this primate beginning at two to ten days of age, depending upon the maturational status of the individual

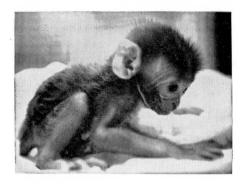

FIG. 1. Response to cloth pad by one-day-old monkey.

animal at birth. The macaque infant differs from the human infant in that the monkey is more mature at birth and grows more rapidly; but the basic responses relating to affection, including nursing, contact, clinging, and even visual and auditory exploration, exhibit no fundamental differences in the two species. Even the development of perception, fear, frustration, and learning capability follows very similar sequences in rhesus monkeys and human children.

Three years' experimentation before we started our studies on affection gave us experience with the neonatal monkey. We had separated more than 60 of these animals from their mothers 6 to 12 hours after birth and suckled them on tiny bottles. The infant mortality was only a small fraction of what would have obtained had we let the monkey mothers raise their infants. Our bottle-fed babies were healthier and heavier than monkey-mother-reared infants. We know that we are better monkey mothers than are real monkey mothers thanks to synthetic

diets, vitamins, iron extracts, penicillin, chloromycetin, 5% glucose, and constant, tender, loving care.

During the course of these studies we noticed that the laboratory-raised babies showed strong attachment to the cloth pads (folded gauze diapers) which were used to cover the hardware-cloth floors of their cages. The infants clung to these pads and engaged in violent temper tantrums when the pads were removed and replaced for sanitary reasons. Such contact-need or responsiveness had been reported previously by Gertrude van Wagenen for the monkey and by Thomas McCulloch and George Haslerud for the chimpanzee and is reminiscent of the devotion often exhibited by human infants to their pillows, blankets, and soft, cuddly stuffed toys. Responsiveness by the one-day-old infant monkey to the cloth pad is shown in Figure 1, and an unusual and strong attachment of a six-month-old infant to the cloth pad is il-

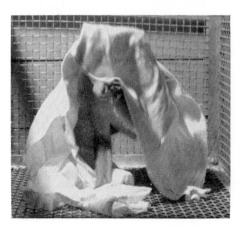

FIG. 2. Response to gauze pad by six-month-old monkey used in earlier study.

lustrated in Figure 2. The baby, human or monkey, if it is to survive, must clutch at more than a straw.

We had also discovered during some allied observational studies that a baby monkey raised on a bare wire-mesh cage floor survives with difficulty, if at all, during the first five days of life. If a wire-mesh cone is introduced, the baby does better; and, if the cone is covered

FIG. 3. Cloth mother surrogate.

with terry cloth, husky, healthy, happy babies evolve. It takes more than a baby and a box to make a normal monkey. We were impressed by the possibility that, above and beyond the bubbling fountain of breast or bottle, contact comfort might be a very important variable in the development of the infant's affection for the mother.

At this point we decided to study the development of affectional responses of neonatal and infant monkeys to an artificial, inanimate mother, and so we built a surrogate mother which we hoped and believed would be a good surrogate mother. In devising this surrogate mother we were dependent neither upon the capriciousness of evolutionary processes nor upon mutations produced by chance radioactive fallout. Instead, we designed the mother surrogate in terms of modern human-engineering principles (Fig-

ure 3). We produced a perfectly proportioned, streamlined body stripped of unnecessary bulges and appendices. Redundancy in the surrogate mother's system was avoided by reducing the number of breasts from two to one and placing this unibreast in an upper-thoracic, sagittal position, thus maximizing the natural and known perceptual-motor capabilities of the infant operator. The surrogate was made from a block of wood, covered with sponge rubber, and sheathed in tan cotton terry cloth. A light bulb behind her radiated heat. The result was a mother, soft, warm, and tender, a mother with infinite patience, a mother available twenty-four hours a day, a mother that never scolded her infant and never struck or bit her baby in anger. Furthermore, we designed a mother-machine with maximal maintenance efficiency since failure of any system or function could be resolved by the simple substitution of black boxes and new component parts. It is our opinion that we engineered a very superior monkey mother, although this position is not

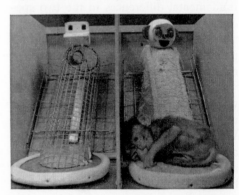

FIG. 4. Wire and cloth mother surrogates.

held universally by the monkey fathers.

Before beginning our initial experiment we also designed and constructed a second mother surrogate, a surrogate in which we deliberately built less than

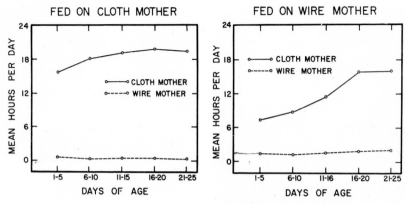

FIG. 5. Time spent on cloth and wire mother surrogates.

the maximal capability for contact comfort. This surrogate mother is illustrated in Figure 4. She is made of wire-mesh, a substance entirely adequate to provide postural support and nursing capability, and she is warmed by radiant heat. Her body differs in no essential way from that of the cloth mother surrogate other than in the quality of the contact comfort which she can supply.

In our initial experiment, the dual mother-surrogate condition, a cloth mother and a wire mother were placed in different cubicles attached to the infant's living cage as shown in Figure 4. For four newborn monkeys the cloth mother lactated and the wire mother did not; and, for the other four, this condition was reversed. In either condition the infant received all its milk through the mother surrogate as soon as it was able to maintain itself in this way, a capability achieved within two or three days except in the case of very immature infants. Supplementary feedings were given until the milk intake from the mother surrogate was adequate. Thus, the experiment was designed as a test of the relative importance of the variables of contact comfort and nursing comfort. During the first 14 days of life the monkey's cage floor was covered with

a heating pad wrapped in a folded gauze diaper, and thereafter the cage floor was bare. The infants were always free to leave the heating pad or cage floor to contact either mother, and the time spent on the surrogate mothers was automatically recorded. Figure 5 shows the total time spent on the cloth and wire mothers under the two conditions of feeding. These data make it obvious that contact comfort is a variable of overwhelming importance in the development of affec-

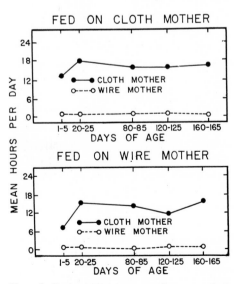

FIG. 6. Long-term contact time on cloth and wire mother surrogates.

Look Magazine Photo

Emil Schulthess

THE HIPPOPOTAMUS

This is the skin some babies feel
Replete with hippo love appeal
Each contact, cuddle, push, and shove
Elicits tons of baby love.

THE RHINOCEROS

The rhino's skin is thick and tough,
And yet this skin is soft enough
That baby rhinos always sense,
A love enormous and intense.

Ylla

Sponholtz

THE ELEPHANT

Though mother may be short on arms,
Her skin is full of warmth and charms.
And mother's touch on baby's skin
Endears the heart that beats within.

THE CROCODILE

Here is the skin they love to touch.
It isn't soft and there isn't much,
But its contact comfort will beguile
Love from the infant crocodile.

From All About Snakes,
Random House, Inc.

THE SNAKE

To baby vipers, scaly skin
Engenders love 'twixt kith and kin.
Each animal by God is blessed
With kind of skin it loves the best.

You see, all God's chillun's got skin.

tional responses, whereas lactation is a variable of negligible importance. With age and opportunity to learn, subjects with the lactating wire mother showed decreasing responsiveness to her and increasing responsiveness to the nonlactating cloth mother, a finding completely contrary to any interpretation of derived drive in which the mother-form becomes conditioned to hunger-thirst reduction. The persistence of these differential responses throughout 165 consecutive days of testing is evident in Figure 6.

One control group of neonatal monkeys was raised on a single wire mother, and a second control group was raised on a single cloth mother. There were no differences between these two groups in amount of milk ingested or in weight gain. The only difference between the groups lay in the composition of the feces, the softer stools of the wire-mother infants suggesting psychosomatic involvement. The wire mother is biologically adequate but psychologically inept.

We were not surprised to discover that contact comfort was an important basic affectional or love variable, but we did not expect it to overshadow so completely the variable of nursing; indeed, the disparity is so great as to suggest that the primary function of nursing as an affectional variable is that of insuring frequent and intimate body contact of the infant with the mother. Certainly, man cannot live by milk alone. Love is an emotion that does not need to be bottle- or spoon-fed, and we may be sure that there is nothing to be gained by giving lip service to love.

A charming lady once heard me describe these experiments; and, when I subsequently talked to her, her face brightened with sudden insight: "Now I know what's wrong with me," she said, "I'm just a wire mother." Perhaps she was lucky. She might have been a wire wife.

We believe that contact comfort has long served the animal kingdom as a motivating agent for affectional responses. Since at the present time we have no experimental data to substantiate this position, we supply information which must be accepted, if at all, on the basis of face validity:

One function of the real mother, human or subhuman, and presumably of a mother surrogate, is to provide a haven of safety for the infant in times of fear and danger. The frightened or ailing child clings to its mother, not its father; and this selective responsiveness in times of distress, disturbance, or danger may be used as a measure of the strength of affectional bonds. We have tested this kind of differential responsiveness by presenting to the infants in their cages, in the presence of the two mothers, various fear-producing stimuli such as the moving toy bear illustrated in Figure 13. A

FIG. 14. Typical response to cloth mother surrogate in fear test.

typical response to a fear stimulus is shown in Figure 14, and the data on differential responsiveness are presented in Figure 15. It is apparent that the cloth mother is highly preferred over the wire one, and this differential selectivity is enhanced by age and experience. In this situation, the variable of nursing appears to be of absolutely no importance: the infant consistently seeks the soft mother surrogate regardless of nursing condition.

Similarly, the mother or mother surrogate provides its young with a source

FIG. 13. Typical fear stimulus.

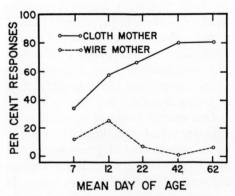

FIG. 15. Differential responsiveness in fear tests.

FIG. 16. Response to cloth mother in the open-field test.

of security, and this role or function is seen with special clarity when mother and child are in a strange situation. At the present time we have completed tests for this relationship on four of our eight baby monkeys assigned to the dual mother-surrogate condition by introducing them for three minutes into the strange environment of a room measuring six feet by six feet by six feet (also called the "open-field test") and containing multiple stimuli known to elicit curiosity-manipulatory responses in baby monkeys. The subjects were placed in this situation twice a week for eight weeks with no mother surrogate present during alternate sessions and the cloth mother present during the others. A cloth diaper was always available as one of the stimuli throughout all sessions. After one or two adaptation sessions, the infants always rushed to the mother surrogate when she was present and clutched her, rubbed their bodies against her, and frequently manipulated her body and face.

After a few additional sessions, the infants began to use the mother surrogate as a source of security, a base of operations. As is shown in Figures 16 and 17, they would explore and manipulate a stimulus and then return to the mother before adventuring again into the strange new world. The behavior of these infants was quite different when the mother was absent from the room. Frequently they would freeze in a crouched position, as is illustrated in Figures 18 and 19. Emotionality indices such as vocalization, crouching, rocking, and sucking increased sharply, as shown in Figure 20. Total emotionality score was cut in half when the mother was present. In the absence of the mother some of the experimental monkeys would rush to the center of the room where the mother was customarily placed and then run rapidly from object to object, screaming and crying all the while. Continuous, frantic clutching of their bodies was very common, even when not in the crouching position. These monkeys frequently contacted and clutched the cloth diaper, but this action never pacified them. The same

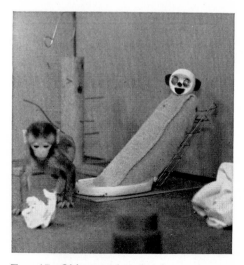

FIG. 17. Object exploration in presence of cloth mother.

FIG. 18. Response in the open-field test in the absence of the mother surrogate.

behavior occurred in the presence of the wire mother. No difference between the cloth-mother-fed and wire-mother-fed infants was demonstrated under either condition. Four control infants never raised with a mother surrogate showed the same emotionality scores when the mother was absent as the experimental

infants showed in the absence of the mother, but the controls' scores were slightly larger in the presence of the mother surrogate than in her absence.

Some years ago Robert Butler demonstrated that mature monkeys enclosed in a dimly lighted box would open and re-open a door hour after hour for no other reward than that of looking outside the box. We now have data indicating that neonatal monkeys show this same compulsive visual curiosity on their first test day in an adaptation of the Butler apparatus which we call the "love machine," an apparatus designed to measure love. Usually these tests are begun when the monkey is 10 days of age, but this same persistent visual exploration has been obtained in a three-day-old monkey during the first half-hour of testing. Butler also demonstrated that rhesus monkeys show selectivity in rate and frequency of door-opening to stimuli of differential attractiveness in the visual field outside the box. We have utilized this principle of response selectivity by the monkey to measure strength of affectional responsiveness in our infants in the baby version of the Butler box. The test sequence involves four repetitions of a test battery in which four stimuli—cloth mother, wire mother, infant mon-

FIG. 19. Response in the open-field test in the absence of the mother surrogate.

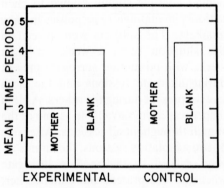

FIG. 20. Emotionality index with and without the presence of the cloth mother.

key, and empty box—are presented for a 30-minute period on successive days. The first four subjects in the dual mother-surrogate group were given a

FIG. 21. Visual exploration apparatus.

single test sequence at 40 to 50 days of age, depending upon the availability of the apparatus, and only their data are presented. The second set of four subjects is being given repetitive tests to obtain information relating to the development of visual exploration. The apparatus is illustrated in Figure 21. The data obtained from the first four infants raised with the two mother surrogates are presented in the middle graph of Figure 22 and show approximately equal responding to the cloth mother and another infant monkey, and no greater responsiveness to the wire mother than to an empty box. Again, the results are independent of the kind of mother that lactated, cloth or wire. The same results are found for a control group raised, but not fed, on a single cloth mother; these data appear in the graph on the right.

Contrariwise, the graph on the left shows no differential responsiveness to cloth and wire mothers by a second control group, which was not raised on any mother surrogate. We can be certain that not all love is blind.

The first four infant monkeys in the dual mother-surrogate group were separated from their mothers between 165 and 170 days of age and tested for retention during the following 9 days and then at 30-day intervals for six successive months. Affectional retention as measured by the modified Butler box is given in Figure 23. In keeping with the data obtained on adult monkeys by Butler, we find a high rate of responding to any stimulus, even the empty box. But throughout the entire 185-day retention period there is a consistent and significant difference in response frequency to the cloth mother contrasted with either the wire mother or the empty box, and no consistent difference between wire mother and empty box.

Affectional retention was also tested in the open field during the first 9 days after separation and then at 30-day in-

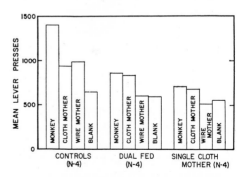

FIG. 22. Differential responses to visual exploration.

tervals, and each test condition was run twice at each retention interval. The infant's behavior differed from that observed during the period preceding separation. When the cloth mother was present in the post-separation period, the babies rushed to her, climbed up, clung tightly to her, and rubbed their heads and faces against her body. After this initial embrace and reunion, they played on the mother, including biting and tear-

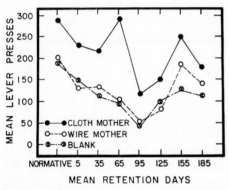

FIG. 23. Retention of differential visual exploration.

ing at her cloth cover; but they rarely made any attempt to leave her during the test period, nor did they manipulate or play with the objects in the room, in contrast with their behavior before maternal separation. The only exception was the occasional monkey that left the mother surrogate momentarily, grasped the folded piece of paper (one of the standard stimuli in the field), and brought it quickly back to the mother. It appeared that deprivation had enhanced the tie to the mother and rendered the contact-comfort need so prepotent that need for the mother overwhelmed the exploratory motives during the brief, three-minute test sessions. No change in these behaviors was observed throughout the 185-day period. When the mother was absent from the open field, the behavior of the infants was similar in the initial retention test to that during the preseparation tests; but they tended to show gradual adaptation to the open-

field situation with repeated testing and, consequently, a reduction in their emotionality scores.

In the last five retention test periods, an additional test was introduced in which the surrogate mother was placed in the center of the room and covered with a clear Plexiglas box. The monkeys were initially disturbed and frustrated when their explorations and manipulations of the box failed to provide contact with the mother. However, all animals adapted to the situation rather rapidly. Soon they used the box as a place of orientation for exploratory and play behavior, made frequent contacts with the objects in the field, and very often brought these objects to the Plexiglas box. The emotionality index was slightly higher than in the condition of the available cloth mothers, but it in no way approached the emotionality level displayed when the cloth mother was absent. Obviously, the infant monkeys gained emotional security by the presence of the mother even though contact was denied.

Affectional retention has also been measured by tests in which the monkey must unfasten a three-device mechanical puzzle to obtain entrance into a compartment containing the mother surrogate. All the trials are initiated by allow-

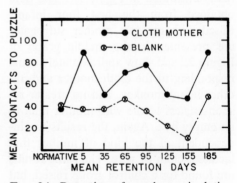

FIG. 24. Retention of puzzle manipulation responsiveness.

ing the infant to go through an unlocked door, and in half the trials it finds the mother present and in half, an empty compartment. The door is then locked and a ten-minute test conducted. In tests given prior to separation from the surrogate mothers, some of the infants had solved this puzzle and others had failed. The data of Figure 24 show that on the last test before separation there were no differences in total manipulation under mother-present and mother-absent conditions, but striking differences exist between the two conditions throughout the post-separation test periods. Again, there is no interaction with conditions of feeding.

The over-all picture obtained from surveying the retention data is unequivocal. There is little, if any, waning of responsiveness to the mother throughout this five-month period as indicated by any measure. It becomes perfectly obvious that this affectional bond is highly resistant to forgetting and that it can be retained for very long periods of time by relatively infrequent contact reinforcement. During the next year, retention tests will be conducted at 90-day intervals, and further plans are dependent upon the results obtained. It would appear that affectional responses may show as much resistance to extinction as has been previously demonstrated for learned fears and learned pain, and such data would be in keeping with those of common human observation.

The infant's responses to the mother surrogate in the fear tests, the open-field situation, and the baby Butler box and the responses on the retention tests cannot be described adequately with words. For supplementary information we turn to the motion picture record. (At this point a 20-minute film was presented illustrating and supplementing the behaviors described thus far in the address.)

We have already described the group of four control infants that had never lived in the presence of any mother surrogate and had demonstrated no sign of affection or security in the presence of the cloth mothers introduced in test sessions. When these infants reached the age of 250 days, cubicles containing both a cloth mother and a wire mother were attached to their cages. There was no lactation in these mothers, for the monkeys were on a solid-food diet. The initial reaction of the monkeys to the alterations was one of extreme disturbance. All the infants screamed violently and made repeated attempts to escape the cage whenever the door was opened. They kept a maximum distance from the mother surrogates and exhibited a considerable amount of rocking and crouching behavior, indicative of emotionality. Our first thought was that the critical period for the development of maternally directed affection had passed and that these macaque children were doomed to live as affectional orphans. Fortunately, these behaviors continued for only 12 to 48 hours and then gradually ebbed, changing from indifference to active contact on, and exploration of, the surrogates. The home-cage behavior of these control monkeys slowly become similar to that of the animals raised with the mother surrogates from birth. Their manipulation and play on the cloth mother became progressively more vigorous to the point of actual mutilation, particularly during the morning after the cloth mother had been given her daily change of terry covering. The control subjects were now actively running to the cloth mother when frightened and had to be coaxed from her to be taken from the cage for formal testing.

Objective evidence of these changing behaviors is given in Figure 25, which plots the amount of time these infants spent on the mother surrogates. Within

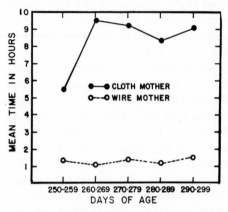

FIG. 25. Differential time spent on cloth and wire mother surrogates by monkeys started at 250 days of age.

10 days mean contact time is approximately nine hours, and this measure remains relatively constant throughout the next 30 days. Consistent with the results on the subjects reared from birth with dual mothers, these late-adopted infants spent less than one and one-half hours per day in contact with the wire mothers, and this activity level was relatively constant throughout the test sessions. Although the maximum time that the control monkeys spent on the cloth mother was only about half that spent by the original dual mother-surrogate group, we cannot be sure that this discrepancy is a function of differential early experience. The control monkeys were about three months older when the mothers were attached to their cages than the experimental animals had been when their mothers were removed and the retention tests begun. Thus, we do not know what the amount of contact would be for a 250-day-old animal raised from birth with surrogate mothers. Neverthe-

less, the magnitude of the differences and the fact that the contact-time curves for the mothered-from-birth infants had remained constant for almost 150 days suggest that early experience with the mother is a variable of measurable importance.

The control group has also been tested for differential visual exploration after the introduction of the cloth and wire mothers; these behaviors are plotted in Figure 26. By the second test session a high level of exploratory behavior had developed, and the responsiveness to the wire mother and the empty box is significantly greater than that to the cloth mother. This is probably not an artifact since there is every reason to believe that the face of the cloth mother is a fear stimulus to most monkeys that have not had extensive experience with this object during the first 40 to 60 days of life. Within the third test session a sharp change in trend occurs, and the cloth mother is then more frequently viewed than the wire mother or the blank box;

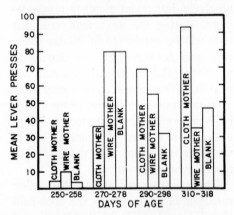

FIG. 26. Differential visual exploration of monkeys started at 250 days of age.

this trend continues during the fourth session, producing a significant preference for the cloth mother.

Before the introduction of the mother

surrogate into the home-cage situation, only one of the four control monkeys had ever contacted the cloth mother in the open-field tests. In general, the surrogate mother not only gave the infants no security, but instead appeared to serve as a fear stimulus. The emotionality scores of these control subjects were slightly higher during the mother-present test sessions than during the mother-absent test sessions. These behaviors were changed radically by the fourth post-introduction test approximately 60 days later. In the absence of the cloth mothers the emotionality index in this fourth test remains near the earlier level, but the score is reduced by half when the mother is present, a result strikingly similar to that found for infants raised with the dual mother-surrogates from birth. The control infants now show increasing object exploration and play behavior, and they begin to use the mother as a base of operations, as did the infants raised from birth with the mother surrogates. However, there are still definite differences in the behavior of the two groups. The control infants do not rush directly to the mother and clutch her violently; but instead they go toward, and orient around, her, usually after an initial period during which they frequently show disturbed behavior, exploratory behavior, or both.

That the control monkeys develop affection or love for the cloth mother when she is introduced into the cage at 250 days of age cannot be questioned. There is every reason to believe, however, that this interval of delay depresses the intensity of the affectional response below that of the infant monkeys that were surrogate-mothered from birth onward. In interpreting these data it is well to remember that the control monkeys had had continuous opportunity to observe and hear other monkeys housed in adjacent cages and that they had had limited opportunity to view and contact surrogate mothers in the test situations, even though they did not exploit the opportunities.

During the last two years we have observed the behavior of two infants raised by their own mothers. Love for the real mother and love for the surrogate mother appear to be very similar. The baby macaque spends many hours a day clinging to its real mother. If away from the mother when frightened, it rushes to her and in her presence shows comfort and composure. As far as we can observe, the infant monkey's affection for the real mother is strong, but no stronger than that of the experimental monkey for the surrogate cloth mother, and the security that the infant gains from the presence of the real mother is no greater than the security it gains from a cloth surrogate. Next year we hope to put this problem to final, definitive, experimental test. But, whether the mother is real or a cloth surrogate, there does develop a deep and abiding bond between mother and child. In one case it may be the call of the wild and in the other the McCall of civilization, but in both cases there is "togetherness."

In spite of the importance of contact comfort, there is reason to believe that other variables of measurable importance will be discovered. Postural support may be such a variable, and it has been suggested that, when we build arms into the mother surrogate, 10 is the minimal number required to provide adequate child care. Rocking motion may be such a variable, and we are comparing rocking and stationary mother surrogates and inclined planes. The differential responsiveness to cloth mother and cloth-covered inclined plane suggests that clinging as well as contact is an affectional variable of importance. Sounds, particularly natural, maternal sounds, may operate as either unlearned or learned affectional variables. Visual responsiveness may be such a variable, and it is possible that some semblance of visual imprinting may develop in the neonatal monkey. There are indications that this becomes a variable of importance during the course of infancy through some maturational process.

John Bowlby has suggested that there is an affectional variable which he calls "primary object following," characterized by visual and oral search of the mother's face. Our surrogate-mother-raised baby monkeys are at first inattentive to her face, as are human neonates to human mother faces. But by 30 days of age ever-increasing responsiveness to the mother's face appears—whether through learning, maturation, or both—and we have reason to believe that the face becomes an object of special attention.

Our first surrogate-mother-raised baby had a mother whose head was just a ball of wood since the baby was a month early and we had not had time to design a more esthetic head and face. This baby had contact with the blank-faced mother for 180 days and was then placed with two cloth mothers, one motionless and one rocking, both being endowed with painted, ornamented faces. To our surprise the animal would compulsively rotate both faces 180 degrees so that it viewed only a round, smooth face and never the painted, ornamented face. Furthermore, it would do this as long as the patience of the experimenter in reorienting the faces persisted. The monkey showed no sign of fear or anxiety, but it showed unlimited persistence. Subsequently it improved its technique, compulsively removing the heads and rolling them into its cage as fast as they were returned. We are intrigued by this observation, and we plan to examine systematically the role of the mother face in the development of infant-monkey affections. Indeed, these observations suggest the need for a series of ethological-type researches on the two-faced female.

Although we have made no attempts thus far to study the generalization of infant-macaque affection or love, the techniques which we have developed offer promise in this uncharted field. Beyond this, there are few if any technical difficulties in studying the affection of the actual, living mother for the child, and the techniques developed can be utilized and expanded for the analysis and developmental study of father-infant and infant-infant affection.

Since we can measure neonatal and infant affectional responses to mother surrogates, and since we know they are strong and persisting, we are in a position to assess the effects of feeding and contactual schedules; consistency and inconsistency in the mother surrogates; and early, intermediate, and late maternal deprivation. Again, we have here a family of problems of fundamental interest and theoretical importance.

If the researches completed and proposed make a contribution, I shall be grateful; but I have also given full thought to possible practical applications. The socioeconomic demands of the present and the threatened socioeconomic demands of the future have led the American woman to displace, or threaten to displace, the American man in science and industry. If this process continues, the problem of proper child-rearing practices faces us with startling clarity. It is cheering in view of this trend to realize that the American male is physically endowed with all the really essential equipment to compete with the American female on equal terms in one essential activity: the rearing of infants. We now know that women in the working classes are not needed in the home because of their primary mammalian capabilities; and it is possible that in the foreseeable future neonatal nursing will not be regarded as a necessity, but as a luxury—to use Veblen's term—a form of conspicuous consumption limited perhaps to the upper classes. But whatever course history may take, it is comforting to know that we are now in contact with the nature of love.

For some of Harlow's revised conclusions on the effect of real mothering, see The heterosexual affectional system in monkeys. *Amer. Psychol.,* 1962, **17,** 1–10 [Ed.].

INFANTILE TRAUMA, GENETIC FACTORS, AND ADULT TEMPERAMENT

Gardner Lindzey, David T. Lykken, and Harvey D. Winston

In spite of a welter of empirical and theoretical activity centering upon the role of infantile experience as a determinant of adult personality it is evident that there are few important issues in this area that have been satisfactorily resolved. Prominent among these open issues is the potential contribution of gene structure to the relation between infantile experience and adult temperament. Although King (1958), has identified gene factors as one of seven major parameters to be considered in studying the relation between infantile experience and adult effects, there is little in the way of compelling empirical findings concerning the role of genetic factors in this setting.

This sparse activity in the world of observation exists in spite of a history of theoretical interest in this issue. There are few general theories of behavior that fail to take into consideration, at least implicitly, the potential impact of constitutional or genetic factors upon early

Reprinted by permission of the American Psychological Association and the authors from the *Journal of Abnormal and Social Psychology,* Vol. 61, 1960.

experience and its consequences. Perhaps the most influential and persistent emphasis upon the role of heredity in this context has been provided by Freud (1905) with his discussions of the determinants of fixation, but his position differs from other personality theorists on this issue primarily in regard to explicitness.

The present study was designed to provide further evidence relevant to this general issue. Because of traditional difficulties involved in using human subjects for studies spanning the life history of the organism and the additional requirement that genetic variation be controlled, it was necessary to use subjects drawn from inbred strains of mice.

While the most unusual aspect of this study inquired into the interaction between gene factors and the effects of infantile trauma, it would be a rash investigator indeed who risked his all on an interaction term. Consistent with this premise is the fact that our study also provides information concerning the general effects of infantile trauma, their situational generality and duration, as well as further evidence regarding the influence of genetic factors upon various measures of temperament.

A word should be said concerning previous results that are relevant to the relation between infantile trauma and emotionality, for here, as well as in connection with the interaction effect we have just discussed, we have made specific predictions prior to the study. Clear evidence of an increase in emotionality in mice as a result of infantile trauma has been demonstrated by Hall and Whiteman (1951), while other investigators working with mice (Stanley & Monkman, 1956) and with rats (Griffiths & Stringer, 1952) have failed to find any significant differences in emotionality between control and traumatized animals. One investigator (Ader, 1957) actually has reported results indicating that treated rats were *less* emotional than control animals. Although these studies have led to conflicting results, the firmness of the findings of Hall and Whiteman (1951), coupled with consistent evidence from human investigations (Bowlby, 1951) and a boost from psychoanalytic theory, led us to predict that early traumatic experience would produce an increase in emotionality (timidity).

In summary, this study was designed to provide information concerning:

(1) The importance of genetic factors as determinants of emotionality, timidity, and activity.

(2) The general effects of infantile trauma, their situational generality, and the duration of these effects through time.

(3) The influence of genetic factors upon the relation between infantile trauma and adult temperament.

Method

SUBJECTS

The (Ss) of this investigation were offspring of breeding animals belonging to four different inbred strains of mice. The parent animals were obtained from a colony maintained by John J. Bittner of the Cancer Biology Laboratories of the University of Minnesota and represent the outcome of many generations of brother-sister matings. The conventional labels for these strains and the approximate number of generations of controlled brother-sister matings are as follows: C57BL/1 or B/1 (51 generations); C3H (93 generations); DBA/8 or D/8 (27 generations); JK (71 generations). The first three strains were selected on the basis of prior information (Lindzey, 1951) indicating diversity in emotionality, while the JK strain was selected because observation of them in the colony suggested that their behavior was quite different from the other strains. They were also selected so that all four strains could be identified easily by their distinctive coat color.

Within each strain the successive litters at birth were assigned alternately to either the experimental or the control group with the restriction that when the second litter by a particular mother was born that it would be given a different assignment than the first litter. This shifting procedure was continued through all litters until the desired number of animals in either the control or experimental group was achieved, and all subsequent litters were then assigned to the other group until the necessary number was reached. Because of the impossibility of predicting survival rates precisely for a period of almost four months, a variable number of animals resulted in the different experimental groups. The smallest number in any single group was 23 while the largest number was 36. The total number of animals included in the study was 259.

Each litter was raised in a separate cage with the mother until 24 days of age, at which time the young were weaned and segregated by sex. Animals were individually identified by an ear punch code, but this operation was not carried out until completion of the first consequent measure in order to avoid the possibility that this relatively traumatic procedure would wipe out the effects of our experimental treatment.

INFANTILE TRAUMA

Control and experimental animals were raised under the same conditions except that at four days of age those animals assigned to the experimental group were on four successive days exposed to an extremely loud, high frequency, auditory stimulus. The procedure followed was essentially the same as that described by Hall and Whiteman (1953) and involved placing the mice on a thin cardboard container in a #1 12-gal. wash tub with a doorbell (#504 Eclipse) fixed to the side. After a 2-min. interval the doorbell was run for 2 min., following which the mice were left in the tub for another two minutes before being returned to their cages. On the first three trials all animals were placed together in the tub, but on the fourth trial they were separated. The procedure for the control animals was precisely the same except that the bell was not rung while they were in the tub.

30-day open field test. Beginning at 30 days of age each mouse was placed for 2 min. in the same type of wash tub in which the auditory trauma had been administered. The tub was brightly lighted by a shielded 150-w. glazed bulb that was placed directly over the tub at a height of approximately 1½ ft. The mouse was left in the tub for 2 min. at the end of which time the incidence of defecation and urination was recorded and the mouse returned to his living cage. This measure was repeated on 10 succes-

sive days. The measure of emotionality was simply presence or absence of defecation and/or urination during each trial.

Stovepipe test. This instrument was devised by Stone (1929) as a measure of timidity or of the "dominance of hiding tendency over hunger," (p. 36) and was used by Hall and Whiteman (1951) in the study referred to earlier. In this measure the mouse was placed in a starting box connected with a **U**-shaped stovepipe (each unit approximately 2 ft. in length) that led to a goal box containing a food receptacle holding wet mash. Thus, all that the mouse had to do to reach the food was to enter the stovepipe, follow the passage, and leave the dark pipe for the more brightly illuminated goal box. The mice were again given 10 trials on successive days, commencing at 70 days of age, and they were run under 22½ hrs. of food deprivation. The measure employed was the total time that it took on the 10 trials for the mouse to enter the goal box. The few mice that on particular trials failed to leave the starting box within 5 min. were on these trials arbitrarily assigned the same time as the mouse that took the longest time in reaching the goal box.

100-day open field test. Commencing at 100 days of age the open field test was repeated for 10 trials with the measure of emotionality consisting of presence or absence of defecation and/or urination summed across the 10 trials for each S. In addition a measure of motility was secured by dividing the wash tub into 12 spaces of equal area and counting the number of spaces that each mouse moved through during the two minute trial and again summing the results of the individual trials over the 10 days.

ANALYSIS OF DATA

The obvious method of statistical analysis for our data was a 2 × 4 analysis of variance and this technique was used for all data except those derived from the first open field test. In the latter case the absence of individual identification made it impossible to summate scores over the 10 trials and, in general, made it virtually impossible to devise a sensitive measure of the interaction hypothesis. Demonstration of strain differences and treatment effects was not particularly difficult, in part because they were relatively evident, and here we have relied upon descriptive presentation and the use of such simple devices as the sign test. The best estimate of interaction that could be devised, however, was to adapt the chi square test and then to apply this test separately to the data for each of the 10 days. This is obviously a somewhat unsatisfactory test of the interaction. We have not hesitated to apply one-tailed tests of significance to data related to directional hypotheses stated in advance of the study.

For purposes of analysis of variance we reduced all groups to the size of the smallest group in order to avoid the complexities of disproportionality. Ss were eliminated on a chronological basis beginning with the animals that were last to complete the procedures. In the case of descriptive presentation of results we have included all animals studied with an appropriate indication of the number in each group.

Results and Discussion

GENE DETERMINANTS OF
TEMPERAMENT

Here we are concerned with strain differences in two open field measures of emotionality, the stovepipe measure of timidity, and an open field measure of motility. The findings are clear and dramatic. No sentient person could observe the data reported in Tables 1–6 and conclude for any one of these attributes that the animals in all the strains could have been drawn from a single common popu-

TABLE 1. PERCENTAGE OF ANIMALS DEFECATING DAILY ON 30-DAY OPEN FIELD TEST

Strain	Treatment	N	Day										Average
			1	2	3	4	5	6	7	8	9	10	
C57BL/1	Control	28	28.6	28.6	32.1	53.6	35.7	39.3	46.4	32.1	28.6	17.9	34.3
C57BL/1	Experimental	25	32.0	36.0	40.0	40.0	60.0	52.0	36.0	40.0	36.0	32.0	40.4
C3H	Control	34	85.3	88.2	82.3	64.7	73.5	70.6	85.3	73.5	73.5	73.5	77.1
C3H	Experimental	39	92.3	92.3	92.3	79.5	82.0	84.6	92.3	94.9	94.9	100.0	90.5
DBA/8	Control	37	64.9	81.1	73.0	70.3	62.2	64.9	62.2	64.9	59.5	67.6	67.0
DBA/8	Experimental	35	54.3	80.0	82.9	80.0	82.9	82.9	74.3	57.1	77.1	71.4	74.3
JK	Control	29	58.6	79.3	82.8	86.2	100.0	89.6	96.5	72.4	93.1	86.2	84.5
JK	Experimental	32	90.6	87.5	84.4	90.6	93.8	96.9	90.6	87.5	87.5	93.8	90.3

lation. In some instances the strains are so different as to show virtually no overlap. In view of the fact that the only known difference between these strains lies in their genetic constitution, it seems a prudent conclusion that genetic factors make a considerable contribution to each of our three measures of temperament.

Our findings are given added weight when coupled with the results of a number of earlier investigations using both rats (Hall, 1938; Broadhurst, 1958) and mice (Lindzey, 1951; Thompson, 1953, 1956; McClearn, 1959), all of which demonstrate wide strain differences on comparable measures. More interesting

collecting the data, and with animals that are not even known to belong to the same subline within the various strains. Even worse, we *do* know that the two samples were drawn from colonies that have been separated long enough to provide ample opportunity for "genetic drift" as well as spontaneous mutation. Given all of these sources of potential variation it is quite surprising to find the consistency of the strains and the measure so great. Thus, we are afforded the luxury of simultaneously gaining confidence in the stability of the organism we are studying and the reliability of our measure.

In general, these findings serve to em-

TABLE 2. CONSISTENCY OF EMOTIONALITY MEASURE IN
1951 STUDY AND PRESENT STUDY

	C57BL	C3H	DBA
Percent Defecation (1951)	37 ($N = 100$)	72 ($N = 100$)	68 ($N = 100$)
Percent Defecation (present study)	34 ($N = 28$)	77 ($N = 34$)	67 ($N = 37$)

than this general congruence is a specific examination of the incidence of defecation on the part of the three strains included in both the present study and the previous investigation by Lindzey (1951). In each study, C57, DBA, and C3H strains were employed and in each case an open field test of emotionality was utilized. In Table 2 the percentage of animals defecating in each strain in the earlier study, and the percentage of defecation over 10 trials in each strain in the present study, are compared. The figures are highly constant in spite of the fact that the data were collected with more than a decade of time intervening, with considerable variation in the details of the open field test, with different persons

phasize again the pervasive impact upon behavior of genetic factors and thus strongly suggest the inadequacy of attempts to formulate or account for behavior that do not direct careful attention to the role of hereditary factors. It is interesting to note that it is not necessary to inbreed selectively for particular characteristics in order to produce clear evidence for the influence of genic factors upon behavior. Inbreeding of the present animals was uninfluenced by the temperament characteristics of interest in the present study, and, in spite of this, we find the particular genetic patterns that have been isolated are dramatically different in their behavioral consequences.

INFLUENCE OF INFANTILE
TRAUMA UPON TEMPERAMENT

What exactly were the effects of the auditory, infantile trauma? The reader will recall our prediction that this experience would lead to an increase of emotionality and timidity. Examination of the data summarized in Table 1 reveals that in spite of the awkwardness resulting from our inability to identify individual animals, there is little doubt that the experimental treatment led to an increase in emotionality as measured by the 30-day test. Inspection of the proportion of experimental and control animals defecating on each of the 10 trials within the four strains reveals that 32 of the 40 comparisons point to the greater emotionality of the traumatized

animals. This incidence of "hits" is well beyond the 1% level of significance, even utilizing the relatively insensitive sign test. Actually, the within-strain results for the C3H animals (on all 10 trials the experimental animals showed a greater proportional defecation) are by themselves significant at below the 5% level using the sign test, while results for the other strains (7 or 8 trials out of 10 in which experimentals defecate more) approach significance.

The results of the stovepipe test, summarized in Table 3, provide suggestive evidence ($p < .10$) for a treatment effect indicating greater timidity (slower in getting to reward) on the part of the traumatized mice. Consistently, we find in Table 4 that at the 100-day open field test there is also a difference in emotion-

TABLE 3. ANALYSIS OF VARIANCE OF STOVEPIPE TEST

Source	df	Sum of Squares	Mean Square	F	P
Treatment	1	2,350,782	2,350,782	1.93	$<.10$ *
Strain	3	241,013,412	80,337,804	65.96	$<.0001$
Interaction	3	10,241,048	3,413,682	2.80	$<.05$
Within (error)	176	214,356,579	1,217,935		
Total	183	467,961,821			

* One-tailed test.

TABLE 4. ANALYSIS OF VARIANCE OF 100-DAY OPEN
FIELD TESTS: EMOTIONALITY

Source	df	Sum of Squares	Mean Square	F	P
Treatment	1	16.5093	16.5093	2.86629	$<.05$ *
Strain	3	679.4458	226.4819	39.3211	$<.0001$
Interaction	3	2.1082	.7027	—	—
Within (error)	176	1013.7287	5.7598		
Total	183	1711.7920			

* One-tailed test.

ality indicating that the treated animals were more emotional. Only in the case of motility, as revealed in Table 5, do we find little indication of treatment effects upon behavior.

pectations and fit very neatly with the results reported by Hall and Whiteman (1951) on the basis of similar experimental operations. However, our results directly contradict the conclusion of Ader

TABLE 5. ANALYSIS OF VARIANCE OF 100-DAY OPEN
FIELD TEST: MOTILITY

Source	df	Sum of Squares	Mean Square	F	P
Treatment	1	14,635.2	14,635.2	1.29	<.50
Strain	3	1,421,619.4	473,873.1	41.8	<.0001
Interaction	3	24,268.4	8,089.5	.071	—
Within (error)	176	1,994,390.6	11,331.8		
Total	183	3,454,213.6			

TABLE 6. MEANS AND SDs FOR STOVEPIPE TEST AND 100-DAY OPEN FIELD TEST

Strain	Treatment	Stovepipe Mean (N = 24)	SD	100-Day Emotionality Mean (N = 23)	SD	100-Day Motility Mean (N = 23)	SD
C57BL/1	Control	2301	1339	4.26	3.40	401.2	135.3
C57BL/1	Experimental	2069	882	4.57	3.19	355.0	165.1
C3H	Control	3322	1669	8.43	1.58	198.2	110.7
C3H	Experimental	4312	1039	9.35	1.05	188.1	85.9
DBA/8	Control	773	436	6.39	2.84	272.5	63.3
DBA/8	Experimental	778	407	6.96	2.71	287.7	99.7
JK	Control	1480	1061	8.87	1.51	163.3	67.1
JK	Experimental	1601	1007	9.48	1.02	133.0	53.7

To summarize, there seems little doubt that subjecting infant mice to a noxious, auditory stimulus of high intensity leads to an increase in emotionality in adulthood and there is some basis for believing that there is also an increase in timidity. There is no evidence, however, that this experience influences motility in an open field setting.

These findings confirm our prior ex-

(1957), based upon an investigation dealing with rats, and are inconsistent with the findings of Griffiths and Stringer (1952), and Hunt and Otis (1955) based on observation of rats, as well as the findings of Stanley and Monkman (1956) derived from the study of mice. There are so many parametric differences between all of these studies (species of animal, nature of trauma, age at trauma, age at consequent measure) that it is probably useless to attempt a rational analysis of the basis for these experimental differences. It is worth note, however, that there is actually no evidence in any study for infantile trauma *decreasing* emotionality. Although Ader has suggested this possibility, his own data, in the only study in which he employed stimuli that could reasonably be considered noxious or traumatic (Ader, 1959), suggest a heightening of emotionality as a result of infantile trauma. Moreover, Ader's attempts to account for the findings of Hall and Whiteman on the basis of the fact that they used seizure-susceptible mice and an infantile trauma identical to that used in producing audiogenic seizures, is not supportable in view of the fact that the present study led to comparable results with strains such as the C57BL/1 and C3H, which are very low in seizure incidence (Lindzey, 1951).

Duration of traumatic effects. Because of the imprecision of our measures and the differences in the form of our data at age 30 days and age 100 days, it is impossible to make any exact estimate of the extent to which the experimental effects may have diminished with the passage of time. However, it is evident that at 30 days, at 70 days, and at 100 days, the influence of the infantile trauma is clearly observable. Whatever may have been lost in intensity, the main effect is still manifest at the time of the last measure. Actually, a close descriptive inspection of the results of the present study, and the results contained in the Hall and Whiteman paper, suggest that there may have been some diminishing of treatment effects by the time of the 100-day test, but there is no firm evidence to support this contention.

Generality of traumatic effects. One obvious and important question has to do with the narrowness with which the effects of the infantile trauma are linked to situations resembling the original traumatic setting. Obviously, the implications of the trauma for the organism are very different if it leads to a generalized response disposition that is elicited in many settings, rather than leading to effects that can be observed only in situations very similar to the original one. Both Beach and Jaynes (1954) and Ader (1959) attempt to account for the increased emotionality following infantile trauma reported by Hall and Whiteman on the basis of the similarity between the traumatic setting and the setting in which emotionality was measured. The results of the present study are quite specific in refuting this proposal, as we secured consistent empirical findings in connection with both Stone's measure of timidity and Hall's open field measure. The stimulus differences between the stovepipe test and the open field test are so profound that if we are willing to concede the possibility of stimulus generalization from the original setting to the stovepipe test, we have already granted tremendous generality to the effects of the trauma. In brief, then, our findings suggest that the results of the infantile trauma are of a relatively general nature and should be discernible in a wide variety of different settings.

IMPACT OF GENETIC VARIATION UPON EFFECTS OF INFANTILE TRAUMA

We have already seen that our behavioral measures of temperament are heavily influenced by genetic variation and that these same measures covary with traumatic, infantile experience. The essential question remaining is whether these two sets of determinants show any interaction. Are the changes in temperament that can be attributed to early infantile experience in part dependent upon the gene structure of the organism undergoing the experience?

It was impossible to devise a completely satisfactory test of the interaction effect for the 30-day open field test of emotionality because the individual animals were not identified. Consequently, the best we could do was to measure the interaction between strain and treatment effects for each of the 10 trials individually. The resulting χ^2 coefficients provide no evidence to support the hypothesis of interaction. It is true that we would have preferred to use a single more sensitive measure of emotionality (incidence of defecation summed over 10 days), and it is possible to speculate that with this increased sensitivity we would have been able to detect an interaction. There is, however, no direct evidence to support this contention.

Our second measure of interaction between strain and treatment effects deals with the stovepipe measure of timidity and, as the results summarized in Table 3 indicate, we found clear evidence for the existence of an interaction. These results suggest that changes in timidity resulting from the infantile trauma are in part dependent upon the strain (genetic makeup) of the mouse. In particular, the C57BL/1 mice seemed much less influenced by the experimental treatment than the other strains. The third test of the interaction hypothesis is presented in Tables 4 and 5, where we find no evidence for an interaction between strain and treatment in effects upon emotionality or motility at the 100-day test.

The simplest conclusion that can be derived from these findings is that there is an interaction between gene factors and infantile trauma for timidity, as measured by the stovepipe test, but not for emotionality or motility. While this finding may ultimately be substantiated, there are certain unsatisfactory aspects to our test of the interaction of strain and infantile trauma in the case of the two emotionality measures and the measure of motility. The test for the 30-day data had to be carried out upon single observations rather than observations cumulated over 10 days and the test of interaction for the 100-day data may have suffered from a diminishing of treatment effects at this stage. It is known that the analysis of variance measure of interaction is not a powerful test and it is possible that interaction could be demonstrated only with more powerful treatment effects or a larger number of Ss. Our failure to find treatment effects upon motility made our interaction measure in this area relatively meaningless.

So far as our hypothesis is concerned, we have obtained evidence for the existence of interaction between strain and infantile treatment effects as predicted, but this relationship was not so general as we had expected. Our conviction concerning the existence of some degree of interaction is strengthened by the results obtained by King (1959), demonstrating an interaction between the effects of infantile handling and membership in different subspecies, and Valenstein, Riss, and Young (1955), suggesting a relationship between the effects of isolation upon sexual behavior and membership in a particular inbred strain. An additional study by King (1957) also provides evidence suggestive of such an interaction, although the experimental treatment (isolation) did not take place in this case until after weaning. The findings indicate that changes in aggressive behavior that were produced by isolation in one mouse strain were not duplicated in a second strain. There is unfortunately, no direct test of the difference between the two strains in treatment effects. Joint consideration of all of these findings provides a relatively firm basis for concluding that the consequences of infantile trauma are in part dependent upon the genetic structure of the organism experiencing the trauma.

What are the implications of such a finding for psychological theory? One may contend that these results, even secured in connection with mere mice or guinea pigs, provide a type of confirmation of Freud's assertion that any attempt to map early experience into adult behavior must allow for the contribution of genetic factors. While such a statement has a rather hollow sound at the level of human behavior because of the little that is known concerning the gene structure of man, it does have some specific empirical implications. For example, our results would suggest that when an investigator works with Ss of unknown or uncontrolled heredity, it is altogether possible to conduct an otherwise exemplary study of the effects of infantile experience and fail to find evidence for such effects. Or, more generally, we may expect that a variety of different empirical findings might be observed in similar studies as a consequence of investigators dealing with Ss of various genetic backgrounds, rather than as a result of faulty experimental technique. In general, this is a finding that makes life more complex for both investigator and theorist, and in an area where there has never been any shortage of complexity.

Summary

This investigation was concerned with the effects of infantile trauma upon adult temperament, the influence of genetic factors upon temperament, and the possibility of an interaction between early experience and gene structure in their influence upon adult behavior.

Four strains of homozygous mice were used in the study, with the infant offspring assigned by litter to either an experimental or control group. In all, 259 mice were studied. The experimental mice, beginning at four days of age, were exposed on four successive days to a noxious, auditory stimulus while the control animals were treated in an identical manner except that they were not exposed to the traumatic stimulus. At 30 days of age all mice were examined for 10 successive days in an open field test of emotionality and beginning at 70 days of age the mice were again observed for 10 successive days in a stovepipe test of timidity. A final measure of emotionality, and a measure of motility, were secured from 10 days of observation in an open field test beginning at 100 days of age.

The data obtained provide clear and compelling evidence for the importance of genetic factors as determinants of emotionality, timidity, and motility. The four strains displayed marked differences in all three attributes. There was also direct evidence for the influence of infantile trauma upon emotionality and suggestive evidence in regard to timidity, but no evidence for such an influence upon motility. The effects of the infantile trauma were enduring, extending at least to an age of 100 days, and were not limited to stimulus situations closely similar to the original traumatic situation. We found evidence of an interaction between the effects of infantile trauma upon stovepipe timidity and genetic factors, but there was no evidence for such an interaction in the case of emotionality. All of our positive findings are supported by evidence supplied by other investigators.

These findings not only demonstrate the central developmental importance of genetic factors and infantile trauma, they also underline the relative complexity of the relationship between infantile experience and adult behavior. Given an interaction between gene factors and infantile trauma it is readily understandable that inconsistent results might be observed by investigators working with heterozygous Ss of unknown gene structure. Finally, we have pointed to the consistency between the present findings and Freud's formulations concerning the role of constitutional factors in the developmental process.

References

ADER, R. Effects of early experience on emotionality. *Amer. Psychologist*, 1957, **12,** 410.

————. The effects of early experience on subsequent emotionality and resistance to stress. *Psychol. Monogr.,* 1959. **73**(2, Whole No. 472).

BEACH, F. A., & JAYNES, J. Effects of early experience upon the behavior of animals. *Psychol. Bull.,* 1954, **51,** 239–264.

BOWLBY, J. *Maternal care and mental health.* Geneva: World Health Organization, 1951.

BROADHURST, P. L. Determinants of emotionality in the rat: III. Strain differences. *J. comp. physiol. Psychol.,* 1958, **51,** 55–59.

FREUD, S. Three essays on the theory of sexuality. (Originally published 1905). In *The standard edition of the complete psychological works of Sigmund Freud.* Vol. 7. London: Hogarth, 1953, Pp. 125–248.

GRIFFITHS, W. J. JR., & STRINGER, W. F. The effects of intense stimulation experienced during infancy on adult behavior in the rat. *J. comp. physiol. Psychol.,* 1952, **45,** 301–306.

HALL, C. S. The inheritance of emotionality. *Sigma Xi Quart.,* 1938, **26,** 17–27.

HALL, C. S., & WHITEMAN, P. H. The effects of infantile stimulation upon later emotional stability in the mouse. *J. comp. physiol. Psychol.,* 1951, **44,** 61–66.

HUNT, H. F., & OTIS, L. S. Restricted experience and "timidity" in the rat. *Amer. Psychologist,* 1955, **19,** 432.

KING, J. A. Relationships between early social experience and adult aggressive behavior in inbred mice. *J. genet. Psychol.,* 1957, **90,** 151–166.

————. Parameters relevant to determining the effect of early experience upon the adult behavior of animals. *Psychol. Bull.,* 1958, **55,** 46–58.

KING, J. A., & ELEFTHERIOU, B. E. Effects of early handling upon adult behavior in two subspecies of deermice, *Peromyscus maniculates. J. comp. physiol. Psychol.,* 1959, **52,** 82–88.

LINDZEY, G. Emotionality and audiogenic seizure susceptibility in five inbred strains of mice. *J. comp. physiol. Psychol.,* 1951, **44,** 389–393.

McCLEARN, G. E. The genetics of mouse behavior in novel situations. *J. comp. physiol. Psychol.,* 1959, **52,** 62–67.

STANLEY, W. C., & MONKMAN, J. A. A test for specific and general behavioral effects of infantile stimulation with shock in the mouse. *J. abnorm. soc. Psychol.,* 1956, **53,** 19–22.

STONE, C. P. Wildness and savageness in rats of different strains. In K. S. Lashley (Ed.), *Studies in the dynamics of behavior.* Chicago: Univer. Chicago Press, 1932. Pp. 3–55.

THOMPSON, W. R. The inheritance of behavior: Behavior differences in fifteen mouse strains. *Canad. J. Psychol.*, 1953, **7**, 145–155.

————. The inheritance of behavior: Activity differences in five inbred mouse strains. *J. Hered.*, 1956, **47**, 147–148.

VALENSTEIN, E. S., RISS, W., & YOUNG, W. C. Experiential and genetic factors in the organization of sexual behavior in male guinea pigs. *J. comp. physiol. Psychol.*, 1955, **48**, 397–403.

DISCOMFORTING THOUGHTS ON "INFANTILE TRAUMA, GENETIC FACTORS, AND ADULT TEMPERAMENT"

Seymour Levine

In a recent issue of this journal Lindzey, Lykken, and Winston (1960) undertook to investigate one of the principal questions concerning the determinants of adult behavior, namely, the interaction between ontogenetic and genetic factors as related to later behavior. There is little question that the problem is important and intriguing; however, as we hope to point out, the study of Lindzey et al. added little but confusion to an area that has its full share of difficulties.

During the past several years there have appeared in the journals a number of papers (Denenberg & Bell, 1960; Levine, 1958, 1959b; Levine, Chevalier, & Korchin, 1956) related to the effects of various infantile experiences with noxious stimuli on later behavior. Several of these papers present data on emotionality using measures similar to those used by Lindzey et al. (1960), namely, defecation, urination, and timidity. The conclusion reached by all of these studies was that infantile experience with noxious stimuli *reduces* emotionality as defined by a significant reduction in

Reprinted by permission of the American Psychological Association and the author from the *Journal of Abnormal and Social Psychology,* Vol. 63, 1961.

autonomic reactivity and increased ambulation. These conclusions are in direct contradiction to that reached by the Lindzey et al. study.

Such conclusions were based on comparisons which unfortunately were irrevocably unavailable to Lindzey et al. (1960). In all of these studies three basic groups were employed, namely, a group subjected to noxious stimulation during infancy, another group which were treated similarly to those receiving noxious stimulation (these two groups of course resemble the Lindzey et al. groups), and a third and critical control group, a group which received *no treatment* during infancy. Both logically and methodologically if one wishes to compare the effects of any treatment such comparisons must be made with a condition of no treatment. This error is more flagrant in view of the numerous reports that have appeared using this specific design when investigating the problem of infantile "trauma" on later emotionality. Thus although in some instances the infant animals subjected to noxious stimulation appear to differ somewhat from their treated controls, when they are compared with totally nontreated animals the effects of noxious stimulation have been to reduce emotionality dramatically. In a recent paper (Levine, 1959a) the following statement appears:

In this study, as in several previous studies, no differences in behavior were observed between the different modes of stimulation. Although some differences have been noted in adulthood between animals that were shocked in infancy and those that were handled, these differences have been transitory, and the magnitude of differences has been much smaller than the differences between stimulated and non-stimulated animals. The evidence obtained thus far has raised the question of what in this area constitutes the major experimental treatment. It appears that the condition of no treatment seems to have the most profound effect upon development and the subsequent emotionality and performance of the animal. Thus far in all of the experiments coming out of our laboratory it has been the non-stimulated infant that has exhibited relatively slower development, *greater* emotionality, and poorer performance in adulthood (p. 245).

Yet Lindzey et al. (1960) interpret their data as confirming their hypothesis that infantile trauma would produce an excessive emotionality. We contend that such an hypothesis is testable only within the strictest limitations if at all, using a design that does not include a nontreated control group. It is indeed difficult to understand how the relevant literature related to this point could have been overlooked since in three of the papers quoted in the references (Ader, 1959; King, 1958; King & Eleftheriou, 1959) reference is made to research in which a nontreated control group design was used. Still in the introduction Lindzey et al. seem to exhibit surprise that "One investigator (Ader, 1957) actually has reported results indicating that treated rats were *less* emotional than control animals," and again state "It is worth note,

however, that there is actually no evidence in any study for infantile trauma *decreasing* [1] emotionality." The evidence speaks for itself when a complete and adequate design is used.

Unfortunately this same major flaw in experimental design has been perpetrated on numerous occasions by several investigators including Ader (1959), Griffiths and Stringer (1952), Scott (1955), and Stanley and Monkman (1956). Perhaps the problem is that the hypotheses that generate these studies start off with assumptions and biases which often result in the omission of "nonessential" control groups.

One cannot preclude the possibility that given certain genetic conditions noxious stimulation can result in increased emotionality. The study by King and Eleftheriou (1959) and more recent investigations by Ginsburg (1960) have indicated that this does occur. Our comments are directed to the point that the Lindzey et al. (1960) study by the very nature of their experimental design could not have demonstrated these relationships. Close inspection of their data casts further doubt upon their conclusions and reveals only marginal levels of significance for the effect they claim to have firmly demonstrated.

It might have been possible to argue that merely placing an infant animal in a washtub for 6 minutes from the fourth to the eighth day could not be sufficient to cause any effect. However, it has been shown on numerous occasions that the simple process of picking up (Levine, 1956, 1959b; Schaefer, 1957) an animal daily during infancy can exert a profound effect on its later behavior and emotionality. In addition the days between 4–8 compare almost directly with

---

[1] The italics in these instances are those of Lindzey, Lykken, and Winston (1960).

the critical periods during which the effects of infantile stimulation appear to have their most profound effect in rats and mice (Denenberg & Bell, 1960; Levine & Lewis, 1959; Schaefer, 1957).

We should like to reaffirm our faith that the problem is an extremely important one and because of its importance demands the utmost of the investigator, and if we may quote again (Lindzey et al., 1960) "this is a finding that makes life more complex for both the investigator and theorist, and in an area where there has never been any shortage of complexity," and albeit this statement is taken out of context it more than amply states the position of the present writer.

Since this critique was written a similar note has appeared by Denenberg (1961).

References

ADER, R. The effects of early experience on subsequent emotionality and resistance to stress. *Psychol. Monogr.,* 1959, **73**(2, Whole No. 472).

DENENBERG, V. H. Comments on "Infantile trauma, genetic factors, and adult temperament." *Psychol. Rep.,* 1961, **8**, 459–462.

DENENBERG, V. H., & BELL, R. W. Critical periods for the effects of infantile experience on adult learning. *Science,* 1960, **131**, 227–228.

GINSBURG, B. E. Genetic control of the ontogeny of stress behavior. Paper presented at the American Psychological Association meeting, Chicago, 1960.

GRIFFITHS, W. J., JR., & STRINGER, W. F. The effects of intense stimulation experienced during infancy on adult behavior in the rat. *J. comp. physiol. Psychol.,* 1952, **45**, 301–306.

KING, J. A. Parameters relevant to determining the effects of early experience upon the adult behavior of animals. *Psychol. Bull.,* 1958, **55**, 46–58.

KING, J. A., & ELEFTHERIOU, B. E. Effects of early handling upon adult behavior in two subspecies of deermice, *Peromyscus maniculatus. J. comp. physiol. Psychol.,* 1959, **52**, 82–88.

LEVINE, S. A further study of infantile handling and adult avoidance learning. *J. Pers.,* 1956, **25**, 70–80.

———. Noxious stimulation in infant and adult rats and consummatory behavior. *J. comp. physiol. Psychol.,* 1958, **51**, 230–233.

———. The effects of differential infantile stimulation on emotionality at weaning. *Canad. J. Psychol.,* 1959, **13**, 243–247. (a)

———. Emotionality and aggressive behavior in the mouse as a function of infantile experience. *J. genet. Psychol.,* 1959, **94**, 77–83. (b)

LEVINE, S., CHEVALIER, J. A., & KORCHIN, S. J. The effects of early shock and handling on later avoidance learning. *J. Pers.,* 1956, **24**, 475–493.

LEVINE, S., & LEWIS, G. W. Critical period for the effects of infantile experience on the maturation of a stress response. *Science,* 1959, **129**, 42–43.

LINDZEY, G., LYKKEN, D. T., & WINSTON, H. D. Infantile trauma, genetic factors, and adult temperament, *J. abnorm. soc. Psychol.,* 1960, **61**, 7–14.

SCHAEFFER, T. The effects of early handling: Infant handling and later behavior in the white rat. Unpublished PhD dissertation, University of Chicago, 1957.

SCOTT, J. H. Some effects at maturity of gentling, ignoring, or shocking rats during infancy. *J. abnorm. soc. Psychol.,* 1955, **51**, 412–414.

STANLEY, W. C., & MONKMAN, J. A. A test for specific and general behavioral effects of infantile stimulation with shock in the mouse. *J. abnorm. soc. Psychol.,* 1956, **53**, 19–22.

CONFUSION, CONVICTION, AND CONTROL GROUPS
Gardner Lindzey, David T. Lykken, and Harvey D. Winston

Levine (1961) is convinced that our study cannot provide a satisfactory answer to any question because it was poorly designed. He asserts that as a result of omitting an essential control group we have observed findings that led to an erroneous conclusion. On the first issue he is flatly wrong, while on the second there is, as yet, insufficient evidence to permit a final answer. In brief, we assert that Levine is confused in regard to the logic of control groups and, further, that his convictions have led him to extrapolate an empirical generalization more broadly than is warranted by existing data.

If we accept Levine's (1961) reasoning that his "untreated" group belongs on the same continuum as our traumatized and nontraumatized groups (an assumption we would question if space permitted), it follows that we have examined the effects upon emotionality of two values of trauma. But, asserts Levine, without the zero point on the trauma continuum it is impossible for us to say anything about the relation between trauma and emotionality. This is simply incorrect! It is perfectly meaningful and legitimate to compare the effect of two nonzero intensities of a particular variable on a dependent measure and the resultant finding stands as an empirical contribution in its own right. Indeed there are few zero points to be found on the psychological scene (cf. S. S. Stevens) and certainly none in Levine's own

Reprinted by permission of the American Psychological Association and the authors from the *Journal of Abnormal and Social Psychology*, Vol. 63, 1961.

research. It is evident that Levine's "untreated group" is not untreated in any absolute sense. Treatment is nothing more than stimulation. All subjects are continuously undergoing treatment from the moment that sensory capacity begins. Our control group had one source of stimulation removed (loud, noxious bell), while Levine's untreated group had another source of stimulation removed (handling prior to weaning). Obviously there are many additional kinds of stimuli (even noxious stimuli) that are a standard part of the laboratory and remain a part of the experience of his untreated control as well as our untreated control. Thus at best his group represents only another point on the trauma continuum, not a zero point, and eventually his findings will have to be fitted into a broader empirical net, just as will ours.

The second important issue has to do with the general relation between infantile trauma and emotionality. Perhaps the major difficulty here is semantic. It is clear to us that Levine uses the terms "infantile trauma" and "emotionality" differently than we do. Consequently, where he sees the existence of direct conflict we see the need for bridging studies to bring two domains of data into some orderly relation. Specifically, we define *infantile trauma* as an intense noxious stimulus administered during infancy while Levine is willing to say that any noxious stimulus, no matter how intense, administered prior to weaning, constitutes an infantile trauma. Thus for him a brief period of daily handling that extends over 20 days of the life of the animal is an infantile trauma, while for us it is neither exclusively infantile nor is it necessarily traumatic. In regard to *emotionality* there is the same difference. We anchor the term specifically in urination/ defecation in an open field situation while Levine is willing to use motility, avoidance learning, and consummatory behavior, as well as other operations, to define emotionality. We feel that our use of the terms "emotionality" and "infantile trauma" is better rooted in past convention than is Levine's usage.

This problem is most clearly revealed in the second paragraph of Levine's (1961) note where he reports that four studies, several using measures similar to ours, have led to results that directly contradict our findings. Let us remember that our dependent measures were timidity (stove-pipe test) and emotionality (urination/defecation) and examine these four studies. Two of them employ as their dependent measures indices of avoidance learning. One employs a measure of water consumption and an index of emotionality consisting of the number of trials on which defecation *and* freezing occur. The fourth study used a measure of defecation on an elevated runway, latency to move on this runway, and a measure of water consumption. To summarize, there is no timidity measure here at all, one study uses an index combining freezing and defecation, which is only a very distant cousin of our urination/defecation measure, and one study uses a somewhat similar defecation measure and *actually finds* with this measure *no treatment effects*—indeed the trend of the data is consistent with *our* prediction. It is difficult to see how observation of no treatment effects can be considered to support Levine's contention that infantile trauma reduces emotionality. It is even harder to see how one can talk about "direct contradiction" when dis-

cussing results based upon measures so different from ours.

In the process of exploring the semantic differences between Levine and ourselves, it has become clear that a critical remark in our paper (Lindzey, Lykken, Winston, 1960, p. 11) concerning Ader's (1959) research was partially a product of language differences and consequently not warranted. Apology is hereby tendered.

There seems no need to comment at length upon the matter of "marginal levels of significance." Such a remark is either too little or too much. Our data are presented explicitly and were subjected to the kinds of analyses that seemed to us most appropriate. We have no doubt that an objective observer given these data would conclude that there was a treatment effect. Moreover, these findings have been repeatedly observed in our laboratory and, as indicated in our paper, they are a replication of findings reported independently by others using the same procedures and comparable subjects. If these findings are indeed replicable, it would seem clear that Levine has some responsibility for modifying his principal generalization if he wishes to extrapolate it so broadly as to include our data.

What of our convictions in regard to the relation between emotionality and infantile trauma? Given our definitions of these terms we feel confident that trauma increases adult emotionality. If we alter the definition of trauma to include the full range of stimulation, we have little doubt that research will eventually reveal a **U**-shaped function linking these two variables. Thus it is quite possible that Levine is right in regard to one portion of this function and that we are right in regard to another segment. It should be added that there are many parameters that can be expected to influence this general relationship and the study of these has only begun.

What can we conclude? First, there is far too little connected evidence to permit an empirical resolution of the general issue. At least as important as additional data is increased semantic clarity and greater information concerning the relation between the various dependent measures employed. Second, in the interests of generalizing his findings broadly, Levine has shown little concern over many important differences between his research and our own and he has demonstrated no interest in the possibility that stimulation and adult emotionality (temperament) may be linked by some reasonably complex function. Third, Levine was incorrect in asserting that our research was incapable of answering any question because we chose to omit his favorite control group.

References

ADER, R. The effects of early experience on subsequent emotionality and resistance to stress. *Psychol. Monogr.,* 1959, **73**(2, Whole No. 472).

LEVINE, S. Discomforting thoughts on "Infantile trauma, genetic factors, and adult temperament." *J. abnorm. soc. Psychol.,* 1961, **63**, 219–220.

LINDZEY, G., LYKKEN, D. T., & WINSTON, H. D. Infantile trauma, genetic factors, and adult temperament. *J. abnorm. soc. Psychol.,* 1960, **61**, 7–14.

EXTINCTION OF THE SMILING RESPONSE IN INFANTS AS A FUNCTION OF REINFORCEMENT SCHEDULE

Yvonne Brackbill

Scheduling of reinforcement has been investigated extensively in relation to the conditioning of non-social responses. The results of these studies indicate in general that a schedule by which reinforcement follows every response is less effective in maintaining performance of that response during extinction than is a schedule by which reinforcement follows only some of those responses (4).

This investigation attempts to extend the study of frequency and patterning of reinforcement to the area of social learn-

Reprinted by permission from the Society for Research in Child Development and the author from *Child Development,* Vol. 29, 1958.

ing and to cortically immature subjects. The purpose of the research is to evaluate the relative efficacy of intermittent as opposed to regular reinforcement upon frequency of smiling in infants.

The use of an instrumental conditioning paradigm in this study is in contrast to past studies of the conditioning of the smiling response (2, 7, 8), all of which, though differing in methodology, have utilized a classical conditioning paradigm in conceptualizing results. The inappropriateness of this framework in accounting for response change over time is most clearly illustrated in the study by Dennis (2).

Method

SUBJECTS

Eight normal infants between the ages of three and one-half to four and one-half months served as Ss. Six were males and two, females. All came from intact middle class homes located within 10 miles of Stanford University.[1]

This particular age range was selected with the consideration in mind that the subject had to be old enough to remain awake for a short time period after feeding, yet not old enough to respond differentially to "mother" vs. "others." Other requirements for selection of Ss were: (a) that the infant not cry so often, with such intensity, and for so long a time that sessions very frequently had to be terminated, with consequent lack of experimental progress; (b) that the infant show an operant rate of at least two responses per five-minute interval; and (c) that the infant be able to maintain a supine position for intervals of five minutes without persistent struggling to regain the prone position.

EXPERIMENTAL PROCEDURE

Ss were assigned to the regularly reinforced (RR) group or to the intermittently reinforced (IR) group in consecutive order of their acceptance as subjects. The first S was assigned to the IR group; the second, to the RR group; and so on.

For both groups, the experimental procedure was divided into three periods: In the first or *operant* period E stood motionless and expressionless at a distance of approximately 15 inches above S, and observed him for eight five-

minute intervals to ascertain the operant level of smiling. In the second or *conditioning* period, reinforcement was meted out, contingent upon S's smile. Specifically, as soon as S smiled,[2] E smiled in return, began to speak softly to S, and picked it up. S was then held, jostled, patted, and talked to for 30 seconds before being replaced in the crib.[3] In the third or *extinction* period, the procedure was again observation without reinforcement, as in the operant period. During extinction, Ss were observed for 13 five-minute intervals.

During all three periods, the basic interval for determining rate of responding was five minutes, and in the discussion to follow, *five-minute interval* (or simply, *interval*) refers to one five-minute period of continuous experimentation. The term *rate of response* refers to number of responses per interval. Also, the terms *response* and *trial* will be used interchangeably.

The two groups of Ss differed in respect to the reinforcement schedules used within the conditioning period. The RR group was maintained on a regular reinforcement schedule during the entire conditioning period. The IR group was maintained on a regular reinforcement schedule until each S had responded at maximum rate (*see below*) for 10 consecutive intervals. Immediately after the tenth interval at maximum rate, Ss were switched to a 2:1 randomized variable ratio reinforcement schedule for a total

---

[1] The author is greatly indebted to Drs. John Anderson and Bruce Jessup for their cooperation in referring subjects.

[2] Interjudge reliability concerning the decision as to whether a smile had or had not occurred was found to be .975, using a total N of 970 such decisions in the formula: twice number of agreements / total number of judgments. This reliability check was done prior to the experiment, with the assistance of Mr. Thomas Milburn.

[3] The reinforcement procedure was recorded on 12 feet of 8 mm. film.

of 60 responses (hence, 30 reinforcements), then to a 3:1 schedule for a total of 45 responses, and finally to a 4:1 schedule for 20 responses. Separate randomizations were used for each subject.

Maximum rate of response was determined as follows. Forty-five seconds were required for the administration of each reinforcement plus its accompanying events. (Five seconds were required for picking *S* up; 30 seconds for reinforcement; five seconds for putting *S* down; and five seconds for recording.) Therefore, no more than six responses could occur and be reinforced during any five-minute interval. *Maximum rate of response* was defined as no fewer than four responses per interval. That particular trial or response that marked the beginning of maximum response rate will be referred to as *criterion*.

Because of intersubject variation in total number of responses to criterion and because it was desired that the experimental results be a function only of reinforcement schedule and not a function of reinforcement schedule plus number of emitted responses, it was necessary to match the two groups for total number of trials during the conditioning period. The method of matching—like the method of group assignment mentioned earlier—was an individual one and was done in consecutive order of admission to the experiment. Specifically, *S* No. 2 (RR group) was matched for total number of trials with *S* No. 1 (IR group); *S* No. 4 was matched with *S* No. 3, and so on.

GENERAL PROCEDURE

Each infant was placed on a schedule of social deprivation during the entire experimental period. Social deprivation was defined as minimized social and body contact between the infant and any other person in its environment, excluding *E*. In effect, this meant elimination of all social and body contacts that were not absolutely necessary for *S*'s well being.

Experimental conditions were kept as standard as possible for all sessions and for all *S*s. *E* always wore a white laboratory coat. *S* was placed in a supine position near the open edge of his crib; placement of *S* and the crib was the same for all sessions. Source of light was standardized, and variance in intensity minimized. At the beginning of each session, *S* was freshly diapered, had just eaten to satiety, and had been awake for from 15 to 20 minutes. During the operant and extinction periods, at the end of every five-minute interval, *S* was placed in a prone position to rest for three minutes. While he was being turned over and during the rest period, *E* was not in his field of vision. During the experimental period, *S* was frequently required to work without rest for two successive intervals, but not for longer.

Typically, there were two to three sessions per day. Length of any one session ranged between 10 and 60 minutes, and was a function of the length of time *S* remained awake. The total number of days spent in experimentation with any one *S* ranged from eight to 16. Because of the very large amount of time per day required for travel, experimentation, and maintenance of rapport with the mother, only one *S* was run at a time.

Results and Discussion

PERFORMANCE DURING THE
OPERANT PERIOD

The two groups did not differ significantly in either mean operant response rate ($t = .29$, 7 df) or total number of responses emitted ($t = .06$, 3 df). For this reason, scores have been combined for graphic presentation (Fig. 1).

Figure 1 also includes a cumulative plot for a ninth, control *S,* who was run, without reinforcement, for an extended operant period of 19 intervals—or roughly three times the length of the operant period for experimental *S*s. These data provide some evidence against the possible explanation that the

Relative stability in response rate is also reflected in Table 2, which contains the individual post-criterion response rates emitted under the regular reinforcement schedule. For the IR *S*s, percentages are based on the 10 intervals of regular reinforcement following criterion. For the RR *S*s, percentages are based on the total number of intervals following criterion. From this table it

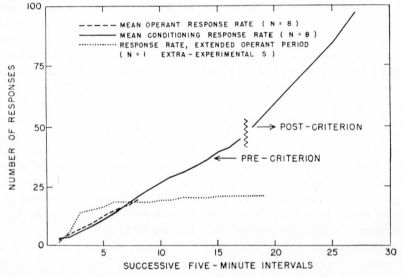

Fig. 1. Cumulative curves showing rate of smiling response during operant and conditioning periods.

mere presence of *E*—and not the reinforcement—is conducive to increased rate of response.

PERFORMANCE DURING THE CONDITIONING PERIOD

For the conditioning period, the total number of responses for each group was 927, while the mean number of responses per subject was 231.7. Mean group response rates are presented in Table 1; the most noticeable features of these data are the abruptness of the change in mean response rate and in variability following criterion.

can be seen that although most *S*s habitually worked at one rate of response, there were interindividual differences in the habitual or "preferred" rate.[4]

[4] One last datum concerning performance during conditioning was provided by *S* No. 8, who gave a clear demonstration of the type of response that Skinner has termed "superstitious behavior" (6). The behavioral sequence was as follows. During reinforcement, *S* kept his left fist doubled in his mouth. When placed in the crib, he withdrew the fist from the mouth and kept it suspended in air for the short time it took him to smile. Then, simultaneously with the beginning of the reinforcement procedure, the fist was promptly rein-

TABLE 1. GROUP RESPONSE RATES DURING OPERANT AND CONDITIONING PERIODS

| | OPERANT RESPONSE RATE | | CONDITIONING RESPONSE RATE | | | | | |
| | | | Preceding Criterion | | For First 10 Intervals Follow-ing Criterion | | For 11th–22nd Intervals Follow-ing Criterion | |
	Mean	σ	Mean	σ	Mean	σ	Mean	σ
Regular Group	2.11	.63	2.70	.47	5.15	.06	5.15	.06
Intermittent Group	2.88	.36	2.43	.44	5.10	.06	6.32 *	1.11 *
							8.12 †	.64 †
							13.00 ‡	1.51 ‡
Combined Groups	2.49	.64	2.56	.50	5.12	.06		

* 2 : 1 schedule.
† 3 : 1 schedule.
‡ 4 : 1 schedule.

PERFORMANCE DURING THE EXTINCTION PERIOD

Two statistical tests were applied to the extinction data in order to test the hypothesis that the IR group would be more resistant to extinction. First, Mc-Nemar's pseudo three-way analysis of variance (5), with blocks representing the experimental variable of reinforcement schedule, was applied to the response frequencies over all 13 extinction intervals. (Summing across 13 intervals, the total number of responses for the IR group was 331; for the RR group, 130.) The resulting F of 17.14, with 1 and 6 df, is significant beyond the .01 level. Second, a mean difference was computed, using the four matched-pair differences in total number of responses during the last six extinction intervals. (In this case, total number of responses for the IR and RR groups were 113 and 3, respectively.) For 3 df the t of 6.77 is significant beyond the .005 level by a one-tailed test.

A noncumulative plot of mean response rates during extinction (Fig. 2), shows some interesting periods of sharp rise in response rate for both groups (interval No. 5 for the RR group; intervals No. 7 and No. 8 for the IR group). The point of occurrence of this "recovery" did not appear to be a function of the length of preceding rest period; e.g., in the IR group, two Ss recovered after a rest of several hours (i.e., at the beginning of a new session), while the other two Ss recovered after a rest of only three minutes (i.e., during a session).

Figure 2 also indicates that every member of the RR group extinguished not to his previous, operant rate of response, but to a zero rate. Coincident

serted into the mouth, the head turned 90 degrees to the left, and the body musculature stiffened. The onset of this stereotyped response coincided with criterion (56th trial). It disappeared for three days during a period of illness (90th through 118th trials), reappeared in full strength with recovery (119th trial), gradually diminished in intensity, and finally disappeared altogether by the 162nd trial.

TABLE 2. INDIVIDUAL RESPONSE RATES DURING CONDITIONING: PERCENTAGE OF
INTERVALS FOLLOWING CRITERION DURING WHICH S EMITTED
FOUR, FIVE, OR SIX RESPONSES PER INTERVAL

	Total Number of Intervals on Regular Reinforcement Following Criterion	Percentage of These Intervals during Which Response Rate Was		
		4	5	6
Intermittent Group				
S No. 1	10	10%	80%	10%
S No. 3	10	20	70	10
S No. 5	10	30	10	60
S No. 7	10	20	40	40
Regular Group				
S No. 2	24	4.2	58.3	37.5
S No. 4	45	13.3	62.2	24.4
S No. 6	31	80.6	19.4	0
S No. 8	22	0	22.7	77.3

with the beginning of zero response rate was a conspicuous behavioral change: S would no longer fixate the discriminative stimulus (E's face). Instead, S's head turned to one side and remained there—an occurence, it might be pointed out, that was in distinct contrast to S's persistent fixation during conditioning. When this occurred, immediately preceding the last extinction interval, E propped S's head with rolled blankets or other material, making it impossible for the infant to turn his head to the left or right more than a few degrees. The "refusal" to fixate persisted even under these conditions; S's eyes then turned toward the ceiling. When withdrawal of reinforcement is conceptualized as frustration-producing (1), this persistent nonfixation may be regarded as an avoidance response that is elicited by continued frustration of the original (approach) response, is incompatible with the original response, and is reinforced by repeated escape from the frustrating situation.

THE RELATION OF PROTEST TO SMILING

As mentioned above, one of the criteria for subject selection was the frequency and intensity of crying. This criterion necessitated continued notations of such behavior during the operant period and first few conditioning intervals. Even after this point, however, E continued to record the incidence of crying, although at the time there seemed to be no particular reason for continuing to collect these data.

In recording crying, one of three types of notation was made, according to the intensity of response. In decreasing order of intensity, the notations were: (a) crying; (b) intense fussing: the same type of muscular and vocal involvement as in crying, but tears appeared only at the corners of eyes and did not course down the cheeks or temples; (c) fussing: considerable muscular and vocal involvement, but less than for the first two categories; no appearance of tears. In the presentation of data and discussions to follow, all three categories will be considered as one and referred to by the generic response term, *protest*.[5]

tinguished with the counter-conditioning of smiling. Specifically, there is a perfect rank correlation between number of trials taken to extinguish the protest response and number of trials to condition-

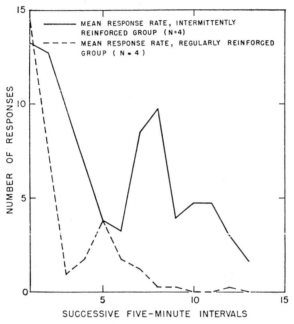

FIG. 2. Noncumulative curves showing mean rates of smiling response during extinction period.

The data concerning protest show that during the conditioning period, as rate of smiling increased, rate of protest decreased—or more properly, protest extinguished—

ing criterion on the smile response. Similarly, during the extinction period, as rate of smiling decreased, rate of protest increased. In this case, the rank order correlation (tau) between rates of emission of the two responses from the beginning of extinction up to the first interval at zero rate of response, is—.69, significant at the .02 level by a two-tailed test. (First appearance of zero response rate was chosen as the referent point for extinction period because it was the closest counterpart of the referent point for the conditioning period, i.e., criterion or beginning of maximum response rate.)

To express these results more gen-

---

[5] It should be noted that interjudge reliability in discriminating protest from nonprotest was not determined. However, as indirect support for the objectivity or reproducibility of these data, the following points should be considered. First, this was a simple discrimination to make; even responses of lowest intensity represented a marked contrast to the infants' typical placid behavior. Second, the total numbers of protests for the two groups were approximately equal. Third, the orderliness of these data was not observed until the end of the experiment, when the results were actually tabulated.

erally, for all *S*s combined, the ratio of protests to smiles during the conditioning period was 1:6.5 preceding criterion, and 1:276 following criterion. During the extinction period, the corresponding ratios were 1:40.5 (preceding first interval at zero rate of response) and 1:2.7 (during and following first interval at zero rate of response). Rates of protest response during operant, conditioning, and extinction periods are shown in Figure 3.

There is a good deal of similarity between these findings and results obtained in a study by Estes (3), in which rats were reinforced for one instrumental response while a previously reinforced, competing response was being extinguished. Estes states that, "These results seem to lend some support to the view that the 'learning' of any one response involves the concurrent extinction of others and that the amount of initial acceleration in a learning curve is deter-

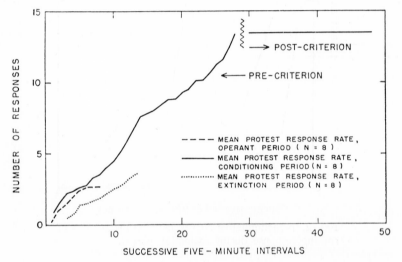

FIG. 3. Cumulative curves showing mean rates of protest response during operant, conditioning, and extinction periods.

One might conceivably object to any interpretation of these correlations on the grounds that they merely reflect the fact that two such responses are mutually exclusive behaviors: an infant cannot protest and smile at the same time. Although this overlooks the important point that all *S*s *changed* in the frequency of emission of both responses, there is a direct answer to such an objection in that the precriterion data show, for every *S*, both part and whole intervals during which neither protest nor smiling occurred at all.

mined to an important extent by the relative initial strengths of all behaviors which may occur in the experimental situation" (3, p. 204).

In the present case, the most important determiner of rate of acquisition of the smiling response appears to be the initial strength of the functionally equivalent, competing protest response. The main difference between procedures is that in Estes' study, the conflicting response was both reinforced and extinguished as an integral part of the experiment, while in the present study only the extinction of the competing response took place during the experiment. Its establishment had already taken place prior to the beginning of the experiment —most probably via reinforcement by maternal care.

Perhaps the most appropriate way of conceptualizing these results is in terms of a habit family hierarchy of two responses for which the initially differing habit strengths were first reversed by selectively reinforcing only the weaker response, and then reversed again by extinguishing that response, allowing for recovery of the first. This leads to the general proposition that rate of acquisition and extinction is a function of the initial discrepancy in habit strength between competing responses.

Summary

This investigation was concerned with the instrumental conditioning of a social response (smiling) in infants. *S*s were two groups of four infants each; one group was maintained on a conditioning schedule of intermittent reinforcement and the other on a schedule of regular reinforcement. The reinforcement consisted of social and body contact between *E* and *S*. The dependent variable was relative resistance to extinction of smiling as a function of the differing reinforcement schedules.

Results confirmed the expectation that intermittent reinforcement is superior in maintaining continued performance of a response during extinction. Further, a negative correlation was found between rates of emission of protest and smiling responses during both conditioning and extinction periods. It was proposed that rate of acquisition and extinction is not only a function of reinforcement schedule but also of initial discrepancy in habit strength between competing responses.

References

1. ADELMAN, H. M., & MAATSCH, J. L. Resistance to extinction as a function of the type of response elicited by frustration. *J. exp. Psychol.,* 1955, 50, 61–65.

2. DENNIS, W. An experimental test of two theories of social smiling in infants. *J. soc. Psychol.,* 1935, 6, 214–223.

3. ESTES, W. K. Effects of competing reactions on the conditioning curve for bar pressing. *J. exp. Psychol.,* 1950, 40, 200–205.

4. JENKINS, W. O., & STANLEY, J. C., JR. Partial reinforcement: A review and critique. *Psychol. Bull.,* 1950, 47, 193–234.

5. MCNEMAR, Q. *Psychological statistics.* New York: John Wiley, 1955.

6. SKINNER, B. F. "Superstition" in the pigeon. *J. exp. Psychol.,* 1948, 38, 168–172.

7. THOMPSON, JANE. Development of facial expression of emotion in blind and seeing children. *Arch. Psychol.,* 1941, 37, No. 264, 1–47.

8. WASHBURN, RUTH. A study of the smiling and laughing of infants in the first year of life. *Genet. Psychol. Monogr.,* 1929, 6, 397–537.

SOCIAL CONDITIONING OF VOCALIZATIONS IN THE INFANT

Harriet L. Rheingold, Jacob L. Gewirtz, and Helen W. Ross

By three months of age the infant gives a well-defined social response to the appearance of adults. He looks at them intently, smiles, becomes active, and vocalizes. This behavior is repeated again and again in sequence. Adults often respond to these acts of the infant; they may only look at the child, but they may also smile to him, touch or caress him, or vocalize in return. Frequently one observes "answering" social and, in particular, vocal play between mother and child. The adults' responses may therefore play an important part in maintaining and developing social responsiveness in the child (Rheingold, 1956). The principles of operant conditioning (Skinner, 1953) suggest that some of these adult responses, functioning as reinforcers, may affect the development of the child's social behavior (Gewirtz, 1956). Thus, smiling in the infant has been shown to respond to conditioning (Brackbill, 1958).

The present study was an attempt to condition vocalizations in infants. Vocalizations were selected for study because they seem to provide an index of the whole social response (Rheingold, 1956). The reinforcing stimulus was a complex of social acts which resembled those an attentive adult might naturally make when a child vocalizes. If temporal contiguity between the infant's vocalization and the reinforcing stimulus, which follows it, brings about an increase

Reprinted by permission of the American Psychological Association and the authors from the *Journal of Comparative and Physiological Psychology*, Vol. 52, 1959.

in the vocalizations, conditioning may be said to have occurred. The possibility that the reinforcing stimulus may also have functioned as an arouser of vocalizations will be considered. In any case, the results of the study should provide further understanding about the development of social responsiveness, as well as of speech.

Method

Two parallel experiments were carried out in sequence. In the first, 11 babies (*S*s) were studied, with one experimenter (*E*) and one observer-recorder (*O*), both women. In the second, 10 other *S*'s and one *S* from Experiment I were studied with the *E* and *O* of the first experiment exchanging roles. An experiment was composed of three successive units in each of which three or four *S*s were studied at one time.

SUBJECTS

The *S*s were 21 infants, all residents almost from birth in the same institution. (We are grateful to Sister Thecla and the staff of St. Ann's Infant Asylum, Washington, D.C., for their generous cooperation.) Their median age was 3.0 months; three-quarters of them were no more than three days older or younger than the median. In each experiment six *S*s were male, five were female. Age was the main criterion for selection. Four possible *S*s were rejected: one seemed immature, two had a very high rate of vocalizing during the first baseline measure, and one was markedly fussy.

The institution offers excellent care

and, as is characteristic of institutions, there are multiple caretakers. In general, the Ss were well developed, healthy, alert, and socially responsive. The Es asked for no modifications in the usual caretaking routines. The caretakers knew that the Es were observing the development of social behavior, but they did not know the details of the experiment. The caretakers' usual behavior toward the Ss appeared not to be modified by the conditions of the experiment.

EXPERIMENTAL CONDITIONS

Baseline. In experimental Days 1 and 2 (first and second Baseline days) E leaned over the crib with her face about 15 in. above S's and looked at him with an expressionless face, while O tallied vocalizations, out of S's sight. The E moved her head as necessary to remain in S's line of vision, a condition which obtained throughout the experiments.

Conditioning. During experimental Days 3 and 4 (first and second Conditioning days), E again leaned over the crib with an expressionless face except that when S vocalized, E made an immediate response and then resumed the expressionless face until the next vocalization. The response, or *reinforcing stimulus,* consisted of three acts executed by E simultaneously, quickly, and smoothly. They were a broad smile, three "tsk" sounds, and a light touch applied to the infant's abdomen with thumb and fingers of the hand opposed. No more than a second of time was required to administer the reinforcer.

At the beginning of the conditioning periods each vocalization was reinforced. Sometimes, as the rate of vocalizing increased, only every second, and later, every third, vocalization was reinforced. In Experiment I, 72% of the reinforcers occurred after *each* vocalization; in Experiment II, 94%. Less frequent reinforcing seemed to depress the rate, at least initially, and, because of the rather severe time restrictions, was abandoned altogether by the end of the study.

Extinction. Experimental Days 5 and 6 (first and second Extinction days) were the same as Days 1 and 2; E leaned over the crib with an expressionless face and made no response to S's vocalizations.

THE VOCAL RESPONSE

Every discrete, voiced sound produced by S was counted as a *vocalization.* A number of other sounds characteristically made by very young infants, e.g., straining sounds and coughs, and the whistles, squeaks, and snorts of noisy breathing, were not counted as vocalizations. Sounds falling under the categories of protests, fusses, and cries (see Emotional Behavior below) were recorded separately. No attempt was made to record the phonetic characteristics of any of the sounds or their duration.

Observer agreement. Agreement between two Os on the number of vocalizations produced by Ss in 3-min. periods was high. Counts for 27 periods, using 13 different Ss, yielded a median percentage agreement of 96 (range, 67 to 100). About half of these reliability measures were obtained at the Ss' cribs, and the rest from tape recordings made during the experiment. These two techniques yielded similar percentages of observer agreement.

The unit of measurement. The unit for statistical analysis was the number of vocalizations an S gave in a 3-min. period. The counts were recorded by half-minutes and these were summed to give the score for the 3-min. period. After a rest period of 2 min., in which both E and O walked away from the baby's crib,

138   SELECTED RESEARCH AREAS

another 3-min. count was made. After a second rest period a third count was made.

In each day nine such 3-min. counts were planned, distributed thus: one block of three in the first part of the morning, the second block of three in the late morning, and the third block of three after the midday meal. The minimum amount of time between blocks was 10 min., although usually an hour or more elapsed.

Actually, nine periods of observations were obtained during only 80% of the 132 subject-days (22 $Ss \times 6$ experimental days). Since three or four Ss were studied at a time, it was not always possible to find nine periods in a day when each was awake, alert, and content. Further, because the experiments were carried out in the nursery which the Ss shared with 12 other infants, the presence and activities of these other babies, and of the caretakers in carrying out their routines, sometimes made it impossible to obtain the desired number of periods.

EMOTIONAL BEHAVIOR

A number of responses which seemed to be "emotional" were recorded during the observation periods. These were: "protests," discrete sounds of a whining nature; "fusses," a series of sounds separated by a catch in the voice, whimpering; "cries" continuous loud, wailing sounds; "persistent looking away from E," rolling of the head from side to side or staring to one side or the other of E; and "marked hand activity," hand play, finger sucking, or face or head rubbing. The last two activities seemed to be attempts to avoid E. Measures of observer-agreement in the recording of these responses were not made.

Each of these responses was given a credit of one for each half-minute in which it occurred. From the sum for each S a mean score was obtained for each experimental day.

Results

SIMILARITY BETWEEN
EXPERIMENTS

Figure 1 presents the means of both experiments for the six experimental days. Each point represents the mean of 11 individual means. It was expected that the effect of the experimental conditions would be similar from experiment to experiment, but the extent to which the slopes of the curves would be congruent was not predicted.

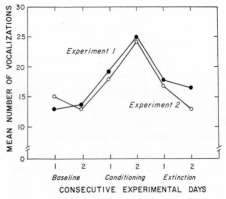

FIG. 1. Mean number of vocalizations on consecutive experimental days.

The amount of similarity between the two experiments was estimated by an analysis of variance (Table 1), using Lindquist's Type VI design (1953). The analysis reveals no evidence of a difference between Experiments. Further, no source of variation involving Experiments is significant. (The difference between the two experiments in second Extinction day means is not significant; it suggests, however, that the less frequent reinforcement in Experiment I may have made the behavior more resistant to extinction.)

Three conclusions may be drawn from such close agreement in the results of two parallel experiments, each using different Ss and different Es: first, we are dealing with some relatively stable characteristics of three-month-old infants;

and, also, in the effect of successive days within conditions ($p < .001$). These effects were assessed by t tests (for paired data) on the amount of change from one day to another in the mean number of vocalizations given by individual Ss. The error term was derived only from the scores for the two days being compared. The tests on the pooled sample (21 df) show that:

TABLE 1. ANALYSIS OF VARIANCE OF EFFECT OF CONSECUTIVE
EXPERIMENTAL DAYS

Source of Variation	df	MS	F
Between Subjects	21		
Experiments (1 vs. 2)	1	1218	0.03
Error	20	45322	
Within Subjects	110		
Conditions (Baseline vs. Conditioning vs. Extinction)	2	71243 (1) [a]	10.63 *
Days within Conditions (1 vs. 2)	1	4205 (2) [a]	1.88
Conditions × Days	2	22917 (3) [a]	9.24 *
Days × Experiments	1	1738 (2) [a]	0.78
Conditions × Experiments	2	2031 (1) [a]	0.30
Conditions × Days × Experiments	2	866 (3) [a]	0.35
Error 1	40	6703	
Error 2	20	2233	
Error 3	40	2481	

[a] Number in parentheses refers to the error term used. The terms were not pooled because of statistically significant differences among them.
* Significant at .001 level.

second, the results may be accepted with confidence; and third, the results of the separate experiments may be pooled for all remaining analyses.

EFFECT OF EXPERIMENTAL
CONDITIONS

Table 1 shows that there was a difference in the effect of the three two-day experimental conditions ($p < .001$),

1. There was no statistically significant difference in the mean number of vocalizations given in a 3-min. period from the first to the second Baseline day ($t = 0.87, p > .30$).

2. The mean number of vocalizations increased from the second Baseline day to the first Conditioning day ($t = 2.69, p < .01$).

3. A further increase occurred from

the first to the second Conditioning day ($t = 3.61$, $p < .001$).

4. On the first Extinction day, vocalizations decreased ($t = 3.19$, $p. < .0025$).

5. The mean number of vocalizations on the second Extinction day was smaller than on the first Extinction day, but the difference was not reliable ($t = 1.35$, $p < .10$).

6. There was no statistically significant difference between the mean number of vocalizations given on the second Extinction day and on the second Baseline day ($t = 1.20$, $p > .20$).

The tests between Baseline days and between Baseline and Extinction days were two-sided tests; the others were one-sided.

If final days within conditions are compared, the differences are more marked: the mean for the second Conditioning day is higher than that of the second Baseline day at $p < .0005$ ($t = 4.80$), and the second Extinction day mean is lower than the second Conditioning day mean at $p < .0005$ ($t = 4.08$). Similar differences occur between the means of experimental conditions, obtained by averaging the first- and second-day results for each condition.

AMOUNT OF CHANGE IN NUMBER OF VOCALIZATIONS

The treatment effects have been found reliable. It seems in order, therefore, to present the means of vocalizations for each day and to calculate the amount of change produced by the experimental conditions. Under baseline conditions the three-month-old infants gave about 13 to 14 vocalizations in a 3-min. period. Individual differences were wide and ranged from 3 to 37 vocalizations. Using the social reinforcer for one day raised the rate to 18 vocalizations, an increase

of 39%. A second day of conditioning elevated the rate to 25, a further increase of 34%. In all, conditioning brought about an increase of 86%. Removing the reinforcer depressed the rate to 17 during the first and to 15 during the second day, the latter approaching very closely the level of baseline performance.

EMOTIONAL BEHAVIOR

Emotional behavior, while striking when it occurred, was observed infrequently. The largest mean for any day in both experiments was 3.0, the smallest was 1.9. The order of the means by experimental days was identical in the two experiments. It was: first Extinction day, second Extinction day, second Baseline day, second Conditioning day, first Conditioning day, and first Baseline day. The greater number of emotional responses during Extinction agrees with the findings of others (e.g., Brackbill, 1958; Skinner, 1953; Verplanck, 1955). Because the responses labeled emotional occurred so infrequently and because observer-agreement measures were not made, no further statistical analysis seemed warranted.

ADDITIONAL FINDINGS

Performance of successive groups. It will be recalled that in any one experimental week the Ss were studied in groups of three or four. Inspection of the results suggests that in such successive group of each experiment an increasing number of Ss conformed to expectation, showing an increase in vocalizations during Conditioning and a decrease during Extinction. The Es apparently became more adept in executing the reinforcer as each experiment progressed.

Performance of individual subjects. Although differences between experimental conditions have been demonstrated for the *S*s as a group, the performance of individual *S*s is of interest. Of the 22 *S*s, 19 showed an increase in vocalizations under Conditioning. For 14 of these 19 the increase was significant at the .05 level, according to the Mann-Whitney Test (1947). Under Extinction, 16 of the 22 *S*s showed some decrease, and for 10 of these 16 the decrease was significant at the .05 level.

Three *S*s departed widely from the group pattern. For two, not only did Conditioning depress the rate of vocalizing, but Extinction restored it to its Baseline rate. The first chewed her thumb more during Conditioning than before or after. The second strained (in an apparent effort to defecate) during Conditioning whenever anyone, *E* or the nurse, leaned over his crib. Both activities precluded vocalizing. Both babies were very active, and it is possible, therefore, that in the very first Conditioning period *E* may have inadvertently reinforced these activities. For the third *S,* in Experiment I the experimental conditions appeared not to affect the frequency of vocalizations. Developmental immaturity seemed the most likely reason, for two weeks later he was studied again in Experiment II (the only *S* to be used in both experiments) with satisfactory results.

Effect of Baseline performance upon Conditioning. The *S*s tended to maintain their relative positions under Baseline and Conditioning. The rank-order coefficient of correlation (R) was .66, $p <$ .0005. Further, the amount of gain under Conditioning was not correlated with original position $(R = .24, \ p > .05)$.

Sex differences. The 12 male *S*s gave slightly more vocalizations during Baseline and gained more under Conditioning than the 10 female *S*s, but the differences were not reliable.

Discussion

The results of these experiments suggest that:

1. Infants' vocal behavior in a social situation can be brought under experimental control; that is, it appears to be conditionable.

2. A social event composed of an everyday complex of acts, performed by an adult who is not a caretaker, can function as a reinforcing stimulus.

3. The incidence of such behavior can be very quickly modified in as young an organism as the three-month-old infant.

ALTERNATIVE EXPLANATION

The question raised in the introduction may now be considered. Did the reinforcing stimulus function as an arouser of vocalizations? Would infants have vocalized more often because of the stimulation it provided, even if it had *not* been made contingent upon the infant's behavior? Or, did some part of the reinforcing stimulus (say, the smile) act as a social "releaser"? The findings appear to be compatible with the conclusion that conditioning occurred: The rate of vocalizing continued to rise on the second day of Conditioning; the rate did not fall to the Baseline level on the first day of Extinction; it continued to fall on the second day of Extinction; and *S*s with low Baseline rates of vocalizing gained under Conditioning, although for them there was often a relatively long time interval (30 sec. or more) between the reinforcing stimulus and the occurrence of the next vocalization. Still, the decisive answer to the question must await an experiment in which the reinforcing stimulus is administered with equal frequency, but never directly after the infant vocalizes.

NATURE OF THE REINFORCER

The results seem to show that some everyday behavior of adults can function as a reinforcing stimulus for an infant. One would like to know from what sources its reinforcing properties arise. In the simplest case, the smiles, sounds, and caresses of adults may be reinforcing only because they provide a change in stimulation. Further information on this matter could be obtained by working with the separate parts of the reinforcing stimulus, one by one; by substituting for them lights or sounds dispensed by a machine; or by using a reinforcer of a less "affectionate" nature than the one used here appears to be. On the other hand, even for the three-month-old infant the smiles, sounds, and caresses of the adults may function as conditioned reinforcers because of their past association with caretaking acts.

It is possible that the Ss of this study, living in an institution, may have had a less rich experience with adults. Institutional babies were used as Ss only because they were more readily available, because more of them could be studied at one time, and because the complicating variable of differences in maternal care could be bypassed. They did not appear however to be "starved" for attention or affection. Indeed, the attendants were often observed responding to babies when they vocalized. While it is possible that mothers would respond more often, in the absence of a comparative study we believe that infants in general would respond as these infants did.

RELATION OF RESULTS
TO THEORIES OF SPEECH

Since this study was limited to the vocalizing of infants in a social situation, attempts to reconcile the results with theories which account for all classes of prelinguistic utterances (babbling is the class frequently mentioned) cannot be complete. Thus, nothing in the findings of this study is incompatible with, for example, Holt's theory (1931) that the sound which the child hears himself make has reinforcing properties; with Lewis' theory (1951) that the adult's speech calls forth the infant's speech (a kind of imitation); or with Piaget's theory (1952) that vocalizing is perpetuated for its own sake by the processes of assimilation and accommodation. These may be labeled circular theories, for they do not postulate the necessity for any class of events prior to the moment when the infant responds to his own or another's vocalization. The theories of Miller and Dollard (1941) and of Mowrer (1950), on the other hand, are based upon the infant's associating the gratification of his needs and the accompanying vocalizations of the caretaker. Again, the results do not contradict this possibility.

The present study, however, does demonstrate the operation of still another principle: that the speech of the infant, if only in a social situation, can be modified by a response from the environment which is contingent upon his vocalizing. Hence, what happens *after* the infant vocalizes has been shown to be important.

SIGNIFICANCE OF RESULTS

On the basis of the results of these experiments it is seen that responses of adults which do not involve caretaking can affect the vocalizing of the young in a social setting. If the results can be extended to life situations, then mothers might be able to increase or decrease the vocal output of their children by the responses they make when the children vocalize. Other kinds of social behavior in addition to vocalizing behavior should respond similarly to conditioning. Brackbill (1958) has shown that smiling in the four-month-old infant may be increased when followed by a social response from an adult. It is likely that still other kinds of social behavior in babies, such as showing an interest in people, reaching out to them or turning away, perhaps even fear of the stranger, may also be affected by the responses adults make to them.

Summary

Infants often vocalize as part of the response they give to the appearance of an adult. The central question of this study is: Can the frequency of vocalizing be increased if the adult makes a social response contingent upon it?

The Ss were 21 normal infants, three months of age, living in an institution. Eleven of them were studied in Experiment I with one E; 10 different Ss and one S from Experiment I were studied in Experiment II with a different E.

During the first and second Baseline days E leaned over S with an expressionless face, and the number of vocalizations was tallied. During the next two days, the first and second Conditioning days, E reinforced vocalizations by simultaneously smiling, clucking, and touching S's abdomen. During the last two days, the first and second Extinction days, E returned to Baseline conditions.

The results indicated that: (a) there was no difference between Experiments, (b) Conditioning raised the rate of vocalizing above the Baseline level, (c) while Extinction lowered it until it approached the Baseline level.

The results suggest that the social vocalizing of infants, and, more generally, their social responsiveness may be modified by the responses adults make to them.

References

BRACKBILL, Y. Extinction of the smiling response in infants as a function of reinforcement schedule. *Child Develpm.*, 1958, **29,** 115–124.

GEWIRTZ, J. L. A program of research on the dimensions and antecedents of emotional dependence. *Child Develpm.*, 1956, **27,** 205–221.

HOLT, E. B. *Animal drive.* London: Williams & Norgate, 1931.

LEWIS, M. M. *Infant speech: A study of the beginnings of language.* (2nd ed.) New York: Humanities Press, 1951.

LINDQUIST, E. F. *Design and analysis of experiments in psychology and education.* Boston: Houghton Mifflin, 1953.

MANN, H. B., & WHITNEY, D. R. On a test of whether one of two random variables is stochastically larger than the other. *Ann. Math. Statist.*, 1947, **18,** 50–60.

MILLER, N. E., & DOLLARD, J. *Social learning and imitation.* New Haven: Yale Univer. Press, 1941.

MOWRER, O. H. *Learning theory and personality dynamics.* New York: Ronald, 1950.

PIAGET, J. *The origins of intelligence in children.* New York: Int. Univer. Press, 1952.

RHEINGOLD, H. L. The modification of social responsiveness in institutional babies. *Monogr. Soc. Res. Child Develpm.*, 1956, **21,** No. 63 (No. 2).

SKINNER, B. F. *Science and human behavior.* New York: Macmillan, 1953.

VERPLANCK, W. S. The control of the content of conversation: Reinforcement of statements of opinion. *J. abnorm. soc. Psychol.*, 1955, **51,** 668–676.

CHAPTER 2

Studies of Perception and Personality

Selective Perception

PERCEPTUAL DEFENSE REVISITED   Gerald S. Blum

Probably no concept in psychology has enjoyed such dizzy popularity in a short span of time as perceptual defense. The word "dizzy" is used advisedly, for what other concept has led to so much experimental work, occasioned such far-flung polemics emanating from places like New South Wales in Australia (4), and been cast aside by its very creators —all within a half-dozen years or so?

Bruner and Postman were responsible to a great extent for the original impetus given to the concept. From their work on motivational factors in perception, they advanced the formulation of perceptual defense as an "unconscious mechanism of resistance to recognition of threatening stimuli." The concept quickly caught the psychologist's fancy. Lately, however, while many others have been eagerly climbing on the bandwagon, there have been two notable defections—namely the drivers, Postman and Bruner. In two recent articles Postman (7, 8) has vociferously denounced the concept, while Bruner has more quietly directed his interests to what he himself has described as the "cold" variables of cognition.

At this point it seems appropriate to examine Postman's revised position. In one article (8) entitled, "Is There a Mechanism of Perceptual Defense?" Postman, Bronson, and Gropper report an ingenious experiment showing that recognition thresholds for taboo and neutral words can be significantly affected by manipulating variables like familiarity of the words themselves, and the set given to the subject in terms of facilitating or inhibiting overt verbal report. From these findings that recognition thresholds can be varied by altering factors other than the emotional significance of the stimulus words, they conclude that the experimental results to date have failed to lend support to the concept of perceptual defense. Having thus cast doubt on the McGinnies type of experiment using word recognition, Postman proceeds to criticize other researches, such as those by Rosenstock (9) and Eriksen (3), as follows:

In other studies in which complex stimuli materials such as sentences and pictures were used, the evaluation of the relative familiarity and structural difficulty of the neutral and critical stimuli is so difficult that the threshold differences cannot be interpreted as evidence for a defensive process (7, p. 299).

The next group of studies taken to task in the paper, "On the Problem of

Reprinted by permission of the American Psychological Association and the author from the *Journal of Abnormal and Social Psychology*, Vol. 51, 1955.

Perceptual Defense," are those which make use of independent personality assessment, such as the Lazarus, Eriksen, Fonda (5) experiment on auditory perceptual recognition. Postman states:

Similar difficulties of interpretation arise in studies which correlate sensitivity to critical stimuli with independent personality measures of the subjects. Even though the personality measures purport to classify subjects in terms of their proneness to defensive reactions, it does not follow that the threshold differences observed do, in fact, represent different degrees of perceptual defense (7, p. 299).

He goes on to make the excellent point that a rigorous operational definition of defense would have to anchor the concept in *antecedent* as well as in consequent conditions.

Then, in the interests of what he describes as theoretical parsimony, he attempts to apply the Bruner-Postman hypothesis theory to the phenomena of perceptual defense. In Postman's own words:

A hypothesis is defined as a predisposition of the perceiver to organize stimulus cues in specific ways. Such hypotheses are anchored on the antecedent side in conditions of stimulus input and specified conditions of the organism (including drives and motives) and on the consequent side in systematic perceptual responses (discriminations, verbal reports, etc.). Hypotheses vary in strength, i.e., they vary in the amount of stimulation necessary to arouse, confirm or deny them. We have found the concept of hypothesis useful in the analysis of a considerable body of experimental data, including the phenomena of perceptual defense which can now be economically conceptualized in terms of interference among competing hypotheses. "What appears to be perceptual defense results from the dominance of strong alternative

hypotheses rather than from active repression of the inimical or dangerous. In the presence of partial information, strong hypotheses incompatible with the threatening stimulus may be evoked. . . . If this is the case, the subject will appear to be defending himself against perception. . . . If, however, hypotheses related to the negative stimuli are strong, the opposite of defense will appear to operate." Thus, the demands of theoretical parsimony led us to abandon perceptual defense as a special principle of perception and to fit the phenomena to which it referred into a broader theoretical context (7, p. 300).

It should be noted, though, that an element of caution also finds a place:

It may, of course, be argued that stimuli such as those used by McGinnies and ourselves are not appropriate for testing the hypothesis of perceptual defense. Such may or may not be the case; the possibility of future positive evidence cannot, of course, be excluded. At the present, however, perceptual defense has, at best, the status of an unconfirmed hypothesis (8, p. 223).

The study described below represents an attempt to control for Postman's incisive criticisms within the design of an experiment.

Hypothesis

The following hypothesis was set up for experimental test: *Subjects predisposed to use the mechanism of repression in conjunction with a given conflict will, when confronted subliminally with a conflict-relevant stimulus, show defensive behavior directly traceable to the perceptual process itself.*

Method

SUBJECTS

Seventeen advanced graduate students in clinical psychology, all of whom were thoroughly familiar with the Blacky Pictures (1) and had known the experimenter for some time.

APPARATUS

For the perceptual task a tachistoscope designed by Gerbrands of Arlington, Massachusetts, was employed. The Ss were tested individually with stimuli presented at a speed of .03 sec. Illumination of the adapting field was 1.57 footlamberts, of the test field 0.85 footlamberts.

PROCEDURE

1. *Assessment of conflict and defense:* Each S was seen individually over a period of several weeks and given the following instructions for the measures listed below. The sequence of presentation was varied systematically in accordance with a prearranged plan.

a. Free Recall (administered at various points in sequence): "I would like to find out how familiar you are with the Blacky Pictures themselves. So what I want you to do is to describe as many of the pictures as you can. First give me the *name* of the psychosexual dimension which the picture is supposed to represent and then describe the *physical* characteristics of the picture in as much detail as you can. All right, go ahead."

b. Timed Recall (always later in sequence than Free Recall, at intervals ranging from one to six weeks, with other tasks sometimes intervening): "I'd like to try you out on another task. This time I want you to name as many of the Blacky Pictures as you can, just as *rapidly* as possible. Just give me the name of the picture as fast as you can. Any order is all right. Ready, go ahead!"

c. Problem Ranking I (administered at various points in sequence): "What I'd like you to do now is rather personal.

If you'd rather not do it, that's okay. The task is to rank these 11 areas (sheet containing names of Blacky Pictures handed to S) according to how you see them as problems in yourself. Just your impressions, without spending much time on it. Of course your responses will be coded and kept completely confidential. Rank 1 stands for the greatest problem; Rank 11 for the least problem."

d. Problem Ranking II (always directly following Problem Ranking I, at intervals ranging from one to three weeks): "Now I'd like you to do the same thing you did a while back. Just rank these 11 areas according to how you see them as problems in yourself. Remember, Rank 1 stands for the greatest problem and Rank 11 for the least."

The assessment of conflict in these sophisticated subjects naturally posed a problem. Since they were familiar with the administration and scoring of the Blacky Pictures, a special method of analyzing their recall and problem-ranking responses was devised in advance of the actual experiment. The following list contains the conflict indicators, which were used additively to provide a numerical score for every subject on each of the Blacky dimensions.

(1) Content (Free Recall): errors in description; slips; excessive doubting or uncertainty about content.

(2) Detail (Free Recall): overly detailed elaboration; overly brief description.

(3) Intrusion (Free or Timed Recall): premature insertion of picture if regular Blacky sequence is generally followed; first three pictures given if sequence not followed.

(4) Delay (Free or Timed Recall): delayed placement of picture if regular sequence is generally followed; last three pictures given if sequence not followed (last two if only ten are given; last one if only nine).

(5) Perseveration (Free or Timed Recall): returning to picture mentioned earlier.

(6) Pause (Free or Timed Recall): long pause just preceding or during picture.

(7) Aside Comment (Free Recall): aside comment to self or experimenter during description of a picture.

(8) Problem Ranking I vs. II: a picture placed three or more ranks apart on the two separate administrations.

Based upon the above system, an individual was considered to have conflict on a given Blacky dimension if his conflict score on that picture reached two or more points.

In addition to the necessity for determining the existence of conflict, the hypothesis calls for a measure of repression. The Free and Timed Recall tasks were, of course, readily suited to this. An S was considered to exhibit repression on a dimension if he forgot the picture or its label in either of the recall procedures, provided he also received a conflict score in that area. The latter requirement was included to minimize the possible influence of forgetting due to nonemotional factors.

2. *Perceptual task:* The perceptual task was also introduced at various points in the testing sequence—sometimes preceding the recall and problem-ranking measures, sometimes following, and other times placed between them. During this session S was first told: "Before going ahead with the tachistoscopic procedure, I'll fill you in briefly on all the pictures along with the dimensional labels." (Following list is read to S:)

Oral eroticism: Blacky nursing from Mama.

Oral sadism: Blacky shaking Mama's collar.

Anal sadism: Blacky defecating between Mama's and Papa's houses.

Oedipal intensity: Blacky watching Mama and Papa make love.

Masturbation guilt: Blacky discovering sex.

Castration anxiety: Blacky watching knife falling on Tippy's tail.

Identification process: Blacky scolding the toy dog.

Sibling rivalry: Blacky watching Mama and Papa pet Tippy.

Guilt feelings: Blacky cringing before a superego figure.

Ego ideal: Blacky dreaming about a male dog.

Love object: Blacky dreaming about a female dog.

Next, S was seated in front of the tachistoscope and familiarized with the apparatus. These instructions followed: "Now I'm going to flash some Blacky Pictures very quickly, at a fraction of a second. There will be four pictures shown simultaneously at each flash—one at the Left, Right, Bottom and Top. The same picture will never appear twice in any one pattern and the patterns themselves will be different from flash to flash. What I want you to do is to tell me which picture you think is in each of the four positions. Even though the speeds will be too fast for you to recognize any picture clearly, make four judgments each time. When I say, 'Ready,' focus on the dark spot at the center of the screen. That will give you the best chance to see all four positions. I'll flash the pictures right after the 'Ready' signal. Also, keep your head in the headpiece until I tell you to sit back and relax. That will keep your eyes adapted to the light. Okay? Let's begin." Forty-eight flashes (6 patterns repeated 8 times) at .03 sec. were presented, so that S made a total of 192 picture calls. A short rest was given after each series of six flashes.

Afterward Ss uniformly stated that they were unable to recognize any of the pictures. Many spontaneously suggested that the same results would have been obtained simply by asking them to name four pictures 48 times, since the stimuli themselves were so faint. Some confessed somewhat sheepishly that they had tried to keep a mental count in order to call each of the 11 pictures equally and thereby not give away their personal dynamics! But despite their familiarity with the Blacky Pictures, their sophistication with respect to psychoanalytic theory, and their knowledge of perception research, one aspect of the procedure eluded all of them completely. This was the crucial element in the experimental design—the fact that the same four pictures were shown over and over. The four pictures actually presented in the tachistoscope (positions rotated) were Oral Eroticism (I), Oral Sadism (II), Masturbation Guilt (V), and Identification Process (VII). These particular four were selected only because they had been used in an earlier study (where they had been combined in terms of physical qualities) and the stimulus patterns were still available (2).

EXPERIMENTAL DESIGN

Based on the above procedures, the following conditions were abstracted. Note that these abstractions are derivations from the actual procedures.

Experimental Conditions:
1. Present Pictures: Conflict plus Repression
2. Present Pictures: Neutral (no conflict, no defense)

Control Conditions:
3. Absent Pictures: Conflict plus Repression
4. Absent Pictures: Neutral

In terms of the hypothesis that defensive behavior can be traced directly to the perceptual process itself, the prediction

was made that pictures in Condition 1 would be undercalled in comparison with Condition 2, but that no difference would appear between the parallel Conditions 3 and 4. The prediction that subjects would show this avoidance response (undercalling) to present pictures relating to areas of conflict and repression involved the assumptions that (a) the subliminal stimulus would activate the conflict; and (b) the necessity to verbalize the conflict area at the conscious level (by calling it) would elicit defensive behavior.

The control aspects of this design bear careful scrutiny. We note that opportunity for perception of the stimulus is present only in the experimental conditions (1 and 2), since the pictures in Conditions 3 and 4 are never flashed. The antecedents of the situation are tied down via the prior assessment of conflict and repression—identical antecedents (same conflict and forgetting scores) existing for 1 and 3, and for 2 and 4. Any possible differential characteristics of the pictures, such as physical properties, familiarity, etc., are controlled by virtue of the fact that the same pictures occur within Conditions 1 and 2, and within 3 and 4. Also, the subjects themselves overlap in the various conditions, for a given S may be represented by different pictures in several conditions. The set is obviously invariant across conditions since only one task is involved. Finally, selective verbal report is not an issue because of the identity between 1 and 3 and between 2 and 4. Thus, the factors which Postman has questioned in earlier studies of perceptual defense—specification of antecedent conditions, familiarity, set and selective verbal report—are controlled so that the influence of the perceptual process itself can be tested.

Results

Table 1 presents the results of the study. The column headed "Number of Subjects" refers to the number of individuals from among the total group of 17 who were able to be represented in each condition. The uneven numbers are due to the fact that all 17 did not have pictures falling into all four conditions, e.g., only six Ss obtained conflict and repression scores on one or more of the present pictures. The N's refer to indi-

uli are actually present (Condition 1) in comparison to the same pictures unaccompanied by conflict and defense (Condition 2). This difference between disturbing and neutral pictures does not obtain when the stimuli are absent (Condition 3 vs. 4). Furthermore, examination of the range of calls per picture in Condition 1 reveals that *every picture was called less often than the purely chance mean of 17.46* (*S*'s 192 calls equally divided among the 11 Blacky Pictures), whereas approximately half

TABLE 1. MEAN FREQUENCIES OF PICTURE CALLS

Conditions	No. of Ss	Mean Number of Calls per Picture	
{ 1. Present Pictures: Conflict + Repression	6	9.42 }	$t = 3.83$ *
{ 2. Present Pictures: Neutral	14	17.12 }	$p <$ .001
{ 3. Absent Pictures: Conflict + Repression	5	15.20 }	N.S.
{ 4. Absent Pictures: Neutral	14	16.69 }	

* Owing to the small and uneven number of entries, it was not possible to include the correlational term in computing t. However, inspection of the scattergram reveals, if anything, a slight positive trend, so that the significance of the results can be accepted with confidence. A one-tailed test was used to determine the p value.

viduals rather than pictures to avoid inflating the size of the sample spuriously, so that in the few cases where an *S* had two or more pictures falling within any condition, a mean of his calls on those pictures was used. The column headed "Mean Number of Calls per Picture" gives the number of calls for pictures in each condition averaged across the individuals represented in that condition. The relevant comparisons in terms of the design are between the experimental set of conditions (1 vs. 2) and the control set of conditions (3 vs. 4).

From Table 1 we see that the predictions are confirmed. Pictures representing areas of conflict and repression are significantly undercalled when the stim-

of the pictures in the other three conditions fall above and half fall below the chance mean. In other words, there are no exceptions to the pattern of undercalling within Condition 1.

Two interesting sidelights also deserve mention. Though the hypothesis deals only with the combined effect of conflict and repression, the data lend themselves to a further breakdown of the effect of conflict alone. Fourteen individuals showed conflict but no defense on present pictures. Their mean number of calls per picture is 17.68, which conforms closely to the chance expectancy. Therefore the conclusion is warranted that an avoidance response cannot be expected solely from the existence of conflict, but requires as an essential component the predisposition to avoid, namely repression. A comparable analysis of the effects of forgetting alone, without accompanying conflict, was not possible because only one case fell into that category.

A second sidelight concerns some further evidence on the level of perceptual discrimination. The positive results in Table 1 already imply that the subjects were unconsciously perceiving the stimuli presented tachistoscopically. Their subjective reports show that the phenomenon was not a conscious one. From the data we can derive an additional clue bearing on the level of discrimination. By confining our attention to calls of the four pictures which were actually present (ignoring calls on the remaining seven), we can check on the accuracy of the position (Left, Right, Top, or Bottom) assigned to the present picture. The group's obtained accuracy of 29.3 per cent is only slightly better than the chance expectancy of 25 per cent. However, the large number of judgments involved enables the difference between these two percentages to achieve statistical significance ($p < .01$). Individual subjects range in accuracy from 17 per cent to 44 per cent.

Discussion

Now to recap the implications of these results and to see how well the Bruner-Postman hypothesis theory fits the facts. First of all, perceptual defense can be traced directly to the perceptual process itself. With the variables of familiarity, set, and selective verbal report all controlled, an avoidance response to a subliminal stimulus has taken place. Apparently the subject makes an unconscious visual discrimination which somehow cues off an avoidance reaction. The threatening stimulus must actually be

provided by the environment in order for this defensive response to be instigated. With respect to antecedent conditions, we now know that it takes a combination of conflict in an area *plus* a predisposition to repress that conflict to produce the avoidance. Conflict alone has no discernible effect.

According to Postman, "What appears to be perceptual defense results from the dominance of strong alternative hypotheses rather than from active repression of the inimical or dangerous." In the present experiment, then, we would be forced to say that S's hypothesis was weaker in Condition 1 than Condition 2. Possibly someone might want to argue that an individual has stronger hypotheses about areas in which he has no conflicts (Condition 2) than areas in which he is conflicted and has already developed a response predisposition (Condition 1). This is a difficult position to maintain. The competing hypothesis theory becomes even weaker when we compare Conditions 1 and 3. Here the hypothesis strength is obviously equal, since both deal with conflict and repression. If the two are both *weak,* then the appearance of a stimulus in Condition 1 (picture actually flashed) would make it stronger than Condition 3. Hence the prediction would have to be that pictures in Condition 1 would be called more often than those in 3—the opposite of what actually occurred, since pictures in Condition 1 were called significantly less than those in 3($t = 1.93\ p < .05$). If, on the other hand, the two are both *strong,* then Condition 1 should have *more* calls than any of the other three, for Postman states specifically that when hypotheses related to negative stimuli are strong, the opposite of perceptual defense will appear to operate.

About the only even remote way we

can try to reconcile the hypothesis theory with our data is to say that the individual in Condition 1 has a *strong hypothesis not to perceive* the negative stimulus, and the response of not perceiving is tripped off by the actual appearance of that stimulus in the tachistoscope. Having gone this far, we are confronted once again with what would have to be a $64 question for Postman—Why does the individual develop a hypothesis not to perceive—a question easily answered if we look to psychoanalytic theory and perceptual defense.

In conclusion, the results of the present study seem to be incompatible with the proposed rejection of the concept of perceptual defense. The "competing hypothesis" theory, which Postman has advocated as a more parsimonious substitute, does not appear to fit the data. Perhaps a more temperate position is called for by our currently limited knowledge of the relationship between personality and perception. The field is ripe for continued intensive, experimental exploration under relevant, carefully controlled conditions. Before we are willing to run the time-honored risk of throwing the baby out with the bath, we should at least make certain that the baby has first been washed.

Summary

Recently the concept of perceptual defense has become the subject of considerable controversy. Prominent in these discussions is Postman's revised position, which maintains that "what appears to be perceptual defense results from the dominance of strong alternative hypotheses rather than from active repression of the inimical or dangerous." In the present study the following hypothesis was submitted to experimental test: *Subjects predisposed to use the mechanism of repression in conjunction with a given conflict will, when confronted subliminally with a conflict-relevant stimulus, show defensive behavior directly traceable to the perceptual process itself.*

The procedures included:

(1) Seventeen advanced graduate students in clinical psychology were assessed for conflict and defense related to dimensions of the Blacky Pictures, by means of a series of recall and problem-ranking methods.

(2) The Ss were given the perceptual task of naming four Blacky Pictures flashed simultaneously at a tachistoscopic speed well below conscious awareness. All 11 pictures were called in varying frequencies over 48 trials, but none of the Ss caught on to the fact that the same four pictures were flashed in every trial. This procedure permitted the establishment of four conditions:

Present Pictures: Conflict plus Repression
Present Pictures: Neutral
Absent Pictures: Conflict plus Repression
Absent Pictures: Neutral.

In accordance with the predictions, pictures in Condition 1 were called significantly less than those in Condition 2, whereas no difference occurred in the comparison of Conditions 3 and 4. Thus, with the variables of selective verbal report, familiarity, set, and antecedent conditions all controlled, an avoidance response directly traceable to the perceptual process was obtained.

The seeming incompatibility of these findings with the Bruner-Postman "hypothesis theory" explanation of perceptual defense was reviewed, with the conclusion that current attempts to abandon perceptual defense in the interests of "theoretical parsimony" may very well be premature.

References

1. BLUM, G. S. *The Blacky Pictures: a technique for the exploration of personality dynamics.* New York: Psychological Corporation, 1950.

2. ———. An experimental reunion of psychoanalytic theory with perceptual vigilance and defense. *J. abnorm. soc. Psychol.,* 1954, **49,** 94–98.

3. ERIKSEN, C. W. Perceptual defense as a function of unacceptable needs. *J. abnorm. soc. Psychol.,* 1951, **46,** 557–564.

4. HOWIE, D. Perceptual defense. *Psychol. Rev.,* 1952, **59,** 308–315.

5. LAZARUS, R. S., ERIKSEN, C. W., & FONDA, C. P. Personality dynamics and auditory perceptual recognition. *J. Pers.,* 1951, **19,** 471–482.

6. McGINNIES, E. M. Emotionality and perceptual defense. *Psychol. Rev.,* 1949, **56,** 244–251.

7. POSTMAN, L. On the problem of perceptual defense. *Psychol. Rev.,* 1953, **60,** 298–306.

8. POSTMAN, L., BRONSON, W. C., & GROPPER, G. L. Is there a mechanism of perceptual defense? *J. abnorm. soc. Psychol.,* 1953, **48,** 215–224.

9. ROSENSTOCK, I. M. Perceptual aspects of repression. *J. abnorm. soc. Psychol.,* 1951, **46,** 304–315.

RESPONSE SUPPRESSION IN PERCEPTUAL DEFENSE

Robert B. Zajonc

Recent theorizing maintains that the phenomenon of perceptual defense can be accounted for in terms of response processes. Elevated thresholds to taboo words are now generally regarded as reflecting a response bias deriving from either previous experience (Goldiamond & Hawkins, 1958), set (Postman, Bronson, & Gropper, 1953), or conflict (Brown, 1961), rather than a defensive perceptual blocking. Although the core of the issue deals with the relative contributions of the stimulus and response to the perceptual defense effect, studies attempting to evaluate such relative contributions have been rather few (Mat-

Reprinted by permission of the American Psychological Association and the author from the *Journal of Experimental Psychology,* Vol. 64, 1962.

thews & Wertheimer, 1958; Neisser, 1954). It is the purpose of this experiment to determine the extent to which both recognition threshold and the galvanic skin response (GSR) are influenced by the stimulus and to what extent by the response, using a procedure first suggested by Garner, Hake, and Eriksen (1956). First, threshold and GSR data for a set of taboo and neutral words were obtained by means of standard methods. Secondly, a paired-associate list was constructed using the previously exposed words as stimulus terms and a new set of taboo and neutral words as response terms. Some taboo stimuli were paired with taboo, others with neutral response terms. Neutral stimuli too, were sometimes paired with neutral and sometimes with taboo response terms.

All Ss learned the paired-associate list to a criterion. The third step consisted of a repeated threshold and GSR assessment of the original stimuli. Now, however, one group was required to indicate recognition as before, i.e., by reading out loud the word presented tachistoscopically, and another by saying the appropriate response term which they have learned in the previous paired-associate task. Thus, the second group was given an opportunity to indicate recognition by means of responses whose emotional significance was either positively or negatively correlated with the emotional significance of the stimulus.

Method

SUBJECTS

Forty male Ss, all enrolled at the University of Michigan, participated in the experiment. They were randomly assigned to two experimental groups consisting of 20 Ss each. The Ss were paid $1.25 per hour for participation in the experiment.

APPARATUS

Gerbrands' transparent mirror tachistoscope with an instant start fluorescent lamp circuit was employed to present stimuli. Skin resistance changes were observed by means of a Lafayette Psychogalvanometer Model 603-A.

MATERIALS

Stimulus words were printed in black 2 in. block letters and presented in the center of the exposure field on grey 10 x 12 in. cards (54.5% reflectance). Stimulus-response pairs in the paired-associates task were shown in the same manner. Twelve taboo and 12 neutral words were selected from McGinnies'

(1949) original list of 18 words to which equivalent neutral and taboo stimuli were added. Half of the taboo and half of the neutral words were used as stimuli in the threshold assessment and as stimulus terms in the paired-associate training task. The remainder of the list was used as response terms in the paired-associate task. Three taboo stimuli were paired with three taboo responses, three taboo stimuli were paired with three neutral responses, three neutral stimuli were paired with three taboo responses, and three neutral stimuli with three neutral responses. These sets of words will be referred to as the TT, TN, NT, and NN sets. The 24 words were Apple, Broom, Candy, Chair, Child, Floor, Music, Rains, River, Shelf, Stove, Trade, Balls, Belly, Bleed, Fairy, Filth, Hymen, Kotex, Penis, Pubic, Raped, Vomit, Whore.

PROCEDURE

As briefly outlined above, the procedure consisted of two recognition threshold and GSR assessment sessions separated by an intervening paired-associate learning task. The Ss were divided into two groups of 20 Ss each, one of which was required during the second threshold assessment session to indicate recognition in terms of the stimuli presented (Group S), the other in terms of the response terms paired with the stimuli (Group R).

Thresholds were obtained by the ascending method of limits in .01-sec. steps beginning with .05 sec. below S's threshold to a neutral training word. The intertrial intervals were approximately 30 sec. Some of the words were shown more than once in order to eliminate pre-recognition guesses during the second threshold assessment, when full knowledge of the list was already available to *S*s. For those words data from the first presentation alone were included in the analysis. The criterion of threshold was the first correct recognition of the word in Group S and the first emission of the correct response term in Group R.

The *S* was seated with his head against the eye-pieces and with his hand to which electrodes were affixed lying relaxed on the table. A rest period of 1 min. was given after the first threshold assessment session and after the paired-associate training.

The tachistoscope was operated by an adult male and the psychogalvanometer by an adult female. The GSR readings were taken in terms of reduction in resistance from the basal resistance level, which was adjusted for each stimulus exposure. Only those reactions which occurred within 5 sec. following stimulus exposure, and only those for which the resistance returned to the immediate neighborhood of the pre-exposure level were recorded. GSR readings were taken on every presentation of the stimulus word. Since some *S*s recognized the word on the fourth exposure, only two pre-recognition trials and the recognition trial were considered. Thus, for each *S* three GSR scores were computed for each set of stimuli, and for the purposes

of analysis all were converted to standard scores with a mean of 50 and *SD* of 10 for all 40 *S*s.

The paired-associate task was conducted using a 2-sec. interval for the presentation of the stimulus and a 2-sec. interval for the presentation of the pair, with 20 sec. between trials. All terms were presented tachistoscopically. The order of the stimuli was randomly altered from trial to trial. Three consecutive correct anticipations of the entire list were used as the criterion.

Results

RECOGNITION THRESHOLD AND GSR BEFORE PAIRED-ASSOCIATE TRAINING

Mean recognition thresholds obtained before paired-associate training are shown in Table 1. The analysis of variance for these results showed that the only significant effect is due to the difference between taboo and neutral words ($F = 17.08$, $P < .001$). Although the mean recognition thresholds for Group R are somewhat higher than those for Group S, this difference is not significant. Also, no significant differences were obtained between taboo words to be later used with taboo responses (TT) and taboo words to be later used with

TABLE 1. MEAN RECOGNITION THRESHOLDS (SEC.) BEFORE
PAIRED-ASSOCIATE TRAINING

| Group | Later PA Conditions | | | | Words | |
	TT	TN	NT	NN	All Taboo	All Neutral
S	.219	.228	.193	.198	.223	.196
R	.234	.233	.206	.213	.234	.210
Both	.227	.231	.200	.206	.229	.203

neutral responses (TN). Nor was there any difference between neutral words to be later used with taboo responses (NT) and neutral words to be later used with neutral responses (NN).

The GSRs are shown in Fig. 1. Again considerable rise in the GSR on the recognition trial ($F = 32.94, P < .001$). No significant differences between TT and TN words as well as between NN and NT words were found for either of the two groups.

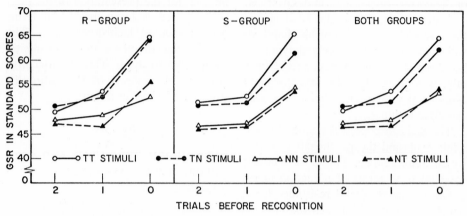

FIG. 1. GSR before paired-associate training.

no difference between the experimental groups was found. It is evident from the results that on all trials taboo words exceed neutral words in GSR ($F = 30.99$, $P < .001$). It is also clear that there is a

PAIRED-ASSOCIATE LEARNING

Average number of trials to learn the four sets of associations are presented in Table 2. The means represent the

TABLE 2. MEAN TRIALS AND ERRORS TO CRITERION IN
PAIRED-ASSOCIATE LEARNING

	Pairs				Words			
Group	TT	TN	NT	NN	Taboo Stimuli	Neutral Stimuli	Taboo Responses	Neutral Responses
Group S								
Trials	4.56	5.62	4.37	5.13	5.09	4.75	4.47	5.38
Errors	4.55	7.10	3.70	6.10	5.83	4.90	4.13	6.60
Group R								
Trials	4.21	4.95	4.48	4.28	4.58	4.38	4.35	4.62
Errors	2.90	5.00	3.80	3.55	3.95	3.68	3.35	4.28
Both								
Trials	4.39	5.29	4.43	4.71	4.84	4.57	4.41	5.00
Errors	3.73	6.05	3.75	4.83	4.89	4.29	3.74	5.44

number of trials which Ss required to learn a given association to a criterion of three correct anticipations, averaged for the three items in each set. Shown in Table 2 is also the average number of errors for each set of pairs. The results indicate that the four sets of associations

ulus word, the TN stimuli should, during the subsequent threshold and GSR assessment of Group R, be more handicapped than NT stimuli. The differences between these pairs in both trials to criterion and average number of errors are significant at the .001 level.

TABLE 3. ANALYSIS OF VARIANCE FOR DATA IN TABLE 2

Source	df	Trials to Criterion		Errors	
		MS	F	MS	F
Treatments (A)	1	8.06	.83	96.09	1.09
Words	3	6.69	6.03 *	48.54	6.23 *
S Component	1	3.11	3.27	14.40	2.68
R Component	1	13.40	8.93 **	115.60	11.73 **
$B_1 \times B_2$	1	3.57	4.12	15.62	1.92
Treatment × Words	3	1.78	1.60	13.45	1.73
$A \times B_1$	1	.24	.25	4.23	.79
$A \times B_2$	1	3.93	2.62	24.03	2.44
$A \times B_1 \times B_2$	1	1.18	1.37	12.10	1.49
Error (b)	38	9.76		88.91	
Error (w)	114	1.11		7.79	
$Ss \times B_1$	38	.95		5.38	
$Ss \times B_2$	38	1.50		9.85	
$Ss \times B_1 \times B_2$	38	.86		8.13	

* Significant at the .01 level.
**Significant at the .001 level.

were not learned at the same rate (see Table 3). In particular, the TN pairs seem to be the most difficult, and the TT easiest. The analysis of variance presented in Table 3 shows a significant effect due to differences between word sets, which is primarily due to the type of response. In general, pairs with a taboo response require fewer trials and lead to fewer errors than pairs with neutral responses. Of particular importance to the present experiment is the difference between the TN and NT pairs. If speed of learning and number of errors reflect the degree to which a given response has become attached to the stim-

RECOGNITION THRESHOLD AND GSR AFTER PAIRED-ASSOCIATE TRAINING

Group R. Table 4 shows recognition thresholds for the four sets of words for the condition in which Ss indicated recognition by means of the response term acquired during the paired-associate training. It is apparent that, compared with those obtained before the paired-associate training, the thresholds to all the words are considerably reduced. It is also clear that no longer does the recognition threshold totally depend on the stimulus. There is a considerable effect due to the response which S utilizes in indicating recognition. It should be pointed out that S's ability to give evidence of recognition, not by means of a word which is presented but by means of a response previously learned, depends on the degree to which these responses were fixated. It will be recalled that the learning of the four types of associations was not uniform. In particular there was a considerable difference between the TN and the NT pairs, in favor of the latter.

Moreover, the examination of the results on paired-associate learning disclosed significant effect due to individual differences. The F-ratios evaluating the individual difference effect were 8.79 for trials to criterion, and 11.41 for errors, which for the degrees of freedom given are significant well beyond the .001 level. We would expect a more reliable test of the relative contributions of the stimulus shown and of the response given from Ss who learned these responses well.

TABLE 4. MEAN RECOGNITION THRESHOLDS (SEC.) IN GROUP R AFTER PAIRED-ASSOCIATE LEARNING

Group	PA Pairs				Words			
	TT	TN	NT	NN	Taboo Stimuli	Neutral Stimuli	Taboo Responses	Neutral Responses
Rapid Learners	.151	.138	.145	.138	.145	.142	.148	.138
Slow Learners	.178	.180	.174	.172	.179	.173	.176	.176
All Ss	.165	.159	.160	.155	.162	.158	.163	.157
Adjusted Means for All Ss	.168	.153	.160	.157	.161	.159	.164	.155

TABLE 5. ANALYSIS OF VARIANCE FOR DATA IN TABLE 4

Source	df	MS	F
Groups (Rapid vs. Slow) (A)	1	24,945	6.72 *
Words	3	338	2.54
S Component (B_1)	1	466	2.13
R Component (B_2)	1	546	5.00 *
$B_1 \times B_2$	1	1	<1.00
Groups $\times$ Words	3	131	<1.00
A $\times$ B$_1$	1	35	<1.00
A $\times$ B$_2$	1	536	4.91 *
A $\times$ B$_1$ $\times$ B$_2$	1	122	1.67
Error (b)	18	3,711	
Error (w)	54	133	
$Ss \times B_1$	18	218	
$Ss \times B_2$	18	109	
$Ss \times B_1 \times B_2$	18	73	

* Significant at the .05 level.

Group R was therefore divided at the median number of trials to criterion, and the recognition thresholds for the rapid and slow learners are shown in Table 4, and the analysis of variance in Table 5. It is clear from Table 4 that slow learners manifest considerably higher recognition thresholds for *all* the words. The difference between groups is significant at better than the .05 level. It appears that the slow learners' recognition threshold depends primarily on the type of stimulus presented, while that of rapid learners on

bottom of Table 4. Analysis of covariance performed on these results disclosed a significant effect due to the response component ($F = 8.78$ for 1 and 17 df) and no effects due to stimulus.

The GSR data shown in Figure 2 follow a similar pattern. Again, as compared with the results obtained before paired-associate training, the GSRs are weaker. The analysis of variance (Table 6) shows a significant effect due to the differences between words which seems to be a function of the stimulus and of

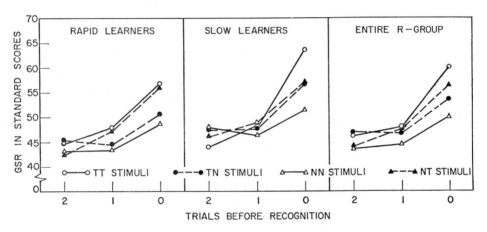

FIG. 2. GSR after paired-associate training (Group R).

the response which they were required to make. However, the Groups x Stimulus x Response interaction was not significant. The overall results, however, indicate that the effects due to the stimulus component were not significant while those due to the response were significant. Further support for the conclusion that recognition threshold depends primarily on the type of response required is obtained when the data are adjusted for differences in learning the four types of associations. The mean recognition thresholds, adjusted by means of the regression equation relating the former to the number of trials, are shown at the

the response component as well. The results of both groups combined indicate that on the second pre-recognition trial the GSRs do not follow any particular pattern. However, the curves for the rapid learners show a pattern of particular interest. On the second pre-recognition trial the GSRs seems to depend primarily on the stimulus component; their order is TN, TT, NN, and NT. As the *S*s approach recognition the stimulus effect is gradually replaced by the response effect and the GSRs are ordered according to the response. One may interpret this result to mean that stimulation present two trials before recognition is probably too weak to call out strong anticipatory partial responses. As soon as the stimulation gains in strength and

learners was 47.55 and for slow learners 50.53, but as is evident from Table 6 this difference was not significant.

TABLE 6. ANALYSES OF VARIANCE FOR DATA IN FIG. 2 AND 3

Source	df	Group R		Group S	
		MS	F	MS	F
Groups (Rapid vs. Slow) (A)	1	522.4	1.19	161.7	<1.00
Words	3	171.1	6.35 **	78.6	3.48 *
S component (B_1)	1	149.6	7.03 *	227.0	7.73 *
R component (B_2)	1	356.5	10.57 **	2.5	<1.00
$B_1 \times B_2$	1	7.3	<1.00	6.3	<1.00
Trials (C)	2	2,235.6	28.97 ***	942.5	12.57 ***
Groups × Words	3	9.6	<1.00	26.1	1.16
$A \times B_1$	1	.3	<1.00	16.9	<1.00
$A \times B_2$	1	27.8	<1.00	51.4	1.92
$A \times B_1 \times B_2$	1	.8	<1.00	10.1	<1.00
Words × Trials	6	136.7	5.44 ***	38.6	3.08 **
$B_1 \times C$	2	87.8	4.27 *	79.0	4.71 *
$B_2 \times C$	2	319.6	12.47 ***	6.6	<1.00
$B_1 \times B_2 \times C$	2	2.8	<1.00	30.4	4.94 *
Groups × Trials	2	25.3	<1.00	39.4	<1.00
Groups × Words × Trials	6	32.6	1.30	22.2	1.77
$A \times B_1 \times C$	2	77.5	3.77 *	36.7	2.19
$A \times B_2 \times C$	2	5.7	<1.00	4.8	<1.00
$A \times B_1 \times B_2 \times C$	2	14.7	<1.00	25.1	4.09 *
Error (b)	18	439.1		441.1	
Error (w)$_1$: Ss × Words	54	27.0		22.6	
Ss × B_1	18	21.3		29.4	
Ss × B_2	18	33.7		26.8	
Ss × $B_1 \times B_2$	18	25.9		11.6	
Error (w)$_2$: Ss × Words × Trials	36	77.2		75.0	
Error (w)$_3$: Ss × Words × Trials	108	25.1		12.6	
Ss × $B_1 \times C$	36	20.6		16.8	
Ss × $B_2 \times C$	36	25.6		14.7	
Ss × $B_1 \times B_2 \times C$	36	29.2		6.2	

* $P < .05$.
** $P < .01$.
*** $P < .001$.

becomes capable of evoking some parts of the learned response, the autonomic reactions lose their dependence upon the stimulus and begin to be dominated by the response component.

The mean GSR reactions for rapid

Group S. The principal purpose of the paired-associate learning task was to enable Ss to give evidence of recognition of the stimulus words without having to say them. However, it is possible to argue that the training simultaneously produced temporary changes in the emotional quality of the stimulus words. Thus, taboo stimuli which were paired with neutral responses could, by virtue of the repeatedly reinforced association, have become emotionally "neutralized." Similarly, conditioning a taboo response to a neutral stimulus word might have affected the emotional quality of the latter.

shown in Table 7, and the analysis of variance for these results has shown effects only due to the stimulus component. It is of interest to note that as was the case in Group R slow learners in Group S also showed somewhat higher recognition thresholds than rapid learners. However, this difference failed to reach an acceptable level of significance.

TABLE 7. MEAN RECOGNITION THRESHOLD (SEC.) IN GROUPS AFTER
PAIRED-ASSOCIATE TRAINING

Group	PA Pairs				Words			
	TT	TN	NT	NN	Taboo Stimuli	Neutral Stimuli	Taboo Responses	Neutral Responses
Rapid learning	.153	.151	.143	.141	.152	.142	.148	.146
Slow learners	.167	.175	.154	.162	.171	.158	.160	.168
All Ss	.160	.163	.149	.152	.161	.150	.154	.157

These eventualities are of course quite remote because of the small number of conditioning trials involved. If conditioning of the type suggested has in fact taken place then the recognition thresholds and the GSR data should show the same patterns in Groups S and R. The average recognition thresholds for Group S are

Neither do the GSR results shown in Fig. 3 suggest any conditioning effect. Besides the increase in reactions over trials, the only significant effect is that due to the stimulus component. The analysis of variance in Table 8 shows an F ratio significant at the .05 level for the stimulus component. On the trials

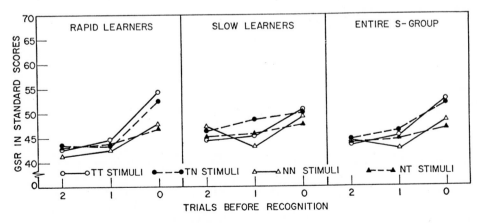

FIG. 3. GSR after paired-associate training (Group S).

TABLE 8. ANALYSIS OF VARIANCE FOR DATA IN TABLE 7

Source	df	MS	F
Groups (Rapid vs. Slow) (A)	1	10,160	3.12
Words	3	896	3.03
S component (B_1)	1	2,532	5.34 *
R component (B_2)	1	157	<1.00
$B_1 \times B_2$	1	0	<1.00
Groups × Words	3	150	<1.00
$A \times B_1$	1	131	<1.00
$A \times B_2$	1	419	1.68
$A \times B_1 \times B_2$	1	1	<1.00
Error (b)	18	3,088	
Error (w)	54	296	
$Ss \times B_1$	18	474	
$Ss \times B_2$	18	250	
$Ss \times B_1 \times B_2$	18	164	

* Significant at the .05 level.

immediately preceding recognition there is a slight but not significant response effect for rapid learners. Also, as observed before, the GSRs of rapid learners are somewhat less than those of slow learners (45.69 and 47.16, respectively), but this difference is decidedly not reliable.

Discussion

The evidence presented failed to disclose perceptual effects of any significance. The recognition threshold was found to be a function not of what S saw but what he had to say. Moreover, GSR data follow an identical pattern. The GSRs were found to be produced not by the stimulus alone, but depended primarily on the response required of S. The results are best accounted for by Brown's (1961) competing response theory. Irrespective of the stimulus, if the responses were in conflict with an inhibitory tendency, that is, if S had to make a vulgar response, both recognition threshold and GSR were elevated. Stimuli arousing no response conflict failed to produce differential thresholds and GSRs irrespective of their "emotionality." Further support for the response competition hypothesis is seen in the GSR data. In general, the differences in the GSRs were found to increase over trials, reaching their peak upon recognition. To the extent that the GSRs reflect response conflict, one would expect that with increasing exposure time both the positive and the negative tendencies increase, thus generating a stronger conflict.

There is evidence in the data that recognition threshold and GSR are also subject to variation as a result of not only a conflict between a positive and negative tendency, but also as a result of a conflict between competing excitatory tendencies. First we note that both are markedly reduced after familiarization with the stimuli. Before paired-associate learning the response alternatives available to Ss are many, and all of these are in competition. The training reduces them to 12, thus reducing the extent of response competition involved. Secondly, consistent differences in the overall recognition threshold and GSR reactions between the rapid and slow learner were found. If one views the speed of the paired-associate learning and the mean number of errors as an index of the amount of response competition present, these results become quite meaningful.

It is not claimed here that the perceptual defense phenomenon has been disproven. But if the phenomenon is empirically demonstrable its proof must be established by experimental methods other than those commonly used. Perhaps Blum's (1954) forced choice technique of threshold assessment holds best promise since it eliminates possible effects due to the response process.

Summary

The role of stimuli and responses in perceptual defense was examined by first obtaining recognition thresholds and GSRs to taboo and neutral words. Subsequently, Ss learned a paired-associate list with the original words serving as stimulus terms and a new set of words as response terms. Half of the neutral stimuli were paired with neutral and half with taboo responses. The same was true of taboo stimuli. Following training, recognition thresholds and GSRs were again measured with one group required to indicate recognition by means of response terms and another by means of stimulus terms. Both recognition threshold and GSR were found to depend primarily on the response required of the Ss in indicating recognition.

References

BLUM, G. S. An experimental reunion of psychoanalytic theory with perceptual vigilance and defense. *J. abnorm. soc. Psychol.*, 1954, **13**, 94–99.

BROWN, J. S. *The motivation of behavior.* New York: McGraw-Hill, 1961.

GARNER, W. R., HAKE, H. W., & ERIKSEN, C. W. Operationism and the concept of perception. *Psychol. Rev.*, 1956, **63**, 149–159.

GOLDIAMOND, I., & HAWKINS, W. F. Vexierversuch: The log relationship between word frequency and recognition obtained in the absence of stimulus words. *J. exp. Psychol.*, 1958, **56**, 457–463.

MATHEWS, A., & WERTHEIMER, M. A "pure" measure of perceptual defense uncontaminated by response suppression. *J. abnorm. soc. Psychol.*, 1958, **57**, 373–376.

McGINNIES, E. Emotionality and perceptual defense. *Psychol. Rev.*, 1949, **56**, 244–251.

NEISSER, U. An experimental distinction between perceptual process and verbal response. *J. exp. Psychol.*, 1954, **47**, 399–402.

POSTMAN, L., BRONSON, W. C., & GROPPER, G. L. Is there a mechanism of perceptual defense? *J. abnorm. soc. Psychol.*, 1953, **48**, 215–224.

THE AUTOKINETIC WORD TECHNIQUE

Allan Rechtschaffen and Sarnoff A. Mednick

It is often assumed that as the structure of stimulus situations decreases, perception becomes more and more influenced by idiosyncratic variables in the perceiver. The autokinetic effect—the apparent movement of a pin point of light in a totally dark room—was utilized to explore the minimum limits of structure which a situation may have and still elicit interpretable responses of a projective nature. The subjects (Ss) were placed in the autokinetic situation and told that words would be written by a moving light. The light was actually held stationary throughout the experiment.

Nine Ss, six male and three female college students, were tested individually as follows: Ss were seated in a totally dark room 8 ft. from the point of origin of a dim light source of approximately 1 mm. diameter. They were given a set of standard instructions which indicated essentially that this was a test of their ability to see words written by a point of light in a dark room. The Ss were encouraged to guess at what a word might be whenever they could not make out every letter of the word clearly. Each S participated in two sessions of 20 exposures each. Duration of exposure was varied randomly using 15, 30, 45, and 60 sec. exposures. Each session lasted approximately 30 min., with a 3-min. rest after the first 10 exposures. To encourage productivity, Ss were praised whenever they saw a word. Only the

Reprinted by permission of the American Psychological Association and the authors from the *Journal of Abnormal and Social Psychology*, Vol. 51, 1955.

standard phrases "very good" and "you're doing fine" were used, and at no time was S told that he got a word right or wrong.

All Ss reported words being written by the point of light. Word production per S ranged from 2 to 43; the group's total production was 122 words. As might be expected, word production varied with exposure time, the 15, 30, 45, and 60 sec. exposure times yielding respectively 14%, 19%, 24%, and 43% of the group's total. Rate of word production increased as the sessions continued. The first 10 exposures of both sessions produced only 30% of all the words seen, while the last 10 exposures of both sessions produced 70% of the total output. Similarly, the second session produced more words than the first, with 74% of the total word output being reported in the second session. Thus while rate of word production seems limited, it apparently can be increased with increased exposure time, length of session, and number of sessions.

Responses ran the gamut from such "unloaded" single words as "and," "on," and "the" through material seemingly related to the immediate situation to material of a very projective, personal variety. Generally, the more productive the S, the more personalized the material seemed.

The most striking example of reference to the immediate situation was given by a male S. During an intermission he told E that he wished to finish the experiment very quickly, because he had an examination to take in a short while. Following this, on the last 10 exposures of the session, he gave these re-sponses: "leave; on; 1 (just the letter); read; after; out; rid; see; 1 (just the let-ter); run." When later questioned, he said he had no idea at the time that what he saw was related to his desire to leave. He seemed genuinely astonished when shown the connection and said that he was not consciously thinking of leaving while he saw the words written.

Material which apparently transcended the immediate situation came from two females who were tested with exposure times of up to 3 min. following the ex-periment proper. One of these Ss, after giving several responses of a very highly personal nature, indignantly demanded of E, "Where did you get all that infor-mation about me?" The other S pro-duced this paragraph:

When men are tired and depraved, they become mean and callous individuals. When men learn to master their souls, the world will be a more humane and tolerant place in which to live. Men should learn to control themselves.

Since there is little in the stimulus situ-ation to "determine" the nature of the re-sponse, the technique may have useful-ness in experimental work where it is desired to elicit idiosyncratic material without having to account for variables associated with the objective, physical stimulus.

PERCEPTION OF DISTURBING AND NEUTRAL WORDS THROUGH THE AUTOKINETIC WORD TECHNIQUE

Sarnoff A. Mednick, Alan Harwood, and Jack Wertheim

The Autokinetic Word Technique (AWT) presents a situation in which the subject (S) is placed in a completely darkened room and asked to read and report words and sentences being written by an apparently moving but actually motionless point of light. A previous study (1) indicates that Ss do indeed re-port the perception of words and sen-tences. The use of the term "perception" is perhaps debatable, but the authors feel justified in its use by the similarity of present operations to those involved in the study of such illusions as the Necker cube.

Reprinted by permission of the American Psy-chological Association and the authors from the *Journal of Abnormal and Social Psychol-ogy*, Vol. 55, 1957.

One of the important uses to which the AWT may appropriately be put is the investigation of nonautochthonous perceptual variables. In this study, it was hypothesized that in the AWT situation "disturbing" words would be perceived with greater latency and less frequency than "neutral" words.

Method

A word association test (WAT) of 40 words was administered to 12 male and 12 female paid volunteer college stu-dents. All of the words used were drawn from the recent Minnesota standardiza-tion of the Kent-Rosanoff Word As-sociation Test on a college population (2). They all have a Thorndike-Lorge AA rating (3), indicating that they are commonly used in the English language. On the basis of probability of response (2), five disturbing and five neutral words were picked for each S from his WAT results. In cases where, due to ties, a decision could not be made solely on the basis of probability, the latency of the response served as the deciding factor. The median probability and latency of responses to the disturbing words were .001 and 2.10 sec., respectively; the median probability and latency of responses to the neutral words were .622 and 1.30 sec., respectively.

The Ss were then introduced to the AWT situation and instructed that we were going to write sentences with the point of light. (These Ss had had two hours of previous experience in the AWT situation in another study.) Before each sentence was written they were informed that they would be given one of the words in the forthcoming sentence. This word might appear at the beginning, middle, or end of the sentence. The S was to inform E when he saw this word.

Ten trials were then given in which the stationary pinpoint of light was turned on for 90 seconds along with a cheap electric motor that produced a convincing, variable noise. On five of the trials, neutral words from the WAT were the suggested words. Disturbing words from the WAT were the suggested words on the other five trials. Whenever S reported seeing the suggested word during the 90-second period, his response latency was noted. When the light was turned off, S was asked to report the complete sentence that had apparently been written by the point of light. E was present in the blacked-out room with S, who was seated approximately nine feet from the point of light.

Results

The two major measures of this study were (a) whether or not S reported perceiving a suggested word, (b) the latency of his reported perception. Of the 10 suggested words, Ss reported failing to see a mean of 3.73 words. Ss failed to see a mean of 2.09 of the five disturbing words and a mean of 1.64 of the five neutral words. This difference, evaluated by the paired replicates test (4), was significant at the .01 level. Thus, S failed to report seeing more of the disturbing than neutral words.

The mean latency of report of perception of the suggested words was 58.6 seconds. The perceived disturbing words had a mean latency of 64.4 seconds. The perceived neutral words had a mean latency of 52.7 seconds. The difference between these values was significant at the .01 level by the paired replicates test. Postponement of the report of perception of the disturbing word could be the result either of a simple unfilled delay of response or of the perception of many words preceding the disturbing word. The mean number of words preceding the suggested word was 1.02 words. The disturbing words were preceded by a mean of 1.08 words; the neutral words were preceded by a mean of .96 words, a difference that is not significant. The delay of report of perception of disturbing words cannot therefore be attributed to the perception of other intervening words.

The mean number of words reported in the sentences built around the disturbing and neutral words were 2.54 and 2.64, respectively. This difference, evaluated by the paired replicates test, was not significant.

Summary and Conclusions

Disturbing and neutral words were selected individually for Ss by means of a word association test. It was then suggested to these Ss that an apparently moving but actually motionless point of light in a completely darkened room (autokinetic effect) would write a sentence containing a given word. The given word was either a disturbing or neutral word.

The Ss reported perceiving fewer of the disturbing words. Those disturbing words that were perceived had a greater latency than perceived neutral words.

References

1. RECHTSCHAFFEN, A., & MEDNICK, S. A. The autokinetic word technique. *J. abnorm. soc. Psychol.*, 1955, **51,** 346.

2. RUSSELL, W. A., & JENKINS, J. J. *The complete Minnesota norms for responses to 100 words from the Kent-Rosanoff Word Association Test.* Office of Naval Res. Tech. Report No. 11, 1954, Contract No. N8.

3. THORNDIKE, E. L., & LORGE, I. *The teachers word book of 30,000 words.* New York: Teachers College, 1944.

4. WILCOXON, F. *Some rapid approximate statistical procedures.* New York: Amer. Cyanamid Co., 1949.

Subception

AUTONOMIC DISCRIMINATION WITHOUT AWARENESS: A STUDY OF SUBCEPTION

Richard S. Lazarus and Robert A. McCleary

Introduction

This paper is a report of an experiment which extends and supports findings which we have previously described in an interim report (13). The results indicate that at tachistoscopic exposure speeds too rapid for correct recognition, subjects are able to give discriminatory responses as measured by their galvanic skin response (GSR). This perceptual process was called by the authors *subception*. The data also suggest that it is important to control for the verbal response preferences of the subjects when evaluating their perceptual accuracy.

A number of considerations prompted the coining of the new term, subception. Despite the inadvisability of recklessly increasing the "deadwood" in the psychological vocabulary, we know of no other term that precisely defines a *process by which some kind of discrimination is made when the subject is unable to make a correct conscious discrimination.* We rejected "subconscious perception" (the only standard terminology that occurred to us) for several reasons.

Reprinted by permission of the American Psychological Association and the authors from the *Psychological Review*, Vol. 58, 1951.

In the first place, the word "subconscious" or "unconscious" is replete with controversial implications, none of which are pertinent to the present case. We particularly wished to avoid the psychoanalytic notions concerning the subconscious, and the alternate notion that the subconscious is one level of awareness —on the inattentive fringe of consciousness, so to speak. Secondly, although there is less quarrel with the word perception, it too often implies awareness on the part of the perceiving organism. In fact, three of the four definitions of perception in Warren's dictionary use the term "awareness." Even if one believes that awareness is not necessary for perception and thus regards subception as simply a special case of perception, we feel that it is a sufficiently unique case to require a unique term. There is, of course, some intrinsic value in using a single word rather than a more cumbersome phrase to identify this perceptual process.

The original impetus for this study came from the recent interest in the role of needs in perceptual behavior. It has been reported frequently that stimuli of different need significance may have different recognition thresholds (1, 6, 10,

12, 14, 19, 20, 24). Although theorizing in this field has lacked precision and completeness, it is possible to find two general frames of reference which have been used to interpret the "need in perception" observations. The first might be identified as the "response availability" approach. The second could be termed the "dynamic" point of view. Both views are by no means incompatible.

Writers who have preferred to use the concept of response availability have pointed out that, for different individuals, some words have greater frequency of occurrence than others (2, 7). Differences in this response availability could act in two ways to produce differential recognition thresholds, depending in part upon the degree of ambiguity of the stimulus material. On the one hand, the subject is more likely to make use of minimal cues from words which are more readily at his disposal than from those which are not. This aspect of the concept appears to be very much like the old notion of attention or set. On the other hand, if the cues are so minimal that the subject appears to be guessing, the presence of certain words in his response repertoire will increase the statistical probability of these words being correctly identified.

Other workers, notably the clinically oriented writers, have implied the unconscious participation of the individual in actively selecting and rejecting the presented material in accordance with his needs (6, 8, 10, 14, 15). For example, McGinnies (14), summarizing some of the work in this area, states, "It seems well established, then, that the perceptual 'filtering' of visual stimuli serves, in many instances, to protect the observer as long as possible from an awareness of objects which have unpleasant emotional significance for him."

In elaborating this type of approach, Eriksen (6) and Lazarus et al. (10) have talked about such variables as type of ego defense and the acceptability of the need—factors which, they believe, can influence the degree to which the subject is able to verbalize and recognize the stimulus material.

Whatever the merits of these two points of view may be, the latter approach, which we have loosely called "dynamic," places its proponents in the difficult position of having to postulate some process of discrimination occurring prior to the ability of the subject to report correct recognition. More specifically, if the observation that a subject can recognize the word "sacred" at faster exposure speeds than the word "income," is attributed to their differential need value, it would be necessary to assume that the subject is somehow identifying the significance of the two words before he is able to report recognition of them. The purpose of the present experiment was to attempt to test this assumption. We have asked the question, "Can subjects make discriminatory responses even when they are not able to report the stimulus correctly?"

There have been other attempts to get at the problem of "discrimination without awareness." Miller (16), in a paper reporting an experiment of his own, reviewed investigations of this problem over a period extending from 1863 to 1938. Miller's experiment, and all the studies he mentioned, differ from the present research in some important ways. For example, Miller showed that accuracy of discrimination was better than chance below the subjects' "limen of awareness." His criterion of discrimination was the correctness of the subject's verbal statement. In the present experiment we are asking whether a discrimination can be made when recognition, as defined by a correct verbal report, is impossible. The problems are therefore not the same. A second major difference in the Miller experiment lies in the fact that whether or not a subject was actually performing below his "threshold" was entirely a subjective and statistical matter. The subjects' limens were obtained by the method of limits. In the present experiment, as you will see, a subject is judged to be operating below his "threshold" when his verbal report is wrong. The danger in Miller's approach is emphasized by the earlier findings of Perky (18), who showed that subjects could not tell the difference between real images which were slightly supraliminal and impressions which were imaginary.

There are several other experiments which are relevant here because of their use of conditioning procedures or the galvanic skin response. A novel approach has been used by Redlich (21) and Levine (11). By the use of hypnotically induced anesthesia, or patients with hysterical anesthesias, these investigators showed that subjects gave psychogalvanic responses to stimuli applied to an anesthetic area. Scott (22) conditioned a finger-withdrawal response during a trance state and tested for the persistence of the conditioned response during the post-trance amnestic period. Presenting mean scores for the eight subjects, he concluded that there was some residual conditioning in the post-trance period, even though the subjects remembered nothing of the conditioning trials and consequently were not "aware" of the significance of the conditioned stimulus.

A different line of attack has been the attempt to condition responses to stimuli which, by various criteria, are below the subject's psychophysical threshold. Sil-

verman and Baker (23) used subliminal alternating current as the conditioned stimulus and paired it with several kinds of emitted responses in human subjects. Although the authors saw some evidence of eye-wink conditioning in three out of ten subjects, the results do not warrant positive conclusions on a statistical basis. Newhall and Sears (17) conditioned finger-withdrawal to a supraliminal light stimulus and tested for conditioned responses at and below the psychophysically determined limen. They reported obtaining conditioned responses with stimuli which were below the limen, and "in several instances visual stimuli that were individually reported unperceived, had evoked the conditioned response." This latter observation was incidental to the main interest of the experiment, and Newhall and Sears stated that they believed the problem of whether a conditioned response could occur without consciousness of the stimulus was still open to question.

In this vein it might be possible to have the conditioned stimulus well above the subject's sensory threshold but, by proper training procedures, have the subject unaware of the fact that the stimulus was a conditioned one. This was the idea behind the work of Diven (5). He used the GSR for his response and masked the conditioned nature of the stimulus by applying the unconditioned stimulus after a 12-second delay. During the delay the subjects free associated to the conditioned stimulus. Most of the subjects reported no awareness of the relationship between the conditioned and unconditioned stimulus, and yet showed conditioned GSR's. Since the confounding effect of stimulus generalization in this experiment cannot be evaluated, Diven's results, showing conditioning without awareness, remain inconclusive.

A more recent study which attempted

to demonstrate discrimination prior to correct recognition was reported by McGinnies (14). Using tachistoscopic presentation and employing a method which was in some respects similar to the present study, he found that subjects gave GSR's which were greater for emotional words than for neutral words, before the words had been consciously recognized. A crucial shortcoming of the experimental design was that the subjects could have been motivated to withhold their report of the socially taboo words (such as *whore, bitch, raped,* etc.) even after some suspicion of their meaning was present. In other words, the GSR during the pre-recognition trials could very well have been an emotional response to recognized words which were not yet reported.

This matter of withholding of reports was treated at some length by Howes and Solomon (7), who also attempted an interpretation of McGinnies' findings based on their notions of word-frequency as a determiner of perceptual accuracy. We have briefly discussed this kind of theoretical orientation under the heading of "response availability." McGinnies (15), in a reply to the note of Howes and Solomon, handled the specific word-frequency criticisms adequately but was unable to explain away the possibility that the subjects were motivated to withhold their report of the taboo words. McGinnies wrote, "It must be admitted that this possibility does, in fact, constitute one of the knottier problems in this kind of research." The experimental design in our experiment was planned to unravel this knot, because the present authors are in agreement with Howes and Solomon that the danger of withholding responses is indeed crucial to McGinnies' conclusion.

Considering the approaches used and the data reported, the authors believe that previous research has not satisfactorily demonstrated that a process of discrimination can operate prior to conscious recognition and in the absence of the possibility of the correct verbal report.

Procedure

In the present experiment, we recorded the subject's GSR by means of an AC bridge apparatus.[1] Dry silver recording electrodes, $\frac{1}{4}''$ square, were attached to the right forefinger and right middle finger tip of the subject. GSR's were read directly as peak deflections on a Ballantine Electronic Voltmeter. These readings were converted into actual impedance changes by substituting a variable resistance box in the circuit in place of the subject, and matching the Voltmeter readings obtained when the subject was in the circuit, with the phase angle of the bridge set at zero. We could read pure impedance change because the AC bridge was designed so that the subject's apparent capacitance change could be balanced out during the experiment by operating a dial that kept a Lissajous figure closed when the phase angle of the subject and the bridge were exactly equated. This impedance change (ohms) was then transformed into admittance change (mhos) in keeping with physiological (4) and statistical (9) suggestions as to the most meaningful unit of measure for the GSR.

We presented the stimulus words on a beaded screen seven feet from the subject by means of a projection tachistoscope. This arrangement allowed for a variation of exposure speeds from $\frac{1}{150}$ second to one second. The illumination and range of exposure speeds varied

---

[1] The authors are indebted to Thomas G. Arnold, at present in the Department of Medicine, The Johns Hopkins Hospital, for the design and development of the GSR apparatus used in this research.

from subject to subject depending upon his perceptual performance and, once established, were held constant for each subject. Five different exposure speeds were selected for each subject such that the slowest speed resulted in near 100 per cent accuracy of recognition of the syllables. In all cases, the fastest exposure speed resulted in accuracy of recognition which did not differ significantly from chance.

Five-letter nonsense syllables were used as the stimuli to minimize as far as possible differences in familiarity. Moreover, the use of nonsense syllables precluded the possibility that subjects would have any motivation to withhold their report. This was, you will recall, a crucial inadequacy in the experiment by McGinnies (14). Ten syllables were presented: YILIM, ZIFIL, GAHIW, GEXAX, JEJIC, JIVID, YUVUF, ZEWUH, VAVUK, VECYD.

The procedure for each subject can be divided into three parts.

1. *Equation period*. After practice at recognition we presented each subject with the ten nonsense syllables tachistoscopically. The syllables were randomized for both order of presentation and exposure speed. Even at speeds where accurate recognition was impossible, each subject was required to make a choice verbally from the ten syllables which he knew made up the stimulus material being presented to him. To aid in this choice each subject used, in succession, ten different lists of the syllables. Each list was in a different order to preclude list-order preference on the part of the subject. After 100 presentations (each of the ten syllables having been flashed twice at each of the five exposure speeds), we divided the ten syllables into two groups of five each, equated for both the number of times the subject used the syllables in the entire 100 responses and the number of times they were correctly recognized. In all cases it was possible to make this two-group division with a high degree of equality. Also, in this phase of the experiment, we noted the exposure speed at which near 100 per cent accuracy of recognition occurred, and used it as the slowest speed in the final test period.

2. *Conditioning period*. In this part of the experiment we employed a one-second exposure speed for all syllable presentations. The GSR was conditioned to the five experimental syllables using electric shock as the unconditioned stimulus. Partial reinforcement was employed, with one-third of all presentations of the five experimental syllables being shocked in random order. During this conditioning period each of the ten syllables was presented an equal number of times to prevent unequal familiarity. This procedure was continued until consistent conditioned responses to the five experimental syllables were established. We instructed subjects not to report during the conditioning trials but merely to identify to themselves the syllables presented to them. This was done to avoid associating the shock with the subject's verbal report and thus influencing his response preference during the final test period. We instructed the subjects at the beginning of the conditioning trials that when they were shocked it would be two or three seconds following presentation of the experimental syllables. This allowed us to read the GSR before the shock was applied. They were further instructed that they would never be shocked after any presentation of the five control syllables.

3. *Final test period*. The procedure of random presentation of the syllables used during the Equation Period was re-

peated here. The exposure speeds were set so that the subject had near 100 per cent recognition at the slowest of the five exposure speeds. This time, however, GSR's were recorded during the time between the tachistoscopic flash and the subject's verbal report. We told the subject to delay his report until signalled, which was about five seconds after the tachistoscopic flash. This delay was used to prevent the verbal report from contaminating the GSR, and the signal was not given until the GSR was recorded for each syllable presentation.

During this final period no shock was paired with any of the syllables. Because of the rapid exposure speeds used in this period, we had feared that reinforcement at this point would result in extinction of the clear-cut GSR discrimination acquired during the Conditioning Period. This inability to use reinforcement in the final phase, however, created no special difficulties. As a result of the instructions and the prior experience with partial reinforcement, the subject's expectancy of being shocked—and consequently the "conditioned GSR"—was maintained throughout the syllable presentations without further use of shock. We had found with preliminary subjects that in the absence of this continuing expectancy of shock, the GSR promptly disappeared. This is in keeping with the findings of Cook and Harris (3).

The following raw data were recorded during the Final Test Period:

(1) The syllable flashed.

(2) The exposure speed of the syllable.

(3) The subject's verbal choice from the ten possible syllables (whether or not he was correct and whether he reported a "shock" or whether he reported a "non-shock" syllable).

(4) The subject's GSR for each syllable presentation.

Results

The results of this experiment can be discussed under three main headings: (1) The galvanic skin responses during the Final Test Period; (2) the relations between response frequency and the accuracy of report for various syllables; and (3) the effect of electric shock on the perceptual thresholds.

GSR data. By far the most striking finding to be reported here concerns the autonomic activity of the subjects in the Final Test Period. These GSR data are shown in the bar graphs in the figure. The average GSR's are put in various columns on the basis of certain criteria. The first main division is dependent upon whether or not the syllable flashed had been associated with shock during the Conditioning Period; this is the Stimulus Category ("shock" vs. "non-shock"). The other breakdown is based on the nature of the subject's verbal report; this is the Response Category. There are three kinds of responses in each of the two stimulus categories: "WS" means that the report was wrong and a "shock" syllable was given by the subject; "WN" indicates that the report was wrong and a "non-shock" syllable was given; "RS" and "RN" signify responses of the appropriate stimulus category which were right. "Response N" refers to the number of separate GSR's contributing to the mean for each column.

The two "MW" (*mean wrong*) *bars are the important GSR measures to note.* These represent the average GSR of the "WS" and "WN" categories for each of the two types of stimuli. Therefore these "MW" columns give the average GSR (equated for both "shock" and "non-shock" responses) when the subject was not able to perceive (*i.e.,* report) the

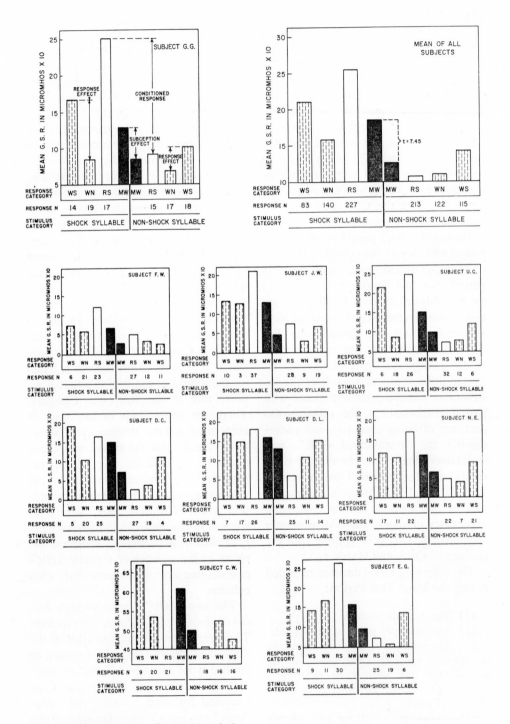

FIG. 1. GSR data from final test period.

flashed syllable. It was necessary to average the GSR's associated with wrong responses because the verbal report itself had an effect on the GSR. You will notice that this "response effect" can be seen in the bar graphs as larger GSR's when the subject used a "shock" syllable as his report. By averaging "WS" and "WN" categories, this "response effect" was effectively controlled.

In every subject the "MW" column is larger when the stimulus presented was a "shock" syllable, and you will recall that in this "MW" category the subject was not able to perceive the syllable correctly. This is the *subception effect.* It is summarized in the bar graph entitled "Mean of All Subjects." Student's "t" for this difference is 7.45, which is significant far below the one per cent level of confidence for eight degrees of freedom. The subception effect was found at all five tachistoscopic exposure speeds when wrong responses were made. It was smallest at the speeds which resulted in either very low or very high accuracy. The systematic increase in the effect as a function of decreasing exposure speed which was suggested in the interim report was not substantiated with further data. *There seems to be little doubt that subjects can make autonomic discriminations when they are unable to report conscious recognition.*

Response frequency. Since this experiment provided a limited multiple-choice response situation for the subjects, it was possible to obtain some information about the importance of response frequency in relation to perceptual accuracy. A product moment correlation was obtained between the number of times each syllable was used and the number of times it was correctly reported. This was done separately for both the Equation Period and Final Test

Period data. Statistical independence of the arrays was achieved by subtracting the number of times each syllable was right from the number of times it was given as a response. These correlations were $+.61$ and $+.67$ respectively. With ten syllables, neither of the relationships is significant. They do suggest, however, that in this kind of situation perceptual accuracy may bear some close relation to frequency of usage. This finding gives some added substance to the arguments to consider statistical response preference as an important variable in some perceptual recognition experiments. These data are relevant to the concept of "response availability" discussed earlier in this paper.

Perceptual accuracy. There is one final observation to be made from our results. Although the major purpose of this experiment was not to study the effect of a need variable on perceptual accuracy, it was possible to analyze our data for such an effect. Since the experimental and control lists of syllables were equated for accuracy and frequency of use during the Equation Period and one of the lists was associated with electric shock, it was possible to see whether the shock had any effect on final perceptual performance. The data were analyzed in two ways to get at this problem. The accuracy for "shock" and "non-shock" syllables was compared both with and without a statistical correction [2] for response preference. In both cases no

---

[2] We are indebted to Dr. Alphonse Chapanis for assisting us in formulating this statement of our correction procedure:

$$A_c = R_A - R_{A_G,} \qquad (1)$$

where

A_c = corrected accuracy score

R_A = number of correct responses to syllable *A*

significant differences were found between "shock" and "non-shock" syllables. However, it might be noted that when no correction for response frequency was

R_{AG} = number of correct responses to syllable A in which the subject was guessing

$$R_{AG} = G_A p_A. \qquad (2)$$

where

G_A = number of responses to syllable A in which the subject was guessing

p_A = probability of the subject using syllable A when he is guessing

Equation (2), however, involves two unknowns, R_{AG} and G_A, and cannot be solved. But note that

$$W_A = G_A q_A, \qquad (3)$$

where

W_A = number of wrong responses to syllable A

$q_A = (1 - p_A)$ = probability of the subject not using syllable A when he is guessing, and here we have two known quantities, W_A and q_A. Thus

$$G_A = W_A/q_A. \qquad (4)$$

Substituting this value of G_A in (2) gives

$$R_{AG} = [W_A/q_A]p_A = W_A[p_A/q_A]. \qquad (5)$$

This value of R_{AG} may be substituted in (1) to give the final equation

$$A_C = R_A - W_A[p_A/q_A]. \qquad (6)$$

As you will probably notice, this is the precise form of the correction used in "true and false" and "multiple-choice" examinations. In these cases, however, a theoretical value of p is used. For example, in a series of "multiple-choice" questions having four items, $p_A = \frac{1}{4}$, and

$$A_C = R_A - W_A[\tfrac{1}{4}/\tfrac{3}{4}] = R_A - W_A/3.$$

In the present study, we used an empirical value of p_A such that

$$p_A = \frac{A_w}{W},$$

where

A_w = the total number of times that A was used as a wrong response

W = the total number of wrong responses

made, seven out of nine subjects showed a greater accuracy for the "shock" syllables and a higher frequency of usage for the "non-shock" group. On the other hand, when the correction was made, there was (for one subject) a reversal from higher accuracy for "shock" syllables to higher accuracy for the "non-shock" syllables. Correcting for this preference actually reversed the apparent accuracy picture for this subject. Although the other subjects did not show such a marked change when response frequency was taken into account there were in most cases some changes in the relative accuracy of the two lists of syllables. This result further supports the correlations found between response frequency and perceptual accuracy. We believe that this is an important methodological point. Where there is any possibility of unequal preference for the stimulus material, it is important to attempt some such correction before conclusions about accuracy of recognition are practical.

Discussion

The major finding of the present research, the subception effect, has implications not only for perceptual theory, which we have mentioned earlier, but may also have relevance in the field of personality and clinical psychology. The unconscious determination of behavior is a concept of considerable importance in present-day clinical thinking. In so far as autonomic activity can be regarded as a form of behavior, we believe that we may have here an experimental instance of such an unconscious process. The field of psychosomatic medicine is, of course, specifically concerned with autonomic activity as a response to threat or conflict situations. Moreover, clinical observations in this area have emphasized the inability of many patients to identify the stimulus situation to which their symptom is presumably a response. The findings in this experiment might eventually help to throw light on these observations. This kind of mechanism is all the more suggestive when coupled with the possibility that "recognition thresholds" might be subject to influence by the "needs" of the individual.

One may ask whether there are meaningful individual differences in "subception" which could be predicted from information about the psychological characteristics of the individual. For example, would people with hysterical personalities show more subception than obsessive-compulsive personalities? Along these lines the kind of procedure employed in the present experiment might be regarded as one possible tool for the study of the perceptual side of different clinical conditions.

There is nothing in our data which suggests the mechanism of the subception effect. It is clear that the subject was unable to detect minimal cues that "tipped him off" that a "shock" syllable was being presented even though the cues were not sufficient to permit precise report of the syllable in question. The subjects showed no tendency to report correctly the "shock" or "non-shock" nature of the syllables on which they were wrong.

Howes and Solomon's attempt (7) to explain McGinnies' GSR data in terms of response probability concepts does not apply here. They say, "Only the most probable word could be reported after each exposure, but GSR's could occur to any word of high probability that had been conditioned previously to the GSR." What they appear to mean is that when a taboo word was flashed at a subthreshold level, there would be a finite possibility that this taboo word would "cross the subject's mind" as one of his pre-recognition guesses, and, even though not reported as the subject's most probable guess, would still have been present as a possibility and thus be able to produce a GSR. Conversely, they argue that when a neutral word was flashed at a subthreshold level, the probability of a taboo word occurring as a pre-recognition possibility was relatively much less likely. Thus, on a statistical basis, a GSR was much less apt to occur. The multiple-choice response situation used in this present experiment, however, encourages equal probability for any of the words to occur as pre-recognition guesses and thus invalidates this kind of interpretation. As a matter of fact, it turned out that when the subject was reporting incorrectly, there were many more non-shock responses to shock syllables than the reverse.

Summary

1. GSR evidence is presented to indicate that at tachistoscopic exposure speeds too rapid for conscious discrimination (as measured by the subject's inability to report which stimulus was presented), the subject is still capable of making a discrimination. We suggest that the level of perceptual activity indicated by this finding be called *subception*.

2. It is important to control for unequal preference for stimulus material before drawing conclusions about the accuracy of perceptual recognition.

3. Pairing some of the stimuli with electric shock does not result in a change in the frequency with which they are accurately identified at various exposure speeds.

4. Some of the implications of this experiment for perceptual and clinical theory are discussed.

References

1. BRUNER, J., & POSTMAN, L. Emotional selectivity in perception and reaction. *J. Personality*, 1947, **16**, 69–77.

2. COFER, C. Personal communication.

3. COOK, S. W., & HARRIS, R. E. The verbal conditioning of the galvanic skin reflex. *J. exp. Psychol.*, 1937, **21**, 202–210.

4. DARROW, C. W. The significance of the galvanic skin reflex in the light of its relation to quantitative measurements of perspiration. *Psychol. Bull.*, 1934, **31**, 697–698.

5. DIVEN, K. Certain determinants in the conditioning of anxiety reactions. *J. Psychol.*, 1937, **3**, 291–308.

6. ERIKSEN, C. W. Perceptual defense: The elevation of perceptual recognition thresholds as a function of unacceptable needs. Unpublished Ph.D. dissertation, Stanford University, 1950.

7. HOWES, D. H., & SOLOMON, R. L. A note on McGinnies' "Emotionality and perceptual defense." PSYCHOL. REV., 1950, **57**, 229–234.

8. KLEIN, G. S., & SCHLESINGER, H. Where is the perceiver in perceptual theory? *J. Personality*, 1949, **18**, 32–47.

9. LACEY, O. L. *et al.* An analysis of the unit of measurement of the galvanic skin response. *J. exp. Psychol.*, 1949, **39**, 122–127.

10. LAZARUS, R. S., SHAFFER, G. W., FONDA, C. P., & HEISTAD, G. T. Clinical dynamics and auditory perception. Paper given at APA meetings, September, 1950.

11. LEVINE, M. Psychogalvanic reflex to painful stimuli in hypnotic and hysterical anesthesia. *Johns Hopk. Hosp. Bull.*, 1930, **46**, 331–339.

12. McCLELLAND, D. C., & LIBERMAN, A. M. The effect of need for achievement on recognition of need-related words. *J. Personality*, 1949, **18**, 236–251.

13. McCLEARY, R. A., & LAZARUS, R. S. Autonomic discrimination without awareness: An interim report. *J. Personality*, 1949, **18**, 171–179.

14. McGINNIES, E. Emotionality and perceptual defense. PSYCHOL. REV., 1949, **56**, 244–251.

15. ——, Discussion of Howes and Solomon's note on "Emotionality and perceptual defense." PSYCHOL. REV., 1950, **57**, 235–240.

16. MILLER, J. G. Discrimination without awareness. *Amer. J. Psychol.*, 1939, **52**, 562–578.

17. NEWHALL, L. M., & SEARS, R. R. Conditioned finger retraction to visual stimuli near the absolute threshold. *Comp. Psychol. Monogr.*, 1933, **9**, No. 43.

18. PERKY, C. W. An experimental study of imagination. *Amer. J. Psychol.*, 1910, **21**, 422–452.

19. POSTMAN, L., BRUNER, J., & McGINNIES, E. Personal values as selective factors in perception. *J. abnorm. soc. Psychol.*, 1948, **43**, 142–154.

20. POSTMAN, L., & SOLOMON, R. L. Perceptual sensitivity to completed and incompleted tasks. *J. Personality*, 1950, **18**, 347–357.

21. REDLICH, F. C. Organic and hysterical anesthesia. *Amer. J. Psychol.*, 1945, **102**, 318–324.

22. SCOTT, H. D. Hypnosis and the conditioned reflex. *J. gen. Psychol.*, 1930, **4**, 113–130.

23. SILVERMAN, A., & BAKER, L. E. An attempt to condition various responses to subliminal electrical stimulation. *J. exp. Psychol.*, 1935, **18**, 246–254.

24. VANDERPLAS, J. M., & BLAKE, R. R. Selective sensitization in auditory perception. *J. Personality*, 1949, **18**, 252–266.

SUBCEPTION: FACT OR ARTIFACT? Charles W. Eriksen

Several years ago Lazarus and Mc-Cleary (6) reported an experiment in which GSR's were conditioned to one group of nonsense syllables and not to another group. They found that a tachistoscopic exposure of a conditioned nonsense syllable resulted in a larger GSR than presentation of a nonconditioned syllable, even when the duration of the exposure was too rapid for correct verbal identification. Lazarus and McCleary termed this effect "subception," which they defined as "a process by which some kind of discrimination is made when the subject is unable to make a conscious discrimination." These authors do not clarify the nature of this process, but their definition and their interpretation of their data imply that the autonomic nervous system, under certain circumstances at least, is capable of making more accurate discriminations among stimuli than exist in the individual's awareness.

This interpretation of their data has received criticism, and alternative interpretations have been offered. Bricker and Chapanis (1) have shown that, following an incorrect verbal response to a tachistoscopically exposed stimulus, the mean number of additional guesses required to name the stimulus correctly was significantly less than would be expected on the basis of random guessing. They argue from this finding that, even when the stimulus was incorrectly responded to, subjects obtained fragmentary cues that limited the number of plausible interpretations or responses. If a conditioned nonsense syllable is among

Reprinted by permission cf the American Psychological Association and the author from the *Psychological Review*, Vol. 63, 1956.

the plausible responses, they expect the GSR to be greater than if the plausible responses contained only non conditioned syllables. Since the exposure of a conditioned syllable would always or nearly always result in this syllable being among the plausible responses, GSR's would then be expected to average larger on such trials than on trials where a nonconditioned syllable was presented.

Howes (3) has also presented an account of the subception effect based upon a statistical model of discrimination. His alternative to a subception process is the hypothesis that "at any specified moment the GSR accompanying an observer's report is proportional to the probability that that report will be a shock [conditioned] syllable" (p. 99).

Both Howes (3) and Bricker and Chapanis (1) have dealt with important aspects of the subception phenomena, but they have not succeeded in coming to grips with certain logical fallacies and operational limitations of the subception experiment. In fact, the present author has heard it argued on several occasions that the Bricker and Chapanis experiment actually confirms the subception process: "After all they demonstrated unconscious discrimination, since they showed that even when the subject was unable to report the correct stimulus, if you forced him to 'guess' he was right more often than would be expected by chance." Even Howes does not attempt to refute the subception interpretation, but presents his statistical model as an alternative description (a model, incidentally, which one could use as a sophisticated account of unconscious discrimination, since Howes does not provide the operations for determining whether the distribution of response probabilities in a subject is represented in awareness or not).

It seems to the present author that much of the confusion and controversy over subception and problems in "awareness" in general is due to unclear formulations of the questions, and to failure to consider the converging operations (2) necessary to permit interpretations of data in terms of unconscious discrimination. It is the purpose of the present paper to reformulate and reanalyze the subception experiment in terms of partial correlation between the stimuli and the two responses, and to show that, when so conceived, the Lazarus and McCleary results are not only consistent with but would be predicted by well-known experimentally derived facts. It is a further purpose of the paper to make clear that the invoking of a subception process to explain the Lazarus and McCleary results was not only unnecessary but was unjustified from the experimental operations employed.

THE SUBCEPTION EFFECT AS
A CASE OF PARTIAL CORRELATION

The results of the Lazarus and Mc-Cleary experiment can be stated in terms of partial correlation.[1] The essence of their experimental design was the requirement that the subject make two concurrent discriminated responses to the perceptual stimulus, namely, a GSR and a verbal response. They found that when the verbal response was held constant, the partial correlation between the stimulus and the GSR was significantly greater than zero. This partial correla-

tion was termed the subception effect by the experimenters, and its occurrence was attributed to the operation of unconscious discrimination.[2]

However, before we can accept this interpretation, we need to examine the general circumstances under which such a partial correlation could occur. We can define the general case of what Lazarus and McCleary have termed the subception effect as the case where the partial correlation between the stimulus and one response, with the second response held constant, is some positive value greater than zero and less than one. The general circumstances under which such a partial correlation would be obtained are where the two responses, R_1 and R_2, are each correlated with the stimulus, but less than perfectly and less than perfectly correlated with each other. In other words, we have a case where each response or response system has a finite error term associated with it, and these error terms are less than perfectly correlated between the two response systems. These conditions are not only sufficient but actually determine that a positive partial correlation will be obtained between the stimulus and either response with the remaining response held constant.

It should be noted that these are essentially the conditions that obtained in the Lazarus and McCleary experiment. They arranged the tachistoscopic duration of stimulus exposures so that the verbal report of the subjects was only about 50 per cent accurate, or so that the correlation of the verbal response with the stimulus was considerably less than

---

[1] The term correlation as used in this paper does not refer to any particular correlation statistic. For this discussion, however, it will be assumed that all correlations are positive or nonmetric.

[2] The distinction between the subception effect and the subception process previously made by Howes (3) will be observed in this paper.

perfect. The GSR in their experiment was also less than perfectly correlated with the stimulus. From previous research we know that the GSR is an unstable response, and the Lazarus and McCleary data also show that large GSRs were obtained to nonconditioned syllables. Since these investigators actually obtained a significant partial correlation between the stimulus and the GSR, we know that the remaining condition (less than a perfect correlation between the two responses) must have existed.

When we formulate the results of the Lazarus and McCleary experiment in partial correlation terms, it becomes possible to state clearly and concisely what their experiment demonstrated. They succeeded in showing that both the verbal response and the GSR are each, at least to a degree, independently correlated with the stimulus and are partially independent of each other. In other words, the GSR is at least partly determined by the stimulus and the intervening perceptual process, and not solely by the verbal response.

The nature of the Lazarus and McCleary result can be seen more clearly if we diagram two possible relations between the verbal response and the GSR.

A. Stimulus → Perceptual

    Process → Verbal Response →

       GSR

B. Stimulus → Perceptual

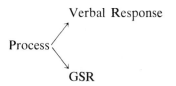

In A we have the condition where the GSR is dependent upon the verbal response to the perception, while in B we have two parallel response systems, each separately dependent upon the perceptual processes. If the relation between verbal response and GSR was as diagrammed in A, it would not have been possible for Lazarus and McCleary to have obtained their results. Such a relation between verbal response and GSR would permit less than a perfect correlation between them owing to error that might exist in the GSR, but it would have been impossible to have obtained a true correlation between the GSR and the stimulus with the verbal response held constant. The fact that these investigators found a partial correlation between the stimulus and GSR when the verbal response was held constant demands a relationship similar to that diagrammed in B, unless their results are to be attributed to sampling fluctuation.

SOME FACTORS CONTRIBUTING TO INDEPENDENCE BETWEEN GSR'S AND VERBAL RESPONSES

It should be carefully noted that the demonstration that both the verbal response and the GSR are independently related to the stimulus is not the same as demonstrating unconscious perception or discrimination. All we have evidence for so far is the presence of two parallel response systems, neither of which is perfectly reliable, and whose error terms are not perfectly correlated.

In view of the neurophysiological differences between verbal responses and GSR's, it is not surprising that the two response systems are not perfectly correlated. Not only are there differences in the latencies for the central nervous system and autonomic nervous system responses, but the motor systems also differ. Any differences in the neurophysiology of the responses allow, theoretically at least, certain physiological variables to affect one response system without affecting the other.

The existence and effect of such physiological variables upon responses were formally recognized by Hull (5) in his principle of behavior oscillation. This principle acknowledged certain random variations in responses and response strength that Hull felt might be attributed to transitory variation in physiological states. He has described the empirical evidence for this principle (5), along with evidence indicating that this type of response error was apt to be uncorrelated between different responses; he referred to the latter as *asynchrony of oscillation*. The fact that Hull found it necessary formally to recognize noncorrelated errors between different responses indicates that their presence in the subception effect is not a novel event.

While the principle of behavior oscillation attests to the empirical basis for assuming noncorrelated error terms between the verbal and autonomic response systems, it does not specify variables that might differentially affect the two systems. However, certain differences in the nature of verbal and autonomic responses suggest some psychological variables that might be expected to produce errors in verbal responses independently of the GSR.

The GSR is essentially a single response varying only in magnitude, and is analogous to a verbal response system with only a single verbal response that can vary in response strength. If the verbal response system contains two or more responses, this permits new variables that may affect the verbal discrimination while leaving the GSR unaffected.

Let us take as an example an experiment in which we have two nonsense syllables, one of which has been conditioned as a stimulus for a GSR. In addition, our subject in this experiment has two verbal responses, one for each nonsense syllable. If we now expose the nonsense syllables tachistoscopically, at durations too short for errorless discrimination, we could reasonably expect some disagreement in the errors made in the response systems. The two verbal responses might not be of the same response strength, so that one of them might be evoked more often than the other. Also, on some trials on which the correct response would have the greatest habit strength to the exposed stimulus, the incorrect response with less habit strength to that stimulus might actually be evoked, due to response competition and behavior oscillation. Response variables such as differing habit strengths and competition could contribute to errors in the verbal responses while leaving the GSR unaffected.

EFFECT OF THE NUMBER
OF RESPONSE CATEGORIES
UPON THE SUBCEPTION EFFECT

If the number of response categories in one response system is limited relative to the other response system, the correlation between the two response systems will be reduced, as will also the correlation of the restricted response system with the stimulus. This situation will also contribute to a large partial correlation between the stimulus and the unrestricted response system. In comparing verbal responses with GSR's we are comparing a response system with a discrete distribution with one that for all practical purposes is continuously distributed. If the number of verbal response categories is too few, we run the risk of spuriously reducing the correlation between the verbal response and the stimuli, and of increasing the partial correlation between the stimuli and the GSR.

As an example, let us suppose an experiment in which we have 10 different-sized squares, to the largest of which we have conditioned a GSR. If the squares are now presented to the subjects one at a time, in accord with stimulus generalization (4, 8) we would expect the magnitude of GSR to vary with the square size, the largest magnitude occurring to the largest square and the smallest magnitude to the smallest square. In addition to recording the GSR on each stimulus presentation, let us also require the subject to make a verbal judgment of the square size, for which we allow him two response categories, "large" and "small." If our subject called the five largest squares "large," we would have no indication from his verbal behavior that he could discriminate among these five squares. Yet we might reasonably expect that the magnitude of GSR would vary with square size within this single verbal response category. In this case we would have a large partial correlation between the stimuli and the GSR when the verbal response was held constant.

Few would be willing to accept the results of our hypothetical experiment as demonstrating unconscious discrimination, without the control operation of permitting the subject to use at least 10 verbal responses. Yet a similar situation prevailed in the Lazarus and McCleary experiment, which contributed an unknown amount to the subception effect they obtained. In their experiment subjects were allowed to use only one of 10 nonsense syllables as a response. While 10 response categories may seem like an adequate number, their adequacy depends upon the complexity of the perceptual stimulation the subjects are to receive.

While we tend to act as though the perceptual stimulus presented to a subject in a tachistoscopic exposure of a nonsense syllable was the nonsense syllable itself, this is not the stimulus perceived by the subject. If it were, there would be no point in using the tachistoscope. When the nonsense syllable SIDAK is tachistoscopically exposed for a short duration and the subject is instructed to report just what he perceives (and is allowed the freedom of the English language for responses), we tend to get responses such as "I saw an 's' followed by what seemed to be two blurred letters, then an 'a' and a 'k.' " If, however, the subject is instructed implicitly or explicitly to respond in terms of a preselected list of nonsense syllables, we obtain the response "sidak" or some other nonsense syllable from the permitted list that has the correct sequence of letters. A second exposure of this nonsense syllable might result in the subject's perceiving all of the letters. If the subject's responses were restricted to preselected nonsense syllables, both exposures might lead to the same verbal response of "sidak," whereas with greater response freedom we would be able to distinguish two different perceptual experiences.

The manner in which verbal response restriction could have contributed to the subception effect obtained by Lazarus and McCleary can be illustrated as follows. Assume that a subject has been exposed to the nonsense syllables VAVUK, YUVUF, BEKUM, and LUFED, and that a GSR has been conditioned to only VAVUK. If now the conditioned syllable VAVUK is tachistoscopically exposed for a short duration, the subject under conditions of free report might respond by saying that he saw only a dark blur with an impression of a "u" somewhere in the blur. A second exposure of the conditioned syllable might produce the report that it looked like a blur again, but that the next to the last letter was a "u." To a third exposure the response might be that he saw blurred letters with a "vu" in the center. If the subject in our example was constrained to respond with one of the four nonsense syllables, all three exposures might well have led to the response "yuvuf."

There is reason to believe that stimulus generalization of the GSR would occur to these fragmentary tachistoscopic perceptions (7). If so, the magnitude of the GSR would increase progressively through these three exposures as the subject's perception, as revealed by free report, became more similar to the conditioned syllable. In this case the magnitude of the GSR would correspond quite closely with the free verbal report. However, if the subject was permitted to use only nonsense syllables as responses, he might group these three different perceptions under a single response. Thus, we have the same condition that existed in our hypothetical experiment on square sizes. We have forced the subject to group what may be differentially reportable perceptions under a common verbal response. We have experimentally constrained or reduced the precision of the verbal response system while leaving the GSR unconstrained; a condition which will increase the partial correlation between the stimuli and the GSR while artifactually reducing the correlation of the stimuli with the verbal responses.

CONSCIOUS AWARENESS AS
A DISCRIMINATED VERBAL RESPONSE

It is recognized that there is nothing incompatible between the formulation of the subception effect as a partial correlation and an interpretation of unconscious discrimination. After all, such a partial correlation may be what we have in mind at times when we refer to unconscious discrimination. Variables such as behavior oscillation and response competition which produce noncorrelated errors between two response systems may be among the reasons that all discrimination is not conscious. But it should be clear from the previous section that if one wishes to take this position, it is necessary that he demonstrate that the observed partial correlation is not solely due to artificial restrictions upon the verbal discriminatory system.

Implicit in the Lazarus and McCleary definition of subception is the equation of conscious awareness with a discriminated verbal report. Such a definition of awareness requires an operational control of any experiment attempting to demonstrate unconscious discrimination. This control consists of showing that the experiment provided the subjects with enough different verbal responses to identify separately each perceptual discrimination they were capable of making. In our hypothetical experiment on square sizes, it would not be justifiable to conclude that our subjects were only capable of making two verbal discriminations of size in the range of sizes tested. Before such a conclusion could even begin to be justified, we would need to run a control condition where subjects were permitted to use 10 or more different verbal responses.

To accept Lazarus and McCleary's conclusion that discrimination was shown by the GSR in the absence of conscious awareness, we must be prepared to assume that a language consisting solely of 10 nonsense syllables is sufficient to describe the entire realm of subjective awareness. In fact, however, the tenability of such an assumption has been disproven by Bricker and Chapanis (1). In addition to recording the subject's first response to a tachistoscopic exposure of a nonsense syllable, they also required the subject to give several alternative guesses. These guessing sequences constitute an increase in the number of verbal responses permitted the subjects. When these guessing sequences were taken into account, it was found that verbal discrimination was significantly greater than was indicated when only the subject's initial response was used. In other words, if only the subject's initial response was considered, the amount of conscious discrimination (as defined by Lazarus and McCleary) would be significantly underestimated.

Summary

The present paper has shown that the subception effect reported by Lazarus and McCleary can be formulated as a partial correlation between the GSR and the stimulus with the verbal response held constant. The general case where such a partial correlation would be obtained is where both the GSR and verbal response are independently correlated with the stimulus, but not perfectly, and the error terms in these two response systems are not perfectly correlated with each other. Several sources of noncorrelated error between the GSR and the verbal response systems were considered.

It was argued that the Lazarus and McCleary experiment did not contain the necessary operations and controls to permit an interpretation of their data in terms of discrimination without verbal awareness. Such an interpretation requires the demonstration that the number of verbal responses available to the subject was sufficient to reflect all the discrimination he was capable of making. The 10 nonsense syllables permitted the subjects as responses in the Lazarus and McCleary experiment were not sufficient to determine the subjects' verbal discrimination capacity.

References

1. BRICKER, P. D., & CHAPANIS, A. Do incorrectly perceived tachistoscopic stimuli convey some information? *Psychol. Rev.,* 1953, **60,** 181–188.

2. GARNER, W. R. Context effects and the validity of loudness scales. *J. exp. Psychol.,* 1954, **48,** 218–224.

3. HOWES, D. A statistical theory of subception. *Psychol. Rev.,* 1954, **61,** 98–110.

4. HULL, C. L. The problem of primary stimulus generalization. *Psychol. Rev.,* 1947, **54,** 120–134.

5. ———. *Principles of behavior.* New York: Appleton-Century, 1943.

6. LAZARUS, R. S., & McCLEARY, R. A. Autonomic discrimination without awareness: a study of subception. *Psychol. Rev.,* 1951, **58,** 113–122.

7. PAVLOV, I. P. *Conditioned reflexes.* (Trans. by G. V. Anrep) London: Oxford Univer. Press, 1927.

SUBCEPTION: FACT OR ARTIFACT?
A REPLY TO ERIKSEN   Richard S. Lazarus

In the January, 1956 issue of this Journal, an interesting critique was offered (2) of the subception experiment reported some years ago by Lazarus and McCleary (4). This is not the first such article which has appeared on the subject. Indeed, there have been several (1, 3, 7), and there have been a few reports of experiments which duplicate and extend the findings of the original study (5, 8). The recent article by Eriksen calls for some examination of the arguments.

In the Lazarus and McCleary experiment, tachistoscopically exposed nonsense syllables which had been associated with painful electric shocks stimulated larger GSR's than nonshocked syllables even when the exposure speeds were too rapid for the subject to identify them correctly. This effect was termed "subception," and a process of autonomic discrimination in the absence of the ability to report conscious recognition was suggested.

Eriksen analyzes the data in the subception study as an instance of partial correlation. He suggests that the subception effect involves a positive correlation between the stimuli and the GSR's and between the stimuli and the verbal responses. The fact that a correlation remains between the stimuli and the GSR even when the relationship between the stimuli and the verbal responses is partialed out is the subception effect itself.

The kernel of Eriksen's argument lies

in his analysis of the number of categories in the two response systems. He points out that the subject is restricted in his verbal response at each presentation of the stimulus to a choice of one of ten syllables. However, no such restriction applies to the GSR system. Thus, if a subject correctly identified some of the letters of the stimulus, but not enough to perceive the entire stimulus correctly, his verbal response might not reflect the partial discrimination which had occurred although the information could trigger the GSR. Such conditions would increase the likelihood of a partial correlation which would favor GSR discrimination in the absence (partialling out) of verbal discrimination.

Eriksen's argument leads him to discard the subception process as an artifact of the statistical conditions imposed by the experimenters. He analyzes these conditions as though there were no doubt that the GSR system is indeed continuous and unrestricted in the functional sense. In his discussion there is the hidden assumption that the subject can really use all of the categories of the GSR theoretically available to him. The measurement which we obtain from the GSR may be continuous, but we do not know the nature of the process underlying the GSR, and the extent to which it is actually restricted or unlimited. The continuity of the measured response may be determined by a discontinuous process. The argument then becomes a matter of which assumptions one wishes to make about the process underlying the measurements themselves.

Reprinted by permission of the American Psychological Association and the author from the *Psychological Review*, Vol. 63, 1956.

In his article, Eriksen makes the following statement about the Lazarus and McCleary formulation of subception:

These authors do not clarify the nature of this process (subception), but their definition and their interpretation of their data imply that the autonomic nervous system, under certain circumstances at least, is capable of making more accurate discriminations among stimuli than exist in the individual's awareness (2, p. 74).

The same kind of statement is made in the critique of subception by Murdock (7, p. 571): "Perhaps the proper conclusion to be drawn from their study [Lazarus and McCleary's] and that of McGinnies as well is simply that the GSR is more accurate and/or sensitive than verbal reports as a measure of recognition."

It is not at all necessary to assume that the physiological response system of the organism is a more precise mirror of the physical stimuli than the verbal response system. A perfectly logical alternative is that the autonomic response system reflects the presence or absence of danger—that is, the shock or non-shock consequences of the stimulus—even though the level of discrimination is not sharp enough to identify the specific components of the stimulus. In this event, the process does not involve a one-to-one correspondence of the autonomic response with the stimulus, but a categorical one. Such a relationship may be based upon the direct response of the organism to the stimulus, or may be mediated by a process of inference in which the nature of the stimulus is built up from the stimulus elements. The latter is exactly what Bricker and Chapanis seem to be suggesting with respect to the verbal response system. The subject uses partial information about the stimulus to make an inference which may turn out to be wrong and not even verbalizable.

Thus, a number of conceptual alternatives arise in our attempts to interpret the data of subception. (a) The autonomic response system may mirror directly the stimulus properties, independent of verbal activity. (b) Alternatively, it may reflect a process of inference about the affect-laden aspect of the stimulus. In the latter case, the autonomic response might or might not depend upon elements of information being articulated verbally. There might be enough information getting through to the verbal sphere to identify the danger, but not enough to perfectly articulate the total stimulus. We are sometimes frightened without being able, at the moment, to indicate verbally what we are frightened of.

There is a most interesting aspect to Eriksen's proposal which is not carried to its logical end. Eriksen implies that, in order truly to demonstrate subception, the number of verbal response categories must be equivalent to the number of GSR categories, or, more pertinently, that the number of verbal categories be no less than the number of discriminations that can be made to the stimuli. He is thus suggesting an experiment which would reflect such a condition—with the implication, it seems, that the subception effect could not then be demonstrated.

Eriksen's argument is based on a statistical rather than a psychological analysis of the problem. It could be also argued that restriction in one response system (verbal) in contrast to the other (autonomic) is quite close to the conditions prevailing in actual life, and that what we refer to as "lack of awareness" can be dependent upon (although not necessarily identical with) just such restriction in the verbal processes. Let me elaborate this point because I think that it gets to the heart of Eriksen's position.

The properties of language are such that it always represents a discrete distribution of responses in relation to the stimulation from the physical world, while the physiological response has no such restriction. Consider, for example, the physical quality of color in relation to the verbal response system which we use to describe it, and the sensory physiology of the organism which also responds to it. We define color in terms of wavelengths of light which are distributed in a continuous pattern. But we do not have language to identify each discriminable difference in wavelength. There are large gaps in the physical stimulus as it is reflected in the verbal categories, red, yellow, green, etc., even when we made much finer gradations such as chartreuse or aquamarine. This same point may be made for all verbal categories, whether they are applied to simple physical events or to complex social events. Furthermore, anthropological data tell us that additional categories of verbal response can be acquired which emphasize certain stimulus aspects of the physical and social world that are functional for one culture and not another.

By extension, the inability of a person to communicate (and hence to give evidence of being aware of certain stimuli) arises partially from the restrictedness of his language. By this postulate, therefore, discrimination without awareness (and perhaps many processes which are called unconscious) is a function of the restriction of one of the response systems involved, the verbal one. If one makes the dynamic assumptions of the clinician, then the response system is restricted through the operation of cer-

tain hypothetical ego processes. In terms of reinforcement learning theory the verbal response system is limited in accordance with rewards and punishments. But the inability of the person to categorize verbally the events to which he is responding can still be viewed as depending upon the condition of verbal response restriction.

From this standpoint, subception is an appropriate empirical model of what actually happens in nature instead of being an artifact of the conditions imposed upon the subject by Lazarus and McCleary. It is quite reasonable and compatible with experience to propose that the individual responds discriminatively to stimuli prior to his being able to articulate the stimulus verbally, although it is likely that discrimination at the autonomic level is quite a different process from that which we usually refer to as perception. The latter involves verbalization and hence awareness. Surely such discrimination takes place in children long before the child can describe his experience through language. How the organism can discriminate the stimulus subverbally is as much an unsolved problem, of course, as how the discrimination can be articulated in speech.

I do not know whether it can be maintained that the autonomic system is a better reflector of the stimulus than the verbal response system. However, organisms unable to use language often seem able to discriminate some stimuli better than man, and the absence of a cerebrum may even result in facilitated discrimination. For example, there are few instances of pigeons being hit by automobiles, although in our large cities they are certainly exposed to this danger. Moreover, a decerebrate frog can apparently catch flies better as a result of his decerebration. It is clear that verbal responses are not necessary for extremely sensitive discriminations, although they surely function importantly in what we call perception. Why reify verbal responses in psychology as though their absence makes discriminative behavior impossible? The subception effect suggests not that autonomic discrimination is better than verbal perception, but that it can be prior or responsive to aspects of the stimulus which are not verbally articulated.

Of the papers which have dealt with the subception effect, none have questioned the existence of the phenomenon. The issue has been how this effect should be regarded. I have discussed here a number of issues which might lead to experiments pertinent to the clarification of the nature of subception. Let us take the more important theoretical possibilities and consider briefly some of the kinds of data which might be useful in each case.

(1) Does the subception effect depend upon the limitation in the number of categories in the verbal response system? This is Eriksen's statistical proposal, and experimentally it would involve extending the number of verbal response categories to equal more nearly the number of categories discriminable in the stimulus. Even if the subception effect were not found under these conditions, however, the question would remain as to whether these conditions actually apply in nature. If there is greater isomorphism between the stimulus object and the GSR than between the stimulus object and the verbal response system, then Eriksen is merely affirming that the subception experiment takes advantage of the way in which man is actually constructed to show autonomic discrimination in the absence of verbal articulation.

(2) Does the GSR mirror the stimulus object directly or does it result in discrimination through some global process of inference about the threat or nonthreat meaning of the stimulus? One possibility here is to "condition" each syllable to different intensities of shock. If the GSR mirrors the object fairly closely, then it will respond differentially to each syllable. If the discrimination is in terms of gross categories, like danger versus no danger, then differentiation between GSR responses should not occur.

(3) Does the GSR discrimination depend at all upon the ability of the subject to verbalize the nature of the stimulus? One approach to this question could require the subject to identify only the shock or nonshock nature of the stimulus rather than asking him to identify the specific syllable. If the subception effect were found here as well (GSR discrimination in the absence of verbal articulation of the shock or nonshock categories), then one might argue that the GSR discrimination does not depend upon verbal identification of the danger. This finding would not be crucial, however, since one could argue that partial information about the stimulus (e.g., combinations of letters) is used by the subject in making an inference from which the GSR discrimination is made, even though the subject could not correctly categorize at the verbal level. However, I believe that this latter problem can never be resolved since the elimination of this possibility cannot be made without also eliminating the variation between stimuli from which discriminations are made.

In regard to this third issue, one other experimental approach occurs to me. I am intrigued by the possibility that aphasic patients with loss of the ability to articulate visual stimuli verbally might nonetheless show GSR discrimination. Language in aphasia has recently been discussed by Werner (9) from a genetic frame of reference. In his microgenetic experiments Werner notes that "stimuli aroused 'feelings of word meanings,' inner experiences of the semantic sphere of the linguistic forms; these were apparently prior to any specific visual articulation of words." In reviewing other work on the problem, he cites the classic example of the subject who reported the word "cigar" as "smoke" which suggests that the correct word was sought by means of a meaning sphere rather than in terms of the visual articulation of word elements. It seems to me that the subception type of experiment could be performed with aphasics, and perhaps even with mutes who cannot use words in articulating stimuli. Should autonomic discrimination be shown in such instances, it would be difficult to dismiss the idea that discrimination of meanings can take place prior to or independent of verbal articulation of the stimulus object.

I am aware that the subception experiment of Lazarus and McCleary does not really prove the existence of autonomic discrimination without awareness any more than the Bricker and Chapanis experiment disproves it. No experiment really *proves* anything, although the experimentation is important in determining whether the empirical consequences of a theory are consistent with it. Psychologists find great, and I believe often fruitless, sport in examining data which arise out of theoretical frameworks which have real fertileness for generating hypotheses and in showing that these data can be explained, *post hoc,* by some other system. Of course it can. In this sense, Eriksen's argument misses the point, as do those of Bricker and Chapanis, of Murdock, and of Howes. The issues dealing with such postulates as perceptual defense (6) and the process of subception cannot be decided solely on the basis of laboratory experiments. These issues have to be cast in the much broader frame of one's entire conceptual view of human behavior. One question which we must consider is the extent to which a view is both fruitful of hypotheses and consistent with the observations of events in nature itself. The nature of the subception process remains a theoretical question. The conditions which define its operation certainly can be clarified by further experimentation.

References

1. BRICKER, P. D., & CHAPANIS, A. Do incorrectly perceived tachistoscopically stimuli convey some information? *Psychol. Rev.,* 1953, **60,** 181–188.

2. ERIKSEN, C. W. Subception: fact or artifact? *Psychol. Rev.,* 1956, **63,** 74–80.

3. HOWES, D. A statistical theory of subception. *Psychol. Rev.,* 1954, **61,** 98–110.

4. LAZARUS, R. S., & MCCLEARY, R. A. Autonomic discrimination without awareness: a study of subception. *Psychol. Rev.,* 1951, **58,** 113–122.

5. LOWENFELD, J. Verbal inhibition in subception. Paper read at Eastern Psychol. Ass., Atlantic City, March, 1952.

6. MCGINNIES, E. Emotionality and perceptual defense. *Psychol. Rev.,* 1949, **56,** 244–251.

7. MURDOCK, B. B., JR. Perceptual defense and threshold measurements. *J. Pers.,* 1954, **22,** 565–571.

8. RUBENFELD, S., & GUTHRIE, G. M. Stimulus generalization and subception. Paper read at Eastern Psychol. Ass., Atlantic City, March, 1952.

9. WERNER, H. Microgenesis and aphasia. *J. abnorm. soc. Psychol.,* 1956, **52,** 347–353.

ACCURACY OF BRIGHTNESS DISCRIMINATION AS MEASURED BY CONCURRENT VERBAL RESPONSES AND GSRs

Don E. Dulany, Jr., and Charles W. Eriksen

Subliminal perception experiments usually demonstrate that some response discriminates accurately below the threshold for a verbal response which the investigator identifies with awareness. Running through the several criticisms of this conclusion is the objection that the psychophysical assessment of the two responses is not comparable. Lack of comparability is especially objectionable, as Eriksen (1958) and Goldiamond (1958) have pointed out, when a phenomenal report procedure admitting several sources of extraneous error or control marks the threshold for awareness and a relatively uncontaminated accuracy judgment provides the measure of "subliminal accuracy." In the classical method of constant stimuli, the O is asked to give a phenomenal report of the presence or absence of a sensory experience on each trial. It has become clear that not only stimulus values but also the O's disposition to say Yes or No determine that report. For the typical undergraduate, wary of being thought hallucinated, the prudent response when unsure is No. This or any other kind of negative response bias can act to raise the phenomenal report threshold. Swets, Tanner, and Birdsall (1955) have shown that by placing "values" on true positives and true negatives and "costs" on false positives and false negatives in various combinations, the O's "operating level" or threshold varies accordingly. Other

Reprinted by permission of the American Psychological Association and the authors from the *Journal of Abnormal and Social Psychology*, Vol. 59, 1959.

sources of nonsensory control—response category and serial effects—affect the phenomenal report to a significantly greater degree than the forced-choice verbal response (Blackwell, 1952, 1953; Goldiamond, 1958). Moreover, Eriksen (1958) has found striking individual differences in discrepancy between phenomenal report and forced-choice thresholds. The implication of this finding is that each O has his own criterion for the report of a sensory experience and that with the phenomenal report procedure, the threshold of awareness has substantially different meaning from O to O.

Eriksen (1956) and Howes (1954) have discussed an additional objection to comparing the accuracy of a discrete verbal response with the accuracy of a continuous GSR. When the O has only a limited number of discrete verbal responses with which to characterize a sensory experience, information may be lost that is not lost to the continuous GSR.

The object of the present study is to compare the discriminative accuracy of the GSR and verbal response when assessed by the same forced-choice psychophysical procedure.

Method

SUBJECTS

The Os were eight male undergraduates paid for their service.

DESIGN

Each O began the experiment with 10 one-hour sessions devoted to brightness discrimination. Ten hours, we had observed, put the O well along on a practice asymptote. Following these practice sessions, GSRs were conditioned to a light stimulus using electric shock as an US. Psychophysical functions for both verbal response and GSR were then obtained concurrently using a forced-choice procedure essentially like that of Blackwell (1953). With this procedure stimulus magnitudes are presented by the classical method of constant stimuli. On each trial, however, rather than a phenomenal report of the presence or absence of a sensory experience, O reports in which of several intervals the stimulus increment appeared; in this experiment, in which of two time intervals the light appeared. The time interval with the larger GSR for the trial was taken to be the GSR's "choice." In this way a discrete index of GSR association with a stimulus was obtained on every trial and the psychophysical measurement of GSR and verbal response became comparable. On the assumption that saying First or Second, as well as presence or absence of the stimulus and greater or lesser GSR, dichotomously indexes a continuous variable, tetrachoric correlation was computed as a measure of the association of the stimulus with each kind of response.

SETTING AND APPARATUS

The O was seated in a $6' \times 4' \times 6'$ light proof room contained within the main experimental room. Four feet in front of his face was a circular field of light $6''$ in diameter with a homogeneous illumination level of 16.40 foot-candles. The test stimuli were presented directly above a fixation point in the center of this field.

The light source was a 300-watt G.E. projection bulb encased in a metal box and cooled by a blower. On one side of the box, an aperture permitted light to pass into a system of lenses, through a light tunnel and then illuminate the circular field presented to O. Through a second aperture at right angles to the first, the light could pass through a $\frac{1}{64}''$ hole, then through a circular wedge and by a system of prisms and mirrors be reflected through the light tunnel to the position of the test patch on the circular field. Each test stimulus was $.6'' \times .2''$ in area and could be varied in intensity by positioning of the circular wedge. A Stoelting stimulus timer controlled a buzzer designating the stimulus intervals and also a shutter which in turn controlled the onset and duration of the test stimulus.

GSRs were recorded with the Stoelting Deceptograph modified so that direct reading of O's basal resistance level could be obtained. Contact was made by sponge electrodes soaked in saline solution and fastened to the sole of O's foot.

Electric shock was produced by a Harvard inductorium set for a faradic stimulation and supplied by a 3-volt DC source.

PROCEDURE

Practice sessions. At practice as well as later experimental sessions, O was allowed a 10-min. adaptation period before psychophysical judgments began. Four Os were trained by the phenomenal report method during the practice sessions, the other four by the forced-choice method and phenomenal report method alternately. Practice effects of the two procedures upon the forced-choice discrimination had been found not to be appreciably different.

In the phenomenal report procedure O was instructed that he was to say "Yes" when he observed the test light and "No" when he did not. Test lights were presented for 3 sec., the interval marked by a muffled buzzer that sounded throughout. Five seconds elapsed between presentations. Each practice session consisted of a total of 240 judgments composed of 24 judgments of each of nine different stimulus intensities plus a blank interval. The frequency of Yes responses to the blank interval defined O's false alarm rate.

In the forced-choice procedure O was instructed that the test light would occur in one of two 3-sec. intervals, each signaled by a buzzer. He was to report at the end of the trial whether the light appeared in the first or second interval. Three sec. elapsed between intervals with a 5-sec. pause between the end of the second interval and the beginning of the next trial. Twenty-four presentations of each of nine stimulus intensities comprised a practice session.

For both procedures, order of presentation of the nine stimulus intensities and the blank interval was randomized, with the restriction that each stimulus and the blank occur twice within each block of 20 trials. In neither procedure was a doubtful category of response permitted. Practice sessions were run on consecutive days at approximately the same time of day for each O with the exception that Os were not available for Sunday running.

GSR Conditioning and Psychophysical Assessment. GSR conditioning began for each O on the day following his tenth practice session. On each trial the buzzer sounded and the light appeared at an intensity that O had reported Yes between 90 and 100% of the time during practice in the phenomenal report procedure. The first seven presentations of the light were reinforced with a moderate electric shock to the forearm. After the

seventh trial, partial reinforcement was gradually adopted until by the twentieth trial, O was on a 30% reinforcement schedule. Blank intervals with the buzzer alone were inserted to extinguish GSR to the buzzer and insure a discriminated response to the light. Conditioning trials continued until an unmistakable conditioned response occurred on nonreinforced presentations of the light, and little or no response occurred during the blank interval with the buzzer alone. An effort was made to condition to a maximum, halting before adaptation began.

Immediately after conditioning, psychophysical functions for concurrent forced-choice verbal response and GSR were obtained. The forced-choice procedure of this session was identical with that of the practice sessions with two exceptions: On each trial, maximum magnitude of GSR to each of the two stimulus intervals was recorded; and instead of the blank stimulus interval, a reinforced presentation of the light stimulus at conditioning intensity occurred twice among every 20 judgments. Since the GSR values to be compared occurred only a few seconds apart, drift in the GSR baseline was not a problem.

To insure adequate GSR conditioning Os submitted to as many as three sequences of conditioning and psychophysical assessment. The criterion adopted was a significant ($p < .05$) positive tetrachoric correlation between presence of a greater GSR and presence of the stimulus computed over the nine stimulus intensities (108 judgments). Four Os met this criterion at the second session and four more at the third session. Another three Os did not meet the criterion by the third session and were dropped from the experiment.

A correction was made for possible

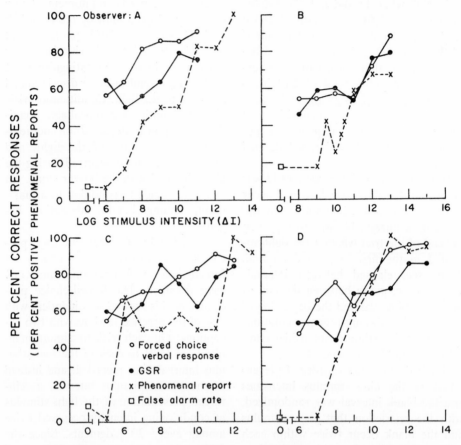

FIG. 1. Percentage of correct verbal responses and GSRs, and percentage of positive phenomenal reports as a function of log stimulus intensity. On this scale, 2 = −.72 log foot-candles and each scale unit equals .08 log foot-candles.

first or second position biases in GSR. Maximum GSR occurring four seconds after the beginning of each stimulus interval was converted to micromhos of conductance change. The average GSRs at first and second interval for successive series of 20 judgments were plotted for each O. Curves were fitted to these two sets of points and the difference between the two curves for a judgment became the bias correction for that judgment. This correction was probably unnecessary since analysis of the data without it yielded almost identical results.

Results and Discussion

For Os A through D the psychophysical functions for GSR and forced-choice verbal response (see Fig. 1) [1] are those obtained during the second experimental

_____

[1] Due to apparatus difficulty, data were usable at only six stimulus values for the first two Os (A and B) and at eight stimulus values for the second two Os (C and D). The effect of this loss of data was to restrict the range of accuracy such that for the first three Os, accuracy did not excel 93% for either response. This restriction does not seem critical.

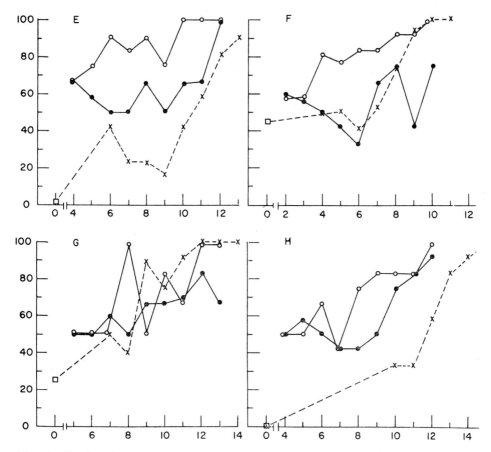

<small>Fig. 1. Continued.</small>

session; for the remaining Os, those obtained during the third experimental session. Phenomenal report curves come from each O's final practice session and are included for rough comparison. We have chosen to present individual psychophysical functions because any method of arriving at composite curves is likely to introduce artifacts critical for this experimental problem.

Our first concern is to know whether either GSR or verbal response shows superior discriminative accuracy when assessed under comparable forced-choice conditions. For seven Os analyzed individually, the r_t of forced-choice verbal response and stimulus computed across all stimulus values was greater than that of the GSR and the stimulus. To evaluate the significance of this difference, $r_t s$ for both kinds of response were converted to Fisher's z and averaged over Os. The resulting $r_t s$ for the forced-choice verbal response are .647 and for the GSR .423. The t for this difference is 2.73, which with 7 df is significant beyond the .05 level. Over a range of stimulus values producing from chance to 99% accuracy the verbal response was the better discriminator.

Since the more common contention is that it is the threshold range that is the area of greater GSR sensitivity, this analysis was repeated over the three lowest stimulus values. For six Os the forced-choice verbal response was more highly correlated with the stimulus than was the GSR. For one O, the GSR correlation with the stimulus was higher, and for the other neither correlation was appreciable ($-.06$ and $.01$). Averaging by means of Fisher's transformation yields a mean r_t of .371 for the forced-choice verbal response as compared with a mean r_t of .309 for the GSR. A t of 1.51 for this comparison falls short of the .05 level. There is no evidence of superior discriminative accuracy for either response in this range.

We have chosen not to speak of thresholds and their comparisons. The very concept of threshold has been subjected to critical analysis (Tanner & Swets, 1954; Swets, Tanner, & Birdsall, 1955) and may be dispensable. Any empirical concept of the threshold is statistical and most are, in some degree, arbitrary. At least some of the confusion surrounding the concept of subception can be laid to inconsistent conceptions of what constitutes a threshold. Instead, individual curves are presented for visual inspection. If there is a single number for each of these functions that can be most meaningfully compared, it should be the inflection point of each curve where it begins to depart from a chance baseline. This ought to be the point at which the response begins to show discriminative accuracy. For the forced-choice verbal response and the GSR, the chance line is 50%; for the phenomenal report, the usual estimate for the chance line is the false alarm rate. Although all three inflection points agree rather well, there is some tendency for the inflection to occur earlier for the forced-choice verbal response than for either of the other responses (Os A, D, G). Most important, in seven cases the inflection point of the curve for the forced-choice verbal response is below that of the GSR. These comparisons are entirely consistent with the tetrachoric analysis.

The substance of this finding is that when discrete indices of both the verbal response and the GSR are compared, the GSR is no better, and considering a wide range of stimuli presented, is the inferior discriminator. Since the verbal response as manifested is normally discrete it is interesting in any case to compare similar measures. But the generality of the finding is as good as the assumption that verbal response tendency—excitatory potential, a priori probability—is continuously distributed.[2] Otherwise the GSR could be said to suffer from an unfair restriction placed upon it. In the course of ordinary experience it could be the very continuity of whatever the GSR indexes that makes it a better discriminator than the discrete verbal response. The assumption of continuity of response strength, however, is common for nonlinguistic instrumental responses and well supported. It is also an assumption made by Skinner (1957) and Osgood (1957) in their treatments of verbal behavior. The specific assumption of continuity of verbal response tendency in psychophysical measurement is supported by the experiments of Bricker and Chapanis (1953), Murdock (1954), and Tanner, Swets, and Birdsall (1955). These experiments show that when the initial response is

---

[2] When the accuracy of the continuous GSR is compared with the accuracy of some discrete verbal response taken to be an index of sensory awareness (e.g., Lazarus & McCleary, 1951), the measures are not comparable if either the sensory or verbal response dimension is continuous.

incorrect, a subsequent guess or ranking of possible responses agrees with the stimulus with greater than chance expectancy. When the correct response is not raised to evocation strength, the stimulus still increases its probability of occurrence as revealed by subsequent measures. With this assumption basic to his statistical theory of subception, Howes (1954) has been able to deduce the relevant experimental facts. At each trial of the present experiment, GSR strength in micromhos change for the two stimulus intervals may show any ratio marked by the extremes of 0 to 1 and 1 to 0. It seems entirely reasonable that verbal response tendency expressed in p values is distributed in the same way.

There is an important question whether these training procedures permitted both the GSR and the verbal response to attain their greatest accuracy. These Os had experienced 10 hours of verbal judgment and were in all cases clearly at an asymptote. Training with the electric shock did not, and for practical reasons, could not be extended through 10 hours. What the GSR accuracy would have been after 10 hours of training we do not know. With the possibility of adaptation or some general disorganization from long periods of shock, there was concern that accuracy would eventually decline. Conditioning was halted at what appeared to be an asymptote, but because of the instability of the GSR a "maximum of accuracy" is difficult to recognize and a true asymptote may not exist. This difficulty obviously limits the usefulness of the GSR as an index of autonomic or emotional sensitivity. Our conditioning procedures have, however, been more extensive than is typical of experiments in this area. We do have clear evidence that conditioning occurred and was maintained in the

significant r_ts for GSR and stimulus and in the psychophysical functions for the GSR, which are in fact curves of generalization from the point of conditioning, a clear and visible stimulus light. Moreover, seven of eight Os met a criterion of 80% correct GSR "judgments" and the other exceeds 75% accuracy during the assessment series. With 1 in every 10 occurrences of the stimulus associated with shock during psychophysical assessment, it was unlikely that the GSR would suffer appreciable extinction, and apparently it did not.

There are, of course, features of the measurement of GSR and verbal response that are not identical here but they seem inherent in the measurement of these responses. Any error in the GSR measuring instrument subtracts from the correlation of GSR and stimulus. And similarly sources of unidentified error for the verbal response will reduce the stimulus-verbal response association. As Eriksen (1956) has shown, there is an appreciable degree of independence between the errors in verbal responses and GSRs. Variables that will influence the accuracy of verbal responses will not concurrently affect the GSR accuracy, at least not to the same extent. Moreover, even though extraneous sources of error in the verbal response may be minimized with the forced-choice technique, many for the GSR—muscle movement, transient fears and discomforts—cannot so easily be ruled out. It is these latter that seem to place the main limits on the accuracy of the GSR.

The subception hypothesis is usually taken to mean that one can, with some response or another, discriminate stimulus values too weak to produce awareness. This hypothesis has not been convincingly tested and it is not tested here. The forced-choice verbal response is not what most would intuitively identify with awareness. And, in fact, numerous studies have reported accuracy excelling chance of some kind of forced-choice response at stimulus intensities that do not provoke the O to say "I can see it" or its equivalent (see Adams, 1957; and Goldiamond, 1958 for reviews). The current objection to these studies (Goldiamond, 1958) is a reassertion of the old argument that reports of private experience are suspect, offered with new documentation that phenomenal reports are under the control of nonsensory variables (Blackwell: 1952, 1953; Tanner & Swets, 1954; Swets, Tanner, & Birdsall, 1955). Until more acceptable techniques for manipulating or indexing awareness are available, it seems more sensible to ask what response systems show greatest discriminative accuracy under comparable conditions of measurement.

Summary

In many subliminal perception experiments some response shows discriminative accuracy at stimulus values below the threshold of awareness determined by classical psychophysical techniques. The procedure is objectionable because the threshold measure admits extraneous variance that the measure of "subliminal accuracy" does not. The measures are not comparable for another reason when one response is the GSR and the other a verbal response because the former is continuous and the latter, as manifested, is discrete. This experiment compares the discriminative accuracy of GSR and verbal response when assessed by the same forced-choice psychophysical technique, a procedure that obtains a discrete index of both responses.

1. Over a range of stimulus values producing from chance (50%) to approximately 99% accuracy of judgment, the verbal response showed significantly higher correlation with the stimulus than did the GSR.

2. Within the range of stimulus values producing from chance to approximately 70% accuracy of judgment, neither response was significantly more accurate than the other.

References

ADAMS, J. K. Laboratory studies of behavior without awareness. *Psychol. Bull.*, 1957, **54**, 383–405.

BLACKWELL, H. R. The influence of data collecting procedures upon psychophysical measurement of two sensory functions. *J. exp. Psychol.*, 1952, **44**, 306–315.

———. Psychophysical thresholds: Experimental studies of methods of measurement. *Engng. Res. Bull.*, Univer. of Michigan, 1953, **36**, 1–227.

BRICKER, P. D., & CHAPANIS, A. Do incorrectly perceived stimuli convey some information? *Psychol. Rev.*, 1953, **60**, 181–188.

ERIKSEN, C. W. Subception: Fact or artifact? *Psychol. Rev.*, 1956, **63**, 74–80.

———. Unconscious processes. In *Nebraska symposium on motivation*. Lincoln: Univer. Nebraska Press, 1958.

GOLDIAMOND, I. Indicators of perception: I. Subliminal perception, subception, unconscious perception: An analysis in terms of psychophysical indicator methodology. *Psychol. Bull.*, 1958, **55**, 373–412.

HOWES, D. H. A statistical theory of the phenomenon of subception. *Psychol. Rev.*, 1954, **61**, 98–110.

LAZARUS, R. S., & MCCLEARY, R. A. Autonomic discrimination without awareness: A study of subception. *Psychol. Rev.*, 1951, **58**, 113–122.

MURDOCK, B. B., Jr. Perceptual defense and threshold measurements. *J. Pers.*, 1954, **22**, 565–571.

OSGOOD, C. Motivational dynamics of language behavior. In *Nebraska symposium on motivation*. Lincoln: Univer. Nebraska press, 1958.

SKINNER, B. F. *Verbal behavior*. New York: Appleton-Century-Crofts, 1957.

SWETS, J. A., TANNER, W. P., Jr., & BIRDSALL, T. G. The evidence for a decision-making theory of visual detection. *Tech. Rep. No. 40, Electronic Defense Group.* Ann Arbor: Univer. of Michigan, 1955.

TANNER, W. P., JR., & SWETS, J. A. A decision-making theory of visual detection. *Psychol. Rev.*, 1954, **61**, 401–409.

CHAPTER 3
Anxiety and Stress

Anxiety As a Personality Variable

DRIVE THEORY AND MANIFEST ANXIETY

Janet A. Taylor

In recent years a number of studies involving human Ss have been devoted to testing the implications of certain Hullian notions concerning the relationship between performance in learning situations and level of total effective drive (D). In these investigations drive has been defined in terms of scores on a manifest anxiety scale (41). In view of the growing experimental literature concerning these hypotheses since their initial statement by Taylor (40) and Taylor and Spence (43), an attempt to outline the theory as it is presently conceived by the Iowa group and to evaluate the evidence concerning it seems to be in order.

Before proceeding with these matters, however, certain misunderstandings which have arisen concerning the purpose of this work should be mentioned. First, although groups have been selected exclusively on the basis of scores on the Manifest Anxiety Scale (hereafter designated as MAS) the interest of the Iowa group has *not* been in investigating anxiety as a phenomenon, but rather in the role of drive in certain learning situations. The assumption has been made that anxiety scores are related in some

manner to drive level, but in terms of the major theoretical interests of this group, any other acceptable specification of drive (e.g., hunger) could be used in experimental tests of the hypotheses about the effect of drive level. Further, as Farber (6) has pointed out, no attempt has ever been made to claim that the only difference between individuals receiving different scores on the MAS is in drive level or that all performance differences could be explained by drive. Undoubtedly there are many characteristics other than drive level on which anxious and nonanxious Ss differ; the investigation of these additional properties of anxiety groups and their influence on performance is certainly both legitimate and important, but it simply has not been the interest of the proponents of the drive theory.

A second point that should be clarified has to do with the MAS. The construction of the test was not aimed at developing a clinically useful test which would diagnose anxiety, but rather was designed solely to select Ss differing in general drive level. Thus the question of the scale's "validity" (i.e., its agreement with clinical judgments) is in a sense irrelevant to the experimental purposes for which the test was developed. In light of this, the test might better have

Reprinted by permission of the American Psychological Association and the author from the *Psychological Bulletin*, Vol. 53, 1956.

been given a more noncommittal label, such as a measure of emotionality, although the fact that the items on the scale were selected by clinicians as referring to manifest anxiety as it is described psychiatrically does not make the title completely inappropriate nor a relationship between clinical judgments and MAS scores unexpected. Certainly the generality of the experimental findings with the MAS would be increased if correlations were found with other definitions and such attempts will be discussed in a later section. However, regardless of the results of such studies, it should be clearly understood that "manifest anxiety" has been defined operationally only in terms of test scores and will be so employed, unless otherwise indicated, in the present paper.

Drive Theory

As stated earlier, the purpose of the Iowa group has been to investigate the effects of varying drive level on performance in learning situations. Actual experimentation has involved two independent problems: (a) specification of the conditions under which drive differences are said to appear, and (b) the theory concerning the effects of drive level on behavior once drive has been aroused. The first problem concerns the postulated relationship between the MAS and drive level, the second between drive (or anxiety) level and performance in various situations. Since the two are separate matters, an outline of the theory concerning the influence of drive will be given first and the hypothesized relationship between drive and MAS scores considered at a later point.

According to Hull (15), all habits (H) activated in a given situation combine multiplicatively with the total effective drive state (D) operating at the moment to form excitatory potential $E[E = \mathrm{f}(H \times D)]$. Total effective drive, in the Hullian system, is determined by the summation of all extant need states, primary and secondary, irrespective of their source and their relevancy to the type of reinforcement employed. Since response strength is determined in part by E, the implication of varying drive level in any situation in which a single habit is evoked is clear: the higher the drive, the greater the value of E and hence of response strength. Thus in simple noncompetitional experimental arrangements involving only a single habit tendency the performance level of high-drive Ss should be greater than that for low-drive groups.

Higher drive levels should not, however, always lead to superior performance (i.e., greater probability of the appearance of the correct response). In situations in which a number of competing response tendencies are evoked, only one of which is correct, the relative performance of high and low drive groups will depend upon the number and comparative strengths of the various response tendencies. Predictions concerning the performance of the groups in such complex tasks involve the introduction of additional Hullian concepts: oscillatory inhibition (O) and threshold (L).

The concept of O was introduced by Hull (15) in an attempt to allow for statement, within his system, of the intra-individual variability in behavior that occurs, presumably, because of uncontrolled variations from instant to instant within the organism and in his environment. The value of O is said to vary from moment to moment, the distribution of O values for a group of (like) individuals on any trial forming a normal probability function. O is further assumed to play an inhibitory role, its value being subtracted from excitatory potential (E), thus yielding momentary excitatory potential $(\dot{E})$. In order for $\dot{E}$ to activate a response, it must attain a minimum or threshold value (L), a value that is presumably the same for all similar habit tendencies evoked in a given situation. Thus $R = f(\dot{E}) = f(E\text{-}O\text{-}L)$.

In any task in which a stimulus tends to evoke a number of competing responses the response that will appear on a given occasion will be the one with the highest suprathreshold momentary excitatory strength $(\dot{E})$ at that moment. Other things being equal, of course, the response with the greatest H and hence E value will have a greater probability of occurring than any other response.

Adding the notion of differing drive level to this conception, we see that the probability of appearance of the correct response involves an interaction between drive level and the number and comparative strengths of the correct and incorrect tendencies. When the correct response is weaker (i.e., has less H) than one or more of the competing response tendencies, high-drive groups should be inferior in performance to low-drive Ss. That is, because of the multiplicative relationship between habit strength and drive, the stronger incorrect tendencies gain relatively more E than the correct tendency in the case of high drive Ss than in low drive, thus leading to a greater probability of occurrence of one of the stronger incorrect responses in the high-drive group. Further, the possibility exists that under a high-drive level new competing responses with very weak habit strengths may be brought over the threshold value of E with the consequence that the probability of occurrence of the correct response is lowered relative to that in a low-drive condition.

At the other extreme, the correct response tendency may be highest in the hierarchy and relatively strong when compared to the incorrect. In such a situation, which is comparable to the case in which but a single habit is aroused, the E value for the correct response would be relatively greater than the other responses in the hierarchy for the high-drive group than for the low-drive, leading to the prediction of the superiority of performance of such subjects.

It should be obvious, then, that maximum inferiority of high-drive Ss would be expected when a large number of competing tendencies are present and the correct tendency is both relatively weak and low in the hierarchy. As the strength of the correct tendency increases relative to the incorrect, high-drive groups should become less inferior and eventually superior in performance to low-drive groups. The exact point of equality would be difficult to specify. Even when the correct response is highest (though not strongly dominant) in the hierarchy, high-drive Ss could still conceivably be inferior in some instances since a greater number of suprathreshold tendencies could more than offset the advantage of the relatively higher E value of the correct response for these individuals.[1]

---

[1] In a recent review Child (3) incorrectly interpreted the theoretical analysis outlined above as involving the sudden introduction of O and L for the situation in which the correct response is highest in the hierarchy. These concepts are of course assumed to be operating in all situations, including the noncompetitional one in which but a single response tendency is being evoked. No appeal was made to these constructs in the latter instance, however, since their inclusion would not affect the predictions. Mention might also be made of other constructs in the Hullian system (e.g., I, V, K,

An important consideration that should be noted about making predictions concerning the effect of drive level upon performance in actual experimental situations is that a behavioral analysis of the situation must have been made; only in experimental arrangements in which the results, independent of drive level, permit statements in terms of competing S-R tendencies are deductions from the theory possible. While the majority of investigations designed to test implications of these derivations concerning drive level have utilized tasks for which analyses in S-R terms had already been made and found to be useful, occasionally an experiment appears in which the investigator attempts to evaluate the total theory by comparing groups on a task which is poorly understood (and for which little or no rationale is presented) or which clearly involves the introduction of variables not included in the theory. The accumulation of empirical evidence concerning the performance of different groups in any situation or attempts to incorporate additional variables within any theoretical framework are certainly to be encouraged, but statements that the results of such studies refute or confirm theoretical expectations are unwarranted when there is no evidence that the boundary conditions imposed by the theory are met.

Drive and Anxiety

The use of the MAS to select groups that are postulated to differ in drive level in an experimental situation has rested on the assumption that scores on the scale are in some manner related to

etc.): it has been assumed that these are of equal value for all drive groups and that a consideration of their values would not result in changing any prediction.

emotional responsiveness, which, in turn, contributes to drive level. Two alternative hypotheses have been entertained concerning the conditions under which emotionality is evoked. One is that test scores reflect differences in a chronic emotional state so that individuals scoring high on the scale tend to bring a higher level of emotionality or anxiety "in the door" with them than do Ss scoring at lower levels (40). A second alternative conception is that MAS scores reflect different potentialities for anxiety arousal, high scoring Ss being those who tend to react more emotionally and adapt less readily to novel or threatening situations than do low scorers (28, 37). According to the first hypothesis differences among anxious and nonanxious groups (providing other conditions imposed by the theory are met) should be found whether or not there is any "threat," in the form of noxious stimulation, fear of failure or the like, in the situation. Thus, for example, the performance of anxious Ss should be superior to the nonanxious in both classical defense conditioning, in which a noxious stimulus is employed, and in reward conditioning into which no objective threat has been introduced. In the case of the second conception, differences would be expected in the performance of anxiety groups only in those situations in which some threat is present. Should this be the correct conception, exact specification of the conditions thought to be sufficient to evoke anxiety would be necessary in order to test hypotheses concerning the role of drive. Available evidence suggests that the magnitude of differences among groups may be related to the level of noxious stimulation employed (37), or to stress-producing instructions (10, 19), suggesting that differences in drive level among groups may depend at least in part upon situational factors. However, the picture is complicated by the results of a number of studies in which differences among anxiety groups have been found in the absence of noxious stimulation or instructions designed to produce stress (8, 24, 25, 26, 42).

Most investigators have not explicitly considered this issue, assuming either that anxiety scores reflect a chronic level of emotionality or that factors are present in the typical laboratory experiment that result in different anxiety levels among groups. For purposes of evaluating those studies in which degree of stress has not been under investigation, the assumption will tentatively be made here that in all situations, individuals scoring high and low on the anxiety scale will differ in drive level, for whatever reason. The evidence more directly concerned with the conditions of anxiety-arousal will be considered at a later point.

Experimental Evidence

CLASSICAL CONDITIONING

Classical conditioning is said to be a noncompetitional situation in which but a single response tendency is being acquired; theoretical expectation therefore is that anxious groups will perform at a higher level than nonanxious. The results of a number of studies of eyelid conditioning using groups with extreme scores on the MAS [2] have upheld these predictions, anxious Ss showing a greater

number of CR's than nonanxious (11, 35, 37, 38, 39, 40). In all cases but one (11), these differences were statistically significant, the exception involving the use of only 10 Ss per group, considerably fewer than were employed in other investigations. Data from eyelid conditioning studies performed in the Iowa laboratories and elsewhere (39) are also available from Ss scoring throughout the entire range of anxiety scores rather than only at the two extremes. The relationship between anxiety and conditioning scores has been uniformly found to be monotonic although not always linear, middle-anxiety Ss tending to show a performance level closer to the low-scoring than the high-scoring groups. The magnitudes of the correlation coefficients obtained have been in the neighborhood of .25, thus indicating that relatively little of the variance among Ss can be accounted for in terms of anxiety scores. In view of the low correlation and the monotonic relationship between the two variables, continued use of extreme groups only for research purposes in such situations seems justified.

A conditioning study employing a response other than the eyeblink has also been reported in the literature. An investigation by Bitterman and Holtzman (1) utilized the PGR technique which, like the eyelid situation it will be noted, involves defense conditioning. After dividing a group of randomly selected college students into the upper and lower 50% on the basis of MAS scores, these investigators found a slight but statistically insignificant superiority in conditioning level on the part of their anxious Ss. Since their anxious group included individuals with scores considerably lower than those in the investigations referred to above, this lack of statistical significance is not too surprising.

[2] In almost all of the studies involving the MAS, a comparison has been made of extreme scorers, typically the 20th percentile or below (nonanxious) and 80th percentile or above (anxious) in terms of a standardization group of college students (41). Use of the terms "anxious" and "nonanxious" groups here should be understood to refer to such extremes unless otherwise indicated.

Several studies are available concerning differential conditioning, also in the eyelid situation (11, 34, 36). The predictions derived from the theory in this instance are that anxious Ss should exhibit a greater excitatory strength both to the positive (reinforced) CS and to the negative (nonreinforced) CS and further, that the difference in excitatory strengths of the two stimuli should be greater for the anxious group. By transforming all raw data into excitatory strength values, Spence and his colleagues (34, 36) have attempted to test these predictions in some five separate instances. In each case, the excitatory strength to the positive CS during differential conditioning was significantly greater for anxious Ss, as was expected. The results concerning the remaining two predictions were not so clear-cut. In four out of five independent instances the excitatory strength to the negative stimulus was greater for the anxious Ss but in no case was the difference significant. In all five cases the difference between excitatory strengths was in the expected direction but was significant in only one instance. While the results of these studies tend to lend some support to the theory, somewhat contradictory findings have been reported by Hilgard, Jones, and Kaplan (11). As mentioned earlier, contrary to other studies of simple eyelid conditioning, these investigations found only a slight, statistically insignificant superiority for anxious Ss during training to the positive CS. During differential conditioning, the anxious group continued to exhibit an insignificant superiority to the nonanxious on the positive CS. However, the responses of the anxious Ss to the negative CS were significantly greater as would be expected by drive theory.

STIMULUS GENERALIZATION

Stimulus generalization, to which differential conditioning is related, has been investigated more directly by Rosenbaum (28) and Wenar (48). Rosenbaum found greater responsiveness to generalized stimuli in a spatial situation for an anxious group than for a nonanxious group, as would be predicted by drive theory, but only in the case of Ss given strong intermittent shock during their performance; for groups given a weak shock or buzzer, no significant differences emerged. After training groups of anxious and nonanxious Ss on a key-pressing response to a strong shock, weak shock or a buzzer presented at regular intervals, Wenar (48) measured the reaction time to these stimuli in a test series in which the intervals of presentation were longer or shorter (temporal generalization) than those employed during training. Reaction time was related significantly to both stimulus intensity and anxiety level, response time being quicker as these variables increased.

MAZE LEARNING

The first study to be concerned with demonstrating that the relative performance of anxious and nonanxious Ss is a function of degree of interference within a task was reported by Taylor and Spence (43), who used a type of serial verbal maze. On the assumption that errors in such a situation are largely the result of interfering response tendencies, due to remote associations, etc., it was expected that anxious Ss would make more errors and take more trials to reach a criterion than nonanxious. The results of this study and of a subsequent investigation by Farber and Spence (8) with a stylus maze have confirmed these hypotheses, the greater number of errors and trials to criterion being made by the anxious groups. An additional prediction was also made for these maze data, namely that the degree of inferiority of the anxious Ss in comparison to the nonanxious should be positively related to difficulty of the choice point. In both studies, significant rank-order correlations were obtained between the difference in number of errors between groups on an individual choice point and the difficulty of that point. Although these results tend to confirm theoretical expectation, some discrepancy between prediction and the experimental findings occurred on the easiest choice points. In each investigation, the small number of errors on the easiest two or three points suggests the presence of few interfering tendencies so that the anxious might be expected to be superior in performance. Even here, however, they tended to be inferior.

In addition to the two studies utilizing extreme groups, one study of stylus maze learning involving the entire range of anxiety scores has been reported. After splitting a randomly selected group of college students into 7 anxiety groups according to their MAS scores, Matarazzo et al. (24) found a linear relationship ($r = .25$) between anxiety and trials to the criterion on the maze.

While the investigations reported above have found differences between anxiety groups on maze performance, Hughes, Sprague, and Bendig (14), utilizing extreme groups, failed to duplicate these results with several serial verbal mazes. Different from the Taylor and Spence study in which the typical 2-second rate of stimulus presentation was employed, Hughes et al. used a 4-second rate in all cases. Previous investigations have demonstrated (12) that performance is positively related to the interstimulus interval in serial learning but since the effects of this variable are poorly understood, the implications of the failure to find differences between anxiety groups with the 4-second condition are not clear. One possibility, based on the assumption that differences in anxiety level are largely determined by situational factors, is that under longer time intervals, stress upon Ss, and hence upon differences in emotionality between anxious and nonanxious, is minimized.

VERBAL LEARNING

Rather than attempting to demonstrate an interaction between anxiety level and degree of interference by examining individual items within a single task, as was done in the maze studies, Montague (25) formed three different lists of serial nonsense syllables which, because of varying degrees of formal intralist similarity and association value of the syllables, presumably differed in the amount of intralist interference. A significant interaction was found between anxiety and list, an anxious group being significantly superior in performance to nonanxious on the list for which similarity was low and association value high, and the position being reversed for groups given a list of high similarity and low association value. Similar findings have been reported by Lucas (19) in a study in which Ss were asked to recall lists of consonants read to them. As the number of duplicated consonants within a list was increased, anxious Ss showed a significant decrease in the amount recalled while the performance of the nonanxious was not affected.

While a number of investigators have

employed serial learning tasks, from the point of view of testing the implications of drive theory, the paired-associate technique seems to be preferable. Whereas intralist interferences due to such factors as remote associations are inherently part of serial learning and are thus difficult to manipulate, the use of discrete S-R pairs permits more precise control of the number and strength of the response tendencies elicited by each stimulus. Turning to the investigations that have employed this paired-associate arrangement, several studies have attempted to minimize the presence of competing response tendencies and thus to demonstrate the performance superiority of anxious Ss. In one, Taylor and Chapman (42) chose nonsense syllables with low formal similarity, in an attempt to provide a noncompetitional arrangement in which each stimulus tended to evoke only its own response. As expected, on two lists for which such low similarity obtained, anxious Ss were significantly superior in performance to nonanxious. Similar superiority of anxious Ss has been reported by Spence (33) on an adjective list in which the association between each S-R pair was presumed to be initially strong and minimum similarity existed among pairs. In a second part of this investigation, an attempt was made to maximize the number of competing tendencies by having a high degree of synonymity among stimuli. As predicted, an anxious group in this case was inferior.

The initial strength of association between S-R was also manipulated by Ramond (26) in an investigation involving a variation of the standard paired-associate technique. Each stimulus, an adjective, had connected with it two response words, one judged to be highly associated with the stimulus and the other with no discernible association. Each type of response was correct for half of the items. When the low association responses were correct, anxious Ss were expected to perform at a lower level than nonanxious because of the greater interference of the strong, incorrect response for this group. The results confirmed this prediction. Theoretical expectations for the situation in which the stronger response was correct are not so clear-cut since the arrangement of the list made it likely that as learning took place the low association responses would interfere occasionally with the high association response because of stimulus generalization. Thus, while anxious Ss might be expected to be superior early in learning, they might lose this superiority as the weak responses are learned and provide competition. The results lent some support to these expectations, anxious Ss first being superior and then inferior to nonanxious although the over-all difference between groups did not reach statistical significance.

Anxiety Scores and Their Relationship to Stress

As was indicated earlier, two alternative hypotheses have been entertained concerning the difference between Ss scoring high and low on the MAS with respect to anxiety: that such groups have different levels of chronic anxiety or that the groups instead differ in their emotional reactiveness to anxiety-evoking stimuli present in a situation.

The studies of verbal learning just discussed indicate that whether due to chronic or situational factors, differences between high and low scoring Ss cannot be said to be produced only when stress is deliberately introduced into the situation, either by means of noxious stimulation as in the case of defense conditioning or by the administration of stress-provoking instructions (e.g., reports of failure). Consideration of the studies into which some threatening stimulation has been introduced may, however, throw some light onto the question as to whether differences in anxiety among groups could depend, at least in part, on situational variables.

Should situational factors play a role in determining differences in emotionality among anxiety groups, the strength of the UCS in classical conditioning might be expected to be related to such group differences. A comparison of three experiments of eyelid conditioning from the Iowa laboratory involving a relatively strong, medium, and mild UCS, respectively, was made by Spence and Farber (35). Examination of the mean conditioning scores reveals that while intensity of the UCS tended to be related to performance, the magnitude of the difference between anxious and nonanxious remained relatively constant under the different intensities. Different results were obtained by Spence and his associates (37) in a study specifically undertaken to evaluate the effect of the strength of noxious stimulation on anxiety groups. In this investigation the Ss, selected without reference to their anxiety scores, were conditioned with a relatively weak UCS, but one group was given occasional electric shocks between trials, another threatened with shock, and a third trained under neutral conditions. These latter Ss, run under neutral conditions, gave fewer CR's than the other groups, especially in earlier trials. When Ss were later divided into the upper and lower 50 per cent according to anxiety scores, it was found that while the high-scoring group conditioned without shock or threat of shock exhibited only a slight, statistically insignificant su-

periority in conditioning performance, the difference between anxiety groups was highly significant for Ss with whom shock or threat of shock was employed.

The previously mentioned studies of stimulus generalization by Rosenbaum (28) and Wenar (48) were also concerned with variations in the intensity of noxious stimulation, in both cases a buzzer and two intensities of shock being employed. While Rosenbaum found a significant difference between groups only when strong shock was used, Wenar's results (with a somewhat different experimental arrangement) indicated a greater responsiveness for the anxious group under all three conditions. Furthermore, the magnitude of the difference between groups was unaffected by stimulus intensity.

Turning to verbal learning, Deese, Lazarus, and Keenan (4) have reported a study in which the effect of electric shock on serial learning was investigated. Here it was found that nonanxious groups given intermittent shocks performed at a significantly lower level than a nonanxious control group run under neutral conditions. In contrast, the performance of the anxious groups remained relatively constant, Ss run under shock not differing from their control group. Further, when all conditions were combined, the performance of the anxious was significantly superior to the nonanxious.[3] Thus, while the differences be-

---

[3] Although, presumably, the serial list was of relatively low intralist similarity, it is difficult to tell from the writers' description what drive theory would have predicted concerning the performance of the anxiety groups, independent of the stress factor. In a second, parallel, experiment involving a more difficult list (12 consonant syllables composed of only 5 consonants) presented for a standard 12 trials Lazarus, Deese, and Hamilton (17) found no differences among groups either as a function

tween groups increased under shock, they were due to the disruptive effect of the shock on the *nonanxious* Ss.

Quite in contrast to the results of Deese *et al.* are the findings obtained by Gordon and Berlyne (10) in an investigation of verbal learning utilizing psychological stress rather than noxious stimulation. After being told that the tasks were measures of intelligence and that their performance on a paired-associate list was above average, anxious and nonanxious groups did not differ significantly in amount of negative transfer on a second paired-associate list. An anxious group told that their first list performance was below average, however, exhibited significantly more negative transfer than did a comparable nonanxious group. Finally, in the Lucas study (19) mentioned earlier in which the recall of consonant lists varying in number of duplications was investigated, the effects of varying numbers of reports of failure to meet expected standards were also studied. While nonanxious Ss increased the amount recalled with greater numbers of failure experiences, the anxious groups did significantly worse.

As may be seen, the available evidence does not present a clear-cut picture with respect to the effects of stress. Summarizing first those investigations involving noxious stimulation, the results indicate that with one exception (4) the performance of all Ss tends to be affected in the same direction as is found with an increase in anxiety (MAS) level. The magnitude of the difference between anxious and nonanxious Ss either remains constant with greater degrees of stimulation or is increased. The data from the two studies employing psychological stress (in both cases defined by telling S he had failed to achieve adequate standards on an intelligence test) have revealed somewhat different relationships. In both instances (10, 19) the performance of anxious Ss under stress was significantly worse than the anxious group tested under neutral conditions while the performance of nonanxious Ss was in one case the same and in the second better than the control group. Thus, the magnitude of the difference between anxiety groups was greater under stress than under neutral conditions.

The available evidence suggests then that situational sources of stress may play a role in determining the difference in anxiety level between Ss scoring at the extremes of the MAS. Whether the differences between groups in the verbal learning studies into which no objective stress had been introduced by the experimenter reflect chronic anxiety level or unidentified sources of threat remains an open question. Speculating on this point, to many college sophomores psychology experiments per se may be seen as somewhat threatening, particularly when the task could be interpreted as reflecting on their personality or intelligence. It is perfectly possible that in experimental arrangements involving no noxious stimulation or stress-inducing instructions which call upon skills not

---

of anxiety scores or of shock-no-shock conditions. While these results appear superficially to be contradictory both to drive theory (which would expect inferiority of anxious Ss) and to the results of the first study with respect to the influence of shock, inspection of their data indicates that all groups averaged only about one correct response per trial. Since so little learning took place it is not surprising to have no differences in performance among groups. For this reason it is felt that the study does not provide very meaningful evidence on the effects of either anxiety level or shock on task performance.

particularly valued by college students, differences between groups might disappear.[4]

Using the results of these studies involving stress to attempt to determine the source of anxiety differences between high- and low-scoring Ss or, for that matter, to test drive theory, involves the assumption that the only effect of stress in any situation is to increase drive level or, at least, that anxious and nonanxious groups do not respond differentially to stress except with respect to anxiety or drive. Although no systematic exploration has been made of the relationship between degree of noxious stimulation and performance on various types of tasks, an examination of the general literature concerning the effect of such stimulation in nonverbal, noncompetition situations lends some credibility to this assumption (32). It is important to note that with one exception (4) the studies of the effects of noxious stimuli on anxious and nonanxious Ss have employed tasks of this type.

In contrast, the literature concerning studies of psychological stress (e.g., ego-involving instructions, reports of failure), most of which have employed quite complex tasks, suggests that factors other than or in addition to drive level are involved. The variety of roles or effects that stress may have in addition to the motivational one has been discussed by Lazarus, Deese, and Osler (18) and more recently by Farber (7). Particu-

larly pertinent to the present discussion is the finding that there are wide individual differences in response to such stress, some individuals improving in performance, others decreasing, and still others being unaffected. The direction of the effect of stress has further been related to several personality variables (18). The Ss scoring at the extremes of the MAS continuum may react to such stress with characteristically different patterns as well. Thus, it is possible that with increasing degrees of stress, differences between anxious and nonanxious other than drive may be aroused and become responsible, at least in part, for the discrepancy between the performance levels of such groups.

Unfortunately, the two available studies involving psychological stress do not permit an evaluation of this suggestion (nor of the possibility that stress of any type, physical or psychological, may have a similar effect in tasks of sufficient complexity). Both, it will be recalled, used learning tasks of such a type that an increase in drive level might be expected to result in deterioration of performance. Thus, it could be argued that the anxious were "threatened" (had their drive level increased) by the stress instructions and hence deteriorated in performance in comparison to their neutral control group while the fact that the nonanxious under stress did not show a similar inferiority merely indicates that they were emotionally unaffected by the stress conditions. The only hint that more might be involved than drive level is contained in the Lucas study in which nonanxious improved with a greater number of failure experiences while the anxious became worse. Such a finding suggests further that these additional factors, if any, might act in the direction of

---

[4] A study of classical reward conditioning of the salivary response by Bindra, Paterson, and Strzelecki (On the relation between anxiety and conditioning, *Canad. J. Psychol.,* 1955, 9, 1–6) which appeared after this review was written confirms this suggestion. No difference was found between anxious and nonanxious groups.

interfering with the performance of anxious Ss and of facilitating the performance of nonanxious. Additional research upon the effects of stress on anxiety groups, particularly with tasks of different levels of complexity is certainly needed to provide information about these possibilities.

The suggestion that at least psychological stress may have other than drive effects on anxious and nonanxious Ss in complex tasks bears some resemblance to the empirical predictions proposed by Sarason and Mandler and their associates (22, 23, 29) for the performance of groups selected by a different measuring instrument, a questionnaire of "test anxiety," designed to select individuals reacting with different degrees of anxiety to intelligence tests and course examinations. These investigators hypothesized that such high-anxious individuals react to an experimental situation represented as a test of intelligence or the like (thus, according to their conception, creating stress) not only with more anxiety or drive than low-anxious but also, as a result of past learning, have evoked by their anxiety irrelevant response tendencies which interfere with task performance. Under increasing stress (such as reports of failure) the performance of high-anxious Ss worsens because of the arousal of a greater number of these irrelevant tendencies, offsetting the facilitating effects of drive; the performance of the low-anxious, however, improves with greater stress due to an increasing drive level, unaccompanied by irrelevant tendencies. Such a theory, although predicting the same results as would be expected from the notions being put forward here about the effect of stress on the performance of anxious and nonanxious in complex tasks, differs from these suggestions in several ways.

In contrast to drive theory, Sarason and Mandler seem to imply that other things being equal, heightened drive always results in raising performance, independent of the type of task involved. Further they propose that the effect of stress is to evoke certain disruptive response patterns in addition to drive only for high-anxious Ss while the suggestion of the present writer is that additional factors may be elicited under stress for both anxiety extremes although their effects on performance may be in the opposite direction.

Although Sarason and his colleagues have confined their interests to "test anxiety" and its effects, primarily, on intelligence-test items under stressful conditions, Child (3) has proposed that all the work done with Ss scoring at the extremes on the MAS, independent of whether stress is introduced, could be more plausibly explained by such an interference theory. These task-irrelevant responses are always present in anxious Ss, as well as a higher drive level, Child states, but they disrupt performance only in complex situations "where the subject is already in conflict between various response tendencies relevant to the task [so that] the presence of irrelevant response tendencies heightens the conflict and interferes with performance to a greater extent than increased drive improves it" (3, p. 154).

It would appear to the present writer that a theory that attempts to attribute all inferiority of performance to irrelevant tendencies would either be forced to predict that anxious Ss would always be inferior to nonanxious in such complex tasks as verbal learning (since it seems hard to maintain that even with verbal materials having little intratask interference, irrelevant extratask responses could not interfere with performance) or, if already obtained results are to be explained, that anxiety level and its correlated irrelevant response tendencies would shift up and down abruptly from task to task and even from stimulus to stimulus within a task as the number of competing response tendencies directly elicited by a stimulus varied. Tieing the number of extratask responses to the number of intratask interferences would seem merely to be adding one more variable to those considered by drive theory without making different predictions in the situations to which drive theory has been thought to be applicable.

It is interesting to note that the suggestions being proposed here concerning the possible role of response as well as drive differences in the performance of anxious and nonanxious Ss in stress situations leads to a different prediction than do Child's hypotheses in certain cases. According to the present writer, on verbal tasks in which anxious Ss are demonstrated to be superior to nonanxious under neutral conditions, the introduction of stress might be expected to minimize this difference between groups or even to reverse its direction, the performance of anxious Ss being lower than under neutral conditions and the nonanxious possibly being higher. Child, while perhaps also expecting nonanxious Ss to be better under stress than under neutral conditions, would be forced to predict that an anxious group under stress would be the same as or even superior to its neutral control group rather than worse. That is, the fact that under neutral conditions the anxious Ss perform at a higher level than nonanxious would indicate, according to Child, that this was a situation in which making irrelevant responses does not interfere with task performance, the difference between groups in favor of the anxious being due,

then, to their higher drive. While stress might increase the drive level of anxious Ss and hence the magnitude or number of the task-irrelevant responses, these latter would still not compete with task-relevant responses since the task is the same.

Still another interpretation of the relationship between anxiety and stress has been suggested, the predictions of which are quite opposed to any of those previously discussed. On the basis of their findings with serial learning that the performance of nonanxious groups deteriorated with shock while that for the anxious did not, Deese, Lazarus, and Keenan (4) suggested that the MAS measures not so much anxiety as how individuals defend themselves against anxiety, and further, that MAS scores are related to the hysteria-psychasthenia continuum. The latter proposal arose from the finding that (with overlapping items excluded) there was a positive correlation of .40 between the MAS and the Psychasthenia (Pt) scale on the MMPI and a —.23 correlation between the MAS and the Hysteria (Hy) scale. By assuming that nonanxious Ss are hysterical individuals who are unable to maintain their defenses in the face of objective inescapable stress (e.g., shock, as opposed to psychological stress), and therefore are greatly disturbed by it while the anxious are psychasthenic and therefore react to objective threat coolly and intellectually, they believe their results become intelligible. The same explanation has been offered by Eriksen (5), who found that Ss scoring high on the Hy scale exhibited more stimulus generalization in an investigation involving shock than did high Pt Ss. These results, Eriksen stated, were inexplicable in terms of drive theory. In attempting to evaluate these hypotheses (and leaving aside any questions of the clinical validity of the various measures employed) it might be well to inject a historical note. In developing a scale for the selection of Ss, the present writer deliberately attempted to include items descriptive of overt or manifest anxiety and avoided including items describing behavior not itself "anxious" but said to be a defense against an internal anxiety precisely because it was the purpose of the scale to select Ss differing in functioning anxiety level in the experimental situation; to the extent that defenses were effective in keeping anxiety at a minimum, inclusion of "defense items" on the scale would have been self-defeating.

The conflict between the hypothesis of Eriksen, Deese, et al., and the assumptions made by drive theorists in using the MAS is not whether some individuals scoring low on the scale are potentially anxious individuals with good defenses, but rather whether the introduction of special conditions such as shock so affect a sufficient number of low scoring Ss as to wipe out or reverse the direction of difference in drive or emotionality between low- and high-scoring groups that exists under neutral conditions. If Ss are thus affected, drive theorists must either abandon the MAS for a different selective instrument, or restrict themselves to testing groups in situations in which defenses are assumed to be operating.

An examination of the available evidence suggests that no modification of the postulated relationship between anxiety scores and drive level needs be made at the present time (if it is understood that the purpose of drive theory is to investigate the effects of drive once in operation rather than the development of a comprehensive theory of anxiety as a personality phenomenon). That is, the

results of Deese et al. (4) seem deviate; no other investigation involving noxious stimulation (since psychological stress does not assault hysterical defenses) has obtained results that would be expected if the anxiety level of low scoring Ss increased up to or beyond that of the high scoring Ss. If such stimulation has any differential effect at all, it appears to be in the direction of increasing the anxiety of the anxious group proportionately more than the nonanxious. Examining the Eriksen results and accepting them as reliable, there seems to be no firm basis for suggesting that drive theory would have predicted more stimulus generalization for the high Pt group than the high Hy. Such a claim rests on the assumption that all nonanxious Ss would be low Hy and all anxious high Pt. The magnitude of the reported correlation coefficients, particularly between the MAS and the hysteria scale does not make this assumption seem too reasonable. Even if high Hy Ss do become disturbed under nonescapable stress, a sufficient number of Ss could remain in the nonanxious group who were "genuinely" nonanxious, or whose defenses remained intact, to have a nonanxious group exhibit less stimulus generalization than the anxious. More relevant than such armchair argument, however, are Rosenbaum's (28) results. Using an experimental arrangement very similar to Eriksen's, Rosenbaum found, it will be recalled, more stimulus generalization for anxious than nonanxious, and even more important, that the difference between groups was significant only under the conditions of strong shock.

MAS and Clinical Measures of Anxiety

As was indicated earlier, the meaning of the term "anxiety" as used in the studies attempting to determine the relationship between drive and performance has been only in terms of MAS scores. While such pure operationism is methodologically sound, the generality of these results would be considerably expanded were a relationship established between the MAS and more common clinical definitions of anxiety. Most valuable would seem to be a comparison of scale scores with observers' ratings of overt behavior since other diagnostic tests of anxiety are themselves purported to be indicators of such behavior. Fortunately, several studies relating MAS scores and observational data have been carried out. In the first of these investigations, reported by Gleser and Ulett (9) of Washington University, a psychiatrist rated 151 normal individuals and 40 psychiatric patients with overt anxiety as a prominent symptom after an hour interview with each subject. Ratings were made on an 8-point scale of anxiety-proneness, defined as the tendency for overt anxiety symptoms to appear in a stressful situation. For the total group the correlation between these ratings and MAS scores was .61. Other similar studies by the Washington group (45, 46) with more restricted samples indicated lower coefficients. In a study of 110 male students, involving the judgments of two psychiatrists, the ratings correlated .28 and .29 with MAS scores for the two raters, while the interjudge reliability was .28 (46). All correlations were significant. Lastly the Washington group reported a coefficient of .40 between the ratings of a single psychiatrist and anxiety scores for 141 normal Ss (45).

Operating in a student-counseling-center setting, Hoyt and Magoon (13) asked experienced counselors to rate their own clients ($N = 289$) into one of three groups: high, medium, or low

manifest anxiety. Comparing the mean MAS scores for each of the resulting anxiety groups, an extremely significant chi square was found, while the contingency coefficient, used as an estimate of the r to be expected if the variable had been continuous, was .47. Using a still different criterion of clinical anxiety, Kendall (16) had pairs of nurses rate TB patients on their ward on a 7-point rating scale for each of nine aspects of manifest anxiety. Selecting from the 93 patients so rated the upper and lower 27% in terms of MAS scores, Kendall compared the difference in mean over-all anxiety ratings for the two groups and found it to be statistically insignificant; taking only the upper and lower 13% on the MAS, a very significant t between mean ratings was obtained.

Finally, a study by Buss, Wiener, Durkee, and Baer (2) represents one of the few investigations utilizing hospitalized psychiatric patients. Each of their 64 patients was interviewed and then rated by four psychologists on nine aspects of directly observed and reported anxiety. Correlations between judges' pooled ratings and MAS scores ranged between .16 to .68 for these various aspects; the correlation with an over-all rating of anxiety was .60.

The variation in the training of the raters, opportunity for observation, rating scales, and populations from which the subjects were drawn makes it difficult to formulate any statement about the "validity" of the MAS. To the extent that all of these observational criteria are themselves correlated and are agreed to be clinically acceptable indices of manifest anxiety, there does seem to be some relationship between MAS and observed behavior. These results suggest, then, that the experimental results obtained with the anxiety scale might also hold for groups selected according to clinical criteria. Such studies as have been reported about the performance of clinically selected anxious groups on comparable tasks tend to confirm this suggestion (1, 20, 30, 47).

In addition to the experimental studies of the performance of anxious and non-anxious groups already discussed, a number of other investigations have reported differences in the behavior of anxious and nonanxious Ss, ranging from indications of number of food aversions (31) to performance in problem-solving tasks (21, 49). The exclusion of these many experiments from consideration here, due to the limited purpose of this paper—that of assessing the evidence directly relevant to drive theory—points up what has not always been fully appreciated about this theory. It is an extremely restricted one, referring only to the effects of drive level (rather than all characteristics of anxious and nonanxious individuals) in relatively simple learning situations. The major prediction of the theory, that there is an interaction between anxiety level and task complexity, seems to be fairly well substantiated by experimental evidence, although more exact deductions have either not been tested as yet or have not fared as well. Whether the theory can be successfully applied to more complex situations than those for which it originally seemed appropriate, as some have attempted to do, or whether additional variables can be added to it and thus broaden its usefulness remains for future research to determine.

References

1. BITTERMAN, M. E., & HOLTZMAN, W. H. Conditioning and extinction of the galvanic skin response as a function of anxiety. *J. abnorm. soc. Psychol.*, 1952, **47**, 615–623.

2. BUSS, A. H., WIENER, M., DURKEE, A., & BAER, M. The measurement of anxiety in clinical situations. *J. consult. Psychol.*, 1955, **19**, 125–129.

3. CHILD, I. L. Personality. *Annual Rev. Psychol.*, 1954, **5**, 149–170.

4. DEESE, J., LAZARUS, R. S., & KEENAN, J. Anxiety, anxiety-reduction, and stress in learning. *J. exp. Psychol.*, 1953, **46**, 55–60.

5. ERIKSEN, C. W. Some personality correlates of stimulus generalization under stress. *J. abnorm. soc. Psychol.*, 1954, **49**, 561–565.

6. FARBER, I. E. Anxiety as a drive state. In M. R. Jones, (Ed.), *Nebraska symposium on motivation*. Lincoln, Nebraska; Nebraska Univer. Press, 1954.

7. ———. The role of motivation in verbal learning and performance. *Psychol. Bull.*, 1955, **52**, 311–327.

8. FARBER, I. E., & SPENCE, K. W. Complex learning and conditioning as a function of anxiety. *J. exp. Psychol.*, 1953, **45**, 120–125.

9. GLESER, GOLDINE, & ULETT, G. The Saslow Screening Test as a measure of anxiety-proneness. *J. clin. Psychol.*, 1952, **8**, 279–283.

10. GORDON, W. M., & BERLYNE, D. E. Drive-level and flexibility in paired-associate nonsense-syllable learning. *Quart. J. exp. Psychol.*, 1954, **6**, 181–185.

11. HILGARD, E. R., JONES, L. V., & KAPLAN, S. J. Conditioned discrimination as related to anxiety. *J. exp. Psychol.*, 1951, **42**, 94–99.

12. HOVLAND, C. I. Experimental studies in rote-learning theory: III. Distribution of practice with varying speeds of syllable presentation. *J. exp. Psychol.*, 1938, **23**, 172–190.

13. HOYT, D. P., & MAGOON, T. M. A validation study of the Taylor Manifest Anxiety Scale. *J. clin. Psychol.*, 1954, **10**, 357–361.

14. HUGHES, J. B., II, SPRAGUE, J. L., & BENDIG, A. W. Anxiety level, response alternation, and performance in serial learning. *J. Psychol.*, 1954, **38**, 421–426.

15. HULL, C. L. *Principles of behavior.* New York: Appleton-Century, 1943.

16. KENDALL, E. The validity of Taylor's Manifest Anxiety Scale. *J. consult. Psychol.*, 1954, **18**, 429–432.

17. LAZARUS, R. S., DEESE, J., & HAMILTON, R. Anxiety and stress in learning: the role of intraserial duplication. *J. exp. Psychol.*, 1954, **47**, 111–114.

18. LAZARUS, R. S., DEESE, J., & OSLER, SONIA F. The effects of psychological stress upon performance. *Psychol. Bull.*, 1952, **49**, 293–317.

19. LUCAS, J. D. The interactive effects of anxiety, failure, and interserial duplication. *Amer. J. Psychol.*, 1952, **65**, 59–66.

20. MALMO, R. B., & AMSEL, A. Anxiety-produced interference in serial rote learning with observations on rote learning after partial frontal lobectomy. *J. exp. Psychol.*, 1948, **38**, 89–101.

21. MALTZMAN, I., FOX, J., & MORRISSETT, L., JR. Some effects of manifest anxiety on mental set. *J. exp. Psychol.*, 1953, **46**, 50–54.

22. MANDLER, G., & SARASON, S. B. A study of anxiety and learning. *J. abnorm. soc. Psychol.*, 1952, **47**, 166–173.

23. ———. The effect of prior experience and subjective failure on the evocation of test anxiety. *J. Pers.*, 1953, **21**, 336–341.

24. MATARAZZO, J. D., ULETT, G. A., & SASLOW, G. Human maze performance as a function of increasing levels of anxiety. *J. gen. Psychol.*, 1955, **53**, 79–96.

25. MONTAGUE, E. K. The role of anxiety in serial rote learning. *J. exp. Psychol.*, 1953, **45**, 91–96.

26. RAMOND, C. Anxiety and task as determiners of verbal performance. *J. exp. Psychol.*, 1953, **46**, 120–124.

27. ROSENBAUM, G. Stimulus generalization as a function of experimentally induced anxiety. *J. exp. Psychol.*, 1953, **45**, 35–43.

28. ———. Stimulus generalization as a function of clinical and experimentally induced anxiety. Unpublished doctor's dissertation. State Univer. of Iowa, 1950.

29. SARASON, S. B., MANDLER, G., & CRAIGHILL, P. G. The effect of differential instructions on anxiety and learning. *J. abnorm. soc. Psychol.*, 1952, **47**, 561–565.

30. SCHIFF, E., DOUGAN, C., & WELCH, L. The conditioned PGR and the EEG as indicators of anxiety. *J. abnorm. soc. Psychol.*, 1949, **44**, 549–552.

31. SMITH, W., POWELL, ELIZABETH K., & ROSS, S. Manifest anxiety and food aversions. *J. abnorm. soc. Psychol.*, 1955, **50**, 101–104.

32. SPENCE, K. W. Learning and performance in eyelid conditioning as a function of the intensity of the UCS. *J. exp. Psychol.*, 1953, **45**, 57–63.

33. ———. Current interpretations of learning data and some recent developments in stimulus-response theory. In *Learning theory, personality theory, and clinical research. The Kentucky symposium.* New York: Wiley, 1953.

34. SPENCE, K. W., & BEECROFT, R. S. Differential conditioning and level of anxiety. *J. exp. Psychol.*, 1954, **48**, 399–403.

35. SPENCE, K. W., & FARBER, I. E. Conditioning and extinction as a function of anxiety. *J. exp. Psychol.*, 1953, **45**, 116–119.

36. ———. The relation of anxiety to differential eyelid conditioning. *J. exp. Psychol.*, 1954, **47**, 127–134.

37. SPENCE, K. W., FARBER, I. E., & TAYLOR, ELAINE. The relation of electric shock and anxiety to level of performance in eyelid conditioning. *J. exp. Psychol.*, 1954, **48**, 404–408.

38. SPENCE, K. W., & TAYLOR, JANET A. Anxiety and strength of the UCS as determiners of the amount of eyelid conditioning. *J. exp. Psychol.*, 1951, **42**, 183–188.

39. ———. The relation of conditioned response strength to anxiety in normal, neurotic and psychotic subjects. *J. exp. Psychol.*, 1953, **45**, 265–272.

40. TAYLOR, JANET A. The relationship of anxiety to the conditioned eyelid response. *J. exp. Psychol.*, 1951, **41**, 81–92.

41. ———. A personality scale of manifest anxiety. *J. abnorm. soc. Psychol.*, 1953, **48**, 285–290.

42. TAYLOR, JANET A., & CHAPMAN, J. P. Paired-associate learning as related to anxiety. *Amer. J. Psychol.*, 1955, **68**, 671.

43. TAYLOR, JANET A., & SPENCE, K. W. The relationship of anxiety level to performance in serial learning. *J. exp. Psychol.*, 1952, **44**, 61–64.

44. ———. Conditioning level in behavior disorders. *J. abnorm. soc. Psychol.*, 1954, **49**, 497–502.

45. ULETT, G. A., GLESER, GOLDINE, LAWLER, A., & WINOKUR, G. Psychiatric screening of flying personnel. IV. An experimental investigation of development of an EEG index of anxiety tolerance by means of photic stimulation—its validation by psychological and psychiatric criteria. *USAF Sch. Avia. Med. Proj. Rep.*, Aug., 1952, Proj. No. 21-37-002.

46. ULETT, G. A., GLESER, GOLDINE, STARR, P., HADDOCK, J., LINGLEY, L., & LAWLER, A. Psychiatric screening of flying personnel. V. Further studies towards the development of an electroencephalographic screening technique *USAF Sch. Aviat. Med. Proj. Rep.*, Aug., 1953, Proj. No. 21-0202-007.

47. WELCH, L., & KUBIS, J. The effect of anxiety on the conditioning rate and stability of the PGR. *J. Psychol.*, 1947, **23**, 83–91.

48. WENAR, C. Reaction time as a function of manifest anxiety and stimulus intensity. *J. abnorm. soc. Psychol.*, 1954, **49**, 335–340.

49. WESLEY, E. L. Perseverative behavior in a concept-formation task as a function of manifest anxiety and rigidity. *J. abnorm. soc. Psychol.*, 1953, **48**, 129–134.

MEDIATED GENERALIZATION AND THE INCUBATION EFFECT AS A FUNCTION OF MANIFEST ANXIETY

Martha T. Mednick

One of the earliest and most widely cited studies attempting to verify clinically observed phenomena in the experimental laboratory was reported by Diven (6). In order to test some notions about

Reprinted by permission of the American Psychological Association and the author from the *Journal of Abnormal and Social Psychology*, Vol. 55, 1957.

the nature of anxiety, he conditioned a psychogalvanic response (PGR) to the word "barn" and measured autonomic reactivity to other rural words. Responsivity to the rural words was found to be greater than to a group of nonrural words, and this was considered to be evidence for the generalization of anxiety. In addition, conditioned autonomic activity tended to increase as a direct function of the length of a rest pause preceding extinction. This was called the "incubation effect." White, Cameron, and others (20, 4, 11), in their discussion of anxiety, deal with these aspects of the Diven study at length.

The Diven findings on verbal generalization may be interpreted in terms of recent attempts to explain clinical phenomena on the basis of learning theory. The study may be regarded as an instance of mediated generalization (MG), a concept discussed by Cofer and Foley (5), which may be illustrated, using Diven's verbal stimuli, as follows:

Barn + shock	elevated PGR
Barn	elevated PGR
Cow (a rural word)	Barn elevated PGR

"Barn," the implicit common or mediating term elicited by "cow," elicits an elevated PGR.

MG has been used in attempts to understand the role of covert symbolic processes in the determination of behavior. Dollard and Miller (7) placed considerable emphasis on this process in their discussion of personality development in terms of learning theory. These writers also used the concept of anxiety incorporated into the Hullian system by assuming that an anxiety response has drive properties and contributes to the total drive state of an organism. Some verification of this hypothesis concerning the drive properties of anxiety has been achieved through studies of the performance on learning tasks of human Ss separated on the basis of response defined anxiety by means of extreme scores on the Taylor Manifest Anxiety Scale (MAS) (17). The results of a number of studies have supported predictions based on the assumption that MAS scores are related to drive level (18).

Dollard and Miller argued further that generalization varies directly with drive and, hence, with anxiety. While stimulus generalization (generalization along a physical continuum of similarity) has been shown to vary with primary drive in animal studies (3, 12) and with anxiety (13), such a relationship has not been clearly demonstrated with MG. Lacey (9), replicating Diven's study and results, found that generalization tended to vary directly with MAS scores, but the group differences did not reach significance. The Lacey study must be interpreted with caution since the conditioning procedures utilized were somewhat irregular; the CS-UCS interval was 15 sec., filled with S associating aloud to the CS. This method was utilized in the interest of maintaining S's unawareness of the CS-UCS contingencies.

The incubation effect described above was the other major finding reported by Diven. Bindra and Cameron (1) also studied this effect during the presentation of noxious stimulation rather than under a conditioning and extinction paradigm. These investigators concluded that there appeared to be a genuine incubation effect but that little is known of its exact nature or its relation to other variables.

The present study was an attempt to reproduce Diven's and Lacey's findings with respect to the generalization and incubation of a conditioned autonomic response and to examine the relationship of mediated generalization to manifest anxiety. An emphasis was placed on an empirical choice of generalization stimuli. It should be noted that generalization words were chosen by Diven and Lacey on a rational basis. It was felt that additional work in this area would profit by a pre-experimental demonstration of the associational relationship of the generalization stimuli to the CS by making it possible to order the stimuli along a rough continuum and to attempt to obtain a gradient of MG.

Method

SUBJECTS

Two groups of 45 Ss each were chosen from introductory psychology classes at Northwestern University on the basis of extreme scores on the Heineman form of the MAS (8). Forty-five individuals (15 males and 30 females) receiving scores of 64 and above on the scale were included in the high anxious group (HA), and the 45 Ss scoring 49 or below (35 males and 10 females) were designated as the low anxious group (LA). In addition, three LA and four HA Ss were tested, but because they showed no evidence of conditioning, they were excluded from further consideration. Ss were assigned to the various conditions by a noninvolved person so that E had no knowledge of MAS scores during the experiment.

APPARATUS

Galvanic measures were made from a standard Stoelting polygraph. Basal readings, taken directly from a dial on the instrument, were recorded periodically. At random intervals during the presentation of the experimental stimuli, an artificial resistance of 1000 ohms was thrown into the machine. This provided a standard measuring unit for each record. The verbal stimulus materials were presented to S by means of a tape recorder via earphones. A loud raucous noise which served as the UCS was also presented by means of the tape recorder. A measure of the intensity of the test stimuli revealed no differences between stimuli.

VERBAL STIMULUS MATERIALS

In constructing the stimulus materials, the results of a recent study by Russell and Jenkins (15) were utilized. These investigators administered the 100 words from the Kent-Rosanoff Word Association Test to 1,007 college students. A single association was elicited to each of the words and the frequency of each association determined. For the present study, the word that was chosen as the CS appeared (in varying degrees of frequency of association) as a *response* to a number of different Kent-Rosanoff stimulus words. Thus, the words "dark," "heavy," "soft," and "lamp" all had as a common response the word "light." "Light" was therefore designated as the CS in the present study and the words to which it had been associated as the generalization test words.

TABLE 1. PERCENTAGE OF INDIVIDUALS ASSOCIATING THE WORD "LIGHT" TO GENERALIZATION WORDS

Sample	N	Generalization Words			
		Dark	Lamp	Heavy	Soft
Minnesota	1007	83	63	58	.86
North-western	174	66	59	47	.1
Minnesota [a]					
HA	28	86	50	54	0
LA	28	82	61	57	0
North-western					
HA	25	60	60	32	4
LA	25	64	60	60	0

[a] Personal communication from Dr. Shirley Jahnson, University of Minnesota.

Table 1 presents the percentage of individuals in the Minnesota group who responded to each generalization test word with the word "light." A list of 40 of the 100 Kent-Rosanoff stimulus words containing all of the test words was also administered to a sample of Northwestern University students; the percentage of individuals responding with the word "light" to the test words in this group can also be seen in Table 1. Since it is important to show that HA and LA individuals do not differ from each other with respect to these associational frequencies, the relevant data are included in Table 1. No important differences were found between these two groups.

The stimulus materials used during the conditioning trials consisted of the CS and a list of 24 neutral words (a neutral word being one to which the CS was not given as an association by the Minnesota group). Each of the neutral words was repeated three times in differing orders, while the critical word, "light," was presented on 14 occasions. Thus, the training series consisted of 72 presentations of neutral words and 14 randomly spaced presentations of the CS. The raucous buzzer followed the CS on 9 of the 14 occasions it was presented. This partial reinforcement procedure was followed for two reasons: as an attempt to prolong extinction, and to allow the trials on which the CS was presented without the UCS to serve as a test for conditioning. The test stimulus list, used for measures of generalization and extinction, consisted of the CS, the four generalization stimuli, and three neutral stimuli. This series was repeated eight times with the order of the four generalization words and one of the neutral words ("square") being counterbalanced so as to avoid positional effects. The remaining two neutral words were included so as to increase the number of

words heard by S between the other words. The time between the presentation of each word in both the conditioning and test series varied from 8 to 12 secs., thus allowing some time for return of S's response to a basal level.

CONDITIONING TRIALS

The Ss in all groups received the same conditioning procedure. The experiment was conducted in a semi-soundproof room that offered relative freedom from distraction. The earphones effectively eliminated other distracting noises. Each S was seated in a comfortable broadarmed easy chair with electrodes and earphones attached to him. Initial instructions, designed to acquaint S with the nature of the apparatus, were given by E. A cloth screen shielded the apparatus from S's view. Additional instructions informing S about the stimuli to be presented were on tape and heard by S over the earphones. These indicated that a buzzer and words were to be presented at various intervals and that S's task was merely to remain quiet and listen since his physiological reactions were being studied. No mention was made of the relationship of the buzzer to the appearance of any specific word.

Following the instructions, 15 "adaptation" words were presented to allow S to adjust to the apparatus before conditioning was attempted. These adaptation words were immediately followed by the conditioning series.

TEST-EXTINCTION TRIALS

Each of the two anxiety groups was divided at random into three subgroups for the extinction procedure. One subgroup (Condition I) underwent a regular extinction procedure immediately following the conditioning series. There was no interruption between training and extinction, no additional instructions were given, and Ss remained attached to the apparatus. The second subgroup (Condition II) had the electrodes and the earphones removed with instructions from E that they would be allowed to rest; S remained in the chair with E seated out of sight behind the screen. After a lapse of 10 min., S was reattached to the apparatus for the extinction procedure. The Ss were readapted to the point where deflections had mainly ceased before the tape recording was again turned on. The third subgroup of Ss (Condition III) was allowed to leave following training and instructed to return exactly 24 hrs. later for the remainder of the experiment. Prior to his final dismissal, each S was asked to report whether he knew which word had been followed by the buzzer.

Results

Raw ohms resistance data were obtained from the records by measuring the heights of galvanic deflections, using the 1000 ohm artificial deflection as the measuring unit. Following the method suggested by Lacey and Siegal (10), ohms resistance was then transformed into conductance units, micromhos (M), by use of the formula, $M = 10^6 (1/r)$. Due to the skewed nature of the data, median measures and appropriate nonparametric statistics were used throughout the analyses. In cases where analysis of variance by ranks was used, the obtained chi-square values were converted to F values (19).

As noted above, there were unequal proportions of males and females in the two anxiety groups so that the anxiety and sex variables were confounded. In order to evaluate the possible effects of sex on conditioning, subgroups of 23 males and 23 females equated for MAS

scores were compared as to the amount of conditioning demonstrated. The differences were not significant (chi square = 1.8). There was thus no evidence that sex was a variable influencing conditioning in this study.

Another preliminary analysis was made in order to see whether the three incubation groups were equally conditioned before the commencement of extinction. An analysis of variance by ranks demonstrated that these groups did not differ significantly ($F = .848$).

It should also be noted that of the 90 Ss, 89 were able to state that "light" had been the word followed by the buzzer.

CONDITIONING

The responsivity to the five conditioning test trials (those occasions on which the CS was not accompanied by the buzzer) represented a measure of conditioning. As can be seen from Fig. 1, the HA

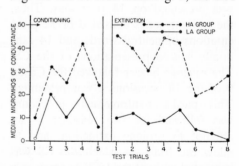

FIG. 1. Median amplitude of conditioned responses at each test trial during conditioning and during immediate extinction (extinction data for condition I only).

group responded with greater amplitude on all test trials than did the LA group. A total conditioning score for each S was obtained by summing the amplitudes of all five of his conditioned responses (CRs) during training. The differences between groups in total scores, evaluated by means of chi square, were significant (chi square = 4.8, $p < .05$ for 1 df).

GENERALIZATION

The tests for generalization were based on the amplitude data of the first extinction series because of the great increase in the number of response failures in the later series. The word "square" was used as the neutral stimulus in all comparisons since the order of presentation of this neutral word was counterbalanced. As may be seen in Fig. 2, the median

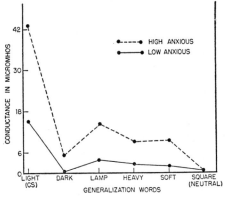

FIG. 2. Median amplitude of response to each word for HA and LA Ss.

amplitude for the test words tended to be higher than for the neutral word in both groups. With respect to the degree to which the test words were associated with the CS "light," the most strongly associated word "dark" elicited less responsivity than would be predicted on the basis of association alone. The remaining three stimuli roughly followed the expected pattern, with "lamp" having the greatest reactivity.

In order to test the significance of the observed differences in responsiveness between the individual words, the data for all 90 Ss were combined and the differences in reactivity to the test words evaluated by means of chi square. The resulting values are reported in Table 2. All the associated words elicited sig-

nificantly greater reactivity than did the neutral word "square," thus demonstrating that generalization had taken place.

TABLE 2. CHI-SQUARE ANALYSES BETWEEN WORDS FOR ALL Ss COMBINED
(All at 1 df)

Word Pair	χ^2	p
Light-Lamp	17.28	<.001
Lamp-Dark	5.28	<.05
Lamp-Heavy	2.78	n.s.
Lamp-Soft	2.37	n.s.
Dark-Square	4.65	<.05
Heavy-Square	10.32	<.01
Soft-Square	12.00	<.01

Turning to the relative performance of the two groups, examination of Fig. 2 reveals that the HA group showed consistently greater median amplitudes than the LA group. In order to obtain a total generalization score, the amplitudes of responses to all four test words were summed for each S. A chi square with respect to this overall score demonstrated the HA group to have significantly more generalization reactivity than the LA group (chi square = 9.3, $p < .05$ for 3 df).

Since the PGR amplitude of the HA Ss was significantly greater than the LA group during conditioning, this fact might be invoked to explain the obtained differences in generalization. In order to see whether these differences in generalization between the HA and LA groups could be demonstrated independently of this initial difference in conditioning level, two subgroups of 24 Ss each, one from the HA and one from the LA group, were matched on the basis of their total amplitude score in conditioning. A chi-square analysis between these subgroups of total generalization scores proved to be significant (chi square = 14.96, $p < .01$ for 2 df).

A final comparison was made among the incubation groups. These three groups, it will be recalled, all received identical training and differed only in the amount of time allowed to lapse before commencing with the regular test-extinction procedure. As previously mentioned, it was demonstrated that these groups, referred to as Condition I (no rest interval), Condition II (10-min. rest interval), and Condition III (24-hr.

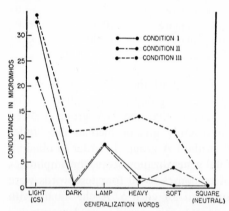

FIG. 3. Median amplitude of response to each word for each condition, HA and LA Ss combined.

interval) were equally responsive at the end of training; any subsequent differences are thus attributable to the rest-interval variable. Fig. 3 summarizes the generalization data of these three conditions for the HA and LA groups combined. An analysis of variance by ranks, testing the differences between Conditions I, II, and III, was significant ($F = 15.0$, $p < .01$ for 2 and 8 df). Inspection of Fig. 3 shows that this significant difference may be attributed to the consistently greater amplitude of Condition III, Conditions I and II being more or less similar at each of the generalization test points. It seemed possible that the

amount of incubation time might affect the HA Ss differently from the LA Ss. The same test between incubation conditions was therefore repeated for the LA and HA groups separately. For the HA group, the difference between Conditions I, II, and III did not reach significance ($F = .455$), but significance was reached for LA Ss ($F = 8.5$, $p < .05$ for 2 and 8 df). The significance of differences between conditions reported above could thus be traced in large part to differences in the LA group.

EXTINCTION

The generalization data reported above represented the first of the eight series of test trials. The nature of all eight series makes it possible to follow the extinction of the CR. Only extinction of responses to the CS will be described since the test words extinguished very rapidly following the first series. Table 3 presents the median PGR amplitude at each extinction series for the CS for all groups and subgroups in the study. When the total HA and LA groups are considered, it may be seen that the HA group tended to maintain greater responsivity than the LA group until both groups finally demonstrated a median responsivity of zero. This greater responsivity was found to some degree in all three extinction conditions, but was most marked in Condition I where extinction immediately followed training. It might also be noted that contrary to the other conditions, the median PGR amplitude of the Condition I HA Ss did not approach zero by the end of the series, indicating that the CR did not completely extinguish.

Discussion

The results of this study confirm Diven's and Lacey's findings with respect to generalization. An inspection of

TABLE 3. MEDIAN AMPLITUDE AT EACH EXTINCTION SERIES FOR
INCUBATION AND ANXIETY SUBGROUPS

	Extinction Series							
	1	2	3	4	5	6	7	8
Cond. I								
LA	10.0	12.0	7.5	13.0	13.5	5.0	3.5	1.0
HA	45.0	40.0	30.0	44.0	42.5	19.5	23.0	28.0
Total	32.5	22.0	13.0	28.0	23.0	6.0	13.0	10.0
Cond. II								
LA	19.0	11.5	23.0	12.0	7.0	2.5	3.5	0
HA	50.0	21.0	9.5	0	9.5	0	0	0
Total	21.5	13.0	19.0	8.0	8.0	0	0	0
Cond. III								
LA	37.0	17.0	8.0	9.0	3.5	0	0	0
HA	29.0	25.5	11.5	8.0	2.5	0	0	0
Total	34.0	22.0	9.0	9.0	4.0	0	0	0
Total Group								
LA	15.0	12.5	9.0	11.0	8.0	4.5	2.0	0
HA	43.0	33.5	20.5	17.5	10.5	1.0	0	0

the generalization data also seem to indicate that reactivity followed a rough gradient, i.e., autonomic responsivity varied directly with the degree of association of the test stimuli to the CS ("light").

Turning to the conditioning data, some comment may be made regarding the conditioning curves themselves. Although it is apparent that conditioning took place, the curves (Fig. 1) are irregular, responsivity being less at the end than in the middle of training. Such generally declining response curves have also been reported by Bitterman and Holtzman (2) and may be at least partly a function of adaptation. In the present study, an explanation in terms of the training procedure also suggested itself. It will be recalled that the CS was presented alone without the buzzer on irregularly spaced trials during training. Thus, conditioning test Trial 1 followed one UCS;

two presentations of the UCS intervened between Trial 1 and Trial 2, one UCS between Trials 2 and 3, three between Trials 3 and 4, and one between Trials 4 and 5. Trials 2 and 4, consequently, had two and three UCS presentations immediately preceding them, whereas Trials 3 and 5 had only one. Inspection of Fig. 1 reveals that the irregularity is contributed to by a decline in responsivity on Trials 3 and 5. It is possible that the decline of responsivity on these trials was at least partly related to their having fewer intervening presentations of the UCS; that is, presentation of the CS alone might have acted as an extinction trial, the effects of extinction still being noticeable when only one presentation of the UCS intervened between two test trials.

With respect to the anxiety variable, previous research using the MAS has shown that HA Ss exhibit both a higher level of performance in conditioning and extinction and higher gradients of SG (2, 18, 13). To the extent that SG and MG are affected by the same variables, HA Ss were expected to show more MG than LA Ss. The expected conditioning and extinction differences were found, and the expectation with respect to MG was also confirmed. It is particularly of interest, in view of the groups' differences in conditioning, that generalization differences were sustained between HA and LA subgroups equated for conditioning performance level. This supports the Dollard and Miller treatment of MG and SG as subsidiaries of the class of phenomena called generalization.

The extinction data of the group as a whole are somewhat at variance with those of other investigators (2) who reported consistently greater PGR responsivity during extinction for HA Ss than LA Ss. In the present case, this difference held up only through the fifth extinction series, after which it diminished sharply. However, it is important to note that Group I was the only group receiving immediate extinction and hence is the only one directly comparable to those of the earlier studies. An examination of Fig. 1 reveals that under Condition I, HA Ss showed greater responsivity throughout and also more resistance to extinction than the LA Ss. This result, then, supports the earlier finding. The data also suggest that an unsuspected effect of the rest interval was to speed extinction for the HA group and thus diminish the differences between the two anxiety conditions.

The incubation of anxiety has been accepted as a fairly meaningful and reliable clinical phenomenon. If an individual learns an anxiety reaction with respect to a particular stimulus situation and after a long interval returns, as it were, to the scene of the provocation, the anxiety is thought of as becoming more and more enhanced with the passage of time. As indicated, there is some experimental evidence to support the assertion of such an effect. However, the findings of this study are not completely in line with this contention. In keeping with others' results, a 24-hr. interval between training and extinction operated to increase galvanic responsivity. This effect was short-lived, however, lasting only for the first extinction series. The 10-min. interval did not result in any PGR increase. This suggests only that recovery from adaptation may be involved and that a 10-min. interval is an insufficient amount of time for the recovery to show its effect.

MG has been demonstrated to be useful in the experimental study of learning and thinking (16). The main finding of this study, the demonstration of a gradient of MG and its relationship to manifest anxiety, indicates that this may also be a useful concept in the study of pathological disturbances of thinking and learning.

Summary

The present study was designed to investigate the phenomena of mediated generalization and the incubation effect. An investigation was also made of the relationship of mediated generalization to level of manifest anxiety as measured by the Taylor Manifest Anxiety Scale (MAS).

Two groups of 45 Ss each were chosen on the basis of extreme scores on the MAS. A conditioned PGR was first established by repeated pairings of a critical word (CS) with a raucous buzzer. Tests of mediated generalization were made following training, using as generalization stimuli, words to which the CS was associated as determined by free associations of a standardization group. In order to investigate the incubation effect the *S*s were divided following training into three subgroups differing in the length of the rest interval between conclusion of training and the institution of extinction trials (immediate extinction, 10-min. interval, and 24-hr. interval).

The results indicated heightened responsivity towards words associated with the CS, thus indicating that mediated generalization had taken place. It was also found that extreme MAS scores were directly related to the magnitude of mediated generalization responsivity. In agreement with reports of other investigators, level of manifest anxiety was found to be directly related to conditioning responsivity as well as to resistance to extinction.

Increased PGR reactivity was found following the 24-hr. pre-extinction interval (i.e., an incubation effect), but the influence of this effect was short-lived being confined to the early part of extinction. The 10-min. delay prior to extinction did not result in galvanic activity which was significantly greater than that found with the immediate extinction condition.

References

1. BINDRA, D., & CAMERON, L. Changes in experimentally produced anxiety with the passage of time: incubation effect. *J. exp. Psychol.*, 1953, **45**, 197–203.

2. BITTERMAN, M. E., & HOLTZMAN, W. H. Conditioning and extinction of the galvanic skin response as a function of anxiety. *J. abnorm. soc. Psychol.*, 1952, **47**, 615–623.

3. BROWN, J. S. The generalization of approach responses as a function of stimulus intensity and strength of motivation. *J. comp. Psychol.*, 1942, **33**, 209–226.

4. CAMERON, N., & MAGARET, ANN. *Behavior pathology.* Cambridge, Mass.: Riverside Press, 1951.

5. COFER, N., & FOLEY, J. P. Mediated generalization and the interpretation of verbal behavior: I. Prolegomena. *Psychol. Rev.*, 1942, **49**, 513–540.

6. DIVEN, K. E. Certain determinants in the conditioning of anxiety reactions. *J. Psychol.*, 1937, **3**, 291–308.

7. DOLLARD, J., & MILLER, W. *Personality and psychotherapy.* New York: McGraw-Hill, 1950.

8. HEINEMAN, C. E. A forced choice form of the Taylor Anxiety Scale. *J. consult. Psychol.*, 1953, **17**, 447–454.

9. LACEY, J. I., SMITH, R. L., & GREEN, B. A. Use of conditioned autonomic responses in the study of anxiety. *Psychosom. Med.*, 1955, **17**, 208–217.

10. LACEY, O. L., & SIEGAL, P. S. An analysis of the unit of measurement of the galvanic skin response. *J. exp. Psychol.*, 1949, **39**, 122–127.

11. MURRAY, H. A. *Explorations in personality.* New York: Oxford, 1938.

12. ROSENBAUM, G. Temporal gradients of response strength with two levels of motivation. *J. exp. Psychol.*, 1951, **41**, 261–267.

13. ———. Stimulus generalization as a function of clinical and experimentally induced anxiety. Unpublished doctoral dissertation. State Univer. of Iowa, 1950.

14. ———. Stimulus generalization as a function of level of experimentally produced anxiety. *J. exp. Psychol.*, 1953, **45**, 35–43.

15. RUSSELL, W. A., & JENKINS, J. J. The complete Minnesota norms for responses to 100 words from the Kent-Rosanoff Word Association Test. The role of language in behavior. *ONR Tech. Rep.*, No. 11, 1954.

16. RUSSELL, W. A., & STORMS, L. H. Implicit verbal chaining in paired associate learning. The role of language in behavior. *ONR Tech. Rep.*, No. 10, 1954.

17. TAYLOR, JANET A. A personality test of manifest anxiety. *J. abnorm. soc. Psychol.* 1953, **48**, 285–290.

18. ———. Drive theory and manifest anxiety. *Psychol. Bull.* 1956, **53**, 303–320.

19. WALKER, H. M., & LEV, J. *Statistical inference.* New York: Henry Holt, 1953.

20. WHITE, R. W. *The abnormal personality.* New York: Ronald Press, 1948.

THE RELATION OF ANXIETY (DRIVE) LEVEL
TO PERFORMANCE IN COMPETITIONAL AND
NONCOMPETITIONAL PAIRED–ASSOCIATES LEARNING

Kenneth W. Spence, I. E. Farber, and Howard H. McFann

Conditioning studies involving some form of noxious stimulation have revealed that level of performance is a function of the intensity of the unconditioned stimulus (13, 17). One interpretation that has been given of this finding is that the more noxious the stimulus the higher is the level of the emotional response (state of emotionality) of S (21, 22). Level of emotionality, in turn, is one of the factors assumed to determine the total effective drive level of the organism. This concept of drive level or D is one of the important intervening variables determining response strength in S-R theory.

Another line of evidence indicating that noxious stimulation and its after-effects determine level of response are the studies (3, 15, 16) which have shown that the level of consummatory

Reprinted by permission of the American Psychological Association and the authors from the *Journal of Experimental Psychology*, Vol. 52, 1956.

response (eating, drinking) is significantly increased for a period of time if Ss are shocked just prior to being placed in the food or water situation. These investigators have interpreted their findings as reflecting the perseveration of the emotional state produced by the preceding shocks, which is assumed to increase response strength through increase in level of D.

Similar motivational properties have been demonstrated in the case of non-noxious stimuli which, in the previous history of S, have been associated with a noxious stimulus. Mowrer (12) and Miller (10) have assumed that such prior training establishes a conditioned emotional (fear) response to the previously neutral stimulus. Studies such as those of Amsel (1), Kalish (8), and Brown, Kalish, and Farber (4) have demonstrated that the presence of these conditioned fear arousing stimuli can intensify coincident stimulus-response tendencies.

Accepting the notion that the degree of emotionality of S, produced either by unconditioned or conditioned stimuli, affects level of response, and interpreting this effect within the framework of our theoretical system as reflecting level of D, a series of experiments was initiated a number of years ago which attempted to manipulate degree of emotionality in a quite different manner (20, 21, 22, 23). In the first of these studies (23) a test was developed which was aimed at differentiating Ss in terms of the degree to which they admitted having overt symptoms of emotionality. The test was in the form of a personality inventory, the items of which were judged by clinical psychologists to differentiate persons in terms of their emotional responsiveness. Unfortunately, the scale was called a test of "manifest anxiety," which has led to all manner of investigations designed to ascertain whether it is a valid test of *real* anxiety! We shall continue to refer to it as an anxiety scale (A scale) but with no assumption other than that it differentiates degrees of emotional responsiveness and level of D.[1]

Turning now to the role of drive in learning situations, the effect of variations in the level of D will, according to the theory, depend upon the nature of the learning task. As has been pointed out on a number of occasions (18, 19), the implications of a theory are a joint function of the laws or hypothetical relations postulated in the theory *and* what are called the initial or boundary conditions of the behavior situation. In simple classical conditioning, in which there is but a single response tendency, an increase in the strength of D results in a higher level of E, and hence implies a stronger response $(R = f(E) = f(H \times D))$. In more complex learning situations involving a hierarchy of competing responses, however, the effect of drive level variation will depend upon this initial response hierarchy and the relative position in it of the response that is to be learned.

In general, the greater the number and strength of the competing, incorrect responses relative to the correct response, the more detrimental should a high drive be to performance level, at least in the early stages of learning. Making use of the known fact that anticipatory and perseverative tendencies in serial learning produce strong competing response tendencies, a test of this implication has been made in three studies, one involving a verbal maze (24), one a stylus maze (6) and one rote serial learning (11). All three experiments provided evidence supporting the implication that the high-anxious Ss would be inferior to Ss scoring at the low end of the scale.

In these serial learning experiments, however, one has little or no knowledge of the relative strength of the correct

---

[1] One sort of criticism of our experiments has revealed a serious misunderstanding of their purpose and underlying logic. It is that since there is not independent evidence that the test really measures emotionality, and there is evidence that the test scores correlate with other personality indices, it cannot legitimately be *assumed* that differences on the test reflect differences in drive level (D). To repeat again the reasoning of these experiments, the *hypothesis* is set up that the test scores reflect differences in emotionality and hence differences in D. This hypothesis is then tested by deriving, with the aid of other parts of the theory of learning, implications concerning differences to be expected in conditioning and various other types of learning situations. Confirmation of these deductions lends support to the theory, including the hypothesis about the relation of the anxiety scale scores to D. Obviously they don't prove the theory, just as any theory is never proved in science.

and incorrect S-R tendencies. On the assumption that the incorrect, competing responses are based on theoretical remote associations or generalized response tendencies, it is possible, as Montague (11) did, to vary the similarity of the nonsense syllables employed, and thus to manipulate, theoretically, the strength and number of competing S-R tendencies. We were interested, however, in designing a learning situation in which it would be possible to manipulate in some better known manner the strengths of both the correct and the competing, incorrect S-R tendencies. Minimization of the latter would provide a situation in which Ss with high drive level would be expected to perform better than those with a low drive, whereas if we maximized the relative strengths and number of competing, incorrect S-R tendencies, the opposite result should obtain. The present study describes two such learning situations and presents the findings of a separate experiment with each.

Theoretical Analysis of Paired-Associates Learning

The situation selected for the experiments was paired-associates learning. In this type of learning situation, S is required to learn to respond to a stimulus word or nonsense syllable by anticipating a paired response syllable or word. By using different orders of presentation of the paired words the development of remote associations, so prominent in serial learning, is minimized.

Paired-associates learning may be conceived as consisting of a set or series of more or less isolated S-R associations or habit tendencies ($S_1 - R_A$, $S_2 - R_B$, $S_3 - R_C$, etc.) that become established as a consequence of the training procedure. Theoretically, if these stimulus-response items were entirely isolated from one another so that the only existent associative tendencies were between each stimulus word and its own paired response word, then Ss with relatively high drive would be expected to perform at a higher level in learning such a series than Ss with a lower drive strength. Essentially, the situation is similar to that of classical conditioning, except that instead of one S-R tendency being conditioned, a number of different S-R tendencies are being established simultaneously. While it may not be possible to obtain complete isolation among the S-R items, it is known how, on the basis of existing experimental knowledge, to approach this limiting condition with its minimal competition among S-Rs. Similarly, it is known how to vary the conditions so as to increase the amount of competition among them.

One of the most important factors determining the degree of isolation of the paired S-Rs is that of generalization, which, in turn, is a function of the degree of synonymity and/or formal similarity among the stimulus and response words. If this factor is minimal, there will be little or no generalized tendency for S_1 to elicit other responses than R_A, S_2 to elicit responses other than R_B, etc.

A second factor that enters into such paired-associates learning is the strength of the associative connection between any stimulus word and any response word. As the result of past experience, words tend to become associated with other words to varying degrees, and for each word the hierarchy of associative strengths tends to be similar for individuals in the same culture. Such differences in the strength of associative connections between words in a language are exemplified by the word association data of Kent and Rosanoff (9).

It is readily apparent that one may also take advantage of this factor to control not only the extent to which each stimulus word will tend to elicit its own paired word but also will tend to elicit response words other than the one with which it is paired. Thus, we could pair each stimulus word with a response word with which it tends, as the result of past verbal experiences, to be highly associated and, at the same time, make sure that the associative connections between each stimulus word and each of the non-paired response words are low or non-existent. Such a condition would obviously help further to minimize the likelihood of competing response tendencies of any appreciable strength for each stimulus-response pair. A list of paired associates in which the paired words have high initial associative connections and in which the degree of synonymity of the stimulus and response words is minimal would thus provide a learning situation in which high-drive (high-anxious) Ss should perform at a higher level than low-drive (low-anxious) Ss.

Contrariwise, we may construct a paired-associates list with a high amount of competition in which the opposite finding should occur; that is, the high-anxious Ss should perform more poorly than the low-anxious. There are a number of different ways in which such competition may be introduced, one of which will be described here.

Beginning with four stimulus-response pairs having high associative connections, the remaining eight pairs are formed as follows. For each of the four original stimulus words two synonymous stimulus words are selected and paired with response words with which they have little or no associative strength. Thus, for each triad of synonymous

stimulus words, two are paired with response words with which they are weakly associated, if at all, and one is paired with a highly associated word, as follows:

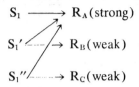

$$S_1 \longrightarrow R_A \text{(strong)}$$
$$S_1' \dashrightarrow R_B \text{(weak)}$$
$$S_1'' \dashrightarrow R_C \text{(weak)}$$

The stimulus words S_1' and S_1'', being highly synonymous with S_1, also have a high initial associative connection with R_A. As a result, the learning of the pairs involving these stimuli, i.e., $S_1' - R_B$ and $S_1'' - R_C$ would involve a strong competing response tendency, one, in fact, that is stronger than that to its paired response. In the case of these paired words, then, we would expect the anxious Ss to be poorer than the non-anxious.

The implications of the theory with respect to the relative performance of high and low drive Ss on the four stimulus-response pairs of the list that have strong original connections (e.g., $S_1 - R_A$) are more involved. At the very beginning of learning the performance of the high-drive Ss should be superior to that of low-drive Ss, just as in the case of the first, noncompetitional list. If properly chosen, these stimulus words should have little if any initial associative tendencies to R_B or R_C. However, once Ss begin to learn the other pairs, (e.g., $S_1' - R_B$, $S_1'' - R_C$) there should develop a generalized habit for S_1 to evoke R_B and R_C (principle of generalization of associative or habit strength). Since the excitatory potential (E) from S_1 to these responses (R_B and R_C) would reach super-threshold values sooner for the high-drive group than for the low-drive group we should expect these responses to intrude or block the correct response (R_A) earlier (and more frequently) in the case of the high-drive group. Thus, we would be led to predict that the initial superiority of the high-drive group on the strongly associated pairs should tend to disappear during training. Evidence with respect to these theoretical expectations was sought in the following experiments.

Experiment I

Since all of our previous experimental studies with verbal learning had involved comparison of high- and low-anxious Ss, in situations in which there were strong competing responses, we were interested, first, in testing the prediction that a noncompetitive verbal learning situation would reveal a superior performance on the part of high-anxious Ss, as has been found in the case of simple classical conditioning. Accordingly, Exp. I involved a paired-associates list in which there was a minimum of competition among the paired words and in which the associative connections between the paired words were initially high.

METHOD

Subjects. The Ss were 20 men and 20 women enrolled in an introductory psychology course, an equal number of each sex having scored in either the upper 20% or lower 20% of scores on the A scale. All were naive with respect to the experimental task.

Apparatus. A Hull-type memory drum was employed to present the lists of paired-associates learning material. The successive stimulus items of each list were exposed every 4 sec., including

TABLE 1. NONCOMPETITIVE AND COMPETITIVE TEST LISTS
USED IN EXP. I AND II

Noncompetitive: Exp. I		Competitive: Exp. II	
Stimulus	Response	Stimulus	Response
Adept	Skilful	*Barren	Fruitless
Barren	Fruitless	Arid	Grouchy
Complete	Thorough	Dessert	Leading
Distant	Remote	*Little	Minute
Empty	Vacant	Petite	Yonder
Frigid	Arctic	Undersized	Wholesome
Insane	Crazy	*Roving	Nomad
Little	Minute	Gypsy	Opaque
Mammoth	Oversize	Migrant	Agile
Pious	Devout	*Tranquil	Placid
Roving	Nomad	Quiet	Double
Stubborn	Headstrong	Serene	Headstrong
Tranquil	Quiet		
Urgent	Pressing		
Wicked	Evil		

* S-R terms in the competitive test list that were taken from the noncompetitive list of Exp. I.

a 1.67-sec. anticipation interval, with a 4-sec. rest interval between successive presentations of a list. The practice list (15 paired nouns) was used to acquaint S with the procedure and to provide maximal and minimal performance criteria. The test list, shown in Table 1, consisted of 15 pairs of two-syllable adjectives from Haagen's word list (7), and was constructed in such a manner as to maximize closeness (strength) of association between paired stimulus-response words. Meaningful intralist associations and formal similarities were minimized. Thus, no beginning letter or suffix was repeated within the stimulus or response list and no stimulus-response pair began with the same letter or had the same suffix. Both lists were presented to S in three different orders to avoid serial learning.

Procedure. All Ss served individually under the same experimental conditions. Immediately following the reading of the instructions describing the method of learning, S received six trials on the practice list followed by a 2-min. rest period. During this rest period S was moved to a seat before the screen containing the drum with the test list. Following this interval, S was run to a criterion of two successive perfect trials on the test list.

On each trial, correct anticipations, errors, and overt intrusions were recorded. An error consisted in either making no response or an incorrect response (an overt intrusion) during the anticipation interval.

The Ss were discarded on the basis of their scores on the practice list if they failed to make a single correct response, or if they made 50 or more correct responses during the six practice trials. Only one S was discarded on the basis of

these minimal and maximal performance criteria, and he was replaced by another.

RESULTS

The mean number of correct anticipations made on the practice list was 14.0 for the high-anxious group and 13.7 for the low-anxious group. These values are to be compared with a mean of 14.7 for a more extensive sample of 267 high-anxious Ss that have been run on the same list and a mean of 13.8 for a sample of 255 low-anxious Ss. Thus, it will be seen that the difference between the present samples in favor of the high group is somewhat smaller than in the more extensive samples.

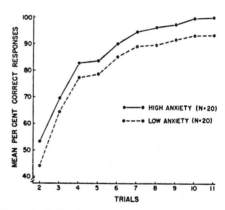

FIG. 1. Paired-associates learning as a function of anxiety under conditions of minimal interpair competition and high initial stimulus-response associative strength.

Learning curves on the test list for the high- and low-anxious groups in terms of the mean percentage of correct anticipations made on Trials 2–11 are presented in Fig. 1. As may be seen, the curves rise rapidly, with that for the high-anxious group starting and remaining consistently above the curve for the low group.

Data on learning in terms of errors and trials to the criterion of mastery are presented in Table 2. It will be observed that the high-anxious Ss were superior to the low-anxious Ss in the case of both measures. The results of an analysis of variance gave Fs for the anxiety variable which were significant at the .01 level for the trial measure and the .05 level in the case of the error measure. In both instances the Anxiety $\times$ Sex interaction was less than one, indicating that the difference between high- and low-anxious Ss held for both sexes.

TABLE 2. NONCOMPETITIVE TEST LIST

Group	N	Trials		Errors	
		Mean	SD	Mean	SD
High-anxious	20	8.95	2.75	20.95	10.49
Low-anxious	20	12.60	4.67	32.50	20.91

Experiment II

In contrast to Exp. I, a portion of the list of paired associates used in Exp. II involved learning in which competing response tendencies initially stronger than the correct responses were present. Our theory would lead us to expect that the high-anxious Ss would perform more poorly than the low-anxious Ss on these paired associates.

METHOD

Subjects. The Ss were all men, 10 of whom scored in the lowest 20% of scores on the A scale and 9 of whom were above the 80th percentile. Three additional Ss failed to meet the criteria established for the learning of the practice list and were discarded.

Apparatus and procedure. The memory drum, instructions, and practice list were exactly the same as those used in the first experiment. Likewise, the procedure was identical, the Ss first receiving six trials on the practice list and then being shifted to the test list, which they were required to learn to a criterion of two successive perfect trials.

The test list of paired adjectives employed in this experiment is given in Table 1. As may be seen, it consisted in part of four paired adjectives (marked by an asterisk) based on the test list of Exp. I. The associative connections between the words of these pairs were very high. For each of the stimulus words of these four pairs two synonymous adjectives were selected as stimulus words by means of Haagen's study. Each of these eight stimulus words was paired with an adjective with which it had little or no associative connection. The data for these two different kinds of paired associates (those with high and those with low associative connections) were treated separately, since the theoretical predictions with respect to them differ.

RESULTS

The high-anxious Ss averaged 15.8 correct anticipations on the practice lists as compared with 14.2 for the low Ss. This difference in favor of the high group was somewhat larger than that for the more extensive samples (see Results section for Exp. I). The difference is not, however, a significant one.

Figure 2 presents learning curves for the high and low groups in terms of the percentage of correct anticipations made on successive pairs of trials. The two lower curves represent the performance on the eight weakly associated word pairs that had strong competing responses, while the two upper curves are for the four pairs in which the words were initially highly associated.

As our theory predicted, the performance curve for the highly anxious Ss was below that of the low-anxious Ss in the case of the eight word pairs that involved competition. However, the difference in number of errors for Trials 2–23 was not significant ($t = 1.56$). In accord with the deduction concerning the four stimulus-response pairs of the list that had high associative connections, we find,

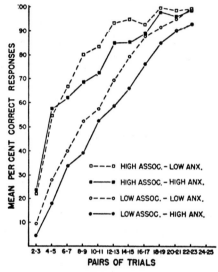

Fig. 2. Paired-associates learning as a function of anxiety under conditions of high interpair competition. Word pairs of both high- and low-association value were interspersed within the same training list, but were analyzed separately.

as predicted, that the performance of the high-anxious Ss was initially superior to that of the low-anxious Ss, although the difference was very slight, and, also, that there was a reversal later in the learning. It should be noted, further, that the differences between the two groups of Ss for the two types of paired associates were opposite in nature at the *beginning* of learning. Thus, the high-anxious Ss did better than the low-anxious Ss on the four word pairs involving no competition

at the same time that they were doing more poorly on the eight word pairs involving competition.

A final set of data pertains to the number of trials required to learn the total list. This measure was, of course, determined primarily by the eight difficult word pairs involving competition. The mean for the low-anxious group was 18.4, with that for the high group being 23.3. The difference was significant at the .05 level ($t = 2.48$). Thus we see that, whereas the high-anxious Ss showed the superior performance in Exp. I, the low-anxious Ss were superior in Exp. II.

Discussion

From a theoretical standpoint the most interesting finding of this investigation is that the high-anxious Ss performed in a superior manner to the low-anxious Ss in Exp. I. In our previous studies that have involved learning situations more complex than classical conditioning (e.g., 7, 28), high-anxious Ss performed more poorly than low-anxious Ss. We ascribed these results to the presence of strong competing responses (anticipatory and perseverative tendencies) that develop in serial learning tasks. In the first paired-associates task reported here (Exp. I) such competing responses were minimized by controlling for generalization as described in the introductory section. The fact that the correct responses had high initial associative connections with their respective stimuli also assured a greater initial differential, *with higher drive strength,* between the excitatory strengths of the correct responses and the excitatory strengths of any incorrect, competing responses, i.e., $E_+ - E_- = D(H_+ - E_-)$. The fact that the high-anxious Ss were superior right from the start is in agreement with our analysis. Furthermore, it may be predicted that if the associative connections between the stimulus and response items were low or nonexistent at the beginning of training (and providing competition were minimized by the methods described), there would be no initial difference between anxious and nonanxious groups, but one would develop in favor of the anxious Ss as learning progressed.

On the other hand, when strong response tendencies in competition with the correct response were provided by means of the methods used in Exp. II, this advantage of high- over low-anxious Ss in paired-associates learning disappeared and the low-anxious Ss actually required significantly fewer trials ($P = .05$) to learn than did the high-anxious Ss.

One final series of comments concerns the interpretation of these studies relating anxiety to learning that has been offered by Child (5). Child would explain the inferior performance of anxious Ss in situations involving competing responses elicited by the task stimuli in terms of task-irrelevant responses made to the anxiety, i.e., irrelevant responses that interfere with performance in the task. Although Child has expressed the view that our interpretation had overlooked the role of such responses, we were actually well aware of such a possibility, and have for some time been interested in the role of such task-interfering responses, which we think of as being elicited by the drive stimuli (s_D) resulting from the emotional (drive) state.[2]

That such distracting, task-interfering

responses will under certain conditions occur we have no doubt. One of the real difficulties is to know when and to what extent they function. From our point of view they are a nuisance, in the sense of a difficult-to-control factor that acts to obscure the role of D in competing response situations. Accordingly, with our primary interest in these studies being in the role of D rather than s_D, we have deliberately attempted to employ conditions in which such interfering responses would be at a minimum. So far as we have been able to observe, our high-anxious Ss have not tended to engage in distracting irrelevant activities to any greater extent than our low-anxious Ss. Possibly the reason for this is that our experimental situations have not been so stressful as to provide the degree of emotionality that would elicit much of this kind of behavior.

The findings of Ramond's study (14) are of some interest in this connection. He employed a choice-learning situation in which S had to learn to choose one of two alternative response words for each of 16 stimulus words. In half of the items the associative connection of the correct response word was stronger than that of the incorrect response word, and in the other half, the incorrect response was the stronger. It was found that under the condition in which the incorrect response was stronger, the anxious Ss did significantly worse than the nonanxious Ss, but under the reverse condition there was not a significant difference in over-all performance, although the anxious Ss started out better and subsequently became poorer than the nonanxious Ss in the later portion of the learning. Since the task-interfering behavior, if there was any, would presumably be equal for the two kinds of learning items, which were intermixed with each other

---

[2] In this connection attention is called to the fact that the series of studies by Amsel and his colleagues (1, 2, 3) which have been concerned with investigating the differential effects of D and the interfering responses elicited by s_D originated in this laboratory.

in the list, the relatively inferior performance of the anxious Ss with one set of items must be accounted for by some other factor than distracting, task-interfering responses. Our explanation would be that the greater drive level of the anxious Ss increased the unfavorable difference in the competing excitatory potentials in the direction of the incorrect responses and thus led to a greater likelihood of occurrence of such erroneous responses.

It is interesting to speculate in connection with Ramond's findings that both mechanisms (D and s_D) were operative, the two acting jointly to lower the performance of the anxious Ss relative to that of the nonanxious Ss in the case of the items in which the incorrect response was the stronger, while their effects were opposed in the case of the other type of item. Thus, whereas higher D would tend to give an advantage to the anxious Ss in the case in which the correct response was the stronger, interfering responses elicited by the cue aspects of anxiety would favor the nonanxious Ss. If this interpretation is correct, we see that the effects of the interfering activities must have become greater as the learning proceeded.

In concluding, attention should be directed to the point that Child's theorizing is not opposed to ours. Both operate within the framework of Hullian S-R theory. Our experiments have merely been somewhat more restricted in interest, being mainly centered on the role of D in determining behavior, rather than in the other possible functions of anxiety, including its drive cue (s_D) aspects.

Summary

On the basis of the assumption that the A scale measures degree of emotionality and, hence, level of D, and the further assumption that the effect of variations in the level of D upon performance in learning depends upon the position in the response hierarchy of the responses to be learned, different predictions were made concerning the relative performance of high- and low-anxious Ss in two different verbal learning situations. In the case of a list of paired associates having a minimum of generalization among the S-R pairs, and, therefore, little competition among responses, it was predicted that highly anxious Ss would perform better than nonanxious Ss. In the case of a list in which competing, incorrect responses could be expected to be stronger than correct responses, it was predicted that highly anxious Ss would perform more poorly than nonanxious Ss.

In Exp. I, using a noncompetitive list, the anxious Ss made significantly fewer errors and required significantly fewer trials to reach the learning criterion than did the nonanxious Ss. In Exp. II, using a list mainly composed of highly competitive items, anxious Ss required significantly more trials to reach the criterion.

The necessity of minimizing the possible confounding effects of responses elicited by the drive stimuli (s_D) resulting from emotionality when one studies the effects of drive level (D) upon learning performance is strongly emphasized.

References

1. AMSEL, A. The combination of a primary appetitional need with primary and secondary emotionally derived needs. *J. exp. Psychol.*, 1950, **40**, 1–14.

2. AMSEL, A., & COLE, K. F. Generalization of fear-motivated interference with water intake. *J. exp. Psychol.,* 1953, **46,** 243–247.

3. AMSEL, A., & MALTZMAN, I. The effect upon generalized drive strength of emotionality as inferred from the level of consummatory response. *J. exp. Psychol.,* 1950, **40,** 563–569.

4. BROWN, J. S., KALISH, H. I., & FARBER, I. E. Conditioned fear as revealed by magnitude of startle response to an auditory stimulus. *J. exp. Psychol.,* 1951, **41,** 317–328.

5. CHILD, I. L. Personality. *Annu. Rev. Psychol.,* 1954, **5,** 149–171.

6. FARBER, I. E., & SPENCE, K. W. Complex learning and conditioning as a function of anxiety. *J. exp. Psychol.,* 1953, **45,** 120–125.

7. HAAGEN, C. H. Synonymity, vividness, familiarity, and association value ratings of 400 pairs of common adjectives. *J. Psychol.,* 1949, **27,** 453–463.

8. KALISH, H. I. Strength of fear as a function of the number of acquisition and extinction trials. *J. exp. Psychol.,* 1954, **47,** 1–9.

9. KENT, G. H., & ROSANOFF, A. J. A study of association in insanity. *Amer. J. Insanity,* 1910, **67,** 37–96; 317–390.

10. MILLER, N. E. Learnable drives and rewards. In S. S. Stevens (Ed.), *Handbook of experimental psychology.* New York: Wiley, 1951. Pp. 435–472.

11. MONTAGUE, E. K. The role of anxiety in serial rote learning. *J. exp. Psychol.,* 1953, **45,** 91–98.

12. MOWRER, O. H. A stimulus-response analysis of anxiety and its role as a reinforcing agent. *Psychol. Rev.,* 1939, **46,** 553–565.

13. PASSEY, G. E. The influence of intensity of unconditional stimulus upon acquisition of a conditional response. *J. exp. Psychol.,* 1948, **38,** 420–428.

14. RAMOND, C. K. Anxiety and task as determiners of verbal performance. *J. exp. Psychol.,* 1953, **46,** 120–124.

15. SIEGAL, P. S., & BRANTLEY, J. J. The relationship of emotionality to the consummatory response of eating. *J. exp. Psychol.,* 1951, **42,** 304–306.

16. SIEGAL, P. S., & SIEGAL, H. S. The effect of emotionality on the water intake of the rat. *J. comp. physiol. Psychol.,* 1949, **42,** 12–16.

17. SPENCE, K. W. Learning and performance in eyelid conditioning as a function of the intensity of the UCS. *J. exp. Psychol.,* 1953, **45,** 57–63.

18. ———. Current interpretations of learning data and some recent developments in stimulus-response theory. In *Learning theory, personality theory, and clinical research.* New York: Wiley, 1954. Pp. 1–21.

19. ———. *Behavior theory and conditioning.* New Haven: Yale Univer. Press, 1956.

20. SPENCE, K. W., & FARBER, I. E. Conditioning and extinction as a function of anxiety. *J. exp. Psychol.,* 1953, **45,** 116–119.

21. SPENCE, K. W., FARBER, I. E., & TAYLOR, E. The relation of electric shock and anxiety to level of performance in eyelid conditioning. *J. exp. Psychol.,* 1954, **48,** 404–408.

22. SPENCE, K. W., & TAYLOR, J. A. Anxiety and strength of the UCS as determiners of the amount of eyelid conditioning. *J. exp. Psychol.,* 1951, **42,** 183–188.

23. TAYLOR, J. A. The relationship of anxiety to the conditioned eyelid response. *J. exp. Psychol.,* 1951, **41,** 81–92.

24. TAYLOR, J. A., & SPENCE, K. W. The relationship of anxiety level to performance in serial learning. *J. exp. Psychol.,* 1952, **44,** 61–64.

SUPPLEMENTARY REPORT: THE RELATIONSHIP OF INDUCED MUSCULAR TENSION TO MANIFEST ANXIETY IN LEARNING O. Ivar Løvaas

The present study investigated the possibility of reproducing the characteristic features of the performance of Ss scoring high on the A scale as determined by Spence, Taylor, and Ketchel (1956), by inducing muscular tension experimentally in randomly selected Ss. The learning task employed had been shown by Spence, Taylor, and Ketchel (1956) to discriminate between Ss who score high and low on the A scale.

Method

The Ss were 12 randomly selected, experimentally naive, male graduate students in psychology. A "tension" group (6 Ss) learned a set of paired adjectives while pressing a Smedley hand dynamometer during the actual trials; a "no tension" group (6 Ss) learned the set without any induced muscular tension.

A presentation device showed each stimulus word of a pair for 1.7 sec., then showed the response word for 2.3 sec., after which the stimulus word of the next pair immediately appeared. Inadequacies in the apparatus allowed an SD of about .1 sec. in the various exposure times. Intervals between trials were 10 sec.

A dynamometer was located on each side of the exposure window, about 25 in. apart and about 20 in. from S. The handles were padded. Tension was induced only in the preferred hand. The dynamometer pointer closed a circuit to light a bulb located 2 in. above one corner of the exposure window, when-

Reprinted by permission of the American Psychological Association and the author from the *Journal of Experimental Psychology,* Vol. 59, 1960.

ever S's pressure was ±3 lb. of the required pressure. During the learning trials each "tension" S squeezed this handle at half the maximal pressure exerted during the 30th sec. of a grip-pressure pretest. The tension signal light was kept on by S during each trial. The Ss in the "no tension" group merely gripped the handle, and contact on the dynamometer allowed a pressure of only 3 lb. to turn the light off.

In order to avoid incentive motivation differences between the groups all Ss were told that they would work for a predetermined number of trials, that if they got all correct one time they should attempt to get all correct again, and that they should do their best on each trial. A practice session of six trials on 10 paired nouns, with use of the dynamometers begun on Trial 3, was followed after 1 min. by a reading by S (aloud) of a nonpaired list of the adjectives to be learned. Errors of pronunciation were corrected. The set of adjectives was then learned by the anticipation method until S achieved two errorless trials or for a maximum of 33 trials. Pairs were shuffled after each presentation.

The set of adjectives used is presented by Spence, Taylor, and Ketchel (1956, Table 1, p. 307) along with the theoretical rationale and predictions for the performance of high- and low-drive Ss on these pairs. Four out of the 10 pairs have stimulus and response words that are highly associated (high-associated pairs) and six pairs are such that the stimulus word tends to elicit more than one response word (competing pairs). Performance of high-drive Ss should be inferior to low-drive Ss on the competing pairs. On the four highly associated pairs, high-drive Ss should show superior performance initially. With increased training, they should increasingly give response words *other* than those originally paired with the stimulus words. The initial superiority of the high-drive Ss should disappear when these pairs become characterized by much response competition.

Results

Figure 1 shows the learning curves for the "tension" and "no tension" groups on the four highly associated pairs and on the six competing pairs. The insert in Fig. 1 is a rough reproduction of the curves from the study by Spence, Taylor, and Ketchel (1956). They used the same set of paired adjectives but employed Ss scoring high and low on the Taylor Manifest Anxiety Scale. As can be observed, results from the two studies are strikingly similar. The results are consistent with the hypothesis that the performance of Ss who score high on the A scale can be approximated by Ss assumed to score lower on the A scale working under induced muscular tension.

Further support for the drive properties of induced muscular tension is to be found in the significant experimental Condition $\times$ Trials (2 through 10) interaction on the highly associated pairs ($F = 3.93$; $P < .01$). The interaction analysis was carried only through Trial 10 in order to preserve homogeneity of variances since many Ss reached mastery

beyond the trial and because previous studies (Spence, Taylor, & Ketchel, 1956; Spence, Farber, & McFann, 1956) had demonstrated that the reversal of superiority between high- and low-drive groups took place by Trial 5. On the Spence, Farber, and McFann assumption (1956, p. 299) that the highly associated pairs become characterized by an increase in response competition with increase in trials, the significant experimental Condition $\times$ Trials interaction supports induced muscular tension as a D variable.

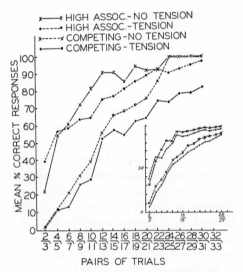

FIG. 1. Paired-associate learning as a function of induced muscular tension ("tension") and no induced tension ("no tension"). The insert shows the results of Spence, Taylor, and Ketchel (1956) employing the same paired associates, but with high-anxious (replacing "tension") and low-anxious (replacing "no tension") Ss.

References

SPENCE, K. W., FARBER, I. E., & McFANN, H. A. The relation of anxiety (drive) level to performance in competitional and noncompetitional paired-associates learning. *J. exp. Psychol.*, 1956, **52**, 296–305.

SPENCE, K. W., TAYLOR, J., & KETCHEL, R. Anxiety (drive) level and degree of competition in paired-associates learning. *J. exp. Psychol.*, 1956, **52**, 306–310.

CONSTRUCT VALIDITY AND THE TAYLOR
ANXIETY SCALE   Richard Jessor and Kenneth R. Hammond

Construct validity (9, 31) is an important new concept which has immediate implications for both psychometrician and experimentalist. Most important is the increased emphasis which construct validity places upon the role of theory in the validation of psychological tests. The aims of the present paper are two: (*a*) to consider the directive role of theory in the construction of psychological tests; and (*b*) to examine certain methodological issues which arise from the more explicit use of theory in test construction. For illustrative purposes we have chosen to make a critical analysis of the Taylor Anxiety Scale (*A* scale) and the research (14, 26, 27, 28, 30) in which it has been employed to establish the independent variable of drive (Hull's *D*).

The nature of the *A* scale and the results of the studies in which it has been used are well enough known so that only a brief description is necessary here. The scale is a self-report inventory consisting of 50 manifest-anxiety items and 175 buffer items, both groups of items taken almost entirely from the Minnesota Multiphasic Personality Inventory (MMPI). The research studies, concerned with testing the assumption that the *A* scale measures drive level, have evaluated the energizing property of *D*. They have indicated that, where the correct response in an experimental learning situation has a high probability of occurrence, the high scorers on the *A* scale perform better than the low scorers. Where the experimental situations are such that there are competing responses or the incorrect responses are equally likely of occurrence at the outset, the high scorers perform less adequately than the low scorers. Both findings are consistent with the Hullian assumption that all habit tendencies elicited in a given situation are multiplicatively affected by the level of drive at the time. These findings have provided the basis for inferring that the *A* scale is, therefore, a measure of drive.

The Use of Theory in Test Construction

Cronbach and Meehl state that "Construct validation takes place when an investigator believes that his instrument reflects a particular construct to which are attached certain meanings. The proposed interpretation generates specific testable hypotheses which are a means of confirming or disconfirming the claim" (9, p. 290). These authors take as the starting point of their discussion the presence of an already existing test or scale purporting to measure or thought to measure a particular variable. They are concerned with the methods of establishing the construct validity of a test after the test has been devised. The present authors, on the other hand, are concerned with the process of devising a scale or test so that it will be consistent with the procedures of construct validation. Our contention is that the test situation itself, and the kinds of test behavior it elicits, must be coordinated to the theory in exactly the same manner as the experiments aimed at validating the test. The Iowa experiments with the *A* scale were designed to fit the paradigm required by the Hullian framework—i.e., they were

Reprinted by permission of the American Psychological Association and the authors from the *Psychological Bulletin*, Vol. 54, 1957.

designed to measure learning, to control probability of occurrence of correct responses, to control other significant sources of drive variation, etc.—in order to make inferences to that framework. The same logic requires that the A scale itself should likewise have been designed so that performance on it might be a basis for inferring drive independently of the outcome of subsequent experiments.

Emphasis on the need for theoretical derivation of psychological tests may be found in recent work by Peak (22) and Butler (5). Their general contention is that the theory or the properties of the construct should determine the nature of the test itself as well as the nature of experiments which establish the construct validity of the test. Peak asserts that "The design of objective instruments and procedures requires . . . a theory about the characteristics and relationships of any variable to be measured . . ." (22, p. 296). She offers an enlightening example of this point: "If, for example, [the investigator] sets out to devise a measure of hostility with a knowledge of the psychoanalytic theory of defense mechanisms, the questions asked and the behavior observed will be very different from that which would seem relevant if manifest expressions of hostility were regarded as the only appropriate data" (22, p. 247).

Butler (5) has recently called attention to the preoccupation of psychometricians with the formal requirements of testing at the cost of ignoring the role of psychological theory in developing tests. He finds it astonishing that there is ". . . no personality inventory for which the content, the form of the items, and the psychometric methods applied have been dictated by a formal psychological model" (5, p. 77). The remainder of his

article is a programmatic effort to use Tolman's theoretical model as the source of hypotheses about the nature of psychometric items most likely to provide useful intervening or independent variables.[1]

The important point here, which relates this discussion to construct validity, is that the psychological, or theoretical, model has implications for the psychometric, as well as for the experimental, procedure. It is an artifact of tradition that theories have been utilized to derive experiments but not to derive tests. Yet construct validity makes the same set of demands on both the psychometric and experimental approaches. Each approach requires that behavior take place under specified and controlled conditions. There seems to be no fundamental reason why theories should make unequivocal demands on the experiment and permit the test to satisfy psychometric requirements only.

The difficulties in moving from theories to empirical conditions, or from theories to classes of observable behaviors, are, of course, apparent. Peak (22) acknowledges that there is no simple methodological prescription for meeting the requirements of theories. Cronbach and Meehl (9) call attention to the absence in psychology of a formal calculus which can provide rigorous implicit definitions of primitive terms and give them empirical meaning. Nevertheless, as they point out (9, p. 294), a theoretical network, though admittedly vague and

---

[1] Although it is not the purpose of this article to examine examples of tests whose items have been derived from theoretical models, the reader may refer to one such test which will serve as an illustration. The test was derived by Liverant (20) from Rotter's social learning theory (24) in order to measure the construct of need value.

sketchy, does exist and provides constructs with whatever meaning they do have.

This network, which guides attempts at construct validity, should play also the *prior* role, we suggest, of guiding test development. Such procedure would have important implications for the adoption of strategy in subsequent construct-validation attempts where the outcome proves to be negative and the investigator has to decide where to lay blame—on the test or the theory—and decide which to revise or discard.

The Development of the Taylor Anxiety Scale

With the foregoing considerations in mind, we return to an examination of the development of the *A* scale. The general question we are asking about the *A* scale is: In what way are the form of the scale, the item selection procedure, the item content, and the nature of the responses elicited by the scale coordinated to or derived from the Hullian framework as indicants of drive. Nowhere, to our knowledge, is this made explicit or is a suitable answer to be found; yet this is precisely what our point of view would demand.

FORM OF THE SCALE

The issue in this section lies in the coordination between the inventory self-report form of the *A* scale and the Hullian construct of drive. In Hullian theory, drive level is coordinated to both antecedents and consequents. The antecedents are generally conditions, e.g., food deprivation, shock, etc., which establish internal states that the organism seeks to avoid. The consequents of drive level are activity or level of energy expenditure. It is clear that the inference of drive level from the *A* scale is contingent

upon consequents; i.e., drive level in this case is a response-inferred construct, since no control or manipulation of conditions antecedent to the *A*-scale responses has been accomplished. Although there has been some general criticism of response-inferred constructs (18, 25), it is clear that Brown and Farber (4) do not consider such criticism fully warranted with respect to inferring drive. They note (according to Farber) that while ". . . more data than those provided by the topography of a response are needed to enable one to identify the extent of its dependence upon one rather than another of its many determinants, this does not mean that there are *no* criteria of drive applicable to responses" (12, p. 26). This is an important statement; yet the obvious fact is that such criteria are nowhere presented in a manner which would coordinate inventory self-reports to drive. Their statement suggests the future possibility of reliance on inventories, but a query still has to be raised as to whether the Hullian concept of drive can, in terms of its present definition, be at all coordinated to self-report verbal responses on any inventory.

SELECTION OF ITEMS

If one is concerned only with the predictive validity of a test, the matter of item content is relatively unimportant, for the empirical item-criterion correlations provide criteria for the final selection of items. However, when a test-developer insists (cf. 28, p. 84; 13, p. 324) that his purpose includes more than the prediction of a particular criterion performance and that the test items are intended to be indicators of a construct, then item content becomes highly important, and item-criterion correlations only are insufficient.

No one can say precisely what the specific steps relating empirical operations to a construct should be, since these must vary with the nature of the construct and the intent of the investigator. However, it is possible to assert that the chain of empirical operations should meet at least one criterion. This criterion is made explicit by Cronbach and Meehl as follows: ". . . unless the network . . . [of constructs and hypotheses] exhibits explicit, public steps of inference, construct validation cannot be claimed" (9, p. 291). We take this to mean that all the methodological links in the development of a test must be scrutinized for their "explicit, public," and therefore objective and retraceable, character. No test can be more objective than the most subjective link in its development.

Therefore, test items which are intended to indicate a construct should be selected by rational (rather than intuitive) means. This means that an item should be scrutinized for its logical relationship to a construct and that the grounds for choice of an item should be explicit and public. The difficulty of deriving a series of items will depend on the scope, precision, content, etc., of the construct to be measured; but there should be no need to resort to a procedure which relies on implicit and private (i.e., undefended or unexplained) judgments or ratings. A single explicit (and sound) argument for an item is better than an implicit rating of an item by many judges, because the former is a retraceable (and thereby self-corrective) step while the latter is not. (Once the choice of items has been made, the empirical criterion for inclusion may well be interitem correlations since the concept may specify a unitary function.) In any case, high interobserver agreement is no substitute for logical validity.

This point needs emphasis because clinical psychologists and psychiatrists are often used as judges in the development of tests. Since their judgments are usually obtained on an intuitive basis (the judges are rarely asked to deduce the items according to the logical requirements of a concept), a hazard is created (in reference to construct validity) which cannot be overcome by appeal to authority (cf. 16).

The hazard introduced by the intuitive procedures usually involved in judging is exemplified in the lack of explicit relationship between A-scale items and drive properties. As pointed out above, Taylor's concept of drive was intended to be identical with Hull's. Yet the procedure for selecting items apparently was *not* to scrutinize them for their logical relationship to drive. Rather, the items were selected on the basis of clinical impression of how well they fit Cameron's (7) definition of anxiety. But why Cameron's definition of a concept when it is Hull's concept of drive which is to be given empirical content? An examination of Cameron's definition leads us to conclude that there are no obvious reasons for choosing his definition rather than any other.

Subsequently the test was shown to discriminate to some extent between psychiatric patients and normals. Taylor reports that, "In an attempt to determine the relationship between the anxiety-scale scores and manifest anxiety as defined and observed by the clinician, the anxiety scores for groups of normal individuals and psychiatric patients were compared" (29, p. 290). The empirical situation at this point is as follows: The scale can now be said to be representative of certain clinicians' judgments about patients, i.e., the scale is a quick device for reaching the same decision as certain clinicians about the manifest anxiety of patients. Unfortunately, it is by no means

difficulties in demonstrating the reinforcing properties of manifest anxiety, "It is quite possible that this sort of demonstration can be accomplished, but to the best of my knowledge no one has yet done so" (12, p. 27). The requirements of construct validation would certainly favor the exploration of this "far-separated, independent section of the network."

Other sections of the "phenotypic space" also require investigation, particularly the effect of manipulation of antecedent conditions on the A-scale responses themselves. Atkinson (1) asks whether scores on the A scale would increase if anxiety were experimentally increased. The possibility of employing conditions, e.g., shock, suggested by other research concerned with establishing or increasing drive, becomes apparent. To summarize, the point is that construct validity requires investigation of diverse properties of the construct. One reason for making this requirement is to lower the likelihood of finding acceptable alternative inferences which can encompass such diversity. This leads us to the next major issue.

DISCONFIRMATION OF ALTERNATIVE INFERENCES

Confirmation of an inference is also established to the extent that other inferences are not equally applicable. Beck states that "Confirmation can come only from the disconfirmation of all alternative hypotheses through the evidential denial of at least one consequent of each alternative . . ." (2, p. 377). In the light of this criterion, the inference of drive from the A-scale studies is not secure. Various investigators have made alternative inferences about what the Taylor scale measures. Three of these

alternatives will be mentioned here.

(a) Most prominent is the controversy raised by Hilgard (17), and by Child (8). They consider an equally plausible hypothesis to be that the A scale measures only different ${}_sH_R$'s rather than different drive levels. Hilgard has concluded that anxiety responses or anxiety-related responses, e.g., stronger defensive or avoidance habits, can account equally well for the data. Certainly, on the face of it, the scale measures nothing other than differential response systems (assuming veridicality). Farber has been explicit in acknowledging an associative component in what the A scale measures, but he insists that it is the drive component which is inferable from the research. Overlooking the possibility, as suggested by Postman (23), that there are no operational means for separating these two components, our immediate purpose is to indicate that alternatives to the drive inference have, at the very least, as yet not been disconfirmed.

(b) Recent studies (6, 15, 19) have also suggested another alternative hypothesis, namely that the scale measures intellectual (habit?) differences rather than drive. While the implications of intelligence as an explanation for the A-scale findings are not yet clear, these empirical findings should be considered. Certainly the obtained correlations between A-scale scores and intelligence (if they are not fortuitous) are not referable to any property of drive as thus far defined.

(c) Finally, the near-perfect correlation between the A scale and the MMPI psychasthenia scale (3, 11), and correlations with other neurotic inventories (10), raises further questions as to whether *any* neurotic inventory would yield similar experimental findings, and, if so, in what way neuroticism in general is coordinated to drive level.

For the test to meet fully the requirements of construct validity, these alternative inferences must be disconfirmed.

The Conditional Definition of Anxiety as Drive

To illustrate a further methodological point concerning construct validity, let us assume our argument concerning the A scale to be valid: that when it was used in connection with the test of the Hullian hypothesis that drive energizes $_sH_R$'s, the A scale had neither logical nor empirical foundation as a measure of drive. This raises the question of whether the studies achieved a definition of drive or tested the Hullian hypothesis.

The first step in the experiment was to identify high and low scorers on the A scale. (Note that no theoretically relevant meaning can be given to any score at this point because no logical or empirical tie can be made to the Hullian concept of drive.) The next step was to perform the experiment in the eyelid conditioning arrangement. Results conforming to expectations were obtained. The researchers had then obtained a *conditional definition* of the concept of drive. The definition is of this form: if a high scorer is placed in a conditioning arrangement, then a high scorer has a high drive if, and only if, the high scorer conditions more rapidly than a low scorer conditions. Farber puts this as follows: ". . . the question of the validity of the Taylor scale *as a useful definition of general drive level* is answered by the accuracy of the prediction of relations between this scale and specified behavior variables, under conditions such that variation in the behavioral variables can be reasonably attributed to differential drive levels" (13, p. 325). Thus,

it appears that the researchers were attempting to achieve a conditional definition of drive.

The investigators assert, however, that the experimental situation provided both a definition of drive and a test of the Hullian hypothesis under consideration at one and the same time. This procedure introduces an ambiguity. If the results are negative, does it mean that the definition of the concept is faulty, or the hypothesis relating the variables? A difficulty remains if the results are positive, since the hypothesis is proved only by asserting the definition. That is, if we ask how the experimenter knows that he actually varied drive, he can only reply that the results are meaningful *if* the A scale measures drive. However, as we have pointed out, the construction of the A scale has not been coordinated to drive, the scale has not been employed in testing the diverse properties of drive, nor have "reasonable" alternative inferences about the A-scale scores been disconfirmed. Therefore the experimental results alone are not sufficient support for the assumption that the A scale measures drive.

The problem of the definition of drive is directly analogous to the problem of the definition of reinforcement. Meehl (21) points out that the reason why the Law of Effect is not circular is that conditional definitions of reinforcers are made independently of the test of the Law of Effect. For example, Meehl presents the following "special law": "On schedule M, the termination of response sequence R, in setting S, by stimulus S^1 is followed by an increment in the strength of S.R." (21, p. 60). In the studies involving the A scale, however, M (the A scale) is not defined by the investigators in terms of an independently observed "schedule," but only in terms of the response sequence in the experiment.

When a construct implies a relationship between variables, these variables must be designated independently of any test of that relationship.

Summary

Construct validity emphasizes the directive role of theory in test validation; the intent of this paper has been to emphasize the directive role of theory in the construction of psychological tests.

Our position is that the psychometric, as well as the experimental, procedure must be coordinated to the hypothetical properties of the construct to be measured. In this way the test situation is made parallel to the experimental situation—the conditions of both being clearly derived from theory, and the behavior elicited in both being clearly relevant to the theory.

The above points, as well as certain methodological issues arising from the explicit use of theory in test construction—the investigation of diverse properties of a construct, disconfirmation of alternate inferences, conditional definitions—were illustrated through a critical examination of the Taylor Anxiety Scale. Our conclusion was that the A scale has only a tenuous theoretical and empirical coordination to the Hullian construct of drive. The experiments which have relied on the A scale may be considered to have attempted thus far a conditional definition of drive rather than to have demonstrated the hypothesis that drive energizes habits.

Our intent has not been to single out a particular test for criticism. We recognize that much work is being done on further construct validation of the A scale. Such work, we hope, will answer some of the questions we have raised, questions which we feel are of importance for psychometrics as a whole.

References

1. ATKINSON, J. W. Comments on Professor Farber's paper. In *The Nebraska symposium on motivation.* Lincoln, Nebr., Nebraska Univer. Press, 1954. Pp. 51–55.

2. BECK, L. W. Constructions and inferred entities. In H. Feigl & M. Brodbeck (Eds.), *Readings in the philosophy of science.* New York: Appleton-Century-Crofts, 1953. Pp. 368–381.

3. BRACKBILL, G., & LITTLE, K. B. MMPI correlates of the Taylor Scale of Manifest Anxiety. *J. consult. Psychol.,* 1954, **18,** 433–436.

4. BROWN, J. S., & FARBER, I. E. Emotions conceptualized as intervening variables —with suggestions toward a theory of frustration. *Psychol. Bull.,* 1951, **48,** 465–480.

5. BUTLER, J. M. The use of a psychological model in personality testing. *Educ. psychol. measmt,* 1954, **14,** 77–89.

6. CALVIN, A. D., ET AL. A further investigation of the relationship between manifest anxiety and intelligence. *J. consult. Psychol.,* 1955, **19,** 280–282.

7. CAMERON, N. *The psychology of behavior disorders.* New York: Houghton Mifflin, 1947.

8. CHILD, I. L. Personality. *Ann. Rev. Psychol.,* 1954, **5,** 149–171.

9. CRONBACH, L. J., & MEEHL, P. E. Construct validity in psychological tests. *Psychol. Bull.,* 1955, **52,** 281–302.

10. DAVIDS, A. Relations among several objective measures of anxiety under different conditions of motivation. *J. consult. Psychol.,* 1955, **19,** 275–279.

11. ERIKSEN, C. W., & DAVIDS, A. The meaning and clinical validity of the Taylor

Anxiety Scale and the hysteriapsychasthenia scales from the MMPI. *J. abnorm. soc. Psychol.*, 1955, **50**, 135–137.

12. FARBER, I. E. Anxiety as a drive state. In *The Nebraska symposium on motivation.* Lincoln, Nebr.: Nebraska Univer. Press, 1954. Pp. 1–46.

13. ———. The role of motivation in verbal learning and performance. *Psychol. Bull.*, 1955, **52**, 311–327.

14. FARBER, I. E., & SPENCE, K. W. Complex learning and conditioning as a function of anxiety. *J. exp. Psychol.*, 1953, **45**, 120–125.

15. GRICE, G. R. Discrimination reaction time as a function of anxiety and intelligence. *J. abnorm. soc. Psychol.*, 1955, **50**, 71–74.

16. HAMMOND, K. R. Probabilistic functioning and the clinical method. *Psychol. Rev.,* 1955, **62**, 255–262.

17. HILGARD, E. R. Theories of human learning and problems of training. In *Symposium on psychology of learning basic to military training problems.* Panel on Training and Training Devices. Res. & Develpm. Bd, 1953.

18. JESSOR, R. Phenomenological personality theories and the data language of psychology. *Psychol. Rev.,* 1956, **63**, 173–180.

19. KERRICK, JEAN S. Some correlates of the Taylor Manifest Anxiety Scale. *J. abnorm. soc. Psychol.*, 1955, **50**, 75–77.

20. LIVERANT, S. The use of Rotter's social learning theory in the development of a personality inventory. Unpublished doctor's dissertation, Univer. of Colorado, 1956.

21. MEEHL, P. E. On the circularity of the law of effect. *Psychol. Bull.*, 1950, **47**, 52–75.

22. PEAK, HELEN. Problems of objective observation. In L. Festinger & D. Katz (Eds.), *Research methods in the behavioral sciences.* New York: Dryden Press, 1953. Pp. 243–300.

23. POSTMAN, L. J. Comments on papers by Professors Brown and Harlow. In *Current theory and research in motivation.* Lincoln, Nebr.: Nebraska Univer. Press, 1953. Pp. 55–58.

24. ROTTER, J. B. *Social learning and clinical psychology.* New York: Prentice-Hall, 1954.

25. SPENCE, K. W. The nature of theory construction in contemporary psychology. *Psychol. Rev.,* 1944, **51**, 47–68.

26. SPENCE, K. W., & TAYLOR, JANET A. Anxiety and strength of the UCS as determiners of the amount of eyelid conditioning. *J. exp. Psychol.*, 1951, **42**, 183–188.

27. SPENCE, K. W., & FARBER, I. E. Conditioning and extinction as a function of anxiety. *J. exp. Psychol.*, 1953, **45**, 116–119.

28. TAYLOR, JANET A. The relationship of anxiety to the conditioned eyelid response. *J. exp. Psychol.*, 1951, **41**, 81–92.

29. ———. A personality scale of manifest anxiety. *J. abnorm. soc. Psychol.*, 1953, **48**, 285–290.

30. TAYLOR, JANET A., & SPENCE, K. W. The relationship of anxiety level to performance in serial learning. *J. exp. Psychol.*, 1952, **44**, 61–64.

31. Technical recommendations for psychological tests and diagnostic techniques. *Psychol. Bull. Suppl.,* 1954, **51**, 2, Part 2, 1–38.

METHODOLOGICAL CONSIDERATIONS IN THE CONSTRUCT VALIDATION OF DRIVE-ORIENTED SCALES

Donald H. Kausler and E. Philip Trapp

Studies concerned with the dynamogenic effects of anxiety, as measured by the Taylor Manifest Anxiety Scale (MAS), on learning and performance (e.g., Spence & Farber, 1953; Spence, Farber, & McFann, 1956; Taylor & Chapman, 1955; Taylor & Spence, 1952) have typically regarded the MAS as a discriminating measure of generalized drive (D). Evidence for the validity of the test is considered present whenever extreme groups, assigned on the basis of test score, perform in the direction hypothesized by related D theory. The particular theory involved has been treated in detail by Farber (1955), Taylor (1956), and Spence (1958).

Construct Validity and the MAS

Experimental validation of a test within a theoretical framework represents an attempt at construct validation. Basic to construct validation, as conceived by Cronbach and Meehl (1955), is the existence of a nomological network that relates the construct to observables and to other constructs. Extending the validity of a construct would involve, according to Cronbach and Meehl (1955), ". . . elaborating the nomological network in which it occurs, or of increasing the definiteness of the components" (p. 290). They further stated that the validation of a test claiming to measure a construct would require the existence of a nomological net surround-

Reprinted by permission of the American Psychological Association and the authors from the *Psychological Bulletin,* Vol. 56, 1959.

ing that construct. The recent article by Spence (1958) attempted, in fact, to describe the nomological net surrounding the construct of emotionally based D.

In their criticism of the construct validity of the MAS, Jessor and Hammond (1957) questioned the extensiveness to which various aspects of the nomological net surrounding D have been investigated experimentally and alternative inferences disconfirmed. They accurately noted that MAS studies have concentrated specifically on the energizing component of D and have generally ignored other, perhaps equally important, aspects of the net. The Jessor and Hammond criticism is certainly germane not only to the MAS but to other scales purporting to measure D.

The present writers, moreover, are inclined to the critical view that even those studies dealing with the dynamogenic aspects of the net encompassing D have, in general, contributed little to a systematic construct validation of the MAS and other D-oriented scales. The literature in the area fairly abounds with studies yielding conflicting or equivocal results. Experiments on serial and paired-associates learning, in particular, have been conspicuously contradictory in their findings. On one hand, Spence, Farber, and McFann (1956), Spence, Taylor and Ketchel (1956), Taylor and Chapman (1955), Taylor and Spence (1955), and others (Montague, 1953; Ramond, 1953) have reported evidence consonant with the nomologies present in the D net; on the other hand, Saltz and Hoehn (1957), Katchmar, Ross, and Andrews

(1958), Sarason (1957a, and 1957b). Hughes, Sprague, and Bendig (1954), and others have provided evidence against the expectations of the theory. The present writers contend that a major difficulty hampering and confusing research in this area has been the tendency to confound interactional effects within the nomological net with certain methodological problems inherent in the research design. The express purpose of this paper is to point out some of these pertinent methodological problems and to suggest some possible ways of resolving them.

Methodological Problems in the Nature of the Task

According to the proponents of D theory, both D level and the relative strengths of competing responses must be accounted for in predicting the effect of D upon performance. Taylor (1956), for example, explicitly stated the position as follows: "In situations in which a number of competing response tendencies are evoked, only one of which is correct, the relative performance of high and low drive groups will depend upon the number and comparative strengths of the various response tendencies" (p. 304). In simple learning situations such as conditioning where a single response tendency is to be acquired, the prediction from D theory is straightforward. High D groups are predicted to condition at a faster rate than low D groups. Considerable experimental evidence would seem to support this prediction based upon the MAS. In verbal learning, and especially paired-associates learning, the prediction would be based upon the amount of interference or competition within the list. D theory would predict that with little intratask interference a high D group should be superior to a low

D group; however, on tasks involving considerable intratask competition, the low D group would be predicted to be superior. The validity of these nomologies within the D net, incidentally, has been questioned by Hill (1957) on purely theoretical grounds.

Because of the D level-response competition interaction that has been postulated to operate within the nomological net, research relating D level as measured by D-oriented scales (chiefly the MAS) to performance on paired-associates tasks requires a "control" over the degree of competition within the task. The empirical results of such studies would then represent evidence for a construct validation of the scale. A crucial condition, therefore, in these validity studies is the degree to which E has controlled intratask interference. The typical procedure is to select nonsense syllables or adjectives in such a way that the similarity of the material and the association value of the material within the list can be conveniently manipulated. Similarity is usually manipulated by varying the letter content of items within the list, and association value is regulated by selecting syllables from Glaze's (1928) or Hull's (1933) tables with previously calibrated association values. By such manipulations, E derives a list which he considers representative of either a competitional or noncompetitional task. As Saltz and Hoehn (1957) point out, this procedure confounds amount of intratask competition with the difficulty of the task. They contend that an increase in response competition is accompanied by an increase in difficulty of the list. They conducted several studies in which they attempted to partial out difficulty from competition. As a result, their findings failed to support D level-response competition theory.

In manipulating lists of nonsense syllables or adjectives in terms of similarity and association value for purposes of varying intratask interference and/or controlling for task difficulty, E seems to be operating under the basic premise that competition within a list is independent of D as measured by his D-oriented scale. We seriously question this premise particularly as it applies to the association value of nonsense syllables and adjectives. The calibrations of Glaze and Hull, it may be recalled, were based upon groups undifferentiated on any D dimension. It does not seem unreasonable to suspect that performance on D scales and number of associations to nonsense syllables may have some covariance. If true, lists constructed from such calibrations would not be comparable lists in terms of competition and difficulty for high and low D groups selected on the basis of scale score. Some adequate empirical demonstrations of independence between these variables are clearly needed.

Methodological Problems in Drive Measurement

Another important methodological problem encountered in construct validation studies on D-oriented scales pertains to the conditional definition of D which the use of such scales involves. These difficulties have been discussed by Jessor and Hammond (1957). They concluded with the statement: "When a construct implies a relationship between variables, these variables must be designated independently of any test of that relationship" (p. 169). The methodology commonly employed in studies involving D scales and complex learning tasks has departed grossly from this important qualification. The scale has been employed both to establish the validity of the construct (D) and simultaneously to establish the construct validity of the scale. Under such confounding dual purposes, failure of the data to fulfill the predicted outcome cannot be taken as substantive evidence for either an absence of construct validity in the scale or for an incorrect nomological net. The results of such studies serve mainly to confuse and cloud the issue.

As a way out of this protracted dilemma, the writers suggest that research in this area begin to utilize experimentally induced D states as controls for evaluating the effects of response-inferred D states. We further recommend positive, nonemotional, approach drives in preference to negative, emotional, avoidance drives, such as shock or threat of shock, which are fraught with so many unsettled theoretical problems in their own right. The nomological net surrounding the positive drives is more clearly defined and has received wider empirical support than is generally the case for the negatively based drives.

Since experimentally induced D would be considered as contributing to generalized D, predictions based on this form of D should be comparable to those based on D inferred from performance on a scale. For example, groups performing under high and low incentive conditions should be at least partially equated with high and low D groups selected on the basis of MAS scores. Predictions of this nature would extend beyond mere rate of acquisition in complex learning and would include such diverse phenomena as intentional versus incidental learning, positive and negative transfer, extinction, etc. The kind of controls advocated here would not, of course, eliminate from consideration other interpretations pertaining to the construct validity of D scales. Predictions concerning emotionally based D upon an interfering response theory, as exemplified by Sarason and Mandler (Mandler & Sarason, 1952; Sarason, Mandler, & Craighill, 1952), or upon a habit theory, as exemplified by Hilgard (1953) and Child (1954), would be difficult to test discriminately by any method. The procedure propounded here has as its basic merit the elements for establishing a more well-defined baseline in an area besieged with many intricacies.

Two alternatives are suggested here for providing the type of control discussed above. The first consists of a replication of a carefully designed, well-conceived experiment in which an experimentally induced positive D had been manipulated and clear-cut results obtained. The replication would consist of repeating the task and procedure as closely as possible with groups selected as high and low scorers, respectively, on the D scale to be validated. Such replication would require a preliminary demonstration that competition within the material to be learned showed no covariance with score on the scale. A study in preparation by the writers exemplifies this approach. It consisted of a replication of a study by Bahrick (1954) in terms of material learned and procedure followed, but was extended to a different D dimension. Bahrick had demonstrated that a high incentive (financial reward) group displayed significantly greater intentional learning but significantly less incidental learning than a low incentive (no financial reward) group. The learning task consisted of the serial learning of geometric forms. Since the nature of the task is one that probably involves little intratask competition, it should differentiate high and low D groups selected by MAS score in a similar manner. That is, D theory would predict that

high scorers on the MAS should show greater intentional learning but less incidental learning than low scorers.

We found, as in the Bahrick study, that the high D group (now identified by MAS score), comparable in intelligence and sex distribution to the low D group, displayed a significantly higher rate of intentional learning. Unlike the Bahrick study, however, the low D group did not display superior incidental learning. The results would therefore seem to conflict with the finding by Silverman and Blitz (1956) that high scorers on the MAS showed significantly less incidental learning on a serial list of nonsense syllables with low association values than low scorers. Silverman and Blitz interpreted their findings in terms of interfering responses correlating with anxiety. Unfortunately, the lack of information concerning the comparability of the list of syllables for the two groups and the lack of control groups performing on the same task under more operationally defined D conditions make it difficult to evaluate such results as either supporting or rejecting the construct validity of the MAS.

The second suggested alternative follows in a natural vein from the first. Studies that are directed at the construct validity of D scales should include within their research design, whenever possible, comparable groups performing the same task as the experimental groups but under varying levels of an experimentally induced approach D. The performance of such control groups would then provide a more adequate basis for evaluating the effects of D inferred from scores on a D scale. A recent study by Katchmar, Ross, and Andrews (1958) illustrates this point nicely. They compared rate of learning for a coding task between groups differentiated in D level in terms of MAS anxiety, ego involvement, and failure-induced stress. Their design is certainly excellent as far as making relative comparisons between these three variations of emotionally based D. In their discussion, however, they state the results for high and low MAS scorers do not support the theoretical formulation of Taylor and Spence. Thus they are inferring that the study does not support the construct validity of the MAS. In our opinion, a more adequate test of the construct validity of the MAS in their study would require two additional control groups, consisting of more clearly defined high and low D groups, where D is manipulated experimentally in a nonemotional, positive, approach direction.

Summary

Experimental studies directed at establishing the construct validity of D-oriented scales, such as the Taylor MAS, are beset with theoretical and methodological problems that make it difficult to interpret their results. This is particularly true in studies that relate response-inferred, emotionally based D to verbal learning. As a partial answer to these problems, the writers contend that studies employing verbal tasks should require a prior demonstration of comparability of the task for extreme groups identified by D scale performance. This need is dictated by the emphasis placed on the interaction between D level and intratask competition in contemporary D theory. The writers further contend that research in this area requires information collected from control groups performing on the same task as the D scale groups under high and low D conditions that represent clearly defined, experimentally induced motivational states. The information thus provided would serve as a baseline for evaluating the evidence for or against the construct validity of the D-oriented scale.

References

BAHRICK, H. P. Incidental learning under two incentive conditions. *J. exp. Psychol.,* 1954, **47,** 170–172.

CHILD, I. L. Personality. *Ann. Rev. Psychol.,* 1954, **5,** 149–171.

CRONBACH, L. J., & MEEHL, P. E. Construct validity in psychological tests. *Psychol. Bull.,* 1955, **52,** 281–302.

FARBER, I. E. The role of motivation in verbal learning and performance. *Psychol. Bull.,* 1955, **52,** 311–327.

GLAZE, J. A. The association value of nonsense syllables. *J. genet. Psychol.,* 1928, **35,** 255–267.

HILGARD, E. R. Theories of human learning and problems of training. In *Symposium on psychology of learning basic to military training problems.* Panel on Training and Training Devices. Res. & Develpm. Bd., 1953.

HILL, W. F. Comments on Taylor's "Drive theory and manifest anxiety." *Psychol. Bull.,* 1957, **54,** 490–493.

HUGHES, J. B., SPRAGUE, J. L., & BENDIG, A. W. Anxiety level, response alternation, and performance in serial learning. *J. Psychol.,* 1954, **38,** 421–426.

HULL, C. L. The meaningfulness of 320 selected nonsense syllables. *Amer. J. Psychol.,* 1933, **45,** 730–734.

JESSOR, R., & HAMMOND, K. R. Construct validity and the Taylor Anxiety Scale. *Psychol. Bull.,* 1957, **54,** 161–170.

KATCHMAR, L. T., ROSS, S., & ANDREWS, T. G. Effects of stress and anxiety on performance of a complex verbal-coding task. *J. exp. Psychol.,* 1958, **55,** 559–564.

MANDLER, G., & SARASON, S. B. A study of anxiety and learning. *J. abnorm. soc. Psychol.*, 1952, **47**, 166–173.

MONTAGUE, E. K. The role of anxiety in serial rote learning. *J. exp. Psychol.*, 1953, **45**, 91–96.

RAMOND, C. Anxiety and task as determiners of verbal performance. *J. exp. Psychol.*, 1953, **46**, 120–124.

SALTZ, E., & HOEHN, A. J. A test of the Taylor-Spence theory of anxiety. *J. abnorm. soc. Psychol.*, 1957, **54**, 114–117.

SARASON, I. G. The effect of anxiety and two kinds of failure on serial learning. *J. Pers.*, 1957, **25**, 283–392. (a)

————. Effect of anxiety and two kinds of motivating instructions on verbal learning. *J. abnorm. soc. Psychol.*, 1957, **54**, 166–171. (b)

SARASON, S. B., MANDLER, G., & CRAIGHILL, P. G. The effect of differential instructions on anxiety and learning. *J. abnorm. soc. Psychol.*, 1952, **47**, 561–565.

SILVERMAN, R. E., & BLITZ, B. Learning and two kinds of anxiety. *J. abnorm. soc. Psychol.*, 1956, **52**, 301–303.

SPENCE, K. W. A theory of emotionally based drive (*D*) and its relation to performance in simple learning situations. *Amer. Psychologist*, 1958, **13**, 131–141.

SPENCE, K. W., & FARBER, I. E. Conditioning and extinction as a function of anxiety. *J. exp. Psychol.*, 1953, **45**, 116–119.

SPENCE, K. W., FARBER, I. E., & MCFANN, H. H. The relation of anxiety (drive) level to performance in competitional and non-competitional paired-associates learning. *J. exp. Psychol.*, 1956, **52**, 296–305.

SPENCE, K. W., TAYLOR, J., & KETCHEL, R. Anxiety (drive) level and degree of competition in paired-associates learning. *J. exp. Psychol.*, 1956, **52**, 306–310.

TAYLOR, JANET A. Drive theory and manifest anxiety. *Psychol. Bull.*, 1956, **53**, 303–320.

TAYLOR, JANET A., & CHAPMAN, J. P. Paired-associate learning as related to anxiety. *Amer. J. Psychol.*, 1955, **68**, 671.

TAYLOR, JANET A., & SPENCE, K. W. The relationship of anxiety level to performance in serial learning. *J. exp. Psychol.*, 1952, **44**, 61–64.

Anxiety Induced through Experimental Stress

ULCERS IN "EXECUTIVE" MONKEYS   Joseph V. Brady

Physicians and laymen alike have long recognized that emotional stress can produce bodily disease. Psychic disturbances can induce certain skin and respiratory disorders, can set off attacks of allergic asthma and may even play a part in some forms of heart disease. Of all the body's systems, however, the gastrointestinal tract is perhaps the most vulnerable to emotional stress. The worries, fears, conflicts and anxieties of daily life can produce gastrointestinal disorders ranging from the "nervous stomach," which most of us know at first hand, to the painful and often disabling ulcers which are the traditional occupational disease of business executives.

Emotional stress appears to produce ulcers by increasing the flow of the stomach's acid juices. The connection between emotional disturbance, stomach secretion and ulcers is well documented. A recent study of 2,000 Army draftees, for example, found that those who showed emotional disturbance and excessive gastric secretion during their initial physical examination developed ulcers later on under the strains of military life.

But not every kind of emotional stress produces ulcers, and the same kind of stress will do so in one person and not in another. Experimental investigation of the problem is difficult. Animals obviously cannot provide wholly satisfactory experimental models of human mind-body interactions. They can, however, be studied under controlled conditions, and it is through animal experiments that we are finding leads to the cause of ulcers as well as to the effect of emotional stress on the organism in general.

Various investigators have succeeded in inducing ulcers in experimental animals by subjecting them to physical stress. But the role of the emotional processes in such experiments has been uncertain. Experiments on dogs by George F. Mahl of Yale University Medical School indicate that a "fear producing" situation lasting many hours increases the animals' gastric secretions, but these animals do not develop ulcers. William L. Sawrey and John D. Weisz of the University of Colorado produced ulcers in rats by subjecting them to a conflict situation: keeping them in a box where they could obtain food and water only by standing on a grid which gave them a mild electric shock. But this experiment, as Sawrey and Weisz themselves pointed out, did not prove conclusively that emotional stress was the crucial factor in producing the ulcers.

Our studies of ulcers in monkeys at the Walter Reed Army Institute of Research developed somewhat fortuitously. For several years we had been investi-

vestigation showed that stress brought about dramatic alterations in the hormone content of the animals' blood, but a more extensive study of 19 monkeys was brought to a halt when many of them died.

At first we considered this merely a stroke of bad luck, but the post-mortem findings showed that more than bad

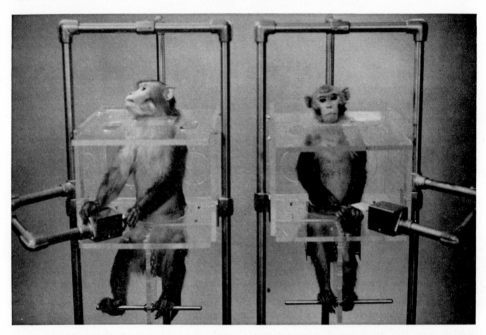

Conditioning experiment involves training monkeys in "restraining chairs." Both animals receive brief electric shocks at regular intervals. The "executive" monkey (*left*) has learned to press the lever in its left hand, which prevents shocks to both animals. The control monkey (*right*) has lost interest in its lever, which is a dummy. Only executive monkeys developed ulcers.

gating the emotional behavior of these animals. In some of our experiments we had been keeping monkeys in "restraining chairs" (in which they could move their heads and limbs but not their bodies) while we conditioned them in various ways. Since these procedures seemed to impose considerable emotional stress on the animals, we decided that we ought to know something about their physiological reactions. Preliminary in-

luck was involved. Many of the dead monkeys had developed ulcers as well as other extensive gastrointestinal damage. Such pathological conditions are normally rare in laboratory animals, and previous experiments with monkeys kept in restraining chairs up to six months convinced us that restraint alone did not produce the ulcers. Evidently the conditioning procedures were to blame.

One of the procedures which showed

a high correlation with ulcers involved training the monkey to avoid an electric shock by pressing a lever. The animal received a brief shock on the feet at regular intervals, say, every 20 seconds. It could avoid the shock if it learned to press the lever at least once in every 20-second interval. It does not take a mon-

of the shocks. To test this possibility we set up a controlled experiment, using two monkeys in "yoked chairs" in which both monkeys received shocks but only one monkey could prevent them. The experimental or "executive" monkey could prevent shocks to himself and his partner by pressing the lever; the con-

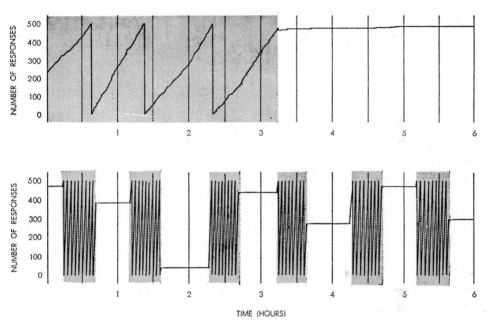

TIME (HOURS)

Responses of monkeys were recorded automatically. Slope of the lines shows the rate of lever-pressing (*vertical lines indicate resetting of stylus*). Upper chart shows responses of an executive monkey during the last half of a six-hour avoidance session (*grey area*) and the first half of a six-hour rest period; shocks were programmed every 20 seconds. Monkeys kept on this schedule developed ulcers. Lower chart shows responses during a 30-minutes-on, 30-minutes-off schedule with shocks programmed every two seconds. Monkeys on this schedule failed to develop ulcers, despite more intense activity and presumably greater psychic stress.

key very long to master this problem; within a short time it is pressing the lever far oftener than once in 20 seconds. Only occasionally does it slow down enough to receive a shock as a reminder.

One possibility, of course, was that the monkeys which had developed ulcers under this procedure had done so not because of the psychological stress involved but rather as a cumulative result

trol monkey's lever was a dummy. Thus both animals were subjected to the same physical stress (*i.e.,* both received the same number of shocks at the same time), but only the "executive" monkey was under the psychological stress of having to press the lever.

We placed the monkeys on a continuous schedule of alternate periods of shock-avoidance and rest, arbitrarily choosing an interval of six hours for each period. As a cue for the executive monkey we provided a red light which was turned on during the avoidance periods and turned off during the "off" hours. The animal soon learned to press its lever at a rate averaging between 15 and 20 times a minute during the avoidance periods, and to stop pressing the lever when the red light was turned off. These responses showed no change throughout the experiment. The control monkey at first pressed the lever sporadically during both the avoidance and rest sessions, but lost interest in the lever within a few days.

After 23 days of a continuous six-hours-on, six-hours-off schedule the executive monkey died during one of the avoidance sessions. Our only advance warning had been the animal's failure to eat on the preceding day. It had lost no weight during the experiment, and it pressed the lever at an unflagging rate through the first two hours of its last avoidance session. Then it suddenly collapsed and had to be sacrificed. An autopsy revealed a large perforation in the wall of the duodenum—the upper part of the small intestine near its junction with the stomach, and a common site of ulcers in man. Microscopic analysis revealed both acute and chronic inflammation around this lesion. The control monkey, sacrificed in good health a few hours later, showed no gastrointestinal abnormalities. A second experiment using precisely the same procedure produced much the same results. This time the executive monkey developed ulcers in both the stomach and the duodenum; the control animal was again unaffected.

In a series of follow-up experiments which is still in progress we have tried to isolate the physiological and psycho-logical factors which produce the "laboratory ulcers." For example, one of our groups suggested that the "social" interaction between the two monkeys might be important. Certainly the most casual observation showed that considerable "communication" was going on between the two animals, who were seated within easy chattering distance of each other. We therefore studied several pairs of animals isolated from each other in sound-proof "telephone booths." Unfortunately isolation failed to protect the executive monkeys, for they continued to develop ulcers.

More recently, however, we have found a factor or group of factors which does seem to be critical in producing ulcers. What we have learned seems to pivot on our chance selection of six hours as the interval for shock-avoidance and for rest in the conditioning procedure. We made this discovery when we sought to improve on the results of our experiments. Though laboratory animals can rarely be made to develop ulcers, we had come upon a procedure that seemed to produce ulcers "to order." The only uncertainty was the length of exposure required. This varied greatly among individual monkeys; some came down with ulcers in 18 days, others took as long as six weeks. If we could develop a technique guaranteed to produce ulcers in, say, 10 days, we could stop the shock-avoidance sessions on the eighth or ninth day, apply various therapeutic measures and study the monkey's response to them.

It seemed reasonable to assume that we might induce ulcers more rapidly and dependably by simply increasing the stress on the animals. We therefore put several monkeys on an 18-hours-on, six-hours-off schedule. After a few weeks one of the animals died, but of tuberculosis, not ulcers. The rest continued to press their levers week after week with no apparent ill effects. Finally, when it began to seem as if we might have to wait for the animals to die of old age, we sacrificed them—and found no gastrointestinal abnormalities whatever!

We put another group on an even more strenuous schedule: 30 minutes on and 30 minutes off, with the shocks programmed for every two seconds rather than every 20. Again one of the animals died, this time of a generalized virus infection unrelated to ulcers. The others, after weeks of frantic lever pressing, showed no gastrointestinal changes.

We had to conclude that the crucial factor was not the degree or even the frequency of stress but was to be sought in the relationship between the length of the stress period and that of the rest period. The six-hours-on, six-hours-off schedule had produced ulcers (and occasionally other somatic disorders) despite individual differences in monkeys, variations in diet and maintenance routines and gross alterations in preliminary physiological tests. No other schedule we had tried produced ulcers at all.

This unexpected finding suggested that we should investigate what was going on in the monkeys' stomachs during the conditioning procedure. A standard technique for investigating gastric processes in experimental animals makes use of an artificial opening, or fistula, in the animal's abdominal and stomach walls through which the contents of its stomach can be sampled. Such fistulas have played an important role in expanding our knowledge of the gastrointestinal system. In the early 19th century the famous U. S. Army surgeon William Beaumont made the first systematic study of the digestive process with the cooper-

ation of a young Canadian who had a fistula due to an imperfectly healed gunshot wound. More than a century later Stewart G. Wolf, Jr., and Harold G. Wolff at the Cornell University Medical

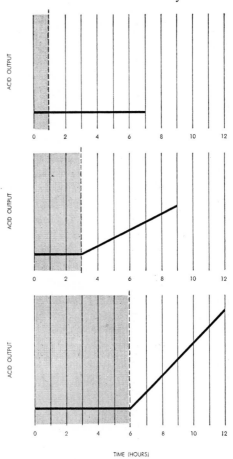

Stomach acidity of executive monkeys, as shown in these highly simplified charts, did not increase during avoidance sessions (*grey*) but rather during the subsequent rest periods. The greatest increase followed a six-hour session; no rise followed a one-hour session.

College, with the help of a man who had a similar injury, conducted a pioneer investigation of the relationship between emotional stress and ulcers. They found that situations which produced feelings of anxiety or aggression in their subject stepped up his gastric secretions and engorged his stomach wall with blood. Physiological changes of this sort, they believed, are the precursors of ulcers.

Edwin Polish of our department of neuroendocrinology has been studying the stomach acidity of some of our executive monkeys by means of artificial fistulas. His measurements, though far from complete, seem to provide one possible explanation of the results of our experiments.

The stomach secretions of the executive monkeys do indeed become considerably more acid, but not (as one might expect) during the avoidance periods. When the animals are actually pressing the levers the acidity of their stomachs rises little. The significant increase in acidity begins at the end of the avoidance session and reaches a peak several hours later, while the animal is presumably resting. This finding suggests a close relationship between the formation of ulcers and the cyclic character of the six-hours-on, six-hours-off procedure. Emotional stress, it appears, must be intermittent—turning the animal's system on and off, so to speak—if it is to cause ulcers. Continuous emotional stress seems to permit a stable adjustment (at least for a while) under which ulcers do not develop. It is tempting to consider the analogy of the vacuum tube or light bulb which seems to last much longer under conditions of continuous current than when it is subjected to frequent heating and cooling.

Like most analogies, this one limps badly and has its limitations. For example, our experiments show that periodic stress does not always bring on ulcers, and Polish's findings are consistent with this. His measurements indicate that the greatest increase in acidity occurs after a six-hour avoidance session. After a three-hour session acidity rises, but less sharply; after a one-hour session it does not rise at all. Periodic emotional stress apparently causes ulcers only if its period coincides with that of some natural rhythm of the gastrointestinal system.

Obviously our knowledge of the physiological and psychological processes which produce ulcers is far from complete. Our understanding of even the relatively well-controlled experiments I have described is just beginning to progress beyond the primitive level. We have yet to discover why emotional stress steps up the stomach's acidity later rather than immediately. We are still looking for a method of producing ulcers at will, in days rather than weeks. Eventually we hope to learn to detect an incipient ulcer before the animal collapses, by examinining the subject's blood, urine and other secretions, thus making post-mortem examinations unnecessary.

There are many other questions about the effects of emotional stress which we have not yet begun to investigate. Really thorough examination of the experimental animals might well show other types of damage of which we are at present unaware. The two monkeys which died of causes unrelated to ulcers, for example, may have succumbed because their resistance had been lowered in some way by psychological stress. It would be surprising to find physical processes wholly unimpaired in monkeys who have been on a 30-minutes-on, 30-minutes-off schedule for several weeks. The opportunity to bring psychosomatic relationships under experimental scrutiny in the laboratory seems to open broad horizons for research into the causes and alleviation of this poorly understood class of ills.

THE PHYSIOLOGY OF FEAR AND ANGER

Daniel H. Funkenstein

When the late Walter B. Cannon, by his historic experiments nearly half a century ago, showed a connection between emotions and certain physiological changes in the body, he opened a new frontier for psychology and medicine. His work, coupled with that of Sigmund Freud, led to psychosomatic medicine. It also made the emotions accessible to laboratory measurement and analysis. Within the last few years there has been a keen revival of interest in this research, because of some important new discoveries which have sharpened our understanding of specific emotions and their bodily expressions. It has been learned, for instance, that anger and fear produce different physiological reactions and can be distinguished from each other. The findings have given us a fresh outlook from which to study mental illnesses.

The best way to begin the account of this recent work is to start with Cannon's own summary of what he learned. Cannon found that when an animal was confronted with a situation which evoked pain, rage or fear, it responded with a set of physiological reactions which prepared it to meet the threat with "fight" or "flight." These reactions, said Cannon, were mobilized by the secretion of adrenalin: when the cortex of the brain perceived the threat, it sent a stimulus down the sympathetic branch of the autonomic nervous system to the adrenal glands and they secreted the hormone. Cannon graphically described the results as follows:

"Respiration deepens; the heart beats more rapidly; the arterial pressure rises; the blood is shifted away from the stom-

ach and intestines to the heart and central nervous system and the muscles; the processes in the alimentary canal cease; sugar is freed from the reserves in the liver; the spleen contracts and discharges its content of concentrated corpuscles, and adrenin is secreted from the adrenal

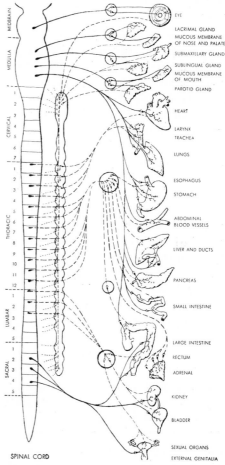

EYE
LACRIMAL GLAND
MUCOUS MEMBRANE OF NOSE AND PALATE
SUBMAXILLARY GLAND
SUBLINGUAL GLAND
MUCOUS MEMBRANE OF MOUTH
PAROTID GLAND
HEART
LARYNX
TRACHEA
LUNGS
ESOPHAGUS
STOMACH
ABDOMINAL BLOOD VESSELS
LIVER AND DUCTS
PANCREAS
SMALL INTESTINE
LARGE INTESTINE
RECTUM
ADRENAL
KIDNEY
BLADDER
SEXUAL ORGANS
EXTERNAL GENITALIA

MIDBRAIN
MEDULLA
CERVICAL 1 2 3 4 5 6 7
THORACIC 1 2 3 4 5 6 7 8 9 10 11 12
LUMBAR 1 2 3 4 5
SACRAL 1 2 3 4 5

SPINAL CORD

The autonomic nervous system is represented by this diagram. The parasympathetic branches, arising from the brain and sacral vertebrae, are indicated by solid lines; the sympathetic branches, arising from the thoracic and lumbar vertebrae, are shown by dashed lines.

267

medulla. The key to these marvelous transformations in the body is found in relating them to the natural accompaniments of fear and rage—running away in order to escape from danger, and attacking in order to be dominant. Whichever the action, a life-or-death struggle may ensue.

"The emotional responses just listed may reasonably be regarded as preparatory for struggle. They are adjustments which, so far as possible, put the organism in readiness for meeting the demands which will be made upon it. The secreted adrenin cooperates with sympathetic nerve impulses in calling forth stored glycogen from the liver, thus flooding the blood with sugar for the use of laboring muscles; it helps in distributing the blood in abundance to the heart, the brain, and the limbs (*i.e.,* to the parts essential for intense physical effort) while taking it away from the inhibited organs in the abdomen; it quickly abolishes the effects of muscular fatigue so that the organism which can muster adrenin in the blood can restore to its tired muscles the same readiness to act which they had when fresh; and it renders the blood more rapidly coagulable. The increased respiration, the redistributed blood running at high pressure, and the more numerous red corpuscles set free from the spleen provide for essential oxygen and for riddance of acid waste, and make a setting for instantaneous and supreme action. In short, all these changes are directly serviceable in rendering the organism more effective in that violent display of energy which fear or rage may involve."

Cannon recognized that among all these physiological changes there were a few which could not be ascribed directly to the action of adrenalin. He therefore postulated that the hormone was supplemented by two additional substances from the sympathetic nerves. An active agent, distinguishable from adrenalin, was eventually identified in 1948, when B. F. Tullar and M. L. Tainter at length succeeded in preparing the optically active form of the substance. It proved to be a second hormone secreted by the adrenal medulla. Called nor-adrenalin, it differs markedly from adrenalin in its physiological effects. Whereas adrenalin elicits profound physiological changes in almost every system in the body, nor-adrenalin apparently has only one important primary effect: namely, it stimulates the contraction of small blood vessels and increases the resistance to the flow of blood.

An animal exhibits only two major emotions in response to a threatening situation: namely, rage and fear. A man, however, may experience three: anger directed outward (the counterpart of rage), anger directed toward himself (depression) and anxiety, or fear. In studies of physiological changes accompanying various emotional states among patients at the New York Hospital, H. G. Wolff and his co-workers noticed that anger produced effects quite different from those of depression or fear. For example, when a subject was angry, the stomach lining became red and there was an increase in its rhythmic contractions and in the secretion of hydrochloric acid. When the same subject was depressed or frightened, the stomach lining was pale in color and there was a decrease in peristaltic movements and in the hydrochloric acid secretion.

The experiments of Wolff, the evidence that the adrenal medulla secreted two substances rather than one and certain clinical observations led our group at the Harvard Medical School to investigate whether adrenalin and nor-adrenalin might be specific indicators which distinguished one emotion from another. The clinical observations had to do with the effects of a drug, mecholyl, on psychotic patients. We had been studying their blood-pressure responses to injections of adrenalin, which acts on the sympathetic nervous system, and mecholyl, which stimulates the parasympathetic system. On the basis of their blood-pressure reactions, psychotic patients could be classified into seven groups (see charts). This test had proved of value in predicting patients' responses to psychiatric treatments, such as electric shock and insulin: certain groups responded better to the treatments than others. But more interesting was the fact that psychotic patients with high blood pressure reacted to the injection of mecholyl in two distinctly different ways. In one group there was only a small drop in the blood pressure after the injection, and the pressure returned to the usually high level within three to eight minutes. In the other group the blood pressure dropped markedly after the injection and remained below the pre-injection level even after 25 minutes. Not only were the physiological reactions quite different, but the two groups of patients also differed in personality and in response to treatment. Thirty-nine of 42 patients whose blood pressure was sharply lowered by mecholyl improved with electric shock treatment, whereas only three of 21 in the other group improved with the same treatment. Further, the two groups showed distinctly different results in projective psychological tests such as the Rorschach.

All this suggested that the two groups of patients might be differentiated on the basis of emotions. Most psychotic patients in emotional turmoil express the

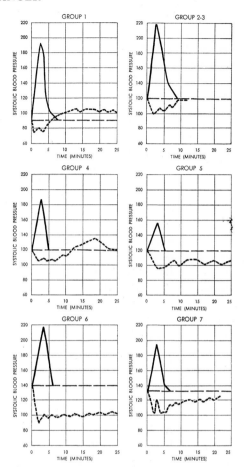

Seven groups of psychotic patients were distinguished on the basis of their blood pressure after injection with adrenalin or mecholyl. In these six charts the basal systolic blood pressure of the patients is indicated by the broken horizontal line. The solid curve shows their response to adrenalin; the broken curve, their response to mecholyl. Groups 2 and 3 are combined because the difference between them is too slight to show in the graph. The mecholyl response for Group 7 is incomplete because of experimental difficulties.

same emotion constantly over a period of days, weeks or months. Psychiatrists determined the predominant emotion expressed by each of 63 patients who had been tested with mecholyl, without knowing in which physiological group they had been classified. When the subjects' emotional and physiological ratings were compared, it turned out that almost all of the patients who were generally angry at other people fell in Group N (a small, temporary reduction of blood pressure by mecholyl), while almost all those who were usually depressed or frightened were in Group E (sharp response to mecholyl). In other words, the physiological reactions were significantly related to the emotional content of the patients' psychoses.

The next step was to find out whether the same test could distinguish emotions in normal, healthy people, using medical students as subjects. They were studied at a time when they were under stress—while they were awaiting the decisions of hospitals on their applications for internships. As the competition among the students for the hospitals of their choice is keen, the period just prior to such announcements is a time of emotional turmoil for the men. A group of students who responded to this situation with elevated blood pressure was given the standard dose of mecholyl. The results were the same as for the psychotic patients: students who were angry at others for the situation in which they found themselves had a Type N physiological reaction; those who felt depressed (angry at themselves) or anxious showed a Type E physiological reaction. The reaction was related only to their temporary emotional state; after the internships were settled and their blood pressures had returned to pre-stress levels, all the students reacted the same way to the injection of mecholyl.

It was at this point that we undertook to investigate the comparative effects of adrenalin and nor-adrenalin. A group of workers at the Presbyterian Hospital in New York had shown that injections of

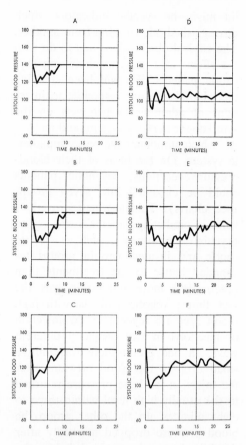

Type *N* response to the injection of mecholyl is traced by the heavy line in the charts on the left. The broken line represents the basal blood pressure. The response is shown for three kinds of subject: (A) healthy individuals under stress who respond with anger toward others, (B) healthy individuals whose blood pressure has been elevated with nor-adrenalin and (C) psychotic individuals with elevated blood pressure and anger toward others.

Type E response to the injection of mecholyl is similarly traced by the heavy line in the charts on the right. In these charts the response is shown for three different kinds of subject: (D) healthy individuals under stress who respond with anger directed inward, or depression, (E) healthy individuals whose blood pressure has been elevated with adrenalin and (C) psychotic individuals with elevated blood pressure and depression.

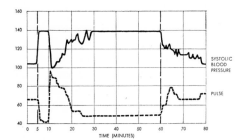

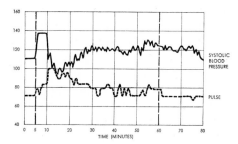

Effect of nor-adrenalin was observed by administering an infusion of the hormone for 60 minutes. After 5 minutes the blood pressure of the subject rose. After 10 minutes mecholyl was injected and the blood pressure fell. Then it rose in a Type N response.

Effect of adrenalin was observed by the same procedure. After the injection of mecholyl the systolic blood pressure of the subject remained depressed in a Type E response.

nor-adrenalin and adrenalin produced two different types of rise in blood pressure, one due to contraction of blood vessels and the other to faster pumping by the heart. Upon learning of this work, we designed experiments to test the hypothesis that the two types of elevated blood pressure, differentiated by us on the basis of mecholyl tests, indicated in one instance excessive secretion of nor-adrenalin and in the other excessive secretion of adrenalin. Healthy college students were first given a series of intravenous injections of salt water to accustom them to the procedure so that it would not disturb them. Then each subpect was tested in the following way. He was given an injection of nor-adrenalin sufficient to raise his blood pressure by 25 per cent. Then, while his blood pressure was elevated, he received the standard dose of mecholyl, and its effects on the blood pressure were noted. The next day the subject was put through the same procedure except that adrenalin was given instead of nor-adrenalin to raise the blood pressure.

Ten students were studied in this way, and in every instance the effect of nor-adrenalin was different from that of adrenalin (see charts). When the blood

pressure was elevated by nor-adrenalin, mecholyl produced only a small drop in pressure, with a return to the previous level in seven to 10 minutes. This reaction was similar to the Type N response in psychotic patients and healthy students under stress. In contrast, when the blood pressure was elevated by adrenalin, mecholyl produced the Type E response: the pressure dropped markedly and did not return to the previous level during the 25-minute observation period.

These results suggested, in the light of the earlier experiments, that anger directed outward was associated with secretion of nor-adrenalin, while depression and anxiety were associated with secretion of adrenalin. To check this hypothesis, another series of experiments was carried out.

A group of 125 college students were subjected to stress-inducing situations in the laboratory. The situations, involving frustration, were contrived to bring out each student's habitual reaction to stresses in real life; that the reactions actually were characteristic of the subjects' usual responses was confirmed by interviews with their college roommates. While the subjects were under stress, observers recorded their emotional reactions and certain physiological changes—in the blood pressure, the pulse and the so-called IJ waves stemming from the action of the heart. This test showed that students who responded to the stress with anger directed outward had physiological reactions similar to those produced by injection of nor-adrenalin, while students who responded with depression or anxiety had physiological reactions like those to adrenalin.

There remained the question: Does the same individual secrete unusual amounts of nor-adrenalin when angry and of adrenalin when frightened? Albert F. Ax, working in another laboratory in our hospital, designed experiments to study this question. He contrived laboratory stressful situations which were successful in producing on one occasion anger and on another occasion fear in the same subjects. His results showed that when a subject was angry at others, the physiological reactions were like those induced by the injection of nor-adrenalin; when the same subject was frightened, the reactions were like those to adrenalin. This indicated that the physiology was specific for the emotion rather than for the person.

In all these experiments the evidence for excessive secretion of nor-adrenalin and adrenalin was based on the physiological changes being similar to those which can be produced by the intravenous injection of nor-adrenalin and adrenalin. Since the substances involved have not been identified chemically, and the evidence is entirely physiological, at the present time we prefer to limit ourselves to the statement that the reactions are *like* those to the two hormones. However, nothing in our experiments would contradict the hypothesis that these substances are actually adrenalin and nor-adrenalin.

What is the neurophysiological mechanism whereby different emotions evoke different adrenal secretions? Although no conclusive work in this area is yet available, some recent investigations suggest a possible answer. U. S. von Euler in Sweden found that stimulation of certain areas of the hypothalamus caused the adrenal gland to secrete nor-adrenalin, whereas stimulation of other areas caused it to secrete adrenalin. These areas may correspond to those which the Nobel prize winner W. R. Hess of Zurich stimulated to produce aggressive behavior and flight, respectively, in animals. The experiments suggest that anger and fear may activate different areas in the hypothalamus, leading to production of nor-adrenalin in the first case and adrenalin in the second. Until more experiments are made, these possibilities must remain suppositions.

Some of the most intriguing work in this field was recently reported by von Euler. He compared adrenal secretions found in a number of different animals. The research material was supplied by a friend who flew to Africa to obtain the adrenal medullae of wild animals. Interpreting his findings, J. Ruesch pointed out that aggressive animals such as the lion had a relatively high amount of nor-adrenalin, while in animals such as the rabbit, which depend for survival primarily on flight, adrenalin predominated. Domestic animals, and wild animals that live very social lives (*e.g.,* the baboon), also have a high ratio of adrenalin to nor-adrenalin.

These provocative findings suggest the theory that man is born with the capacity to react with a variety of emotions (has within him the lion and the rabbit), and that his early childhood experiences largely determine in which of these ways he will react under stress.

Stated in another way, the evolutional process of man's emotional development is completed in the bosom of the family. We have found in other studies that individuals' habitual emotional reactions have a high correlation with their perceptions of psychological factors in their families.

This entire series of experiments yielded data which can be understood in the frame of reference of psychoanalytical observations. According to theory, anger directed outward is characteristic of an earlier stage of childhood than is anger directed toward the self or anxiety (conflicts over hostility). The latter two emotions are the result of the acculturation of the child. If the physiological development of the child parallels its psychological development, then we should expect to find that the ratio of nor-adrenalin to adrenalin is higher in infants than in older children. Bernt Hokfelt and G. B. West established that this is indeed the case: at an early age the adrenal medulla has more nor-adrenalin, but later adrenalin becomes dominant.

Paranoid patients show a greater degree of regression to infantile behavior than do patients with depression or anxiety neurosis. And it will be recalled that in our tests paranoid patients showed signs of excessive secretion of nor-adrenalin, while depressed and anxious patients exhibited symptoms of adrenalin secretion.

These parallels between psychological and physiological development suggest further studies and some theories for testing. Standing on the shoulders of Cannon and Freud, we have extended our view of human behavior and discovered fertile new fields for exploration.

THE PHYSIOLOGICAL DIFFERENTIATION BETWEEN FEAR AND ANGER IN HUMANS   Albert F. Ax

Simultaneous multiple recording of several physiological reactions during emotional changes may serve several purposes. The primary purpose is to add to our understanding of the precise nature of the total emotional reaction, which has not been adequately studied. From the psychological point of view, the details of the physiological state constitute an essential part of the conditions existing at the time of observation.

Multiple recording contributes more

Reprinted by permission of the journal and author from *Psychosomatic Medicine*, Vol. 15, 1955.

than the mere addition of variables for observation. The quantitative patterns of these differentially influenced processes (such as blood pressure, heart rate, sweating, skin temperature) provide a qualitative description of the emotional state at the physiological level and may be diagnostic of the type of emotional reaction. This characteristic of being differentially influenced by varying emotional states was an essential consideration in selecting which variables to record. Other criteria for selecting the variables were that they be available for continuous recording and that recording them would not seriously disturb the subject.

The multiple-variable approach for studying physiological states may provide answers to three different questions:

(1) Can individuals be classified in terms of their physiological reaction syndromes, which are paradigmed by the psychosomatic diseases?

(2) Can the physiological reactions serve as an emotional or motivational indicator during psychological observation? This is a classical use of physiological reactions made by psychologists.

(3) The third approach seeks for patterns of physiological reaction which may be diagnostic of the primary emotional states. It seeks to examine, for example, Cannon's hypothesis that fear and anger are essentially similar physiological reactions.

This paper reports a study of the latter type of polygraph research: that is, the physiological differentiation of two emotional states. Fear and anger were selected for study as being the two emotional states most often described as being identical physiological states. Although Cannon's theory that "fight and flight" excitement states have similar visceral patterns has been demonstrated to be generally true, there has always existed the possibility that a closer inspection of the physiological reaction patterns might reveal a differentiation or subtyping of the excitement states.

There have been hints deriving from both theoretical and experimental sources that question the hypothesis of the undifferentiated physiological state. Magda Arnold (1), arguing from both neurological evidence and a reconsideration of published experimental data, concluded that fear is a strong arousal state of the sympathetic branch of the autonomic nervous system, whereas anger is a strong arousal state of both the sympathetic and parasympathetic branches of the autonomic nervous system. Wolf and Wolff have described increases in motility, secretion, and vascular dilatation of the viscera associated with anger or resentment and decreases in these functions during anxiety and depression. Mittleman and Wolff, in a study of finger temperature changes during psychoanalytical therapy, reported that decreases in temperature were associated with periods of anxiety and discussions of unpleasant topics, while during sexual excitement there were increases in finger temperature.

None of these studies, however, clearly demonstrated that these reported differences in physiological response might not be due either to different intensities of arousal or merely to the unique response patterns of a single individual. Accordingly, for this study it was planned to select an adequate sample and to record simultaneously with the emotional arousal a number of physiological reactions which could produce "patterns" of response.

Procedure

The variables recorded are shown in Fig. 1. The Grass eight-channel electroencephalograph was used as the main recorder and amplifier. Since the Grass has only $A. C.$ amplifiers, modulated $A. C.$ envelopes were used for all continuous variables. The transducers can be briefly described.

(1) The electrocardiogram was recorded directly from ear and leg leads.

(2) The ballistocardiogram, as an index of stroke volume, was produced by a crystal phono pickup imbedded in a wooden block lying across the subject's ankles. A small lead weight on the end of the stylus converts the pickup into an efficient ac-

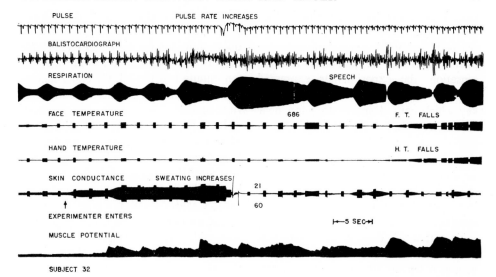

FIG. 1. The variables recorded in this study. The Grass eight-channel electroencephalograph was used as the main recorder and amplifier. Since the Grass has only *A.C.* amplifiers, modulated *A.C.* envelopes were used for all continuous variables.

celerometer which responds to the ballistic reaction of the body to ejection of blood from the heart.

(3) Respiration was recorded from thorax and abdominal pneumograph tubes activating an inductance tambour.

(4 and 5) Face and finger skin temperatures were detected by V-611 Western Electric thermistors in an *A. C.* bridge using the electroencephalograph for recording the imbalance.

(6) The skin conductance, as the index of sweating of the volar surfaces of two fingers of one hand, was also measured by a bridge using 60-cycle *A. C.*

(7) Finally, at the bottom of the chart is the integrated muscle potential index from the frontalis muscle picked up by sponge electrodes and integrated and recorded as a modulated 60-cycle envelope. Systolic and diastolic blood pressures were taken every minute by a nurse.

The room temperature was held constant at 23° C. ± 0.1° C.

The subject reclined in the testing room on a rigid table covered by a hair mattress. The nurse and experimenter were also in this room. The polygraph and operator were in an adjacent room.

The subjects were recruited through newspaper advertisements and a state employment agency. The only criteria for inclusion were that they must be free from any illness and within the age limits of 21 and 55 years. The average age was 27 years; 22 were men and 21 women. They were paid $3.00 for 2 hours. Only those whose blood pressure did not exceed 140/90 after 20 minutes' rest were included.

The subjects were told that this was a study of the physiological differences between people with hypertension and those without hypertension, that their only task was to relax on the bed and listen to their preferred music for about an hour. A rest period of 25 minutes preceded the stimulus periods. The stimulation periods of fear and anger were alternated so that 22 subjects received the fear stimulation first and 21 subjects received the anger stimulation first.

The fear stimulus consisted of a gradually increasing intermittent shock stimulus to the little finger which never reached an intensity sufficient to cause pain. When the subject reported the sensation, the experimenter expressed surprise, checked the wiring, pressed a key which caused sparks to jump near the subject, then exclaimed with alarm that this was a dangerous high-voltage short circuit. The experimenter created an atmosphere of alarm and confusion. After five minutes from the time the subject reported the shock, the experimenter removed the shock wire, assuring the subject that all danger was past, that the short circuit had been found and repaired. A ten- to fifteen-minute recovery period with music separated the fear and anger stimuli.

The polygraph operator was the key figure for the anger situation. He was described to the subject as not the regular operator but one who had been fired for incompetence and arrogance, but due to the sickness of the regular operator he had to be employed for that day. Thus he was labeled as a suitable target for hostility by the subject.

At the beginning of the anger stimulus, the operator entered the room stating he must check the wiring because some of the calibrations might be off. The experimenter objected but agreed to go into the other room and operate the polygraph. The operator shut off the music, criticized the nurse, and told the subject sarcastically that it would have helped if he had been on time. He checked the electrodes, roughly adjusted the subject, and criticized him for moving, noncooperation, and other behavior. After five minutes of abuse, the operator left and the experimenter returned, apologizing for this rude behavior. The experimenter reassured the subject and urged him to relax once more. After ten minutes the experimenter interviewed the subject for a five-minute period, questioning his memory and feelings for the first interruption; following another ten-minute rest period, the experimenter questioned him about the second interruption.

Remarks made by subjects either just after the stress stimulus or during the interviews illustrate their feeling states. Just after the operator left the room following the "anger" stimulus, one female subject said, "Well! It's easy to see he is not an educated man." A male subject said, "Say, what goes on here? I was just about to punch that character on the nose." Examples of fear reactions were also clearly genuine. One woman kept pleading, "Please take the wires off. Oh! Please help me." Another said during the interview that she had prayed to be spared during the fear episode. A man said, "Well, everybody has to go sometime. I thought this might be my time."

Some subjects used rather far-fetched rationalizations to limit or prevent fear. One man with great assurance said, "I wasn't really worried because I knew these wires were much too small to be dangerous." One subject did not report the shock for several minutes. The experimenter noticed an involuntary twitching and asked about it. The subject said, "Oh, I thought that was just part of the experiment."

The records for 6 subjects were not included in this study because it was immediately decided, purely on the basis of the interview and observation before seeing the polygraph data, that these subjects did not become either sufficiently angry or frightened to justify comparison.

For all variables the maximum rises and falls during the stimulus period and the following two minutes (a total of seven minutes) were recorded as deviations from the resting level just prior to the stimulus period. Systolic and diastolic *blood pressures* recorded every minute were scored in millimeters of mercury. The *heart rate* was averaged for a six-second interval in selecting the maximum and minimum points. The *ballistocardiograph* score was the average voltage for approximately ten beats, covering exactly either two or three complete respirations.

Respiration was scored for changes in rate, amplitude, and inspiration/respiration ratio. Five consecutive breaths whose volume was judged to be maximum were selected for measurement. The I/R ratio and amplitude showed no significant difference for fear and anger. An index of volume, composed of the product of rate times amplitude, showed a significant difference which, however, was less significant than rate alone. Hence, rate was chosen as the variable to represent respiration.

Both *face temperature and hand temperature* were expressed in log units with the zero of the scale at 15° C., which is approximately 1° C. below the wet bulb thermometer temperature for the conditions of the experiment. Thus, if the finger were covered with perspiration and blood flow were zero, the temperature on the log units scale would approximate zero.

The *sweating index* was the skin conductance, which is the reciprocal of the resistance component of the impedance. Two aspects of conductance were scored:

(1) the skin conductance rise as the maximum increase in conductance above the resting level just prior to the experimental period;

(2) the number of increments per unit time in skin conductance of at least 1 micromho, which must have increased at least one micromho in three seconds.

One score for *muscle tension* was the maximum change in muscle potential which was averaged over a fifteen-second interval. The second muscle tension score was the average number of potential peaks per unit time. A peak was defined as an increment which doubled its size within three seconds.

Results

In Table 1 are tabulated the means, standard deviations, differences of means for anger and fear, the t of the differences, and the null probabilities for the fourteen variables. In Fig. 2, these means are graphed in standard score units. The black bars represent the changes during the anger stimulus, and the white bars the changes during the fear stimulus. The + signs indicate increases in the variable, and the − signs decreases. Seven of the variables show significant differences between anger and fear. Four of the variables—diastolic blood pressure rises ($DBP+$), heart rate falls ($HR-$), number of galvanic skin responses ($\#GSR$), and muscle tension increases ($MT+$)—have greater average reactions for anger. Three variables—skin conductance increases ($SC+$), number of muscle tension peaks ($\#MTP$), and respiration rate increases ($RR+$)—have greater average reactions for fear.

It is of value to combine and express quantitatively these differences between the reactions of anger and fear, and also to provide a means of testing the significance of the combined differences. The difference between fear and anger which we wished to describe was not an amplitude difference but only the qualitative difference, which would be revealed in the profile shape with all aver-

TABLE 1. CHARACTERISTICS OF THE RAW SCORES

| | Means | | σ | | | | |
	A	F	A	F	MA − MF	t	Prob t
DBP+	17.83	14.49	9.33	7.97	3.34	2.47	.02
HR−	6.02	3.98	3.72	3.41	2.04	3.66	<.01
FT−	.00498	.00414	.00390	.00366	.000842	1.22	>.10
HT−	.0497	.0448	.0320	.0208	.00489	.841	>.10
#GSR	11.56	4.74	7.84	5.08	6.82	5.60	<.01
MT+	4.35	13.34	3.12	2.08	1.01	2.54	.02
BC−	22.6	18.4	38.9	40.3	4.2	.79	>.10
BC+	173.2	142.8	178.5	134.4	31.56	1.15	>.10
SBP+	19.19	20.35	8.58	11.77	−1.16	.68	>.10
HR+	25.79	30.32	14.19	17.69	−4.53	1.59	>.10
SC+	9.41	14.81	18.88	10.42	−5.40	5.2	<.01
#MTP	10.45	13.17	7.88	7.94	−2.72	2.19	.04
FT+	.00294	.00348	.00382	.00317	−.00054	.87	>.10
RR+	2.31	6.00	3.99	6.50	−3.69	3.46	<.01

age amplitude differences eliminated. Although there was no significant average amplitude difference between the fear and anger profiles, this factor was completely eliminated by the following procedure, illustrated for 1 subject in Table 2.

Standard scores based on the mean and standard deviation for both anger and fear combined were computed for these seven variables for the 43 subjects. The scores of each profile were then summed across the seven variables.

The difference between these two sums $(F - A)$ was obtained and divided by 7 to obtain the average difference in amplitude for this subject. This average difference was then subtracted from each score of the fear profile to produce the corrected fear profile (Fc). The average amplitude of this corrected fear profile was now identical to the average amplitude of the anger profile. In the next step, each of these corrected fear scores was subtracted from its corresponding anger score $(A - Fc)$. The mean of the

TABLE 2. SAMPLE OF METHOD FOR COMPUTING THE PROFILE DIFFERENCE SCORES

	A > F				A < F		
Subject 1.	DBP+	HR−	MT+	#GSR	SC+	RR+	#MTP
F	−.470	1.077	−.657	− .700	1.381	− .018	1.146	ΣF	1.759
A	−.696	2.962	−.955	.377	.685	−1.667	.399	ΣA	1.105
Fc	−.563	.984	−.750	− .793	1.288	− .111	1.053	F − A	.654
A − Fc	−.133	1.978	−.205	1.170	− .603	−1.556	− .654	M$_{f-a}$	.093
	Σ$_{a>f}$		M$_{a>f}$		Σ$_{a<f}$		M$_{a<f}$	M$_{a>f}$ − M$_{a<f}$	
	2.810		.702		−2.813		−.938	1.640	

differences for the four variables whose average amplitude was greater for anger was obtained ($M_{a > f}$, which for Subject 1 is .702). Likewise, the mean of the differences for the three variables whose average amplitude was less for anger was obtained ($M_{a < f} = -.938$). This latter mean difference was subtracted from the former [.702 − (−.938)] to produce the *profile difference score* of 1.640, which is a sum composed of the differences ($A - F$) between those variables which are greater for anger plus the negative differences $-(A - F)$ between those variables which are greater for fear.

It might appear more direct merely to have summed the seven absolute differences and called it a "profile shape difference score." The difficulty with such a score is that even by the null hypothesis of no average difference between the shapes of the two profiles, the sum would have a mean of finite value of unknown distribution. Obtaining its theoretical distribution is complicated by intercorrelation of the variables.

The more useful profile difference score obtained, as described above, by subtracting the mean ($F > A$) differences from the mean ($A > F$) differences produces a distribution with a theoretical mean of zero, assuming the null hypothesis of no difference in shape between the anger and fear profiles. The reason the theoretical mean of this distribution of *profile difference scores* is zero is because it is a sum of seven distributions, each of which has a theoretical mean of zero, each being a distribution of differences of standard scores whose means are zero.

The actual distribution of the *profile difference scores* deviated very significantly from the theoretical one derived from the null hypothesis. Forty-two of the forty-three scores were positive,

whereas the null expectation is that approximately half would be positive and half negative. The mean of the distribution was 1.087 with a t of 10.24, which indicates that the null hypothesis may be rejected with a high degree of confidence.

Discussion

It could be argued that the assignment of variables to the anger-greater-than-fear category and to the fear-greater-than-anger category on the basis of their mean differences would, of necessity, produce positive profile difference scores. There are, however, two legitimate methods for assignment of variables to the category: (1) by an hypothesis independent of this data; and (2) by inclusion of only those variables which have differences sufficiently great to establish with confidence their correct category. Both methods were employed in this study. The data from the first 16 subjects were examined and found to have the pattern relationships described here for the total group. The hypothesis is not completely independent, however, because the original 16 subjects are included in the total. The second principle of including only those variables showing significant differences bears the burden of our thesis. The fact that 50 per cent of the variables show significant differences around the .99 level of confidence constitutes the evidence that there is a difference in physiological reaction pattern to the two stimulus conditions here labeled "anger" and "fear." The individual *profile difference score* is a quantitative measure of the difference in reaction made by the individual for the two stimulus situations. It might be considered an index of emotional differentiation expressed in the physiological reaction.

The differences found can hardly be

due to amplitude differences of the two emotional states, since some reactions were greater for fear and others were greater for anger. The differences remained when the profiles were equated for amplitude.

Possible interference effects due to the sequence of one stimulus situation following the other were controlled by stimulating half of the group first to anger and half of the group first to fear.

There was no selection of subjects which could have corrupted the results, since the only subjects eliminated were those 6 deemed not to have been both angered and frightened purely on the basis of the interview and observation, without reference to the physiological reactions.

An argument with some relevance may be raised. Possibly the differences found are not the result of two different emotional reactions, but related somehow to differences in the procedure and behavior of the subject during the two stimulus situations. Possibly there was more talking or small movements during one stimulus period than during the other. The two procedures were made as similar as possible. Close scrutiny of the records and of the wire recordings reveals no such systematic difference.

The use of two aspects of one variable, such as maximum rise in skin conductance ($SC+$) and the number of rises in skin conductance ($\#GSR$), or the maximum change in muscle tension ($MT+$) and the number of peaks in muscle tension ($\#MTP$) might be questioned. If two aspects of one variable were merely reciprocals of each other, they would be equally discriminative of the two states, but the second would contribute no additional discrimination over the first. Product moment correlations between maximum rise in skin conductance and number of rises in skin conductance were $-.05$ for fear and $+.38$ for anger. Correlations of muscle tension change with number of muscle tension peaks were $+.07$ for fear and $+.16$ for anger, which indicates almost a complete lack of dependence between them. The $+.38$ correlation between maximum changes in skin conductance and number of rises in skin conductance during anger probably indicates a small tendency for those subjects with the larger sweating response to make these responses more frequently but only during anger. The complete lack of substantial negative correlation certainly removes any question of these two aspects being merely reciprocals of each other.

A rather surprising finding is the general lack of correlation between the varibles. The intervariable correlations are found in Table 3. Very few approach significance, and those are quite small compared to the self-correlations for fear and anger, which average .53. This lack of correlation among the physiological reactions fits a general hypothesis underlying this study: that is, that there is marked uniqueness in physiological expression of emotion. Evidence which further supports this thesis is the significantly larger between-subjects variance (9.68), as compared with the within-subjects variance (4.00), which has an F ratio of 2.42, significant at the 99 per cent level of confidence. (It was determined that neither distribution differed significantly from normal.) This finding is in essential agreement with results reported by Lacey and by Malmo (5, 6, 7, 8), in which various types of autonomic responses are described as being characteristic either of the individual or of a special diagnostic group. This well-established specificity of autonomic-response pattern in a sense highlights the

TABLE 3. CORRELATIONS FOR ANGER AND FEAR FOR THE VARIABLES WHICH DISTINGUISHED SIGNIFICANTLY BETWEEN ANGER AND FEAR

		DBP+	HR−	#GSR	MT+	SC+	#MTP	RR+
DBP+	A		−.17	.32	−.12	.38	.10	.16
		.51a						
	F		−.11	−.10	−.08	−.03	.08	.22
HR−	A			−.09	−.09	−.04	−.16	−.00
			.49a					
	F			−.01	.10	.13	.06	.01
#GSR	A				−.28	.38	.00	−.12
				.42a				
	F				−.06	−.05	.14	−.16
MT+	A					−.17	.16	.24
					.64a			
	F					−.06	.07	−.04
SC+	A						.06	.25
						.77a		
	F						−.09	−.29
#MTP	A							−.01
							.52a	
	F							−.06
RR+	A							.26a
	F							

a The self-correlations are between anger and fear.

present findings of uniformity of response, which is characteristic of a specific emotional state experienced by many different individuals. If the physiological response pattern which is diagnostic of a specific emotional state could be measured for each individual as a deviation from his characteristic response pattern, much greater accuracy of specific emotional diagnosis might be expected.

Another interesting finding was the consistently larger correlations (neglecting sign) between the variables for anger than for fear. The mean of the fear correlations .090 and for anger .157, the difference being significant at the 96 per cent level of confidence, the t being 2.25 for 20 degrees of freedom. One might interpret this greater tendency for higher correlation of the physiological reactions during anger to indicate a greater organization or integration during anger than during fear. Such an interpretation might be examined in terms of the evolutionary theory of the struggle for survival. Possibly successful attack would usually require greater mobilization and organization of the individual's resources than would flight. The paralysis of extreme fear might exemplify almost complete lack of effective integration.

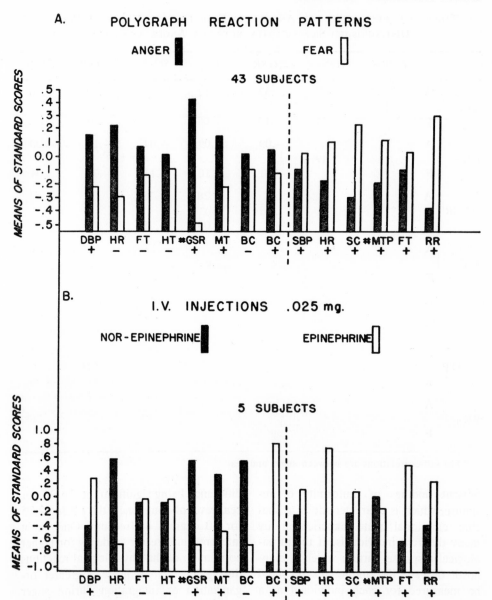

FIG. 2. The polygraph reactions, in standard score units, to the two stress situations called "anger" and "fear."

In speculating as to a possible integrating factor for these two different physiological reaction profiles for fear and anger, it was noticed that the fear profile resembled that produced by an injection of epinephrine while the anger profile more nearly resembled that of a combined epinephrine and nor-epinephrine reaction. Goldenberg reported that injections of nor-epinephrine produce a larger rise in diastolic blood pressure and a larger fall in pulse rate and stroke volume, while epinephrine produces a larger rise in systolic blood pressure, pulse rate, and stroke volume. Since the chief action of nor-epinephrine appears to be that of general vasoconstriction while that of epinephrine is one of increased cardiac output and reflex vasodilatation, we might predict that face temperature and hand temperature falls would be greater in nor-epinephrine, while face temperature rises would be greater for epinephrine. We know of no data which would suggest what to expect for muscle tension, respiration, or sweating changes.

The bar graph (Fig. 2) is arranged so that the eight variables in which the mean reactions were greater for anger are placed left of the dotted vertical line, and the remaining six variables in which the mean reactions were greater for fear are placed right of the dotted vertical line. The only variable in which the empirical data are in reversal to theory (of anger being like nor-epinephrine and fear like epinephrine) is the ballistocardiograph increases. This difference (although not statistically significant) may be explained by the fact that heart rates, on the average, were faster for fear, which could have reduced auricular filling of the heart and thus have reduced the stroke volume for fear as compared to anger. Another possible explanation is that since anger is presumed to be a state of combined epinephrine and nor-epinephrine, the epinephrine may have succeeded in dominating the ballistocardiograph variable.

The patterns obtained for fear and anger argue against the proposal by Arnold that anger differs from fear in that the parasympathetic system is strongly aroused in anger. Our findings that diastolic blood pressure rises and skin temperature falls were greater in anger and that face temperature rises were less in anger are each contrary to that of a general parasympathetic reaction. None of the values obtained, except the insignificantly greater rise of the stroke volume index during anger, on the other hand, is inconsistent with the hypothesis of a combination epinephrine- and nor-epinephrine-like reaction for anger and an epinephrine-like reaction for fear.

Conclusions

The results of this experiment indicate that two stimulus conditions which appeared to the experimenter and to the subjects as being properly termed "anger-producing" and "fear-producing" were accompanied by simultaneously recorded physiological reaction patterns which, on the average, were clearly different for the two stimuli for this sample of 43 subjects. These results do not refute Cannon's hypothesis of a unitary visceral excitement reaction but merely reveal a further differentiation in physiological reaction pattern. The patterns obtained for fear and anger are suggested as being similar to those produced by injections of epinephrine and a combination of epinephrine and nor-epinephrine. The intercorrelations of the physiological variables were significantly higher for anger than for fear, which was interpreted as indicating greater integration during anger.

These results provide further evidence for the psychophysiological unity of the organism in the sense that even the finest nuances of psychological events may be found to have a corresponding differentiation at the physiological level.

Summary

Forty-three subjects were stimulated in the laboratory to "fear" and "anger," during which the following physiological reactions were recorded:

(1) heart rate,
(2) ballistocardiogram,
(3) respiration rate,
(4) face temperature,
(5) hand temperature,
(6) skin conductance, and
(7) integrated muscle potential.

The scores used were the maximum rise and maximum fall from the preceding resting level and the number of responses of a critical value per unit time. Of the 14 scores thus obtained, 7 showed significant discrimination between anger and fear. Diastolic blood pressure rises, heart rate falls, number of rises in skin conductance, and muscle potential increases, were greater for anger than for fear, whereas skin conductance increases, number of muscle potential increases, and respiration rate increases were greater for fear than for anger. *Profile difference scores,* computed from appropriate combinations of these differences, were found to be greater than zero in 42 of the 43 cases and to have a mean which deviated very significantly from zero, which rejects the null hypothesis that there is no difference in physiological reaction between anger and fear.

The patterns obtained for anger and fear argue against the Arnold proposal that anger is a strong reaction of both the sympathetic and parasympathetic branches of the autonomic nervous systems, whereas fear is but a sympathetic reaction.

Another finding was the very low correlations among the physiological reactions and the significantly higher intercorrelations for anger than for fear, which was interpreted as indicating greater physiological integration during anger.

Between-subject variance was significantly greater than within-subject variance, which supports the findings of Lacey and Malmo that there is considerable specificity in physiological response patterns.

The physiological response patterns of anger were suggested as being similar to those produced by injections of epinephrine and nor-epinephrine combined, and those of fear as being similar to injections of epinephrine.

References

1. ARNOLD, M. "An excitatory theory of emotion." In: REYMERT, M. L. (ed.): *Feelings and Emotions.* New York, McGraw-Hill, 1950, Chap. 2.

2. CANNON, W. B. *Bodily Changes in Pain, Hunger, Fear, and Rage.* New York, Appleton, 1920.

3. GOLDENBERG, M., *et al.* The hemodynamic response of man to nor-epinephrine and epinephrine and its relation to the problem of hypertension. *Am. J. Med. 5:*792, 1948.

4. LACEY, J. I. Individual differences in somatic response patterns. *J. Comp. Physiol. Psychol. 43:*338, 1950.

5. MALMO, R. B., and SHAGASS, C. Physiologic studies of reaction to stress in anxiety and early schizophrenia. *Psychosom. Med. 11:*9, 1949.

6. MALMO, R. B., SHAGASS, C., and DAVIS, H. D. Specificity of bodily reactions under stress. *Proc. A. Res. Nerv. & Ment. Dis. 29:*231, 1950.

7. MALMO, R. B., SHAGASS, C., and HESLAM, R. M. Blood pressure response to repeated brief stress in psychoneurosis: A study of adaptation. *Canad. J. Psychol. 5:*167, 1951.

8. MALMO, R. B., SHAGASS, C., and SMITH, A. A. Responsiveness in chronic schizophrenia. *J. Person.* 19:359, 1951.

9. MITTELMAN, B., and WOLFF, H. G. Emotions and skin temperature: Observations on patients during psychotherapeutic (psychoanalytic) interviews. *Psychosom. Med.* 5:211, 1943.

10. WOLF, S., and WOLFF, H. G. *Human Gastric Function.* New York, Oxford, 1947.

AUTONOMIC FEEDBACK: THE PERCEPTION OF AUTONOMIC ACTIVITY

George Mandler, Jean M. Mandler, and Ellen T. Uviller

During the past several years there has been an increasing concern with the measurement and manipulation of the anxiety variable in human subjects. This interest is in contrast to May's summary in 1950: ". . . the problem of human anxiety has been absent from the strictly experimental specialties of psychology . . . (and) . . . has largely been omitted from the other branches of academic and theoretical psychology as well." (8, p. 99).

The measurement of anxiety has largely relied on the use of self-rating scales such as the Manifest Anxiety Scale (10) and the Test Anxiety Questionnaire (7). These scales have depended for their construction on some a priori definition of anxiety. In the case of the Manifest Anxiety Scale, this definition leaned heavily on the identification of symptoms consonant with Cameron's specification (2). For the Test Anxiety Questionnaire, the defining operations for item choices were even more vaguely dependent on an intuitive appreciation of the anxiety concept. The point need not be labored that these item choices depend to a large extent on the rather nebulous agreement as to what anxiety "really is." Such an agreement would be easily reached if the anxiety concept were securely anchored in a theoretical framework which provided invariant indices. Such indices are not available for anxiety as an individual difference variable in human subjects. Neither psychoanalytic theory nor the neo-Hullian formulation, to cite the two most frequently used models, provide clear-cut definition for the identification of the variable in human subjects.

This lack of specification for a variable which is subsumed under the emotions is not a novel problem in psychology. In 1890, William James issued a plea for a unified theoretical basis for emotional variables:

But as far as 'scientific psychology' of the emotions goes, I may have been surfeited by too much reading of the classic works on the subject, but I should as lief read verbal descriptions of the shapes of the rocks on a New Hampshire farm as toil through them again. They give one nowhere a central point of view, or a deductive or generative principle. They distinguish and refine and specify *in infinitum*

Reprinted by permission of the American Psychological Association and the authors from *The Journal of Abnormal and Social Psychology,* Vol. 56, 1958.

without ever getting on to another logical level (3, p. 448).

More recently Brown and Farber (1) have suggested a lucid solution for this problem within a Hullian framework. Their formulation, however, is not intended to make the definition of any particular emotional variable more specific. It appears, for the present, to be valuable to specify objective variables which are independent of any general solution for a theory of the emotions. In particular, it is suggested that the concept of anxiety has frequently been used in a global and complex fashion, subsuming many different constituent variables.

The study to be presented here is the first in a series of investigations of one such variable, that of autonomic feedback. Autonomic feedback is defined as the relationship between autonomic response and the subject's reported perception of such response-induced stimulation. While this feedback phenomenon encompasses a variety of different visceral as well as skeletal effects, the major source of stimulation is associated with the activity of the autonomic nervous system. We suggest that this phenomenon represents one variable which has frequently been described as part of the anxiety complex. We will take a position of theoretical neutrality on its specific relationship to anxiety. The study of autonomic feedback may be theoretically useful and empirically productive whether or not it is related to the anxiety concept. However, the three major sources of this concept do stem from general considerations of emotions and anxiety:

(1) Autonomic feedback is related to James' position that so-called emotional states can best be described as perceptions of bodily (physiological) activities. It is also related to Lange's (and more recently Wenger's) (4, 11) definition of emotions as patterns of physiological response.

(2) In the psychoanalytic literature, insofar as it has stayed close to Freud's original formulations, anxiety is primarily a perceptual or ego phenomenon. It is the subject's report of a subjective state, rather than the objective occurrence of any symptoms, which defines anxiety.

(3) The anxiety scales mentioned above contain an appreciable number of items related to the subjective report of physiological events.

The first question to be raised concerning the problem of autonomic feedback is a simple one. What is the relationship between the occurrence of autonomic response and the subject's reported perception of such activity?

Physiological events are, in the daily life of the human organism, private events. They stimulate receptors, primarily kinesthetic ones, and are therefore one of the prior conditions for the subject's report of their occurrence. However, the report of the perception of these events is necessarily couched in words which have a different history than do those words which report the perception of public, external events. Skinner (9) has presented several arguments for the nonacceptability of such emotional terms for psychological science; they are primarily based on an analysis of the conditions of reinforcement for such words as "anxious," as compared with the conditions of reinforcement for such words as "red" or "table." Briefly, the contingency between the public event or object and the occasions of reinforcement for the terms applied to them is under the control of the reinforcing community. Such control is not possible for the acquisition of mental or emotional terms. A child will be reinforced for the use of the term "table" whenever in the presence of a table; he may be reinforced for the use of the term "anxious" or "angry" under a variety of internal stimulating conditions which are unknown to the reinforcing community. The result is a wider variability in the use of the latter as compared with the former class of terms.

Under such conditions, it is unwise to expect a simple relationship between the observation of autonomic activity—once made public—and the subject's report of its occurrence. In this initial study we use a twofold approach to the problem of report, and then, given a presumably reliable measure of report, we relate it to autonomic activity.

An examination of the relationship between self-report and autonomic activity is also relevant to the validity of one of the assumptions underlying the anxiety scales mentioned above. It is often tacitly assumed that the report of these subjects is veridical. That is to say, a subject who reports a high degree of subjective anxiety or of symptoms indicative of such anxiety does in fact exhibit these symptoms. However, two different states of affairs may account for a report of considerable internal response: (a) The high scoring subject may actually exhibit a greater amount of symptoms or autonomic activity than the low scoring subject, or (b) the high scoring subject may not differ from the low scoring subject in reactivity but be more sensitive to and more likely to report small changes in autonomic response.

The study will attempt to deal with this issue by examining the level of autonomic reactivity in two groups of subjects, those who report a high as against a low degree of autonomic feedback.

Method

DESIGN

A questionnaire dealing with the frequency and intensity of autonomic self-perceptions was administered to 166 Ss. The 19 highest scoring Ss and the 13 lowest scoring Ss were exposed to an intellectual stress situation. Subsequently, they were interviewed as to their autonomic perceptions during the stress experience and ranked on the basis of this interview. The records of the 14 Ss who obtained high scores on both the questionnaire and the interview and the 9 Ss who scored low on both instruments were then examined for level of autonomic reactivity.

QUESTIONNAIRE CONSTRUCTION

The Autonomic Perception Questionnaire (APQ) consists of three sections. The first section requires free response descriptions by the Ss of their states of feeling and reactions when (a) in a state of anxiety and apprehension and (b) in a state of pleasure. The Ss were instructed that when later questions referred to anxiety or pleasure, they should understand by those terms the state which they described in this section. The second section consists of 30 graphic scale items, each of which deals with the perception of bodily activity. These items cover seven areas of bodily reaction: heart rate, perspiration, temperature changes, respiration, gastrointestinal disturbance, muscle tension, and blood pressure. An item is composed of such questions as: "When you feel anxious, how often are you aware of any change in your heart action?" with a 14.5 cm scale, the end points of which are marked "Never" and "Always." S can mark the scale at any point. For scoring purposes, the scale is divided into 10 equal intervals, and the S is assigned a score from zero to nine for each item. Of the 30 self-rating scales, 21 relate to feelings when in a state of anxiety, and nine relate to the state of pleasure.

The third section of the questionnaire consists of 70 MMPI items. Fifty are from the Manifest Anxiety Scale, and an additional 20 were selected from the MMPI as dealing with reports of internal bodily stimulation. These 20 items, together with 14 contained in the MAS, make up a new 34-item Body Perception Scale (BPS).

The questionnaire was administered to 166 Harvard College students (primarily sophomores) as part of a course requirement. Prior to the administration of the questionnaire, Ss were asked to indicate whether they would be willing to volunteer for subsequent sessions, without being informed of the nature of these sessions.

THE STRESS SITUATION

The Ss for the stress experiment were selected on the basis of their total score on the 21 anxiety items of the APQ. Of the 25 highest scoring and the 25 lowest scoring Ss who were requested to participate in another individual session, 19 Highs and 13 Lows kept their appointments. Volunteering did not affect the selection of Ss and showed no differential tendency in participation.

The stress situation consisted of three tasks with concomitant physiological recording. S was seated with his back to the experimenter and the recording apparatus, facing a wall on which the task materials were presented. After a 20-minute adaptation period, S was told that he was to be given a series of standardized intelligence tests which should present no difficulty to the average col-

lege student. The tasks, a logical reasoning test, a vocabulary test, and a verbal maze, were designed to be extremely difficult, and no S was able to complete any of them satisfactorily. They were presented to all Ss in the same order:

(1) The reasoning test consisted of 15 items. S was presented with a series of propositions. He was then given 15 statements and was required to indicate the truth or falsity of these deductions from the propositions. The mean number correct on this test was 7.2 (out of 15).

(2) The vocabulary test consisted of 10 items, each of which presented a word and a choice of five definitions. The mean number correct was 2.6 (out of 10), which indicates the difficulty of the task.

(3) In the Verbal Maze, S was presented with a series of choice points consisting of 2, 3, 4, or 5 letters. Each particular combination of letters had one correct choice which permitted S to go on to the next choice point. A trial consisted of 12 such choice points, which were repeated for every trial. After four trials, S was told that he was doing very badly (which every S was in fact) and then was given two more trials.

PHYSIOLOGICAL MEASURES

A six-channel Grass polygraph was used to obtain measures of autonomic activity.[1] The basic equipment consisted of a Grass pen-recorder, driven by standard Grass D.C. amplifiers. Five channels were used in the present study:

(1) *Heart rate.* A cardiotachometer gives either a direct reading of the conventional EKG record, or a tachometer record which supplies a reading of interbeat intervals which can be directly translated into beat-to-beat changes in heart rate.

(2) *Psycho-galvanic response.* Pream-

---

[1] Major credit for the instrumentation goes to Albert Grass and Walter Bird of the Grass Instrument Company, Quincy, Massachusetts.

plification was supplied by a Fels Dermohmmeter,[2] which incorporates an automatic range reset feature. The subject current is 70 microamps. Cup electrodes were used on the S's palms.

(3) *Respiration*. A standard pneumograph and a Grass PT-5 pressure transducer were used.

(4) *Face temperature*. A Tele-Thermometer [2] with a thermistor probe placed on S's cheek was employed.

(5) *Blood volume*. A Waters oximeter, measuring changes in the opacity of the earlobe, was used as a pickup. The major variable contributing to change in opacity is assumed to be blood volume, which in turn is related to pressure changes.

Results and Discussion

Questionnaire and interview data. Table 1 shows the intercorrelations between the two parts of the APQ (Anxiety and Pleasure), the MAS (Manifest Anxiety Scale) and the BPS (Body Perception Scale). All correlations except that between Pleasure APQ and BPS for volunteers, are significant at the .01 level or better. The highest correlation is that of .70 between the MAS and the BPS. When the 14 overlapping items are removed from the BPS, the correlation drops to .60. The hypothesis that the

TABLE 1. INTERCORRELATIONS AND MEANS FOR QUESTIONNAIRE SCALES

	Anxiety APQ		Pleasure APQ		MAS		BPS
Anxiety APQ	—						
Pleasure APQ	.50	.45	—				
MAS	.52	.51	.31	.28	—		
BPS	.52	.52	.20	.37	.67	.73	—
Mean Volunteers	81.6		25.7		17.51		6.46
(N = 74)							
Mean Nonvolunteers	81.6		22.8		16.34		6.24
(N = 92)							

Note.—The first correlation given is for volunteer Ss, the second for nonvolunteer Ss.

POSTEXPERIMENTAL INTERVIEW

Following the stress situation, the S was given a structured interview to elicit his perceptions of autonomic changes during stress. Eight questions tapped areas similar to those used in the Autonomic Perception Questionnaire. The interview was scored by assigning values of two, one, and zero to the Ss' responses, corresponding to reports of much, little, or no autonomic feedback.

[2] Obtained from the Yellow Springs Instrument Co., Yellow Springs, Ohio.

Manifest Anxiety Scale is significantly related to Ss' report of internal perceptions is sustained. The Anxiety APQ, the major concern in this investigation, shows consistent correlations around .50 with the three other scales. This finding supports the view that the questionnaire has some communality with other anxiety-related measures. Of special interest are the positive correlations shown by the Pleasure APQ, indicating that Ss who report more internal stimulation do so whether the reference is to pleasurable or to anxiety-arousing situations. Whether this is an autonomic or a perceptual phenomenon or a function of response set is, of course, open to question. Finally, there are no significant differences between volunteers and nonvolunteers on either correlations or scale means. This may be related to the fact that Ss volunteered before being aware of the nature of the tests to be taken.

As indicated above, the 19 highest scoring and the 14 lowest scoring Ss on the Anxiety APQ participated in the stress situation. The range of their postexperimental interview scores extends from 0 to 16, which is the same as the theoretical range. The mean score for the high APQ Ss was 7.2; for the low APQ Ss, it was 4.1 ($p < .05$). This finding suggests some validity in the APQ, which taps the Ss' general perception of autonomic reactions. The specific report of autonomic reactions in a stress situation is related to the more general APQ score.

The interview scores of the 32 Ss were divided at the median. Fourteen of the 19 high APQ Ss were also high on the interview rating, while nine of the 13 low APQ Ss were also low on the interview rating. The 23 Ss who showed concordance in their questionnaire and interview scores were selected for the following analysis of autonomic responses.[3]

PHYSIOLOGICAL FINDINGS

For purposes of analysis, the polygraph record was divided into ten reaction periods which represented various aspects of the test process: initial instructions, instruction periods for each test (three periods), and test presentations (six periods). The choice of measures of

autonomic activity was dictated by two considerations. The first was previous utility in other studies. Since there are no such measures as the *best* indicator of changes in heart rate, PGR, etc., it was considered to be most efficient to describe the reactivity on any one channel of autonomic activity in terms of more than one measure. The second consideration was dictated by theoretical reasons. Since our primary interest was in autonomic perception, we attempted to select those response aspects which are most likely to be the basis of perceptual discriminations. Such indices as total increase in autonomic response and the variability of responses were considered to fulfill this criterion. The following measures were used:

Heart rate:
(1) The mean autonomic lability score [4] for the first and last reaction periods.
(2) The variability of mean heart rate over all ten periods. Means were based on the initial 60 sec. of each of the 10 reaction periods.
(3) Total raw increase in heart rate from base level to the highest level attained.
PGR:
(1) Number of PGR responses during the total record. A response was defined as a change in resistance of 400 ohms or more.
(2) Mean of the two largest responses occurring during reaction periods two through ten.[5]
(3) Total increase in conductance over the entire record.
Respiration:
(1) Increase in respiration rate from the base level to the highest level attained.
(2) The variability of mean respiration

---

[3] While a study of the discordant Ss is certainly of interest, such an investigation was postponed due to the small number of Ss in the discordant cells. Further work on this problem is in progress.

[4] The autonomic lability score, developed by Lacey (4), evaluates stress levels corrected for differences in base levels.

[5] The first reaction period was eliminated since it always included the largest drop in resistance, primarily as a function of shifting S from the resting period to the task situation.

rate based on the initial 60 sec. of each of the ten reaction periods.

(3) Change in the standard deviation of inspiration size from reaction period one to reaction period ten.

Temperature:

(1) Magnitude of the largest *increase* in temperature regardless of the reaction period in which it occurred. Measured from the base reading of the reaction period.

(2) Magnitude of largest *decrease* in temperature, similar to 1.

(3) Range over the entire record.

(4) Autonomic lability score of the final temperature reading, using the base period as the initial level.

Blood volume:

(1) The three largest oximeter responses over the total record.

(2) The number of responses over the total record.

(3) The variability of response frequency based on ten reaction periods.

In order to test the major hypothesis concerning differences in autonomic reactivity between high and low perceivers, an over-all rank order was established for each channel. This order was achieved by summing the ranks on each constituent measure and then establishing a new rank order based on these sums. Similarly, a total reactivity rank order was established, based on all five channels. Table 3 presents these ranks for the two groups. The rank difference between the two groups is significant for three channels (heart rate, PGR, and respiration) as well as for the over-all total reactivity score. As expected, the latter shows the best differentiation between the two groups. It should be pointed out that no significant differences were found between the two groups in base levels on any autonomic channel.

TABLE 2. INTERCORRELATIONS AMONG MEASURES WITHIN CHANNELS

Heart Rate:	1 vs. 2	.75	Respiration:	1 vs. 2	.49
	1 vs. 3	.84		1 vs. 3	.03
	2 vs. 3	.93		2 vs. 3	.43
PGR:	1 vs. 2	.27	Blood Volume:	1 vs. 2	.52
	1 vs. 3	.71		1 vs. 3	.14
	2 vs. 3	.47		2 vs. 3	−.00
Temperature:	1 + 2 vs. 3	.58			
	1 + 2 vs. 4	.32			
	3 vs. 4	.47			

Table 2 shows the intercorrelations among these various measures within channels. They indicate that the heart rate, PGR, and temperature measures have the highest intrachannel consistency, while respiration and blood volume measures show much less communality. In general, these correlations confirm the statement that no one measure derived from any autonomic channel is likely to be representative of general reactivity in that channel.

Thus, Ss who consistently *report* a high autonomic reactivity also show high autonomic reactivity when compared with Ss who report little autonomic feedback.

Table 3 also indicates the large variability in ordering from channel to channel. This is consistent with Lacey's previous finding of autonomic response specificity (5). We do not know, however, whether perceptual specificity is related to autonomic specificity, i.e.,

TABLE 3. SUBJECTS' RANKS ON FIVE CHANNELS AND TOTAL REACTIVITY

Subjects	Variables					Total Reactivity
	Heart rate	PGR	Temper- ature	Respira- tion	Blood Volume	
High Perceivers:						
1	9	19	7.5	11	—	13.5
2	5	1	15	—	4	3
3	3	10	2	2	—	1
4	16	14	19	3	3	10.5
5	1	15	16	10	5.5	8
6	21	5	13	5	17	16.5
7	2	9	1	13	2	2
8	—	6	11.5	4	—	5
9	13	4	7.5	12	9	7
10	4	12	21	7	13	12
11	8	—	17	8	11	10.5
12	12	7	5.5	14.5	—	9
13	15	11	4	16	15	16.5
14	6	2	14	6	5.5	4
Low Perceivers:						
1	10	20	10	18	1	15
2	17.5	21	5.5	22	14	20.5
3	11	3	3	17	7	6
4	17.5	17	20	1	19	19
5	20	13	11.5	9	18	18
6	19	22	23	14.5	10	22
7	14	8	9	19	8	13.5
8	7	18	18	21	16	20.5
9	22	16	22	20	12	23
Significance of Difference between Groups						
(White's T test)	$p < .01$	$p < .01$	$p > .05$	$p < .05$	$p > .05$	$p < .01$

Note.—Missing ranks indicate non-usable polygraph records. In these cases the total ranks are based on prorated estimates.

whether differential report of a particular channel is also related to differential autonomic behavior within that channel. Such a comparison is not possible when extreme Ss are selected on the basis of *total* APQ scores.

Initially, the question was raised whether Ss who report a high level of autonomic activity differ in intensity of autonomic response or whether they over-react to autonomic stimulation. Up to this point, the results tend to favor the former interpretation. However, it is possible to evaluate the second hypothesis more directly from the data.

As was indicated earlier, the APQ contains questions relating to all five channels tested in this study. On the basis of their scores on these questions, Ss can be assigned ranks on the perception of these channels similar to the ranks presented in Table 3. Whenever an S's rank on the *perception* of a particular autonomic channel is higher than his rank on autonomic *response*, he may be said to be overestimating his autonomic reactivity; when these ranks are reversed, he may be thought of as underestimating his reactivity. By this procedure, Ss can be classified as to their general tendency, i.e., in all five channels, to over- or to underestimate their autonomic activity. Twenty-two of the 23 Ss could be classified in this manner. Table 4 shows the

TABLE 4. AUTONOMIC PERCEPTION AND ESTIMATION TENDENCIES

	Number of Ss Showing Discrepancies between Perception and Reactivity	
	Perceptual Over-estimation	Perceptual Under-estimation
High Perceivers	9	4
Low Perceivers	1	8

distribution of these Ss among the high and low APQ groups. The significant chi square ($p < .01$) indicates that high perceivers tend to overestimate their reactivity while low perceivers tend to underestimate. In relation to the initial question, it appears that both processes appear to be operating. Ss who report high autonomic feedback not only show a high degree of autonomic reaction but also tend to overestimate that stimulation; similarly, low perceivers show less activity and also underestimate it.

Further studies are in progress to answer some of the questions arising from this investigation:

1. What is the relationship between autonomic feedback and autonomic re-activity for an unselected population, i.e., when dealing with the full range of perceptual and autonomic scores rather than with selected extremes.

2. What is the relationship between task performance and autonomic feedback? In the present study, the tasks were deliberately constructed to be of such great difficulty that no useful individual differences in performance could be observed.

3. What is the relationship between this perceptual-autonomic aspect of the anxiety phenomena and other behavioral indices?

4. Can response specificity be demonstrated in both the perceptual and the autonomic systems?

Summary

Two groups of Ss were selected who showed consistency in their report of autonomic activity (autonomic feedback). High perceivers were Ss who reported a high level of autonomic feedback in anxiety situations in general and also reported such a high level in a specific stress situation. Low perceivers were Ss who reported a low degree of autonomic feedback in both situations. The results showed:

1. Positive correlations between scores on an autonomic perception questionnaire and other paper-and-pencil tests of anxiety reactions.

2. High perceivers showed significantly greater autonomic reactivity than low perceivers.

3. High perceivers tended to overestimate their autonomic responses, while low perceivers tended to underestimate them.

References

1. BROWN, J. S., & FARBER, I. E. Emotions conceptualized as intervening variables—with suggestions toward a theory of frustration. *Psychol. Bull.,* 1951, **48,** 465–495.

2. CAMERON, N. *The psychology of behavior disorders: A bio-social interpretation.* Boston: Houghton Mifflin, 1947.

3. JAMES, W. *The principles of psychology.* Vol. II. New York: Henry Holt, 1890.

4. LACEY, J. I. The evaluation of autonomic responses: Toward a general solution. *Annals N. Y. Acad. Sci.,* 1956, **67,** 123–164.

5. LACEY, J. I., BATEMAN, D. E., & VAN LEHN, R. Autonomic response specificity: An experimental study. *Psychosom. Med.,* 1953, **15,** 8–21.

6. LANGE, C. *The emotions.* Denmark, 1885. (Trans. by H. Kurella) Leipzig: Theodor Thomas, 1887.

7. MANDLER, G., & SARASON, S. B. A study of anxiety and learning. *J. abnorm. soc. Psychol.,* 1952, **47,** 166–173.

8. MAY, R. *The meaning of anxiety.* New York: Ronald Press, 1950.

9. SKINNER, B. F. The operational analysis of psychological terms. *Psychol. Rev.,* 1945, **52,** 270–277.

10. TAYLOR, JANET A. A personality scale of manifest anxiety. *J. abnorm. soc. Psychol.,* 1953, **48,** 285–290.

11. WENGER, M. A. Emotion as visceral action: An extension of Lange's theory. In M. L. Reymert (Ed.), *Feelings and emotions.* New York: McGraw-Hill, 1950.

INTRINSIC MOTIVATION AND PSYCHOLOGICAL STRESS
William Vogel, Susan Raymond, and Richard S. Lazarus

In the theoretical approach to psychological stress recently proposed by Lazarus and Baker (1956, 1957), two problems were emphasized. On the one hand, an individual's pattern of motivation was regarded as determining the potency of any situation in producing stress. On the other hand, once a stress reaction is aroused, the person's behavior depends upon his method of coping with the disturbance. Factors both of motivation and of cognitive control therefore need to be included in the systematic study of psychological stress.

Some experimental efforts to examine this point of view have recently been reported (Lazarus, Baker, Broverman, & Mayer, 1957; Vogel, Baker, & Lazarus, 1958), mainly involving the manipulation of motive strength both by its experimental arousal and by selection of Ss with differing degrees of some relatively enduring motivational trait (intrinsic motivation). The present paper is mostly restricted to the experimental analysis of the role of intrinsic motivation.[1] It deals with three main issues.

Reprinted by permission of the American Psychological Association and the authors from *The Journal of Abnormal and Social Psychology,* Vol. 58, 1959.

---

[1] This article is the first of two which actually represent a single experimental effort to study simultaneously the role of intrinsic motivation and cognitive control factors in psychological stress.

First and most important is the role of type of motivation in determining whether a stress state occurs. An excellent recent review of research in the area of ego involvement has been presented by Iverson and Reuder (1956). We propose that any typical stressor situation will produce a state of stress only if it threatens important ego-motivations of the S. Thus, if the experiment casts doubt on the intellectual adequacy of an S who has little motivation to achieve intellectually, there will be little or no stress. In this study we selected Ss who were primarily either achievement motivated or affiliation motivated, exposing them to an achievement stressor and an affiliation stressor condition. Our expectation was that a state of stress would occur only if the stressor condition communicates with the predominant motive pattern.

The second issue concerns the relation of the stress state to task performance. The problem is a complicated one, and the evidence from the literature suggests that there is no simple relationship between stress and performance (Lazarus, Deese, & Osler, 1952; McClelland, 1951); sometimes there appears to be facilitation of performance and at other times there is impairment. It has been shown that facilitation or impairment is partly a function of the S's cognitive structure (Broverman & Lazarus, 1958). Others (Sarason & Mandler, 1952) have suggested that one should expect no change, facilitation, or impairment in performance, respectively, depending upon the compatibility of the stressor-produced responses with the required task operations. Our present approach to the problem includes the use of two different types of tasks, a perceptual-motor task (the McKinney Reporting Test: McKinney, Strother, Hines, & Al-

lee, 1951), and a more conceptual task (scrambled words). We hypothesized that a stress state would increase perceptual motor output (a frequent finding in other research [Lazarus et al., 1952]) but would impair conceptual operations. In the case of the former, increased affect should be compatible with greater motor output, while in conceptual operations, the affect should result in interference.

Finally, we chose one infrequently used additional variable, the S's past history of success or failure in his predominant motivational sphere, that is, achievement or affiliation, because such success or failure might determine the nature of the S's apprehension of the present stressor situation, or might reflect personality characteristics associated with the ability to master stressful experiences. Previously successful Ss, on both above bases, should be less readily disturbed by the stressor conditions.

Method

SELECTION OF SUBJECTS

The assessment of achievement motivation and of affiliation motivation was accomplished by means of a variety of techniques which were devised to screen a large group of Ss, selecting for the experiment only those with clear manifestations of the desired motive traits. The selection plan involved an attempt to obtain ideal cases who were either highly motivated toward achievement and disinterested in affiliation, or highly motivated toward affiliation and disinterested in achievement. These Ss were further subdivided into successful and unsuccessful groups so that four groups of 10 Ss each were ultimately created:

affiliation oriented [2] successful, affiliation oriented unsuccessful, achievement oriented successful, and achievement oriented unsuccessful. Let us consider the six techniques devised to select Ss with these characteristics.

Academic achievement in relation to aptitude. This index was based on the S's academic class standing in relation to his performance on the American Council on Education college aptitude test. Both distributions were expressed in standard score form, and the difference between the paired scores identified some Ss whose aptitude was greater than achievement (underachievers) and some who were relatively high in academic achievement compared with aptitude (overachievers).

Amount of study. Each S was required to indicate on a chart, on which half-hour intervals each day for a whole week were arrayed, what he had done during these intervals the previous week. Each half-hour space had to be filled in. To serve as a guide, a number of activities were illustrated on the margin of the chart, including organized school athletics, dating, school club activity, studying, relaxing alone, bull sessions, cards, etc. From this it was possible to obtain information about the amount of time the S spent studying or in some closely related activity, and the amount of social activity he had engaged in.

Values questionnaire. Each S was given a 15-item test, each question to be answered true or false. The test was constructed so that achievement values were pitted against affiliation values. For ex-

ample, Item 4 stated, "Competition is bad, it kills friendship"; Item 8 was, "I would rather be voted 'most likely to succeed' than 'most popular guy on campus'"; and Item 11 read, "People who study a lot seem pretty one-sided, they don't have too many friends." The answer "true" to Items 4 and 11 suggests stronger affiliation than achievement values, while a "true" for Item 8 suggests the reverse.

Social attainment scale. A shortened adaptation of the Worcester Social Attainment Scale (Phillips & Cowitz, 1953) was prepared on which the S was required to indicate memberships in social organizations, teams or school organizations, officerships held, jobs held, community activity, and so on. It was possible by means of this questionnaire to estimate the degree of accomplishment of Ss in affiliative activities compared with activities that were aimed at academic or occupational achievement.

Sociometric scale. Since all of the selection techniques were administered in group, it was possible to ask each boy, in turn, to stand while the others rated him on a five-point scale concerning how well they knew him and how well they liked him. Thus, we could determine (*a*) how well an S was known by his peers, (*b*) how well he was liked by his peers, (*c*) how well he himself knew others in the class, and (*d*) to what extent he liked them.

Teachers' ratings. Each S had been asked to give the names of three teachers whom he felt knew him best. Each of the teachers was given a scale upon which he rated the S's aptitude, his academic effort, his desire for warm affiliative relationships with others, and his success at achieving warm affiliative relationships. The categories on the scale were arranged so that they represented

---

[2] Henceforth we shall use the term "oriented" to refer to the groups designated in terms of the behavioral criterion of motivation, and "motivation" when we are clearly referring to the inference of a motivated state or disposition.

different degrees of affiliative and achievement striving and the successfulness of the S in satisfying these needs.

During the initial selection procedures, 185 students at the Worcester Academy, a private college preparatory school in Worcester, Massachusetts, were used as Ss.[3] The boys had been asked to cooperate by their school authorities. They ranged in age from 16 to 19 years with an occasional student over 20. They were told that they were to be tested by two Clark University psychologists but were given no explanation by the school regarding the purpose of the tests. They were initially tested in three groups of just over 60 boys each, all on the same morning. The group sessions lasted approximately 90 minutes. The Ss were told the purpose of the testing was to select a small number of students who were to be used in further experimentation.

The six techniques for assessing achievement as opposed to affiliation motivation were utilized in such a way as to produce 40 experimental Ss who represented as pure cases as could be obtained. Twenty achievement oriented and 20 affiliation oriented Ss were selected, with half of each of these groups being the most successful or the most unsuccessful individuals within their particular motive pattern. The distribution for each trait was converted into standard scores, and Ss for each subgroup were taken from the upper parts of the distribution on each relevant trait.

For example, to be in the achievement oriented, successful group, the S had to

be in at least the top 25% of the group on the criterion of the study hours, as well as in the upper 25% on the index of overachievement. In addition, the teachers had to agree that these Ss worked hard and, in their judgment, achieved a performance level in school commensurate with or beyond their ability. Disagreements in the teachers' ratings, or between criteria, required discarding the case. Ss in this group were also at the bottom half of the distribution with respect to evidence of affiliative orientation as displayed in the sociometric scale and in the teachers' ratings of social interest as well as in evidence of social activity on the social attainment scale. Finally, such an S was also required to be in the upper 25% in terms of achievement orientation on the self-report values questionnaire. The ten Ss who best fitted these criteria were selected for the achievement oriented, successful group, and the other cases were discarded. Each additional group was selected in the same general fashion.

The intercorrelations between the various indices may be examined for the light they throw on the validity of the preselection procedures. The inference that an S has strong affiliative motivation, for example, does not depend upon there being a high relationship between the criteria, since each may contribute some independent source of variance. For one S, the main avenue for attempted gratification of the motive may be in social club activities, while for another it may rest with informal conversation in the dormitories. Nonetheless, it would be supportive to our assumptions if there were a sensible pattern of relationships between the indices. Table 1 shows the pattern of intercorrelations, excluding the teachers' judgments which could not be used for correlation pur-

[3] We wish to express our great appreciation to William S. Piper, Headmaster of the Worcester Academy, and R. L. W. Smyth, assistant in Admissions, for their valuable assistance in conducting this study at their school.

TABLE 1. INTERCORRELATIONS BETWEEN CRITERIA FOR THE SELECTION OF
AFFILIATION VERSUS ACHIEVEMENT MOTIVATION

	B	C	D	E	F	G	H
A	+.629 *	*+.391*	*+.171*	*+.023*	*−.055*	*+.184*	*−.021*
	+.559	+.272	+.375	−.466	−.328	−.035	−.256
B		*+.265*	*+.269*	*+.051*	*−.016*	*+.059*	*−.058*
		+.014	+.137	−.234	−.376	+.099	−.182
C			*+.364*	*−.041*	*+.087*	*+.231*	*−.091*
			+.617	−.281	−.212	+.354	−.376
D				*−.030*	*−.200*	*+.043*	*+.089*
				+.268	−.227	+.199	−.444
E					*+.073*	*+.056*	*+.161*
					+.490	+.094	+.426
F						*+.091*	*+.165*
						−.143	+.481
G							*−.097*
							−.281

Note.—Key:

A How well S said he knew others, on sociometric rating test
B How well S said he liked others, on sociometric rating test
C How well others knew a subject, on sociometric rating test
D How well others liked a subject, on sociometric rating test
E Achievement-affiliation values test (see write-up on test construction.)
F Study hours
G Ratings on social attainment scale
H Overachievement index

* When $N = 40$, an r of .312 is significant at the .05 level, and an r of .403 is significant at the .01 level. When $N = 161$, an r of .169 is significant at the .05 level, and an r of .224 is significant at the .01 level. The italicized r's are based upon an N of 161. The nonitalicized r's are based upon the 40 selected subjects.

poses because of their particular form (a pattern analysis was needed for this index rather than a scale). The r's are presented separately for the 40 selected cases, and for the total sample of usable records with an N of 161.

Space limitations prevent an elaborate discussion of these interesting intercorrelations. A brief examination of the table, however, reveals that there are significant correlations between the criteria, and that those which were employed to differentiate affiliative and achievement motivation tend to be negative, while those which were used within a motive pattern are positively related. The pattern of intercorrelations gives some empirical support to the assumptions underlying our use of the various criteria to select ideal types in the affiliative versus achievement directions.[4]

PHYSIOLOGICAL MEASURES OF THE STRESS STATE

The main criterion of the arousal of stress was based upon autonomic changes usually associated with emotions. Ss were told at the beginning of the experiment that the relationship between bodily activity and work was being investigated, and that during the experiment their pulse, blood pressure, and galvanic skin response were to be measured. Approximately five minutes was spent adapting the S to the measuring devices and chatting amiably. Measures of the physiological reactivity were recorded periodically in all three of the eight-minute experimental conditions, GSR readings taken at the first and third minutes of any particular condition, pulse at two minutes, and systolic and diastolic blood pressure

[4] We have not included the McClelland type (McClelland, Atkinson, Clark, & Lowell, 1953) of fantasy n achievement as a preselection criterion because the fantasy measure is subject to the influence of many internal as well as external conditions, leaving the exact status of the measure in doubt (Lazarus, Baker, Broverman, & Mayer, 1957). We did present some of the TAT pictures to the 40 preselected Ss, once under "neutral conditions" before the experiment proper, and then again under "aroused conditions" following the stressor condition. None of the relationships between these means and any of the dependent variables in the study are significant. Moreover, few significant relationships with other preselection criteria appeared. The two significant relationships were with the social attainment scale and aroused n achievement ($r = +.33$), and the overachievement index and aroused n achievement ($r = -.38$). Each of these relationships are, in a sense, in the opposite direction from expectation. It seems to us that insufficient attention has been paid to the conditions under which the n achievement score measures achievement motivation.

at four minutes. This same procedure for all three measures was repeated twice in each of the three experimental conditions. The apparatus and method used in obtaining the physiological measures was identical to a previous published study exploring a similar problem (Vogel et al., 1958).

With respect to the statistical treatment of the physiological data, regression equations of the two experimental conditions, respectively, on the practice condition were employed according to formulas provided by Lacey (1956), thus removing the effect of the base level (obtained under the practice condition). It is our belief that such a procedure is the most suitable one for the present experimental design, and is probably superior to the one reported in our previous research (Vogel et al., 1958).

Aside from the problem of base level, a second issue in simultaneously dealing with several measures or channels of physiological response concerns the means of combining measures to provide a single index of physiological reactivity. One technique, recommended by Lacey, involves taking the most reactive physiological channel for each S across all conditions and employing that channel as his index of physiological reactivity. A second alternative is to average the standard scores for each measure, systolic and diastolic blood pressure, pulse, and GSR, for all three conditions. The third alternative is a variant of the first in which the most reactive measure in each condition is retained for analysis, thus occasionally employing a different physiological channel for the same S under different conditions. The first and third techniques conform best to Lacey's (1952) evidence and concepts of autonomic response specificity.

Since there are theoretical advantages

and disadvantages to each method in the present experiment, analyses were performed with all three methods. Occasionally the data are reported with respect to one physiological method of measurement, while in other instances another method has been presented because more striking relationships were obtained with it.

In our earlier work (Vogel et al., 1958), the most meaningful results were obtained with the first method, that of Lacey. In the present study we obtained intercorrelations between the three physiological measures, with an N of 40, separately for the ego-involvement and stressor conditions. Under the ego-involvement condition, Lacey's method of using the most reactive channel (ignoring conditions) correlates $+.90$ with the method of using the highest channel for each condition, and $+.57$ with the simple average of all channels. The measure based on the highest channel for each condition correlates $+.73$ with the average for all channels. Under the stressor condition, the pattern is similar, the respective correlations being $+.96$, $+.65$, and $+.73$. All of these relationships are highly significant and substantial in magnitude, and in the context of confusion in the literature over which type of approach to employ, it is possible to argue for a certain amount of interchangeability between them. Most commonly, the direction of relationships with one method is the same as that found with another, although, at times, the significance level changes.

TASKS

In an earlier related study (Vogel et al., 1958), the McKinney Reporting Task (McKinney et al., 1951) had been employed. It consists of a long series of circles containing three symbols in various quantities in each. The S's task is to count as quickly and accurately as possible the number of symbols of each kind that each circle contains. This task was also employed in the present study.

In addition to this rather simple perceptual-motor task, a second task was also employed in which the S had to unscramble a set of scrambled words as quickly and as accurately as possible. In order to examine performance on these two tasks under comparable psychological conditions, Ss in each experimental condition worked on them alternately, with four one-minute periods of each.

EXPERIMENTAL CONDITIONS AND PROCEDURE

The entire experiment took place in two sessions. The first session comprised the preselection testing; the experimental procedure proper took place two months later. Ss were tested individually over a two-week period. The Ss selected from the initial testing were sent letters requesting their cooperation and indicating that they would receive pay at the rate of $1 an hour. All of the Ss solicited in this way appeared for the experiment. The first condition of the experimental session may be identified as the practice period (following accustoming the S to the physiological apparatus) in which the S was given first the McKinney Reporting Test and the scrambled words task in alternating fashion, with the instructions that he was obtaining practice on two different types of task in order that he might get used to them. Through this point the treatment accorded all Ss was precisely the same.

Each of the four pre-selected groups had been subdivided into two matched groups which from this point on were given different treatments: on the one hand, an affiliation stressor condition, and on the other hand, an achievement stressor condition. In other words, half of the achievement oriented Ss were exposed to an achievement stressor and half to an affiliation stressor. Similarly, half of the affiliation oriented group were exposed to an achievement stressor and half to an affiliation stressor.

Following the practice condition, the ego-involvement condition was introduced. For the achievement stressor treatment, Ss were told that the testing, for which they had been selected, measured their capacity for successful academic and occupational achievement. To lend credence to these instructions the experimenter ostensibly read them from a copy of the *Journal of Educational Psychology*. The instructions were as follows:

The sole purpose of the Clark University study is to measure degree of academic and intellectual ability. It has already been shown in previous research that persons who are outstanding in general intellectual attainment, as well as those who are outstanding in their college studies, do superior work on both parts of the test. Further work is now being carried out with the test. For instance, psychologists have found they can best discover which preparatory students will become academic successes in college by checking both physiological reactivity during the test, as well as performance on both the scrambled words and reporting task sections of the test.

The affiliation stressor treatment, on the other hand, included the following instructions which emphasized capacities for warm affiliative relations with other people. These instructions were pasted into, and ostensibly read to the S from, a copy of the *Journal of Personality:*

The sole purpose of the Clark University study is to determine which persons have the qualities which make warm, friendly personalities. The measures are not related to intellectual or social attainment, but are concerned with identifying those attributes which make a person warm and friendly in interpersonal relations. It has already been shown during this research that people who have these particular qualities do superior work on both parts of the test. For instance, psychologists have found that they can best discover which preparatory students have these qualities of warmth and friendliness by checking the S's physiological reaction during the test, as well as the S's performance on both scrambled words and reporting task sections of the test.

At this point certain aspects of the tasks were changed. The symbols on the McKinney Reporting Test were suddenly made to assume relevance. For the affiiliation stressor treatment, the symbols represented "friend," "acquaintance," and "enemy"; for the achievement stressor treatment they represented "honors," "pass," "flunk." With respect to the scrambled words task, in the practice session both groups had received the same innocuous scrambled words such as "truck," "window," "breeze," etc. Now in the ego-involvement condition, all the words were need related. The achievement stressor treatment involved such words as "fail," "poorest," "teacher," "school"; the affiliation stressor treatment included such words as "mother," "company," "lonely." The words given the two groups were matched for frequency in terms of the Thorndike-Lorge List (1944), for word length, and method of scrambling. During the ego-involvement condition, Ss performed the tasks just as they had done during the practice session with eight minutes of work, one minute alternately on each task, beginning with the McKinney Reporting Test.

Following the ego-involvement session, the experimenter examined each S's performance and initiated the failure-stressor condition by informing him that he had failed the test very badly. The achievement stressor and affiliation stressor treatments involved different threatening statements, related to the need state being assaulted. For the achievement-stressor treatment, Ss were told that their prospects for college and future successes were poor, and it was suggested that it might be worth trying again. For the affiliation stressor treatment, the person was identified as a person who lacks capacity for warm, friendly relationships compared with others. It was admitted that he might have a need for friendly relations but he was just not warm and friendly as a person. It was implied that all the information obtained by the experimenter supported this conclusion. Following these statements, the task performance was resumed exactly as in the ego-involvement condition, except that every two minutes the experimenter, examining the S's work, extemporaneously criticized its poor quality.

Results

In our presentation of the results, we shall separately examine the data pertinent to the three issues cited at the outset. First, we consider the proposition that stress depends upon the relationship between the stressor condition (achievement- or affiliation-stressors) and the predominant intrinsic motive of the S.

THE ROLE OF INTRINSIC
MOTIVATION IN DETERMINING
STRESS REACTIONS

The empirical consequence of our proposition that stress depends upon the relevance of the stressor condition to the motive pattern can be examined by comparing the Ss who are achievement oriented with those who are affiliation oriented in respect to physiological arousal

TABLE 2. PHYSIOLOGICAL AROUSAL AS A FUNCTION OF TYPE OF INTRINSIC MOTIVATION AND THE NATURE OF THE EXPERIMENTAL CONDITIONS

Groups and Conditions	Highest Channel [a] (Lacey)	Highest Channel for Each Condition [b]	Average for All Measures [c]
Achievement Motivation			
Achievement Oriented Conditions	60.7	62.3	54.1
Affiliation Oriented Conditions	57.2	59.3	50.6
Affiliation Motivation			
Achievement Oriented Conditions	58.6	60.1	51.9
Affiliation Oriented Conditions	63.1	64.0	52.8

Note.—There is a significant main effect source of variation when the ego-involvement condition is compared with the stressor condition. These figures are derived by summing across these two conditions because the patterns shown here are comparable within the ego-involvement and stressor conditions and tend to be significant in each case. This breakdown is simpler and more to the point in examining the role of motivation in determining arousal under stressor conditions.

[a] $F = 5.58$; significant at less than .05 level.
[b] $F = 5.00$; significant at less than .05 level.
[c] $F = 2.88$; not significant.

under the two types of ego-orienting conditions. Table 2 presents these data. We have presented the physiological reactivity as determined by the various subject-condition interactions, in terms of each of the three procedures for combining physiological measures discussed in the procedure section.

While the trends for each of these procedures are similar, there are significant interactions between type of motive orienting condition and motive pattern for the first two, but not for the third. In other words, when the achievement oriented group is presented with achievement oriented conditions (conditions

duces no significant interactions. The pattern is the same for both experimental conditions, and it occurs regardless of the method of combining physiological indices, although it is more striking and statistically significant with some methods than with others.

THE RELATION OF THE STRESS STATE TO TASK PERFORMANCE

There does not exist a simple relationship between the stress state and performance, a finding that was expected in

TABLE 3. PERFORMANCE AS AN INTERACTIVE FUNCTION OF STRESS RELEVANCE AND PHYSIOLOGICAL REACTIVITY UNDER THE STRESSOR CONDITION

		Percent Items Correct		
Group	N	McKinney Reporting Test	Scrambled Words	Both Tasks Combined *
Motivation Relevant Stressor				
High Physiological Reactivity	10	50.56	61.34	55.95
Low Physiological Reactivity	10	39.46	48.51	43.98
Motivation Irrelevant Stressor				
High Physiological Reactivity	10	49.58	51.06	50.32
Low Physiological Reactivity	10	45.34	56.98	51.16

Note.—The index of physiological reactivity here is based on averaging the measures in each channel and making a median split. The other methods produce only comparable trends.
* F for interaction $= 6.34$; significant at below .05 level.

that pose a relevant threat to the central motive state of the S), there is a high degree of autonomic reactivity. On the other hand, when the achievement oriented group is exposed to a nonrelevant threat (the affiliation oriented conditions), there is a low degree of reactivity. Similarly, when the affiliation oriented group is exposed to affiliation orientation, the physiological reaction is greater than when this group is exposed to an achievement-orienting condition. A further analysis of these results in which the ego-involvement condition is separated from the stressor condition pro-

the light of the literature on stress and performance and on the basis of previous research by Vogel et al. (1958), where it was found that performance depended upon the interplay of motivation and somatic reactivity. Moreover, we have hypothesized different effects of the stress state depending upon whether the task was essentially perceptual-motor or conceptual in character. In the present study, no significant relationships were found between performance and the motivation variable alone, or between performance and the relevance of the stressor conditions to intrinsic motivation.

However, as has been previously found in similar research (Vogel et al., 1958), significant effects in performance were obtained when stress relevance and physiological reactivity were studied in interaction.

If we combine performance on both the McKinney Reporting Test and the Scrambled Words Task in terms of percentage of items correct during the stressor condition, we find that when the S is exposed to a stressor condition relevant to his intrinsic motivation, his per-

arately, as well as combined. This finding replicates one previously reported (Vogel et al., 1958) with the McKinney Reporting Test where it was argued that Ss who were aroused even when it is inappropriate or, conversely, unaroused when they should be aroused, showed inadequate performance functioning. It should be noted that in the over-all analysis of variance, no significant effects were contributed by type of stressor or type of motivation by themselves. Therefore it was possible to combine them in

TABLE 4. PERFORMANCE AS A FUNCTION OF STRESS RELEVANCE
AND TYPE OF TASK * [a]

		Ego-involvement		Stressor	
Group	N	McKinney	Scrambled Words	McKinney	Scrambled Words
Motivation Relevant Stressor	20	55.06	45.98	57.94	53.49
Motivation Irrelevant Stressor	20	52.25	55.70	54.10	56.31

Note.—Performance measured by number items attempted. Similar trends are found for percentage items correct.
* Interaction F (motivation $\times$ tasks $\times$ conditions) is significant below .05 level.
[a] Essentially the same pattern of results is found if high and low physiological reactivity or arousal is substituted for the motivation relevance categories.

formance is good if he also responds to the stressor condition with a *high* degree of physiological reactivity. However, under stress relevant conditions and with a *low* degree of physiological reactivity, performance is likely to be poor. On the other hand, when the stressor is irrelevant to the predominant intrinsic motivation and there is a high degree of physiological reactivity, performance is less adequate than when there is a low degree of physiological reactivity. These data are presented in Table 3 with the McKinney Reporting Test and the Scrambled Words Task shown sep-

the form of motivation-relevance categories.

An interesting relationship between stress relevance and performance as a function of type of task appears in Table 4. These data deal with our hypothesis that stress will facilitate certain sensory-motor functions but interfere with conceptual ones. It will be seen that a motivation relevant stressor is associated with low performance output on the conceptual task (scrambled words) compared with a motivation irrelevant stressor. The reverse pattern, however, holds for the perceptual-motor task (Mc-

Kinney Reporting Test). A motivationally relevant stressor is associated with higher output than a motivationally irrelevant stressor. It should also be noted parenthetically that the same kind of relationship is found with degree of physiological reactivity as the means of S classification; physiological arousal and motivational relevance have been shown to be related in Table 2. Moreover, type of stressor and type of motivation separately produced no significant effects, making the combined categories of motivation relevance appropriate.

TABLE 5. SUCCESSFULNESS AT MOTIVE GRATIFICATION IN RELATION TO PHYSIOLOGICAL AROUSAL

Group	N	Physiological Arousal [a]	
		Ego-involvement	Stressor
Successful	20	55.43	64.28
Unsuccessful	20	52.17	67.68

[a] The method of combining physiological measures here is the use of the highest channel (Lacey's method). With this method the interaction $F = 4.49$; significant below the .05 level. With the use of the highest channel for each condition, the F is 3.43 approaching significance. The data are comparable in direction with a simple averaging of physiological measures, but do not reach statistical significance.

PAST SUCCESS AND FAILURE AND THE STRESS REACTION

At this point it should be recalled that both the affiliation oriented and achievement oriented Ss were divided into those considered successful in gratifying these needs and those who were unsuccessful. By means of the factorial design, it was possible to study the contribution of this variable to the arousal of a state of stress.

Table 5 demonstrates that degree of success in fulfilling one's predominant motivations is a significant factor in determining the degree of affective arousal. Successful people are more readily aroused in the ego-involvement condition (minimal threat) than unsuccessful people, but, in turn, their increase in physiological arousal under the stressor condition (strong threat) is less than for the unsuccessful group. Further analysis has shown that there is no interaction between success and stress relevance, or success and the nature of the motive pattern. Moreover, there was no significant effect of past degree of success on any of the performance measures.

Summary

Three issues were explored experimentally in this study. One dealt with the proposition that the arousal of a state of stress depends upon intrinsic motive states in the individual as well as the nature of the stressor conditions. A second was concerned with the relations between a stress state and task performance. The proposal was made that stress would tend to improve sensory-motor output and impair conceptual performance on the basis of different amounts of interference. The third involved the importance of the S's past history of success or failure in a particular motivational direction in determining whether a stress state would be aroused.

One hundred and eighty-five preparatory school students were used as a general subject pool and were given a battery of tests and procedures in order to select two groups differing in predominant motive pattern. Twenty Ss were selected as strongly oriented toward achievement as opposed to affiliation, and 20 with the reverse pattern, representing as ideal cases as it was possible to select to contrast the two types of predominant motivations. Subjects were additionally divided into those who were successful and those who were unsuccessful within their motive sphere, and arranged in a factorial design. Half of the achievement oriented Ss were exposed to an achievement oriented type of stressor condition and half to an affiliation stressor condition. The affiliation oriented group was similarly divided and given the two stressor treatments. The arousal of stress was studied by means of autonomic reactions, including pulse, blood pressure, and GSR.

The results clearly support the view that the arousal of stress depends upon the relationship between the motive pattern and the type of stressor condition. The relative effect of stress on a sensory-motor task was facilitative, while on a conceptual task it produced impairment. Successful subjects were more easily aroused by minimally threatening conditions than unsuccessful subjects, and less disturbed by more severe stressor conditions.

In general, the research suggests the importance in stress research and theory, of such factors as intrinsic motivation, the type of task, and the S's past history of success or failure within the relevant motivational sphere.

References

BROVERMAN, D., & LAZARUS, R. S. Individual differences in task performance under conditions of cognitive interference. *J. Pers.*, 1958, **26,** 94–105.

IVERSON, M. A., & REUDER, M. E. Ego-involvement as an experimental variable. *Psychol. Rep.*, 1956.

LACEY, J. I. Autonomic response specificity and Rorschach color responses. *Psychosom. Med.*, 1952, **14,** 256–260.

————. The evaluation of autonomic responses: Toward a general solution. *Ann. N. Y. Acad. Sci.*, 1956, **67,** 123–164.

LAZARUS, R. S., & BAKER, R. W. Personality and psychological stress—A theoretical and methodological framework. *Psychol. Newsltr.*, 1956, **8,** 21–32.

————. Motivation and personality in psychological stress. *Psychol. Newsltr.*, 1957, **8,** 159–193.

LAZARUS, R. S., & BAKER, R. W., BROVERMAN, D. M., & MAYER, J. Personality and psychological stress. *J. Pers.*, 1957, **25,** 559–577.

LAZARUS, R. S., DEESE, J., & OSLER, S. J. The effects of psychological stress upon performance. *Psychol. Bull.*, 1952, **49,** 293–317.

McCLELLAND, D. C. *Personality*. New York: Dryden, 1951.

McCLELLAND, D. C., ATKINSON, J. W., CLARK, R. A., & LOWELL, E. L. *The achievement motive*. New York: Appleton-Century-Crofts, 1953.

McKINNEY, F., STROTHER, G. B., HINES, R. R., & ALLEE, R. A. Experimental frustration in a group test situation. *J. abnorm. soc. Psychol.*, 1951, **46,** 316–323.

PHILLIPS, L. & COWITZ, B. Social attainment and reactions to stress. *J. Pers.*, 1953, **2,** 270–283.

SARASON, S. B., & MANDLER, G. Some correlates of test anxiety. *J. abnorm. soc. Psychol.*, 1952, **47,** 561–565.

THORNDIKE, E. L., & LORGE, I. *The teachers' word book of 30,000 words*. New York: Columbia Univer. Press, 1944.

VOGEL, W., BAKER, R. W., & LAZARUS, R. S. The role of motivation in psychological stress. *J. abnorm. soc. Psychol.*, 1958, **56,** 105–112.

A STUDY OF AFFECTIVE RESPONSIVENESS IN A LIE-DETECTION SITUATION   Jack Block

Some years ago, H. E. Jones (9) found a relatively low relationship between the intensity of the galvanic skin response (GSR) and the amount of overt emotional expression when both were measured simultaneously in nursery-school children. Although stimuli which *on the average* elicited strong autonomic responses were also found to evoke a great deal of observable emotional expression, *for individual children* the correlation over situations between GSR activation and outward emotionality was quite low.[1] Since the measures employed were highly reliable, the low relationship within individuals between internal and overt manifestations of emotions suggested that stable individual differences exist in the patterning of emotional expression.

This provocative finding was repeated and extended by Jones in a further study (10). Here, one hundred adolescents were available who, in the course of participating in a longitudinal study, had experienced eleven test situations where GSR recordings were gathered. The 20 individuals who were highest in the average magnitude of their GSRs and the 20 who were lowest were selected, and

Reprinted by permission of the American Psychological Association and the author from *The Journal of Abnormal and Social Psychology*, Vol. 55, 1957.

[1] The correlation over the 22 situations between the group's average GSR and the average rating on overtness of response was .83 and .80 in the initial and retest experiments. For individual children, the correlation averaged .20 and .25 in the two separate tests.

the independently rated overt behavioral characteristics of the two groups compared.

The "high reactives" were rated as less assertive, less animated, less talkative, and less attention-seeking than the "low reactives," all of these differences occurring at the .01 level of significance. The high reactive group was also evaluated as more calm, more deliberative, more good-natured, more cooperative, and more responsible than the low reactives, who were judged as irritable, excitable, impulsive, and immature.

Jones suggested that the high reactives are introversive characters, while the low reactives represent the psychoanalytic concept of "impulse neurosis" (2). The process of socialization is the agent causing the child to shift from undifferentiated, externalizing modes of expression to complex, internalizing avenues of affect discharge.

It is important to note that Jones also observed the presence of two additional patterns of emotional expression. He identified a "generalizer" type, consisting of children who respond at both overt and internal levels simultaneously, and a "reciprocal" type, represented by children who sometimes respond overtly but with little GSR reactivity and who at other times evidence a highly reactive GSR but with little overt response.

The work by Jones has been summarized here because it is surprisingly little known and because it served as a springboard for the present experiment. His results have implications for conceptions of the nature and etiology of psychopathy and for a more general understanding of the place and process of affect in personality.

The present study aimed at an independent verification and extension of Jones's findings. It contrasts with the previous work in several ways: the subject sample used was older and probably more homogeneous with respect to intelligence, interests, and socioeconomic level; there was only one GSR recording session; the more stressful circumstance of lying was employed as the stimulus situation; and finally, objective test measures as well as ratings were available for comparison with GSR reactivity.

Method

SUBJECTS AND EXPERIMENTAL PROCEDURE

Seventy male applicants to a medical school underwent an 18-hour assessment program at the Institute of Personality Assessment and Research. In age they ranged from 19 to 32 years with a mean at 22. Intellectually, the group was at a very superior level. Their socioeconomic level was clearly middle class.

Each of the subjects (Ss) was observed in a wide variety of personality revealing situations, ranging from charades and stress interviews to standardized psychodramas and dinnertime conversation. One of the procedures each S experienced was the lie-detection situation. At his scheduled time, S entered the experimental room where he was greeted by the experimenter (E) and seated before the imposing apparatus. A pneumograph was attached around S's chest, his left thumb was inserted into a pulse pressure recording device, and electrodes were attached to his right hand. Only the GSR circuit of the apparatus was in fact operative during the

experiment, the respiration and pulse transducers being employed for their dramatic effect only.[2]

The E conducted a short interview, inquiring about the origins of S's medical interests, his professional aspirations, the nature of his father's occupation, and so on, while an assistant adjusted the apparatus. S was then informed that the apparatus was a lie detector and that his skill as a liar was to be investigated.

The S selected a number ranging from 1 to 5 without informing E of his choice. The E then queried S a number of times over each possibility, employing a fixed but unsystematic order of interrogation. To each question, S was instructed to say "no," even where denial meant a lie. Questioning was varied in phrasing and accentuation so as to maintain the interpersonal aspects of the essentially standard stimulus situation. At the end of the series of 30 questions, S informed E as to his actual choice. In two additional replications, S selected an alternative (one of six months, one of six colors) and, again, E repeatedly interrogated him as to his choice. Again, S denied all possibilities, including the one he had in fact chosen. The temporal relations of stimuli and responses were recorded by noting E's questions on S's GSR record.

It was found that some Ss displayed a diffuse and unselective GSR responsivity and some were relatively unreactive; most were selectively responsive, the GSR tending to appear only after the lie. Over the three trials, an accommodation effect was usually observed as the S adapted to the situation.

---

[2] Although there is some controversy among practitioners as to the suitability of the GSR as a lie detector under actual field conditions, there appears to be agreement as to its validity in experimental contexts (8, 11).

Two raters judged the GSR records for amount of reactivity and selected the 20 most highly reactive individuals and the 20 least reactive individuals. Reactivity was judged primarily on the basis of the number of GSRs the subject manifested without further quantification of the size or duration of the response. Ratings were employed rather than a simple count because of the necessity to evaluate occasional movement and instrument artifacts. Classification of Ss into the categories was highly reliable, 36 of the 40 criterion cases being selected by both raters. The disagreements were resolved by mutual consent of the raters. Categorization of Ss into the two GSR criterion groups occurred before the examination of any other data. The results to be reported in the next section are based upon the comparison of the two groups, Reactors and Nonreactors, on a number of measures.

Results

INTELLECTUAL DIFFERENCES

Intelligence is a powerful determiner of behavior, and its role in any particular context requires evaluation. Accordingly, the Reactors and Nonreactors were compared on measures defining various aspects of intellectual functioning. These included the Medical College Admissions test, grade-point average, a college vocabulary test (5), the Gottschaldt test (3), and a measure of originality based upon three of the Guilford tests of originality (6).

On none of these measures did the differences between the two groups approach significance. There is no evidence that such differences as may exist between the two groups can be ascribed to intellectual factors as these are ordinarily understood and measured.

DIFFERENCES ON RATING MEASURES

At the end of assessment, each S was evaluated by each staff psychologist. One of the means employed for codifying staff impressions of each S was the Q-sort method of personality description (13); another was the Gough Adjective Check List (4).

TABLE 1. Q ITEMS DISTINGUISHING BETWEEN THE REACTOR AND NONREACTOR GROUPS

Characteristic of Reactors:

10. His anxiety and tension find outlet in bodily symptoms and dysfunction; anxiety and tension are converted into somatic symptoms	.05
11. Is protective of those close to him	.05
14. Is readily dominated by others; submissive	.05
19. Seeks reassurance from others	.05
30. Gives up and withdraws where possible in the face of frustration and adversity	.05
40. Is vulnerable to real or fancied threat; generally fearful; is a worrier	.05
70. Behaves in an ethically consistent manner	.05
74. Lets other people take advantage of him; allows exploitation	.05

Characteristic of Nonreactors:

94. Expresses his hostilities directly	.01
96. Values his own independence and autonomy	.01
1. Critical, not easily impressed, skeptical	.05
62. Tends to be rebellious and non-conforming	.05

A comprehensive 115-item Q set was used which included items oriented toward highly inferential features of the personality system as well as toward the more readily observable aspects of the individual.[3] Five psychologists, none of whom had observed the S's behavior in the lie-detection situation, Q sorted each S. These data, combined into a composite by equally weighting the ratings of each judge, codified the impressions and evaluations of these staff members with respect to the subject. Because the psychologist raters had no information as to the behavior of the S in the test situation, the Q-sort data provide a totally independent source of information as to the personality characteristics of each S.

The comparison of the Q ratings for Reactors with the ratings for Nonreactors revealed twelve items differentiating at or beyond the .05 level of significance. These are listed in Table 1.

TABLE 2. ADJECTIVES DISTINGUISHING
BETWEEN THE REACTOR AND
NONREACTOR GROUPS
(.05 level of significance)

Characteristic of Reactors:

Cautious	Idealistic
Dependent	Mannerly
Dreamy	Suggestible

Characteristic of Nonreactors:

Clever	Leisurely
Cool	Opportunistic
Evasive	Practical
Independent	Realistic
Ingenious	

A separate group of seven staff psychologists employed the Adjective Check List in their characterization of each S. These data, when summed across raters and analyzed, served as a cross check on

[3] A copy of the Q set employed is available from the writer.

and amplification of the Q findings. The adjectives differentially characterizing the Reactors and Nonreactors at or beyond the .05 level of significance are presented in Table 2.

It is clear from the nature of the differentiating Q items and adjectives that the two groups differ along some version of the psychological dimension suggested by Jones. The Reactors are perceived as withdrawing, worrying individuals who turn their anxieties toward internal routes of expression. The Nonreactors are evaluated as independent, aggressively direct, and relatively nonconforming, all of these being visible rather than inward or covert expressions of impulses.

INVENTORY ITEMS DIFFERENTIATING
THE GROUPS

A number of personality inventory items (from the Minnesota Multiphasic Personality Inventory and the California Psychological Inventory) distinguished between the two groups. Summarizing their import, it would appear that the Reactors introspect relatively often, are sometimes radically subject to their moods and impulses, and are very much concerned with the appropriateness of their behavior in social contexts. In contrast, the Nonreactors indicate an absence of rumination and a self-control of their behavior. Also expressed is a preference for autonomy and a difficulty with representatives of authority.

SOME TEST MEASURES
DIFFERENTIATING THE GROUPS

All Ss experienced the rod-and-frame procedure developed by Witkin (14). Here the S is placed in a totally dark room before a luminescent square tilted from the vertical. He revolves, via a suitable control, a rod centered within the frame until he perceives the rod as at the true vertical (or horizontal). In the blackness of the experimental room, the only external cue to verticality is the misleading frame. An alternative basis for judgment is available from internal, proprioceptive gravitational cues. In the present study, the Reactors proved to be more affected by the external frame of reference than were the Nonreactors ($p < .05$). That is, the Reactors were more externally oriented and more open to outside influence in the presence of uncertainty than were the Nonreactors, who lent greater credence to their proprioceptive cues.

A rather curious result emerges from a comparison of the behavior of the two groups in the Crutchfield independence-of-judgment experimental procedure (1). Here the subject is exposed to a group consensus about a problem which differs from what the S perceives as the correct or preferred solution. The extent to which S conforms to the group opinion in his manifested choice provides a measure of independence found by Crutchfield to be richly related to character structure.

In the present analysis, Reactors and Nonreactors did not differ in amount of independence as expressed by their choice behavior. But subjects also expressed their subjective confidence in their judgments. The Reactors, although actually conforming no more than Nonreactors, proved to be less confident about their course of action ($p < .001$). Independence (or conformity) in the Reactor thus appears to have a different psychological base than in the Nonreactor. It might even be said that manifesting independence in the face of uncertainty and doubts, as did the Reactors, required more courage than equivalent behavior where subjective doubt does not prevail, as among the Nonreactors. Although the classification into Re-

actors and Nonreactors was based solely upon the evaluation of the GSR, some evidence for the physiological generality of reactivity may be adduced from a subsequent finding. Following a stressful psychodramatic situation (7), it was found that the systolic blood pressure of Reactors was raised significantly more than that of the Nonreactors ($p < .01$).

Discussion

The present results, taken together with those of Jones and others, provide reasonable evidence that electrodermal responsiveness is related to personality structure and behavior. While in both studies, the number of significant relationships is small considering the multiple tests of significance, the consonance of both sets of data argues for their psychological stability. The placing of these data within a conceptual frame of reference is another matter.

An interpretation of the findings in terms of the notion of externalization-internalization simply does not serve. The externalizing-internalizing dimension has been only informally conceptualized, but it appears to be concerned with whether need tensions are discharged via external, action modes of expression or whether needs are routed internally into cognitive and visceral channels of discharge. Implicit here is the assumption that there exists a reciprocal relationship between overt motor response and cerebral or autonomic activity. That is, overt motor response *displaces* internal activity and *vice versa*. Jones' finding, supported by Seymour (12), that there are "generalizers," individuals whose expression of need states is simultaneously overt and covert, upsets such a notion. Observations of a culture like the Italian, where emotion is vigorously displayed but also apparently internally experienced, also weigh against the reciprocal theory of externalization-internalization. Clearly, an additional dimension or a reformulation of the concept is required in order to encompass the various patterns of emotional expression which have been noted.

It is suggested here that an important distinction is being obscured in the definition of externalization-internalization by opposing overt motor response on the one hand against cognitive *and* visceral channels of discharge on the other. The italicization of *and* is important, for it is precisely this conjunction which may be inappropriate. From an instrumental point of view, cognitive activity *and* motor behavior are both means to drive reduction, whereas autonomic, visceral reaction serves no such function. Autonomic activity appears instead to be an expression of an affective state and does not in and of itself bring about a significant reduction of the disturbing emotional charge. Tension reduction is brought about only by appropriate cognition, fantasy, or motor behavior, not by autonomic arousal.

If this reformulation appears a tenable one, then externalizing-internalizing can be redefined as a way of characterizing the direction or orientation of an individual's response to the impelling affective disequilibrium. GSR lability, from this point of view, is simply a convenient index of the tensional state, of whether an individual has anxiety or affect in a given situation or whether he does not have anxiety or emotion in that situation. It has no implication, however, for the direction of the response precipitated by the emotion. Since affective responsiveness may eventuate in motor as well as cognitive behavior, the dilemma previously posed by the "generalizer" no longer exists.

The dimension distinguishing between the Reactors and Nonreactors in the present study, may be the dimension of affective responsiveness without regard for just how the individual copes with emotional states. There has been little direct investigation of affective responsiveness although it is known that there are great differences in the extent to which individuals experience affect and have their self-percept brought forward into consciousness as a conditioner of behavior. Some individuals experience too much affect, e.g., anxiety neurotics, and are thereby incapacitated. But others do not experience sufficient emotion, sufficient in relation to a normative criterion, and therefore do not react on the basis of an implicit but culturally shared set of behavioral premises. Because they operate from a different premise system, these individuals are more likely to emit behavior which is inconceivable to the affectively responsive observer. Such people include the primary psychopath, certain forms or stages of the schizophrenic reaction and, in general, those individuals identified by psychiatrists as possessing "flattened affect."

Summary

Seventy Ss, during the course of an assessment program, experienced a lie-detection situation where GSR reactions were recorded. The twenty most reactive subjects and the twenty least reactive subjects were selected and compared on a variety of measures. Reactors appeared to be more dependent, dreamy, idealistic, and suggestible; Nonreactors were evaluated as relatively cool, evasive, opportunistic, and independent. The findings were related to the previous work of Jones, and a reformulation of the notion of externalization-internalization was offered.

References

1. CRUTCHFIELD, R. S. Conformity and character. *Amer. Psychologist*, 1955, **10**, 191–198.

2. FENICHEL, O. *The psychoanalytic theory of neurosis.* New York: Norton, 1945.

3. GOTTSCHALDT, K. Uber den einfluss der erfahrung auf die wahrnehmung von figuren. *Psych. Forsch.*, 1926, **8**, 261–317; 1929, **12**, 1–87.

4. GOUGH, H. G. *The adjective check list.* Berkeley: Univer. California Printing Department, 1952.

5. GOUGH, H. G., & SAMPSON, H. *The college vocabulary test.* (Form A). Berkeley: Univer. of California Inst. of Personality Assessment and Research, 1954.

6. GUILFORD, J. P., WILSON, R. C., CHRISTENSEN, P. R., & LEWIS, D. J. A factor-analytic study of creative thinking: I. Hypotheses and descriptions of tests. *Reports from the Psychol. Lab.*, No. 3, Los Angeles: Univer. of Southern California, 1951.

7. HARRIS, R. E., SOKOLOW, M., CARPENTER, L. G., FREEDMAN, M., & HUNT, S. P. Response to psychologic stress in persons who are potentially hypertensive. *Circulation*, 1953, **7**, 874–879.

8. INBAU, F. E. *Lie detection and criminal interrogation.* (2nd ed.) Baltimore: Williams & Wilkins, 1948.

9. JONES, H. E. The galvanic skin response as related to overt emotional expression. *Amer. J. Psychol.*, 1935, **47**, 241–251.

10. ———. The study of patterns of emotional expression. In M. L. Reymert (Ed.), *Feelings and emotions: the Mooseheart Symposium.* New York: McGraw-Hill, 1950.

11. MACNITT, R. D. In defense of the electrodermal response and cardiac amplitude as measures of deception. *J. crim. Law and Criminol.*, 1942, **33**, 266–275.

12. SEYMOUR, R. B. Personality correlates of electrodermal resistance and response. Unpublished doctor's dissertation, Univer. of California, 1950.

13. STEPHENSON, W. *The study of behavior.* Chicago: Univer. of Chicago Press, 1953.

14. WITKIN, H. A., LEWIS, H. B., HERTZMAN, M., MACHOVER, K., MEISSNER, P. B., & WAPNER, S. *Personality through perception.* New York: Harper, 1954.

CHAPTER 4

Expression of Conflict through Fantasy

THEMATIC APPERCEPTION TEST: SOME EVIDENCE BEARING ON THE "HERO ASSUMPTION"

Gardner Lindzey and Dagny Kalnins

From its very moment of origin, the Thematic Apperception Test has been intimately associated in the minds of most users with the assumption that there are certain characters in each story that clearly reflect attributes of the storyteller, while other figures are more revealing of the storyteller's perceptions of the individuals who populate his personal world. In an empirical discipline, however, the length of time that a belief has been held entitles it to no special consideration, and it is therefore quite natural that this assumption should be challenged.

Objections to the hero assumption were particularly prone to occur because of the intimate relation between an individual's own attributes and that which he perceives in the outer world. Thus, it is commonly assumed, with considerable supporting evidence, that an individual who is highly aggressive will perceive more hostility in the world around him than an individual who is less aggressive. This association between internal and external tends to disrupt and blur the easy distinction implied by the original assumption. It should be mentioned that Murray, who initially formulated this assumption, was fully aware of the complexity of the relation

Reprinted by permission of the American Psychological Association and the authors from *The Journal of Abnormal and Social Psychology*, Vol. 57, 1958.

between the individual's inner and outer worlds and never intended that the test interpreter should slavishly maintain a rigid distinction between "hero" and "other." In fact, the manual originally published with the test (12) contains a lengthy discussion of various complications that under special circumstances make it necessary to modify or abandon the assumption of a single hero or identification figure.

Even accepting the fact that ultimate precision will surely depend upon some more complicated set of assumptions than those we are here concerned with, it is still an interesting question whether the interpreter of the TAT can go further with the assumption of a distinction between hero and non-hero than he can with the assumption that all figures in the story are equally revealing of the "own characteristics" of the storyteller. Although endless rational arguments can be introduced bearing on the choice between these assumptions, what we need most is not logical inference nor emotional polemic but controlled empirical evidence. In this spirit, the present paper is intended to outline the results of two small investigations designed to provide some very tentative findings that bear upon the utility of employing the distinction between hero figures and non-hero figures in interpreting Thematic Apperception Test protocols.

In the first study, we began with the

very simple notion that if "heroes" were more indicative of characteristics of the subject (*S*) than were "other figures," the *S* should perceive them or react to them differentially. Given this reasoning, we proceeded to administer the TAT to a number of *S*s, conducted an individual inquiry in which we tried to assess the reaction of the storyteller to each of the figures in his stories, and then looked for differences in reaction to those figures independently rated as identification figures as opposed to those that were not rated as identification figures.

In the second study, we were able to examine certain quantitative shifts that occurred in TAT stories following a frustration experience within the framework of the hero assumption and within the framework of the assumption that all figures are equally indicative of characteristics of the storyteller.

It should be clearly understood that in these studies we are *not* asking whether the simple assumption of a single hero in each story is the most fruitful assumption that can be made. What we *are* asking is whether this is a more fruitful assumption than the opposite extreme, the assumption that all figures in the story are equally revealing of the storyteller's characteristics. There are many fine gradations between these extremes, and a shrewd observer with a facile pen can complicate the assumptions endlessly. Some of the many alternative assumptions have been considered in an earlier paper by one of the present authors (6), and his presentation has been examined critically by Piotrowski in several subsequent papers (13, 14). What is needed now, however, is not further complexity or rational elaboration but rather a statement of assumptions with sufficient explicitness so that they lead to clear empirical consequences, followed by a careful testing of these consequences.

The findings presented here are, at most, a beginning on the road to clarifying the kinds of underlying processes that operate in the construction of imaginative stories. Their sole virtue lies in the fact that they make clear under controlled circumstances something about the relative merit of two widely divergent and yet defensible assumptions concerning the process of interpreting imaginative protocols.

Subject Reactions to Hero and Non-Hero Figures

If the assumption of a hero in each story whose attributes are especially revealing of the *S*'s psychological makeup is to prove defensible, it seemed to us that we should be able to show that the *S* reacted differently to hero figures than he did to those figures judged not to be hero figures. In particular, we reasoned that if heroes were carriers of storyteller attributes, the *S* should see these figures as more similar to himself than the non-hero figures, or else he should react with a violent denial of any similarity or resemblance between himself and the hero figures. This conclusion was derived from the assumption that the TAT revealed both conscious attributes and unconscious or unacceptable attributes of the *S,* coupled with the further reasoning that when a figure represented a conscious quality of the storyteller, he would accept and report the similarity, while under circumstances where there was an unacceptable impulse or quality involved, he would tend to deny strongly any similarity between himself and the figure.

Consequently, the hypothesis to be tested in this study asserts that story-characters independently judged to be hero figures are seen by the S as similar to himself or as having no self-similarity whatsoever, while figures independently judged *not* to be hero figures are more often seen by the storyteller as resembling others or else as representing stereotyped or fictional characters. It seems clear that the assumption that all figures are equally revealing of the storyteller provides no basis for predicting any difference in S reaction to hero and non-hero figures.

PROCEDURE

A shortened version of the TAT consisting of Cards 2, 5, 7GF, 9GF, 10, and 18GF was administered in a small group setting to 30 Syracuse University undergraduate females. Use of group administration seemed warranted in view of the results of an earlier investigation (7) comparing individual and group administration. The Ss had volunteered to participate in the study from an introductory course in psychology. After completion of the group test, individual appointments were made for each S within 48 hours from the time of the original test. During the individual interview, each S was asked to tell as much as she could concerning the factors that led to her creating each of the stories she had constructed. In addition, for each character in each of the stories, she was required to make a judgment of how similar the character was to herself and how similar it was to other people whom she had known. The responses of the Ss permitted us to categorize each character in terms of similarity to self (thought of as self, could be self, some similarity to self, denial of similarity to self) and similarity to other (thought of as other, similar to other). The characters were also classified in a general stereotype category

when the S reported that the figure represented some general fictional character or when she reported no resemblance to anyone and could not say what had influenced her to create this character.

The stories were independently analyzed in order to identify the hero and non-hero figures in each story. Two raters with no shared practice and with only a few general scoring principles were able to reach complete agreement on the identity of the hero figure (or the absence of a hero) in 90 per cent of the 180 stories rated.

The analysis of these data posed certain thorny problems as the most obvious and pertinent arrangements of the data led to more observations than subjects and thus made customary statistical analysis inappropriate. In view of this difficulty, we followed the convention of presenting the data descriptively in what seems to us the most revealing manner and then, in addition, performing certain further analyses that permit the application of the usual tests of significance.

In order to reduce the number of observations to the number of Ss, we adopted a procedure for each of the three relevant areas of response (similarity to self rather than other, denial of similarity to self, stereotype) that permitted us to assign to each S a score representing the extent to which his six stories fitted with or deviated from the predicted pattern. Thus, if the first story that the individual told found him identifying the judged hero of the story as resembling himself, while the non-hero figures were judged to be similar to others, a score of one would be assigned. If a non-hero figure was judged to be similar to the self, while the hero figure was not judged to be similar to the self, a score of minus one was assigned. If the hero and non-hero figures were treated in identical fashion, a score of zero was entered. The total score for each *S* consisted of the sum of the individual scores for his six stories and could theoretically vary from plus six (confirmation of the hypothesis in every story) to minus six (negation of the hypothesis in every story). This procedure provided three sets of scores representing the extent to which the stories and inquiry responses of the individual *S*s conformed to our predictions in regard to similarity to self versus other, denial of similarity to self, and stereotyped response.

of the predictions made in advance of the study. Figures independently rated as heroes tend to be perceived as more similar to the storyteller than non-hero figures, or else are denied any similarity to the storyteller. On the other hand, non-hero figures, when compared to hero figures, tend more often to be identified as similar to some person other than the storyteller or else are classified as stereotyped. If the categories implying various degrees of similarity to self are combined into a single category and the same operation is performed for categories representing similarity to others, it is then possible to examine the association

TABLE 1. SUBJECT REACTIONS TO HERO AND NON-HERO FIGURES

| Reactions | Frequencies | | | | Total |
| | Hero | | Non-Hero | | |
	Observed	Chance Expectancy	Observed	Chance Expectancy	
Self	3	2.46	3	3.54	6
Could Be Self	14	7.38	4	10.62	18
Similar to Self	21	11.07	6	15.93	27
Denial of Self	29	24.19	30	34.81	59
Other	9	11.07	18	15.93	27
Could Be Other	33	36.08	55	51.92	88
Stereotype	78	96.76	158	139.24	236
Total	187		274		461

RESULTS

The general results of the study are summarized in Table 1, where we find the distribution of hero and non-hero figures in each of the categories having to do with similarity to self and to other as well as the stereotype category. A comparison of the frequencies actually obtained with those that would be expected by chance alone makes it evident that the trend of these data is in support

between the hero and non-hero distinction and similarity to self and other in a single 2 × 2 table. In Table 2, the outcome of such a procedure is represented, and there is clear evidence for association between the hero designation and perceived similarity to the self. It is, of course, not legitimate to perform the usual statistical analyses because of the lack of independence of observations. However, any such test applied to this array of findings would indicate the predicted association at a highly significant level. In general, these findings hold true not only for the over-all distribution reported in Table 1, but they are also sustained when the same distribution for each of the six cards is examined separately.

TABLE 2. SIMILARITY TO SELF AND OTHER OF HERO AND NON-HERO FIGURES

	Hero	Non-Hero
Similar to Self	38	13
Similar to Other	42	73

The results of our statistical comparison of hero and non-hero figures are presented in Table 3, where it is again made clear that the data tend to support our hypothesis. When heroes and non-heroes are compared in regard to *perceived similarity to self and others,* the scores present a significant deviation from chance in favor of the predicted greater similarity of self to hero figures and of others to figures judged to be non-heroes. The stories of 18 of our Ss revealed the predicted association between self-similarity and hero figures and other-similarity and non-hero figures; for four of the Ss, the hero and non-hero figures were treated in similar fashion, while the remaining eight Ss reversed the prediction. Examination of the tendency to *deny similarity to self* reveals confirmation of our prediction that this would occur more frequently with hero than with non-hero figures. A number of Ss provided no evidence of denial in any of their responses, so there was no possibility of differential perception of the hero and non-hero figures; but in those cases where there was such evidence, 12 of 17 Ss showed a tendency to react with denial to hero figures more often

than to non-hero figures. We also found evidence that non-hero figures were more often categorized as *stereotyped* or unrelated to either self or to other persons than were hero figures. There were nine Ss who revealed no difference in the incidence of hero and non-hero figures who were perceived as stereotyped; but of the remainder, 17 reported the non-hero figures as more stereotyped, and only four saw the hero figures as more stereotyped.

The above findings provide clear confirmation of our predictions and thus support the value of the hero assumption. These same results, however, dramatically underline the shortcomings of this assumption in the face of certain TAT stories. Although the general trend

TABLE 3. CONFIRMATION OF PREDICTIONS CONCERNING DIFFERENCES IN REACTION TO HERO AND NON-HERO FIGURES

Reaction	$\overline{X}$	$s_{\overline{x}}$	t	p
Hero Similarity to Self and Non-hero Similarity to Other	.966 [a]	.343	2.82	<.05
Denial of Similarity to self	.343	.186	2.31	<.05
Stereotype	1.033	.261	3.95	<.01

[a] A positive deviation from zero indicates confirmation of the predicted relation.

of the data fits with the derivation from the hero assumption, there are individual Ss who consistently reverse the prediction; e.g., there are some Ss who characteristically view non-hero figures as like themselves and hero figures as like others. Thus, it seems clear that the actual situation is more complex than a literal application of the hero assumption would imply. Consequently, it becomes an important investigative task for the future to discover something about the types of Ss or stories or both where this assumption may be applied fruitfully, as well as those where some other assumption should be utilized. This same conclusion is supported by the general findings contained in Table 1. While these results support our prediction, it is a group trend that we observe with many individual exceptions.

A very brief summary of our Ss' reports concerning what had provided them with the idea for their stories is contained in Table 4. The results summarized here make clear that in a large number of cases (48 per cent) the Ss indicate only that the story came from their imagination. Next most frequently mentioned as a determinant is the picture or some specific element within it (37 per cent).

TABLE 4. REPORTED SOURCE OF
TAT STORIES

Source	Frequency of occurrence	
	n	%
Imagination	87 [a]	48
Properties of Card	66	37
Autobiographical Events	37	21
Experience of Others	30	17
Reading: Fiction	28	16
Movies, TV	24	13
Reading: Non-fiction	8	4

[a] Total number of stories: 180.

In those cases where the Ss are able to identify a specific experience as having suggested the story, this was less likely to have been a fictional encounter (movies 13 per cent, novels 16 per cent) than an autobiographical event (21 per cent) or general experience and observation

(17 per cent). Only a very small number (4 per cent) of the stories were reported to have stemmed from nonfiction reading.

In summary, the general findings of this study provide modest support for the hero assumption, although they also suggest that in individual cases the data do not mesh smoothly with this assumption. Let us turn now to the second study.

Changes Following Frustration Viewed from the Vantage of the Hero Assumption

As we have already agreed, one of the major difficulties in evaluating the general utility of the hero assumption is posed by the close relation between internal states of the S and his perception of external reality. It is not easy to conceive of circumstances that on a priori grounds seem likely to produce changes in the motivational state of the S which will not be mirrored in changes in his perception of external reality. What we need is to construct a set of conditions under which the hero assumption predicts differential changes in hero and non-hero characteristics while the other assumption, of course, predicts consistent changes for both types of figures.

Such a combination of conditions seemed to exist in connection with a set of data that was part of an earlier study (5). These data consisted of a set of TAT protocols collected before and after a frustration experience together with an appropriate set of control protocols. Most important, a great deal was known about the details of the frustration experience and the Ss' reactions to this situation. This information permitted us to make specific predictions concerning the changes that could be expected if one assumed all figures to be equally representative of the storyteller or if one assumed that there was only one figure, the hero, that reflected personal characteristics of the storyteller.

In brief, the frustration situation was of such a nature that it seemed plausible to expect that the S's hostility toward others would increase, that he would also perceive others as directing hostility or aggression toward him, and finally that he would feel guilty or direct aggression toward himself. All acts of aggression within the TAT stories were analyzed in terms of whether the aggression was directed from (a) hero against other, (b) hero against self, (c) other against hero, or (d) other against other.

The assumption that all figures were equally characteristic of the storyteller implied that there should be a significant increase in aggressive acts of all four types in view of our prior information concerning the increased aggressive tendencies on the part of the storyteller. This assumption clearly suggests that if the S was more aggressive, this tendency should be revealed evenly or equally in all figures within the story. On the other hand, the hero assumption implied that there should be an increase in only three of the four categories. Aggressive acts carried out by the hero against others should increase as a result of the storyteller's increased extrapunitive tendencies. There should also be an increase of aggressive acts carried out by the hero against himself in view of the increased guilt or intrapunitiveness of the storyteller. Finally, there should be an increase in aggressive acts carried out by others against the hero as a result of his perception of the other members of the group as hostile toward him. There was nothing in our analysis of the frustration situation to suggest that the storyteller saw the persons around him as being hostile or aggressive toward each other so we would not predict any change in hostility between non-hero figures. Consequently, we find that the two assumptions agree in predicting significant changes in three of the four categories but are differentiated in their predictions concerning the fourth category.

The reasoning above is readily defensible on rational grounds. The important feature of this derivation, however, is not its invulnerability to logical assault but rather the fact that it was executed prior to analysis of any data except that having to do with a category where no difference was predicted (aggressive acts carried out by heroes against others). In other words, before the fact, the two assumptions, coupled with our detailed knowledge of the frustration situation, seemed to lead to a differentiated prediction which we set out to test. After the fact, there is little doubt that with reasonable motivation and ingenuity either assumption could be rationalized by a sophisticated observer with these or almost any other set of empirical findings.

PROCEDURE

The Ss in this investigation were 40 male undergraduate students of Harvard University who had been selected so that on the Allport-Kramer Prejudice Scale (1) they fell at the extremes of a group of 575 students enrolled in an undergraduate psychology course. This division of the Ss into high and low prejudice groups is of no interest in the present inquiry, and our current analysis overlooks the dimension of prejudice except for the fact that experimental and control Ss were individually matched in terms of prejudice score. The 20 control Ss were also matched with the experimental Ss in age. The Ss were told merely that they were participating in a study of personality structure and development. At the very outset of the study, each S was administered individually a shortened version of the Thematic Apperception Test consisting of Cards 3BM, 8BM, 16, and 20. At the end of approximately two months, the 20 experimental Ss were exposed to an experimentally contrived frustration situation, and immediately following this, they were again given the TAT. The instructions were to make no effort to recall their original story, but if they thought of it first, to put it aside and tell the next story that came to mind. The control Ss were given the TAT under the same conditions except that there was no intervening frustration experience.

The frustration experience has been fully described elsewhere (9), and it is necessary here only to point out that the experience was carefully divorced from the administration of the TAT and that the S was exposed to multiple frustration involving both psychological and complex social motives. The frustration of the latter motives was effected in a group experiment conducted with four confederates, two male and two female, who were ostensibly fellow participants in the study. By disguised manipulation, the experimental S was made to fail repeatedly on the group task, which was presumably related to intelligence; he thereby failed to achieve a sizeable financial reward offered for successful performance, and he also kept the other members of the group from winning financial rewards. At various times beginning immediately after the frustration situation, detailed subjective reports were collected, and these, in addition to objective observations made during the conduct of the experiment, enabled us to describe quite accurately just how the Ss experienced or reacted to this situation.

The TAT protocols were scored simply by counting aggressive acts and then coding them in terms of whether or not they were carried out by the hero of the story and whether or not they were directed toward the hero. The effects of the frustration situation were measured by means of subtracting for each experimental S the number of aggressive acts within each category before frustration from the number of such acts after frustration. From this difference score, we then subtracted the difference between the first and second administration of the test for the matched control S. In other words, the scores that we are concerned with represent the difference between the first and second test administrations for the experimental Ss, corrected by the equivalent shifts shown by the control Ss.

RESULTS

The results of our analysis are summarized in Table 5. Utilizing either assumption, we predicted that aggressive acts by the hero against others, by hero against self, and by others against hero, would increase following frustration. There is confirmatory evidence for all of these predictions. The shift is in the predicted direction in all three cases and is statistically significant at the conventional .05 level for acts involving the hero against others, and others against hero. It is just short of this significance level for acts involving the hero against self.

When we turn to the fourth column of Table 5, we find the data bearing upon the differential predictions derived from the two assumptions. The hero assumption predicted no change, whereas the other assumption predicted a shift similar to that observed for the categories just discussed. The results are surprisingly definitive as the distribution of change scores has a mean of exactly zero; there is no evidence whatsoever of any shift in this category. In other words, the data we have reported provide strong evidence for the superior predictive efficiency of the hero assumption under the single circumstance where the two assumptions differ in their consequences.

sumption so that under known conditions we can apply the kind of complexity in analysis that our findings as well as the convictions of most clinicians, imply is necessary in order to derive consistently sensitive and accurate inferences from the instrument.

TABLE 5. CHANGES FOLLOWING FRUSTRATION IN INCIDENCE OF VARIOUS TYPES OF AGGRESSIVE ACTS

Shift in Score	Hero against Other	Hero against Self	Other against Hero	Other against Other
Increase				
4			xxx	
3	x	x	xxx	x
2	xxxxxx	xxx	xxxxx	
1	xxxxxx	xxxx	xxxxx	xxxxxx
0	xxx	xxxxxxxx	xxx	xxxxxxx
Decrease				
−1	xxx	xxx	x	xxx
−2		x		xxx
−3	x			
$\overline{X}$	.75	.40	1.75	0
$S_{\overline{x}}$	.33	.28	.29	—
t	2.27	1.43	6.89	—
p	$<.02$	$<.10$	$<.005$	—

Discussion

It is clear that the results of these two studies provide some warrant for the continued use of the hero assumption. Our findings suggest that under two circumstances the derivations from this crude assumption fit the observed data better than the derivations that can be made from the easy assumption that all figures in the story are equally revealing of storyteller characteristics. Having agreed to this, however, we must hasten to emphasize the importance of research and formulation that will lead us to a more elaborate statement of the hero as-

There is no discussion of the alternatives to the hero assumption nearly so illuminating as Murray's original analysis of the hero distinction where we find the following special cases proposed:

(1) The identification of subject with character sometimes shifts during the course of the story; there is a *sequence of heroes* (first, second, third, etc.). (2) Two forces of the subject's personality may be represented by two different characters, for example, an antisocial drive by a criminal and conscience by a law-enforcing agent. Here we would speak of an *endopsychic thema* (internal dramatic situation) with two *component heroes*. (3) The subject

may tell a story that contains a story, such as one in which the hero observes or hears about events in which another character (for whom he feels some sympathy) is leadingly involved. Here we would speak of a *primary* and a *secondary* hero. Then (4), the subject may identify with a character of the opposite sex and express a part of his personality just as well in this fashion. (In a man this is commonly a sign of a high feminine component and in a woman of a high masculine component.) Finally, there may be no discernible single hero; either (5) heroship is divided among a number of equally significant, equally differentiated *partial heroes* (e.g., a group of people); or (6) the chief character (hero in the literary sense) obviously belongs to the subject-object situation; he is not a component of the storyteller's personality but an element of his environment. The subject, in other words, has not identified with the principal character to the slightest extent but has observed him as he would a stranger or disliked person with whom he had to deal. The subject himself is not represented, or is represented by a minor character (hero in our sense) (12, p. 7).

Having tentatively identified such special cases is an important contribution, but it is equally essential to provide a careful specification of how one goes about identifying actual stories and figures that should be interpreted in the light of each of these cases. This, it seems to us, is a promising and largely untouched area of research.

There are several tacks which such investigation might follow. First, it is possible that one might be able to discover within-story cues that would be helpful in deciding whether to apply the simple hero assumption or some more complex version. Second, there is the ever present likelihood that knowledge of which assumption would be most fruitful will depend upon further information concerning the S himself. Thus, the appropriate assumption might vary with the cognitive style, character type, cultural background, or intellectual level of the S. Third, depending upon the situational context in which the test is administered, the process of story creation may vary so that different assumptions are warranted. When the test is given in a threatening assessment situation, we might find a different interpretive assumption warranted than when the test is given in a permissive clinical setting, where the S is voluntarily seeking assistance. There are, of course, many other types of questions that might be asked concerning this aspect of the interpretive process. However, if we knew something about the relation between the variants of the hero assumption and variation in the nature of the story, in the characteristics of the S, and in the situational context, we would be tremendously advanced over our present position.

Granted that further research is indicated, do our findings in their present state provide us with useful information? They do! First, as we have indicated, they give modest support for those clinicians and investigators who have habitually employed the hero assumption in their use of the TAT. Second, they provide negative evidence for the various persons working with the instrument who have attempted to eliminate completely the hero assumption in favor of the other alternative we have considered. One may object to these inferences on the grounds that our findings are by no means definitive. Indeed they are not! But, in the absence of definitive findings, one uses the best evidence one can find, and it seems to us that the present studies fit this specification even if only by default.

There remains the interesting question whether our findings have any implications for the research carried out by the many investigators interested in the quantitative study of the TAT who have not employed the hero assumption. What of investigations such as those by Eron (2), Hartman (3), Henry (4), and McClelland *et al.* (11), where there is typically no distinction between hero and other? In spite of the highly tentative nature of our findings, they do seem to imply that these investigators might have demonstrated somewhat greater test sensitivity if they had recognized the difference between characteristics displayed by hero and by other figures in their efforts to relate test attributes to independent measures. This same possibility exists in connection with some of our own research (8, 10) and poses an intriguing problem for further investigation.

Summary

We have conducted two studies designed to test the comparative effectiveness of the assumption that there is customarily a single figure in TAT stories which is particularly revealing of the storyteller's own attributes as opposed to the assumption that all figures in the stories are equally revealing of the subject's characteristics. In the first study, 30 female undergraduate subjects were asked to judge the similarity between themselves and the figures in TAT stories they had created. They also reported on the similarity between these figures and other persons they had known, and described what had led them to tell each story. The results of the study confirmed our prediction derived from the hero assumption that hero figures would more often be identified as similar to self or else denied any similarity to self, while non-hero figures would more often be identified as similar to other persons or else would represent general stereotypes.

The second study examined changes in TAT protocols following a frustration experience. Aggressive acts carried out by heroes against others and against the self, and also aggressive acts carried out by others against the hero, all increased following frustration. There was no change in the incidence of aggressive acts carried out by others against others. The hero assumption had predicted just this pattern of results, while the alternative assumption incorrectly predicted consistent increases in all four types of aggressive acts.

Thus, the results of both studies provide evidence supporting the utility of the conventional assumption of a hero in each TAT story. The findings also suggest, however, that under certain conditions a more complex set of assumptions may be desirable or necessary.

References

1. ALLPORT, G. W., & KRAMER, B. M. Some roots of prejudice. *J. Psychol.*, 1946, **22**, 9–39.

2. ERON, L. D. A normative study of the Thematic Apperception Test. *Psychol. Monogr.*, 1950, **64**, No. 9 (Whole No. 315).

3. HARTMAN, A. A. An experimental examination of the Thematic Apperception Technique in clinical diagnosis. *Psychol. Monogr.*, 1949, **63**, No. 8 (Whole No. 303).

4. HENRY, W. E. The Thematic Apperception Technique in the study of culture-personality relations. *Genet. Psychol. Monogr.*, 1947, **35**, 3–135.

5. LINDZEY, G. An experimental examination of the scapegoat theory of prejudice. *J. abnorm. soc. Psychol.*, 1950, **45**, 296–309.

6. LINDZEY, G. Thematic Apperception Test: Interpretive assumptions and related empirical evidence. *Psychol. Bull.,* 1952, **49,** 1–25.

7. LINDZEY, G., & HEINEMANN, SHIRLEY H. Thematic Apperception Test: Individual and group administration. *J. Pers.,* 1955, **24,** 34–55.

8. LINDZEY, G., & NEWBURG, A. S. Thematic Apperception Test: A tentative appraisal of some "signs" of anxiety. *J. consult. Psychol.,* 1954, **18,** 389–395.

9. LINDZEY, G., & RIECKEN, H. W. Inducing frustration in adult subjects. *J. consult. Psychol.,* 1951, **15,** 18–23.

10. LINDZEY, G., & TEJESSY, CHARLOTTE. Thematic Apperception Test: Indices of aggression in relation to measures of overt and covert behavior. *Amer. J. Orthopsychiat.,* 1956, **26,** 567–576.

11. McCLELLAND, D., ATKINSON, J. W., CLARK, R. A., & LOWELL, E. L. *The achievement motive.* New York: Appleton-Century-Crofts, 1953.

12. MURRAY, H. A. *Thematic Apperception Test Manual.* Cambridge: Harvard Univer. Press, 1943.

13. PIOTROWSKI, Z. A. The Thematic Apperception Test of a schizophrenic interpreted according to new rules. *Psychoanal. Rev.,* 1952, **39,** 230–251.

14. ———. TAT newsletter. *J. proj. Tech.,* 1952, **16,** 512–514.

SOCIALIZATION OF AGGRESSION AND THE PERCEPTION OF PARENTS IN FANTASY   Jerome Kagan

Research on both the prediction and determinants of overt aggression in children has usually focused on the intensity of aggressive motivation as a major antecedent variable. For example, in studies attempting to predict overt aggression from related fantasy it has been usual practice to correlate a broad index of fantasy aggression with a category of overt aggressive behavior like fighting or delinquent activity. The implicit hypothesis seems to be that frequency of fantasy aggressive acts is an index of aggressive drive and should be positively correlated with occurrence of overt aggression. Most of these studies failed to find a positive and linear relation between these two variables (7, 11, 15, 16). However, re-

Reprinted with permission of the Society for Research in Child Development and the author from *Child Development,* Vol. 29, 1958.

cent investigators (5, 9, 12, 13) have stressed that aggressive motives are conflictful and subject to inhibitory influences and they have attempted to measure the strength of these avoidance or inhibition tendencies. In these more recent studies evaluation of fantasy indices of aggression anxiety significantly improved the power of the fantasy behavior to predict occurrence of overt aggression.

The present research utilized hypotheses concerning the child's acquisition of inhibitions on aggression to predict types of fantasy content that should be related to overt aggression in young boys. Current theorizing about the developmental determinants of aggressive behavior suggests that a perception of the parent as hostile and nongratifying influences the child's predisposition to aggressive behavior in two ways. It has been assumed that these conditions increase aggressive motivation and, in addition, are contrary to the conditions which motivate the learning of prohibitions on aggression. With respect to the latter, it is suggested that an important motive for the acquisition and practice of parental prohibitions on aggression is anxiety over anticipated loss of parental love. The more intense the anxiety over this anticipated loss the stronger will be the response of adhering to the prohibitions of the parents. That is, the child trades the gratification derived from being aggressive for the continued love of his parents. Mahler (10) has stated,

Education, from the simplest gradual domestication and training of the infant up to the learning of skills and high scholastic achievement, can be compared with a continual barter in which the child is brought to give up infantile, egoistic and increasingly unacceptable, immature and objectionable behavior in return for tangible or intangible premiums, symbolizing love (p. 45).

It is hypothesized that the degree of anxiety generated by anticipation of loss of parental love depends, in part, on (a) the degree to which the child feels dependent on the parent for support in time of need and (b) the degree of nurturance given the child. These two variables are apt to be positively related and difficult to assess separately since a child should gradually extinguish on dependent overtures to parents if requests for support and nurturance were not gratified to some extent. Furthermore, an excessively nurturant and indulgent mother tends to prevent independent behavior from developing and the strength of the child's dependent tendencies remains at a high level. The position taken here is that the combination of a dependent child and a nurturant parent is most apt to generate anxiety over the anticipation of withdrawal of nurturance since the child feels he requires continued parental support. Thus, a dependent child who perceived the parents as nurturant would be highly motivated to adopt the prohibitions of the parents since disobedience should elicit anxiety over possible rejection. On the other hand, the child who was minimally dependent on the parent and who perceived the parent as hostile and nongratifying should feel less anxiety over anticipation of loss of love for such a loss would be viewed as less dangerous. Such a child would be minimally motivated to adopt and practice parental prohibitions. Existing data support these ideas. Several research reports suggest both a positive relation between maternal rejection and overt aggression in the child and an inverse relation between maternal overindulgence and the child's aggressive activity (1, 3, 8, 19). In a more recent study based on interviews with middle and working class mothers (17), Sears *et al.* found, for boys, a positive relation between dependency on the mother and a measure of the child's conscience and an inverse relation between maternal rejection and degree of conscience development. The authors conclude, "the pattern most calculated to produce 'high conscience' should be that of mothers who are usually warm and loving and then, as a method of control, threaten this affectionate relationship" (p. 388).

One final set of statements must be made explicit before the specific predictions can be stated. First, among young boys one can differentiate between unprovoked and justified aggression (8, 14). Although the former is generally punished by parents, the latter is often approved and encouraged by peers and family, and the young boy learns that aggression is expected and justified when he is attacked by his social environment. If it is further acknowledged that most boys encounter situations in school justifying some form of aggressive retaliation, then chronic and consistent absence of aggressive behavior would indicate very strong inhibitory responses on overt aggression.

On the basis of the above discussion it was predicted that in comparing extremely aggressive and nonaggressive boys the former should perceive the parents as less gratifying and more hostile and show less dependent behavior toward the parents than the latter.

In this study the major technique used to measure the child's perception and relationship to his parents was a fantasy situation in which the child told stories to pictures specially devised to suggest themes of dependence on adults, nurturance from adults, anger between a child and parent, and parental punishment. It was expected that nonaggressive boys would report more dependency and parental nurturance themes and fewer themes involving anger between parent and child than a group of extremely aggressive boys.

A major problem in assessing the fantasy involved the question of whether certain fantasy content is or is not representative of the child's environmental behavior and experiences. Some investigators (15, 18) have implied that fantasy is apt to be representative of the child's environment and behavior when the fantasy behaviors and events are not goal states that are usually prohibited and/or frustrated. Parental anger and hostility are not usually regarded as desired goals, and dependent behavior toward an adult is not strongly prohibited in children. In this regard, Kagan and Mussen (6) found a significant positive relation between dependency themes on the TAT and overt dependent behavior among a group of male college students. It is therefore suggested that the specific fantasy content under study might be dominated by themes and actions representative of reality.

Procedure

The subjects were 118 boys (Ss) drawn from seven classes (grades one through three) in a Columbus, Ohio, public school. Their ages ranged from 6–1 to 10–2 with a median age of 7–0. The school population was predominantly middle class, the majority of the fathers being skilled laborers and tradesmen. Before initiating interviews with each S the experimenter (E) spent several hours with each of the seven classes in order to become familiar with the children. After introductory games had established rapport in the interview, the E introduced the fantasy task with the following statement:

Let's play a guessing game now. I have some pictures here and I want you to guess what's happening in the picture. You have to make up a story to tell what you think is going on in the picture.

Thirteen pictures were administered, nine of which illustrated either a man or woman interacting with a small boy. The remaining four showed boy-boy interactions and are not relevant to this report. The nine adult-child pictures, in the order of their presentation, were as follows:

1. A boy is sitting on a chair holding a broken shoe lace and a woman is standing in the background.
2. A crying boy is sitting on the floor and a woman is standing behind the boy, looking down at him.

3. A boy with bowed head is standing near a bicycle which is turned over and a man is looking down at the boy.

4. A boy with bowed head is approaching a man sitting in a chair.

5. A boy is walking away from a woman who has her hands over her mouth.

6. A boy is holding his hand out to a man who is standing with one hand in his pocket.

7. A boy is crying and a woman is bending over the boy.

8. A boy with a cut on his arm is crying and a woman is standing in the background with her back to the boy.

9. A boy is crying and a man is standing in back of the boy looking down at him.

After the pictures were administered the E asked each S some questions, three of which are relevant for this report:

1. Who is the boss in your house, your mother or your father?

2. If your mother said one thing and your father said something different who would you listen to, your mother or your father?

3. Let's make believe you were bad at home and your mother and father were both home, who would punish you, your mother or your father?

Each S was rated by one person, his teacher, on a five-point scale for the following behaviors: (a) tendency to start fights at the slightest provocation and (b) tendency to hold in his anger and not to express it overtly. These two behaviors were selected in order to obtain a check on the consistency of the ratings. It was assumed that an S with a low rating on (a), i.e., never starts fights, would receive a high rating on (b), i.e., always holds in his anger. If the raters were consistent, there should be a high negative correlation between the ratings on these two variables. The product-moment correlation was $-.94$.

On the basis of the teacher ratings a group of 21 extremely aggressive boys (Group A) and 21 extremely nonaggressive boys (Group NA) were chosen from the entire sample. These two groups were composed of the three most and three least aggressive Ss in each of the seven classes. The Ss in both groups had been given extreme ratings on both variables.

Although the fantasy stories were scored for a large variety of themes, only the following content categories appeared with considerable frequency to the nine adult-child pictures.

1. *Dependency*—themes in which a child sought help from an adult with a problem situation.

2. *Nurturance*—themes in which a child was given unsolicited help with a problem; an adult showed concern for a child's welfare or a child was given money, food or gifts.

3. *Anger to a parent*—themes in which a child expressed anger toward a parent.

4. *Parental anger to a child*—themes in which a parent was angry with a child.

5. *Punishment*—themes in which a parent physically punished a child by spanking, slapping, hitting.

The themes were scored independently by the E and a graduate student in psychology without knowledge of the behavior ratings of the Ss. Percentage of agreement was high for each category and the over-all percentage of agreement for these five categories was 93 per cent.

Results

FANTASY DATA

1. *Dependency*. Occurrence of dependency themes was more frequent for the nonaggressive Ss with 9.5 per cent of Group A and 33.3 per cent of Group NA reporting one or more dependency themes ($p = .07$). All probability values are for one tail and were evaluated by the exact method described by Fisher (2).

2. *Nurturance.* There was no significant difference between the groups with respect to nurturance themes: 57.1 per cent of Group A and 61.9 per cent of Group NA reported this type of theme. However, one of the nurturance categories, "adult concern for a child's welfare," did tend to differentiate the groups with respect to the role of the person who showed this concern. The Ss in Group NA labeled the concerned adult as either a mother or father while the aggressive Ss described the concerned adult as a policeman, maid, stranger, or other nonparent figure. For the 15 Ss who told themes of adult concern, 28.6 per cent of Group A and 87.5 per cent of Group NA labeled the concerned adult as a parent ($p < .05$). One might infer from this finding that nonaggressive Ss were more likely than the aggressive ones to perceive the parents as nurturant figures. Supportive data from a study with older boys will be presented later.

3. *Parental anger.* As predicted, more of the Ss in Group A than in Group NA told one or more stories depicting parental anger toward a child (72.6 per cent versus 38.1 per cent; $p < .02$).

4. *Anger to parent.* The number of Ss in each group telling themes involving anger toward a parent also differentiated the two groups with 38.1 per cent of Group A and 9.5 per cent of Group NA telling one or more of these themes ($p < .05$).

5. *Punishment.* There was no significant difference between the groups on frequency of punishment themes: 52.4 per cent of each group reported one or more of these themes. It is possible that parental punishment is not a sensitive indicator of the gratifying or rejecting nature of the parent-child relationship, for Hollenberg and Sperry (4) also found a very low correlation between ratings of maternal frustration and punitiveness on the basis of interview data.

INTERVIEW DATA

1. *Child's perception of the boss of the family.* Two of the Ss in Group A had no father living with them and they were excluded from the statistical computations. To the question "Who is the boss in your house, your mother or your father?" more of the nonaggressive Ss answered "Mother" (42.9 per cent versus 10.5 per cent; $p < .05$).

2. *Child's preference for obedience.* To the question "If your mother said one thing and your father said something different who would you listen to, your mother or your father?" 57.1 per cent of Group NA and 26.3 per cent of Group A answered "Mother" ($p < .05$).

3. *More punitive parent.* To the question "Let's make believe you were bad at home and your mother and father were both at home, who would punish you, your mother or your father?" 47.6 per cent of the Ss in Group NA and 21.1 per cent of those in Group A viewed the mother as the major punitive agent ($p = .09$).

Discussion

The aggressive boys produced less themes in which the child showed dependent behavior toward adults or a parent showed concern for a child's welfare and more themes in which the parent-child interaction was characterized by anger. These data tend to support the prediction of a correlation between overt aggressive behavior and fantasy content depicting a hostile parent-child interaction and weak dependent tendencies toward the parent. If the fantasy can be regarded as representative of reality, these results may be interpreted as partial validation for the hypothesis that prohibitions on aggressive behavior are more likely to be learned and practiced when the child is dependent on his parents and perceives them as nurturing and gratifying. Under these conditions the child should be anxious over possible loss of parental gratifications if he fails to adopt the parental prohibitions on aggressive behavior.

The answers to the three direct questions seem compatible with this interpretation. The nonaggressive boys were more likely to describe the mother as the major punitive agent, the parent they would be likely to obey, and "the boss" in the home. This perception of the mother as the dominant figure in the home suggests that the nonaggressive boys would be more likely than the aggressive ones to fear alienation from the mother and therefore more likely to adopt and practice her prohibitions on aggression. If it is further assumed that middle class mothers are apt to place stronger prohibitions on overt aggression than the fathers, the positive relation between fear of alienation from the mother and absence of overt aggression tends to support the hypothesis of the paper. It is sometimes stated that one measure of degree of identification in a child is the degree to which prohibited motives have become socialized, and this process has sometimes been labeled "conscience" development. However, the child may use either his mother, father, or other figures as models for identification. The present relation between strong inhibition of aggression and a perception of the mother as authoritarian, suggests that a measure of "conscience" development is not necessarily an index of intensity of identification with the same sex parent.

As mentioned earlier, data from a research project at a military school [1] furnished some support for the finding that

_____

[1] These data were obtained while the author was collaborating on the Medical Research Project, U. S. Army Hospital, West Point, New York, and the author wishes to thank Lt. Col. William Hausman for permission to report these data. The conclusions are those of the author and should not be construed as representing those of the Department of the Army.

when a fantasy stimulus suggested nurturance from an adult to a child figure, aggressive Ss were not apt to label the older figure as a parent despite the fact that this interpretation was quite congruent with the external stimulus.

From a total entering class of 683, 170 boys wrote stories to selected TAT cards. The dependent measure of overt aggression for this sample of older adolescent males (age range 17 to 22) was the number of demerits accrued by each boy for violations of regulations during the first five months at the school. The distribution of demerits for the entire class of 683 was divided into quartiles and 29 of the Ss who wrote TAT stories fell in the lowest demerit quartile (low on violations) and 29 were in the highest demerit quartile (high on violations). Analysis of the stories written to TAT card 7 BM which involved nurturance from the older to the younger man (63 per cent of the themes) revealed that 70.0 per cent of the low aggressive men and 31.3 per cent of the high aggressive men labeled the older nurturant figure as the father of the younger one ($p < .05$).

Additional data from a succeeding first year class at the same school furnish similar results. The entire class of 765 subjects wrote short stories to specially devised pictures, two of which illustrated an adolescent male and an older man. The first depicted a boy standing in front of a seated man and the second depicted an adolescent male sleeping in a bed with an older man leaning over the sleeping boy. Approximately one third of the group told stories to each picture in which the older figure nurtured the younger one. The demerit distribution for the entire class was standardized, divided into quartiles and each S assigned a score of 1 to 4 depending on the demerit quartile into which he fell. Comparison of the mean demerit score between the Ss telling themes of nurturance from a father versus themes of nurturance from a nonparent figure revealed that for each picture the latter group had a higher demerit score ($p < .15$). Although these differences are not highly significant, the results are in the expected direction. One reason for the rather low significance value could be that both of these pictures were less suggestive of a nurturant relation between the adult and the boy than card 7 BM of the TAT. In any case, the results from these three independent studies all suggest that when a fantasy stimulus is congruent with an interpretation of a nurturant relation between a parent figure and younger male, failure to label the adult figure as a parent is positively correlated with overt aggressive behaviors. One might infer that failure to label the nurturant adult as a parent reflects a perception of the parent as nonnurturant.

Although this report has focused on the socialization of aggression, it is believed that anxiety over anticipated loss of nurturance acts as a motive for the socialization of other behaviors, e.g., sexuality and passivity, which also are subject to parental prohibitions. In addition to the partial validation of the hypotheses regarding the socialization process, a second implication of these data concerns the possible predictive power of these fantasy categories with respect to overt aggression. The findings tend to affirm the initial statement that fantasy content which is theoretically related to inhibition of aggression may be a more sensitive predictor of overt aggressive tendencies than the usual practice of summing the number of aggressive acts that a subject includes in his fantasy productions.

Summary

It was predicted that the fantasy stories of extremely aggressive boys would contain more hostility between parent and child and less dependency on adults than the stories of nonaggressive boys. The prediction was based on the assumption that minimal dependency on parents and a perception of them as hostile would oppose the adoption and practice of parental prohibitions on aggressive behavior, while dependent tendencies and a perception of the parent as nurturant should facilitate socialization of aggressive motives. Individual interviews were held with 118 boys, ages 6–1 to 10–2, in which stories to pictures and answers to direct questions were obtained. Teachers rated the aggressive behavior of the children and the data for the 21 most aggressive and the 21 least aggressive boys were reported. The results showed that more of the nonaggressive boys produced themes of dependency on adults and more of the aggressive boys told stories involving anger between parent and child. In answers to direct questions the nonaggressive children perceived the mother rather than the father as the major punitive agent and the parent they would be most apt to obey. This result indicated that the nonaggressive boys were more anxious about alienation from the mother than from the father. It was suggested that anxiety over alienation from the mother should lead to relatively strong inhibitory responses with respect to aggressive behavior since mothers are apt to be less permissive of aggression than fathers.

References

1. BALDWIN, A. L., KALHORN, JOAN, & BREESE, FAY H. Patterns of parent behavior. *Psychol. Monogr.,* 1945, **58**, No. 3.

2. FISHER, R. A. *Statistical methods for research workers.* (7th Ed.) Edinburgh: Oliver & Boyd, 1938.

3. HATTWICK, B. W. Interrelations between the pre-school child's behavior and certain factors in the home. *Child Develpm.,* 1936, **7**, 200–226.

4. HOLLENBERG, ELEANOR, & SPERRY, MARGARET. Some antecedents of aggression and effects of frustration on doll play. *Pers. Sympos. Topical Issues,* 1951, **1**, 32–43.

5. KAGAN, J. The measurement of overt aggression from fantasy. *J. abnorm. soc. Psychol.,* 1956, **52**, 390–393.

6. KAGAN, J., & MUSSEN, P. H. Dependency themes on the TAT and group conformity. *J. consult. Psychol.,* 1956, **20**, 29–32.

7. KORNER, ANNELIESE F. *Some aspects of hostility in young children.* New York: Grune & Stratton, 1949.

8. LESSER, G. S. Maternal attitudes and practices and the aggressive behavior of children. Unpublished doctor's dissertation, Yale Univer., 1952.

9. ———. Conflict analysis of fantasy aggression. *J. Pers.,* 1958, **26**, 29–41.

10. MAHLER, M. S. Ego psychology applied to behavior problems. In N. D. C. Lewis & B. C. Pacella (Eds.), *Modern trends in child psychiatry.* New York: International Universities Press, 1945. Pp. 43–56.

11. MURRAY, H. A. *Thematic apperception test manual.* Cambridge: Harvard Univer. Press, 1943.

12. MUSSEN, P. H., & NAYLOR, H. K. The relationships between overt and fantasy aggression. *J. abnorm. soc. Psychol.,* 1954, **40**, 235–240.

13. PITTLUCK, PATRICIA. The relation between aggressive fantasy and overt behavior. Unpublished doctor's dissertation, Yale Univer., 1950.

14. RADKE, MARIAN J. The relation of parental authority to children's behavior and attitudes. *Univer. Minn. Inst. Child Welf. Monogr. Series,* 1946, **22**.

15. SANFORD, R. N., ADKINS, M. M., MILLER, R. B., COBB, E. A., & others. Physique, personality and scholarship: a cooperative study of school children. *Monogr. Soc. Res. Child Develpm.,* 1943, **8**, No. 1.

16. SEARS, R. R. Relation of fantasy aggression to interpersonal aggression. *Child Develpm.,* 1950, **21**, 5–6.

17. SEARS, R. R., MACCOBY, ELEANOR E., & LEVIN, H. *Patterns of child rearing.* Evanston, Ill.: Row, Peterson, 1957.

18. TOMKINS, S. S. The present status of the thematic apperception test. *Amer. J. Orthopsychiat.,* 1949, **19**, 358–362.

19. UPDEGRAFF, RUTH. Recent approaches to the study of the preschool child. *J. consult. Psychol.,* 1939, **3**, 34–36.

ACHIEVEMENT MOTIVE AND TEST ANXIETY CONCEIVED AS MOTIVE TO APPROACH SUCCESS AND MOTIVE TO AVOID FAILURE

John W. Atkinson and George H. Litwin

Since 1950 there have been an increasing number of studies using thematic apperceptive (or equivalent) measures of n Achievement (McClelland, Atkinson, Clark, & Lowell, 1953; Atkinson, 1958; French, 1958) and the Mandler-Sarason Test Anxiety Questionnaire (TAQ) (Mandler & Sarason, 1952; Sarason, Mandler & Craighill, 1952; Mandler & Cowen, 1958), which amply demonstrate that knowledge of motivational differences enhances prediction of achievement related performances. The reader who is familiar with this literature will have noted that studies of n Achievement show it to be a motive that generally enhances performance in achievement situations while studies of Test Anxiety show it to be a motive that normally produces decrements in achievement test performance. Interpretations of the results of studies that have employed only a measure of n Achievement have often included some reference to Ss having low n Achievement scores as apparently more fearful of failure (Atkinson, 1953; Brown, 1953; Moulton, Raphelson, Kristofferson, & Atkinson, 1958). On the other hand, studies that have employed only the measure of Test Anxiety (Mandler & Sarason, 1952; Sarason & Mandler, 1952; Sarason, et al., 1952) have viewed the behavior of Ss having low Test Anxiety scores as less conflicted and more task oriented. One

Reprinted by permission of the American Psychological Association and the authors from *The Journal of Abnormal and Social Psychology*, Vol. 60, 1960.

might be tempted to think that these two sets of research findings overlap completely and that the measures employed merely tap opposite ends of a single motivational variable. This would seem a plausible inference in light of the correlation of —.43 between the two measures reported by Raphelson (1957) in a study that also showed each to be related in the expected direction to a physiological index of manifest anxiety in a stressful test situation.

The position taken here, however, is that the measure of n Achievement obtained from thematic apperception (McClelland, et al., 1953; Atkinson, 1958) or the French Test of Insight (French, 1955, 1958; French & Thomas, 1958), a very similar projective instrument, and the measure of Test Anxiety obtained from the self-knowledge scale developed by Mandler and Sarason are not measures of the same variable. Rather, it is assumed that these particular measures of n Achievement indicate the strength of a motive to approach success, while Mandler-Sarason Test Anxiety scores indicate the strength of a motive to avoid failure.

A theoretical model explaining how these two motives influence risk taking (i.e., selection) and level of performance in achievement test situation has been presented by Atkinson (1957, 1958) elsewhere. It provides a basis for testing assumptions about what is being measured by the two instruments. According to the theory, when a person's motive to achieve success is stronger than his motive to avoid failure, the resultant of the conflict is always positive; i.e., approach motivation, no matter what the level of difficulty of the task. An individual so motivated is most attracted to tasks of intermediate difficulty where the subjective probability of success is .50. Here the resultant positive motivation is strongest. However, if the motive to avoid failure (which is presumed to be a disposition to become anxious about failure under achievement stress) is stronger, then the resultant of the approach-avoidance conflict is avoidant motivation for all levels of difficulty. The maximum strength of avoidant motivation, i.e., the strongest anxiety about failure, occurs when tasks are of intermediate difficulty. Hence, according to the theory, a person so motivated finds all achievement tasks unattractive, particularly ones of intermediate difficulty. He performs them only when constrained by social pressures (otherwise he would "leave the field"),[1] and he performs them inefficiently; i.e., he suffers a performance decrement as a consequence of conflict engendered by competing avoidant tendencies, to the extent that his anxiety is aroused (Sarason, et al., 1952).

The present study tests several hypotheses derived from the theoretical model and simultaneously, the assumptions that (a) n Achievement, as measured by thematic apperception or a similar projective instrument, is a positive disposition to approach success and that (b) what has been called Test Anxiety is a disposition to avoid failure. The dependent variables are: goal setting (level of aspiration) when individuals are confronted with tasks which differ in difficulty (ring toss from distances ranging from 1 to 15 ft.); persistence at an achievement task when it is not clear that success has been attained (length of time spent working on a final examination); and efficiency of performance, or level of accomplishment (score on the final examination).

The hypotheses are as follows: Persons in whom the motive to achieve success is stronger than the motive to avoid failure (a) more often select tasks of intermediate difficulty, (b) work for a longer time on the final examination, and (c) get higher scores on the final examination than persons in whom the motive to avoid failure is the stronger motive. Hence, given the previously stated assumptions about the meaning of measures derived from the two tests, it is expected that n Achievement scores obtained from the French Test of Insight should be positively related to preference for intermediate risk, persistence, and efficiency of performance, and that scores from the TAQ should be negatively related to these same variables. Predictions should be enhanced when Ss are simultaneously classified as high or low on both measures.

A secondary interest is to explore the behavioral correlates of another measure called n Achievement which is obtained from the Edwards Personal Preference Schedule (1954). To date, there have been strong indications that direct (i.e., assent or preference) and indirect (i.e., imaginative or projective) methods of measuring achievement motivation do not yield comparable results. DeCharms, Morrison, Reitman & McClelland (1955) have found this to be true when a direct and indirect method of measuring n Achievement were compared in terms of predictions to behavior. Birney (see Mc-

---

[1] "Social pressures" reduce to other kinds of motivation, extrinsic to achievement, for performing the tasks (e.g., desire for social approval), which are not normally measured in experiments of this sort.

Clelland, 1958a) has found that measures of n Achievement obtained from thematic apperception and the Personal Preference Schedule (PPS) are uncorrelated ($r = -.002$, $N = 300$). This absence of relationship between the two measures is also reported by Marlowe (1959), who found, in addition, that the thematic apperceptive measure of n Achievement was positively related to peer group ratings of achievement related behavior, while the measure obtained from the PPS was not.

In summary, the purpose of this investigation is to examine the construct validity (see Cronbach & Meehl, 1955) of three contemporary measures of achievement related motives. Predictions concerning the behavioral correlates of the measures employed are generated by a theory that conceives the achievement motive and the motive to avoid failure as independent, latent, directional dispositions and states the conditions *under* which and the degree *to* which they are aroused and manifested in overt action.

Method

SUBJECTS

The Ss were male students enrolled in a sophomore-junior level psychology course at the University of Michigan in the fall of 1957. The data were collected in the laboratory sections of the course. The instructors served as Es.[2] There were 49 Ss on whom both the measures of n Achievement and Test Anxiety were available. Not all of these Ss, however, appeared for all of the later data collection sessions. In all comparisons, the largest possible number of Ss is used, even though this results in slight fluctua-

tions in the size of samples among the various comparisons.

MEASURE OF n ACHIEVEMENT AND TEST ANXIETY

Early in the semester Ss were administered, under neutral classroom conditions, a Test of Insight developed by Elizabeth French (1958). The test consists of 10 short verbal statements about people which Ss are asked to analyze. Both Forms I and II of the Test of Insight were used, half of the Ss getting each form. The interpretations of behavior, which are very similar to TAT stories, were scored for n Achievement (according to the method of content analysis described by McClelland, et al. 1953; Atkinson, 1958) by a scorer whose reliability had been established above .90 on training materials.[3] The distribution of n Achievement scores for each form was broken at the median. Ss above the median were classified as high in n Achievement and those below as low in n Achievement.

Test Anxiety scores were obtained from the Mandler-Sarason TAQ (see Mandler & Cowen, 1958). The TAQ were distributed in class and Ss were asked to complete them outside of class and to return them the following week. The questionnaires were scored by dividing each scale into intervals, assigning a score of 1–4 for each scale, and summing the scale scores to obtain the Test Anxiety score. This scoring method correlates very highly with that originally described by Mandler and Sarason ($r = .94$, $N = 50$), and differs from that recently described by Mandler and Cowen only in

---

[2] We wish to acknowledge the assistance of Joseph Veroff and Lawrence Littig.

[3] We wish to acknowledge the assistance of Lois Hendrickson who scored the protocols. Because many of the interpretations had no achievement imagery, the Unrelated Imagery category (UI) was scored 0 instead of −1.

that it uses 4 intervals instead of 10. The distribution of Test Anxiety scores was dichotomized at the median. The PPS developed by Edwards (1954) was administered to *S*s in class. The distribution of PPS n Achievement scores was also dichotomized at the median.

GOAL SETTING IN MODIFIED RING TOSS GAME

Several weeks after the individual difference measures had been obtained, *S*s played a ring toss game. Four games were set up in the room when they entered, one on each side, one in the front, and one in the back of the room. Each game consisted of a wooden peg 2 in. in diameter and 12½ in. high mounted on a round wooden base, a ring 10 in. in diameter, and 15 lines marked on the floor at one ft. intervals. A number was marked on the floor next to each line. The closest line was one ft. from the target and numbered 1; the farthest line was 15 ft. from the target and numbered 15.

The *S*s were told: "Today you are going to play a ring toss game. You will have an opportunity to take 10 shots at the target from any line you wish. You may move after each shot or shoot from the same line. Someone will record your shots and get your code number when you finish. We want to see how good you are at this." The instructor then kept track of the shots and hits of the first few *S*s, and these *S*s then kept score for the rest of the class. Two of the ring toss games were used by men and two by women. There was a good deal of informal banter during the session. No attempt was made to interfere with or to control the lifelike situation. Only the results for men are considered here since there remain unresolved questions concerning the validity of measures of n

Achievement and Test Anxiety when applied to women.

DATA FROM FINAL EXAMINATION

The final examination in the course from which the *S*s were drawn was a multiple choice and short answer test held several months later. It was scheduled to last from 9:00 to 12:00 a.m. Most of the students did not take the full three hours. As each student left the examination room after turning in his exam, and when he was out of sight of students still working on the exam, he was handed a card with the time written on it and asked to write his code number on it. The code number made it possible to relate the amount of time spent working on the exam to the individual difference measures, to goal setting behavior in the ring toss game, and to the final examination scores. The data were transcribed into a score for each *S* which represented the number of minutes spent working on the final examination.[4]

Results

DESCRIPTIVE ANALYSIS OF GOAL-SETTING DATA

The *S*s were classified simultaneously as high or low n Achievement and Test Anxiety. It follows from our assumptions about the two measures that the group classified high n Achievement-low Test Anxiety should be more strongly motivated to approach success than to avoid failure. The low n Achievement-high Test Anxiety group, on the other hand, should be more strongly motivated

---

[4] Because of overflow in the main examination room, 20 to 30 students took the examination in a different room. A constant of 5 min. was subtracted from the score of these students since they began the examination about 5 min. later.

to avoid failure than any other group. The other two groups, the high n Achievement-high Test Anxiety group and the low n Achievement-low Test Anxiety group should be more conflicted or intermediate in resultant motivation.

Figure 1 presents a smoothed curve for each of the four groups describing the percentage of shots taken from each distance. The curves are smoothed by the method of running averages. From Fig. 1

low Test Anxiety group. The curves indicate a relative difference between the motivation groups in preference for intermediate difficulty.

In Table 1, various ways of analyzing the data into easy, intermediate, and difficult regions are explored. The first method (I) is to divide the range of distances into equal geographic thirds. This is the method employed by Atkinson, et al. (1959) in an earlier study. The sec-

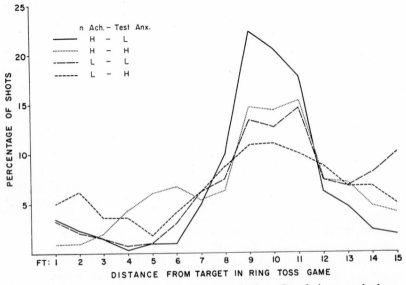

Fig. 1. Percentage of shots taken from each line. Graph is smoothed according to the method of running averages, for Ss classified as high or low simultaneously in n achievement and test anxiety, H–L ($N = 13$), H–H ($N = 10$), L–L ($N = 9$), L–H ($N = 13$).

it can be seen that all four groups show some preference for the distances around 9–11 feet. However, Ss high in n Achievement and low in Test Anxiety prefer this region most strongly, while the low n Achievement-high Test Anxiety group shows the weakest preference for it. The other two groups are between these two as predicted. At both the closest and farthest distances, the low n Achievement Test Anxiety group takes more shots than the high n Achievement-

ond method (II) is to use the obtained distribution of shots to determine the easy, intermediate, and difficult regions. Use of the obtained distribution of shots to define degrees of difficulty was suggested by McClelland (1958b) in an investigation of risk taking in children. The obtained distribution was first broken into approximate thirds (II-A) and then into the approximate interquartile range and extreme quarters (II-B) to show the effect of widening the region of intermediate difficulty. The third method (III) takes the middle third of distance around the obtained median of 9.8 feet.

Examination of Table 1 shows that all of the methods yield comparable results. The high n Achievement-low Test Anxiety group consistently takes the greatest

Test Anxiety group fall between the two extreme groups as expected.

EFFECTS OF n ACHIEVEMENT AND TEST ANXIETY

It is desirable to express the goal setting tendency of each person as a single score in statistical tests. An Aver-

TABLE 1. PERCENTAGE OF TEN RING-TOSS SHOTS TAKEN BY Ss SIMULTANEOUSLY CLASSIFIED HIGH AND LOW IN n ACHIEVEMENT AND IN TEST ANXIETY USING ALTERNATIVE CRITERIA FOR DEFINITION OF DEGREE OF DIFFICULTY (OR RISK)

Basis for Definition of Three Degrees of Difficulty (or Risk)	Distance in Feet	Motivation (n Achievement Test Anxiety)			
		High-Low $N = 13$	High-High $N = 10$	Low-Low $N = 9$	Low-High $N = 13$
I. Using Geographic dis-	1–5	8%	15%	9%	21%
tance: Equal Thirds	6–10	70	55	49	43
	11–15	22	30	42	36
II. Using Obtained Distribu-	1–8	22	31	28	39
tion of Shots:	9–10	55	39	30	25
A. Approximate Thirds	11–15	22	30	42	36
B. Approximate Inter-	1–7	11	26	18	32
quartile Range vs. Ex-	8–11	73	48	48	41
treme Quarters	12–15	16	26	34	28
III. Using Both Obtained Dis-	1–7	11	26	18	32
tribution of Shots and	8–12	82	60	58	48
Geographic Distance:	13–15	7	14	24	20
Middle Third of Dis-					
tance about the Obtained					
Median Shot (9.8 ft.)					

percentage of shots from the intermediate region and the low n Achievement-high Test Anxiety group consistently takes the least number of shots from the intermediate region. The difference between the percentage of shots taken by these two groups from the intermediate distances ranges from 27% to 34%. The high n Achievement-high Test Anxiety group and the low n Achievement-low

age Deviation score, which was found by Litwin (1958) to be the most consistent measure across tasks of the tendency of persons to prefer intermediate risk, was used. An Average Deviation score was computed for each shot as follows: Distance of shot-Mdn. distance of all shots/ Average Deviation of all shots. The Average Deviation score for each S was the mean of his scores (irrespective of sign) on the 10 shots. A low Average Deviation score means that shots were taken from intermediate distances; a large score means that shots were taken from very close or very far back in relation to the median of all shots.

In Table 2 the performance of Ss high and low in n Achievement is summarized for the three dependent variables: ring toss Average Deviation score; minutes spent working on the final exam; and the score on the final exam. From Table 2 it

also shows the percentage of Ss falling above or below the combined group median in each case; 60–64% of the high n Achievement group fall in the predicted cell, and 64–68% of the low n Achievement group fall in the predicted cell.

Table 3 presents the same information for the high and low Test Anxiety groups. Again, all the results are as predicted. The high Test Anxiety group tends to have higher Average Deviation

TABLE 2. MEDIAN SCORE ON THREE DEPENDENT VARIABLES FOR Ss CLASSIFIED HIGH OR LOW IN n ACHIEVEMENT AND PERCENTAGE OF Ss ABOVE OR BELOW THE COMBINED GROUP MEDIAN

Variable	Item	n Achievement		High vs. Low [a]
		High	Low	
Risk Taking: Average	N	23	22	
Deviation Score in	Mdn.	.63	.91	$U = 177.5$
Ring Toss Game	% below Combined Group Mdn.	61	36	$p = .04$
Persistence: Minutes	N	25	19	
Spent Working on	Mdn.	164.9	154.0	$U = 156.5$
Final Exam.	% above Combined Group Mdn.	60	32	$p = .03$
Efficiency: Final Exam	N	25	19	
Score	Mdn.	101	85	$U = 152.5$
	% above Combined Group Mdn.	64	32	$p = .02$

Note.—The slight fluctuation in N is explained in the Method section.
[a] Mann-Whitney U Test. All tests of significance are one-tailed tests.

can be seen that the high n Achievement group tends to have lower Average Deviation scores, i.e., to show a greater preference for intermediate risk, to spend more time working on the final exam, and to have higher final examination scores than the low n Achievement group. The differences between the two groups were tested by the Mann-Whitney U test. Since the direction of differences was predicted in each case, one-tailed tests were made. The differences between the high and low n Achievement groups are all statistically significant. Table 2

scores, i.e., to show greater avoidance of intermediate risk, to leave the final exam sooner, and to have lower final examination scores than the low Test Anxiety group. Mann-Whitney U tests were computed on the differences between the motivation groups; one-tailed tests were made. The groups differ significantly in Average Deviation scores ($p = .04$). For both the number of minutes spent working on the final exam and final examination scores the probability of the difference in the predicted direction is .06. It can be seen that 59–64% of the low Test Anxiety group, and 59–68% of the high Test Anxiety group fall in the predicted cells in relation to the combined group median.[5]

In Table 4, Ss are again simultaneously classified on n Achievement and Test Anxiety. The high n Achievement-low Test Anxiety group is seen to have the lowest Average Deviation score (i.e., the greatest preference for intermediate risk), to spend the most time working on the final exam, and to have the highest

for intermediate risk), to leave the final exam the earliest, and to have the lowest final examination scores. The high n Achievement-high Test Anxiety group and the low n Achievement-low Test Anxiety group generally fall between the two extreme groups as predicted. Mann-Whitney U tests of the differences between the high n Achievement-low Test Anxiety group and the low n Achievement-high Test Anxiety group employing one-tailed alternative hypotheses are

TABLE 3. MEDIAN SCORE ON THREE DEPENDENT VARIABLES FOR Ss CLASSIFIED HIGH OR LOW IN TEST ANXIETY AND PERCENTAGE OF Ss ABOVE OR BELOW THE COMBINED GROUP MEDIAN

| Variable | Item | Test Anxiety | | High vs. Low [a] |
		High	Low	
Risk Taking: Average	N	23	22	
Deviation Score in	Mdn.	1.00	.63	$U = 177$
Ring Toss Game	% below Combined Group Mdn.	35	64	$p = .04$
Persistence: Minutes	N	22	22	
Spent Working on	Mdn.	154.8	165.2	$U = 176$
Final Exam	% above Combined Group Mdn.	32	64	$p = .06$
Efficiency: Final Exam	N	22	22	
Score	Mdn.	91.0	101.5	$U = 177$
	% above Combined Group Mdn.	41	59	$p = .06$

Note.—The slight fluctuation in N is explained in the Method section.
[a] Mann-Whitney U Test. All tests of significance are one-tailed tests.

final examination scores. The low n Achievement-high Test Anxiety group tends to have the highest Average Deviation scores, (i.e., the weakest preference

[5] When only the extreme quartiles are compared, as is common in research using the Test Anxiety Questionnaire, the percentage of groups ($N = 11$) falling into predicted cells is increased somewhat to 63–72%. The median split is used here both because the N is relatively small to begin with and also to call attention to the relative sensitivities of the various measures of achievement related motivation when applied to the same dependent variables.

all statistically significant. When the percentage of Ss in each of the motivation groups falling above or below the combined group median is computed, 67–77% of the high n Achievement-low Test Anxiety group are correctly placed, and 69–75% of the low n Achievement-high Test Anxiety group are correctly placed. Simultaneous classification on both approach and avoidance motives clearly improves the prediction.

The examinations were graded A+ (excellent) to E (failure) before this analysis was even begun. It is of interest to note that the median final examination score for the high n Achievement-low Test Anxiety group (102.3) was a B — grade on the final exam, and that 67% of this group received B— or better on the exam while only 7% received a grade of D or E. On the other hand, the median final examination score for the low n Achievement-high Test

THE MEASURE CALLED n ACHIEVEMENT ON THE PPS

Table 5 presents the results for Ss classified as high or low on PPS n Achievement. The only statistically significant result is for the ring toss Average Deviation scores, and here it is directly opposite to what would be ex-

TABLE 4. MEDIAN SCORE ON THREE DEPENDENT VARIABLES FOR Ss SIMULTANEOUSLY CLASSIFIED HIGH OR LOW IN n ACHIEVEMENT AND TEST ANXIETY AND PERCENTAGE OF Ss ABOVE OR BELOW THE COMBINED GROUP MEDIAN

Variable	Item	n Achievement Test Anxiety				High-Low vs. Low-High [a]
		High-Low	High-High	Low-Low	Low-High	
Risk Taking: Average	N	13	10	9	13	
Deviation Score in	Mdn.	.48	1.03	.88	.93	$U = 42.5$
Ring Toss Game	% below Combined Group Mdn.	77	40	44	31	$p < .025$
Persistence: Minutes	N	15	10	7	12	
Spent Working on	Mdn.	165.3	157.5	148.3	154.5	$U = 40.5$
Final Exam	% above Combined Group Mdn.	73	40	43	25	$p < .01$
Efficiency: Final Exam	N	15	10	7	12	
Score	Mdn.	102.3	96.5	91	82.5	$U = 47.5$
	% above Combined Group Mdn.	67	60	43	25	$p < .025$

Note.—The slight fluctuation in N is explained in the Method section.
[a] Mann-Whitney U Test. All tests of significance are one-tailed tests.

Anxiety group (82.5) was a D grade; 58% of this group received a D or an E on the final exam and only 25% received a grade of B— or better.[6]

pected if the test measured the strength of motive to achieve success as conceived in the risk taking theory. The high PPS n Achievement group have significantly

[6] These results are viewed as consistent with the idea that highly anxious individuals suffer a performance decrement on achievement tests (Sarason, et al., 1952). It may be argued that unmeasured differences in ability and not differential anxiety are responsible for the result. Perhaps Ss score high on Text Anxiety because they have performed badly in the

past (also as a consequence of low ability). The argument is plausible, but so also is the alternative. Accordingly, finding that Ss who score high on Test Anxiety also score low on some independent test of academic ability would be expected since ability is always measured under the very kind of stressful test conditions that produce performance decrements in anxious Ss. Experimental evidence higher Average Deviation scores, (i.e., greater avoidance of intermediate risk) than the low PPS n Achievement group ($p = .02$). Two-tailed alternative hypotheses were used here since there is little evidence in previous research to support any assumptions about what this test measures. For neither time spent working on the final examination nor final examination scores are the differences between the two PPS n Achievement groups statistically significant. The

Since the PPS n Achievement measure behaves as if it were a measure of the motive to avoid failure (at least in the risk taking game), the PPS n Achievement measure was substituted for the Test Anxiety measure in a simultaneous classification with n Achievement (French Test of Insight). The high n Achievement-low PPS n Achievement group ($N = 11$) had 82% of its Ss below the combined group median for Average Deviation score, the low n

TABLE 5. MEDIAN SCORE ON THREE DEPENDENT VARIABLES FOR Ss CLASSIFIED HIGH OR LOW IN PPS n ACHIEVEMENT AND PERCENTAGE OF Ss ABOVE OR BELOW THE COMBINED GROUP MEDIAN

Variable	Item	PPS n Achievement		High vs. Low [a]
		High	Low	
Risk Taking: Average	N	22	21	
Deviation Score in	Mdn.	.97	.50	$U = 137.5$
Ring Toss Game	% below Combined Group Mdn.	36	62	$p = .02$
Persistence: Minutes	N	24	20	
Spent Working	Mdn.	157.5	163.0	$U = 223.5$
on Final Exam	% above Combined Group Mdn.	42	55	$p = .70$
Efficiency: Final	N	24	20	
Exam Score	Mdn.	100.0	89.5	$U = 181.5$
	% above Combined Group Mdn.	58	40	$p = .17$

Note.—The slight fluctuation in N is explained in the Method section.
[a] Mann-Whitney U Test. All tests of significance are one-tailed tests.

trends are inconsistent. If anything, Ss having high PPS n Achievement scores do not work as long on the exam but get better grades than those having low scores.

(e.g., Sarason, et al., 1952) which shows that anxious Ss perform as well or better than nonanxious Ss under nontest conditions but more poorly under achievement test conditions makes the motivational interpretation plausible pending the discovery by someone of a method of isolating the motivational and aptitudinal influences on the usual so-called test of ability.

Achievement-high PPS n Achievement group ($N = 10$) had 30% of its Ss below the combined group median. The difference between these two extreme groups was very significant ($U = 16$, $p = .01$ in this direction), larger than the comparable difference shown in Table 4 when Test Anxiety is used to assess the tendency to avoid failure!

When Ss were classified on all three of the measures, n Achievement, Test Anxiety, and PPS n Achievement, striking differences were noted. The high n

Achievement-low Test Anxiety-low PPS n Achievement group ($N = 7$) had 100% of its Ss below the combined group median for Average Deviation score while the low n Achievement-high Test Anxiety-high PPS n Achievement group ($N = 8$) had only 25% of its members below the combined group median. The difference between these two groups was highly significant ($p = .001$).

INTERCORRELATION OF VARIABLES

Spearman rank order correlations were used to ascertain the degree of intercorrelation among the independent and dependent variables. The three measures of achievement related motives were not significantly related. The correlations between the several measures were as follows: Test Anxiety and PPS n Achievement, .11 ($N = 47$); PPS n Achievement and n Achievement, $-.05$ ($N = 47$); Test Anxiety and n Achievement, $-.15$ ($N = 47$).

The three dependent behavioral variables, however, tended to be positively related to one another. The index of risk taking preference, Average Deviation score (low scores given high ranks), and the measure of persistence, time spent working on the final exam, were correlated .34 ($N = 40$, $p < .05$); number of min. spent working on the final exam and final examination score were correlated .27 ($N = 40$, $p < .10$); the Average Deviation score (low scores given high ranks) and final examination scores were correlated .19 ($N = 40$, $p < .25$). A more substantial relationship is evident between the two behavioral indices of motivation, risk taking and persistence, that are not strongly influenced by academic ability, than between either of these measures and exam performance which is strongly influenced by ability.

Discussion

CONSTRUCT VALIDITY OF THREE TESTS

These results yield support for the assumptions stated earlier regarding the nature of the variables being measured by the French Test of Insight and the Mandler-Sarason TAQ. Since Litwin (1958) reports directly comparable risk taking results when using thematic apperception to assess achievement motivation, it can be concluded that n Achievement scores obtained from thematic apperception or the Test of Insight indicate the strength of a motive to approach success. Test Anxiety scores yield results consistent with the assumption that the variable involved is a disposition to avoid failure. This assumption is not at variance with Mandler and Sarason's (1952; Sarason, et al., 1952) explanation of the performance decrement shown by anxious persons under achievement stress: the anxious person's performance suffers when task-irrelevant (avoidant) responses interfere with task-relevant (approach) responses.

The results concerning efficiency of performance, or level of accomplishment, under achievement-oriented conditions replicate earlier findings concerning n Achievement (Atkinson & Reitman, 1956; French, 1955) and Test Anxiety (Mandler & Sarason, 1952; Sarason, et al., 1952). The positive relationship between n Achievement and persistence at a task replicates an earlier finding by French and Thomas (1958) and is further evidence of the tendency also noted in recall of interrupted tasks (Atkinson, 1953). To our knowledge, this is the first study to relate Test Anxiety to a measure of persistence. The relationship of Test Anxiety to risk taking or goal setting behavior was first noted by Vitz (1957), and Litwin (1958) has recently replicated the present risk taking findings using several different tasks.

The results concerning the measure of n Achievement obtained from the Edwards PPS are nebulous. This is the third occasion on which no relationship has been found between this direct preference measure and an indirect or projective measure of n Achievement. The observed tendency of persons having high PPS n Achievement scores to avoid intermediate risk, as if they were in fact more strongly motivated to avoid failure than to achieve, dramatically reinforces the statement that *different methods of assessing human motives do not yield comparable results* (see McClelland, 1958a). The inconsistency and lack of statistical significance of the other results pertaining to the PPS measure of n Achievement make it very difficult to understand just what is being measured by this test. One suggestive lead is provided by some unpublished results obtained by Charles Seashore.[7] He had Ss judge the social desirability of all the statements on the PPS on a seven point scale about three months after taking the test and found a correlation of .47 ($N = 50$) between PPS n Achievement score and judged social desirability of the achievement statements. One might conclude from this that although the paired items are equated for *average* social desirability, individual differences in scores obtained from this test can be considered measures of individual differences in what is deemed socially desirable. This conclusion is supported by a recent study by Corah, Feldman, Cohen, Gruen, Meadow, and Ringwall (1958) in which

judged social desirability of items within pairs on the PPS correlated highly with the item selected. Arguing in a similar vein, McClelland (1958a) has suggested designating measures obtained by direct preference or assent methods as "values," e.g., *v* Achievement (see also deCharms, et al., 1955), in order to avoid the inevitable confusion that arises in trying to reconcile research findings involving variables assessed by different methods but gratuitously called by the same name.

In terms of the theoretical conception of risk taking and achievement related behavior presented in detail elsewhere (Atkinson: 1957, 1958) and the assumptions regarding the variables measured here, the present findings provide considerable evidence of construct validity for the n Achievement scores obtained from the French Test of Insight and for Test Anxiety scores interpreted as measures of the strength of a disposition to be anxious about, and hence motivated to avoid, failure. However, until national norms are available for each of these measures, the crude designations as "high" and "low" of groups who stand above or below the median score in a college population are at best crude estimates of relative strength.

THE RELATIONSHIP OF n ACHIEVEMENT AND TEST ANXIETY

The zero order correlation between n Achievement and Test Anxiety reported here is at variance with Raphelson's (1957) earlier report of a negative correlation. Yet the results may not, in fact, be inconsistent. In the present study the projective measure of n Achievement was presented under *neutral* classroom conditions, and the results show that persons having high n Achievement scores are as likely as not also to have high Test Anxiety scores. In Raphelson's study,

---

[7] Personal communication, Sept., 1958.

the n Achievement scores were obtained from thematic apperceptive stories written by Ss under *achievement orientation* during a rest period in the middle of a rather stressful test situation. The results of Martire (1956) and Scott (1956) clearly point to the possibility that persons who are strong in *both* achievement motive and motive to avoid failure may inhibit or distort the expression of achievement related imagery when anxiety about failure has been actively aroused in them by threatening situational cues. If so, it would be expected that persons classified high n Achievement (on the basis of *neutral* thematic apperceptive or Test of Insight scores) and also high in Test Anxiety should express less achievement related imagery when anxiety about failure is aroused. This state of affairs would induce the negative correlation between the measures reported by Raphelson.

Given only high (above the median) n Achievement scores, one can assume that the achievement motive is relatively strong in relation to an unmeasured motive to avoid failure; given low n Achievement scores, one can assume that the motive to achieve success is relatively weak in relation to an unmeasured motive to avoid failure. When the motive to avoid failure is also measured, using the Test Anxiety Questionnaire, and Ss having high n Achievement scores but also having high Test Anxiety scores are segregated, we then have more reason to be confident that our inference of relatively stronger motive to achieve success in the remaining high n Achievement-low Test Anxiety group is correct, as the present results indicate. Similarly, segregating Ss who have low scores on both n Achievement and Test Anxiety leaves a group low in n Achievement and high

in Test Anxiety in whom we have more reason to be confident that the motive to avoid failure is relatively stronger. Yet in a group of college students it is unlikely that these are all persons in whom the absolute strength of motive to avoid failure is greater than the absolute strength of achievement motive. We find that this group does not actually *avoid* intermediate risk, as would be expected if the avoidance motive were stronger than the approach motive. Instead we find only a relatively weak preference for intermediate risk, in comparison with other groups. Presumably, most persons in whom the avoidant motive is actually stronger in an absolute sense are eliminated long before they reach college. The findings of Miller (1951), Eysenck (1955), and Eysenck and Himmelweit (1946) concerning extremely high levels of aspiration set by persons diagnosed as neurasthenic and extremely low levels of aspiration among persons diagnosed as hysteric represent the pathological extremes in avoidant motivation which may appear very rarely in college groups. The present research used all available Ss and made its cutting point in the distributions at the median. Perhaps the choice of more extreme groups of Ss, as has been common in research with the Mandler-Sarason test, would produce such avoidant groups even in a college population. The small number of Ss in the present investigation precluded this possibility.

THE MEASURE OF SUBJECTIVE
PROBABILITY OF SUCCESS

An issue of fundamental importance that is treated rather inadequately here is the measurement of subjective probability of success. Strong assumptions are made concerning how the chances of success must appear to *S*s as they approach the ring toss game. It is implicitly assumed here, as in an immediately preceding study (Atkinson, et al., 1959) which made the point explicit, that the probability of success must have appeared closer to 1.00 than to .50 at 1 ft. and closer to 0 than to .50 at 15 feet. The zone of intermediate risk or intermediate difficulty, i.e., where probability of success approximates .50, must therefore fall somewhere in between.

The actual probabilities of success obtained from the shots taken by *S*s in this experiment, while not altogether relevant since it is probability of success as it appears to *S*s at the beginning of the game that is required to test hypotheses from the risk taking theory, do nevertheless provide some support for the assumptions made. At 1 ft., the actual probability of success was 1.00. At 15 ft., it was 0. And at 7 ft., the actual probability of success was .52. However, the average observed probability of success was only .23 between 8 and 12 ft. where most shots were taken by the high n Achievement-low Test Anxiety group.

Some data collected by Litwin (1958) in a follow-up study illuminate the problem somewhat. Litwin found that when *S*s were asked to estimate their chances of hitting from each line in an 18 ft. game before performing, the average reported probability of success was nearest to .50 at 11–12 feet. This was two-thirds of the distance from the easiest to the most difficult line. In the present experiment, the modal point of shots by the high n Achievement-low Test Anxiety group was 9–10 ft., two thirds of the distance from 1 ft. to 15 feet. The *S*s in Litwin's study approached the game with overly optimistic expectancies of success. In all likelihood the same thing occurred

in the present experiment, though no evidence can be presented to support the claim.

Summary

It is assumed that measures of n Achievement obtained from the French Test of Insight (and thematic apperception) indicate the strength of a motive to achieve success and Mandler-Sarason Test Anxiety scores indicate the strength of a motive to avoid failure. Given these assumptions and a theory of motivational determinants of risk taking behavior, the following hypotheses are investigated: persons in whom the motive to achieve success is stronger than the motive to avoid failure (*a*) should prefer tasks of intermediate difficulty, (*b*) should show greater persistence in working at an achievement related task, and (*c*) should show more efficiency, or a higher level of accomplishment, than persons in whom the motive to avoid failure is stronger than the motive to achieve success.

Results on 49 college men regarding distance of shots in a ring toss game, time spent working on a final examination, and score on the final examination support the hypotheses and hence the construct validity of the two measures of motive strength.

Relationships between these behavioral variables and the variable called n Achievement on the PPS do not support the inference that strength of motive to achieve success is being measured by this test.

The three measures of achievement related motives are not correlated. These results highlight the importance of discovering why different methods of measuring apparently the same human motive do not yield comparable results.

References

ATKINSON, J. W. The achievement motive and recall of interrupted and completed tasks. *J. exp. Psychol.*, 1953, **46**, 381–390.

————. Motivational determinants of risk-taking behavior. *Psychol. Rev.*, 1957, **64**, 359–372.

ATKINSON, J. W. (Ed.) *Motives in fantasy, action, and society.* Princeton: Van Nostrand, 1958.

ATKINSON, J. W., BASTIAN, J. R., EARL, R. W., & LITWIN, G. H. The achievement motive, goal-setting, and probability preferences. *J. abnorm. soc. Psychol.*, 1960, **60**, 27–36.

ATKINSON, J. W., & REITMAN, W. R. Performance as a function of motive strength and expectancy of goal attainment. *J. abnorm. soc. Psychol.*, 1956, **53**, 361–366.

BROWN, R. W. A determinant of the relationship between rigidity and authoritarianism. *J. abnorm. soc. Psychol.*, 1953, **48**, 469–476.

CORAH, N. L., FELDMAN, M. J., COHEN, IRA S., GRUEN, W., MEADOW, A., & RING-WALL, E. A. Social desirability as a variable in the Edwards Personal Preference Schedule. *J. consult. Psychol.*, 1958, **22**, 70–72.

CRONBACH, L. J., & MEEHL, P. E., Construct validity in psychological tests. *Psychol. Bull.*, 1955, **52**, 281–302.

DECHARMS, R. C., MORRISON, H. W., REITMAN, W. R., & McCLELLAND, D. C. Behavioral correlates of directly and indirectly measured achievement motivation. In D. C. McClelland (Ed.), *Studies in motivation.* New York: Appleton-Century-Crofts, 1955.

EDWARDS, A. L. *Edwards Personal Preference Schedule.* Manual. New York: Psychological Corp., 1954.

EYSENCK, H. J. A dynamic theory of anxiety and hysteria. *J. ment. Sci.*, 1955, **101**, 28–51.

EYSENCK, H. J. & HIMMELWEIT, H. T. An experimental study of the reactions of neurotics to experiences of success and failure. *J. gen. Psychol.*, 1946, **35**, 59–75.

FRENCH, ELIZABETH G. Some characteristics of achievement motivation. *J. exp. Psychol.*, 1955, **50**, 232–236.

————. Development of a measure of complex motivation. In J. W. Atkinson (Ed.), *Motives in fantasy, action, and society.* Princeton: Van Nostrand, 1958.

FRENCH, ELIZABETH G., & THOMAS, F. H. The relation of achievement motivation to problem-solving effectiveness. *J. abnorm. soc. Psychol.*, 1958, **56**, 45–48.

LITWIN, G. H. Motives and expectancy as determinants of preference for degrees of risk. Unpublished honors thesis, Univer. of Michigan, 1958.

McCLELLAND, D. C. Methods of measuring human motivation. In J. W. Atkinson, (Ed.), *Motives in fantasy, action, and society.* Princeton: Van Nostrand, 1958. (a)

————. Risk-taking in children with high and low need for achievement. In J. W. Atkinson (Ed.), *Motives in fantasy, action, and society.* Princeton: Van Nostrand, 1958. (b)

McCLELLAND, D. C., ATKINSON, J. W., CLARK, R. A., & LOWELL, E. L. *The achievement motive.* New York: Appleton-Century-Crofts, 1953.

MANDLER, G., & COWEN, JUDITH E. Test anxiety questionnaires. *J. consult. Psychol.*, 1958, **22**, 228–229.

MANDLER, G., & SARASON, S. B. A study of anxiety and learning. *J. abnorm. soc. Psychol.*, 1952, **47**, 166–173.

MARLOWE, D. Relationships among direct and indirect measures of the achievement motive and overt behavior. *J. consult. Psychol.*, 1959, **23**, 329–332.

MARTIRE, J. G. Relationships between the self concept and differences in strength and generality of achievement motive. *J. Pers.*, 1956, **24**, 364–375.

MILLER, D. R. Responses of psychiatric patients to threat of failure. *J. abnorm. soc. Psychol.*, 1951, **46**, 378–387.

MOULTON, R. W., RAPHELSON, A. C., KRISTOFFERSON, A. B., & ATKINSON, J. W. The achievement motive and perceptual sensitivity under two conditions of motive arousal. In J. W. Atkinson (Ed.), *Motives in fantasy, action, and society*. Princeton: Van Nostrand, 1958.

RAPHELSON, A. C. The relationship between imaginative, direct verbal, and physiological measures of anxiety in an achievement situation. *J. abnorm. soc. Psychol.*, 1957, **54**, 13–18.

SARASON, S. B., & MANDLER, G. Some correlates of test anxiety. *J. abnorm. soc. Psychol.*, 1952, **47**, 810–817.

SARASON, S. B., MANDLER, G., & CRAIGHILL, P. G. The effect of differential instructions on anxiety and learning. *J. abnorm. soc. Psychol.*, 1952, **47**, 561–565.

SCOTT, W. A. The avoidance of threatening material in imaginative behavior. *J. abnorm. soc. Psychol.*, 1956, **52**, 338–346.

VITZ, P. The relation of aspiration to need achievement, fear of failure, incentives, and expectancies. Unpublished honors thesis, Univer. of Michigan, 1957.

CHAPTER 5

Resolution of Conflict: Defense Mechanisms

Studies of Repression

AN EXPERIMENTAL ANALOGUE OF REPRESSION
I. HISTORICAL SUMMARY   Anchard F. Zeller

Introduction

At the heart of the theoretical psychoanalytic structure is the concept of repression, which is the mechanism by which painful or unpleasant material is excluded from consciousness and motor expression. In his earlier writings Freud (17) stressed the importance of repression as the primary ego defense but in his later works he revised his concept by pointing out that repression is only one of several mechanisms which the ego may utilize in an effort to avoid unpleasantness. The ego may indulge in flight, it may resort to condemnation, in which case the material remains conscious, or it may resort to repression.

Repression is of two kinds: first, primal or archaic repression which denies entrance into consciousness of some archaic idea attached to instinctual strivings which are unacceptable to the ego, and second, after-expulsion or repression proper which pushes from consciousness material which, although once conscious, has in some way become associated with primally repressed material. Repression is not forgetting. It is an active process which requires the exertion of constant

Reprinted by permission of the author from the *Psychological Bulletin*, Vol. 47, 1950.

energy by the ego. This is true for both primal repression and after-expulsion. Repression may be complete or partial. If it is complete there is very little hope of investigating it experimentally. If it is partial the repressed material may remain as it was, ready to reappear in consciousness if the repression is removed, or the force attached to it may manifest itself in consciousness in the form of neurotic symptoms. Incomplete repression lends itself more readily to experimental investigation. From the standpoint of the clinician, after-expulsion is of more importance than primal repression, since most observed cases of repression are examples of incomplete after-expulsion. That is, an individual is unable to recall material which he has at one time known but which has in some way become unacceptable, but the memory for which may be restored by appropriate treatment. Although seldom explicitly stated, this is the concept of repression which has served as a basis for most of the experiments in the field. A great many experiments have been designed, first, to demonstrate the phenomenon and second, to quantify the factors involved. Such a demonstration must of necessity fulfill three requirements. First, it must demonstrate that the material in question has been learned by the individual. Second, it must demonstrate that the introduction of an inhibiting factor causes inability to recall or a significant decrease in the recall of the material. Third, it must show that the removal of the inhibiting factor results in the reinstatement of the ability to recall the material. As will be shown in this review of the literature there has as yet been no clear cut laboratory demonstration which includes all of these steps.

Experimental Studies
of Repression

Questionnaire method. The first experimental attack was made by F. W. Colgrave (10) in 1898 when he administered a questionnaire to a group of school children which contained the question, "Do you recall pleasant or unpleasant experiences better?" He concluded from his results that pleasant items were better recalled than unpleasant. As critics have pointed out, the questionnaire method is not a highly valid measure, but a start had been made. Kowalewski (30) and again Susukita (81) as late as 1935 also utilized the questionnaire in the study of this problem.

Associations with sensory stimuli. In 1905 Gordon (20), working in Külpe's laboratory, initiated another type of attack on the problem by associating sensory stimuli with material to be learned and later testing recall. She used colored figures paired with protocols, and administered a recognition test after three weeks. She found no difference between pleasant, unpleasant, and indifferent items. Tait (82), using color recognition, found a slight superiority for memory associated with pleasant colors. Anderson and Bolton (1) tested the recognition and recall of odors with nonsense

names attached and found little difference between pleasant, unpleasant, and indifferent items. Gordon (21) again attacked the problem in 1925, this time using pleasant and unpleasant odors followed by a memory test. Again she found no difference between memory for pleasant and unpleasant items. Kenneth (28) used odors as a free association stimulus. He found more pleasant than unpleasant associations, but the results are not especially relevant to repression. Frank and Ludvigh (16) paired odors with nonsense syllables and found that pleasant associations were recalled oftener. The most complete experiment on memory value of pleasant and unpleasant items was conducted by Ratliff (55) using sensory stimulation paired with numbers. Three types of sensory stimuli, odors, colors, and consonant chords, were paired with the numbers. He found that with visual and auditory stimulation the pleasant was recalled more often than the unpleasant, but for olfaction the unpleasant recall was superior.

Recall of experience. Another approach extensively used to study the relation of affect to memory was initiated by Kowalewski (31) in 1908 when, the day following a Christmas vacation, he instructed his students, "Write down whatever pleased you yesterday." His results indicated more pleasant than unpleasant experiences. A recall ten days later gave similar results. He interpreted his results to mean that the pleasant is better retained than the unpleasant. As critics were quick to point out, however, he assumed that pleasant and unpleasant experiences were equal in number, which assumption has more recently been proven erroneous. Other investigators employing the recall of holiday experiences have been Wohlgemuth (91), Meltzer (40, 41, 43), Jersild (27),

Cason (8), Waters and Leeper (87) Menzies (44), O'Kelly and Steckle (48), and Steckle (79). The studies of Wohlgemuth (91) and Cason (8), two of the best controlled, indicate no difference between recall of pleasant and unpleasant associations when the fact that there are actually more pleasant than unpleasant experiences is taken into account, while the results of the other investigations indicate only a slight tendency for greater recall of pleasant experiences.

Kowalewski (30, 31) concluded from his results that the recall of affective material is related to personality types. He interpreted his data to mean that optimists remember proportionally more pleasant experiences while pessimists tend to remember proportionally more unpleasant experiences. This possibility has been investigated by Meltzer (40, 43), O'Kelly and Steckle (48), and Steckle (79) with inconclusive results. Flugel in 1917 (see Flugel, 1925, 14) attempted to establish an "Algedonic Ratio" of pleasant to unpleasant for the individual. This was again attempted by Meltzer (41) in 1930.

Other experiments which have used the recall of past experience have been conducted by Gordon (22) and Thompson (83) who used the recall of childhood experiences. Gordon found no evidence for a greater percentage of pleasant recall, but Thompson found evidence for a pleasant-unpleasant differential in favor of the pleasant.

Discrete associations. In addition to the experiments in which preceding events have been recalled and re-recalled, a number of experiments have utilized other methods to test memory for affectively toned experience. Peters (49) had subjects answer to a stimulus word with an experience. He found 65 per cent of total recalls were pleasant in nature. Peters and Nemecek (50) used the same technique with comparable results. Griffitts (24) asked for responses to stimulus words and found a difference in favor of pleasant associations. Stagner (77) in a well-controlled experiment in which a single pleasant and unpleasant event were recorded, together with their associations, found what he called evidence for an active repression when the events were again presented to the subjects with instructions to recall the associations.

Reaction time. The effect on reaction time of various affectively toned material has been investigated by Birnbaum (5), Tolman (84), Tolman and Johnson (85), Baxter, Yamada and Washburn (4), Morgan, Mull and Washburn (46), and Smith (76). All but Birnbaum found positive results, viz., pleasant tone decreases reaction time.

Memory for word lists. The number of experiments using this method has been large. Chaney and Lauer (9), Lynch (36), Cason (8), Stagner (78), Balken (2), Bunch and Wientge (6), Silverman and Cason (75), White and Ratliff (90), Carter (7), White (89), Gilbert (18), Lanier (33), and Pintner and Forlano (51) have all worked with this type of material, using periods of recall up to two years. None of these experiments has given a conclusive answer to the problem. They have all tended to show, however, that the problem of affect and recall is not a simple one, but rather a very complex phenomenon depending on many factors, such as sex, age, social status, intelligence, etc. (see Gilbert, 1938).

Miscellaneous studies. A few other studies have been conducted which do not readily fall into the above categories. Laird (32) asked his subjects to write the names of ten friends and check those liked and disliked. Later he asked the subjects to list ten names as fast as possible. A comparison of the two lists indicated that some subjects tended to list more disliked persons in the second list than did others. He interpreted his results in terms of optimistic and pessimistic personality types but found no evidence for repression. Fox (15) had his subjects learn pleasant and unpleasant sonnets and found those preferred were better retained. Stone (80) used photographs to which names liked or disliked by the subjects were attached. He found that those associated with pleasant names were better recalled. McMullin (39) found evidence that interpolated activity of an affective nature could produce differences in the amount of retroactive inhibition.

Review articles or discussions of various aspects of pleasant-unpleasant experiments have been presented by Meltzer (42), Moore (45), Sears (64, 67, 68, 69), Gilbert (19), McGeoch (37), Rapaport (54), and Prentice (53). As can be seen from the experiments reviewed so far, very little has been contributed to an understanding of the problem of repression as outlined by Freud. Of the experiments mentioned so far, the score stands 32 to 14 in favor of more effective recall of pleasant than of unpleasant experiences, with 5 experiments having neutral results. These results, however, can not be taken as an indication of repression.

As Meltzer (42) has pointed out, most of the experiments before 1930 were conducted on the false assumption that the pleasant and unpleasant events were of equal frequency. Henderson (25) as early as 1911, however, recognized the fallacy and interpreted this as failing to support the idea that the un-

pleasant was repressed. Myers (47) also argued that we do not forget the disagreeable, but that there are more agreeable than disagreeable experiences in life. Flugel (14) also recognized this as did Griffitts (24) and Wohlgemuth (91). In none of the studies has any attempt been made to restore recall when repression has been assumed as basic to the pleasant-unpleasant differential. In most cases repression has been equated to differential forgetting, whereas it could have been more reasonably interpreted as differential learning. In most cases repression has not been conceived as the dynamic process outlined by Freud, and in no case has an adequate test been designed.

Frame of reference. There have, however, been a number of studies which have recognized the importance of learning set. Following the work of Bartlett (3) a number of studies have been conducted in which controversial material about which the subjects were known to have specific opinions was presented and then recalled later. As early as 1928 Zillig (93) gave both men and women a number of selections to read, the content of some being favorable and others being unfavorable to women. The women recalled a much greater percentage of favorable items about themselves than the men did about the women. Studies following the same plan have been conducted by Watson and Hartmann (88) using theistic and atheistic material, Seeleman (70) using attitude toward the negro, Edwards (11) with pro- and anti-New Deal material, Levine and Murphy (34), pro- and anti-communistic literature and Postman and Murphy (52) using United Nations vs. Axis power attitudes. Wallen (86) used his subjects' own opinion of themselves, compared with bogus group opinions, and found they remembered the items which agreed with their own opinions better than those which did not. Shaw (73) and Shaw and Spooner (74) repeated the same experiment with modifications and obtained comparable results. All these studies indicate that attitude and preconceptions influence memory. Edwards (12) has presented an argument in favor of a "frame of reference" determinant in forgetting, regardless of whether the material is intrinsically pleasureful or otherwise. Steckle (79) presents a similar argument. Again, however, it should be noted that the analysis is of differential forgetting, not of an active, removable repression.

Specific studies. There have been a number of experiments based on different approaches to the problem which have shown considerably more insight into the nature of the problem and more imagination in the design of the experiment. Koch (29) using a number of psychology students had them rate their satisfaction with grades on quizzes. Five weeks later a recall test of the grades indicated the grades with the most affect, either positive or negative, were better recalled. In 1936 Sears (64) presented an excellent review of functional abnormalities of memory in which he pointed out that none of the experiments had fulfilled the conditions of a true test of repression, since the fundamental assumption of the experiments had been that pleasantness and unpleasantness of an intellectual or sensory nature is equivalent to unpleasantness in terms of ego threat. In 1937 Sears (66) presented a study in which subjects were given two tasks, learning nonsense syllables and sorting cards. A list of syllables was learned, followed by success or failure at card sorting, and this was in turn followed by the learning of a second list. The second list learned by the successful card sorters was significantly better than the learning of the same list by those who failed at card sorting. Sears interprets this as evidence of repression. It might be pointed out that the difference could well be attributed to lesser motivation rather than to an active repression. No attempt was made to remove the repression.

One of the better demonstrations of repression has been given by Huston, Shakow, and Erickson (26) using the technique developed by Luria (35) in which the "associations of higher central nervous system processes are associated with voluntary movement so that the conflicts in the former are disclosed in the latter." The subjects were hypnotized and were told that they had participated in some event in a manner out of keeping with their normal standard of ethics. Stimulus words, some neutral and some related to the suggested experience, were read to the subjects who had a post-hypnotic amnesia for the suggestions. There were significant differences in reaction to the words associated with the hypnotic suggestions. The subjects were then rehypnotized and the suggestion removed. Retests indicated the effects had disappeared. This experiment comes close to a demonstration of repression, but the use of hypnosis as a repression medium makes it difficult to interpret.

Flanagan (13) and Sharp (71) at the University of Chicago used sexual and profane word pairs, respectively, and found significant differences in the learning and recall of the two types of material. It should be pointed out in this connection that no attempt was made to equate the affective and control material for difficulty in learning, and the experimental situation was such that embarrassment over the nature of the material to be reproduced undoubtedly contributed a great deal to the results. Sharp (72) in 1938, using neurotic subjects and material taken from case histories, found curves of retention which would indicate that pleasant material is more readily recalled after a time while unpleasant material is repressed (forgotten).

McGranahan (38) in an interesting interpretation of the Freudian concept, points out that repression is a process which can be carried out more efficiently at a conscious level by a well-integrated personality. To demonstrate this, he forbade his subjects to name a color on penalty of being shocked. The subject then answered to a series of stimulus words to which color responses are common. The well-integrated individuals "repress" the color responses while those who fear the shock make more color responses.

In 1930 Meltzer (42) concluded after a critical review of the studies on feeling and memory that the difficulty with repression studies was that the investigators were looking for universal responses. Rosenzweig (56, 57, 58), and Rosenzweig and Mason (61) pointed out that the lack of acceptable results in previous studies was due to a lack of clear understanding of the problem. They further point out the fallacy of assuming that sensory pleasantness and unpleasantness is the same as conative pleasantness and unpleasantness. Further, repression operates on a conative type of material which is negative in hedonic tone, the negative affect being determined by the conflict of the material with ego-supporting drives, such as self-respect, etc. They cite the experiments of Zeigarnik

(92) as a prototype of the repression experiment and set up a series of investigations in which children were allowed to complete one half of the tasks and fail on one half. Recall was better for the completed tasks. Varying the task set, Rosenzweig (59, 60) found that ego-involvement led to recall of completed tasks, while task orientation led to better recall of uncompleted tasks. Two experiments conducted by Sarason and Rosenzweig (62, 63) in connection with Rosenzweig's triadic hypothesis further attempted to correlate repression with hypnotizability and impunitive reactions to conflict. Rosenzweig interprets his evidence as lending support to his hypothesis.

Gould (23) designed an experiment which came close to a test of repression. The subject was required to choose one of two tasks. The choice supposedly revealed a good or bad character trait of the subject, the character traits "revealed" having been predetermined by the investigator regardless of the task chosen. The subject was then told what the choice revealed about him and was allowed to complete the task, then make another choice until six had been chosen. The subject was then asked to list all of the tasks. Following this, the nature of the experiment was explained to the subject. As an incidental remark, Gould notes that after the explanation some of the subjects remembered more of the tasks than before.

Summary and Conclusions

A review of the literature shows that there has been no experiment which has fulfilled the criterion of a laboratory test of repression. Most experiments have been directed toward testing the relationship between affect and recall. The majority of experiments have been found to fall in eight categories:

(1) Questionnaire method: this was the earliest used method and is unsuited to the problem.

(2) Associations with sensory stimuli: the chief criticism of this method was that it assumed the equivalence of sensory unpleasantness with ego unpleasantness.

(3) Recall of experiences: many of these experiments have assumed actual numbers of pleasant and unpleasant experiences to be equal.

(4) Discrete associations: association tests have in general shown more pleasant associations.

(5) Reaction time: these experiments have shown shorter reaction time with pleasant material.

cally formulated, namely, that *no test of repression can be considered adequate until the removal of the repression factor has resulted in the restoration to consciousness of the repressed material.* Any experiment which does not include this crucial step is not complete and the results can be attributed to other factors such as set, differential learning, differential motivation, practice, etc. rather than to active repression.

A proposed experimental design to test the hypothesis that repression proper is a process which inhibits recall without, however, destroying the memory for the subject matter, and that the memory can be restored by the elimination of the repression factor is presented below.

	Control		*Experimental*
I.	Step 1. Learning	=	Learning
	Step 2. Retention Test	=	Retention Test
	Time Interval		
II.	Step 3. Retention Test	=	Retention Test
	Step 4. Neutral Task		Repression
	Step 5. Retention Test	>	Retention Test
	Time Interval		
III.	Step 6. Retention Test	>	Retention Test
	Step 7. Neutral Task		Removal of Repression
	Step 8. Retention Test	=	Retention Test

(6) Memory for word lists: this method, the most frequently used, has yielded nothing significant.

(7) Frame of reference: these studies have shown a selective effect of attitude on memory.

(8) Specific studies: these studies, specifically reviewed in the article, while showing a clearer conception of the problem, have failed to demonstrate repression.

All reviews and criticisms of the problem have agreed that no adequate test of repression has been made. In most studies the repression has been conceived as differential forgetting. The most significant criticism has not been specifi-

If the hypothesis is supported, the results indicated in the design can be expected. Any other results, although not disproving repression, would cast real doubt on the validity of the concept.

The design involves two equated groups, a control and an experimental group. The individuals in each group are exposed to some material (Step 1) which they are to learn. Their degree of mastery is then measured with a retention test (Step 2). This satisfies the first requirement of an experimental test of repression proper, namely that the material be learned.

After a time interval another test of

retention of the originally learned material is administered to the individuals in both groups (Step 3). Up to this point the performance of the groups should show no significant difference. At this point the procedure varies. The individuals in the experimental group are subjected to an ego threat associated with some activity while the individuals in the control group perform the same activity with no induced affect (Step 4). After this another retention test of the originally learned material is administered (Step 5). If the average retention in Step 5 is significantly better for the control group, the second criterion of an adequate experimental test of repression has been met.

After another time interval the subjects are again asked for a measure of retention of the originally learned material. (Step 6). This is followed by the same activity associated with the ego threat in Step 4, only this time there is no ego threat for either the experimental or the control group. Restoration of memory following the change in ego value of the task would constitute the third and crucial step in the experimental demonstration of repression proper.

Bibliography

1. ANDERSON, A. C., & BOLTON, F. J. The inhibition of the unpleasant. *J. abnorm. soc. Psychol.*, 1925, **20**, 300–302.

2. BALKEN, E. R. Affective, volitional and galvanic factors in learning. *J. exp. Psychol.*, 1933, **16**, 115–128.

3. BARTLETT, F. C. *Remembering: a study in experimental and social psychology.* New York: Macmillan; Cambridge, Eng.: Univ. Press, 1932.

4. BAXTER, M. F., YAMADA, K., & WASHBURN, M. F. Directed recall of pleasant and unpleasant experiences. *Amer. J. Psychol.*, 1919, **30**, 300–302.

5. BIRNBAUM, K. Ueber den Einfluss von Gefühlsfaktoren auf die Assoziationer. *Monatsch f. Psychiat. u. Neurol.*, 1912, **32**, 95–123.

6. BUNCH, M. E., & WIENTGE, E. The relative susceptibility of pleasant, unpleasant, and indifferent material to retroactive inhibition. *J. exp. Psychol.*, 1933, **9**, 157–178.

7. CARTER, H. D. Effect of emotional factors upon recall. *J. Psychol.*, 1936, **1**, 48–55.

8. CASON, H. The learning and retention of pleasant and unpleasant activities. *Arch. Psychol., N. Y.*, 1932, No. 134. Pp. 96.

9. CHANEY, RUTH, & LAUER, A. R. The influence of affective tone on learning and retention. *J. educ. Psychol.*, 1929, **20**, 287–291.

10. COLGRAVE, F. W. Individual memories. *Amer. J. Psychol.*, 1898–99, **10**, 228–255.

11. EDWARDS, A. L. Political frames of reference as a factor influencing recognition. *J. abnorm. soc. Psychol.*, 1941, **36**, 34–61.

12. ———. The retention of affective experiences—a criticism and restatement of the problem. *Psychol. Rev.*, 1942, **49**, 43–53.

13. FLANAGAN, D. E. The influence of emotional inhibition on learning and recall. Unpublished Master's thesis, Univer. Chicago, 1930.

14. FLUGEL, J. C. A quantitative study of feeling and emotion in everyday life. *Brit. J. Psychol.*, 1925, **15**, 318–355.

15. FOX, C. The influence of subjective preference on memory. *Brit. J. Psychol.*, 1922–23, **13**, 398–405.

16. FRANK, J. P., & LUDVIGH, E. J. The retroactive effect of pleasant and unpleasant odors on learning. *Amer. J. Psychol.*, 1931, **43**, 102–108.

17. FREUD, S. Repression. In *Collected papers,* Vol. 4, 84–97. London: Hogarth Press, 1925.

18. GILBERT, G. M. The age difference in the hedonistic tendency in memory. *J. exp. Psychol.,* 1937, **21**, 433–441.

19. ———. The new status of experimental psychology on the relationship of feeling to memory. *Psychol. Bull.,* 1938, **35**, 26–35.

20. GORDON, KATE. Ueber das Gedachtnis fur Affective bestimmte Eindrucke. *Arch. ges. Psychol.,* 1905, **4**, 437–458.

21. ———. Recollection of pleasant and unpleasant odors. *J. exp. Psychol.,* 1925, **8**, 225–239.

22. ———. A study of early memories. *J. Delinqu.,* 1928, **12**, 127–132.

23. GOULD, R. Repression experimentally analyzed. *Character and Pers.,* 1942, **10**, 259–288.

24. GRIFFITTS, C. H. Results of some experiments on affection, distributions of associations and recall. *J. exp. Psychol.,* 1920, **3**, 447–464.

25. HENDERSON, E. N. Do we forget the disagreeable? *J. Phil Psychol. sci. Meth.,* 1911, **8**, 432–438.

26. HUSTON, P. E., SHAKOW, D., & ERICKSON, M. H. A study of hypnotically induced complexes by means of the Luria technique. *J. gen. Psychol.,* 1934, **11**, 65–97.

27. JERSILD, A. Memory for the pleasant as compared with the unpleasant. *J. exp. Psychol.,* 1931, **14**, 284–288.

28. KENNETH, J. H. An experimental study of affects and associations due to certain odors. *Psychol. Monog.,* 1927, No. 37. 64.

29. KOCH, H. L. The influence of some affective factors upon recall. *J. gen. Psychol.,* 1930, **4**, 171–190.

30. KOWALEWSKI, A. *Studien zur Psychologie des Pessimismus.* Wiesbaden, 1904.

31. ———. *Schopenhauer und sein Weltanschauung.* Berlin, 1908.

32. LAIRD, D. The influence of likes and dislikes on memory as related to personality. *J. exp. Psychol.,* 1923, **6**, 294–300.

33. LANIER, L. H. Memory for words differing in affective value. *Psychol. Bull.,* 1940, **37**, 492–493. (Abstract.)

34. LEVINE, J. M., & MURPHY, G. The learning and forgetting of controversial material. *J. abnorm. soc. Psychol.,* 1943, **38**, 507–517.

35. LURIA, A. R. *The nature of human conflicts.* (Trans. by W. H. Gantt.) New York: Liveright, 1932.

36. LYNCH, C. A. The memory value of certain alleged emotionally toned words. *J. exp. Psychol.,* 1932, **15**, 298–315.

37. McGEOCH, J. O. *The psychology of human learning.* New York: Longmans, Green, 1946.

38. McGRANAHAN, D. V. A critical and experimental study of repression. *J. abnorm. soc. Psychol.,* 1940, **35**, 212–225.

39. McMULLIN, T. E. A study of the affective nature of the interpolated activity as a factor in producing different relative amounts of retroactive inhibition in recall and recognition. *J. exp. Psychol.,* 1942, **30**, 201–215.

40. MELTZER, H. The forgetting of pleasant and unpleasant experiences in relation to intelligence and achievement. *J. soc. Psychol.,* 1930, **2**, 217–227.

41. ———. Individual differences in forgetting pleasant and unpleasant experience. *J. educ. Psychol.,* 1930, **21**, 399–409.

42. ———. The present status of experimental studies of the relation of feeling to memory. *Psychol. Rev.,* 1930, **37**, 124–139.

43. MELTZER, H. Sex differences in forgetting pleasant and unpleasant experiences. *J. abnorm. soc. Psychol.*, 1931, **25**, 450–464.

44. MENZIES, R. The comparative memory value of pleasant, unpleasant and indifferent experiences. *J. exp. Psychol.*, 1936, **18**, 267–279.

45. MOORE, E. H. A note on the recall of the pleasant vs. the unpleasant. *Psychol. Rev.*, 1935, **42**, 214–215.

46. MORGAN, E., MULL, H. K., & WASHBURN, M. F. An attempt to test moods or temperaments of cheerfulness and depression by directed recall of emotionally toned experiences. *Amer. J. Psychol.*, 1919, **30**, 302–304.

47. MYERS, G. C. Affective factors in recall. *J. Phil. Psychol. sci. Meth.*, 1915, **12**, 85–92.

48. O'KELLY, L. I., & STECKLE, L. C. The forgetting of pleasant and unpleasant experiences. *Amer. J. Psychol.*, 1940, **53**, 432–434.

49. PETERS, W. Gefühl und Erinnerung; Beiträge zur Erinnerungsanalyse. *Psychol. Arbeit.*, 1911, **6**, 197–260.

50. PETERS, W., & NEMECEK, O. Massenversuche über Erinnerungassoziationen. *Fortschr. Psychol. Anwend.*, 1914, **2**, 226–245.

51. PINTNER, R., & FORLANO, G. The influence of pleasantly and unpleasantly toned words on retention. *J. soc. Psychol.*, 1940, **11**, 147–148.

52. POSTMAN, L., & MURPHY, G. The factor of attitude in associative memory. *J. exp. Psychol.*, 1943, **33**, 228–238.

53. PRENTICE, W. C. H. The interruption of tasks. *Psychol. Rev.*, 1944, **51**, 329–340.

54. RAPAPORT, D. *Emotions and memory.* Baltimore: Williams and Wilkins, 1942.

55. RATLIFF, M. M. The varying function of affectively toned olfactory, visual and auditory cues in recall. *Amer. J. Psychol.*, 1938, **51**, 695–699.

56. ROSENZWEIG, S. The recall of finished and unfinished tasks as affected by the purpose with which they were performed. *Psychol. Bull.*, 1933, **30**, 698. (Abstract.)

57. ———. The experimental study of repression. In H. Murray (Ed.) *Explorations in personality.* New York: Oxford Univ. Press, 1938. Pp. 472–491.

58. ———. The experimental measurement of types of reaction to frustration. In H. Murray (Ed.), *Explorations in personality.* New York: Oxford Univ. Press, 1938. Pp. 585–599.

59. ———. Need-persistive and ego-defensive reactions to frustration as demonstrated by an experiment on repression. *Psychol. Rev.*, 1941, **48**, 347–349.

60. ———. An experimental study of "repression" with special reference to need-persistive and ego-defensive reactions to frustration. *J. exp. Psychol.*, 1943, **32**, 64–74.

61. ROSENZWEIG, S., & MASON, G. An experimental study of memory in relation to the theory of repression. *Brit. J. Psychol.*, 1934, **24**, 247–265.

62. ROSENZWEIG, S., & SARASON, S. An experimental study of the triadic hypothesis: reaction to frustration, ego-defense, and hypnotizability. I. Correlational approach. *Character and Pers.*, 1942, **11**, 1–19.

63. SARASON, S., & ROSENZWEIG, S. An experimental study of the triadic hypothesis: reaction to frustration, ego-defense, and hypnotizability. II. Thematic Apperception Approach. *Character and Pers.*, 1942, **11**, 150–165.

64. SEARS, R. R. Functional abnormalities of memory with special reference to amnesia. *Psychol. Bull.*, 1936, **33**, 229–274.

65. ———. An experimental test of one phase of the hypothecated repression sequence. *Psychol. Bull.*, 1936, **33**, 744. (Abstract.)

66. SEARS, R. R. Initiation of the repression sequence by experienced failure. *J. exp. Psychol.*, 1937, **20**, 570–580.

67. ———. Non-aggressive reactions to frustration. *Psychol. Rev.*, 1941, **48**, 343–348.

68. ———. Survey of objective studies of psychoanalytic concepts. *Soc. Sci. Res. Coun. Bull.* No. 51, 1943.

69. ———. Experimental analysis of psychoanalytic phenomena. In J. McV. Hunt (Ed.), *Personality and the behavior disorders.* New York: Ronald Press, 1944. Pp. 306–332.

70. SEELEMAN, V. The influence of attitude upon the remembering of pictorial material. *Arch. Psychol., N. Y.,* 1940, **36**, No. 258.

71. SHARP, AGNES A. The influence of certain emotional inhibitions on learning and recall. Unpublished Master's thesis, Univ. Chicago, 1930.

72. ———. An experimental test of Freud's doctrine of the relation of hedonic tone to memory revival. *J. exp., Psychol.,* 1938, **22**, 395–418.

73. SHAW, F. J. Two determinants of selective forgetting. *J. abnorm. soc. Psychol.,* 1944, **39**, 434–445.

74. SHAW, F. J., & SPOONER, A. Selective forgetting when the subject is not ego involved. *J. exp. Psychol.,* 1945, **35**, 242–247.

75. SILVERMAN, A., & CASON, H. Incidental memory for pleasant, unpleasant and indifferent words. *Amer. J. Psychol.,* 1934, **46**, 315–320.

76. SMITH, W. W. Experiments on memory and affective tone. *Brit. J. Psychol.,* 1921, **11**, 236–250.

77. STAGNER, R. The redintegration of pleasant and unpleasant experiences. *Amer. J. Psychol.,* 1931, **43**, 463–468.

78. ———. Factors influencing the memory value of words in a series. *J. exp. Psychol.,* 1933, **16**, 129–137.

79. STECKLE, L. C. Again—affect and recall. *J. soc. Psychol.,* 1945, **22**, 103–105.

80. STONE, A. R. The reaction of memory to affective states. *Amer. J. Psychol.,* 1925, **36**, 112–123.

81. SUSUKITA, T. Ueber das Gedächtnis für lust- und unlustbetonte Erlebniss im Alltagsleben. *Tohoku Psychol. Folia,* 1935, **3**, 187–204.

82. TAIT, W. D. Effects of psychophysical attitudes on memory. *J. abnorm. soc. Psychol.,* 1913–14, **8**, 10–38.

83. THOMPSON, R. H. An experimental study of memory as influenced by feeling tone. *J. exp. Psychol.,* 1930, **13**, 462–467.

84. TOLMAN, E. C. Retroactive inhibition as affected by conditions of learning. *Psychol. Monogr.,* 1918, No. 107, 187–195.

85. TOLMAN, E. C., & JOHNSON, I. A note on association time and feeling. *Amer. J. Psychol.,* 1918, **29**, 187–195.

86. WALLEN, D. Ego involvement as a determinant of selective forgetting. *J. abnorm. soc. Psychol.,* 1942, **37**, 20–29.

87. WATERS, R. H., & LEEPER, R. The relation of affective tone to the retention of experiences in everyday life. *J. exp. Psychol.,* 1936, **19**, 203–215.

88. WATSON, W. S., & HARTMANN, G. W. The rigidity of a basic attitudinal frame. *J. abnorm. soc. Psychol.,* 1939, **34**, 314–335.

89. WHITE, M. M. Some factors influencing recall of pleasant and unpleasant words. *Amer. J. Psychol.,* 1936, **48**, 134–139.

90. WHITE, M. M., & RATLIFF, M. M. The relation of affective tone to learning and recalling words. *Amer. J. Psychol.,* 1934, **46**, 92–98.

91. WOHLGEMUTH, A. The influence of feeling on memory. *Brit. J. Psychol.*, 1923, **13**, 405–416.

92. ZEIGARNIK, B. Über das Behalten von erledigten und unerledigten Handlungen. *Psychol. Forsch.*, 1927, **9**, 1–85.

93. ZILLIG, M. Einstellung und Aussage. *Z. Psychol.*, 1928, **106**, 58–106.

AN EXPERIMENTAL ANALOGUE OF REPRESSION
II. THE EFFECT OF INDIVIDUAL FAILURE AND
SUCCESS ON MEMORY MEASURED BY RELEARNING

Anchard F. Zeller

In a recent review article by Zeller (7), the following design was proposed as the necessary framework for an experimental test of the concept of repression proper or after-expulsion:

	Control	Experimental
I.	Step 1. Learning	= Learning
	Step 2. Retention test	= Retention test
	Time Interval	
II.	Step 3. Retention test	= Retention test
	Step 4. Neutral task	Repression
	Step 5. Retention test	> Retention test
	Time Interval	
III.	Step 6. Retention test	> Retention test
	Step 7. Neutral task	Removal of repression
	Step 8. Retention test	= Retention test

The present experiments have followed this design.

Individual Experiment I

RELEARNING 15 SEMI-NONSENSE SYLLABLES

In order to fulfill the conditions outlined it was necessary first to find some kind of neutral material to be learned

Reprinted by permission of the author from the *Journal of Experimental Psychology*, Vol. 40, 1950.

and for which the rate of learning could be quantified. Second, it was necessary to find some kind of interpolated material which could be manipulated by the experimenter so that it would have either neutral, success or traumatic value to the subject. The first condition presented very little difficulty as there is a great variety of relatively neutral verbal material available. The paired associates method was adopted, using as the specific material the control list of Flanagan (1) consisting of 15 paired three-letter semi-nonsense syllables.

The choice of the interpolated material presented more difficulty. It seemed, however, that the best that could be chosen was some type which could be presented in a situation which was so un-structured that the subject was entirely dependent on the examiner for the interpretation of his performance. Further, the material had to be of such a nature that any statement made by the examiner about the subject's success or failure could be readily accepted because apparently confirmed by the objective evidence. After several other methods had been tried and discarded, the medium chosen for the artificial induction of success or failure was imitative tapping using Knox cubes. Knox cubes consist of a set of five one-in. wooden cubes. These were chosen because the task of reproducing a tapping pattern with these blocks appears simple and yet even the best subjects are seldom able to imitate a pattern of eight units. As very few individuals are acquainted with the standard performance level with Knox cubes, there is little chance that the examiner's interpretation would be questioned by the subject.

Material. The material for this experiment consisted, first, of a set of 15 3×5 in. cards on each of which was typed in capitals the syllable pair to be associated; second, a set of stimulus cards on each of which was typed the first of the paired syllables which appeared on the first set; and third, a set of Knox cubes (i.e., five one-in. black cubes). Timing was done by a clock pendulum with a 2.1-sec. swing or with a Waltham 10-sec. sweep stop watch. The only other material required was paper and pencil.

Subjects. The subjects for this experiment were 20 male and female college students who volunteered their services. Although it is not possible to give an accurate figure, at least 50 percent of these volunteered in the hope of eventually obtaining psychological advice. It is

therefore probable that they represent a more emotionally unstable group than a random selection of college students.

Procedure. Each subject was tested individually and privately. In order that the true nature of the experiment might not be revealed to the subject, he was informed that he was participating in a learning experiment in which a number of tests of memory would be used. Following this introduction he learned the list of 15 syllables to a criterion of one perfect trial. This was accomplished by exposing the set of cards with the paired syllables at the rate of 2.1 sec. per card and by then exposing the stimulus set at the same rate and having the subject write the correct response. This was repeated, alternately showing the paired syllable set and then the stimulus syllable set until the criterion was reached. Subjects were required to write the appropriate response on a clean sheet of paper each time. A 2.1-sec. exposure is a relatively short time for a written response so the association had to be made quickly.

Following learning to the criterion, the subject was dismissed with instructions to return in three days (72 hours). No indication was given that the next part of the experiment would in any way be associated with the paired syllables. The first few subjects were arbitrarily assigned to a control or experimental group, but later, in order to equate the groups, the subjects were divided on the basis of rate of learning following the initial experimental session.

When the subject returned 72 hours later he relearned the list of 15 paired syllables by the same procedure to a criterion of one errorless trial. Up to this point all subjects had been treated alike and the two groups had been equated for learning ability. At this point, however, the procedure for the two groups varied drastically. The control subjects were shown the five black cubes, four of which were spaced about one in. apart in a straight line, the fifth being held in the experimenter's hand. (The experimenter sat opposite the subject.) The subject was told, "Here are five blocks, four on the table and one in my hand. With this block [indicating the one held in the hand] I will tap the others in some order, for example [taps blocks in 1, 3, 2, 4, order], and you are then to do the same thing. Do you understand?" The subjects grasped the idea rapidly and exhibited a great deal of interest in the 'test.' The level of the task was adjusted so that the subject very seldom failed. Although he was not told his results for the reproduction of any individual pattern, at the end of 15 min. he was told, "You did all right." The examiner appeared to the subject to be keeping a record of the results, and the subject could observe this at any time. This was carefully placed with the subject's learning sheets. After the 15-min. tapping test the examiner announced, "We will now continue with another phase of the experiment." The cards were again presented and the number of trials to relearn to the criterion recorded. The entire situation was one of pleasantly toned relations and the subjects usually left in a cheerful mood. Each was instructed to return 72 hours later.

The experimental group was treated quite differently. It had been found by preliminary experiments that the most acute emotional disturbance would be caused if the subject could be prevented from becoming angry at the experimenter. This is in keeping with the findings of Rosenzweig (3) and Rosenzweig and Sarason (4, 5) that individuals who react impunitively in a frustrating situation repress, while those subjects who react extrapunitively or intropunitively tend to use other defense mechanisms. Consequently, the experimenter appeared in the role of a very concerned although stern individual. The directions given were the same as in the control situation. "Here are five blocks, four on the table and one in my hand. With this block [indicating the one held in the hand] I will tap the others in some order, for example [tap 1, 3, 2, 1, 4, 2, 4] and you are to do the same thing. Do you understand?" If the subject tapped the blocks from left to right as the examiner did, he had to reverse the pattern since the examiner was on the opposite side of the table. On the other hand, if the subject tapped the blocks in the same direction as the experimenter, his own orientation from left to right was reversed. The first block sequence usually contained seven units which the subject almost surely could not reproduce, or if he could, he was so unsure of himself that he readily believed he had not. Either way he was told by the examiner that he had made a very serious error indicative of poor mental powers. After each failure he was informed that he had failed. The examiner kept score of the successes and failures (all failures) on a sheet which began at seven and ended at fifteen as a score, so that the individual being tested could see himself failing repeatedly at the very bottom of the scale. After a number of failures the examiner elaborately added a new bottom to his scale and informed the individual that he was now working at the eight-year-old level. After a few failures most individuals actually showed a spurt of improvement (which was not indicated to them) compensated for by making the patterns more intricate without increasing their length. Following repeated failure, however, the responses became disorganized. At this point the examiner stopped the experiment temporarily and asked the subject to get hold of himself as he was doing worse than anyone the examiner had ever tested. The subject was informed that no one with such a score could ever hope to get through college and great concern was expressed for the fact that he had such a poor memory. This served to distress the individual still further so that at the end of another few minutes most subjects were sitting on the edge of the chair concentrating all of their attention on the task. The examiner, however, regularly informed the subject of failure after each trial. It was by no means uncommon at this point for the individual's performance to deteriorate to such an extent that he was unable to reproduce even a simple four or five unit sequence. In the last few minutes of the 15-minute period it was, for a few subjects, thought advisable to reduce the tension. In this particular experiment, however, no subject had to be informed of the true purpose at this point.

Following the block tapping test the subject was told that his performance was completely unsatisfactory, that his memory was poor, and that his chances of success were nil. *At no point, however, was any mention made of the nonsense syllables previously learned.*

The subject was then told that it was necessary to continue to another part of the experiment and the syllables were then presented for relearning. As was previously mentioned, a 2.1-sec. interval is relatively short for a written response, so that any decrease in the rapidity of association results in a greatly increased number of trials necessary to reach the criterion. This failure in turn further disorganized the response in all of the subjects. Even when the individual reached

the criterion he showed none of the accompaniments of a successfully completed task, but seemed to remain under some tension. At the completion of the relearning he was told to return in three days to continue the experiment. It was at this point and in this group that the greatest incidence of subjects lost through failure to return occurred. The data on these subjects were omitted entirely in the final analysis. The direction in which they would have influenced the results had they completed the experiment cannot be determined. It could be predicted that their inclusion might have increased the significance of the results at sessions 3 and 4 since they repressed so readily; or if the repression were difficult to remove the significance of the statistics at sessions 5 and 6 might have been reduced.

Seventy-two hours later individuals from both groups returned. The control group was treated exactly as it was the second day, that is, there was first a relearning of the syllables followed by a 15-min. session of block tapping, either neutral or mildly pleasant in tone, again followed by a relearning of the syllables.

The experimental group was treated differently. They were first presented with the syllables to be relearned. This seemed to bring back a great deal of the emotion associated with the previous session, although no effort was made to either mention or avoid mentioning it, the pre-test conversation being held to a minimum. After the relearning, the blocks were again produced but at this point the experimenter restructured the situation. The subject was introduced to the test by very easy stages and was allowed to succeed at every trial. Hope dawned! The experimenter then gave the subject a set of fake norms he had prepared showing an entirely different picture, and told the subject that the experiment was one in motivation, and that only very superior subjects were chosen to participate. It was amazing to see the change in attitude on the part of the subject. As far as the experimenter knows not one subject doubted his (the experimenter's) statement. The entire tone of the relationship was altered. The subject was cooperative, happy, and in some cases almost euphoric. Although it was not possible to keep a genuine record of the individuals' block tapping scores, there is little doubt that the individuals in this group exceeded the control group at this point. Following 15 min. of block tapping (all successes) the next syllable relearning test was administered. The subjects were eager, uninhibited and, as the results show, much better in performance. Seventy-two hours later the individuals from both groups returned for a last test session which lasted only a very few minutes.

RESULTS AND DISCUSSION

The results are presented in Figs. 1 and 2 and in Tables I and II. Fig. 1 [1] presents the data in terms of the number of trials to learn to the criterion, while Fig. 2 presents the same data in terms of the number of syllables recalled at the first presentation of the stimulus set at each learning session.[2] Tables I and

---

[1] For detailed tables of the data of these experiments, order Document 2710 from American Documentation Institute, 1719 N St., N.W., Washington 6, D. C., remitting $0.50 for microfilm (images one in. high on standard 35-mm. motion picture film) or $1.20 for photocopies (6 × 8 in.) readable without optical aid.

[2] Although only two groups were used in the experiment, the experimental group will be referred to as Group III so that the results of this experiment may be directly compared with results in an experiment to follow.

II are presented in terms of P-values, the probabilities that the measured differences are due to chance factors. As can be seen from the figures, the two groups are approximately equal for Session 1 and Session 2. Session 3, which occurred immediately after the first block tapping

TABLE I. EXPERIMENT I. THE t- AND P-VALUES FOR DIFFERENCES BETWEEN THE MEANS OF EXPERIMENTAL AND CONTROL GROUPS RELEARNING 15 SEMI-NONSENSE SYLLABLES

	Test Session					
	1	2	3	4	5	6
t	0.26	0.33	6.43	4.47	1.00	0.00
P	.40	.37	.0001	.001	.17	—

TABLE II. EXPERIMENT I. THE t- AND P-VALUES FOR THE DIFFERENCES BETWEEN THE MEANS OF THE CONTROL AND EXPERIMENTAL GROUPS FOR THE NUMBER OF SYLLABLES RECALLED ON THE FIRST TRIAL OF EACH SESSION (RELEARNING OF 15 SEMI-NONSENSE SYLLABLES)

	Test Session					
	1	2	3	4	5	6
t	0.61	1.20	5.00	4.17	1.00	0.00
P	.28	.13	.0004	.001	.17	—

session, is the first point at which there is a reliable difference. At this point $t = 6.43$. The probability of a difference this large, in the same direction, resulting from chance is less than one in 10,-000. These findings are in keeping with those obtained by Sears (6) and McClelland and Apicella (2). Sears found

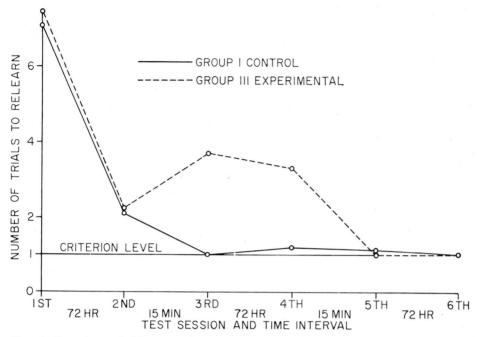

FIG. 1. Experiment I. Mean number of trials to relearn 15 semi-nonsense syllables at each test session.

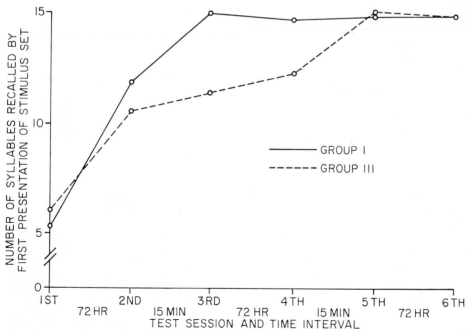

FIG. 2. Experiment I. Mean number of syllables recalled at first presentation of the stimulus set at each test session.

that failure at card sorting affected the learning of nonsense syllables, and Mc-Clelland and Apicella in a very ingeniously designed experiment found that verbal abuse could inhibit the demonstration of learning but that this learning became apparent when the inhibition caused by the abuse was removed. The McClelland and Apicella experiment used card sorting as the original learning and success at pursuitmeter performance as a means of removing inhibition. They explain the improvement in performance in terms of a decrease in anxiety over anticipated failure. In their experiment there is, however, no evidence to warrant a conclusive explanation in terms of repression. That is, the difference between the groups could just as readily be attributed to differences in attitude, set, motivation, or attention, and not to an active repression.

At the next relearning test (4th session) which was administered at the beginning of the third experimental day, there is an absolute difference of 2.1 trials which has a probability of less than eight in 10,000 of being due to chance. Although there is no evidence that the result is not due to forgetting or differences of motivation, such an explanation seems improbable. The results of the fifth session indicate that the removal of the ego threat by success resulted in greatly improved recall. The results of the sixth session indicate that the groups have remained equivalent in performance. The number of subjects at this point was, however, reduced as this last session was incorporated into the design after the experiment had begun.

Taken as a whole it would appear that, in keeping with the original purpose of the experiment, a technique has been found which can be used to induce, in the laboratory under controlled conditions, an emotional experience which fulfills all of the requirements of a Freudian repression sequence. As was pointed out, however, the differential at each stage might be explained in some other manner. For instance, the difference at the third session might be attributed to motivational factors. Although no measure of motivation was attempted, it seemed to the experimenter that the experimental subjects were much more highly motivated than were the members of the control group at this point. A similar point could be made for the 4th session, although here again subjective evaluation would tend to indicate otherwise. Also at the 4th session the experimental group had had on the average more practice than the control group and the passage of time could have served to dissipate any disorganization of response caused by anger or other emotional disturbance. At this point, unless there were repression, it would seem to make sense to predict that the experimental group would either equal or surpass the control group.

Unfortunately, the control group had reached a limit of its measurable learning at the third session, so that it was impossible to determine whether overlearning was taking place. If such were the case, a more delicate measuring instrument might show a difference between the two groups. The results of the fifth session are in keeping with those of McClelland and Apicella (2), who would explain the results in terms of a delayed demonstration of previous learning. They would attribute this to reduced anxiety over anticipated failure. The last relearning shows results which would have been predicted in keeping with any of the above explanations, all subjects having reached the final learning period in theoretically the same emotional condition.

It should be noted that there are several factors which would tend to distort the real picture. One mentioned previously is that the control group reached a criterion level too soon, with the result that no spread was possible. Another is, that the subjects who were in the experimental test group and who 'forgot' to appear for the test on the third day, quite possibly depressed the results. The very fact that they did not appear might indicate that repression had advanced to such a stage that they literally did not remember the appointment! An alternative explanation, of course, is that they remembered only too well and quite consciously avoided returning to have their egos further deflated.

Individual Experiment II

RELEARNING 30 SEMI-NONSENSE SYLLABLES

Although the results from the first experiment in this series were statistically clear cut, alternative interpretations of the data were not excluded. This made it desirable to repeat the experiment with further controls. While the fundamental design of the experiment was not altered, the following changes were made: 1. introduction of a group in which failure on the tapping test was designated as specific to tapping; 2. introduction of a group in which failure was designated by the experimenter to apply to both the tapping and syllables test; 3. lengthening of the list of syllables from 15 to 30 pairs; 4. reduction of the interval between successive testings from three to two days.

The following four groups of 10 sub-

jects each were used in this experiment.

Group I. The control group which suffered no experimentally induced failure. This group is equivalent to the control group in Experiment I.

Group II. A group in which failure at the tapping test was designated by the experimenter as specific to that task. These individuals were told that they had done well on the syllables test. The reason for introducing this group was to determine if failure per se could account for the results obtained in the previous experiment. If so, the results for this group should resemble the results of the experimental group in Experiment I. On the other hand, if the induced failure remained specific to the situation, it should not affect the associated material, namely, the syllables test, so the relearnings for the group should then approximate those of Group I. A further possibility was that the emotions associated with the failure designated as a specific to the block test might show a partial generalization and cause the results of this group to fall midway between Groups I and III. Another possibility was that such specific failure might facilitate relearning (as compensation) so that Group II would surpass Group I.

Group III. This is the same as the experimental group (Group III) of Experiment I. Failure was induced in the block tapping test and by implication into any other activity the individual might undertake, although no mention of the syllable test was made in connection with the block test.

Group IV. This was a group in which the subjects were told they failed during both the tapping test and the syllables test. It was felt that such a procedure would show whether or not failure irradiating from a single type of material would be equivalent to complete failure on all types. If the performance of this group were equivalent to Group III, then it would seem reasonable to interpret the poor performance of Group III to their generalization of failure to the syllables test. If, on the other hand, being informed of failure in both situations was even more traumatic to the subject, relearning could be expected to show more deterioration. In any case, it was felt that the results would cast more light on the mechanism of repression.

Material. The material for this experiment was the same as for Experiment I with the exception of the syllable list which was increased to thirty pairs.

Subjects. The subjects for this experiment were 40 college students of both sexes. All were volunteers, although 20 were paid for their time and 20 were not. Altogether, 48 individuals were used, but for various reasons eight did not complete the experiment. The results of these subjects are not reported. There was no duplication of subjects from the previous experiment in any subsequent experiment.

Procedure. All subjects learned the list of 30 syllables to a criterion of one perfect trial. This was accomplished as in the previous experiment. The groups were equated through the beginning of the second session by the same method as used in Experiment I.

The procedure was the same for all groups through the relearning experience at the beginning of the second test day. Beyond this point the procedure varied in the different groups.

In the block tapping test the experimenter sat opposite the subject. Four blocks were arranged one in. apart in a row. The experimenter said, "Here are five blocks, four on the table and one in my hand. With this block [indicating the one held in the hand] I will tap the others in some order. For example [taps 1, 3, 2, 4, or 1, 3, 2, 1, 4, 2, 4 depending on the group], and you are to do the same thing. Do you understand?"

Group I was given 15 min. of block-tapping exercises. Members of this group were not told their results, but the patterns were kept at such a low level of difficulty that it was obvious to the subject that he was succeeding very well. In addition, he could see, if he wished to, that the examiner was recording success after each reproduced pattern. At the end of the 15-min. period he was told, "You did all right," and a relearning test was administered. He was then told to return in 48 hours. On the third test day the syllables were again learned to the criterion (4th session) and the procedure of the second day duplicated. There was a 15-min. block-tapping period followed by relearning (5th session). Forty-eight hours later each subject returned for the 6th and last session.

The individuals in Group II were treated differently. The first trial at block tapping was on a difficult seven-unit pattern (1, 3, 2, 1, 4, 2, 4) which was almost certain to be beyond the subject's capacity. In any case, even if the subject succeeded, he readily accepted the suggestion that he had failed. As the examiner was across the table from the subject, if the subject tapped the blocks in the same order, his left-right orientation was opposite to that of the examiner and if he changed the orientation so that he also tapped from left to right, the order of the blocks was reversed. Either way he was informed that he had committed a very stupid error. "I am very disappointed in you. Your achievement on the nonsense syllables was so good I am very amazed at your complete lack of ability on this test." After each trial (all were failures) the examiner informed the subject he had failed. A careful score was kept showing repeated failures below the bottom of a scale extending from 7 to 15. After a number of failures, the experimenter informed the subject that he was performing at the level of an eight-year-old, but that it was surprising considering his accomplishment on the syllables test. At this point the examiner stopped the experiment, added a new bottom to the scale and told the subjects to get hold of themselves. The results were usually an improved block performance which seemed to deteriorate very little even though they were repeatedly told that they had failed. Although great concern was shown by the experimenter over the subjects' failure at this task, the subjects, although in most cases worried, seemingly did not get really upset about the situation. Several suggested that they had always had poor mechanical ability and all readily admitted that telephone numbers were easily forgotten. It seemed that the feeling of having succeeded on the syllables acted as a strong ego supporting factor so that apparently little emotional trauma was experienced. At the end of 15 min. a relearning test was administered (3rd session). The subjects seemed very glad to get back to this type of material, as was indicated by such remarks as "This is my meat; I'll really knock this off." These subjects seemed to have reached the stage of accelerated performance noted in the failure group of the previous experiment (see Experiment I), but it did not deteriorate as the performance of individuals in that group did after a few trials with repeated failure. Forty-eight hours later a third relearning test (4th session) was given followed by a 15-min. block-tapping session. At this point the individuals were allowed to suc-

ceed and were informed of their success. Surprisingly enough, several insisted they could not do the block-tapping test and that their mechanical aptitude had always been poor. They even seemed reluctant to give up the dubious distinction of being the only person to ever make such a low score. After this 15-min. session another relearning test (5th session) was given and the subjects were asked to return in 48 hours. At the last session, which lasted only a few minutes, the syllables were again learned (6th session) to a criterion of one perfect trial.

The subjects in Group III were treated exactly the same as the individuals of the failure group in Experiment I. The difficulty of the task was immediately set above their capacity. They were first informed of their stupidity in orienting themselves wrong in tapping the blocks. They failed on every tapping pattern and were informed of their failure. Care was taken to keep an obvious record, and great concern was shown for their lack of memory ability. The subjects responded first with renewed effort and then as failures continued, the behavior became tense and disorganized which resulted in such deteriorated performance that in one case the individual was incapable of tapping three of the four blocks in the proper order. It seemed to the experimenter that the subjects were very highly motivated at this point. The disorganized behavior was fostered by the examiner who, while seeming to be sympathetic, did everything he could to instill a feeling of absolute and complete inadequacy in the subject. Nothing was omitted in the attempt to make the situation as traumatic as possible. As the aim was to make the situation emotionally unbearable for the individual, the specific type of disparagement resorted to depended to a great extent on the reaction of the subject. All were informed of their stupidity, inadequacy, emotional instability, and lack of both concrete and abstract intelligence. No reference was made at any time, however, to the syllable test during the block tapping test. After this a relearning test (3rd session) was administered and no further reference to failure was made after the block test was finished. The subjects had for the most part become so disorganized that they failed on the first trial. This failure seemed to increase the state of tension to such a point that repeated failures were the rule. Following this test the subject was instructed to return in 48 hours to continue the experiment.

On the third experimental day, each subject was again given a relearning test (4th session). At this time the very sight of the examiner seemed to cause a certain amount of uneasiness, and when the subjects were informed that the first task would be to relearn the syllables, this uneasiness increased. Following this the blocks were produced again and the subject given very easy patterns to reproduce. As more and more of these were successfully reproduced, the tension dissipated and the subject became more relaxed and accuracy increased. At this point it was explained that the experiment had been partially one of motivation and that they had been chosen because of their superior ability. A bogus set of norms was exhibited and the subject was allowed to succeed no matter what he did. Although no legitimate records could be kept of block tapping ability owing to the necessity of falsifying the record during experimental sessions, it seems certain that objective measurement would show that the group at this period reached a maximum of achievement. Following the 15-min. period, a

relearning test (5th session) was again administered. Forty-eight hours later the subjects returned for the 6th and final session.

The individuals in Group IV were treated the same as the subjects in all other groups up to the time that the first tapping pattern test was given. After the presentation of the first tapping pattern they were informed not only that their first tapping pattern was incorrect, but that this could have been predicted because of their poor showing on the syllables test. Following this, the procedure observed in Groups II and III was followed fairly closely, although it was possible to add more fuel to the flame by mentioning the failure on the syllables as well as the subject's general low mental ability and specific inability to do well on the blocks. After each tapping test the subject was told, "That is wrong again," with as much resignation in his voice as the experimenter could register. In this group nothing was spared to make the subject feel emotionally uncomfortable. As the subject became more and more disorganized, it was only necessary to let him see the results of his efforts in order to further upset him. After 15 min. of tapping patterns, the 3rd session was given and the subject was asked to return in 48 hours. On the third experimental day, the subjects were again given a relearning test (4th session) followed by another 15-min. block tapping session. As in Groups II and III, these subjects were allowed to succeed, and the experimenter again explained the nature of the experiment, indicating that the subjects in question had been chosen because of their superior mental ability and that they were really doing very well. If possible, the members of this group showed even more relief than those in

Group III. After this a relearning test (5th session) was given and the subject was asked to return in 48 hours. At this time the 6th and last relearning was done by the subject.

RESULTS AND DISCUSSION

The results are indicated in Figs. 3 and 4, and in Tables III and IV. Figure

tween Groups I and II and between Groups III and IV (Table III and Fig. 3). The greatest absolute difference between Groups I and II at any point is only 0.7 at the first test session, the P-value for which is .33. The greatest statistical difference is for the 5th test session, where a difference of .1 had a P-value of .17. Between Groups III and

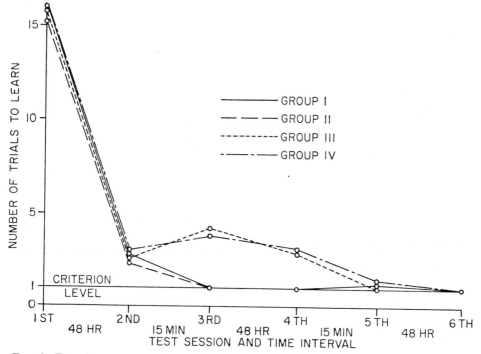

FIG. 3. Experiment II. Mean number of trials to relearn 30 semi-nonsense syllables at each test session.

3 presents the results in terms of the number of trials to learn at each test session, while Fig. 4 presents the same data in terms of the number of syllables recalled at the first presentation of the stimulus cards at each test session. Tables III and IV present the statistical treatment of the data in terms of P.

The change most apparent at first glance is the remarkable similarity be-

IV the greatest absolute difference of .3 at the 4th test session has a P-value of .39, while the greatest statistical difference is indicated by a P-value of .27 for an absolute difference of .1 at the 5th test session.

Since Group II so closely resembles Group I, it would seem reasonable to assume that failure specific to a single, specifically defined situation offers very

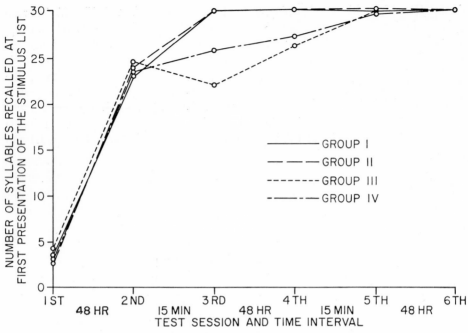

FIG. 4. Experiment II. Mean number of syllables recalled at the first presentation of the stimulus set at each test session.

little threat to an individual's security. An alternate explanation is that being informed of success on syllable reproduction counteracted the effect of being informed of failure at block tapping.

Groups III and IV also show remarkable similarity. The conclusion which seems to be indicated is that failure which is not designated as specific spreads to associated tasks (Group III) and that a number of specific failures (Group IV) are no more disruptive to an individual's performance than a failure generalized from a specific situation. It could reasonably have been expected that the individuals in Group IV would

TABLE III. EXPERIMENT II. P-VALUES FOR THE DIFFERENCES BETWEEN MEANS OF GROUPS RELEARNING 30 SEMI-NONSENSE SYLLABLES

	Test Session					
	1	2	3	4	5	6
Groups I–II	.33	.29	.50	.50	.17	.50
Groups I–III	.47	.41	.0001	.001	.50	.50
Groups I–IV	.50	.42	.003	.001	.27	.50
Groups II–III	.36	.36	.0001	.001	.17	.50
Groups II–IV	.35	.26	.003	.001	.08	.50
Groups III–IV	.48	.35	.39	.38	.27	.50

have done measurably less well than the individuals in Group III. This, however, did not occur.

The experiment on the whole is subject to many of the same criticisms leveled at Experiment I, namely, that the control group (Group I) reached a level of proficiency by the 3rd test session which made it impossible to measure their learning past this point and consequently impossible adequately to compare the groups. Another possibility is that the individuals used as subjects

$P < .003$; Diff. II–III $= 3.2, P < .0001$; Diff. II–IV $= 2.9,$ $P < .003$), can be explained in terms other than repression. The subjects in Groups III and IV may have been emotionally disorganized, or may have just quit trying. This last explanation from the examiner's viewpoint does not seem very likely, however, as the individuals in Groups III and IV appeared to be much more highly motivated than the individuals in the other groups. The differences at the 4th session, which are comparable to those of

TABLE IV. EXPERIMENT II. *P*-VALUES FOR THE DIFFERENCES BETWEEN THE MEANS OF GROUPS FOR THE NUMBER OF SYLLABLES RECALLED ON THE FIRST TRIAL OF EACH SESSION (RELEARNING OF 30 SEMI-NONSENSE SYLLABLES)

	Test Session					
	1	2	3	4	5	6
Groups I–II	.17	.39	.50	.50	.17	.50
Groups I–III	.27	.25	.0001	.0002	.50	.50
Groups I–IV	.36	.24	.0002	.0001	.43	.50
Groups II–III	.07	.35	.0001	.0003	.17	.50
Groups II–IV	.23	.42	.0002	.0001	.39	.50
Groups III–IV	.16	.28	.09	.07	.43	.50

were not representative of college students in general. In spite of the fact that one half of the subjects were paid for their time, the greatest single factor determining their volunteering was the hope of later discussing personal problems. Next, although the overall picture supports the hypothesis that an actively induced repression can be removed with a consequent revival of memory traces, an analysis at any one point leads to several possible explanations. For example, at the 3rd test session the results, although certainly significant (Diff. I–III $= 3.2, P < .0001$; Diff. I–IV $= 2.9,$

the 3rd session, are open to the same interpretation (Diff. I–III $= 1.9, P < .001$; Diff. I–IV $= 2.1, P < .001$; Diff. II–III $= 1.9, P < .001$; Diff. II–IV $= 2.1, P < .001$).

The results for the 5th test session are in keeping with those obtained by McClelland and Apicella (2). At this point the added practice should have resulted in superior performance for Groups III and IV as compared with Groups I and II. Unfortunately the measuring instrument was not delicate enough to discriminate this possible difference.

The results of the 6th test session are

in keeping with any of the previously mentioned explanations.

Apparently the decrease from 72 to 48 hours between experimental days had little effect (compare Figs. 1 and 3).

In any attempt to test experimentally any of the psychoanalytic mechanisms, the experimenter is faced first with the problem of defining the concept and second to designing an experiment to test adequately the concept. It is always possible that somewhere in this process the true meaning of the original concept has been lost. It seems, however, that the concept of repression proper or after-expulsion can be defined as an active process which forces once conscious material from consciousness without destroying the memory for the material, which memory may be restored following the removal of the inhibiting factor. The present design seems adequate to test this hypothesis. Although alternative explanations are possible, it seems reasonable to conclude that the results indicate that an experimental analogue of repression has been produced in the laboratory.

Summary and Conclusions

Two experiments have been conducted to test the hypothesis that repression proper is an active process which inhibits memory for previously known material which has become unacceptable to the individual, but that the memory for the material may be restored by reducing the ego threat associated with the original material. The neutral material consisted of 15 and 30 semi-nonsense syllables respectively for Experiments I and II. Induced failure in reproducing a series of tapping patterns using five one-in. black Knox cubes constituted the ego threat, while success at the same task served to remove the threat. Neutral experience at tapping was the interpolated material in the control group. The results indicate:

(1) That induced failure at a task, when not indicated as specific to that task, serves to reduce the ability to recall previously known material which has become associated with the failure task.

(2) That this reduced ability lasts for a period of time (three days in Experiment I and two days in Experiment II).

(3) That induced success at the same associated task serves to increase the ability to recall the original material.

(4) That implied failure is as disruptive to memory as specific knowledge of failure.

(5) That failure indicated as specific to a given task has no measurable effect on the ability to perform other tasks.

(6) That although other explanations in terms of motivation, interest, or attitude cannot be ruled out, the experiment fulfills the requirements of an analogue of Freudian repression.

References

1. FLANAGAN, D. E. The influence of emotional inhibition on learning and recall. Unpublished Master's thesis, Univ. of Chicago, 1930.

2. MCCLELLAND, D. C., & APICELLA, F. S. Reminiscence following experimentally induced failure. *J. exp. Psychol.*, 1947, **57**, 159–169.

3. ROSENZWEIG, S. An outline of frustration theory. In: J. McV. HUNT (Ed.), *Personality and the behavior disorders*. New York: Ronald Press, 1944.

4. ROSENZWEIG, S., & SARASON, S. An experimental study of the triadic hypothesis: reaction to frustration, ego-defense, and hypnotizability. I. Correlational approach. *Character and Pers.*, 1942, **11**, 1–19.

5. SARASON, S., & ROSENZWEIG, S. An experimental study of the triadic hypothesis: reaction to frustration, ego-defense, and hypnotizability. II. Thematic apperception approach. *Character and Pers.*, 1942, **11**, 150–165.

6. SEARS, R. R. Initiation of the repression sequence by experienced failure. *J. exp. Psychol.*, 1937, **20**, 570–580.

7. ZELLER, A. F. An experimental analogue of repression. I. Historical summary. *Psychol. Bull.*, 1950, **47**, 39–51.

AVOIDANCE CONDITIONING OF VERBAL BEHAVIOR WITHOUT AWARENESS: A PARADIGM OF REPRESSION

Charles W. Eriksen and James L. Kuethe

Several recent experiments have suggested that the principles of learning theory may be profitably applied to the study of language and verbal behavior (2, 4, 6). These studies have shown that the verbal behavior of a subject can be manipulated through the use of differential reinforcement and in many cases the subjects remain unaware that their behavior has been modified, i.e., they are unable to state in what way their behavior has changed or even that it has changed. While these experiments have dealt with overt verbal behavior, it seems reasonable that implicit verbal behavior or thinking might similarly be affected. If so, these experiments have some interesting implications for research on psychological defense mechanisms in that they offer suggestions as to how defenses might be learned and how they might operate.

It is an empirical observation that responses followed by punishment or anxiety tend to be eliminated or replaced by other responses. If thoughts or implicit verbal behavior are considered as responses subject to manipulation by reinforcement, we can expect that thoughts that have become conditioned stimuli for anxiety will be eliminated or replaced by other thoughts. Dollard and Miller (3) have presented a detailed theoretical treatment of defense mechanisms along these lines.

Such a theoretical account of the learning of defense mechanisms would gain support if it could be shown that thoughts or associations that were followed by anxiety were eliminated or replaced. It was our purpose in the present study to determine, first, whether verbal associations that the subject (S) had formed during his life experiences could be changed by punishment in the form of electric shocks, and second, whether these changes in verbal associations could be produced without the S's becoming aware that his behavior had been modified. We also wished to determine if such effects would persist when the experimental task was changed.

Reprinted by permission of the American Psychological Association and the authors from *The Journal of Abnormal and Social Psychology*, Vol. 53, 1956.

Method

The basic technique used in this study was a modified form of the word association test. Here the same set of stimulus words was administered to Ss a number of times in an unbroken sequence. Table 1 shows the 15 stimulus words comprising the association list that was used. It was assumed that each word on this list constituted a stimulus having a hierarchy of associations or responses that had been acquired by S during his life experiences. From a pilot study we had found that when the same word list is repeated a number of times, Ss tend to continue to repeat their original associations. We wished to determine whether strong electric shocks administered every time certain selected associations occurred would result in these responses dropping out and being replaced by other associations.

Prior to beginning the experimental sessions with an S, the E randomly designated five of the stimulus words in the list which were to be the *critical* stimuli for this particular S. During the first trial the S's associations to these five words, whatever they happened to be, were punished by a strong electric shock. Without pause the S was given a second trial on the 15 stimulus words followed by a third trial and so on for a total of ten trials or until the S had reached a criterion of two successive trials without the occurrence of any one of the five punished associations. On each trial the stimulus words occurred in a different sequence. During these succeeding trials on the list, S was administered a strong electric shock every time he responded with one of the five associations that had been shocked on the first trial. Shocks were administered only when these "taboo" associations occurred.

Shocks were administered through ankle electrodes attached to the S's left ankle. The source of the shock came from an inductorium and a 3 v.d.c.

source. Faradic stimulation was used. The intensity of shocks varied slightly between Ss due to such factors as differences in skin resistance, but in all cases it was evident from the S's comments and behavior that the shocks were quite painful.

In order to maximize the opportunities for obtaining "learning without awareness," the Ss were misinformed as to the nature of the experiment and the reason for the electric shocks. They were told that the purpose of the experiment was to determine the maximum speed of mental associations. They were instructed that shocks would occur under two conditions: one, if their association to a stimulus word was too slow for that particular stage of practice; and the second was a condition that the E could not divulge to them in advance, but they might discover it on their own during the session and thus be able to avoid getting the shocks.

TABLE 1. STIMULUS WORDS

Careless	Lovely
Perfect	Hasty
Cheerful	Gawky
Tidy	Rural
Rotten	Thrifty
Costly	Old
Small	Boastful
Polite	

The Ss were instructed to respond to each stimulus word with the first word that came to mind and as quickly as possible. To insure that they understood the nature of the task, several practice words were administered. They were also informed that the same list of words would be repeated over and over, but each time the words would occur in a different sequence. During the experimental session S's association time to each stimulus word was measured to the nearest hundredth of a second by means of an electronic voice key. The timer was started by the sound of E's voice and manually stopped by E when S responded.

At the conclusion of this learning phase of the experiment, Ss were informed that this experiment was over and were then asked to do one more task before leaving. This consisted of chained associations to the stimulus words. The Ss were told that the same stimulus words would be repeated again, but this time they were to say all the words that came to mind and continue doing so until the E said "stop." Fifteen seconds were allowed for chained associations to each stimulus word. Before starting this phase of the experiment, Ss were all carefully instructed that there would be no further electric shocks.

In carrying out the chained associations in this experiment, we were interested in two things. First, we wished to see if the punished association would occur when the S was required to give a large number of responses, and second, we were interested in determining if the effects of punishment would be generalized to a situation somewhat different from the original learning situation, in which the threat of shocks had been removed.

At the conclusion of the chained associations the S was closely interviewed to determine his ability to verbalize the true nature of the experiment and changes in his behavior. All Ss were asked the following questions: Did you discover how to avoid getting shocks? Did you do anything to keep from getting shocked? What did you do? Did you ever find yourself withholding a response word and trying to think of something else to say? (If a positive answer was obtained, S was asked if he could recall any instances where this occurred.) Those Ss who reported deliberately withholding responses and substituting other responses for them were also questioned as to whether they had to continue doing this throughout the experiment.

In addition to the questioning, Ss were shown a list of the stimulus words and asked to indicate which words had been followed by shock and what response word they had given when the shocks occurred.

Subjects. Thirty-one male undergraduate students served as Ss in the experiment. All were obtained from the elementary psychology course at The Johns Hopkins University. As part of the course requirements, they were required to serve as Ss in psychological experiments.

Results

Awareness. On the basis of the interview data it was possible to divide the Ss clearly into high- and low-level-of-awareness groups. The high awareness Ss were able to state the real basis for shocks and to describe what they had done to avoid them. They were also able to identify correctly three or more of the critical stimulus words as well as the response they had given that led to punishment. All reported deliberately withholding punished responses while trying to think of another response to substitute for it. However, they all reported that after a few trials it was no longer necessary to withhold the punished responses deliberately since the new, or safe, response began to occur "automatically."

The low awareness Ss, on the other hand, were unable to state any reasons for the shock other than the misinformation the E had given them prior to the experiment. Occasionally they expressed hypotheses that were quite unrelated to the real basis for shock and which were quite at variance with their actual behavior. They were unable to provide an accurate description of changes in their behavior and all stated that they had not learned how to avoid getting shocks. When asked to indicate which of the stimulus words had been followed by shock, their selection was random. In no case were their selections more than 20 per cent correct.

It was possible to classify eleven of the Ss as having a high level of awareness or insight and another eleven Ss as having a low level of insight. There were another five Ss who could not be clearly placed in either the insight or the noninsight group. These Ss seemed to have a vague idea as to the reasons for shock and what they needed to do to avoid them, but their verbalizations were not definite enough to permit clear-cut decisions. We have labeled these Ss as the partial insight group. The remaining four Ss resisted classification on our insight criteria. Three of these Ss had adopted an incorrect hypothesis concerning the shocks. While their hypotheses were incorrect, they were nonetheless effective in avoiding shocks. For example, two of these Ss had the hypothesis that shocks occured when they gave synonyms and they had changed all of their responses to avoid synonyms. The other two Ss had resorted to using only two response words, such as, "good" and "bad" for all stimulus words. The data from these four Ss were excluded from further analysis.

Since we were successful in obtaining two levels of awareness or insight in our Ss, we have treated insight as an independent variable in the remainder of the data analyses. We have not presented the data for the partial insight group, how-

ever, due to the small number of Ss that fell into this group.[1]

Avoidance learning. Both the insight and noninsight groups were quite successful in learning to avoid the punished associations. As Fig. 1 shows, the number of repetitions of punished responses decreases rapidly for both groups while the number of nonpunished responses

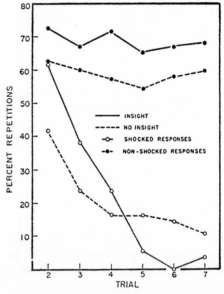

FIG. 1. Percentage of first-trial responses repeated on succeeding trials as a function of punishment.

that were repeated from trial to trial tends to remain constant. For the insight group, a mean of 68.2 per cent of the first-trial, nonpunished response words were repeated on Trial 7 while only 3.6 per cent of the punished responses were repeated on this trial. A *t* test of the difference between these two means resulted in a *t* value of 12.2 which with ten

---

[1] In nearly all of the subsequent comparisons it was found that the partial insight Ss were intermediate between the insight and the noninsight groups although their performance more closely resembled that of the insight Ss.

degrees of freedom was significant beyond the .001 level. The same comparison for the noninsight group shows the mean percentage of repetition of the first-trial, nonpunished responses on Trial 7 to be 60.0 per cent as compared with a mean percentage of 10.9 for the punished responses. The t value of 6.21 is again quite significant ($p < .001$).[2]

While both the insight and noninsight groups show marked and reliable evidence of avoidance learning in this experimental situation, there does not appear to be any reliable evidence of a difference in rate of learning between these two groups. From Fig. 1, it appears that the noninsight group showed a tendency for more avoidance of shocked responses on Trials 2 through 4, but a t test based upon the mean percentage of shocked responses for each S in the two groups summed through these three trials does not approach statistical reliability ($t = 1.42$, $p > .10$). Also the same comparison between the insight and noninsight Ss on Trials 5 through 7 yields a t of 1.44 which is again insignificant ($p > .10$).

From Fig. 1 it appears that the noninsight group tended to give fewer first-

------

[2] An over-all analysis of variance of these data was not justified due to the marked heterogeneity of variance that existed from the early to the late trials and the skewness of the distributions on the late trials. The t tests that have been employed have either been corrected for heterogeneity of variance by the method suggested by Cochran and Cox (1) or the comparisons are between data that show reasonable evidence of meeting the underlying assumptions involved.

As a further precaution all statistical analyses involving percentages in this study were repeated using an arc-sine transformation of the percentages. In no case did the analyses using the transformed data result in significance levels appreciably different from those reported for the untransformed data.

trial responses to the noncritical stimuli than did the insight group. To determine whether this difference was reliable, the mean percentage of first-trial responses given by each S on Trials 2 through 7 was computed. The means of these mean percentages were 68.8 for the insight group and 58.8 for the noninsight group. The resulting t of 1.22 with 20 df does not approach accepted levels of statistical reliability and we cannot conclude that the two groups differ on the repetition of first-trial associations on subsequent trials.

A further confirmation of the lack of effect of insight upon the rate of avoidance learning is found when we compare the number of trials required by the insight and the noninsight groups to reach the criterion of two successive trials without a repetition of a punished response. The results of this analysis are seen in Table 2. As this table shows, the mean number of trials required for both groups is nearly identical and the t

TABLE 2. NUMBER OF TRIALS TO REACH THE CRITERION

Groups	Mean	Variance Estimate	t
Insight	4.18	2.8	.09
Noninsight	4.27	6.8	

Note.—The criterion trials have been omitted from the computations.

test falls far short of acceptable levels of significance.

Reaction times. While there is no evidence of differences in rate of avoidance learning between the insight and the noninsight Ss, there are some marked differences between these two groups in reaction times to stimulus words that have had punished responses (critical stimuli). On each trial the median reaction time to critical and noncritical stimuli was computed for each S. In Fig. 2 the mean of these median reaction times as a function of number of trials is shown for the insight and the noninsight groups. For the noninsight group the mean reaction times for both the five critical and the ten noncritical stimuli decreases as a function of trials. By the last trial the reaction times are virtually the same for both critical and noncritical words.

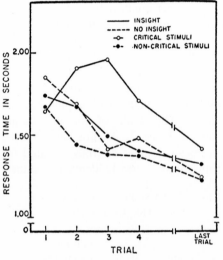

FIG. 2. Reaction times to critical and noncritical stimuli as a function of trials.

For the insight group, however, the relation of reaction times to trials differs for the critical and the noncritical stimuli. The times for the noncritical words decrease with trials as did reaction times for both critical and noncritical words in the noninsight group, but for the critical stimuli there is an initial increase in reaction time. Only on the fourth trial does the mean reaction time to the critical words begin to decrease, and even then it is still longer than the reaction time on the first trial.

In order to evaluate the statistical reliability of the interaction between insight, trials, and critical words that appears in Fig. 2, a modified four-way analysis of variance (insight, critical stimuli, trials, and Ss) was performed. The analysis used was identical to that described by Lindquist as Plan VI (5). The data for this analysis were the median reaction times for critical and noncritical stimuli for each S on each of the first four trials.[3] The summary of this analysis is given in Table 3.[4]

Our main concern in this analysis was whether the trend of reaction times to the critical stimuli as a function of trials in the insight group was reliably different from the trend for the noncritical words and for both critical and noncritical words in the noninsight group. This question can be answered by the triple interaction between groups, critical stimuli, and trials. As is seen in Table 3, this interaction is highly significant ($p <$ .001).

This difference in reaction time to critical and noncritical words between the insight and the noninsight groups provides us with an independent check upon the validity of classifying these Ss as insightful or insightless on the basis of their verbal statements. The increase in reaction time to critical stimuli in the insight group is what might be expected in view of their statements that they deliberately withheld responses that had been punished while they attempted to think of new responses. It should also be noted that the reaction-time data bear out their statements that they soon

[3] Only the first four trials were used in this analysis since a number of the Ss in both groups had reached the avoidance criterion by the end of the fourth trial.

[4] Bartlett's test for heterogeneity of variance did not reach significance at the .05 level.

learned to think of nonpunished responses "automatically" since the reaction times for the last trials closely approach those for the noncritical stimuli.

The analysis in Table 3 also confirms several other effects that are indicated in Fig. 2. Trials are, of course, a significant source of variation, but there is no overall difference between the insight and the

action times decreased at a slower rate for the first three trials than did the reaction times for the noninsight group.

Chained associations. Following the avoidance conditioning on the word-association test, the Ss were informed that there would be no more shocks in the experiment. They were then asked to chain-associate for 15 seconds to each

TABLE 3. SUMMARY OF THE ANALYSIS OF VARIANCE OF THE
REACTION-TIME DATA FOR TRIALS 1–4

Source	Sum of Squares	df	F Ratio	p
Totals	47.32	175		
Trials	1.46	3	.49/.07 = 7.00	<.001
Critical Stimuli	1.49	1	1.49/.21 = 7.09	<.05
Insight	1.03	1	1.03/1.36 = .76	>.10
Subjects	27.13	20	1.36/.07 = 19.42	<.001
Trials × Critical Stimuli	.29	3	.10/.07 = 1.43	>.10
Trials × Insight	.95	3	.32/.07 = 4.57	<.01
Critical Stimuli × Insight	.07	1	.07/.21 = .33	>.10
Trials × Critical Stimuli × Insight	2.06	3	.69/.07 = 9.86	<.001
Within-subject Error terms:				
Pooled Subjects by Trials	4.25	60	.07/	
Pooled Subjects by Critical Stimuli	4.15	20	.21/	
Pooled Subjects by Trials by Critical Stimuli	4.44	60	.07/	

noninsight groups other than the interactions with other variables. The main effect attributed to critical and noncritical words is significant at the .05 level, suggesting that the reaction times to the critical words tended to be somewhat longer during the first four trials. The only other significant effect is the interaction between trials and the insight and noninsight groups. Inspection of Fig. 2 shows that for the insight group, re-

of the stimulus words. In Table 4 we have presented a breakdown of the chained association data for the insight and noninsight Ss in terms of mean number of associations and mean number of first-trial response words repeated as a function of critical and noncritical stimuli.

The data on total associations and on percentage of repetitions of the first trial words were separately analyzed by a modified three-way classification analysis of variance (insight, critical words, and Ss). The analysis for total associations revealed no significant effects. This is apparent from Table 4. However, the analysis of percentage of repetitions of first-trial responses resulted in one significant effect ($p < .01$). More first-trial responses to noncritical stimuli than to critical stimuli were elicited during

TABLE 4. COMPARISON OF GROUPS ON THE AVERAGE NUMBER OF CHAINED ASSOCIATIONS PER STIMULUS AND THE AVERAGE PERCENTAGE OF FIRST-TRIAL RESPONSES

Groups	Mean Number of Associations		Mean Percentage of First-trial Responses Repeated	
	Stimuli		Stimuli	
	Critical	Non-critical	Critical	Non-critical
Insight	4.5	4.4	49	66
Noninsight	4.4	4.5	50	74

chained associations. This finding indicates that the effects of shocks upon the Ss' associations have persisted despite a somewhat different task and the conscious knowledge that electric shocks will no longer occur.

Discussion

In order to explain the phenomena of repression in terms of the principles used in describing avoidance conditioning and the effects of punishment as Dollard and Miller (3) have done, it is necessary to show that implicit verbal behavior or thoughts are analyzable into stimulus-response sequences. It is also necessary

to show that these stimulus-response sequences are learned and modified by the same principles of reinforcement that govern other behavior. In their book, Dollard and Miller have given a plausible treatment of these points.

The results of the present experiment have contributed another step toward an analysis of repression in terms of avoidance conditioning. There are two characteristics of repression that must be demonstrated by any experimental analogue of the repression process. In order for repression to be effective, the anxiety-provoking thought must be prevented from occurring. Thus, the experimental analogue must provide reasonable evidence that the changes in behavior have occurred not only at the overt level but at the covert level as well. Also, since a prominent feature of repression, as clinically observed, is the S's lack of awareness of the repression process, the experimental analogue must demonstrate that the anxiety-provoking thought is eliminated "automatically." That is, the S should not have an awareness of having deliberately and intentionally changed his thoughts.

The results of the present experiment seem to meet these two requirements quite well, especially in the case of Ss in the noninsight group. Not only did these Ss show a marked and rapid decrease in punished associations, but this dramatic change in their associations occurred without verbal awareness on their part. These Ss were unable under intensive questioning to describe what they had done to avoid shocks, and they reported no awareness of having deliberately withheld associations in an attempt to think of a new association.

Fortunately we do not have to rely upon the verbal reports of these Ss alone to support our belief that this avoidance learning occurred without awareness. A comparison of the reaction times for the insight and the noninsight groups lends confirmation to the Ss' verbal reports. The insight Ss who had clear verbal awareness of how to avoid shocks and who reported having tried deliberately to withhold punished associations and think up new ones, were found to show an initial increase in reaction times to the critical stimuli for the first three trials. This increase in reaction time is what would be expected to accompany the implicit behavior that these Ss describe having experienced. For the noninsight group, on the other hand, reaction times to the critical stimuli show a monotonic decrease from the first trial to the last. The reaction times to the critical stimuli in this group are closely comparable to the reaction times to the noncritical stimuli throughout the experiment. The re-action-time data for the critical words in the noninsight group correspond quite well with what would be expected of an "automatic" repression process.[5]

While the verbalizations and the re-action-time data for the noninsight group

---

[5] It is interesting to equate the performance of the insight group with the process of conscious suppression and the performance of the noninsight group with the process of repression as these processes are described by Dollard and Miller (3). In both groups the punished responses were successfully avoided, but in the noninsight group the avoidance occurred "automatically" without awareness and without an increase in reaction times. In the insight group, on the other hand, the avoidance was a deliberate conscious act and was accompanied by increased reaction times while these Ss searched for substitute responses. In the noninsight group the data indicate that the thought itself or the implicit verbal response was initially conditioned while in the insight Ss the overt verbalization was first conditioned and then the thought or implicit response.

strongly indicate that avoidance learning had occurred without awareness, these same data also suggest that the behavior changes occurred at the covert as well as at the overt level. Not only do the Ss from the noninsight group report a lack of withholding of associations, but their reaction-time data also indicate that their overt and covert responses were identical. Had these Ss implicitly responded with punished associations, it seems likely that their association times would have been appreciably longer to the critical stimuli than to the noncritical stimuli. Actually, however, there was little or no difference in the association times to the two classes of stimuli. Even among the Ss in the insight group, the reaction times to critical stimuli had become comparable to the reaction times for noncritical stimuli by the last trial. This finding again corresponds with their verbal report that after a few trials the new associations "came to mind automatically" and they no longer thought of the punished responses.

One further piece of evidence that the shocks had effected associations on the implicit level is to be found in the data on the chained associations. Had these punished associations been present in implicit behavior, we would have expected more of them to have attained overt expression when the threat of punishment was removed. Both groups, however, gave fewer of the punished responses during chained association than would be expected on the basis of the number of first trial responses obtained to the noncritical stimuli.

While it was not the purpose of the present experiment to contribute to the theoretical controversy concerning the manner in which punishment eliminates responses, our data seem to favor an interpretation along the lines of an inhibitory process or decrement in the absolute response strength of the punished responses. An increase in response strength of alternative responses alone does not seem adequate to account for the data obtained from chained associations. Here the *S*s had an opportunity to give a relatively large number of responses to each stimulus. Thus, it could be expected that not only would the stronger responses tend to occur, but there was the opportunity for responses lower in the response hierarchy to occur also. Yet only a few punished responses occurred, a result which is all the more surprising since these punished responses were for the most part initially the dominant response in the hierarchy.

Summary

The *S*s were presented with a 15-item word-association list under the guise that they were taking part in an experiment to determine the limit of speed of associations. They were instructed to respond with the first word that came to mind as quickly as possible after the stimulus word was presented. During the first trial on the list, the *E* administered a strong electric shock immediately after five arbitrarily selected response words. The *S*s were then given a number of further trials on the same 15 stimulus words. Every time an *S* responded with one of the five first-trial punished responses, he received another electric shock. At the conclusion of this phase of the experiment, *S*s were informed that there would be no further shocks. They were then asked to chain-associate to each of the stimulus words.

On the basis of intensive questioning at the conclusion of the experiment, it was possible to classify the *S*s into insight and noninsight groups. The insight *S*s were characterized by having a high degree of verbal awareness as to the basis for the electric shocks and what they had to do to avoid receiving them. The noninsight *S*s had a low level of verbal awareness as to the reasons for the shocks and what they had done to avoid them. Both insight and noninsight groups showed a rapid and marked learning of avoidance behavior. No reliable differences were found between the two groups in terms of rate of learning or on the number of trials to achieve the criterion of two successive trials without the occurrence of a punished response. However, there were clear differences between the two groups in reaction times to stimulus words that had elicited shocked responses. The nature of these differences corresponded with what would be expected from the *S*s' verbalization. Both groups showed a significant decrement in the number of punished responses that occurred during chained associations. The relation of these data to a theory of repression was discussed.

References

1. COCHRAN, W. G., & COX, GERTRUDE M. *Experimental designs*. New York: Wiley, 1950.
2. COHEN, B. D., KALISH, H. I., THURSTON, J. R., & COHEN, E. Experimental manipulation of verbal behavior. *J. exp. Psychol.*, 1954, **47**, 106–110.
3. DOLLARD, J., & MILLER, N. E. *Personality and psychotherapy*. New York: McGraw-Hill, 1950.
4. GREENSPOON, J. The reinforcing effect of two spoken sounds on the frequency of two responses. *Amer. J. Psychol.*, 1955, **68**, 409–416.

5. Lindquist, E. F. *Design and analysis of experiments in psychology and education.* Boston: Houghton Mifflin, 1953.

6. Sidowski, J. B. Influence of awareness of reinforcement upon verbal conditioning. *J. exp. Psychol.,* 1954, **48,** 355–360.

THE REPRESSION HYPOTHESIS STUDIED IN A SITUATION OF HYPNOTICALLY INDUCED CONFLICT

Ruth A. Bobbitt

In recent years, a number of experimental psychologists have tried to rewrite psychoanalytic theory in operational terms. The concept of repression has stimulated a variety of studies (13, 16, 21, 22, 23, 24, 25) that have succeeded primarily in pointing up methodological problems but have contributed little to our knowledge of repression as either a phenomenon or a process. This paper reports a study made ten years ago (3) that still seems pertinent today.

Repression, as a method of ego defense, protects the individual from painful emotional states by keeping ideas that represent certain impulses out of consciousness (7, p. 86). Following Freud's formulation, we may identify the necessary conditions for the development of repression as these: (*a*) An instinctual impulse is aroused; (*b*) gratification of this impulse is in some way unacceptable to the ego of the individual; (*c*) pain (anxiety) has been experienced as the ego demands have been frustrated in gratifying the instinctual tendency (7, p. 84; 9, p. 119); and (*d*) the need to avoid this anxiety is stronger than the instinctual drive (7, p. 85).

Reprinted by permission of the American Psychological Association and the author from *The Journal of Abnormal and Social Psychology,* Vol. 56, 1958.

As a process, repression as conceived by Freud has the following dynamic characteristics:

(1) The repressed is only separated from consciousness (awareness) and is presumably still active in the unconscious. In fact, the extent and degree of repression varies as inhibitory and instinctual propensities fluctuate (7, pp. 89–90).

(2) Generalization of cues and responses often occurs. Cues originally related to the drive may be repressed, but other representations may be admitted to consciousness and acted upon with the accumulated energy of the repressed (7, pp. 86–87). Or, the related ideas may become so associated with the repressed that they must also undergo repression, if the individual is to avoid anxiety (Freud's "repression proper,") (7, p. 86). If repressed impulses are satisfied, it must be through substitute activities. Unless such satisfactions are complete, the need persists, to be expressed through an increasing number of substitute ideas and with "the damming-up consequent on lack of real satisfaction" (7, p. 87).

Since "the motive and purpose of repression is simply the avoidance of 'pain' " (7, p. 92), it follows that repression may be considered successful only to the extent that it does avoid anxiety or pain. It has been noted by Freud (10, pp. 21–22) and by Merrill (16) and

Zeller (23) that unsuccessful, i.e., partial repression, or repression in which at least the affective component has become attached to a substitute idea is most amenable to analysis or experiment. These emotional components become apparent when one considers the dynamics of psychoanalytic therapy in which the aim is to remove repressions. Freud says, ". . . the patient can go on spinning a whole chain of . . . associations, till he is brought up in the midst of them against some thought-formation, the relation of which to what is repressed acts so intensely that he is compelled to repeat his attempt at repression" (7, p. 88). Finally, summarizing the formula for therapy, ". . . all repressions are to be undone; the mental condition is then the same as if all amnesias are removed. When all gaps in memory have been filled in, all the enigmatic products of mental life elucidated, the continuance and even the renewal of the morbid condition is impossible" (8, p. 269).

In this theoretical context, this investigation is specifically concerned with anxiety behavior as the response variable to be measured as a function of degree (completeness) of repression. In terms of the general hypothesis, and apart from therapeutic intervention, the following relationships are predicted: In the absence of either conflict or repression, there should be no anxiety behavior. In conflict with full repression, there should be no anxiety behavior except as the repressive process fluctuates. With incomplete repression, there should be an increase in the scope and intensity of anxiety disturbance. As repression ceases to operate disturbance should reach a maximum and show considerable generalization. Finally, when both repression and conflict are removed there should no

longer be anxiety behavior related to the conflict.

Most of the investigations of repression have utilized some measures of memory as the response variable. Zeller (23, pp. 40–45) recently provided an excellent critical review of these, pointing out the fallacies and inadequacies of each. The kind and amount of feeling tone, emotional disturbance, or ego threat in the experimental situation are seen as important factors. He also stresses that any critical study must demonstrate "restoration to consciousness of the repressed material" upon removal of the repression factor (23, p. 46).

Zeller (23, p. 44) and other writers (16, 22) have noted the Huston, Shakow, and Erickson experiment (13) as one of the better demonstrations of repression, although the use of hypnosis makes interpretation somewhat difficult. The criticism in terms of dependence on hypnosis loses some weight when we consider that results in conformity with the repression hypothesis occur as predicted, and that these results could not have been predicted on the basis of hypnosis alone. The hypnotic approach surely warrants further investigation, if only for the fact that other approaches thus far devised involve variables perhaps even more difficult of appraisal, i.e., learning, motivation, reminiscence, retroactive inhibition, etc. (24, p. 422).

A further consideration in experimental design is the response to be measured as a function of repression. In the case of most of the experiments measuring memory responses, "anxiety" or some form of personal involvement (frustration, incompleteness, unpleasantness) is inferred. In the study of Huston, Shakow, and Erickson (13), however, the responses measured are presumed on the basis of tests of validity to be measures of emotional disturbance or anxiety. The condition of repression is of course also independently validated.

Method

This experiment employs hypnotically induced conflicts as described by Erickson (6) tested according to Luria's association test procedures (13, 15). Experimentally induced conflicts offer opportunity for necessary control. Except when hypnosis has been employed, however, studies of conflict in human subjects (*Ss*) have been too circumscribed and moderate for our purposes. The hypnotic method has been found to have some validity, i.e., the experimenter can define the nature of the conflict, assure the *S*'s susceptibility to and acceptance of it, suggest in general the nature of his reaction to it, create the effects of repression and, finally, remove the hypnotic effects without undesirable residual reactions.

Luria's method for testing emotional disturbance calls for conditioning a voluntary motor pressure of the preferred hand to occur simultaneously with a verbal response. The theory is that an integrated response of low habit strength under voluntary control is notably susceptible to disorganizing effects of emotional disturbance. His report of the general validity of the method has been verified in a group of studies (1, 4, 5, 11, 12, 13, 18, 19, 20).

The design of this experiment is as follows: Under hypnosis, an incident created to arouse a severe state of conflict is related to six selected *S*s. In the waking state, responses to a standard set of 100 association test words are recorded under five experimental conditions: (*a*) before the conflict is induced; (*b*) after induction of the conflict and with posthypnotic amnesia for it; (*c*)

with partial posthypnotic amnesia; (*d*) with full awareness of the conflict as an immediate actuality; and (*e*) after hypnotic removal of the conflict. The association test is composed of "critical" words relating directly to the conflict story; "postcritical" words immediately following critical words, and "neutral" words to which the *S*'s responses were in no way disturbed on a preliminary testing. The three experimental variables are thus subjects (assumed to contain a random effect), types of verbal stimuli and conditions of conflict awareness. The simple factorial design permits evaluation of the three variables in all combinations by means of analyses of variance.

SUBJECTS

*S*s were selected from a group of male junior and senior medical students who had no previous experience with hypnosis, but were willing to serve in a reaction time experiment involving hypnosis. After training, each *S* was rated hypnotizable and capable of complete posthypnotic amnesia.[1] No individuals were accepted whose personalities were rated "extreme" on the basis of a brief Rorschach evaluation, a psychiatric interview and behavior during hypnotic training sessions.

PROCEDURE

The same conflict story and instructions governing degree of awareness were related under hypnosis to each *S*. In outline, the story was this:

In medical school, the *S* has had an experience so disturbing that he had to forget it. As it is recalled, he will reexperience it in detail. He was attending a party and volunteered to borrow a

---

[1] Hypnosis was conducted by three psychiatrists, Drs. Paul Huston, A. W. Freidinger, and F. S. Bobbitt.

car and go for more beer. On his way back, he drove rapidly around a dark corner and felt the car hit something. He feared an accident but did not want to stop since he was in a borrowed car and had been drinking. He rationalized that it had probably been only a bump in the road and drove on. Next morning his fears were confirmed in a newspaper story of a child, near death and hopelessly crippled as the result of a hit and run accident. The details of the account made it clear to him that he was the driver for whom the police were searching. He experienced great panic and conflict about what to do.

Each condition of awareness was induced under hypnosis after review of the story. For the postconflict condition, the hypnotist proved to S under hypnosis that the incident could not have occurred and talked freely with him to assure removal of the conflict. After completion of the experiment, a final hypnotic session assured removal of the conflict; it was suggested also that the S would recall his thoughts and feelings, wanting to talk freely about them when he awakened.

The association test was administered before hypnosis (Condition I), in the waking state after each hypnotic session (Conditions II, III, and IV), and after the conflict was removed (Condition V).

Independent ratings of each S's behavior and introspective accounts were made by two judges, the hypnotist and the E. Unanimous agreement that S had accepted the conflict and with respect to levels of awareness was required.

The 100-word association test, composed of 60 neutral, 20 critical, and 20 postcritical words, was individually constructed for each S. Neutral and postcritical words were selected on the basis

of S's responses to a preliminary test of 210 words. Words were excluded when any measure of response deviated markedly from his mode. Eighty words were then drawn at random from the remaining list. The critical words were either key words in the conflict story (*collision, party, newspaper, borrow*, etc.) or suggested feelings and ideas closely related to it (*criminal, guilty, conflict*, etc.). These words were randomized and distributed at varying intervals among the neutral words. The same order of words was maintained throughout the testing.[2]

The apparatus employed (2, 3) furnished several response measures: verbal reaction time (VRT), time between beginning of verbal response and beginning of voluntary motor pressure (VR-VMP), number of VMP made during a single stimulus-response sequence (#VMP), duration of the first VMP in a stimulus-response sequence (DVMP), number of involuntary motor pressures occurring in a stimulus-response sequence (#IMP), duration of IMP (DIMP), breathing rate (BR), and number of conflict-associated verbal responses obtained during a single testing period (#CAVR). These measures were reliable, as indicated by agreement between two scorers. Reliability coefficients range from .84 to .997 on measured items and percentages of agreement range from .916 to 1.00 on counted items.

Results

The validity of the experimental situation, apart from that of the response measures, is assumed on the basis of

---

[2] Maintaining the same sequence of words throughout the experiment makes likely the operation of practice effects in opposition to the experimental hypotheses. Changing sequence, however, might introduce factors less subject to appraisal.

unanimous judges' ratings and on the consistency among observations and introspective reports. Furthermore, there appears to be descriptive similarity between repression, as postulated here, and the posthypnotic conditions of awareness.

Validity of response measures could be tested more directly. By means of analyses of variance, the three experi-

TABLE 1. RESULTS OF VALIDITY TESTS OF ALL RESPONSE MEASURES SHOWING FOR EACH THE LEVEL OF CONFIDENCE WITH WHICH THE HYPOTHESIS OF NO DIFFERENCE MAY BE REJECTED

Difference Tested	Response Measure [a]							
	VRT	VR-VMP	DVMP	#VMP	BR	#IMP	DIMP	CAVR
1. Between Means for Conflict and Nonconflict Conditions								
a. Critical Words, Conflict Minus Critical Words, Nonconflict	1%	2–5%	5–10%	10–20%	—[b]	5–10%	5–10%	—[b]
b. All Words, Conflict Minus All Words, Nonconflict					20%			
c. All Words, Conflict Minus All Words, Postconflict								10–20%
2. Between Mean Response to Critical and to Neutral Stimulus Words								
a. Critical Words, Conflict Minus Neutral Words, Conflict	1%	5–10%	20%	10–20%	—[b]	10–20%	10–20%	—[b]
b. Critical Words, Nonconflict Minus Neutral Words, Nonconflict	20%	20%	20%	20%	—[b]	20%	20%	—[b]

[a] Response measure:
VRT—Verbal reaction time
VR-VMP—Time between verbal response and voluntary motor pressure
DVMP—Duration voluntary pressure
VMP—Voluntary motor pressure
BR—Breathing rate
IMP—Involuntary motor pressure
DIMP—Duration involuntary pressure
CAVR—Conflict associated verbal response

[b] Response measure could not be tested for this difference.

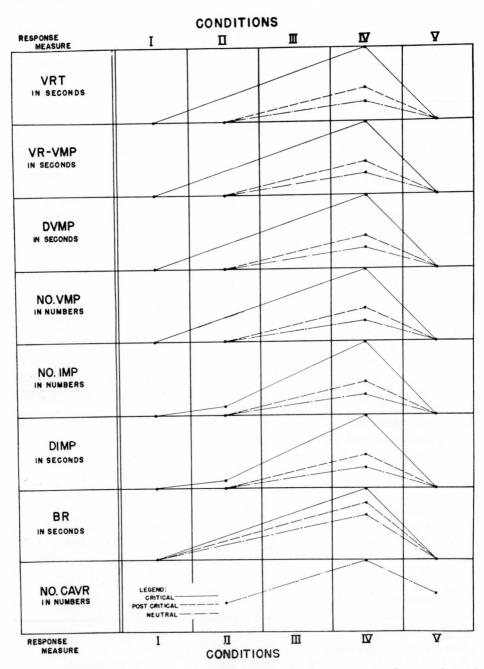

FIG. 1. Hypothetical curves of response measures for the total group by experimental conditions and types of stimuli.

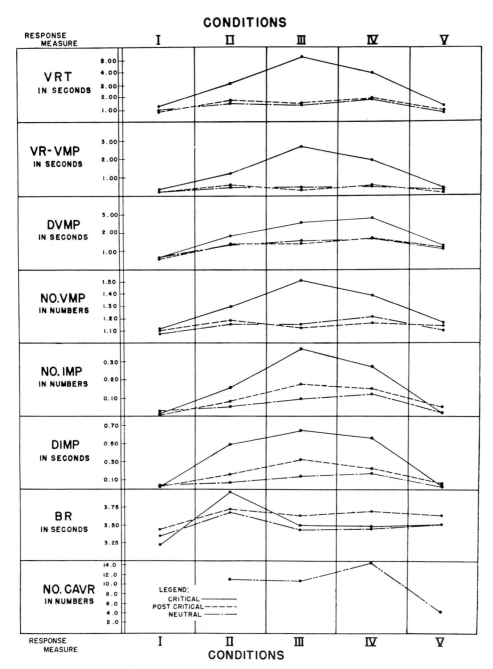

FIG. 2. Means of response measures for the total group by experimental conditions and types of stimuli.

mental variables (subjects, stimuli, and conditions) were tested in interaction with one another (14). Since none of these tests was significant, the specific differences relating to validity and to the experimental hypotheses were tested by the triple interaction variance as the error term.

Table 1 summarizes results of the validity tests.[3] It is seen that (a) all response measures, except BR, tend to differentiate responses in the conditions of conflict from those in conditions of non-conflict (see Lines 1a, 1b, and 1c); (b) all measures but DVMP tend to differentiate between responses to critical and to neutral words under the conflict conditions (Line 2a). Conversely, no difference between responses to these words is shown in the nonconflict conditions (Line 2b). It is interesting to note, in terms of Luria's findings, that VRT and VR-VMP can be considered valid with greater confidence than any of the other measures.

It is now possible to evaluate the findings in relation to the experimental hypotheses. When hypothetical results (Fig. 1) are compared with obtained results for the group (Fig. 2), general conformity is apparent. However, maximum disturbance tends to occur more often in Condition III (partial awareness) than in Condition IV (full awareness), and there is little generalization of disturb-

ance in responses to postcritical and neutral stimuli.

The specific experimental predictions have been subjected to statistical tests reported in Table 2, however, are only those tests warranted by the validity tests (Table 1) and study of Fig. 2. Breathing rate and conflict-associated verbal responses are omitted as are comparisons involving responses to postcritical and neutral words.

(1) There was little disturbance under the condition of conflict without awareness (Table 2, Line 1). Only VRT and DIMP tend to differentiate between these conditions. That there is no particular disturbance in relation to other types of stimuli is evident in Fig. 2.

(2) There is increased disturbance in response to critical words in the condition of partial awareness over the condition of conflict without awareness (Table 2, Line 2) and over the condition of preconflict (Table 2, Line 3). There is also the predicted involvement of more response measures (Table 2, Line 3 in relation to Line 1), but obviously not a significant generalization of disturbance to postcritical and neutral stimuli (Fig. 2).

(3) The predicted further increase (to a maximum) in disturbance under the condition of conflict with full awareness (Table 2, Lines 4 and 5) did not occur. Fig. 2 shows that, for most measures, disturbance in this condition (IV) is somewhere between the other two conflict conditions. For all measures though, responses to critical words are significantly different in the condition of full awareness from those in the preconflict condition (Table 2, Line 6).

(4) All response measures lose their disturbed character when conflict is removed but awareness maintained (Table 2, Line 7). No response measure differs significantly between preconflict and postconflict conditions. With no data available on

---

[3] Tests significant at or below the .05 level of confidence are considered "significant"; those between the .05 and .20 levels are considered "suggestive." This procedure is used to point up consistent trends. The small number of Ss makes necessary large differences, considerable precision and intersubject homogeneity for a high level of statistical significance; requirements difficult of fulfillment in an experiment of this kind.

conflict-associated verbal responses in the preconflict condition, it is not possible to evaluate the significance of the average of four such responses in the postconflict condition (Fig. 2).

not occur in Condition IV. In this connection, it must be considered that:

(1) All obtained differences between conditions of awareness may be due to

TABLE 2. TESTS OF THE "DEGREE OF AWARENESS" HYPOTHESIS SHOWING THE LEVEL OF CONFIDENCE WITH WHICH THE HYPOTHESIS OF NO DIFFERENCE MAY BE REJECTED

(For each response measure, for critical stimulus words only)

Difference between Means	Response Measure					
	VRT	VR-VMP	DVMP	VMP	IMP	DIMP
1. Preconflict Minus Conflict without Awareness	5–10%	20%	20%	20%	20%	10–20%
2. Conflict without Awareness Minus Conflict with Partial Awareness	1–2%	5–10%	20%	10–20%	10–20%	20%
3. Preconflict Minus Conflict with Partial Awareness	1%	1%	2–5%	1–2%	1%	2–5%
4. Conflict with Partial Awareness Minus Conflict with Full Awareness	10–20% [a]	20%	20%	20%	20%	20%
5. Conflict without Awareness Minus Conflict with Full Awareness	20%	20%	10–20%	20%	20%	20%
6. Preconflict Minus Conflict with Full Awareness	1%	2–5%	1–2%	10–20%	2–5%	5–10%
7. Preconflict Minus Postconflict	20%	20%	20%	20%	20%	20%

[a] This tendency is for verbal reaction time to be significantly less disturbed.

Discussion

Two discrepancies, one major and one minor, between the experimental hypotheses and obtained data have been noted. First, maximum disturbance did

chance. However, the consistent statistical, graphic, and introspective results make this a remote possibility.

(2) Contrary to the judges' evaluations and the introspective accounts, there may have been no real difference in awareness between Conditions III and IV.

(3) With development of full awareness, the situation may have had less conflict-value. No S expressed doubt that the accident occurred. Three Ss stated that they feared inevitable punishment and show a general downward trend in disturbance. Two Ss had decided against conscience and in favor of self-protection. One of these showed greatest disturbance in Condition IV, while the other showed somewhat inconsistent increases and decreases in disturbance. One S, whose behavior was much the same in Conditions III and IV, could see no solution to the conflict but was trying to avoid detection.

If there was resolution of conflict in Condition IV, the hypothesis as formulated may be true, but most of the test may have been administered after resolution began and may measure the process of conflict and anxiety reduction instead of reaction to the development of full awareness.

(4) The data may reflect an error in the formulation of the hypothesis concerning degree of awareness. The development of full awareness of a conflict may be accompanied by diminution in disturbance so that maximum disturbance occurs when awareness is at least partial but somewhat less than complete. The peak of disturbance may come with developing awareness, but almost immediately other defenses operate to reduce disturbance (anxiety).

(5) The effects of full awareness may have been counteracted by some habituation factor. Tests of practice effects, i.e., differences between Conditions I and V, do not show significant results (Table 2, Line 7). Tests of abreaction or desensitization cannot be made separate from those of the experimental hypotheses.

The second discrepancy is that the expected generalization of disturbance to postcritical and neutral stimulus words did not materialize to any significant extent. The qualitative findings of Luria and of Huston, Shakow, and Erickson (13, 15) suggest such generalization, while the statistical findings of Gardner (11) do not. Generalization may depend on several factors, two of which should be mentioned here:

(1) The time interval between a verbal response and the succeeding verbal stimulus (in this study, approximately three seconds were allowed to elapse to permit dissipation of disturbance in the appropriate stimulus-response sequence).

(2) The remoteness of postcritical and neutral words from critical subject matter (in this experiment, rather unusual care was taken, in selecting neutral words, to avoid critical implications).

Summary

Based on the Freudian concept of repression, an experiment was designed to test the following specific hypotheses with respect to anxiety behavior:

1. Repression serves to protect the individual from anxiety related to the repressed impulse.

2. The less successful the repression, the greater is the anxiety experienced in relation to conflict between the repressed and the ego demands.

3. Complete failure of repression results in maximum anxiety, a condition which persists until a new repression is instituted or another defense becomes operative.

4. Complete relief from both repression and conflict results in cessation of anxiety.

Through hypnotic induction and control of conflict and degree of awareness, five experimental conditions were produced: (a) preconflict control; (b) conflict with posthypnotic amnesia for the situation; (c) conflict with partial posthypnotic amnesia; (d) conflict with full awareness; and (e) postconflict control. Eight measures of response to a word-association test administered by the Luria method were obtained for six Ss. Each S was tested in the waking state under the five experimental conditions.

For the Ss as a group it was demonstrated that (a) there was a conflict; (b) there was a progressive increase in degree of awareness; and (c) most of the measures of behavior reflected emotional disturbance with some validity.

Results were as predicted except in two respects:

(1) There was not the anticipated maximum disturbance when Ss were made fully aware of the conflict. It is suggested that (a) with failure of repression certain defenses quickly operate to diminish anxiety, or (b) the hypothesis requires reformulation at this point.

(2) Predicted generalization of disturbance to neutral stimulus material did not occur, although there was generalization to an increasing number of response measures. It appears that the testing procedure allowed most disturbances to dissipate in the stimulus-response sequence in which they began.

References

1. BARNACLE, C. H., EBAUGH, P. G., & LEMERE, F. Association motor investigation of the psychoneuroses. *Amer. J. Psychiat.*, 1935, **91**, 925–937.

2. BOBBITT, RUTH A. A new apparatus for the Luria experiment. *J. exp. Psychol.*, 1940, **27**, 578–582.

3. ———. An experimental investigation of certain aspects of the repression hypothesis. Unpublished doctoral dissertation, State Univer. of Iowa Library, 1947.

4. BURTT, H. E. Motor concomitants of the association reaction. *J. exp. Psychol.*, 1936, **19**, 51–63.

5. CROSLAND, H. R. The psychological methods of word-association and reaction-time as tests of deception. *Pub. Univer. Oregon, Psychol. Series I*, 1929, **1**, 104.

6. ERICKSON, M. H. The method employed to formulate a complex story for the induction of an experimental neurosis in a hypnotic subject. *J. gen. Psychol.*, 1944, **31**, 67–84.

7. FREUD, S. Repression. *Collected Papers*, 1915, **4**, 84–97.

8. ———. Early papers and history of psychoanalytical movement. *Collected Papers*, 1924, **1**, 379.

9. ———. *New introductory lectures in psychoanalysis.* New York: W. W. Norton, 1933.

10. ———. *The problem of anxiety.* New York: Psychoanalytic Quarterly Press & W. W. Norton, 1936.

11. GARDNER, J. W. An experimental study of the Luria technique for detecting mental conflicts. *J. exp. Psychol.*, 1937, **20**, 495–506.

12. HOUTCHENS, H. M. A study of mental conflict in delinquent and nondelinquent boys. Master's thesis, Univer. of Iowa, 1935. (Abridged in *J. Juv. Res.*, 1935, **19**, 180–192.)

13. HUSTON, P. E., SHAKOW, D., & ERICKSON, M. H. A study of hypnotically induced complexes by means of the Luria technique. *J. gen. Psychol.*, 1934, **11**, 65–97.

14. LINDQUIST, E. F. *Statistical analysis in educational research.* Boston: Houghton Mifflin, 1940.

15. LURIA, A. *The nature of human conflicts.* (Trans. by W. Horsley Gantt.) New York: Liveright, 1932.

16. MERRILL, R. An experimental study of repression. Unpublished doctoral dissertation, Univer. of Washington Library, 1953.

17. MILLER, N. E., & DOLLARD, J. *Personality and psychotherapy.* New York: McGraw-Hill, 1950.

18. MORGAN, M. I., & OJEMANN, R. H. A study of the Luria method. *J. appl. Psychol.,* 1942, **26,** 168–179.

19. OLSON, D. M., & JONES, V. An objective measure of emotionally toned attitudes. *J. genet. Psychol.,* 1931, **39,** 174–196.

20. REYMERT, M. L., & SPEER, G. S. Does the Luria technique measure emotion or merely bodily tension? *Character & Pers.,* 1939, **7,** 192–200.

21. ROSENZWEIG, S. Investigation of repression as an instance of experimental idiodynamics. *Psychol. Rev.,* 1952, **59,** 339–345.

22. SEARS, R. R. Functional abnormalities of memory with special reference to amnesia. *Psychol. Bull.,* 1936, **33,** 229–274.

23. ZELLER, A. F. An experimental analogue of repression. I. Historical summary. *Psychol. Bull.,* 1950, **47,** 39–51.

24. ———. An experimental analogue of repression. II. The effect of individual failure and success on memory measured by relearning. *J. exp. Psychol.,* 1950, **40,** 411–422.

25. ———. An experimental analogue of repression. III. Effect of induced failure and success on memory measured by recall. *J. exp. Psychol.,* 1951, **42,** 32–38.

A COMPARISON OF "DREAMERS" AND "NONDREAMERS": EYE MOVEMENTS, ELECTROENCEPHALOGRAMS, AND THE RECALL OF DREAMS

Donald R. Goodenough, Arthur Shapiro, Melvin Holden, and
Leonard Steinschriber

The experimental study of dream phenomena has been seriously handicapped by the lack of effective methods for determining when a sleeping person is dreaming. Recently, however, on the basis of an extensive series of experiments (Aserinsky & Kleitman: 1953, 1955; Dement, 1955; Dement & Kleitman: 1955, 1957a, 1957b), Dement and Kleitman (1957b) concluded that this difficulty can be overcome by studying eye movements and brain waves during the course of sleep.

Reprinted with permission of the American Psychological Association and the authors from *The Journal of Abnormal and Social Psychology,* Vol. 59, 1959.

The major findings of these studies were as follows:

(1) There are occasions during sleep when the usual slow drift of the eyes is replaced by rapid conjugate eye movements grossly indistinguishable from the type of eye movements a subject would have, for example, while awake and watching a play.

(2) These eye movements occur during light sleep as defined by electroencephalographic criteria (B or A- stages [Simon & Emmons, 1956]).

(3) Periods of light sleep during which eye movements occur ranged from 3 to 50 min. in duration and tended to occur periodically throughout the course of natural sleep at intervals of 70 to 104 min.

(4) In about 80% of experimental

awakenings from eye movement periods, *S*s reported that they had been dreaming, whereas such reports occurred in only about 7% of awakenings at other times. Furthermore, all *S*s studied were found to have eye movement periods and were able to report the occurrence of dreams following most of the eye movement awakenings.

(5) The duration of an eye movement period preceding an experimental awakening was consistent with subjective estimates of the duration of the dream.

(6) The predominant direction of eye movements (i.e. vertical or horizontal) was related to the direction of movement in the visual imagery of the dream as recalled by the *S*.

These findings are consistent with the proposition that dreams occur during eye movement periods.

If this hypothesis is correct, Dement and Kleitman have discovered a powerful tool for the study of dreams, dreamers, and the process of dreaming. The difference between people who claim that they dream frequently and people who claim that they rarely or never dream is one of the many problems for which this tool provides a method of study.

On the basis of clinical material, observations of sleep talkers, and early studies of the recall of dreams following experimental awakenings (Ramsey, 1953), it has long been clear that many more dreams occur than are usually recalled the morning after. It often has been assumed that the difference between dreamers and nondreamers can be attributed to differences in the recall of dreams rather than to differences in frequency of dream occurrence. This study was designed to check on these hypotheses using the eye movement criteria developed by Dement and Kleitman. More specifically, habitual "dreamers" were compared with habitual "nondreamers" with respect to several char-

acteristics of the eye movement periods as well as the ability to recall dreams following eye movement awakenings and awakenings from periods of ocular quiescence. The study also provides an opportunity to repeat, in an independent laboratory, some of the observations of Dement and Kleitman, on types of *S*s who should offer the most stringent test of the usefulness of the eye movement criteria.

Each of the 60 male college students, who were willing to participate in these studies as paid volunteers, filled out a questionnaire indicating how often they usually recalled dreams. From this number, eight *S*s who stated that they recalled dreams almost every night (dreamers) and eight *S*s who stated that they recalled dreams less than once a month (nondreamers) were selected for the laboratory study.

Each of the 16 *S*s slept for three nights in the laboratory (not necessarily consecutively). Each *S* was scheduled to report to the laboratory one hour before his usual bedtime and was awakened for the last time in the morning at his usual hour for rising. The *S* was prepared and instructed during the hour before bedtime. He was told that he would be awakened by a bell; that he could turn off the bell by lifting a bedside phone from its cradle; and that he should report immediately whether or not he had been dreaming and the detailed content of any dream recalled. After practice in the procedure, the *S* was allowed to retire. Electro-oculograms and monopolar frontal, parietal and occipital EEGs were continuously recorded from the time the *S* first went to bed until the final awakening.

The procedures used by Kleitman and Dement (1955, 1957a, 1957b) were followed with few exceptions. Small silver cup electrodes filled with Cambridge Electrode Jelly were attached to the skin by applying U.S.P. collodion and drying with an air jet. Standard frontal, parietal and occipital EEG placements were used. In addition, electrodes were attached to each ear lobe to provide a neutral terminal, to the vertex, and to a point one cm. lateral to the outer canthus of each eye. The individual lead wires were tied together several inches above the vertex and then passed as a single cable to an electrode plug board lying on the floor alongside the bed. A shielded cable led from the plug board through the wall of the bedroom to an eight channel Grass EEG in an adjacent room in which the experimental equipment and *E* were stationed. The *S* was grounded through the shield of the cable and the vertex electrode. Although the bedroom was not soundproof, an attempt was made to keep extraneous noise to a minimum. This attempt was only partially successful.

A recording of a loud bell played through a speaker in the bedroom was used as an awakening stimulus. When the *S* awoke, he answered the bedside phone, automatically terminated the stimulus, and gave his report. *S* could be questioned through an intercom system if the report was not sufficiently clear, but *E* tried not to communicate with *S* after an experimental awakening until the spontaneous report had been completed. All conversation was tape recorded.

An attempt was made to awaken each *S* during at least two eye movement periods and two periods of ocular quiescence per night in counterbalanced order. Two additional awakenings were permitted at the discretion of *E*. However, it was not possible to follow these procedures at all times. In general, the second eye movement period of each night was not interrupted by an experimental awakening.

Nearly all eye movement periods were allowed to continue for at least 5 min., but not longer than 15 min., before an experimental awakening. Awakenings from periods of ocular quiescence always occurred at least 4 min. after the end of any preceding eye movement period.

Criteria for identifying eye movements were identical to those used by Dement and Kleitman. For the purposes of this study, the duration of an eye movement period was measured from the beginning of the first eye movement of the period of light sleep to the last eye movement of the period or to the experimental awakening.

EEG records were inspected and the stage of sleep predominating in each 10-minute period was charted. The times at which each eye movement period began and ended were also recorded. A separate index card was made out for each awakening and for each uninterrupted eye movement period, and the relevant data from the EEG record were noted on one side of the card. All data were rechecked twice and incomplete or incorrectly conducted awakenings were discarded before listening to the tape recordings of the *S*'s report.

The tape recordings were transcribed on the back of the appropriate cards. A "blind" classification of the dream reports was then conducted in terms of the following categories:

D—A dream was recalled in some detail.

ND—The *S* believed that he was definitely dreaming, but could recall no content.

A—The *S* believed that he was awake.

N—The *S* believed that he had been asleep but not dreaming.

The final classification of each report

was determined by agreement between two judges. For purposes of subsequent analyses, reports in the D category were taken as evidence of the recall of a dream. Reports classified as ND, A, or N were counted as no dream recall.

The percentage of the awakenings which led to the report of a dream was computed for each S under the various conditions of the experiment. All means (and tests of significance) to be reported are based on the percentage per S as a

Results

DISTRIBUTION OF EYE MOVEMENT PERIODS

The eye movement periods were distributed throughout the night for both dreamers and nondreamers in the same general pattern described by Dement and Kleitman. Every S had at least one eye movement period every night with one exception. (One S slept only one-

TABLE 1. RECALL OF DREAMS AS A FUNCTION OF TYPE OF DREAMER AND OCULAR ACTIVITY PRECEDING AWAKENING

Type of Awakening	Dreamers			Nondreamers		
	Total N of Awak- enings	N of Awaken- ings Lead- ing to Re- port of a Dream	% Recall of Dreams (Mean per S)	Total N of Awak- enings	N of Awaken- ings Lead- ing to Re- port of a Dream	% Recall of Dreams (Mean per S)
From Eye Move- ment Periods	49	44	93	42	19	46
From Periods of Ocular Quiescence	56	27	53	43	7	17

descriptive unit. For example, an S might recall a dream following 9 out of 10 eye movement awakenings. The S's "score" under these conditions would then be 90%. The mean percentage of recall would be the mean of these scores for all Ss in the group.[1]

---

[1] Dement and Kleitman report their data in terms of percentages, summing over all Ss before dividing the total N of awakenings leading to the report of a dream by the total N of awakenings. Since the total N of awakenings varies from S to S in these studies the two methods need not lead to similar figures, but in our data they are almost identical.

half hour during one of his nights and had no eye movement period that night.) Furthermore, dreamer and non-dreamer groups did not differ significantly in the mean number of eye movement periods per hour asleep (Mann-Whitney U test[2]). The mean number was .6 per hour for both groups, or one eye movement period every 100 min. of time asleep. (Time asleep was measured from the first appearance of sleep spindles in the EEG record to the final awakening.)

---

[2] Reference to the tests of significance used in this study can be found in Siegel (1956).

DREAM RECALL

Every *S*, even if he claimed that he had never dreamt before, was able to report at least one dream during the course of the study. In most cases these reports were given in great detail.

For the entire group of 16 *S*s there were a total of 211 awakenings. However, 21 of these were discarded because of accidents in procedure. Of the remaining 190 awakenings, a mean of 70% of those during eye movement periods and 35% of those during ocular quiescence led to the report of a dream

dreamers had a surprisingly high percentage of recall following awakenings from periods of ocular quiescence, but this fact does not necessarily mean that the eye movement criteria are invalid (see discussion).

In order to check on the possibility that these between-group differences might be a function of differences in time asleep, data on the duration of the sleep periods were examined. Table 2 shows that the dreamers tended to sleep longer per night than nondreamers. This difference was due to the fact that the dreamers usually fell asleep earlier.

TABLE 2. DURATION OF THE SLEEP PERIOD AND RELATED DATA

Subjects	Duration of Sleep Period Mean/Night		Time to Bed Mean	Time First Asleep Mean
	Hrs.	Min.	Hr. A.M	Hr. A.M.
Dreamers	6	:08	12:53	1:08
Nondreamers	5	:10	1:26	2:02
Difference		:58 *	:33 **	:54 *

* $P < .05$ (Mann-Whitney *U* Test).
** Not statistically significant.

(Table 1). This difference was highly significant ($P < .001$, one-tail sign test).

The difference between awakenings from eye movement periods and awakenings from periods of ocular quiescence was large and significant within the dreamer group ($P < .01$, one-tail sign test) and the nondreamer group as well ($P < .05$, one-tail sign test). All but one *S*, a nondreamer, had a greater percentage of recall following awakenings from eye movement periods.

The dreamers had a significantly higher percentage of dream recall for both types of awakenings than the nondreamers ($P < .02$ and .05, respectively, Mann-Whitney *U* test) (Table 1). The

In order to determine whether the between-group differences in time asleep might account for the differences in dream recall, all awakenings during the last 58 min. of sleep each night were discarded for the *S*s of the dreamer group and the data reanalyzed. This operation equalized the mean duration of the sleep period for the two groups. In all, 29 awakenings were affected, 9 eye movement awakenings and 20 awakenings from periods of ocular quiescence. The mean percentage of eye movement awakenings leading to the recall of a dream was not affected by the correction. The significance of the between-group differences was unchanged. However, for the awakenings from periods of ocular quiescence the mean percentage leading to the recall of a dream fell from 53 to 34. The difference between dreamers and nondreamers in dream recall following such awakenings was no longer significant.

The sharp drop in percentage of recall by dreamers following awakenings from periods of ocular quiescence, obtained by discarding data from the last 58 min. of each night of sleep, suggested that dream recall might be less likely in the early hours of sleep. Awakenings during the first four hours of sleep were compared with awakenings after the end of the fourth hour to test this hypothesis. This division of the sleep period resulted in an approximately equal number of awakenings in the two time intervals.

For awakenings from periods of ocular quiescence in the nondreamer group and eye movement awakenings in the dreamer group, too few responses differed from the prevailing trend to warrant statistical analysis. In the dreamer group, where a mean of 53% of the awakenings from periods of ocular quiescence led to the recall of a dream, an analysis was carried out. Six awakenings which followed an eye movement period by less than 10 min. were not included in this analysis since previous work had suggested that dream recall is frequent following such awakenings (Dement & Kleitman, 1957b). For periods of ocular quiescence, a mean of 17% of the awakenings in the early hours of sleep and 67% of the awakenings in the latter part of the sleep period led to dream recall ($P < .05$, two-tail sign test). A similar analysis was carried out for the eye movement awakenings of nondreamers where 46% led to the recall of a dream. No significant difference in dream recall between early and late sleep periods was found.

Dream recall following eye movement awakenings does not seem to be a function of the time at which the awakening occurs, but dream recall following awakenings from periods of ocular quiescence is more frequent in the last half of the sleep period.

EEG PATTERNS DURING EYE MOVEMENT PERIODS

Eye movement periods were classified according to the prevailing EEG pattern during which they occurred. The sleep stages described by Simon and Emmons (1956) were used for this classification.

No rapid conjugate eye movements were observed during EEG's representing deep stages of sleep (C, D, E), although a few low-voltage sleep spindles occurred in some of the eye movement periods. Eye movement periods did occur during the light sleep EEGs which could be classified as A- or B. In order to describe more precisely the EEG records during light sleep, the following procedure was adopted: (*a*) Each 20-sec. interval during an eye movement period was inspected; (*b*) The interval was given an A- classification if any alpha bursts were seen; (*c*) The prevailing sleep stage was taken as A- if more than 50% of these intervals were placed in the A- class. In almost all of the eye movement periods more than 75% or less than 25% of the 20-sec. intervals contained A- bursts. The method of classification thus seemed to reveal a major division in the data.

There seemed to be two distinct types of people among the Ss with regard to the stage of sleep during which eye movements occurred. For some Ss all or most of their eye movements occurred during the A- stage. For other Ss eye movements rarely or never occurred during the A- stage. Six of the nondreamers, but only one of the dreamers, belonged to the A- type. The difference between dreamers and nondreamers was significant ($P < .05$, Fisher's exact probability test).*

Discussion

Our results clearly confirm the basic findings of Dement and Kleitman that rapid conjugate eye movements occur during periods of electroencephalographically light sleep and that an S who is awakened during such a period is likely to recall a dream. However, the data do not conclusively establish that dreams are experienced during and only during eye movement periods.

THE EYE MOVEMENT DEFINITION OF DREAMING

The data are consistent with the proposition that a dream is experienced during every eye movement period. It is certainly easier to account for the occurrence of rapid conjugate eye movements behind the closed lids of a sleeping person if it is assumed that a dream is being experienced. Under this assumption the observed differences in dream recall between eye movement awakenings and awakenings from periods of ocular quiescence would also be expected on the basis of well-known principles of forgetting (i.e., the shorter the time interval between an experience and a test of recall, the greater the likelihood of recall).

The finding that there are some eye movement awakenings which do not lead

---

* Dr. Goodenough has asked that a note be made of a failure to replicate the difference between groups in alpha activity during the eye-movement periods. All other findings have been replicated. [Ed.]

to the recall of a dream is important, but not necessarily inconsistent with the assumption. In fact, some of the most interesting implications of the eye movement definition of dreaming have to do with the forgetting of dreams. In order to identify instances of dream forgetting, it is necessary to know when a dream has taken place. The eye movement criteria provide a working definition of dreaming with which the study of forgetting may be approached.

The proposition that dreams occur only during eye movement periods is more difficult to justify on the basis of the available evidence.

Periods of light sleep without conjugate eye movements sometimes occur, and Dement and Kleitman (1957a) have suggested that dreams are experienced during these periods. In this study there were too few awakenings from light sleep without eye movements to test their suggestion.

The large number of dream reports given after awakenings from deep sleep poses a more serious problem. It is possible to account for these reports, however, without abandoning the assumption that dreams occur only during eye movement periods or light sleep.

It is suggested that dream reports following awakenings from periods of ocular quiescence may refer to dreams which occurred earlier in the night during eye movement periods, or even to the recall of thoughts which the S might have had while falling asleep. This interpretation is based on two reasonable assumptions:

(1) Dement and Kleitman (1957b) found that dreams are often recalled following awakenings which occur less than eight minutes after the end of an uninterrupted eye movement period. These reports presumably reflect recall of dreams

which occurred during the preceding eye movement period. It is assumed that there may be some recall of dreams over much longer periods of time, particularly for the "dreamers" of this study.

(2) If an S is awakened and recalls a dream, it is assumed that he may have difficulty determining whether the dream occurred just before the awakening or at an earlier time.

Such an interpretation seems reasonable on the basis of qualitative observations made in the course of this study. Several of the dream reports given after awakenings from periods of ocular quiescence were very similar in content to earlier reports by the same Ss on the same night following eye movement awakenings. In one case, the S spontaneously said that he wasn't sure whether he was repeating an earlier report or describing a dream that had just occurred.

The data on the percentage of awakenings from periods of ocular quiescence which led to the report of a dream are also consistent with this interpretation. Since awakenings late in the night are necessarily preceded by more dreaming than early awakenings, the finding that dream recall is more frequent in the late part of the sleep period is to be expected.

Under the assumption that the process of recall is impaired in deep sleep, it could be argued that dreams are occurring even though no dream is ever reported following an awakening from such deep sleep. If it is also assumed that eye movements are blocked in deep sleep, it seems possible to account for the findings of these studies. However, we believe that it will prove more fruitful to use the eye movement criteria as a working definition of the dreaming state. The use of this definition apparently leads to interesting and testable hypotheses.

THE FORGETTING OF DREAMS

If it is assumed that dreams are experienced during and only during eye movement periods (or light sleep) our data indicate that the difference between habitual dreamers and habitual nondreamers does not lie in the frequency of dreaming. The groups do differ in the ability to recall dreams even under the conditions of this experiment.[3]

It has often been suggested that massive repression plays an important role in the forgetting of dreams (Freud, 1956). Of course our data do not bear upon this hypothesis, but they suggest a method for future research. Since eye movement periods which lead to the recall of a dream can be distinguished from those which do not, it is possible to study the conditions under which forgetting occurs. It is also possible to study dream content among Ss who do not ordinarily recall their dreams. Such studies may provide a new and useful method for systematic experimental analysis of the mechanism of repression.

Our data suggest another hypothesis that might help to account for failure to report dreams under nonlaboratory conditions.

If a dream is defined as an experience that occurs during sleep, some Ss probably mislabel their experiences. One S (from a different study) said that he was *asleep* and *thinking* when awakened from an eye movement period. In other instances, Ss were not sure whether they had been asleep and dreaming or awake and thinking. Neither type of mislabel-

---

[3] This difference may be reduced through the use of different awakening techniques, however. In more recent studies we have obtained much higher percentage of recall from nondreamers by using improved sound conditioning and a louder awakening stimulus.

ling is very frequent under the conditions of this experiment, but the occurrence of any mislabelling raises some interesting questions.

During the instruction period one of the Ss who said that he never dreamt asked this question: "How will I know if I have had a dream or not?" Although we were somewhat surprised by it at the time, this seems like a reasonable question from a person who has never recalled a dream.

What cues does an S use to judge whether or not he has had a dream?

The popular concept of a dream certainly includes the notion that it is an experience which occurs during sleep. It might also include the following characteristics: (a) The dream is experienced as if something were happening to the dreamer as opposed to an imagined series of events; (b) It is not accompanied by the feeling of control over the content; (c) It is frequently bizarre or internally inconsistent.

The S who said that he was asleep and thinking, apparently felt that he had had an experience during sleep which was not bizarre or internally inconsistent and over which he felt some control, etc. In fact, a large number of the dream reports collected in this study were not bizarre or internally inconsistent, even though they were given in some detail. We doubt that they could be distinguished from reports of some of the hypnogogic reveries or waking fantasies of these Ss. However, most Ss would probably have said that they were dreaming if they had known (or believed) that they were asleep at the time, even if the "typical" content characteristics were not present.

Let us suppose that an S recalls an experience when he awakens in the morning under ordinary conditions. How does he decide whether he was asleep or awake at the time the experience occurred?

In the absence of any other, more decisive, cues, it seems likely that the content of the recalled experience may be used by an S to judge whether he was asleep and dreaming or awake and thinking at the time. For example, if an S recalls an experience that is bizarre or internally inconsistent he might decide, on this basis alone, that he was asleep and dreaming. The following verbatim reports are illustrative:

I am not sure whether I fell asleep. Oh, yes, I was at the beach. I was with my mother and father and a girl next door. She is a friend of the family, not too much a friend of mine. We were talking, and I couldn't sit next to her, so I was somewhat displeased, so I changed to another seat. I started talking to other girls and so did she. I can remember specific conversation. People came up and asked me why I was carrying my bag—clothing bag. I looked in a newspaper for a certain basketball score. Basketball is in the winter. I think I must have been asleep. I wouldn't have been thinking about this if I were awake, I don't imagine. I guess I was dreaming.

From the S who had asked how he could tell whether or not he was dreaming:

I don't know whether I was dreaming or not. I'm not sure whether I was asleep or not. I had a vision in mind of riding down a wide avenue—no story, but moving, as if sitting in an automobile and the various houses and buildings passing by—a vision. I may have thought that or dreamt it.

In the first illustration, the S apparently decided that he was asleep and dreaming on the basis of an internal inconsistency in the content. In the second illustration, no inconsistency appears in the report and the experience is not definitely identified as a dream.

The finding that eye movement periods tend to occur in association with A- EEGs for nondreamers, and B EEGs for dreamers is particularly interesting in the light of the mislabelling hypothesis. If this finding is confirmed by future research, it may clarify the basis for the failure to report dreams in some Ss.

According to the traditional view (Simon & Emmons, 1956) an A- EEG represents a borderline state between drowsiness and sleep. Following this view it might be argued that for many of our eye movement awakenings the S was not actually asleep. Kleitman (1957) discounts this argument as follows:

Just as a "sleep" EEG is without diagnostic significance in the presence of behavioral wakefulness, . . . so is a "wakefulness" EEG, obtained during behavioral sleep. Such an EEG was invariably observed in our laboratory during dreaming, with the Ss unquestionably asleep (p. 357).

While our study was not designed to check on this question, systematically, our impressions are the same as Kleitman's. The errors in subjective judgment cited in the illustrations should not be taken as evidence against Kleitman's contention. These errors occurred with as large a relative frequency in deep sleep as in light sleep. In all, 17% of the awakenings led to the judgment, "I was awake."

An A- EEG record may reflect a lighter stage of sleep than a B EEG record, however. Furthermore, it seems reasonable to suppose that dreams which occur during a very light stage of sleep would not be as bizarre and would seem more like thought or fantasy to the S than would dreams which occur in a deeper stage of sleep. In this view the traditional distinction between the kind of thought processes that usually occur during the waking state and the kind that usually occur during dreams is expanded. Three stages, defined in terms of depth of sleep (or state of cortical functioning) and type of thought processes are proposed.

If the dreams that occur during an A- EEG are less bizarre, etc., and if such content characteristics are important determinants of recall or correct labelling under ordinary conditions, then it is not surprising to find some nondreamers who have most of their eye movement periods during A- EEGs.

There is another interpretation of this EEG difference that may have some merit.[4] Grey-Walter (1953) has identified individual differences in waking EEG records, related to differences in characteristic thought processes. In most adult Ss alpha waves can be observed in waking occipital tracings recorded under relaxed conditions with eyes closed. These waves are usually blocked for a period of time following the sudden presentation of a visual stimulus. The resulting EEG record is similar to (if not identical with) the record obtained during the B stage of sleep. However, in some Ss alpha blocking does not occur. For these Ss, the alpha waves persist despite a sudden visual stimulus. Grey-Walter believes that these Ss tend to think in symbolic terms with little visual imagery. Other Ss have little or no alpha under any conditions. These Ss are believed to use visual imagery extensively, with little recourse to symbolic thought. The majority of people, who show a

---

[4] We are indebted to W. Dement for calling our attention to this possibility.

waking alpha that can be blocked by a visual stimulus, presumably use visual imagery or symbolic thought as the situation requires.

Only one of our Ss had no waking alpha, but, unfortunately, studies of alpha blocking were not conducted. It may be that Ss who have their eye movement periods during the A- sleep stage also show a waking alpha that is resistant to blocking, and characteristically think in symbolic terms, whether awake or asleep. Such continuity between the sleeping and waking states seems reasonable enough on a priori grounds.

Although these hypotheses have been based in part on physiological concepts, personality characteristics of the dreamer may play a crucial role. It is assumed that dreams which occur during A-EEGs are accompanied by some feeling of control over the content. If these hypotheses are confirmed, it would be interesting to explore the possibility that A- dreams may occur in Ss who are overcontrolled more generally in their psychological functioning.

Summary

Habitual dreamers were compared with habitual nondreamers using Dement and Kleitman's "objective method for the study of dreaming." Two groups of Ss were studied, a group of dreamers who reported that they usually dreamt almost every night and a group of nondreamers who said that they dreamt less often than once a month. Continuous recordings of eye movement potentials and EEGs were taken on each S during three nights of natural sleep. Ss were awakened several times each night by the sound of a loud bell and were asked whether or not they had been dreaming.

Periods of rapid conjugate eye movements occurred at intervals throughout the night during light sleep (A- or B stages) for all Ss. Experimental awakenings from eye movement periods led to the recall of dreams more frequently than awakenings at other times. So-called "nondreamers" were less likely to recall a dream than dreamers, but every S studied, even Ss who said that they had never dreamt before, reported at least one dream during the study.

Eye movement periods occurred as frequently for nondreamers as for dreamers. However, there were significant differences between dreamers and nondreamers in the EEG patterns which occurred during eye movement periods.

These findings support the contention of Dement and Kleitman (1957b) that recordings of EEG and eye movement potentials may provide useful objective criteria for determining when a dream is occurring. They also suggest directions for future research on problems relating to the forgetting of dreams.

Since publication of this article, all findings have been replicated except for the difference between groups in alpha activity during the eye-movement periods [Ed.].

References

ASERINSKY, E., & KLEITMAN, N. Regularly occurring periods of eye motility, and concomitant phenomena, during sleep. *Science*, 1953, **118**, 273–274.

———. Two types of ocular motility occurring in sleep. *J. appl. Physiol.*, 1955, **8**, 1–10.

DEMENT, W. Dream recall and eye movements during sleep in schizophrenics and normals. *J. nerv. ment. Dis.*, 1955, **122**, 263–269.

DEMENT, W., & KLEITMAN, N. Incidence of eye motility during sleep in relation to varying EEG pattern. *Fed. Proc.*, 1955, **14**, 37.

DEMENT, W. & KLEITMAN, N. Cyclic variations in EEG during sleep and their relation to eye movements, body motility, and dreaming. *EEG clin. Neurophysiol.*, 1957, **9,** 673–690. (a)

———. The relation of eye movements during sleep to dream activity: An objective method for the study of dreaming. *J. exp. Psychol.*, 1957, **53,** 339–346. (b)

FREUD, S. *The interpretation of dreams.* New York: Basic Books, 1956.

GREY-WALTER, W. *The living brain.* New York: Norton, 1953.

KLEITMAN, N. Sleep, wakefulness, and consciousness. *Psychol. Bull.*, 1957, **54,** 354–359.

RAMSEY, G. Studies of dreaming. *Psychol. Bull.*, 1953, **50,** 432–455.

SIEGEL, S. *Nonparametric statistics for the behavioral sciences.* New York: McGraw-Hill, 1956.

SIMON, C. W., & EMMONS, W. H. EEG, consciousness, and sleep. *Science,* 1956, **124,** 1066–1069.

Studies of Displacement

A CASE STUDY IN A BEHAVIORAL ANALYSIS OF PSYCHOTHERAPY
Edward J. Murray

Psychotherapy is of considerable interest to many psychologists today. This is partly because psychotherapy is the only rational approach to the treatment of neuroses and psychoses. It is also because psychotherapy is a unique source of data about some of the most important and elusive processes of human behavior. Yet, there is much we need to learn about psychotherapy. It is not clear why only some patients improve. Current research using measures before and after therapy, or comparing therapy with no therapy, yields little useful information; such an approach establishes no relationship between what actually occurs during therapy and the outcome. Thus, there is no rationale for gradually improving tactics or understanding the changes in various kinds of patients. In spite of the general descriptions of therapy that are available, it is not clear just what happens between a therapist and his patient. To some extent this is due to the complexity and the number of the events in therapy. In addition, we have to contend with the subjectivity of the therapist's report. What is needed is an objective be-

Reprinted with permission of the American Psychological Association and the author from *The Journal of Abnormal and Social Psychology,* Vol. 49, 1954.

havioral description of psychotherapy. Such a description must be comprehensive enough to capture the important events and yet simple enough to clarify the complexity of the events. With an adequate description of the events in psychotherapy, studies on the prediction of therapeutic progress from psychological tests, as well as studies on the evaluation of therapy using outside criteria, will take on new meaning and exert more influence on therapeutic conduct. The purpose of this paper is to describe a first step which was taken in the direction of an adequate description of psychotherapy.

Many events occur during psychotherapy. Those which are readily observable may be grouped as physiological, gross behavioral, and verbal. All three groups have been studied (e.g., 3, 10) and should be studied further. However, verbal behavior seems to be most critical from many points of view. There have been studies on the grammatical and formal properties of verbal behavior in therapy (e.g., 2), which are interesting in many ways but do not seem to be related to the major theories of personality in any determinate way. The content or meaning functions of verbalization seem much more relevant. The general method for studying such material is called content analysis. The research on psychotherapy done by the Rogers group (10) uses content analysis. However, in content analysis the categories which one selects are determined by theory. The theory guiding the Rogerian content analysis appears to be a vague perceptual schema. The content analysis which we are developing is guided by two other points of view: psychoanalytic theory and learning theory. In this context the most relevant categories are those concerned with motivation and defense. Thus, we propose to study the content of verbal behavior in psychotherapy with respect to underlying motives and defenses. This study illustrates this approach with one psychotherapy patient.

A Case Study

The patient was seen for 17 hours in an outpatient clinic.[1] All hours except the thirteenth were phonographically recorded. The first hour was omitted because it consisted of history taking. The patient was referred by the medical clinic. His complaint was that "he has trouble getting to sleep at night—feels that if he falls asleep he may die. He is tremendously threatened but can't say what he is threatened by." At the time of the first interview the patient was described by the therapist as follows:

The patient is a well built, good looking young man of 24. His family was once well-to-do, he's a college graduate, and he's now working in a real estate firm. . . . His parents were divorced when he was eight after a protracted period of arguments which the patient remembers as painful to him. Apparently his mother was unfaithful and a good deal of the dispute was

about this. The patient also remembers being taunted about his mother's behavior by one of his companions. Before the divorce the entire family moved about and finally lived with the maternal grandmother. He was surrounded by dominating and pampering females. He now relates this to a "complex" of going from person to person for aid. After the divorce he lived with his aunt. His mother remarried, had a child, who is now nine, and moved in with the patient and his aunt, which is the present home situation. His mother was harsh to him and he developed a distaste for her. He wanted to be different from her and rejected her "emotional" kind of living in favor of a "logical and rational approach." He adjusted to school and social relations with boys very easily. He tended, though, to be a teacher's pet in grammar school. He did well in science and math in high school and started out in biology at college. Upon his return to college after the war he changed to the social sciences taking his degree in history. His relations with girls were extremely innocent until he went in the army. He masturbated during adolescence in spite of guilt and fear about it. The army's attitude about masturbation enabled him to overcome a good deal of this guilt. While in the army he went out with a college girl without ever having intercourse, avoiding the kind of girls with whom he might have had sex and avoiding one situation with this girl which might have led to sex. While overseas he did have some sexual relationships. Generally he seems very cooperative and well motivated.

Therapy was mainly supportive but included interpretations about the defensive nature of his physical complaints and the hostility which arose when he became dependent. A permissive attitude toward the expression of hostility was maintained.

After a considerable period of trial and error, two main categories were selected for content analysis: *hostility* and

[1] The author wishes to thank Dr. Larry Hemmendinger of the Veterans Administration Regional Office, Bridgeport, Connecticut, for providing this case material.

defense statements. The hostility category was divided into six subcategories of hostility: (*a*) mother, (*b*) aunt, (*c*) other people, (*d*) general situations and groups, (*e*) the therapist, and (*f*) a vague "at home" (referring to one or more persons in his home). The defense category was composed of: (*a*) intellectual defensive statements which included the patient's views on philosophy, science, current events, etc., and (*b*) complaints about a wide variety of physical symptoms and discomforts. Everything else was considered irrelevant.

The unit scored was called a statement. This was either a simple sentence or the meaning phrases of a more complicated sentence. Each statement was judged as belonging to one of the several categories. The main measure was the number of statements in a given category for each hour. Relationships from hour

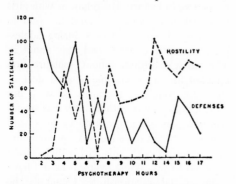

FIG. 1. Frequency of hostility and defense statements throughout therapy.

to hour between categories, and between categories and the behavior of the therapist, were determined.

The record of each hour was played very slowly, and each statement was judged either as belonging to one of the eight categories or as irrelevant. A reliability study with three other judges scoring the same hour showed that the categories were defined in a way which

was precise enough for teaching other people the method. The reliability was high when the eight categories were compared ($r = .86$, .89, and .91; $p < .01$ in all cases), and even higher when the irrelevant category was added ($r = .94$, .95, and .98; $p < .01$ in all cases).

Hostility and Defenses

Expressing hostility was a major problem for the patient. In the summary of the treatment, the therapist says, "his problems today seem centered around dependency and concomitant resentment." However, the therapist did feel that some progress was made in his ability to express his hostility as well as to see its relationship with his dependency. If the patient had trouble expressing hostility, then his hostility must have aroused anxiety. From the theory of conflict (1, 4) we would predict that if hostility is inhibited by anxiety, then, if anxiety is reduced by the permissive attitude of the therapist, the overt manifestations of hostility should increase while the overt manifestations of anxiety should decrease. In this study it is assumed that the hostility statements are the overt manifestation of hostility, and the defense statements the overt manifestation of anxiety. Figure I shows the hostility and defense statements throughout the course of psychotherapy. It can be seen that hostility increases and defenses decrease. Moreover, the hour-to-hour fluctuations show a true reciprocal relationship which strengthens the conflict analysis. The crisscrossing from Hour 4 to Hour 8 takes place in between the part of the therapy when defenses were high and the later part when the expression of hostility was high. The correlation is negative and highly reliable ($r = -.73$, $p < .01$).

However, the objection might be

raised that this is not a dynamic relationship between the two categories because the total number of statements is limited and when one category goes up the other must come down. This is not the case, because, with the exception of one hour, pooled hostility and defense statements never constituted more than 60 per cent of the total statements of one hour. An objection which can be made to this is that there may be nothing unique about the hostility-defense relationship if the residual or irrelevant statements also correlate with either hostility or defenses. This objection is ruled out by the fact that the residual is not correlated with hostility ($r = -.20$) or with defenses ($r = .19$). Another objection which might be raised is that, since the total number of statements varied from hour to hour because of differences in the patient's rate of speech, the length of pauses, and the number of therapist's remarks, the relationship is an artifact of the different totals. That this is not the case is shown in Fig. 2, where the percentage of the total number of hostility and defense statements is plotted.[2] In this form, hostility is still negatively and highly reliably correlated with defenses ($r = -.75$, $p < .01$). Hostility in percentage form correlates very highly with hostility in the frequency form in Fig. 1 ($r = .96$, $p < .01$). This is also true of defenses ($r = .94$, $p. < .01$).

We feel that this result strongly suggests that the patient's anxiety about expressing hostility was decreased as a result of the therapist's activity and/or inactivity. However, this may be limited only to the therapeutic situation; outside observations are needed to demonstrate

---

[2] The results presented in Figs. 3, 4, and 5 also show little change when plotted in percentage form.

any more general conclusion. The verbal changes shown here may or may not be indicative of fundamental emotional change. Here again, other evidence is needed. It is also conceivable that this hostility was a defense against a more anxiety-arousing sexual problem. But in any event, the lawfulness of the change is encouraging for the usefulness of the method.

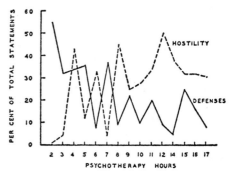

FIG. 2. Percentage of hostility and defense statements throughout therapy.

The Displacement of Hostility

An examination of the occurrence of statements in the subcategories of hostility from hour to hour reveals a sequence of persons toward whom hostility is directed rather than a global display on each hour. Figure 3 shows hostility to mother, aunt, and a combined "others" and "general." The sequence strongly suggests displacement. From a psychoanalytic point of view we would expect the mother to be the recipient of the most basic hostility. Mother, aunt, and others form a meaningful gradient of generalization. The patient's hostility to his mother gradually increased up to Hour 6. The therapist's summary of Hour 6 says, "he revealed that his mother had punished him for masturbating. She also forced food upon him and punished him for not eating promptly. He was 'too little to fight back' but did act in a spiteful way several times. He described other hostilities and retaliations with respect to his mother." The following hour showed little hostility. Then for several hours he expressed hostility to his aunt. This is viewed as primarily a displacement from the mother, although the aunt elicited her own share of hostility. Following this there was a dis-

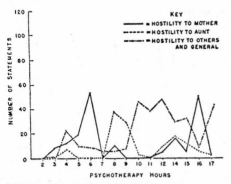

FIG. 3. Hostility statements referring to mother, aunt, and others—general through-out therapy.

placement to other people. We expected the sequence to reverse itself, i.e., after the hostility to others, hostility would be expressed first to the aunt again and finally to the mother again. However, a dramatic external event took place between Hours 15 and 16: his aunt was suddenly taken to the hospital for an emergency cancer operation. The therapist says that during Hour 16, "after considerable struggle he finally stated an ambivalency about the event." Furthermore, his hostility to his mother was increased because she had hinted that if the aunt died, *she* would take over the home.

It should be noted that the learning analysis of displacement (5), which has been confirmed in several animal experiments (6, 7, 9), does not predict sequences of hostility to various objects. Since it is desirable to make such pre-

dictions, we embarked on an extension of displacement theory (8) and an experimental investigation, in collaboration with Mr. Mitchell Berkun, of displacement with animals in a free-choice situation. Suffice it to say that if rats are both rewarded and punished at a given goal so as to establish a conflict, they will still approach that goal part way before displacing to another goal. This is an example of how precise data from psychotherapy can influence theories of behavior based on animal work.

The fact that hostility was directed toward people who were further and further displaced provides an alternative explanation for the general increase in hostility throughout therapy. If expressing hostility to these people aroused less anxiety than expressing hostility to his mother, we would expect more and more hostility as therapy progressed. Probably *both* displacement and a general reduction of anxiety because of the treatment operated to permit hostility to increase. The hostility expressed to the patient's mother in Hour 16 was much stronger and was concerned with much more recent events than was the hostility in Hour 6. Thus, there was a therapeutic effect. Indeed, expressing hostility to relatively unimportant people may be therapeutically valuable because it is less fearful. In learning theory terms, fear is extinguished in the displaced situation and these extinction effects are generalized back to the fear in the primary conflict situation. In the experiment mentioned above, the rats returned to the original goal after making unpunished goal responses in the displaced situation.

Defenses

The two defense categories seemed to operate as alternate members of a defensive armamentarium. In Fig. 4 it can be seen that the intellectual defense was high at the outset and decreased throughout the first part of therapy. This intellectual defense was never interpreted. The physical complaint defense increased

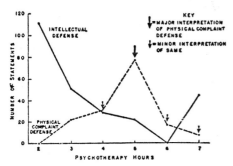

FIG. 4. The interaction of intellectual and physical complaint defenses and the effects of interpretations during the first portion of therapy.

as the intellectual defense decreased. After the major interpretation in Hour 5, the physical complaint defense dropped off sharply. In Hour 6 both defenses were low, and this hour proved to be especially fruitful, as was noted above. This expression of hostility also increased his anxiety, and the following hour was a dull one. Moreover, with the physical complaint defense interpreted, the non-interpreted intellectual defense increased in a compensatory way in this subsequent hour. Both defenses decreased during the rest of psychotherapy and show no distinguishing features as far as the number of responses is concerned. The interpretation of the physical complaints may have functioned as a punishment, or may have established insight. Further indices are needed to distinguish between the two possibilities.

There is also a possibility that the two defenses had different functions. The intellectual defense was more assertive and self-aggrandizing. It may have been a

way of telling the therapist that he was masculine or mature. On the other hand, the physical complaints had a pleading and ingratiating tone. This defense may have been motivated by feminine or dependent needs. However, both may be viewed as motivated by anxiety and both served the function of avoiding talk about conflict areas.

Fortunately, we examined another case which showed some striking similarities to this one. The general personality picture was the same as the present case. In addition, the two chief defenses were similar to the physical complaints and intellectualizations characterizing our present case. The second patient had physical complaints, although he had more insight into their psychogenesis. A category comprising physical complaints and more psychologically phrased feelings of tension, conflict, and blocking was defined. The intellectual defense

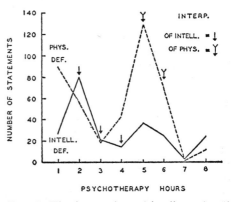

FIG. 5. The interaction of intellectual and physical complaint defenses and the effects of interpretations throughout the therapy of a second patient.

was quite similar to the first case. Figure 5 shows the course of physical, etc. defensive statements and intellectual defensive statements throughout the eight hours of therapy. This second patient began with physical complaints which decreased from Hour 1 to Hour 3 without interpretation. As the physical complaints decreased, the intellectual defense increased. This was interpreted in a punitive way in Hour 2 and, less severely, in Hours 3 and 4. Both defenses were low in Hours 3 and 4 and it was in these hours, both in our opinion and in the unsolicited opinion of the therapist, that the most important hostile material came out. In Hour 5 it was the uninterpreted defense—physical complaints—that showed the greatest increase. In this case, the therapist then proceeded to interpret the physical complaint defense on Hours 5 and 6. Both defenses were low for the last two hours.

This second case in a sense provides a natural experimental control for the first case. In the first case intellectual defenses were highest at first and decreased without interpretation; in the second case this was true of physical complaints. In the first case physical complaints supplanted intellectual defenses; in the second case intellectual defenses supplanted physical complaints. In the first case the physical complaints met with the disapproval of the therapist; in the second case this was true of intellectualizations. In both cases the punitively interpreted defenses decreased. In both cases important hostile material emerged when both physical complaints and intellectualizations were low. In both cases the expression of hostility was followed by an upswing in the uninterpreted defense. These results strengthen our belief that the physical complaints and intellectualizations are alternate defenses against anxiety. They also tend to confirm the general conflict analysis we have made. The increase in defenses after the expression of hostility may be related to the "negative therapeutic effect" (1). We may also tentatively formulate the hypothesis that,

with this kind of patient, uninterpreted (or unpunished) defenses have a greater probability of occurrence when anxiety is increased than interpreted (or punished) defenses. It is obvious that much more evidence is needed before making any definite conclusions.

Summary and Conclusions

In our present state of knowledge about psychotherapy, final conclusions should be avoided. Therefore, it is with trepidation that we approach the task of making a comprehensive summary statement about our illustrative case. This is true even though the therapy was brief and the changes were probably not fundamental. We might ask about the success of this case. The therapist does not sound optimistic in his summary: "The patient now has insight into his problems but can't extricate himself from them. Because of a general character weakness it is improbable that short term therapy will be of much more value." But our feeling is that it is important to understand what has happened during these interviews, whether or not the therapy was eminently successful. We feel that our objective description aids in this. Here is a tentative recapitulation of the case in terms of the data presented in this study.

The patient began treatment with a good deal of anxiety and subsequent defensiveness. His defensiveness decreased as a result of a combination of permissiveness about hostility and punitiveness about defenses on the part of the therapist. As this occurred he expressed strong hostility to his mother. This expression of hostility led to an increase in anxiety and defensiveness. The defense which increased was the one not previously punished by the therapist. Subsequently, hostility was displaced further and further away from his mother. Hostility to displaced objects was stronger because it aroused less anxiety. It is possible that because of the unpunished expression of hostility to the displaced objects, the patient was able later in therapy, when environmental factors precipitated it, to express hostility about his mother much more strongly, at least in the therapeutic situation.

Although this integration involves several assumptions, we feel it is strongly supported by the data. It will be noted that the statements made in the summary concern motivational and defensive shifts. This is what the categories were set up to measure. Other events, such as the establishment of insight, require other kinds of categories. Thus, we offer no evidence to support the therapist's opinion that the patient understood the relationship between his hostility and his dependency at the end of therapy.

This preliminary study has been presented to illustrate the kinds of results which can be obtained by studying psychotherapy carefully and quantitatively. We feel that it also demonstrates the applicability of principles derived from animal and human experimentation to complex human behavior. On the other hand, it is only data as clear as these that will stimulate experimental work and modify existing theories. We also hope that this study has indicated some of the difficulties involved in a behavioral analysis of psychotherapy. Cases do not miraculously become comparable when studied quantitatively. New cases are expected to present as many problems as they solve. Nor do we feel that all of the important events in psychotherapy can be described by this method. Indeed, many important things in this case have been ignored. But, as this method becomes more refined, and as equally objective measures are added to it, we feel that our understanding of psychotherapy, and human behavior in general, will be furthered.

References

1. DOLLARD, J., & MILLER, N. E. *Personality and psychotherapy.* New York: McGraw-Hill, 1950.

2. GRUMMON, D. L. An investigation into the use of grammatical and psychogrammatical categories of language for the study of personality and psychotherapy. Unpublished Ph.D. dissertation, Univer. of Chicago, 1950.

3. LASSWELL, H. D. Certain prognostic changes during trial (psychoanalytic) interviews. *Psychoanal. Rev.,* 1936, **23**, 241–247.

4. MILLER, N. E. Experimental studies of conflict. In J. McV. Hunt (Ed.), *Personality and the behavior disorders.* New York: Ronald, 1944. Pp. 431–465.

5. ———. Theory and experiment relating psychoanalytic displacement to stimulus response generalization. *J. abnorm. soc. Psychol.,* 1948, **43**, 155–178.

6. MILLER, N. E., & KRAELING, DORIS. Displacement: greater generalization of approach than avoidance in a generalized approach-avoidance conflict. *J. exp. Psychol.,* 1952, **43**, 217–221.

7. MILLER, N. E., & MURRAY, E. J. Displacement and conflict: learnable drive as a basis for the steeper gradient of avoidance than of approach. *J. exp. Psychol.,* 1952, **43**, 227–231.

8. MURRAY, E. J. Displacement in psychotherapy. Paper read at East. Psychol. Ass., Boston, 1953.

9. MURRAY, E. J., & MILLER, N. E. Displacement: steeper gradient of generalization of avoidance than of approach with age of habit controlled. *J. exp. Psychol.*, 1952, **43**, 222–226.

10. ROGERS, C. R. *Client-centered therapy.* Boston: Houghton Mifflin, 1951.

DISPLACEMENT AS A FUNCTION OF CONFLICT

Edward J. Murray and Mitchell M. Berkun

The concept of displacement has long played an important role in the theory of neurosis. As early as 1894, Freud (2) said that phobias and obsessions were substitutes for unbearable sexual ideas. He saw sex as a form of energy which could be *displaced* from one idea to another, like an electric charge. This displacement mechanism operates in dreams (3) and in slips of the tongue (4). Hostile impulses, desires for prestige, and other nonsexual drives may also be expressed through displacement.

The basic concept is that an impulse arouses too much anxiety to be admitted into consciousness or to be expressed directly. Therefore, a state of conflict exists. One way of resolving the conflict is to displace the impulse. This may be done in several ways: A man may unconsciously hate his father but dream of killing a policeman. Or, he may be conscious of hating his father but substitute quarreling with him for murdering him. Finally, he may be aware only of an ambition to be better than his father. Thus, displacement may take place from one stimulus to another, from one response to another, or from one drive to another. However, it is not clear from psychoanalytic theory

Reprinted by permission of the American Psychological Association and the authors from *The Journal of Abnormal and Social Psychology*, Vol. 51, 1955.

just why a displaced form of an impulse is less anxiety arousing. Why can the man dream of killing a policeman but not his father?

Recently Miller (6) has attempted to answer this question by relating displacement to the learning theory concept of generalization. If a response has been learned to one stimulus it may be elicited by similar stimuli. This is *generalization*. The more similar the generalized stimulus is to the original stimulus, the more

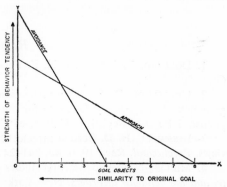

FIG. 1. Tendencies to approach and avoid displaced goals as a function of similarity to original goal.

likely it is to elicit the response. This is called the gradient of generalization. Miller assumes that a tendency to approach a goal object will be generalized to other goal objects. This tendency to approach may be based on hunger, thirst, sex, hostility, or any other drive. However, a tendency to avoid a goal object based on fear will also generalize to other goal objects. The key assumption is that the generalization gradient of avoidance is steeper than that of approach. In Fig. 1, we have the case where a tendency to avoid a particular goal object (e.g., goal 0) is greater than an approach tendency toward that goal. A state of conflict exists, which prevents a goal response at that point. However, since avoidance falls off more rapidly than does approach as the goal objects become less similar, there are some goal objects for which approach is greater than avoidance. Responses can occur at any of these goals. But it is at goal 4 that responding will occur with greatest frequency, since it is there that the net difference between approach and avoidance is greatest. Displacement takes place at an intermediate, rather than an extremely distant, point for this reason. Miller's theory of displacement has been tested and verified by a number of animal experiments (6, 8, 12).

A theory of conflict itself has also been proposed by Miller (5, 7). The assumptions about the approach and avoidance gradients in the conflict theory are identical with those of the displacement theory. However, while displacement refers to a dimension of similarity between goal objects, the conflict theory applies to the dimension of *nearness* to one particular goal object, as is shown in Fig. 2. Miller has applied the theory of displacement to the situation where a rat is afraid to eat at one goal but will eat at another (8). On the other hand, conflict theory has been applied to the situation where a rat is afraid to eat at a particular goal but still faces that goal (5). In this situation the rat will approach the goal along a line to the point where avoidance becomes greater than approach. In Fig. 2 this is the intersection point of the two lines.

The theory of displacement seems to have a great deal to offer in understanding complex human behavior. An attempt to apply the theory to events in psychotherapy has been made by Murray (10, 11), and to problems in social attitudes by Berkun (1). However, it soon became evident that the theory as it has been formulated does not adequately account for displacement phe-

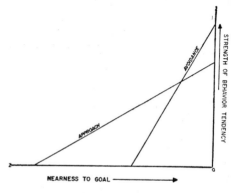

FIG. 2. Approach and avoidance tendencies with respect to a goal as a function of nearness to that goal.

nomena on the human level. For example, Murray (11) counted the number of hostile statements about a patient's mother, aunt, and other, relatively unimportant people in each of 15 recorded psychotherapy hours.

Figure 3 shows the percentage of statements in each of these categories for each hour of therapy. One might have expected from displacement theory that the patient would begin with the least important and least anxiety-arousing people and work toward the most important person: the mother. Actually, the reverse occurred. The patient expressed mild hostility about his mother, then hostility about his aunt, and then hostility about the other, relatively unimportant people. Later he returned to his mother and expressed much stronger hostility about her. The hostility was considered stronger

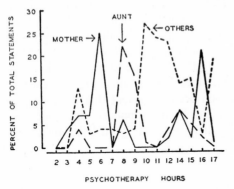

FIG. 3. The percentage of the total number of statements in each hour in the content categories of hostility-mother, hostility-aunt, and hostility-others made by the patient during the course of psychotherapy (from Murray [11]).

because it was about more recent events and was expressed in a louder, angrier voice.

What seems to have happened is this: the patient was afraid to express strong hostility about his mother. He gradually came *nearer* to expressing the strong hostility, but finally reached the point where anxiety was too great. This is the conflict point: hour 6. At this point, the conflict was resolved by displacement to statements about the aunt, who was similar, but less anxiety arousing. Eventually, the conflict point with respect to the aunt was reached, and again the conflict was resolved by displacement. Now the facts become understandable if we think in terms of two dimensions: (*a*) *nearness*, in terms of how overt or how strong the hostility becomes, and (*b*) the *similarity* between the person or goal object toward whom the hostility is expressed and the person for whom the hostility is intended.

Essentially, conflict and displacement are operating simultaneously.

The present theory was formulated to account for the simultaneous operation of conflict and displacement. This can be done by considering the three-dimensional model in Fig. 4. The vertical (Y) axis represents strength of a behavioral tendency. The X axis represents the dimension of similarity of goals to an original goal, at point 0. The Z axis represents nearness to the goal. Thus, the model may be viewed as a combination of Miller's displacement and conflict

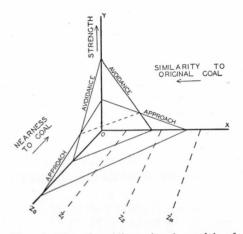

FIG. 4. The three-dimensional model of conflict and displacement. The original goal, where approach and avoidance tendencies were learned, is at point 0. The plane $0XY$, identical with Fig. 1, shows the decrement in approach and avoidance tendencies toward goals less and less similar to the original goal. The plane $0YZ$, identical with Fig. 2, shows decrements in approach and avoidance tendencies as a function of nearness to the goal. The vertical axis, $0Y$, represents the strength of the behavioral tendency to approach or avoid a goal.

theories. The approach tendency is now viewed as a surface determined by the approach line in plane $0XY$ and the approach line in plane $0YZ$. So, too, is there an avoidance surface. According to the assumptions of the theory, the avoidance surface is steeper and may intersect the approach surface. Thus, between the origin and the line of intersection of the two surfaces, avoidance is greater than approach. The intersection line, shown dotted, represents the locus of conflict points for all goals. In Fig. 4 the surfaces have been drawn as planes. This is only for the sake of visual simplicity. Actually a more detailed use of the model might require curved surfaces.

The properties of the model may become clearer if it is applied to a concrete experimental situation. Suppose the origin represents a goal at which an animal has been both rewarded with food and punished with electric shock. Let the line Z_0 represent the alley along which the rat had to run to get to the goal. Now let the lines Z_1, Z_2, and Z_3 represent other alleys which also lead to goals but which are less and less similar to the original alley and its goal. If the animal is now placed at Z_0, the model predicts that he will approach toward the primary goal until the point is reached where avoidance is greater than approach. He will oscillate around the point in the alley where the two surfaces intersect, and then will displace into alley Z_1. Now, the intersection point in alley Z_1 is closer to the goal (which is on the X axis) than it was in Z_0. Therefore, the animal will advance closer to the goal. Eventually, the conflict point in Z_1 will be reached, and the animal will displace into alley Z_2. The animal should go all the way down and make a goal response in Z_2, since in this alley (see figure) approach is always higher than avoidance. It must be noted that if the animal should displace from Z_1 to Z_0, he will enter a zone where the avoidance is higher. Therefore, he

should hastily retreat either back into Z_1 or back up alley Z_0 away from the goal.

As the animal approaches any of the goals, a certain amount of fear extinction will take place. Moreover, if he actually makes a response at one of the displaced goals, a great deal of fear extinction should occur, providing he receives no punishment. As fear is extinguished, the entire model will change. The avoidance surface will be *lowered,* which will result in the intersection line being pushed closer to the origin along both the nearness and similarity dimensions. The consequence of this is that, if the animal is again placed at Z_0, he will move closer to the goal in that alley than previously. Also, after displacement, he will be able to make a goal response at a point on the X axis much closer to the origin. He may make it in alley Z_1. Eventually, the extinction of fear will so reduce the avoidance surface that a goal response at the origin will be made! Thus, the responding in the displaced alleys will be therapeutic, in the sense of gradually eliminating the conflict in the original alley.

An animal experiment was designed to test some of the predictions generated by this model. The apparatus is shown in Fig. 5. For some animals, the wide, white alley represents Z_0; for others the narrow, black alley represents Z_0. Both approach and avoidance training were given in this "original" alley and the subsequent behavior of the rats observed.

Method

Apparatus. The white, gray, and black alleys shown in Fig. 5 were 7, 5, and 3 in. wide respectively. Each was 48 in. long and 6 in. high, with wooden sides, a galvanized iron floor, and a hardware cloth cover. The windows, 2½ in. square, were placed 0, 1, 2, and 3 ft. from the starting point. The two dividing walls, containing the windows, could be removed entirely or be replaced by windowless walls.

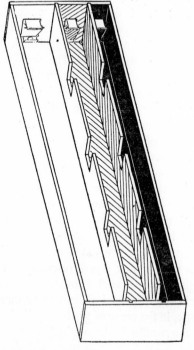

<figure>FIG. 5. The wide-white, medium-gray, and narrow-black alleys in which rats were trained and tested.</figure>

Each food cup was covered by a metal shield which had to be pushed back by the rat to expose the food. The shields were 2⅜, 1¾, and 1 in. wide and painted respectively white, gray, and black.

The rats could be shocked when they completed the circuit between the painted shield and the painted floor with a current of 480 volts and an amperage determined by the unmeasured resistance of the paint.

Subjects. Since a preliminary study showed that rats have a strong black

preference, the following selection procedure was used to cancel this out.

Eighteen male, albino rats of the Sprague-Dawley strain and 90 days old were used. Each rat was placed in the apparatus with both dividing walls removed for two 5-min. periods and the total time spent in white, gray, and black areas recorded. The point of entry was first the white alley, then the black alley for half the animals, and the reverse for the other half.

Seven animals were eliminated because of a strong black preference. Of the remaining 11 rats, eight showed a slight preference for the black. These eight rats were subsequently trained in the black alley so that they would have to displace *against* their preference. The remaining three rats showed a slight preference for white. These rats were subsequently trained in the white alley so that they too would have to displace *against* their preference. Thus, the slight initial color preference was set against the hypothesis.

Procedure. The animals were fed Purina Laboratory Chow Checkers for 1 hr. a day, beginning seven days before the training started, in order to establish a hunger rhythm. Feeding came 1 hr. after the usual daily run. Water was available at all times.

An *approach-training* trial consisted in putting the rat gently in the starting end of the alley and allowing him to run to the goal box, push back the shield, and get a pellet of food. The food reward was ½ gm. of a mash consisting of equal weights of ground Purina Laboratory Chow and water. Each animal was given two trials on day 1, four trials on days 2 to 10, and two warm-up trials on day 11, which was the test day. Thus, there were 40 approach-training trials altogether. Three or four minutes elapsed between successive training trials on the same day.

The apparatus contained the windowless walls on trials 1 to 10, to prevent wandering. The walls with windows were inserted during trials 11 to 38. It was noted that there was no tendency to go through the windows. The windowless walls were again inserted for trials 39 and 40, so that there would be no great change when shock trials (which required windowless walls) were started immediately afterward.

The *avoidance training* was all given on day 11, after the two food-reward warm-up trials. The windowless walls were used. The rats were placed at the starting end as usual, but when they ran down and made contact with the food cup they received a shock of 480 volts. They were removed immediately after being shocked, or after 2 min. if they received no shock. They could not get the food without being shocked. Successive shock trials (spaced about 10 min. apart) were given until the rats failed to go more than 18 in. down the alley within the time limit—in other words, three-eighths of the way to the goal.

The *testing* began immediately after the animals reached the above criterion of avoidance. The walls with the windows were now inserted. Each rat was placed at his regular starting position and left in the apparatus for 2 min. or until he made a "goal response" in any one of the three alleys. Food was present behind the shield only in the alley in which the original training was given. There was no shock on any goal box.

Getting the food in the original alley or moving the shield in the other alleys was considered a goal response. Brushing the shield with whiskers and touching the side or top of the food cup were not considered goal responses.

The testing trials were continued until the rats got the food in the original alley. Three trials were given on day 11, and seven trials every day thereafter until the animal reached the criterion.

 ## Results

General. The group results are presented below as they were evaluated statistically on a number of measures related to the main hypotheses. A rat's path was followed with a pencil on a diagram of the apparatus. As a general introduction, the trial-by-trial tracings of a single rat are presented in Fig. 6. Although this

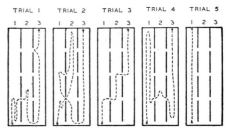

FIG. 6. A single rat's record of trial-by-trial behavior. Original training took place in alley 1; alleys 2 and 3 are the alleys of diminishing similarity. The goals are at the top of the diagram. Each trial was begun by placing the rat at the starting point, shown here by the open circle. The rat was removed when he made a response at a goal, shown by the solid circle.

rat is selected, he shows in a dramatic way what was true for the group statistically. In the first test trial he was put in the alley of original training, alley 1, where he oscillated in conflict. He then displaced to alley 2, the gray alley, advanced toward the goal and then retreated. He entered alley 3, the farthest alley, and went all the way down to make a full goal response. On trial 2 he nearly made a goal response in alley 2 but scampered back and finally made a goal response in alley 3 again. The rat's behavior on trial 3 is a picture-perfect exemplification of the three-dimensional model. The rat went part way down alley 1, displaced into alley 2 and went farther down, displaced into alley 3 and went all the way down to make a goal response. On trial 4 he almost made a goal response in alley 1, but ran back and went to alley 3. On trial 5, the rat went all the way down, made a goal response in alley 1, and got the food. The sequence illustrates the displacement out from the original conflictual alley, the decrease of avoidance in all alleys as a result of the extinction of fear, and the therapeutic result of responding in displaced situations, which enables the rat to resolve the conflict in the original alley.

+Displacement is a resolution of conflict. This hypothesis is confirmed by the fact that 11 of 11 animals left the original alley and entered the gray alley ($p < .001$, by a one-tailed sign test, used throughout). In addition, eight of the 11 animals left the gray alley and entered the farthest alley ($p < .06$). It will be remembered that during approach training the animals showed no tendency to leave the training alley.

The hypothesis is further confirmed by the fact that eight of the 11 animals made a goal response in either the gray or farthest alley before making a goal response in the original alley ($p < .06$). The three rats who made goal responses in the original alley after meeting the criterion were shocked once more when they did so. Subsequently, two of the three made goal responses in either the gray or farthest alleys before making another goal response in the original alley. Thus, with this additional shock, 10 of the 11 animals support the hypothesis ($p < .01$). The eleventh animal had such strong avoidance that he made no goal responses anywhere.

It was also found that generally those animals who did not make a goal response in the gray alley entered the farthest alley and made goal responses there. Only one of the eight rats who entered the farthest alley had previously made a goal response in the gray alley ($p < .04$).

Behavior is governed by intersecting approach and avoidance surfaces. One way in which this was shown was that the animals went farther down toward the goal in the gray alley than in the original alley. Furthermore, they went farther down in the farthest alley than in the gray alley. This is shown in Fig. 7 where

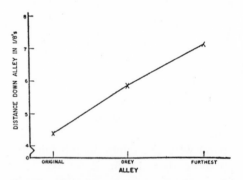

Fig. 7. Mean distance traversed in each alley.

the group average of each rat's average excursion down each alley over all test trials is plotted in terms of one-eighths of the way down. The differences were all highly reliable ($p < .01$).

The rats should also tend to use windows farther down toward the goal when leaving the gray and farthest alleys than when leaving the original alley. In order to show this, the windows were numbered 1, 2, 3, and 4, with 4 being closest to the goal. Each animal was given a score for his leaving the original alley which consisted of the sum of the products of the number of each window times the frequency of leaving via that window. This sum was then divided by the total frequency of exits from the original alley. Simliar scores were obtained for exits from the gray and farthest alleys. The results are shown in Fig. 8. The animals tended to use windows farther down toward the goal when leaving the gray alley than the original alley ($p <$ .05). Similarly they tended to use windows farther down in the farthest alley than the original alley although the difference only approached reliability ($p <$ .10). The difference between the gray and the farthest alleys was in the right direction but not reliable.

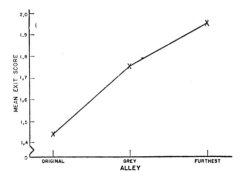

FIG. 8. Mean exit score (see text) for each alley.

The avoidance plane is lowered because of the extinction of fear. The most parsimonious way of showing this was to consider only the trials before any goal responses, displaced included, were made. This eliminated the objection that the results are overloaded because the rats were run until they made goal responses and that they had to show an increase in excursion as a function of the number of trials.

Trials in the first half of testing were compared with trials in the second half of testing for the eight animals who required more than one trial before making a goal response.

The measure used above in Fig. 7 was computed for the first and second halves of testing for each alley. The results are shown in Fig. 9. In the later testing trials the animals go farther down the alleys

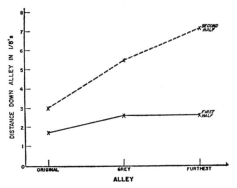

FIG. 9. Mean distance traversed in each alley as a function of displacement, comparing earlier testing trials with later testing trials.

than in the earlier trials but they go proportionally farther down the more displaced the alleys are. The over-all increase for all alleys is highly reliable ($p < .01$).

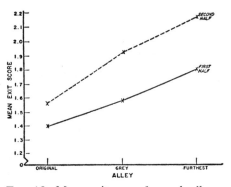

FIG. 10. Mean exit score for each alley as a function of displacement, comparing earlier testing trials with later testing trials.

Similarly, the animals tended to use windows farther down as the number of trials increased. This is shown in Fig. 10 as a somewhat reliable ($p < .05$) over-all increase.

Goal responding in displaced situations will have a therapeutic effect on the original conflict. This is shown simply by the fact that 10 of the 10 animals who made goal responses in the gray or farthest alleys eventually made goal responses in the alley of original training ($p < .001$). Two to 27 trials were required for this. This result, of course, does not evalute the effectiveness of this therapy relative to other methods such as forcing the animal down the training alley.

An Additional Study

In the main experiment the rats were not given food if they made a full goal response in a displaced alley. It is possible that food reward in the displaced alleys would hasten the extinction of fear and thereby the therapeutic effect. On the other hand, the animals might become fixated at the displaced goal and never resolve the original conflict.

In order to make a preliminary test of these hypotheses, 10 rats were retrained. They were given four approach training trials a day for three days. On the fourth day, two warm-up trials were added, making a total of 14 retraining trials. The rats were then retrained for avoidance as in the main experiment. Then half the animals were tested with food reward present in all three food cups, and the other half with food present only in the original alley as in the main experiment.

No differences were found between the two groups. The conditions seemed to have been fulfilled in that the animals in the first group found and ate the food in the displaced goals. However, extinction of fear was much faster during this second experiment for both groups. It may very likely be that a real difference was masked by the interaction with the first study.

Discussion

The experimental results obtained in this study are consistent with the three-dimensional model presented. However, it should be pointed out that the model predicted only the general trend of each rat's behavior. There were many turns and retreats by individual rats which remained inexplicable to the experimenters. Nonetheless, each rat's behavior was primarily in line with the model both graphically and statistically.

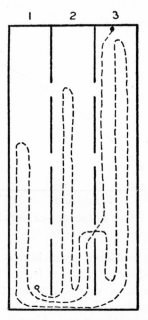

FIG. 11. A sample record, illustrating the general pattern of approaching the goal more closely in the displaced alleys than in the original alley. Each trial was begun by placing the rat at the starting point (shown here by the open circle), and ended by removing him when he made a response at the goal (solid circle).

Many of the rats retraced and doubled back on a single trial. An example is shown in Fig. 11. However, a lawful pattern can be discerned even in this seemingly chaotic result. The rat started out in the original alley, went part way down the gray alley, then farther down the last alley, returned to the original and went part way down, and finally went all the way down in the last alley. But it seems as if an invisible, impassable wall stretched diagonally across the alleys.

The present theory seems to have real value in understanding some of the events in psychotherapy. The model fits the psychotherapy data in Fig. 3 very nicely. Other psychotherapy data on this point are being gathered. There is no implication that this kind of behavior is present in every psychotherapy case or in every psychotherapy hour. However, displacement as a way of resolving conflict does occur, and is recognized by therapists in one way or another. An example of this is presented below in a verbatim excerpt from a psychotherapy hour. A mature therapist, not familiar with the present model, had been seeing the patient three times a week for about five months. This hour had begun with the patient discussing some jealousy he felt toward his wife about their son, as well as an attraction he himself felt toward his daughter. We start with the therapist challenging the patient's denial of the jealousy.

Therapist: And to have asked me—and to have said well you don't think you're jealous of Jimmy would certainly suggest that this were an important, very important item for you.

Patient: I don't feel that way. (pause) Maybe I have a feeling which I have subdued. I don't know because I just recalled that shortly after I got out of the Army, and we moved to the farm, our—there was —a—ah—somebody we knew whose— somebody that Mary knew—I don't know this person very well, a—probably met her, but I don't know her very well. They have —ah—son also about Jimmy's age, and

when the husband came back from the Army, he couldn't adjust to the child. Now, I dunno how it came about. But I know why the reason for it was. And the reason for it was that he was jealous of the child, and it took him a long time to get over it. And—ah—when I had the di—difficulty with Jimmy, in the sense that I felt that I wasn't behaving correctly in hi—in relation to him—that I didn't love him enough —ah—the thought occurred to me that maybe I was jealous. But—ah—it never registered. I mean it never left the impression I mean for thinking, well it is so, I am and I was jealous, or I am jealous of Jimmy. And therefore I—ah—you know to feel that way about it. My impression of my relation to Jimmy have always been that the reason that I don't—didn't—in— seem to feel the love for him that I felt for Ruth was that during the first sixteen months of his life, I was away. I didn't grow up with him. If there was any jealousy of Jimmy it was in relation to his in-laws. Now that is very possible. Although it's something which I also—suppressed. Ah— and the reason I say it's possible 'cause it sort of well-le—le—leaves a—ah—a sort of memory.

T: You're jealous of his in-laws?

P: Of his in-laws yeah. Because he was brought up with them. I still—until I came home—he was born in their hou—hospital and came to their house, and my wife lived with her—parents.

T: Ho—how do you mean you're jealous of his in-laws?

P: Well—ah—when I first came home, and for the first year or so or more than a year, ah—Jimmy was more prone to turn to his grandfather and grandmother than he was to me.

T: Mmmmhnn

P: And, although I understood it, there was a certain amount of—ah—well not bitterness, I wasn't bitter about it, but a certain amount of—a sort of resentment, a mild type of resentment.

T: You make this sound so—ah—

P: Well—

T: So—diluted.

P: Well it was diluted. I mean it wasn't something which I felt keenly enough to be angry at his grandparents, let's say, or with Jimmy himself. I mean I realized that he had grown up with them.

T: Mmmmhnn

P: And, therefore, it was more natural for him to—until he became completely o—overcame his—ah—strangeness to me, and it took quite a long time. Ah—then there was—there was a certain amount of resentment. It wasn't directed against the parents or (stuttering)—dec—was den—ac—actually directed against a certain circumstance which kept me away. And it was a resentment that which in a certain—ah—to a certain kind of effect in itself also in the feeling I had toward people who had remained behind and had made money.

T: Mmmhnn. Your in-laws made money?

P: Yes. My father-in-law made a lot of money from the war. Before the war he was not very much different than I'm—position I'm in today.

T: Mmmmhnn

P: Ah—but—ah—he was over-stocked when the war started. Terribly over-stocked. I know I was in the store, and he had junk. I mean which under normal conditions wouldn't have moved. But—ah—the war came and prices sky-rocketed. I know that there were items that he made seven, eight hundred percent on.

T: And yet, you were only mad at the circumstances?

P: Yes. I didn't blame him for making a profit, but he didn't set the price. I'm not mad at the circumstances only but at the —at the fact that such a situation existed.

T: Yeah. You notice what you've done here?

P: No.

T: You started out saying that you were jealous of your in-laws.

P: Mmmmhnn.

T: And you ended up saying that you —what you really didn't like were the circumstances.

P: I don't understand.

T: Well—

P: I mean I don't un—

T: You—ah—you said that when you say you're jealous of your in-laws, you're really saying that part of your reaction to your in-laws is one of anger.

P: Yeah.

T: That they had something that you didn't have.

P: Yes.

T: Yet, the longer you talked about this, the more you turned away from the idea that you were jealous, resentful to them, and you turned more and more and more to say that you really didn't resent them that you resented the circumstances that caused Jimmy to be raised by them, and that caused them to make money.

The basic resentment may very well have been aroused by the patient's wife. The patient displaced to the in-laws and then to "circumstances." The therapist interpreted the shift from in-laws to "circumstances" and was able to demonstrate to the patient his problem in expressing hostility. It is also interesting that the patient shifted the problem from being jealous because they had taken his role as father to being jealous of their financial success. This may also constitute a displacement to some extent. When speaking of displacement from the wife to the in-laws or from one kind of jealousy to another, we do not mean to imply that the in-law problem and the financial problem were manufactured merely to have an object for displacement. Minor problems are excellent for displacement since their truth can easily be established.

This case has illustrated simultaneous displacement along two dimensions. The dimensions might be called one of *frustrating agents* and one of *drives frustrated*. It is quite conceivable that people tend to displace simultaneously along several dimensions each of stimuli, responses, and drives. This may account for some of the bewildering complexity of free association in psychotherapy.

Summary

(1) Miller's theory of displacement was extended by integration with his conflict theory into a three-dimensional model.

(2) To test deductions from this model rats were first trained to get food at one end of an alley and then shocked while eating until they no longer approached the food cup. They then left this alley and entered other alleys differing slightly from the original alley. Here they went closer to the food end than in the original alley. Tracings of their movements followed a pattern predicted from the model.

(3) After making goal responses in the generalized alleys, the rats returned to eat in the original alley, showing a "therapeutic" effect.

(4) These findings were related to events in psychotherapy.

References

1. BERKUN, M. M. The conflict model and social attitudes. Paper read at East. Psychol. Ass., Boston, April, 1953.

2. FREUD, S. The defence neuropsychoses. In *Collected papers*. Vol. I. London: Hogarth, 1950. Pp. 59–75.

3. ———. *The interpretation of dreams*. New York: Macmillan, 1913.

4. ———. *On the psychopathology of everyday life*. New York: Macmillan, 1914.

5. MILLER, N. E. Experimental studies of conflict. In J. McV. Hunt (Ed.), *Personality and the behavior disorders*. Vol. I. New York: Ronald, 1944. Pp. 431–465.

6. ———. Theory and experiment relating psychoanalytic displacement to stimulus-response generalization. *J. abnorm. soc. Psychol.*, 1948, **43**, 155–178.

7. ———. Comments on theoretical models illustrated by the development of a theory of conflict behavior. *J. Pers.*, 1951, **20**, 82–100.

8. MILLER, N. E., & KRAELING, DORIS. Displacement: greater generalization of approach than avoidance in a generalized approach-avoidance conflict. *J. exp. Psychol.*, 1952, **43**, 217–221.

9. MILLER, N. E., & MURRAY, E. J. Displacement and conflict: learnable drive as a basis for the steeper gradient of avoidance than of approach. *J. exp. Psychol.*, 1952, **43**, 227–231.

10. MURRAY, E. J. Displacement phenomena in animal studies and psychotherapy. Paper read at East. Psychol. Ass., Boston, April, 1953.

11. ———. A case study in a behavioral analysis of psychotherapy. *J. abnorm. soc. Psychol.*, 1954, **49**, 305–310.

12. MURRAY, E. J., & MILLER, N. E. Displacement: steeper gradient of generalization of avoidance than of approach with age of habit controlled. *J. exp. Psychol.*, 1952, **43**, 222–226.

Studies of Identification

MASCULINITY, IDENTIFICATION, AND FATHER-SON
RELATIONSHIPS   Paul Mussen and Luther Distler

By identifying with his parents—i.e., endeavoring "to mold (his) own ego after the fashion of one that has been taken as a model" (S. Freud, 1949, p. 63)—the child begins to acquire his parents' personality characteristics, behavior, values, motivations, and attitudes. Two of the major consequents of the processes of identification are the development of the superego, or conscience, and the acquisition of behavior and personality characteristics appropriate to his own sex (sex-typing).

It has been hypothesized that both boys and girls form their first identification with a female, the mother, because she is likely to be the most gratifying and affectionate person with whom the child has contact (Mowrer, 1950; Sears, Maccoby, & Levin, 1957). Continued identification with the mother is appropriate for a girl, for she must acquire feminine personality characteristics and interests, but the boy "must shift to a masculine identification, sometime in his early years, if he is to develop normally masculine personality" (Sears et al., 1957, p. 373).

Reprinted by permission of the American Psychological Association and the authors from *The Journal of Abnormal and Social Psychology,* Vol. 59, 1959.

According to psychoanalytic theory, the boy's shift to identification with his father begins during the Oedipal phase of development and is motivated by fears and anxieties related to his hostility toward that parent. By identifying with his father, the boy's fears of counter-aggression are reduced and, at the same time, he vicariously obtains his mother's attention and affection. This is the defense mechanism that has been called "identification with the aggressor" (A. Freud, 1937) and "defensive identification" (Mowrer, 1950).

In contrast to this, the developmental hypothesis states that identification with the father depends on a positive, affectionate relationship between father and son (Mowrer, 1950; Payne & Mussen, 1956). If the father is an important source of nurturance, reward, and satisfaction, his responses and characteristics acquire secondary reward value and the boy imitates his father's behavior in order to "reproduce bits of the beloved and longed for parent" (Mowrer, 1950, p. 615).

Although the two hypothesized explanations of the dynamics underlying identification with the father seem to be vastly different from each other, there is some supportive evidence for each of them. The validity of the developmental identification hypothesis has been tested in a number of recent studies (Levin & Sears, 1956; Payne & Mussen, 1956; P. Sears, 1953; Sears et al., 1957; Sears, Pintler, & Sears, 1946). Thus in one study, five-year-old boys with warm and affectionate fathers (as judged by home interviews) showed stronger father identifications than did boys with "cold" fathers (P. Sears, 1953). It has also been reported that adolescent boys who perceive their fathers as nurturant (according to projective tests) are more likely to identify strongly with this parent than are boys who do not perceive their fathers as rewarding (Payne & Mussen, 1956). Moreover, certain characteristics of boys generally regarded as consequents of identification with the father—sex-typed behavior such as aggression (Levin & Sears, 1956), masculine interests and attitudes (Payne & Mussen, 1956), and highly developed conscience (Sears et al., 1957)—tend to be associated with favorable father-son relationships.

The hypothesis of defensive identification is complex one that is difficult to investigate empirically. However, there are extensive clinical observations indicating that, as this hypothesis would predict, many children attempt to reduce their anxieties by adopting the aggressive characteristics of individuals whom they perceive as threatening to them (A. Freud, 1937; Mowrer, 1950).

It is quite possible, of course, that the two hypothesized identification processes are not mutually exclusive but may function together to facilitate the boy's shift from a feminine to a masculine identification (Sears et al., 1957). This view is consistent with that of the role theorists who equate identification with the father with "father role playing" (Brim, 1958;

Cottrell, 1942; Parsons, 1955). These theorists maintain that identification, or role-playing, depends on the *power* of the identificand—a combination of his reward value *and* his threat or punishment potential. More specifically:

Given two . . . persons with whom one interacts and who differ in power over the actor (the identifier), i.e., differ in the degree to which they control rewards and punishments for the actor, one would predict that the actor would adopt many of the characteristics of the powerful as contrasted to the less powerful other person. This follows from the fact that it is more important to the actor to predict the behavior of the powerful figure, that he is motivated more strongly to take his role (i.e., to identify), that rewards and punishments are more impressive and the learning consequently better (Brim, 1958, p. 3).

The present paper reports the results of an investigation that attempted to evaluate the validity of the three hypothesized explanations of identification —developmental, defensive, and role-playing. It was assumed that, for young boys, appropriate sex-typing of interests is an indication of identification with the father, and that amount of identification can be estimated from the degree of sex-typing. The rewarding-nurturant and threatening-punitive qualities of the father were evaluated in terms of the child's *perceptions* of the father, rather than in terms of the father's actual behavior, the criterion used in some previous studies (Levin & Sears, 1956; P. Sears, 1953; Sears et al., 1957).

There were several central questions. How do boys who are strongly identified with their fathers, i.e., highly masculine in their interests, perceive their fathers: as basically nurturant and rewarding, as would be predicted from the developmental identification hypothesis, or as punitive and threatening, in accordance with the defensive identification hypothesis? Or are they viewed as powerful agents of both reward and punishment, as the role-playing hypothesis of identification maintains?

Method

Subjects. According to psychoanalytic theory and observational data, the late preschool period is a critical time in the boy's shift from feminine to masculine identification. For this reason, it seemed best to use kindergarten boys as Ss for this investigation.

Initially, 38 white five-year-old boys in two kindergarten classes of a predominantly middle-class public school [1] were given the IT Scale for Children (ITSC), a projective test of sex-role preference (Brown, 1956). The test consists of 36 picture cards depicting various objects, figures, and activities commonly associated with masculine or feminine roles. The child is given a card with a figure drawing unstructured as to sex and referred to as IT. He is then presented with groups of pictures of toys and with paired choices of activities, and asked to choose what IT would like.

"In using IT the assumption is made that the child will project himself or herself into the IT-figure on the basis of his own or her own sex-role preference, and will attribute to IT the child's own role preference." (Brown, 1956, p. 5). The possible range of scores on the test is from zero, an exclusively feminine score, to 84, an exclusively masculine score.

[1] The authors wish to express their appreciation to A. B. Campbell, Assistant Superintendent of Schools of Berkeley, C. B. Johnson, Principal of the Jefferson School, and C. B. Holmes and E. P. Light, kindergarten teachers, for their cooperation in this study.

The 10 boys with the highest scores (range 79–84, with a mean of 83) and the 10 boys with the lowest scores (range 30–63, with a mean of 53) were selected for further study.[2] The two groups were matched in socioeconomic status, each of them having the same number of upper-lower, lower-middle, and upper-middle class boys. Ten of the Ss, 5 high scorers and 5 low scorers, came from one kindergarten class, and 10 from the other.

Measures of parent-child relations. Between one and four weeks after he had taken the ITSC, each of the 20 boys was

[2] While the Ss were selected only on the basis of masculinity score on the ITSC, there is some suggestive evidence that those scoring low on the test were also somewhat more feminine in personality characteristics. Their teachers rated the Ss on 20 scales of personality characteristics, adapted, with slight modifications, from the Fels Child Behavior Scales. These characteristics were: aggression, affection, cheerfulness, competition, conscience, curiosity, emotional control, gross activity, friendliness, gregariousness, kindness, leadership, obedience, patience, physical apprehensiveness, quarrelsomeness, sensitivity, shyness, suggestibility, and tenacity (Richards & Simons, 1941).

The two groups of Ss differed significantly (at approximately the .02 level) on 4 of the 20 scales. The low scorers rated significantly higher than the highly masculine on: gross activity, friendliness, cheerfulness, and gregariousness. The latter three characteristics are, according to sociological analyses of sex role, specifically assigned to the expressive or feminine role (Brim, 1958; Cottrell, 1942; Parsons, 1955). The relatively high ratings of gross activity among those low in masculinity may also reflect group differences in these social characteristics. Significant positive correlations between the gross activity scale and the cheerfulness and gregariousness scales have been reported previously (Richards & Simons, 1941). Apparently, the child who is expressive, outgoing, and cheerful is quite likely to be seen as more active.

tested individually in a structured doll-play session. Early in the session, the child familiarized himself with three easily manipulated dolls, representing a mother, a father, and a boy doll, and some very simple toy furniture, which were on a low table in the testing room. S was told that these were to be used in a story-telling game in which the examiner would make up the first part of the story and S would complete it.

The examiner then presented, with appropriate manipulations of the dolls, a series of nine incomplete, family situation stories, and the child was asked to complete each one in play. The stories were structured in such a way that the child could depict either or both parents as nurturant and/or punitive. Five of the incomplete stories follow:

(1) The child wants a certain toy. He can't reach it. He goes into the living room to get help. Both Mommy and Daddy are busy reading. What happens?

(3) The child lives on a very busy street. Mommy and Daddy told him never to cross the street alone. The child is playing in the front yard, and Mommy and Daddy are not there. A friend is on the other side of the street playing with his new bike. The child wants to cross the street very much. What happens?

(4) The child is having fun playing with his toys. Mommy and Daddy say "It's time to go to bed now." The child says "I don't want to go to bed now." Then the child throws a toy on the floor and it breaks. What happens?

(5) The child is getting ready to go to school. He has a knot in his shoelace. He can't fix it. What happens?

(8) Let's pretend the little boy had a bad dream. Now the little boy wakes up from his bad dream, screaming. He calls for Mommy or Daddy. Which one does he call for, Mommy or Daddy? Then what happens?

If the child failed to respond to one of the stories or said "I don't know," the story was repeated or the question rephrased. If S did not mention the parents in his play, the examiner asked "What did Mommy or Daddy say or do?" When the child did not designate a specific parent in his response, the examiner inquired "Who did that, the Mommy or the Daddy?" Each doll-play session was completely recorded.

Scoring the doll-play responses. The major hypotheses with which the study was concerned dealt with the relationship between boys' masculinity scores and their perceptions of their fathers. The structured doll-play situation, however, permitted evaluations of the child's perceptions not only of his father but also of his mother and his parents as a unit (when mentioned without specific designation of mother or father) as nurturant and/or punishing. The assumption underlying the use of this technique is that the boy's responses in doll play reveal his own feelings about his parents' treatment of him.

Each story was scored for the presence of nurturance or punishment by the father, mother, or "they" (parents undifferentiated). The stories were scored without the scorer's knowledge of the child's ITSC score.

The following scoring categories were used:

Father Nurturance (FN) score was the total number of stories in which the child character in the stories received help, comfort, attention, or reassurance from the father (e.g., "his Daddy gets it for him" in response to Story 1 described above).

A Mother Nurturance (MN) score was derived by counting the number of stories in which the mother was depicted as nurturant. (For example, in response to the story about the dream, "He calls his Mommy and she says it's just a dream and he can sleep with her.")

They Nurturance (TN) score was the number of stories in which the parents as a unit were nurturant. (For example, *S,* in response to Story 3: "They help him cross the street." *E:* "Who helps, Mommy or Daddy?" *S:* "His Mommy and Daddy.")

Total Nurturance (TotN) score was the sum of the MN (Mother Nurturance), FN (Father Nurturance), and TN (They Nurturance) scores.

The total number of stories in which the father, mother, or "they" disciplined, spanked, criticized, or admonished the child in the story constituted, respectively, the Father Punishment (FP), Mother Punishment (MP), and They Punishment (TP) scores.

Total Punishment (TotP) score was the sum of the FP (Father Punishment), MP (Mother Punishment), and TP (They Punishment) scores.

It should be noted that a given story could be scored for more than one variable. For example, if the mother in the story spanked the child and later comforted him, the story would be scored both Mother Punishment (MP) and Mother Nurturance (MN).

The total number of stories involving relationships with the father, either nurturant or punitive (i.e., FN plus FP) constituted the Father Power (FPow) score. Analogously, Mother Power (MPow) was the sum of the Mother Nurturance (MN) and Mother Punishment (MP) scores.

Results

The three theoretical formulations of the dynamics underlying the shift from feminine to masculine identification, out-

lined above, could be evaluated by determining the relationships between masculinity status and perceptions of parents, as measured by the child's responses in doll play. If the developmental hypothesis is valid, highly masculine boys would perceive their fathers as more rewarding and affectionate or, operationally, would have higher Father Nurturance (FN) scores than boys with low masculinity scores. On the basis of the defensive identification hypothesis, however, it would be predicted that boys who were

TABLE 1. MEAN SCORES OF BOYS HIGH AND LOW MASCULINITY GROUPS ON FAMILY PERCEPTION VARIABLES

Variable	High Masculinity Group	Low Masculinity Group
Mother Nurturance (MN)	2.1	1.7
Father Nurturance (FN)	3.7	2.2
They Nurturance (TN)	.8	.7
Total Nurturance (TotN)	6.6	4.7
Mother Punishment (MP)	1.2	1.5
Father Punishment (FP)	2.8	2.1
They Punishment (TP)	.2	.7
Total Punishment (TotP)	4.2	4.3
Mother Power (MPow)	3.3	3.2
Father Power (FPow)	6.5	4.3

most strongly identified with their fathers —as this is reflected in their highly masculine interests—would regard their fathers as more threatening and punitive, i.e., would have higher Father Punishment (FP) scores than boys whose father identifications are weak. The role-playing hypothesis of identification offers a third prediction. According to this theory, boys with strong tendencies to play the father role or to identify with the father would feel that their fathers were powerful figures and important sources of both rewards and punishments. In terms of the variables of this study, this would mean that highly masculine boys would have higher Father Power (FPow) scores than boys who have not achieved strong masculine identifications.

Since responses to the structured doll-play situation were scored for perceptions of the mother and "they" (parents as a unit) as nurturant-gratifying and/or punitive-threatening, it was also possible to assess the relationships between these variables and strong or weak sex-typing among five-year-old boys.

Table 1 presents the mean scores of the high and low masculinity groups on all the doll-play scores.

In view of the facts that the number of Ss in each group was small and that the distributions of scores on these variables was nonnormal, U tests (Mann & Whitney, 1947) were employed to compare rank transformation scores on all doll-play scores of Ss scoring high and low on the ITSC. The results of these tests and their significance levels are sumarized in Table 2.

It is obvious from this table that the two groups of Ss differ significantly in many of their perceptions of their families. Compared with boys low in masculine identification, as measured by the ITSC, those who were high in this characteristic perceived themselves as receiving more Total Nurturance (TotN) (i.e., more nurturance from all sources combined). Evidently, this difference is primarily attributable to differences in one major component of TotN, the perceptions of father's nurturance, for the two groups differ significantly in Father Nurturance (FN) scores but not in the

Mother Nurturance (MN) or They Nurturance (TN) scores.[3]

This finding seems clearly consistent with the developmental identification hypothesis. It supports the prediction, made on the basis of this hypothesis, that

TABLE 2. DIFFERENCES BETWEEN HIGH AND LOW MASCULINITY GROUPS ON FAMILY PERCEPTION VARIABLES

Variable	U	p	Group with Higher Scores
Mother Nurturance (MN)	45.5	NS	—
Father Nurturance (FN)	23.5	.02	Highs
They Nurturance (TN)	48.5	NS	—
Total Nurturance (TotN)	16.0	.004	Highs
Mother Punishment (MP)	44.0	NS	—
Father Punishment (FP)	30.5	.06	Highs
They Punishment (TP)	34.0	.07	Lows
Total Punishment (TotP)	47.0	NS	—
Mother Power (MPow)	49.5	NS	—
Father Power (FPow)	18.5	.007	Highs

[3] While the use of t tests was not entirely warranted because of the nonnormality of the doll-play scores, these tests were applied to the data of Table 1. The results were very similar to the U test results, i.e., the high and low masculinity groups differed significantly from each other in the variables FN ($p = .01 - .025$), TotN ($p = <.01$), FP ($p = .01 - .025$), FPow ($p = <.005$) and almost significantly in TP ($p = .05 - .10$).

young boys are more likely to identify strongly with their fathers, and thus to acquire masculine interests, if they perceive their fathers as highly nurturant and rewarding.

The data also appear to lend support to the second, or defensive identification, hypothesis, which predicted that high masculine identification would be related to views of the father as threatening and punitive. Highly masculine boys tended to attribute more punishment to the fathers in their doll-play stories than boys low in masculine identification did, although the difference between the two groups in the father punishment score was not quite as marked as the difference in the father nurturance variable.

The third, or role-taking, hypothesis states that the degree of identification and, consequently, sex-role learning varies with the amount of the child's interaction with the identificand and the degree to which the latter has power over him, i.e., controls both his rewards and his punishments. The data of the present study seem to be fully in accord with this hypothesis, since the low and high masculinity groups differ markedly in Father Power (FPow) scores, the high identifiers giving a significantly greater number of these responses. This finding is exactly what would be anticipated, since this score is composed of the FN and FP scores, and the highly identified group scored significantly higher in each of these.

The high and low masculinity groups were not significantly different in any of the variables related to perceptions of the mother. However, compared with those scoring low on the ITSC, high scorers tended to perceive their parents as a unit as less punitive, i.e., tended to have lower They Punishment (TP) scores ($p = .07$). This would seem to be fur-

ther confirmation of the findings of another study which concluded that adolescent "boys who feel comfortable in their relationships with their parents adopt more of their father's behavior and attitudes than boys who experience less favorable parent-child relationships" (Payne & Mussen, 1956, p. 361).

It may be that the boy who scores high in They Punishment (TP) views his family milieu as hostile and unfriendly. While he may not feel that either parent is particularly threatening, he may feel generally rejected, unwanted, and unimportant. Insofar as this is true, the child may be expected to attempt to avoid intensive interactions with his parents. Under these circumstances, he should not identify strongly with his father and, consequently, should not acquire highly masculine interests.

Discussion

The data of the present study indicate that for boys, sex-typing of interests is more directly related to their perceptions of their fathers than to perceptions of their mothers. This finding is in accord with the findings of previous studies (Levin & Sears, 1956; Payne & Mussen, 1956; Sears et al., 1957) as well as with an assumption underlying all three of the identification hypotheses outlined above; namely, that the acquisition of masculine interests, attitudes, and patterns of behavior is primarily determined by the boy's interactions with his father.

Some of the findings of this study lend support to the defensive identification hypothesis; others seem to support the developmental hypothesis. Since the two hypotheses generate predictions that are in some respects diametrically opposed, there are also data that are inconsistent with both hypotheses. Thus, since the developmental hypothesis postulates that identification with the father is dependent upon nurturant rewarding interactions with that parent, the finding that boys also identify with punitive, threatening fathers must be inconsistent with this hypothesis. Conversely, the finding that boys are more likely to identify with a nurturant father is inconsistent with the view of defensive identification or identification with the aggressor.

A high level of masculine identification does not appear to depend on any one specific type of father-son relationship. From the child's point of view, the significant factor seems to be the father's *salience*—his importance in the child's life—rather than the particular techniques he uses in dealing with his child. Thus, as a group, boys who have made substantial father-identifications— reflected in their strongly sex-typed interests—perceived their fathers as both more nurturant *and* more punitive. Hence, masculine sex-role identification cannot be attributed exclusively to either the reward value or the threat potential of the father.

For these reasons, it seems to us that the role theory of identification is most fully consistent with—and most adequately integrates—the present data. The two groups were clearly differentiated on the Father Power (FPow) score, indicating that, compared with the other group, the highly masculine boys had—or at least perceived that they had—more intensive interactions with their fathers. This is exactly what is predicted by the role theory of sex-role identification, which maintains that more interaction with another individual, e.g., the father, leads to greater assimilation of his role.

Moreover, role theory states most explicitly that an individual is most likely to assimilate the role of, or identify with, individuals he sees as powerful. From the child's point of view, the most powerful individual is probably the one who most effectively controls his rewards and punishments. In this way, the theory implies that both reward and punishment strongly influence the course of role learning.

It follows from these postulates of role theory that the boy should be most strongly motivated to imitate or to practice his father's role frequently if he has a great deal of interaction with his father and sees him as a powerful source of rewards and punishments. Under these circumstances, the child gets extensive experience playing the father's role and adopts more of the father's characteristics, including those connected specifically with his sex-role. Our data are substantially in accordance with these theoretical predictions. The highly father-identified Ss—those who had adopted masculine interests and behavior—did in fact perceive their fathers as more interactive with them and as major providers of rewards *and* punishments.

There is also a psychoanalytic hypothesis which these data seem to confirm. In summarizing psychoanalytic writings on identification, Bronfenbrenner (1958) notes that one of the "syndromes of parent-child relationship . . . predisposing the child to incorporate or introject the parent" is "a relationship based on conditional love, in which the parent, willfully or unconsciously, withholds expression of affection as the price of conformity" (p. 128). This means that the boy is most likely to identify with his father if his feelings toward him are affectionate, while the father's love is given conditionally. According to this hypothesis, high nurturance from the father, together with the threat of withdrawal of his love (high FP) would lead to strong father identification. This prediction seems to be verified by the finding that highly masculine boys have relatively high Father Power scores, indicating a high degree of combined father nurturance and father punishment.

The findings may also be conceptualized in terms of general behavior theory. Among those with whom the preschool boy has intimate associations, the father is the one who has the most adequate knowledge of appropriate masculine behavior. If there is a high level of father-son interaction (high FPow scores), the father should frequently, and fairly regularly, reward the son's sex-appropriate responses and punish sex-inappropriate responses when they occur. Consequently, the boy's masculine responses should be relatively rapidly and effectively strengthened, while his sex-inappropriate responses become extinguished. In short, vigorous application of both rewards and punishments by the father facilitate the son's shift from feminine to masculine identification.

On the other hand, the condition of relatively little father-son interaction implies sporadic, and at best ineffective, rewards and punishments by the father. Under these circumstances, the shift in identification may be a difficult one, and the child's acquisition of sex-typed interests and behavior may be considerably retarded.

It seems that the father's use of *both* reward *and* punishment is his most effective method of "teaching" his son masculine behavior. It must be emphasized, however, that the high masculine and low masculine groups also differed significantly in the individual variables relating to perceptions of father reward and father punishment. From this it may be inferred that sex-appropriate behavior may be "taught" primarily by rewarding

appropriate responses *or* punishing inappropriate responses. In short, from the child's point of view, the important factor is the salience of his relationship with his father, not the particular techniques that the father uses in handling him.

Of course, the present data refer *only* to masculinity of interests. Other possible long-range consequents of different processes of identification cannot be evaluated. For example, it is quite possible that boys who learn their sex roles primarily as a result of being punished or threatened by their fathers differ in many ways (e.g., in personality characteristics, self-conceptions, or basic motivations) from those who achieve their masculine identifications by means of developmental identification or through learning based on some combination of reward and punishment by the father. As the data stand, however, we can only state that five-year-old boys may shift from feminine to masculine identification, as measured by the acquisition of masculine interests, as a result of either developmental or defensive identification processes or, as role theory suggests, by some combination of the two.

Summary

The IT Scale for Children (ITSC), a test of sex-typing of interests, was administered to 38 white, middle-class, kindergarten boys. The 10 Ss scoring highest in the test were assumed to have developed the highest degree of male role identification, while the 10 scoring lowest were considered the least strongly identified with this role.

In order to determine the relationship between parental perceptions and degree of masculine identification, each of the 20 boys was tested in a structured doll-play situation. During the session, the child completed, in play, nine incomplete stories involving parent-child relations. Responses were scored in terms of the amount of nurturance, punishment, and power (nurturance plus punishment) attributed to the mother, father, and parents as a unit.

The study was designed to evaluate three hypothesized processes of identification—developmental, defensive, and role-taking. Analysis of the data provided evidence consistent with all three hypotheses. As predicted from the developmental identification hypothesis, young boys who were strongly identified with the male role perceived their fathers as more rewarding and nurturant ($p = .02$) than their weakly identified peers did. According to the defensive identification hypothesis, the strongly father-identified boys perceive their fathers as more punitive and threatening. This hypothesis was also supported ($p = .06$). Boys high and low in masculinity were also clearly differentiated on the Father Power score ($p = .007$). This finding indicates that those who have made substantial male identifications view their fathers as powerful sources of *both* reward and punishment, and is in accordance with role theory, which maintains that the child is most likely to assimilate the role of an individual with whom he has intensive interactions, especially if this individual is powerful. To the present authors, it seems that role theory, with its explicit emphasis on the importance of both reward and punishment in role-learning, best integrates all these data.

References

BRIM, O. G., JR. Family structure and sex role learning by children: a further analysis of Helen Koch's data. *Sociometry*, 1958, **21**, 1–16.

BRONFENBRENNER, U. The study of identification through interpersonal perception. In R. Tagiuri & L. Petrullo (Eds.), *Person perception and interpersonal behavior.* Stanford, Calif.: Stanford Univer. Press, 1958. Pp. 110–130.

BROWN, D. D. Sex role preference in young children. *Psychol. Monogr.*, 1956, **70** (14, Whole No. 421).

COTTRELL, L. S., JR. The analysis of situational fields in social psychology. *Amer. sociol. Rev.*, 1942, **7**, 370–383.

FREUD, ANNA. *The ego and the mechanisms of defense.* London: Hogarth, 1937.

FREUD, S. *Group psychology and the analysis of the ego.* London: Hogarth, 1949.

LEVIN, H., & SEARS, R. R. Identification with parents as a determinant of doll play aggression. *Child Develpm.*, 1956, **27**, 135–153.

MANN, H. B., & WHITNEY, D. R. On a test of whether one of two random variables is stochastically larger than the other. *Ann. math. Statist.*, 1947, **18**, 50–60.

MOWRER, O. H. *Learning theory and personality dynamics.* New York: Ronald, 1950.

PARSONS, T. Family structure and the socialization of the child. In T. Parsons & R. F. Bales (Eds.) *Family, socialization, and interaction process.* Glencoe, Ill.: Free Press, 1955.

PAYNE, D. E., & MUSSEN, P. H. Parent-child relations and father identification among adolescent boys. *J. abnorm. soc. Psychol.*, 1956, **52**, 358–362.

RICHARDS, T. W., & SIMONS, MARJORIE. Fels Child Behavior Scale. *Genet. psychol. Monogr.*, 1941, **24**, 259–309.

SEARS, PAULINE. Child-rearing factors related to playing of sex-typed roles. *Amer. Psychologist*, 1953, **8**, 431. (Abstract)

SEARS, R. R., MACCOBY, ELEANOR E., & LEVIN, H. *Patterns of child rearing.* Evanston, Ill.: Row, Peterson, 1957.

SEARS, R. R., PINTLER, M. H., & SEARS, PAULINE. Effect of father separation on pre-school children's doll play aggression. *Child Develpm.*, 1946, **17**, 219–243.

A COMPARISON OF DIRECT, INDIRECT, AND FANTASY MEASURES OF IDENTIFICATION

James Bieri, Robin Lobeck, and M. David Galinsky

Much discussion has centered about the theoretical formulation of identification in terms of its relationship to introjection (Knight, 1940), aggression (Freud, 1946), and learning (Seward, 1954). A recurrent controversy is whether identification is best construed as a normal process of becoming like a significant other through social learning, or whether identification should be considered defensive behavior stemming from an interpersonal conflict (Sanford, 1955). Our own view is that it is worthwhile to keep in mind two necessary (but not sufficient) aspects of identification. First, some degree of *similarity* between the behavior of a subject and the object of identification is necessary. This aspect of identification is emphasized by those who view identification as a developmental process of social learning (Mowrer, 1953; Seward, 1954), and by those who measure identification empirically in terms of the real or perceived similarity between the object and the subject (Beier & Ratzeburg, 1953; Cava & Raush, 1952; Lazowick, 1955; Livingstone, 1956; Payne & Mussen, 1956; Sopchak, 1952). A second aspect of

Reprinted by permission of the American Psychological Association and the authors from *The Journal of Abnormal and Social Psychology,* Vol. 58, 1959.

identification is the condition that some *degree of involvement* or closeness of relationship must exist or have existed between the object and the subject. Those who emphasize the defensive nature of identification tend to stress this aspect of the concept (Freud, 1946; Sanford, 1955).

Each of these aspects of identification may be assessed with varying degrees of *directness*. By degree of directness we mean the extent to which a person is aware of and focused upon reporting an aspect of his experience, in this case, his relationships with his parents. Thus, we used the interview as a direct technique with which to measure both perceived similarity and involvement as aspects of identification. As an indirect measure of perceived similarity we used Osgood's semantic differential (Osgood, Suci, & Tannenbaum, 1957). Finally, we used the Thematic Apperception Test (TAT) as a fantasy measure (very indirect) of involvement.

Many research studies of identification in recent years have used *indirect* measures of identification. Most of these indirect measures assess identification by the degree of similarity between the way a subject (*S*) fills out an inventory for himself and the way he fills it out for one or both of his parents (Beier et al., 1953;

Cava et al., 1952; Livingstone, 1956; Sopchak, 1952). Other studies using this indirect approach have compared S's responses with those of his parents (Lazowick, 1955; Payne & Mussen, 1956).

Our purposes in this research are twofold. First, we wish to extend the range of empirical measures of identification to include direct and fantasy measures, as well as the more common indirect measures, and to analyze systematically the consistency among these measures. Second, we wish to include several measures of each aspect of identification (i.e., similarity and degree of involvement) and to examine the relationship between these measures. These considerations lead to the following general predictions:

Hypothesis 1. There will be significant positive relationships among the various empirical measures of the perceived similarity aspect of identification.

Hypothesis 2. There will be significant positive relationships among the empirical measures of the involvement aspect of identification.

Hypothesis 3. There will be significant positive relationships between the empirical measures of the perceived similarity and involvement aspects of parental identification.

Method

SUBJECTS

Results for two groups of Ss are presented. The Female group consisted of 30 college undergraduates attending a summer school session of Harvard University. There were two married women in this group. The age range was from 18 to 24 years, with a median age of 19.4 years. The Male group consisted of 60 college students, including 30 attending Harvard College and 30 summer school students at the same institution.

Among the men, there were three married Ss, while the group had an age range of 17 to 29 years, with a median age of 20.5 years. All Ss were paid at existing research rates.

As a result of the intensive nature of the assessment, each S was seen in two experimental sessions. The semantic differential was administered during the first session, while the TAT and interview were reserved for the second session.

EMPIRICAL MEASURES OF IDENTIFICATION

Direct measure. A structured interview centering about S's relationships with his parents formed the basis of the direct measurement of both aspects of identification. This interview consisted of a series of 12 questions discussed with S in a prearranged order. Content for these interview items were suggested in part by the interview schedule used by Adorno, Frenkel-Brunswik, Levinson, & Sanford (1950). All interviews were tape-recorded, with S's consent, and were subsequently transcribed verbatim for scoring purposes.

Two interview questions formed the basis of the direct measures of identification:

(1) Which parent do you feel you are most like at the present?

(2) Which parent did you feel closer to as a child?

The first item ("like") was the direct measure of perceived similarity as an aspect of identification. The second item ("child") was the direct measure of the degree of involvement. The interviewer attempted to obtain as much amplification of each response as was deemed necessary for our scoring purposes. Each of these two questions was interspersed among other items that were not used in this study but had relevance to the parent-child relationship, including topics such as discipline, satisfactions, and conflicts. The interviews varied from 15 to 30 minutes in length, and were always conducted at the end of the last research session so that the effects of discussing this direct material on the indirect and fantasy measures would be minimized.

The over-all responses to the two interview items were scored in terms of one of three general categories: (a) the response clearly indicated one parent as being most relevant to the query (scored M or F); (b) both parents were mentioned as relevant to the question, but one was given greater weight than the other (scored M/F or F/M); (c) neither parent was seen as crucial or relevant to the question (scored 0), or S could not make a choice in the direction of either parent (scored ?).

Responses in Category (a) are exemplified by a statement such as "I'm definitely most like my father" ("like" item) or, "I was closer to my mother as a kid" ("child" item). Category (b) was scored for statements such as, "I'm really like both my parents in some ways, but I guess I'm somewhat more like my mother" ("like" item). Responses in Category (c) might include statements as "I'm like both, but I don't think I'm like one more than the other" ("like" item) or, "I wasn't particularly close to either of my parents as a youngster" ("child" item).

Considering men and women together, 67% of the responses to both interview items fell in Category (a), 20% fell in Category (b), and 13% were scored in Category (c). It is evident that these three categories represent decreasing degrees of decisiveness with which S verbalizes the relative importance of one parent compared to the other in relationship to himself. The fact that 87% of all Ss gave responses in Categories (a) or (b) indicates that such a direct measurement of identification is feasible, whatever its subsequent validity may prove to be.

All scoring of the interviews was done by one person. Interrater reliability was assessed by having a second person independently score 20 randomly selected interviews. Of the 40 responses scored, 87% agreement was found. All five disagreements in scoring were caused by a confusion of Categories (a) and (b). Thus, when these two categories were combined (e.g., M/F responses were considered to be M responses), 100% agreement was achieved.

Indirect measure. The indirect measure of the perceived similarity aspect of identification was Osgood's semantic differential (Osgood et al., 1957). Essentially, this is a seven-point rating scale, each end of the scale being one of a pair of bipolar adjectives. S is asked to rate a person on all nine pairs of adjectives. Adequate reliability of ratings has been demonstrated (Osgood et al., 1957). Our list of adjectives is the same as that used by Lazowick (1955), and contains nine adjective pairings derived from Osgood's factor analysis so as to contain three pairings on each of the three most general factors obtained. Thus, three pairings have to do with potency (strong–weak, heavy–light, and rugged–delicate), three with evaluation (clean–dirty, fresh–stale, and happy–sad), and three with activity (fast–slow, hot–cold, and active–passive). S was asked to rate himself, his father, and his mother on each of these nine dimensions. There was a random ordering of the dimensions for each person rated so as to reduce possible response sets in the ratings. A score of perceived similarity to each parent was obtained by summing the squares of the differences between the rating S gave himself and that he gave a parent on every adjective pairing. For example, a high score for the mother (M score) reflects a perception of greater dissimilarity between S and the mother, while a low M score reflects greater perceived similarity between S and the mother. A second identification score was obtained from the semantic differential by subtracting the M score from the F score, yielding a difference score (D score). Ss with positive D scores were considered to perceive themselves as more like the mother, and Ss with negative D scores were considered to perceive themselves as more like the father.

We consider the semantic differential to be an indirect measure of identification because S is not making a direct and deliberate comparison of himself with one parent in contrast to the other as in the interview.

Fantasy measure. The use of the TAT represented our most extreme indirect assessment of identification. Here we were concerned with the degree of involvement S manifested in his relationships with each parent. Our reasoning in arriving at an objective scoring scheme for the TAT measure of identification involved one central assumption: that in the stories an individual tells to cards depicting an older and younger person in close proximity, the stronger the influence of the parent-child relationship in his current behavior, the more likely that his stories depict an explicit parent-child relationship. Thus, we selected two cards that could be construed as involving a parent-son relationship for males, and two that could depict a parent-daughter relationship for females.

For male Ss, we used from the standard TAT set Card 7BM (older man and younger man) and Card 6BM (older woman and man, commonly called the mother-son card). Standard TAT instructions were given on these two cards, designed to tap involvement in the father-son and mother-son relationships respectively. For female Ss, only Card 7GF of the standard TAT cards was deemed suitable for investigating this aspect of parental identification. This card depicts an older woman sitting on a sofa speaking or reading to a girl next to her. To obtain an appropriate picture for the father-daughter relationship, a modification of the Make-a-Picture-Story Test (MAPS) was devised. A card from the MAPS was selected depicting an empty room containing a closet. To one side was placed a female figure of adolescent or young adult age, while on the other side of the room a figure of an older man was placed. As in the case of males, standard TAT instructions were given for both cards.

The TAT stories were tape-recorded and scored from the transcriptions. Each story was scored on a six-point scale so arranged as to reflect the degree to which the story explicitly contained a parent-child relationship. The following criteria were used in scoring:

5: parent-child relationship explicitly stated in which there is close personal involvement with each other;

4: parent-child relationship with a minimum of personal involvement;

3: two persons who are relatives (but not parent and child) or close personal acquaintances;

2: two persons not related but living in close physical proximity (e.g., landlady and tenant), or two persons with a business and professional relationship (e.g., lawyer and client);

1: two persons together in the story

only incidentally (e.g., man delivering message to woman);

0: only one person mentioned in the story, or both figures are the same person (e.g., young man thinking when he is older).

Such a scoring scheme obviously ignores many of the subtle cues contained in thematic stories. However, it does systematically order the stories in terms of a gradient of explicit parent-child involvement. It has the further advantage of making scoring relatively objective, as reflected in the analysis of interrater reliability. Of 60 stories independently scored by two persons (one of whom scored the stories for all Ss), there was perfect agreement on 48 (80%) of the stories. Further, of the 12 stories on which disagreement existed, 11 scores deviated by a value of only one.

These scores were used in two ways as measures of the involvement aspect of identification. First, all Ss' scores on a particular card could be compared to indicate degree of involvement. Secondly, scores between two cards could be compared so as to indicate the relatively greater involvement with one parent or the other. For this latter purpose, we simply subtracted the score S obtained on the Father card from the score obtained on the Mother card (M-F). We then assumed that the higher the (M-F) score, the greater is the involvement with the mother as compared to the father.

Results

On each of the identification measures used, men and women had very comparable ranges of scores. Since scores on some tests were continuous in nature (semantic differential M and F scores, and TAT) while others were discontinuous (semantic differential D

scores and interview), the relationships stated in our general hypotheses were tested by chi square. The number of Ss used in comparing one measure to another vary in the ensuing tables because none of the neutral scores (those reflecting no parental preferences in response) was used. On continuous measures, scores were dichotomized as close to the median as possible. The interview was dichotomized by grouping responses in the first two scoring categories ([a] and [b] above) on each parent. By combining these two categories we were not only able to maximize the number of Ss used in our analyses, but in addition utilized the 100% scoring reliability for these grouped categories, reported above. One exception was made to this in the case of the question, "which parent did you feel closer to as a child?" Because only nine male Ss were scored for "father," we included in our analysis the nine additional cases in which replies were scored in Category (c), i.e., neither parent.

HYPOTHESIS 1

Our first analysis concerned the prediction that measures of the perceived similarity aspect of identification will be positively associated with each other. Table 1 presents findings comparing the interview "like" question ("Which parent do you feel you are most like at present?") with the three scores of the semantic differential.[1] The results for the Female and Male groups indicate that two of the three measures of identification on the semantic differential are significantly associated in the predicted dir-

---

[1] All probability values in the tables are for a one-tailed test, as the direction of the relationships was predicted. For females, Fisher's exact probability test was used. For males, chi square corrected for continuity was used.

TABLE 1. COMPARISON OF PERCEIVED SIMILARITY MEASURES OF
IDENTIFICATION
(Chi-square analysis)

Interview "like" Item	Semantic Differential					
	F Score		M Score		D Score	
	High	Low	High	Low	Plus	Minus
Female Group						
Mother	8	8	6	10	9	7
Father	5	6	9	2	1	10
p	—		.03		.02	
Male Group						
Mother	14	8	10	12	15	7
Father	12	21	13	20	12	21
p	.05		—		.02	

ection with the "like" item on the interview.

HYPOTHESIS 2

The second analysis centered about the prediction that measures of the involvement aspect of identification will be positively associated with each other. Table 2 compares the findings for the "child" item on the interview ("Which parent did you feel closer to as a child?") with the TAT measures of identification. While none of the predicted relationships was significant for the Female group, it is to be noted that for males two TAT measures of the involvement aspect of identification were significant when compared with responses to the "child" item of the interview. It should be recalled that these findings for men

TABLE 2. COMPARISON OF INVOLVEMENT MEASURES OF IDENTIFICATION
(Chi-square analysis)

Interview "child" Item	TAT					
	Mother Card		Father Card		(M-F) Score	
	High	Low	High	Low	High	Low
Female Group						
Mother	10	4	5	9	8	6
Father	13	3	6	10	9	7
p	—		—		—	
Male Group						
Mother	32	10	14	28	23	19
Father	9	9	10	8	5	13
p	.05		.10		.05	

TABLE 3. COMPARISON OF PERCEIVED SIMILARITY AND INVOLVEMENT
MEASURES OF IDENTIFICATION
(Chi-square analysis)

Interview "like" Item	TAT							
	Mother Card		Father Card		(M-F) Score		Interview "child" Item	
	High	Low	High	Low	High	Low	Mo	Fa
Female Group								
Mother	13	3	6	10	10	6	11	3
Father	8	3	5	6	5	6	2	8
p	—		—		—		.01	
Male Group								
Mother	8	14	8	14	13	9	15	7
Father	16	17	20	13	12	21	23	10
p	—		.07		.08		—	

compare those men who report they were closer to the mother as a child with those who report they were closer to the father or to *neither* parent. When the "neither" category is omitted, no significant relationships are found for the Male group. Thus, our findings for men must be interpreted in terms of males who either were or were not closer to the mother as a child.

HYPOTHESIS 3

The final analysis pertains to the prediction that measures of the perceived similarity aspect of identification (interview "like" item and semantic differential) are positively associated with measures of the involvement aspect of identification (TAT and interview "child"). Of the two perceived similarity measures of identification, only the interview "like" item was associated significantly with one of the involvement measures. From Table 3 we note that in the case of women, the interview "like" item relates significantly to the interview

"child" item. For men, the interview "like" item relates in the predicted direction to two of the TAT involvement measures of identification, the Father card and the (M-F) score. The semantic differential did not relate significantly to any of the involvement measures of identification.

Discussion

Our finding that of the three semantic differential scores only the D score relates significantly for both sexes to the direct perceived similarity measure has implications for studies which utilize indirect measures of identification, such as rating scales or inventories. It suggests that a *comparative* score, comparing *S*'s similarity to one parent in contrast to the other, may be a more fruitful measure of the perceived similarity aspect of identification than a score reflecting *S*'s degree of similarity to either parent alone. Alternatively, if only one parent is used in deriving an identification score based on perceived similarity, the score based on the *same-sex* parent may be more desirable.

While our efforts to relate direct and fantasy measures of involvement met with some success in the case of men (Table 2), for women none of the results relating direct and fantasy measures approached significance. In part, we believe this is because the stimulus material used to elicit fantasy was less adequate for our purposes in the case of women than of men. For males, the two TAT cards depicted a "son" close in age to our Ss, while for females, the Mother card contained a "daughter" who was considerably younger than our female Ss. On the Father card for females, the stimulus material elicited an overly uniform theme in which 70% of the women told stories of a male figure expressing strong anger toward the female figure.

It is possible that the lack of significant findings for women on the TAT is related to the observation often made that parental identifications of women are less consistent than those of men. Sex differences in consistency of parental identification may be analyzed in terms of changes in scores from direct to indirect (or fantasy) assessment levels. In relation to the two aspects of identification we have measured, the findings suggest that, although men are more consistent than women in the involvement aspect of identification (Table 2), both sexes tend to be consistent in the perceived similarity aspect of identification (Table 1).

On the interview "like" and semantic differential D score, 60% and 51% of the men, respectively, perceived themselves as more like the father (Table 1). For women, 69% and 37%, on these two measures, perceived themselves as more like the mother. More detailed analysis of these shifts in identification

between assessment levels reveals further differences between men and women. Of the 22 men who perceived themselves as more like the mother on the interview "like," seven (about one-third) shifted identification to the father on the D score. Conversely, of the 33 men with father identification on the interview "like," 12 (about one-third) shifted identification to the mother on the D score. Women showed a different pattern of shifts. Of the 16 women who stated that they were more like the mother on the interview, seven shifted identification to the father on indirect assessment. Of the 11 women with father identification on the interview "like," only one shifted to the mother on the D score. Thus, the relative inconsistency of the perceived similarity aspect of parental identification is different for both sexes. Women who shift, change from same-sex identification on direct assessment to opposite-sex identification on indirect assessment. Men who shift, change equally from one parent to the other.

Somewhat opposite results emerge on the involvement aspect of identification (Table 2). Here, women who shifted identification from the direct to the fantasy level tended to be equally divided in terms of changing from one parent to the other. For men, of those who changed, 79% stated they were closer to the mother on the interview but scored closer to the father on the TAT (M-F).

We conclude, then, that the relative inconsistency of parental identifications of men and women, as measured by a change in identification scores from the direct to indirect (or fantasy) assessment levels, is a function of two factors. First, consistency varies with the aspect of identification under study. Second, consistency may vary as a function of the particular parental identification established by direct assessment.

Summary

This study was designed to investigate predicted relationships of three levels of directness of assessment (direct, indirect, and fantasy) to two aspects of parental identification, i.e., perceived similarity to a parent and degree of involvement with a parent. Perceived similarity was measured directly by an interview item ("Which parent do you feel you are more like?") and indirectly by the semantic differential. Involvement was measured directly by the interview ("Which parent were you closer to as a child?"), and by fantasy with two cards from the TAT or MAPS depicting a father-child or mother-child relationship. It was predicted that (a) perceived similarity measures would be positively related, (b) involvement measures would be positively related, and (c) since both perceived similarity and involvement are assumed to be components of identification, they should be positively associated with each other. Two groups of college students were used as Ss, consisting of 30 women in one group and 60 men in the other group. The major results are:

(1) For both men and women, the direct (interview "like" item) and indirect (semantic differential) measures of perceived similarity are in general significantly related to each other (Hypothesis 1);

(2) For men, the direct (interview "child" item) and fantasy (TAT) measures of involvement tend to be significantly related (Hypothesis 2);

(3) For neither sex was the direct measure of perceived similarity (interview "like" item) and the fantasy measure of involvement (TAT) significantly associated, although trends in this direction were more apparent for men; for women, the direct measure of involvement (interview "child" item) was significantly related to the direct measure of perceived similarity (interview "like" item) (Hypothesis 3);

(4) The problem of sex differences in consistency of parental identification is analyzed in terms of changes in identification scores from direct to indirect or fantasy assessment levels. It is concluded that both the aspect of identification measured and the specific parental identification made on direct assessment must be specified in drawing conclusions on this point.

References

ADORNO, T. W., FRENKEL-BRUNSWIK, ELSE, LEVINSON, D. J., & SANFORD, R. N. *The authoritarian personality.* New York: Harper, 1950.

BEIER, E. G., & RATZEBURG, F. Parental identification of male and female college students. *J. abnorm. soc. Psychol.,* 1953, **48,** 569–572.

CAVA, E. L., & RAUSH, H. L. Identification and adolescent boys' perception of the father. *J. abnorm. soc. Psychol.,* 1952, **47,** 855–856.

FREUD, ANNA. *The ego and the mechanisms of defense.* New York: International Universities Press, 1946.

KNIGHT, R. P. Introjection, projection and identification. *Psychoanal. Quart.,* 1940, **9,** 334–341.

LAZOWICK, L. M. On the nature of identification. *J. abnorm. soc. Psychol.,* 1955, **51,** 175–183.

LIVINGSTONE, D. The personality correlates of high and low identification with the father. Unpublished doctoral dissertation, Univer. of Houston, 1956.

MOWRER, O. H. *Psychotherapy: Theory and research.* New York: Ronald, 1953.

Osgood, C. E., Suci, G. J., & Tannenbaum, P. H. *The measurement of meaning.* Urbana: Univer. Illinois Press, 1957.

Payne, D., & Mussen, P. H. Parent-child relations and father identification among adolescent boys. *J. abnorm. soc. Psychol.,* 1956, **52,** 358–362.

Sanford, R. N. The dynamics of identification. *Psychol. Rev.,* 1955, **62,** 106–118.

Seward, J. P. Learning theory and identification. *J. genet. Psychol.,* 1954, **84,** 201–210.

Sopchak, A. L. Parental identification and tendencies toward disorders as measured by the MMPI. *J. abnorm. soc. Psychol.,* 1952, **47,** 159–165.

CHAPTER 6

Studies of Three Modes of Personality Organization

The Authoritarian Personality

THE CALIFORNIA F SCALE IN PSYCHOLOGICAL RESEARCH: 1950–1955   H. Edwin Titus and E. P. Hollander

With the publication of *The Authoritarian Personality* (2) in 1950, the commonality of two streams of research interest was established. By applying the tools of "depth psychology" to the study of ideology, this work opened the way for a substantive integration of personality dynamics with social behavior.

While it is too early now to foretell the eventual place accorded this work, it may certainly be said to have left its mark on the contemporary scene. Probably no other single development in recent years has stimulated so much thought and investigation. Since 1950, a veritable cornucopia of research in the authoritarianism area has evidenced itself. Even as the outpouring continues, however, we may reasonably hope to take stock of the accomplishments of this period.

More than any other, the F (Fascism) scale developed by the California group has been widely accepted and widely used as a research variable. It is the purpose of this paper to present an overview of studies using the F scale which have been reported in the literature.

Reprinted with permission of the American Psychological Association and the authors from the *Psychological Bulletin,* Vol. 54, 1957.

Since the scale (Form 40–45) has been modified in one way or another by many of its users, it has occasionally been necessary here to make somewhat arbitrary decisions concerning the inclusion or exclusion of a study. Generally, only those studies which have not changed the scale too severely have been included; thus, data drawn from the A–E scale are not covered, as is true of other extremely short modifications of the original. However, some studies using 12 or more of the most discriminating items of the original have been included. The guiding principle for decisions of inclusion or exclusion has been the intent of gathering together that information which will be most valuable to future users of the F scale and which will contribute most to an understanding of its meaning.

To facilitate presentation and comprehension, studies have been grouped into five major categories, with appropriate subgroupings. Other segmentation schemes may have served better; this procedure offers advantages, but assuredly has limitations as well.

Ideology

It is convenient to distinguish studies with an ideological, or attitudinal, flavor from those striking more deeply at personality characteristics. In this section our focus of attention will be on the former grouping.

PREJUDICE

Despite the fact that the F scale was originally developed as a measure of prejudice, few studies have dealt with its relationship with prejudice per se. Flowerman et al. (23) made a study of the validity of the F scale as a measure of ethnic prejudice for groups geographically removed from those on which the original validity studies were conducted. They found correlations ranging from .30 to .60 between the F scale and prejudice. The subjects were Protestant and Catholic men and women in Minneapolis, St. Paul, and Baltimore. It is unfortunate, at least for comparative purposes, that an interview method was used for determining the subjects' F-scale score, thus making extrapolation to the questionnaire method difficult, if not impossible. The results, however, did tend to support the use of the F scale as a measure of prejudice.

Goldstein et al. (26), using the Allport-Vernon Scale of values, a social distance scale, and a background information questionnaire, investigated the relationship between prejudice and other ideological aspects of the authoritarian syndrome using groups of white, nonsouthern, native-born, Christian students from Princeton and UCLA. Goldstein confirmed that a general tolerance-prejudice factor exists and that an authoritarian syndrome closely associated with prejudice is quite real. It is important to note that this author felt that the approach of Adorno et al. ". . . is tenable though quite unsubstantiated. However, [their] great desire to theoretically unify authoritarianism seems mistaken. . . . The authoritarian syndrome is probably a conglomerate which cannot be entirely explained on the basis of an elaborately unified theory. . . . If this desire [to unify] were kept within reason, abnormality would probably receive less emphasis and the theoretical contribution of the authors would be of greater value" (26, p. 35).

Somewhat by way of contrast, Campbell and McCandless (10) report evidence for the existence of a general factor which tends to unify "most, if not all" attitudes toward those of other ethnic groups. They provide evidence that the F scale correlates substantially with a variety of prejudice measures, including ethnocentrism and xenophobia.

Steckler (60) conducted a study of the authoritarian ideology in Negro college students. Scales were developed to measure anti-Negro attitudes, antiwhite attitudes, and so-called ideological militancy-pacifism. He found a moderate covariance between anti-Negro, antiwhite, and ideological militancy-pacifism on the one hand and F on the other. Steckler suggests that authoritarian components must therefore be involved, to some degree, in this measure. Since the F scale is usually used with white, Christian, nonsouthern Americans, it is difficult to evaluate these data. We have, at present, no evidence to indicate clearly the meaning of F-scale scores for Negroes. Proper evaluation must await further work using F or similar scales with Negro populations.

POLITICAL ATTITUDES

At the time of the 1952 national political conventions, Milton (47) hypothesized that ". . . individuals who preferred MacArthur for President of the United States would obtain higher scores on the F scale . . . than those who preferred other presidential aspirants" (47,

p. 597). To test this contention, he administered the F scale and a questionnaire concerning presidential choice to 390 students at the University of Tennessee. In line with his hypothesis he found that those students who favored MacArthur had significantly higher F-scale scores than those favoring other candidates. In addition, he found that a significant number of the students favoring either Taft or MacArthur were in the upper 25 per cent of F-scale scorers. Milton warns that these data must be interpreted with caution, but suggests that there seems to be evidence ". . . for a speculation that has been offered by many individuals, i.e., voting behavior is influenced, partially, by certain personality attributes of both the voter and the candidate" (47, p. 598).

Gump (28) noticed that newspaper comments in opposition to Truman's dismissal of MacArthur seemed to follow the antidemocratic trends as defined in *The Authoritarian Personality,* and tested the proposition that high F-scale scorers would favor MacArthur (an authoritarian symbol) whereas, the low scorers would tend to favor Truman's action. The statement "MacArthur should have been dismissed" was added to the F scale which was administered to a sample of 405 students at the University of Colorado. The results showed that those favoring MacArthur had significantly ($p < .001$) higher F-scale scores than did those who favored Truman's action. Gump suggests that "Insofar as the F scale measures anti-democratic trends, the hypothesis that there is a relatively high frequency of anti-democratic trends among these college students who opposed the dismissal of General MacArthur is amply supported by the findings" (28, p. 134). This study, like the preceding one, is based on the premise that students with relatively high authoritarian tendencies will be attracted to authoritarian symbols. Since the results were in both cases significant and in the direction predicted, it appears that the F scale may have some value in predicting political trends; however, it is likely that such clear-cut results can be obtained only when individuals who have been clearly presented as authoritarian figures are involved.

FAMILY IDEOLOGY

Huffman (31) has developed a scale for the measurement of "Traditional Family Ideologies" (TFI) which correlates .73 with a shortened version of the F scale. This author suggests that to the degree that the F scale and the TFI scale are valid, the correlation between them would indicate a fair correspondence of what is being measured by the two scales. Since the hypothesis was that the autocratic trends in family ideology could be shown by an attitude-opinion scale, and in turn related to the authoritarian personality variables, these results would seem to indicate some success in demonstrating her hypothesis.

Kates and Diab (37) hypothesized a correlation between attitudes on parent-child relationships and authoritarianism. They administered the F scale, The University of Southern California Parent Attitude Survey, and a number of other scales including the California Ethnocentrism and Politico-Economic Conservatism scales and a scale of ambiguity intolerance, to 172 college students (61 males and 111 females). Of interest here is their finding of a correlation of .21 ($p < .01$) between the F-scale scores and possessive attitudes, for males and females combined. For the sexes separately, they found that the female students' F-scale scores correlated .34 and

.28, ($p < .01$) respectively with dominant and possessive attitudes, whereas for the males the only significant correlation with the F scale was a .29 ($p < .05$) correlation with ignoring attitudes. The authors tentatively suggest, from these and other relationships found, that "strong authoritarian beliefs may be maladjustive in a democratic society since such beliefs are associated with attitudes similar to those held by parents of problem children" (37, p. 16).

TEACHER ATTITUDES

Juul (36) has considered F-scale scores in relation to teacher attitudes toward child behavior. He used a shortened version of an inventory called "How I Teach" to measure teaching attitudes of college seniors in a teacher training curriculum. It was his hypothesis that ". . . many of the concepts and attitudes expressed by teachers and textbooks in courses in child psychology and mental hygiene constitute a serious threat to the equilibrium of the inner world of the authoritarian individual. In organizing his experiences, he is therefore forced to exclude, distort, repress or otherwise fit every situation, event, and person into his framework and need structure" (36, p. 17). As a consequence of this hypothesis it would naturally follow that equalitarian students would tend to get significantly higher scores than authoritarian students on a test of knowledge of child psychology, teaching attitudes, and opinion-teaching practices. As was predicted, he found a negative correlation between "How I Teach" and the F scale. In addition he found that F-scale scores tended to decrease and "How I Teach" scores to increase as a function of the number of courses taken in psychology; however, this relationship was not significant. As a result of his findings, Juul suggests that "In the interest of children, students who display extreme authoritarianism should be encouraged to enter some field of endeavor that does not entail constant contact with children" (36, p. 189). Also he suggests that teachers should be helped to understand the causes of an authoritarian personality and be made aware that many practices within the classroom tend to aggravate these tendencies toward authoritarianism.

ATTITUDE CHANGE

Christie (11), using 182 white inductees in an army basic training center, attempted to find the relationship between involuntary membership in a military society and individual acceptance of authoritarian statements. A modified form of the F scale was given in conjunction with interviews prior to and after completion of six weeks of infantry training. Only a minor increase in acceptance of F-scale items was found upon the second administration of the F scale. However, when the recruits were divided into subgroups on the basis of sociometric data, it was found that those recruits who were more accepted than rejected by both peers and training personnel did shift significantly ($p < .05$) toward higher F-scale scores. The increase in authoritarianism by those recruits who fit better into military life was taken to indicate the importance of situational as well as personality factors in the acceptance of the authoritarian ideology. Although it is no doubt true that situational factors are important, one cannot draw definite conclusions until the problem of the relationship of authoritarianism and military adjustment is better understood.

Levinson and Schermerhorn (39) used the F scale together with several other variables in a study of the emotional-attitudinal effects on its members of a workshop in intergroup relations. In the test given at the beginning of the workshop they found authoritarianism to be somewhat greater (*a*) among Negroes than among whites, (*b*) among teachers as compared to other occupations, (*c*) among Catholics than among "conventional" Protestants, and (*d*) among "conventional" Protestants than among humanistic Protestants (Unitarians and Congregationalists) and Jews. Of particular interest is the fact that they found a significant decrease ($p < .05$) in F-scale scores on the second testing which was done at the end of the workshop. Nevertheless, the over-all trends remained the same, as was demonstrated by a correlation of .75 between the initial and final testings. For those who are interested in changing prejudicial attitudes this study should offer some hope; however, only the fact that these attitudes can be changed in a relatively short period of time has been demonstrated. Data are still needed to provide information concerning the best means of changing these attitudes and perhaps of greater importance, we need data concerning the relative stability of these attitudinal shifts.

A recent study of Wagman (62) seems to shed some light on the problem of method of changing the prejudiced attitudes of relatively authoritarian and nonauthoritarian individuals. It was found that for relatively high F-scale scorers, attitudes of racial prejudice were increased or decreased by use of a technique of authoritarian suggestion. Although a nonauthoritarian information method was effective with low F-scale scorers, it tended to "boomerang" for the high scorers. These findings are provocative and may lead to a greater understanding of attitude change; however, they are not unequivocal. Although in most cases Wagman's results were in the direction predicted, in a number of cases they failed to reach the .05 level of significance.

Personality Correlates

SOCIAL PERCEPTION

Scodel and Mussen (59) report a study intended to give additional information on the characteristics of authoritarian perception. Specifically, they wished to test the hypothesis that ". . . authoritarians, because of their lack of insight into others and their need to consider themselves members of the ingroup, would perceive nonauthoritarian peers to have attitudes and personality characteristics similar to their own" (59, p. 184). They studied 27 pairs of subjects, each consisting of an authoritarian and a nonauthoritarian, as defined by F scores. These pairs were told to discuss such neutral topics as radio, television, and the movies. At the conclusion of these sessions, subjects were given a second administration of the F scale with instructions to respond as they thought their discussion partners would. In line with the hypothesis, the high authoritarians did not perceive their partners as having F-scale scores differing from their own; whereas those with low F-scale scores estimated their partners' scores to be significantly higher than their own, but lower than they actually were. The low F-scale scorers were significantly more accurate in their estimate of their partners' responses on both the F scale (and the MMPI) than were the high F-scale scorers. The results, therefore, are in accord with the hypothesis.

In a study of the stability of the self

concept, Brownfain (9) thought it desirable to distinguish between rigid and stable individuals. Accordingly, he used the F scale to identify rigid individuals so as to eliminate them from his sample; he found the correlation between F-scale scores and his index of stability for this sample of 62 to be $-.25$ ($p < .05$). Thus, in accordance with his expectations, the lower (more stable) a person's score on this index, the higher his F-scale score.

By way of contrast to Brownfain's finding, however, Cowen (19) found that low negative self-concept scores went with high F scores. These results were equivocal. In one group ($N = 34$) he failed to find a significant difference, whereas in another ($N = 47$) he found differences in authoritarianism between high and low negative self-concept scorers to be significant at the .01 level. Cowen suggests the generalization that high scorers, i.e., those with a marked negative self concept, are less predisposed toward authoritarian attitudes.

RIGIDITY

Brown (6, 7, 8) reports a study of the relationship between rigidity and authoritarianism. Since in exploratory studies he failed to verify Rokeach's findings of the relationship between problem-solving rigidity and authoritarianism, he compared their respective procedures and found indications that it might be necessary to arouse some anxiety over achievement before authoritarian subjects would perform rigidly on the Einstellung arithmetic problems. It was hypothesized that this anxiety would be aroused when the testing orientation was ego-involving. Using the ego-involving nature of testing atmosphere as the independent variable, he administered the F scale, the Einstellung arithmetic problems (as a measure of rigidity), and McClelland's projective measure of need for achievement (to provide an index of anxiety over achievement), to a group of college students.

As expected, there was a greater correlation between the score on the Einstellung problems and the F-scale score in the group that was ego-involved than in the group that was relaxed. It is interesting to note that in the group that received an ego-involving orientation, both authoritarianism and rigidity were associated with anxiety over achievement, while in the relaxed group, moderate anxiety scores were associated with high F-scale scores, but not with greater rigidity in problem solving. Brown suggests that these results indicate that the rigidity which is associated with authoritarianism is a kind of defense mechanism which is perceived as warding off personal failures.

Jones (35) has studied the relationship between Necker Cube fluctuation and F-scale performance. Drawings of the Necker Cube were presented to two groups of Naval Aviation Cadets. One group ($N = 251$) was given a set toward reversal, while a second group ($N = 122$) was given a set against reversal. Kendall's rank-correlation procedure was used to compare F-scale scores with the number of reversals reported by each cadet. In the first group, a correlation of $-.144$ (which corresponds to a normal estimate of $r = -.22$) was found when the cube was drawn on the board. Similar results were found when each cadet had a drawing of the Necker Cube on a sheet before him. In both cases the null hypothesis was rejected at the .01 level or better; however, in the second group the rank correlation between the two variables was only $-.017$ (which corresponds to a normal estimate of $r = -.03$). By way of interpretation,

Jones suggests that the authoritarians are intolerant of fluctuation, while the nonauthoritarians are not so disposed. He concludes that "Since the F scale is a measure of authoritarian attitudes, an empirical relationship between the F scale and a perceptual variable speaks strongly for a personal base to authoritarian attitudes. . . . Only by supposing a personal substructure underlying the adoption of authoritarian attitudes can we account for the observed empirical relationship" (35, p. 126).

Because there have been conflicting results concerning whether the authoritarian is more rigid and more intolerant of ambiguity than is the nonauthoritarian, Davids (21) has attempted to clarify the issue. He administered the F scale, the Taylor Manifest Anxiety Scale, ambiguous visual stimuli (the inkblot concepts from McReynold's Concept Evaluation Technique) and ambiguous auditory stimuli (selections from the Azzageddi Test) to a group of twenty male college students selected on the basis of the heterogeneity of their backgrounds. In addition, information was gathered concerning each student's academic achievement and his "ego-structure" (the latter was based on the judgment of a clinical psychologist).

It was found that the F-scale scores correlated positively with manifest anxiety and negatively with academic achievement and ego-structure. All of these correlations were statistically significant. However, contrary to theory and the experimenter's expectations, no significant relationship was found between the F-scale scores and tolerance of either ambiguous visual stimuli or ambiguous auditory stimuli. Also, a direct measure of ambiguity tolerance based on the subject's ratings of their own reactions to the auditory task showed no significant relation with F-scale scores. These data would seem to add more weight to the point of view that intolerance of ambiguity is not part of the authoritarian syndrome. Nevertheless, since various investigators have used different instruments and have employed greatly differing samples, their data cannot be combined to give a clear-cut answer to the problem. At present the available evidence is spotty and equivocal.

NEUROTICISM

Jones (34), in a study of the relationship between manifest anxiety and authoritarianism, administered the F scale and the Taylor Manifest Anxiety Scale to two samples (Ns of 166 and 245, respectively) of Naval Aviation Cadets. For the two samples he found significant rank correlations of .134 ($p < .015$) and .143 ($p < .003$), respectively. Jones notes that while positive correlations were found, nevertheless, they are rather low. This can be explained, he suggests, on the basis of three considerations. First, the F scale measures authoritarian ideology and thus high scores may not always reflect authoritarian personalities, but instead authoritarian inclination. Second, among the low F-scale scorers there may be "genuine authoritarians of some other sort than that measured by the F scale" (34, p. 3). Finally, anxiety may accompany a number of personality disorders, many of which are not in themselves authoritarian. Jones concludes with the view that, if the presence of anxiety may be taken as an index of underlying neurosis, authoritarianism may be regarded as a neurotic form (34, p. 4).

Taking a point of view which is diametrically opposite to Jones' conclusion, Masling (43) suggests that the concept of the authoritarian personality can have utility only when it is devoid of what he considers to be value judgments. Despite the fact that some observers have viewed the authoritarian as neurotic, Masling refers to four studies which have failed to demonstrate that the authoritarian is significantly different from the equalitarian with respect to neuroticism. Of particular interest here is a study which Masling made with Courtney and Greer (18) in which they failed to find a significant correlation between the F scale and the Rotter Incomplete Sentences Test. When high and low F-scale scorers were compared in terms of their incomplete sentences, there was no significant difference between means. Masling concludes that there is a tendency to use the term "authoritarian" as a mild form of profanity to describe undesirable persons. He suggests that the concept be re-examined in the light of these data and be purified of value judgments before further work is done using it as an anchorage for research (43, p. 318).

Stotsky (61) has presented evidence that, although existing data seem to show that there is not a relationship between neuroticism and the F-scale scores, students in psychology classes are learning a neurotic stereotype of the authoritarian. Students ($N = 137$) enrolled in classes of adjustment were presented with the F scale three times. The first time they were told to respond according to their personal opinions; the second time as a "neurotic individual" would; and the third time as "the normal person" would. Critical ratios showed significant ($p < .001$) differences between the means in each of the three possible comparisons. The students rated themselves lower than "normals" and the "normals" lower than the "neurotics." The author suggests that this indicates the presence of a stereotype regarding the authoritar-

ian which follows on the tendency, described by Masling (43), to view "authoritarian" as somehow "bad."

IMPULSIVITY

Sampson (58) undertook an investigation to determine the differences in chance-taking behavior between authoritarians and nonauthoritarians. Using as subjects 93 boys and girls in a high-school college-preparatory program, he conducted two gambling experiments, after which he administered the F scale, a questionnaire concerning behavior in the gambling experiments, and the MMPI.

Contrary to his expectations, no differences were found between authoritarian and nonauthoritarian subjects in their mean chance-taking behavior. Also, he found "no consistent evidences . . . for a relationship between mean chance-taking behavior and impulsivity . . ." (58, p. 96). A significant tendency was found, however, for inconsistency in chance-taking behavior to be associated with low authoritarianism. There was evidence, too, that persons who are inconsistent in their chance-taking behavior obtain higher impulsivity scores. Sampson suggests that "the inconsistent behavior of authoritarian persons may have been due to the pressure of such conflicting factors as their estimation of the most logical behavior according to probabilities, their desire to hold to what they could be sure of, and perhaps to 'hunches' that they might be lucky. The more impulsive, loosely organized behavior of authoritarian persons is interpreted as a resultant of their confusion and conflict in a situation of manifest uncertainty" (58, p. 97). It should be emphasized that these results do not necessarily support the contention that authoritarians are intolerant of ambiguity.

MISCELLANEOUS

Radke-Yarrow and Lande (50) have investigated the relationship of personality and reactions to minority group-belonging. Sixty Jewish men and women of college age were studied. Each subject was given a battery of tests covering personality and group-belonging variables. The F scale was found to be related to reactions of group-belonging: individuals with high F-scale scores were much more anti-Semitic ($p < .001$) and showed more avoidance of group-identification ($p < .03$), than were individuals with low F-scale scores. A comparison of high and low F-scale scorers also revealed that those persons who scored high were more aggressive and less constructive in their reactions to problems arising out of minority-majority group conflicts. Finally, it was found that in this sample the high F-scale scorers also scored high on a scale of social distance.

It is noteworthy that Adelson (1) has developed a scale of Jewish Authoritarianism which correlates .67 with the F scale. This scale is said to be internally consistent and have a corrected odd-even reliability of .79. Adelson has found this scale useful in differentiating certain subgroups within his Jewish college student sample.

Rosen (56) has compared volunteers and nonvolunteers for psychological experimentation. He found that volunteers evidenced significantly lower scores on the F scale than did nonvolunteers. Furthermore, volunteers were found to take significantly longer to complete his questionnaire. It is conceivable, however, that the differences were more a function of interest than of authoritarianism, that

is, the volunteers may have been trying to obtain "better" scores.

Meer (45, 46) has presented evidence concerning the affective content of the dreams of high F-scale scorers as opposed to low F-scale scorers. For his sample of undergraduates, he found that high scorers have more aggression toward outgroup characters than toward ingroup characters ($p < .01$); in the dreams of the low scorers, there was no significant difference in aggression between ingroup and outgroup characters. In addition, he found that high scorers have more friendly acts with ingroup characters than with outgroup characters in their dreams ($p < .05$); no such differences were found for low scorers. Meer indicates that the significant differences obtained support in part the contention that authoritarians cannot tolerate emotional ambivalence.

Interpersonal Behavior

This section is concerned with behavioral correlates of authoritarianism, particularly as they are manifested in personal interactions.

LEADERSHIP

The relationship between authoritarianism and leadership has been the focus of attention in a number of studies. Military and industrial needs for leaders are everpresent, but the Korean war heightened these needs at about the same time that *The Authoritarian Personality* was published. On the surface, at least, there appeared to be a relationship between authoritarian ideology and leadership, especially in the military institution which traditionally has been seen as authoritarian.

Rohde (53) tested the hypothesis that

authoritarians are more likely than equal-itarians to be accepted as followers by their superiors. The F scale was admin-istered to each of 176 aircrew members. In addition, each man was rated by his airplane commander according to three standards: (*a*) willingness to take the man into combat, (*b*) the man's desira-bility as a friend, and (*c*) the command-er's confidence in the man. Contrary to expectation, negative correlations (—.326, —.457, and —.112 respec-tively) were found between these stand-ards and F-scale scores. These results appear somewhat puzzling in light of theoretical considerations regarding au-thoritarianism. One might have expected that leaders would tend to select those individuals who would readily submit to their authority (authoritarian submis-sion).

Further unexpected results were found by Hollander (29, 30) in a study with Naval Aviation Cadets. He hypothesized that (*a*) there would be a significant pos-itive relationship between scores achieved on the F scale and incidence of choice by one's peers for a military leadership position, and (*b*) there would be a sig-nificant difference, with respect to F-scale scores, between the leadership nominees of those "high" on authori-tarianism and those "low" on authoritar-ianism (30, p. 365). A total of 268 cadets from nine consecutively formed sections at the Naval School of Pre-Flight were asked to fill out a leadership nomination form for their section in which they were instructed to pick the three best qualified and the three least qualified to serve in the hypothetical position of "Student Commander." The peer-nomination scores evolved were re-lated to F-scale scores. Correlational analysis revealed a negative relationship

between authoritarianism and peer nomi-nations ($r = -.23$; $p < .01$) which re-mained significant even when intelligence was held constant. Again contrary to ex-pectation, no significant differences were found between those subjects nominated as leaders by others who were respec-tively "high" and "low" on authoritarian-ism. In essence, Hollander suggests that a high F-scale score may indicate a per-son's lack of social intelligence or social perception, thus making him less able to deal effectively with the needs of others and consequently less acceptable to his peers as a leader. Another consid-eration put forth is that there may be real differences between acceptance of the authoritarian ideology and authori-tarian behavior as it is traditionally con-ceived.

Bass *et al.* (5) have hypothesized that personality variables which tend to differ-entiate between high and low authori-tarians would also differentiate between those who score respectively high and low in leaderless group discussions (LGD). The F scale was administered to a group of ROTC students for whom LGD ratings were obtained the previous year. A curvilinear relationship was found between these two variables (eta was significantly greater than Pearsonian *r* at the .01 level). However, the authors note that the obtained Pearsonian *r* of —.16 ($p < .05$) indicates ". . . that there existed a slight, general tendency for those who score higher on the LGD to be more resourceful, flexible, and self-reliant, and less stereotyped, submissive, power oriented, and rigid individuals than those who scored lower on the LGD" (5, p. 127). They report that an inspection of the scatterplot of these data revealed that the extreme authori-tarians did very poorly as a group on the

LGD. Those who achieved maximum success on the LGD were the subjects that tended to be permissive but not overly so. Finally, those who were extremely tolerant tended to score low on LGD, but not as low, however, as the more authoritarian subjects. While these interpretations are worth noting, one may well feel that they are founded more in theory than in the available empirical evidence.

In still another relevant work, Jones (32, 33) has studied authoritarianism as it relates to the perception and evaluation of potential leadership. Ten groups were set up, composed equally of high and low F-scale scorers. Each group was presented with information about a recruit platoon leader by means of a mock interview recorded and played to the subjects. The information given was varied along two dimensions: personal power (forceful or passive) and leadership attitude (autocratic or democratic). Subsequently, they were asked to rate the potential leader on a 30-trait rating scale. Contrary to his prediction, it was found that low authoritarians saw the forceful stimulus person as more powerful and the passive stimulus person as less powerful than did the high authoritarians. In an interpretation similar to Hollander's (30), Jones suggests that this difference may be a function of the relative sensitivity of the lows to personal or internal power cues as compared to the highs who tend to differentiate on the basis of institutional status. The high authoritarians also tend to be more accepting and less critical in their ratings and descriptive comments than do those who obtain low F-scale scores. Moreover, it was found that those respectively high and low in authoritarianism differ in their organization of an impression as measured by differences in the intercorrelations of traits, but this organization was found to be highly dependent on the nature of the stimulus information presented. The lows tended to evaluate leadership on the basis of many different personal and performance qualities, whereas the highs tended to make a clear distinction between the merits of the stimulus person as a leader and his worth as a person. Contrary to Jones's prediction the lows demonstrated a more pervasive "halo effect" than did the highs; however, the lows were seen to be at the same time more sensitive to stimulus cues and generally more critical of the stimulus person.

Medalia (44) has produced the most recent investigation of authoritarianism and leadership. With a sample of airmen ($N = 298$) in Air Force radar squadrons, he tested several hypotheses having to do with the interplay of F scores with leader acceptance and group cohesiveness. He used re-enlistment intent as an index of the latter variable. One of his major predictions was that the correlation between leader acceptance and re-enlistment intent would increase with higher F scores. It was found, however, while there was a considerable increase in correlation between these two variables for the middle level of F-scale scores, as compared to the low level, that the trend did not continue; the correlation was very low for the high F-scale scorers and, in fact, slightly lower than was obtained in the case of the low F-scale scorers (44, p. 211). But beyond this, Medalia has provided data indicating a positive relationship between leader acceptance and the level of unit member authoritarianism. Furthermore, a negative attitude toward re-enlistment was found more often among low authoritarians than among high authoritarians. The central test of the "Frommian compromise" (44, p. 212) raises more questions than it answers, however.

To deal with some of the problems associated with the relationship between authoritarianism and acceptance of military ideology, French and Ernest (25) studied 186 airmen undergoing basic training. The F scale, some items similar to the F scale, and a "military ideology" scale were administered once at the beginning of training and again at the end of six weeks. Half of the subjects were tested under allegedly anonymous conditions, while the other half signed their papers.

In accordance with their hypothesis they found that F-scale scores were related to acceptance of the military ideology. It was also found that the relationship was somewhat stronger when the items dealing with projectivity, sexual goings on, superstition, and so on, were omitted, that is, when only the items dealing with attitudes toward authority, conventionalism, and hard-headedness were used. This may be a clue to reasons for some of the unexpected results found by others. Indeed, it may suggest that the F scale attempts to measure too much, at least insofar as military adjustment and leadership are concerned. It is also of interest that the "F scale responses were found to be unchanged by military training, but subject to increase under the pressure of the combination signing the papers and the first week of training" (25, p. 191).

On theoretical grounds, the use of the F scale in studies of leadership appears entirely appropriate. In point of fact, though, the meaningfulness of the empirical data obtained is not always evident. One may even say that, since both variables are so complex and diffuse, we are correlating one unknown with another.

GROUP BEHAVIOR

In a study by McCurdy and Eber (41), groups with either an authoritarian or democratic orientation were established. In addition, one each of the two kinds of groups was made up of high F-scale scorers while the other was made up of low F-scale scorers. All groups were given the problem of learning the correct pattern of switch order necessary to keep a bulb lit in the center of the table at which they were seated. Contrary to expectation, no significant differences were found between groups, except in the case where errors per unit of time were computed; there the F ratio for the significance of differences was significant at the end of one and two minutes, that is, when the groups were still actively at work trying to solve the problem. The authors suggest that it is possible that the nonsignificant results may have been a function of the disturbance caused by placing authoritarians in a democratic setup. This contention still requires experimental demonstration.

Wells (64) has investigated a number of possible behavioral correlates of the authoritarian personality. He collected detailed records of the behavior of individuals, respectively high and low scorers on the F scale, from observations of small discussion classes. Of his twelve hypotheses, only one was supported by the data; this was the prediction that high F-scale scorers would check more of the complimentary responses on a "Comments on the Course" questionnaire. The over-all conclusion from this study was that perceptual and cognitive differences cannot be clearly translated into behavioral terms. This conclusion adds to the position that there is an incongruity between authoritarian attitudes and authoritarian behavior, as has been suggested elsewhere (30).

Cultural and Subcultural Variations

VARIATION WITHIN THE UNITED STATES

Christie and Garcia (12) noted that inasmuch as a wide range of attitudes and ideologies regarding minority groups are overtly expressed in California, subjects from this population would have greater freedom to select ideologies which are compatible with their need for outlets for aggressive impulses. As a consequence, it seemed reasonable to determine whether similar patterns would be found in a subculture marked by relatively more homogeneous ideologies. They compared, therefore, the F-scale responses of a group of students at the University of California—presumably comparable to the original sample of Adorno et al. (2)—with a college population in an unnamed southwestern city. The latter population, although characterized by similar demographic variables, was said to have had a more limited ideological exposure. They found that the southwestern city sample had significantly higher acceptance of items on the F scale. Furthermore, an item analysis of the F scale indicated that 18 of the thirty items were accepted to a significantly greater extent ($p < .05$) by the southwestern city students (12, p. 469). A cluster analysis of the responses on the F scale yielded three clusters which were similar in both groups, but the remaining four California clusters were not duplicated by the five remaining southwestern city clusters. It was found, too, that the same item often fell in different clusters in the same samples; therefore, it was suggested that interpretation of the meaning of an item must vary between the two subcultures (12, p. 465).

Bass (5) in the study of the LGD mentioned above, under leadership, used as subjects students from the deep South. He found that in general there was not much difference in mean scores between this and the original California group. It was noted, however, that the range in scores for his subjects was quite restricted. This may have served to attenuate the correlation.

Davidson and Kruglov (22) have investigated the possibility that certain background variables have an effect on F-scale scores. They administered the F scale and a background questionnaire to a sample of 492 male students enrolled at the City College of New York. For purposes of comparison, they selected groups of high and low scorers on the F scale (1 SD above and below the mean, respectively). They found no significant differences between high and low scorers with respect to parents' birthplace or occupation, with the exception that significantly more ($p < .05$) students with one foreign-born parent were in the low scoring group. They did find significant differences between high and low scorers with respect to interest in college: significantly more ($p < .01$) of the students majoring in engineering were among the high scorers than were among the low scorers. Also a significantly larger proportion ($p < .01$) of the students majoring in liberal arts were low F-scale scorers. Davidson and Kruglov suggest that some of these background variables may account for similarities and differences among persons exposed to different subcultures.

FOREIGN SAMPLES

Prothro and Melikian (49) set out to determine whether ". . . residence in an authoritarian culture [leads] to greater acceptance of the 'authoritarian' items of the California scale" (49, p. 354). They suggest that this problem has implications regarding the validity of the scale. In addition, their study also attempts to answer the question of whether an authoritarian culture produces other traits found in the antidemocratic personality, such as Politico-Economic Conservatism. Using 22 F-scale items, plus items from other scales, the authors tested 130 subjects (70 Christians and 60 Moslems) at The American University, Beirut, Lebanon. A mean F score of 5.03 was found which was significantly higher than that found in studies with American students. The Moslems had a mean score of 5.15, the Christians 4.86; a *t* between these was significant ($p < .02$).

Since a somewhat abbreviated scale was used, it was not legitimate to make direct statistical comparisons between this sample and American samples. However, the authors suggest that the difference would probably be highly significant. It is interesting to note that in this sample, unlike American samples, the correlation between Politico-Economic Conservatism and the F scale was quite low ($r = .02$). Despite the fact that the F scale was not used in its conventional form, the data clearly indicate a marked cultural variation in F-scale scores and at the same time lend some weight to the validity of the F scale as a measure of authoritarianism.

Another study, this one by Cohn and Carsch (17), used the F scale with a sample of 140 workers in a German cosmetics factory. For this group, a mean score of 5.26 was obtained. "This score is higher than the mean score for any group thus far reported in the literature. . . . If one makes the assumption that these workers are 'fascistic' personalities, then the data appear to support the validity of the F scale" (17, p. 471). The authors also found a negative correlation between educational level and F-scale scores; this is comparable to the trend found with American subjects by Cohn (15), among others.

Studies of the Instrument

Since it is an implicit assumption in studies using the F scale that it is an indirect measure, i.e., one with low "transparency," it seems fitting to consider a paper which deals with this assumption. Cohn (14) cites evidence that the F scale correlates with intelligence and suggests that such a relationship may mean that more intelligent persons are able to penetrate the meaning of the F scale and thus respond in a more acceptable or "proper" way. To test these contentions he administered the F scale twice to a group of 64 college students. On the first administration they were instructed to respond as they thought "highly educated, intelligent people" would; on the second administration they were told to respond as they thought "unskilled laborers of low intelligence" would. The mean scores were 2.39 and 5.45, respectively, for the first and second administrations; this difference was significant at the .01 level. Cohn also correlated the difference in scores with the "Altus Verbal Aptitude Test" and found the relationship to be significant at the .01 level. It was Cohn's conclusion that ". . . the F scale can be faked and therefore cannot be considered an indirect measure.

Furthermore, it would appear that intelligence is related to the ███ to 'fake good' " (14, p. 732).

In a similar vein ███ also suggested that it may be possible that the F scale measures authoritarian submission, because people who have a tendency to respond positively in an ambiguous situation are submissive, rather than because of item content. Leavitt *et al.* (38), taking this study as a starting point, have further investigated this aspect of the F scale. They reworded half of the original items negatively and administered the F scale (half positive and half negative items) to five independent populations. They found generally that with high scorers (based on the unchanged half) there were negative or low positive correlations between the two halves, while with low scorers the correlations between the two halves were fairly high and positive. This was taken to indicate that ". . . the present design of the F scale confounds form and content variables, but in the 'right' direction; that authoritarian people as measured by the scale agree more with authoritative statements; and that, therefore, a portion of the discriminatory power of the F scale derives from its form, rather than its content" (38, p. 221). A somewhat comparable finding has been reported by Mullery *et al.* (48).

Related to this last study, Bass (4) has investigated the hypothesis that one's ". . . performance on the F scale has less to do with the content validity of the items than with the response set to acquiesce to any generalizations about social issues—authoritarian or equalitarian" (4, p. 616). He composed a scale made up of opposites of each of the F-scale items. After having the new scale items rated by a group of students on

their opposition to the original items, he constructed two scales each made up of half new items and half original items. These scales were administered to students in psychology classes.

The tendency for an individual to support both the new items and the original items was taken as a measure of a response set to acquiescence. It was found that there was a greater tendency toward acquiescence as the items became more ambivalent; a factor analysis indicated that about three-fourths of the reliable variance of the F scale could be accounted for in terms of this response set. Bass, therefore, concludes ". . . that a much more parsimonious explanation can be given to account for the positive relations between authoritarianism, misanthropy, xenophobia, and ethnocentrism, where all are measured by scores based on acceptance of generalizations about social affairs. It appears that these correlations may be due primarily to a response set to acquiesce to *any* generalization about social issues" (4, p. 623).

Webster, Sanford, and Freedman (63) have developed a 123-item scale based on the F scale which is said to tap the authoritarian syndrome; it correlates .74 with the F scale, while giving evidence of being harder to fake. Some 677 items drawn from various personality tests including the MMPI and the California Personality Inventory were used in its construction. This new scale is said to be less ideological and more personality-centered than the F scale.

Summary and Conclusions

Some sixty-odd studies involving the F scale (2), reported from 1950 through 1955, were surveyed. It was noted that scores derived from the scale have been used in studies of prejudice, leadership, rigidity, adjustment, and group behavior, among others. Furthermore, the F scale has been found to correlate with intelligence, xenophobia, family ideology, anxiety, re-enlistment intent, and co-operation in experimentation, to name but a few of the multitude of variables to which it has been related.

Without entertaining a broad critique, one may nonetheless be awed by the massive and amorphous area which has been touched upon by F-scale researchers. To comprehend it requires a theoretical substructure which is not yet available, except in kaleidoscope form. But some distinguishable points do stand forth. Notable among these is the evident fact that the F scale correlates most systematically with other paper-and-pencil measures, and least systematically with interpersonal behaviors, particularly as situational conditions are varied.

In this regard, it is well to recall that intelligence and educational level have both been found to relate negatively to the scale. It is not astonishing, then, that a general intelligence factor may operate here to provide the basis for a good many of the r's which have been so zealously garnered. That intelligence underlies some of these relationships, is only part of the story. There is evidence, too, that various response sets may account for still more of the variance involved.

Regarding interpersonal studies, it is clear that relationships found with "leadership," let us say, have not held as the situation was altered. Surely this ought not surprise anyone in light of the newer conceptions of situational determinants. But even more significant, in this picture, is the concomitant inclination to impute a correspondence between ideology, personality, and institutional form so as to view them as having a congruency of "authoritarian" identity. This may be theoretically acceptable, but it is not empirically supportable, at this juncture. Only confusion has derived from this confounding of elements in research undertakings.

The more ultimate questions regarding the scale's place as a personality measure are not readily resolved by recourse to the works covered. Deeper consideration of this issue has been presented elsewhere (13). At this writing, one may say that, if anything, the F-scale literature begs questions about the very definition of such terms as "personality" and "syndrome" themselves.

Today, although much work has been done using the F scale, one might reasonably hesitate to recommend it as a "practical" instrument in applied settings. Many questions still remain to be answered before its use would have much meaning in terms of predicting human behavior. Perhaps the greatest need, if the F scale is to be used still more in research, is for evidence regarding its behavioral implications. Beyond this, adequate studies of the scale qua scale are required; hopeful signs in this direction are to be seen in some of the work reported.

References

1. ADELSON, J. B. A study of minority group authoritarianism. *J. abnorm. soc. Psychol.*, 1953, **48**, 477–485.

2. ADORNO, T. W., FRENKEL-BRUNSWIK, ELSE, LEVINSON, D. J., & SANFORD, R. N. *The authoritarian personality*. New York: Harper, 1950.

3. Aumack, L. The effects of imprisonment upon authoritarian attitudes. *Amer. Psychologist,* 1955, **10**, 342. (Abstract)

4. Bass, B. M. Authoritarianism or acquiescence? *J. abnorm. soc. Psychol.,* 1955, **51**, 616–623.

5. Bass, B. M., McGehee, C. R., Hawkins, W. C., Young, P. C., & Gebel, A. S. Personality variables related to leaderless group discussion behavior. *J. abnorm. soc. Psychol.,* 1953, **48**, 120–128.

6. Brown, R. W. Some determinants of the relationship between rigidity and authoritarianism. Unpublished doctor's dissertation, Univer. of Michigan, 1952.

7. ———. A determinant of the relationship between rigidity and authoritarianism. *J. abnorm. soc. Psychol.,* 1953, **48**, 469–476.

8. ———. Authoritarianism and the achievement motive. *Amer. Psychologist,* 1952, **7**, 311. (Abstract)

9. Brownfain, J. J. Stability of the self-concept as a dimension of personality. *J. abnorm. soc. Psychol.,* 1952, **47**, 597–606.

10. Campbell, D. T., & McCandless, B. R. Ethnocentrism, xenophobia and personality. *Hum. Relat.,* 1951, **4**, 185–192.

11. Christie, R. Changes in authoritarianism as related to situational factors. *Amer. Psychologist,* 1952, **7**, 307–308. (Abstract)

12. Christie, R., & Garcia, J. Subcultural variation in authoritarian personality. *J. abnorm. soc. Psychol.,* 1951, **46**, 457–469.

13. Christie, R., & Jahoda, Marie (Eds.) *Studies in the scope and method of "The Authoritarian Personality."* Glencoe, Ill.: Free Press, 1954.

14. Cohn, T. S. Is the F scale indirect? *J. abnorm. soc. Psychol.,* 1952, **47**, 732.

15. ———. Factors related to scores on the F scale. Unpublished doctor's dissertation, Univer. of Michigan, 1953.

16. ———. The relation of the F scale to a response set to answer positively. *Amer. Psychologist,* 1953, **8**, 335. (Abstract)

17. Cohn, T. S., & Carsch, H. Administration of the F scale to a sample of Germans. *J. abnorm. soc. Psychol.,* 1954, **49**, 471.

18. Courtney, P. D., Greer, F. L., & Masling, J. M. Leadership identification and acceptance. Philadelphia: Institute for Research in Human Relations, 1952. (Rep. No. 1.)

19. Cowen, E. L. The "negative self concept" as a personality measure. *J. consult. Psychol.,* 1954, **18**, 138–142.

20. Crockett, W. H., & Meidinger, T. The effects of F-scale score, similarity, and relevance of information upon accuracy of interpersonal perception. *Amer. Psychologist,* 1955, **10**, 341. (Abstract)

21. Davids, A. Some personality and intellectual correlates of intolerance of ambiguity. *J. abnorm. soc. Psychol.,* 1955, **51**, 415–420.

22. Davidson, Helen, & Kruglov, Lorraine. Some background correlates of personality and social attitudes. *J. soc. Psychol.,* 1953, **38**, 233–240.

23. Flowerman, S. H., Stewart, Naomi, & Strauss, Marian. Further investigation of the validity of "authoritarianism" as predictive of ethnic prejudices. *Amer. Psychologist,* 1950, **5**, 307–308. (Abstract)

24. Freedman, M. B., Webster, H., & Sanford, N. Some psychodynamic correlates of authoritarianism in women. *Amer. Psychologist,* 1955, **10**, 341. (Abstract)

25. French, Elizabeth, & Ernest, R. R. The relation between authoritarianism and acceptance of military ideology. *J. Pers.,* 1955, **24**, 181–191.

26. Goldstein, M. General tolerance-prejudice and the authoritarian syndrome. Unpublished doctor's dissertation, Princeton Univer., 1952.

27. GUBA, E. G., & GETZELS, J. W. The construction of an other-directedness instrument, with some preliminary data on validity. *Amer. Psychologist,* 1954, **9,** 385–386. (Abstract)

28. GUMP, P. V. Anti-democratic trends and student reaction to President Truman's dismissal of General MacArthur. *J. soc. Psychol.,* 1953, **38,** 131–135.

29. HOLLANDER, E. P. An investigation of the relationship between authoritarian attitudes and leadership selection in a military setting. Unpublished doctor's dissertation. Columbia Univer., 1952.

30. ———. Authoritarianism and leadership choice in a military setting. *J. abnorm. soc. Psychol.,* 1954, **49,** 365–370.

31. HUFFMAN, PHYLLIS. Authoritarian personality and family ideology: a scale for the measurement of traditional family ideology. Unpublished master's thesis, Western Reserve Univer., 1950.

32. JONES, E. E. The role of authoritarianism in the perception and evaluation of perspective leaders. Unpublished doctor's dissertation, Harvard Univer., 1953.

33. ———. Authoritarianism as a determinant of first-impression formation. *J. Pers.,* 1954, **23,** 107–127.

34. JONES, M. B. Aspects of the autonomous personality: I. Manifest anxiety. *U. S. Naval Sch. Aviat. Med. Res. Rep.,* 1953, Proj. No. NM 001 058.25.03.

35. ———. Authoritarianism and intolerance of fluctuation. *J. abnorm. soc. Psychol.,* 1955, **50,** 125–126.

36. JUUL, K. D. Authoritarian personality in relation to teachers' attitudes toward child behavior. Unpublished doctor's dissertation, Wayne Univer., 1953.

37. KATES, S. L., & DIAB, L. N. Authoritarian ideology and attitudes on parent-child relationships. *J. abnorm. soc. Psychol.,* 1955, **51,** 13–16.

38. LEAVITT, H. J., HAX, H., & ROCHE, J. H. "Authoritarianism" and agreement with things authoritative. *J. Psychol.,* 1955, **40,** 215–221.

39. LEVINSON, D. J., & SCHERMERHORN, R. A. Emotional-attitudinal effects of an intergroup relations workshop on its members. *J. Psychol.,* 1951, **31,** 243–256.

40. LEVINSON, D. J., & HUFFMAN, PHYLLIS. Traditional family ideology and its relation to personality. *J. Pers.,* 1955, **23,** 251–273.

41. McCURDY, H. G., & EBER, H. W. Democratic versus authoritarian: a further investigation of group problem solving. *J. Pers.,* 1953, **22,** 258–269.

42. MacKINNON, W. J., & CENTERS, R. Authoritarianism, social class, and the "Iron Curtain Situation." *Amer. Psychologist,* 1955, **10,** 350–351. (Abstract)

43. MASLING, M. How neurotic is the authoritarian? *J. abnorm. soc. Psychol.,* 1954, **49,** 316–318.

44. MEDALIA, N. Z. Authoritarianism, leader acceptance, and group cohesion. *J. abnorm. soc. Psychol.,* 1955, **51,** 207–213.

45. MEER, S. J. The relation between authoritarian attitudes and dreams. *Amer. Psychologist,* 1952, **7,** 312. (Abstract)

46. ———. Authoritarian attitudes and dreams. *J. abnorm. soc. Psychol.,* 1955, **51,** 74–78.

47. MILTON, O. Presidential choice and performance on a scale of authoritarianism. *Amer. Psychologist,* 1952, **7,** 597–598.

48. MULLERY, J., *et al.* The F scale and a tendency to agree with contradictory maxims. Unpublished School of Business student paper, Univer. of Chicago, 1954.

49. PROTHRO, E. T., & MELIKIAN, L. The California public opinion scale in an authoritarian culture. *Publ. Opin. Quart.,* 1953, **17,** 353–362.

50. RADKE-YARROW, MARIAN, & LANDE, B. Personality correlates of differential reactions to minority group-belonging. *J. soc. Psychol.*, 1953, **38**, 253–272.

51. RANCK, J. G. Some personality correlates of religious attitude and belief. *Amer. Psychologist,* 1955, **10**, 350. (Abstract)

52. ROBERTS, A. H., ROKEACH, M., & McKITRICK, K. Anomie, authoritarianism, and prejudice: a replication of Srole's study. *Amer. Psychologist,* 1952, **7**, 311. (Abstract)

53. ROHDE, K. J. The relation of authoritarianism of the aircrew member to his acceptance by the airplane commander. *Amer. Psychologist,* 1951, **6**, 323. (Abstract)

54. ROKEACH, M. Dogmatism and opinionation on the left and on the right. *Amer. Psychologist,* 1952, **7**, 310–311. (Abstract)

55. ———. Religious and political commitment in relation to dogmatism and the authoritarian personality. *Amer. Psychologist,* 1955, **10**, 340–341. (Abstract)

56. ROSEN, E. Differences between volunteers and non-volunteers for psychological studies. *J. appl. Psychol.,* 1951, **35**, 185–193.

57. SANFORD, N. Recent developments in connection with the investigation of the authoritarian personality. *Sociol. Rev.* (new series), 1954, **2**, 11–33.

58. SAMPSON, H. An investigation of the relationship of chance-taking behavior to authoritarianism and impulsivity. Unpublished doctor's dissertation, Univer. of California, 1953.

59. SCODEL, A., & MUSSEN, P. Social perceptions of authoritarians and nonauthoritarians. *J. abnorm. soc. Psychol.,* 1953, **48**, 181–184.

60. STECKLER, G. A. A study of authoritarian ideology in Negro college students. Unpublished doctor's dissertation, Western Reserve Univer., 1951.

61. STOTSKY, B. A. The authoritarian personality as a stereotype. *J. Psychol.,* 1955, **39**, 325–328.

62. WAGMAN, N. M. An investigation of the effectiveness of authoritarian suggestion and non-authoritarian information as methods of changing the prejudiced attitudes of relatively authoritarian and non-authoritarian personalities. Unpublished doctor's dissertation, Univer. of Michigan, 1954.

63. WEBSTER, H., SANFORD, N., & FREEDMAN, M. A new instrument for studying authoritarianism in personality. *J. Psychol.,* 1955, **40**, 73–84.

64. WELLS, W. D. Behavioral correlates of authoritarian personality. Unpublished doctor's dissertation, Stanford Univer., 1954.

AUTHORITARIANISM OR ACQUIESCENCE?

Bernard M. Bass

Since the appearance of *The Authoritarian Personality* (1), the F scale has become one of the most widely used

Reprinted by permission of the American Psychological Association and the author from *The Journal of Abnormal and Social Psychology,* Vol. 51, 1955.

social psychological research tools. The authors and most writers subsequently believed that the items of the scale had considered content validity since they were concerned with conventional mores, submission to authority, and power orientation. Empirical validation studies, along with internal consistency analyses, appeared to corroborate these conclusions since the F scale was found to correlate to some extent with other psychometric measures such as rigidity (13), dogmatism (14), and ethnocentrism (1). Yet, the authors regarded the F scale as an "indirect" assessment. Hence, they intimated that it contained more than content validity. Cohn (7), however, showed that college students readily could distort the results, indicating the scale lacked disguise.

Purpose

The present study tested the hypothesis that performance on the F scale has less to do with the content validity of the items than with *the response set to acquiesce to any generalizations about social issues—authoritarian or equalitarian.* Thus, it was proposed that scores on the F scale and any other inventories concerned with generalizations about social relations, morals, prejudice, custom, and status relations are primarily measures of the tendency to *agree with any* opinionated or doctrinaire statements about human affairs. Verification of the hypothesis would cast new light on the findings of correlations between the F and other similarly constructed scales.

Previous Conceptualizations

A number of studies have appeared in the last few years which suggest that a more parsimonious concept than authoritarianism may be used in accounting for personality differences of significance in understanding fascist or antidemocratic tendencies.

Dogmatism, misanthropy, xenophobia, suggestibility, and acquiescence are some of the basic concepts that have been offered.

DOGMATISM

Analyses (13, 14, 15) of the F scale by Rokeach led to the inference that "authoritarianism" as measured by the F scale was a reflection in the personal-social relations area of a more generalized personality trait of dogmatism. Rokeach (14) was able to construct a Dogmatic Personality Scale composed of statements concerning overidentification with a cause, guilt, egocentrism, etc, which correlated .67 with the F scale and .51 with an inventory composed of both reactionary and radical opinionated statements, matched for opposite content, about international affairs, God, socialized medicine, etc.

MISANTHROPY

Sullivan and Adelson (16) suggested that misanthropy might be the desired, more generalized, concept. They found a correlation of .43 between assenting to derogatory statements about ethnic minorities and assenting to derogatory statements about people in general.

XENOPHOBIA

Campbell and McCandless (6) advanced xenophobia as the more basic concept. They found the E and F scales to correlate highly with each other and with a scale measuring a general dislike of others.

SUGGESTIBILITY

Guba and Getzels (10) submitted 19 "inner-directed" and 19 "outer-directed" slogans which were associated with opposing behavioral tendencies to a group of subjects. The subjects tended to accept slogans of either direction or reject both types of slogans. The tendency to accept any type of slogan also correlated significantly with scores on the F scale.

The authors concluded that both their scales were measures of suggestibility implying, then, that scores on the F scale were associated with the tendency to be suggestible.

ACQUIESCENCE

Cohn (8) found a correlation of .41 between the F scale and the tendency to respond "yes" to MMPI items. This implied that acquiescence—the tendency to concur with any statement—could account for some of the variance of the F scale. Acquiescence appeared to explain an unpublished correlational analysis of 13 scales based on 20 aphorisms each by the present author. All the scales, unfortunately, were scored in the same direction on any given scale. The author obtained an intercorrelation matrix which contained only positive correlations although the scales involved items in such diverse and opposite domains as misanthropy and affiliation, aggression and nurturance, and self-abasement and achievement.

Subsequent to the completion of the present study, the author was directed to an Italian publication by Ancona (2) in which he describes the development and use of a scale composed of 15 items from the F scale and 15 "reciprocals" of the same items in order to measure the response set to acquiesce. He obtained significant negative relations between this means of measuring acquiescence and projective measures of the need for achievement (2, 3).

Acquiescence might account also for Hardesty's (12) and Block and Block's (4, 5) results. Hardesty found that more authoritarian subjects tend to react faster in associating words involving abstract social issues. Block and Block reported that subjects who acquiesce and score high on the E scale tend to set norms

earlier in the autokinetic experiment (4), and to accept more readily suggestions from the experimenter (5).

Construction of the G Scale

For each of 29 statements in the original F scale, a statement was placed in a newly constructed scale, henceforth referred to as the G scale. (Ancona [2] labeled a similar independently developed scale, Scale $\frac{1}{F}$.) Each new statement was opposite in meaning—or as opposite as the author could make it— to an original statement of the F scale. In some cases, it was merely enough to insert or remove the word "not" or "no" in the original statement to obtain its opposite. In other cases, extensive revision was necessary.

Each of the statements of the F scale was paired with its opposite in the G scale and presented to a class of 63 students in introductory sociology. To reduce "halo" effect in the ratings, 6 pairs of statements in agreement with each other were interspersed among the 29 pairs of opposing statements.

The subjects were asked to rate each *pair* of statements using the following schedule: 0—Identical in meaning; 1—More similar than opposed in meaning; 2—Neither similar nor opposed in meaning; 3—More opposed than similar in meaning; 4—Completely opposite in meaning.

Table 1 lists the 29 pairs of statements in order of the median of ratings assigned to each pair by the subjects. In the presentation of the pairs of statements to the subjects, the order was randomized and F and G scale items were presented either first or second in random sequence.

The six pairs of similar statements, employed to reduce halo, which are not listed in Table 1 had median ratings of 2.52, 1.90, 1.01, .93, .37, and .16, respectively.

Of the original 29 pairs of F and G items, only the last pair listed in Table 1 had a median "opposition" value which indicated it was regarded by the 63 judges as a pair of statements more similar than opposed in meaning. This pair, which failed to be more opposite than similar, was eliminated from further consideration in the remainder of this study.

Comparison of the F and G Scales

One statement from each of the 28 pairs of opposite statements was placed in either Form 1 or Form 2. If a state-

ment of the F scale was placed in Form 1, its opposite G scale statement was placed in Form 2 and vice versa. Each form contained 28 statements in all, half of which were from the original F scale and half were from the G scale without any paired opposites appearing in the same form.

Subjects. Eighty-four students in various undergraduate psychology classes, who, in general had no previous knowledge of studies using the F scale were administered Forms 1 or 2. Sixty-three of these subjects were given Form 1 first and Form 2 a week later. Twenty-one students received Form 2 first and Form 1 a week later. The standard instructions given by Adorno et al. (1) were used in administering both forms.

TABLE 1. THE PAIRED OPPOSITES OF THE F AND G SCALES IN ORDER OF MEDIAN DEGREE OF OPPOSITION AS RATED BY 63 JUDGES

Median Rating of Degree of Opposition	F Scale	G Scale
3.99	People can be divided into two distinct classes, the weak and the strong.	People cannot be divided into two distinct classes, the weak and the strong.
3.97	The business man and the manufacturer are much more important to society than the artist and the professor.	The artist and the professor are much more important to society than the business man and the manufacturer.
3.97	Familiarity breeds contempt.	Familiarity does not breed contempt.
3.96	Every person should have complete faith in some supernatural power whose decisions he obeys without question.	No person should have complete faith in some supernatural power whose decisions he obeys without question.
3.95	It is best to use some prewar authorities in Germany to keep order and prevent chaos.	It is worst to use some prewar authorities in Germany to keep order and prevent chaos.
3.92	Some people are born with an urge to jump from high places.	No people are born with an urge to jump from high places.
3.91	Human nature being what it is	Human nature being what it is,

Median Rating of Degree of Opposition	F Scale	G Scale
	there will always be war and conflict.	universal peace will come about eventually.
3.87	No weakness or difficulty can hold us back if we have enough will power.	Weaknesses and difficulties can hold us back; will power is not enough.
3.84	The wild sex life of the old Greeks and Romans was tame compared to some of the goings-on in this country, even in places where people might least expect it.	Some of the goings on in this country, even in places where people might least expect it, are tame compared to the wild sex life of the Greeks and Romans.
3.83	Nobody ever learned anything really important except through suffering.	Nobody ever learned anything really important through suffering.
3.78	Homosexuals are hardly better than criminals and ought to be severely punished.	Homosexuals are not criminals and should not be punished.
3.75	Nowadays when so many different kinds of people move around and mix together so much, a person has to protect himself especially carefully against catching an infection or disease from them.	A person does not have to worry about catching an infection or disease just because many different kinds of people move around and mix together a great deal nowadays.
3.73	Sex criminals such as those who rape and attack children, deserve more than mere imprisonment; such criminals ought to be publicly whipped, or worse.	Sex criminals such as those who rape and attack children should be treated as sick people, not publicly whipped or worse.
3.71	When a person has a problem or worry, it is best for him not to think about it, but to keep busy with more cheerful things.	When a person has a problem or worry, it is best for him to think about doing something about it, not be distracted by more cheerful things.
3.67	Wars and social troubles may someday be ended by earthquake or flood that will destroy the whole world.	Wars and social troubles may someday be ended by wisdom and education, not by an earthquake or flood that will destroy the whole world.
3.63	Some day it will probably be shown that astrology can explain a lot of things.	Astrology will never explain anything.
3.55	An insult to our honor should always be punished.	An insult to our honor should be studied, not punished.

Median Rating of Degree of Opposition	F Scale	G Scale
3.51	Young people sometimes get rebellious ideas, but as they grow up they ought to get over them and settle down.	Young people sometimes get rebellious ideas. As they grow up they ought to try to carry them out and not be content to get over them and settle down.
3.51	What this country needs most, more than laws and political programs, is a few courageous, tireless, devoted leaders in whom the people can put their faith.	What this country needs most, more than a few courageous, tireless, devoted leaders in whom the people can put their faith, is better laws and political programs.
3.39	No sane, normal, decent person could ever think of hurting a close friend or relative.	A sane, normal decent person might have to hurt a close friend or relative.
3.33	Nowadays more and more people are prying into matters that should remain personal and private.	Nowadays, not enough investigating of personal and private matters is done.
3.24	Most people don't realize how much our lives are controlled by plots hatched in secret places.	Our lives are not at all controlled by plots hatched in secret places.
3.10	What a youth needs most is strict discipline, rugged determination, and the will to work and fight for family and country.	What a youth needs most is to be free to make up his own mind, to be flexible and to work and fight for what he considers right personally even though it might not be best for his family and country.
2.96	Obedience and respect for authority are the most important virtues children should learn.	Self-reliance, respect for democracy and lack of need to submit to authority are the most important virtues children should learn.
2.93	Science has its place, but there are many important things that can never possibly be understood by the human mind.	Because of science, it will be possible for the human mind to understand most important things.
2.87	There is hardly anything lower than a person who does not feel a great love, gratitude, and respect for his parents.	Many fine people honestly could never bring themselves around to feeling a great love, gratitude, and respect for their parents.

Median Rating of Degree of Opposition	F Scale	G Scale
2.57	If people would talk less and work more, everybody would be better off.	If people would discuss matters more before acting, everybody would be better off.
2.53	A person who has bad manners, habits, and breeding can hardly expect to get along with decent people.	Decent people can get along with a person who has bad manners, habits, and breeding.
1.86	Most of our social problems would be solved if we could somehow get rid of the immoral, crooked, and feeble-minded people.	Most of our social problems would be solved if we could somehow cure or help the immoral, crooked, and feeble-minded people.

TABLE 2. MEAN SCORES ON THE F AND G SUBSCALES AND THEIR COMPOSITES AND THEIR CORRELATIONS BY LEVELS OF OPPOSITION

Midpoint of the Range of Medians of Opposition Ratings	Mean Scores			Standard Deviations		Correlations		
	F Sub-scales	G Sub-scales	Com-posite F + G Sub-scales	F Sub-scales	G Sub-scales	r_{FG}	r_{FT}	r_{GT}
3.95	2.67	2.80	2.73	2.28	1.77	−.52	.64	.32
3.79	2.36	3.31	2.84	2.58	2.05	−.29	.69	.45
3.50	2.89	3.04	2.96	2.52	2.04	−.24	.72	.51
2.88	3.36	3.60	3.47	2.52	1.66	.05	.84	.58
Combined Scale	2.83	3.18	3.00	2.00	1.12	−.20	.85	.34

Method of Scoring. The pairs of statements in opposition were sorted into four "levels of opposition" according to their median rated degree of opposition. Seven pairs of statements were placed at each of the four levels. The midpoint of the range of medians for each of the four levels was 3.95, 3.79, 3.50, and 2.88 respectively.

An F subscale score and a G subscale were obtained for each subject at each of the four levels. This was done by scoring the 7 statements of each scale at each level in the manner outlined by Adorno et al. for the original F scales. Values ranging from +3 for strong agreement with the statement by a subject to −3 for strong disagreement were assigned each response. A constant of 3 was added to eliminate negative values and a subject's total score for a given subscale was divided by 7 to determine his average agreement or opposition to a given set of 7 statements which composed an F or G subscale. A score of 3.0 implied neutrality. Subscale scores could range from 0.0 to 6.0.

SCORING RESULTS

Table 2 presents the mean scores for all subjects on all subscales.

The grand mean value of 3.00 for the entire group confirmed the supposition that the contents of the F and G scales were on the whole opposite in meaning. When added algebraically for the group as a whole, the scales served to cancel each other.

The subjects, all from psychology classes, tended as a group to be more equalitarian than authoritarian on both scales, in that they tended to disagree more with the F scale statements (M = 2.83) and agree more with the G scale statements (M = 3.18). This difference was significant according to the analyses of variance to be described below ($p <$ .01).

Evidence of Response Set to Acquiesce

If no response set existed, then each individual's F scale score when combined with his G scale score, should sum to a constant of 3.00 (ignoring chance fluctuations).

The variance of individuals on combined F and G scores should be attributable to chance if no response set existed. Response set to acquiesce could be inferred if significant differences appeared in total scores based on the addition of the two scale scores. It would mean that some individuals agreed with both F scale statements and opposite G scale statements, while other individuals disagreed with both. Table 3 presents the three-way analysis of variance of these combined F and G scores. The three main effects were: F and G scales

(Scales), the four levels of opposition (Levels), and individual differences (Individuals).

Two of the three first-order interactions, Scales $\times$ Individuals and Scales $\times$ Levels were significant sources of variance ($p <$ .01). ($V_{s \times i}/V_{s \times l \times i} = 3.2$ and $V_{s \times l}/V_{s \times l \times i} = 8.3$). The third interaction, Individuals $\times$ Levels was not significantly different from the higher-order-interaction, Scales $\times$ Levels $\times$ Individuals ($V_{i \times l}/V_{s \times l \times i} = .5$); therefore, the two were combined into a pooled error term. The main effects, Levels, Scales, and Individuals, were then tested for significance using as appropriate error terms; Pooled Error, Scales $\times$ Individuals, and Scales $\times$ Levels. The various F ratios and their significance are shown at the bottom of Table 3.

Of primary concern to this study was the ratio, V_i/V_p of 2.7, which is significant ($p <$ .01). This finding suggested that variations among individuals' composite F + G scores could not be accounted for by chance as estimated by pooled error. Thus, it was inferred that *individuals differ from each other significantly in their tendency to acquiesce to any statements about human interaction—whether for or against authoritarian ideology.* However, this generalization holds only if we ignore fluctuations of individuals from one scale to the other for the ratio $V_i/V_{s \times i}$ of .7 was not significant.

Since the interaction, Individuals $\times$ Levels was not significant, it was inferred that individuals were consistent in their differential tendencies to approve statements at different levels of opposition. Another interesting consistency in the data was the tendency of subjects to acquiesce more to items of both scales which were in less opposition to each

TABLE 3. ANALYSIS OF VARIANCE OF F AND G SCALE SCORES
BY LEVELS OF OPPOSITION

Source	SS	df	V
(s) Scales (F and G)	1114	1	1114.0
(l) Levels of Opposition	2647	3	882.3
(i) Individuals	6156	83	74.2
(s × l) Scales × Levels	870	3	290.0
(s × i) Scales × Individuals	9322	83	112.3
(i × l) Individuals × Levels	4787	249	19.2
(s × l × i) Scales × Levels × Individuals	8658	249	34.8
(p) Pooled (s × l × i) + (i × l)	13,445	458	27.0
Total	33,554	671	

$$F = \frac{V_{i \times l}}{V_{s \times l \times i}} = .5 \qquad F = \frac{V_{s \times l}}{V_{s \times l \times i}} = 3.2 * \qquad F = \frac{V_{s \times l}}{V_{s \times l \times i}} = 8.3 *$$

$$F = \frac{V_s}{V_p} = 41.3 * \qquad F = \frac{V_s}{V_{s \times i}} = 9.9 * \qquad F = \frac{V_s}{V_{s \times l}} = 3.8$$

$$F = \frac{V_l}{V_p} = 32.7 * \qquad\qquad\qquad F = \frac{V_l}{V_{s \times l}} = 3.0$$

$$F = \frac{V_i}{V_p} = 2.7 * \qquad F = \frac{V_i}{V_{s \times i}} = .7$$

* $p < .01$.

other. This tendency could not be accounted for by chance according to the ratio, V_l/V_p of 32.7. (This result will be considered again later in more detail.)

Correlation between Authoritarianism and Acquiescence

At each level of opposition, the F and G subscale scores were correlated with each other. Formula 13.34 in Guilford (11, p. 358) was used to estimate the correlations between F and the total score based on the algebraic sum of F and G. The correlations between the G subscale scores and the combined scores from F and G subscales were estimated in the same way. Table 2 shows these correlations which indicate that F scale scores contributed more to the total or

acquiescence score than the G scale scores. This is consistent with and may be explained by the fact that the corrected split-half reliability of the F scale was .81 while the corrected split-half reliability of the G scale was only .50.

As statements became less opposite in meaning, response set to acquiesce [1] increased consistently according to the correlations listed in Table 2 between F subscale scores and F + G subscale scores and between G subscale scores

---

[1] The response set to acquiesce should not be confused with the tendency to increase in agreement. All subjects increased in their agreement with statements at lower levels of oppositions. But, in addition, individual differences in tendency to agree with all items became more consistent with statements at lower levels of opposition.

and F + G subscale scores. If it can be assumed that statements drawn from less opposite pairs occupy less extreme positions on the authoritarian-equalitarian continuum than those statements drawn from pairs in great opposition, then these results are consistent with Cronbach's (9) generalization that response set increases as items become more ambiguous. The present results suggest that response set to acquiesce increases as statements become more ambivalent. It also is consistent with unpublished results obtained by the author which indicate that decrease in educational level of respondents correlates with the tendency to agree with any fairly abstract aphorisms. (This ambiguity-acquiescence relationship may help to account for the negative correlation obtained by Levinson between the F scale and intelligence test scores [1]).

Content versus Response Set Variance

A multiple centroid factor analysis was performed on the correlation matrix shown in Table 4. (The G scale has been reflected.) The diagonal entries are the

TABLE 4. THE FG CORRELATION MATRIX

Scale	F	G(−)
F	(.81)	.20
G(−)	.20	(.50)

corrected split-half reliabilities of the F and G scales of .81 and .50 respectively. Therefore, the analysis factored the *reliable* variance rather than the common variance of both scales.[2]

---

[2] This analysis was suggested in a letter by Lee J. Cronbach.

The unrotated centroid factor matrix is shown in Table 5.

From the result shown in Table 5, it is inferred that the factor with which the F and G scales correlate equally but opposite in direction concerns authori-

TABLE 5. FACTOR MATRIX

	Factor		
Scale	I Acqui-escence	II Authoritari-anism	r_{11}
F	.77	.47	.81
G	.53	−.47	.50

tarian-equalitarian content. The factor with which both the F and G scales correlate positively is regarded as a factor measuring the tendency to acquiesce to both authoritarian and equalitarian generalities. If these factors are labeled correctly, then it is concluded (ignoring the possibility of content variance unique to the F scale, not found on the G scale) that 59 per cent of the variance of the F scale is accounted for by Factor I, Acquiescence, while only the remaining 22 per cent of the reliable variance of the F scale concerns Authoritarianism as found in Factor II. Thus, three-fourths of the reliable variance of the F scale appears to be a function of acquiescence.

Conclusions

Much has been made of the correlations between the F scale and various measures of ethnocentrism, intolerance, leadership ideology, misanthropy, and xenophobia. The present results suggest that the F scale will correlate highly with *any* set of slogans about social issues where items are all scored in the same direction. For example, if the F scale, along with a series of only favorable generalizations about Negroes—preferably with some degree of ambivalence associated with each—are presented for approval or disapproval, the present results force us to predict that "authoritarians" will turn out to be much more "favorable" toward minority groups than heretofore suspected.

It must be made clear that the results of this study should not lead to rejecting the supposition that the F scale is measuring generalized personality tendencies which have been reported as associated with rigidity, intolerance for ambiguity, and conformity when these latter are measured by means other than concurrence with proverbs, generalizations, and maxims. The results do suggest that a large amount of the variance in the F test measures the generalized trait of *acquiescence,* not *authoritarianism.* Moreover, the results suggest that doubt should be cast on generalizations based solely on correlations between social attitude scales where all statements are scored in the same direction since a large percentage of the covariance may be due to this generalized tendency to acquiesce rather than to the particular contents of the scales.

Summary

The purpose of this study was to test the hypothesis that scores on the F scale and similarly constructed inventories are primarily measures of acquiescence rather than authoritarianism.

For each of the statements of the original F scale, opposite statements were composed to form the G scale. The degree was determined to which each of the statements was in opposition to its mate.

Response set to acquiescence was measured by obtaining each individual's tendency to support *both* F and G scale statements. An analysis of variance disclosed that, if individuals' fluctuations from one scale to another are ignored, they, the individuals, tend to differ significantly from each others in tendency to acquiesce. (Acquiescence is correlated more highly with the results of the F scale—a more reliable scale—than with the G scale.)

It appeared that response set to acquiesce increased as items became more ambivalent.

A factor analysis of the data indicated that approximately three-fourths of the reliable variance of the F scale was associated with an acquiescence factor while only one-fourth was attributable to a content factor of authoritarianism.

It is suggested that a much more parsimonious explanation can be given to account for the positive relations between authoritarianism, misanthropy, xenophobia, and ethnocentrism, where all are measured by scores based on acceptance of generalizations about social affairs. It appears that these correlations may be due primarily to a response set to acquiesce to *any* generalizations about social issues. In turn, this response set may have significance for understanding personality, social attitudes, and problem-solving behavior.

References

1. ADORNO, T. W. *et al. The authoritarian personality.* New York: Harpers, 1950.
2. ANCONA, L. Indagine sulta natura psichica del "Response Set." La "motivazione al successo." *Arch. psicol. neurol. Psichiat.,* 1954, **15,** 23–74.
3. ———. La c. d. motivazione al successo (need for achievement) in termini di

"response set" di acquiescenza e di negativismo. *Arch. psicol. neurol. Psichiat.,* 1954, **15,** 158–168.

_ 4. BLOCK, J., & BLOCK, JEANNE. An investigation of the relationship between intolerance of ambiguity and ethnocentrism. *J. Pers.,* 1951, **19,** 303–311.

5. ———. An interpersonal experiment on reactions to authority. *Hum. Relat.,* 1952, **5,** 91–98.

6. CAMPBELL, D. T., & McCANDLESS, B. R. Ethnocentrism, xenophobia, and personality. *Hum. Relat.,* 1951, **4,** 185–192.

7. COHN, T. S. Is the F scale indirect? *J. abnorm. soc. Psychol.,* 1952, **47,** 732.

8. ———. Factors related to scores on the F (Predisposition to Fascism) Scale. Unpublished doctor's dissertation, Univer. of Michigan, 1953.

9. CRONBACH, L. J. Further evidence on response sets and test design. *Educ. psychol. Measmt.,* 1950, **10,** 3–31.

10. GUBA, E. B., & GETZELS, J. W. The construction of an other-directedness instrument, with some preliminary data on validity. *Amer. Psychologist,* 1954, **9,** 385. (Abstract)

11. GUILFORD, J. P. *Fundamental statistics in psychology and education.* New York: McGraw-Hill, 1950.

12. HARDESTY, F. P. An exploratory investigation of relationships between reaction-time characteristics on a word-association test and authoritarianism. *Amer. Psychologist,* 1954, **9,** 390. (Abstract)

13. ROKEACH, M. Prejudice, concreteness of thinking, and reification of thinking. *J. abnorm. soc. Psychol.,* 1951, **46,** 83–99.

14. ———. Dogmatism and opinionation on the left and on the right. *Amer. Psychologist,* 1952, **7,** 310–311. (Abstract)

15. ———. The nature and meaning of dogmatism. *Psychol. Rev.,* 1954, **61,** 194–204.

16. SULLIVAN, P. L., & ADELSON, J. Ethnocentrism and misanthropy. *J. abnorm. soc. Psychol.,* 1954, **49,** 246–249.

IS THE F SCALE IRREVERSIBLE?

Richard Christie, Joan Havel, and Bernard Seidenberg

One of the most frequently used instruments in the area of personality and attitude measurement is the F scale developed by the authors of *The Authoritarian Personality* (1). It has not always been used judiciously, but many data have been collected in conjunction

Reprinted by permission of the American Psychological Association and the authors from *The Journal of Abnormal and Social Psychology,* Vol. 56, 1958.

with it in hundreds of samples. It has been found to be correlated (significantly) with attitude measures varying from Arab nationalism (24) to Xenophobia (6) (not to neglect Xenophilia! [22]) and with other variables as diverse as Necker cube reversals (15) and amount of out-group aggression in dreams (19).

The F scale was designed as a covert measure at the personality level of incipient fascistic tendencies, although it is more commonly interpreted as a measure of authoritarianism.

A feature of the F scale that has come under recent critical scrutiny is the unilateral wording of its items. These are so phrased that agreement with them is scored as indicative of potential fascism, disagreement as nonfascistic. Most of these criticisms stem from Cronbach's summary of earlier work on response set and his indication of its importance in answering test or scale items (10, 11). Some subjects, it appears, have general tendencies to accept or reject items. Although this susceptibility to respond in a set way may be indicative of a broader factor of acquiescence, it need not manifest itself uniformly. According to Cronbach, response set is more likely to occur when a given item is vague or otherwise lacking in specificity or is in an area with which the individual is unfamiliar. Such considerations are pertinent to many of the items in the F scale which are characterized by nonspecificity of referent and do not make sense when analyzed logically.

Response Set and the F Scale: Some Questions

Although the authors of *The Authoritarian Personality* gave more detail about their research procedures than is customary, they failed to anticipate all the critical questions that might be raised and there are explanatory lacunae. One of these is the failure to explain why F-scale items were unilaterally worded. This is in contrast to an earlier discussion of the explicit rationale for a similar wording of the E (Ethnocentrism)-scale items since it was recognized that this violated recommendations of experts on scale construction (1, p. 59).

Three of the 38 items in the original Form 78 F scale were worded in such a fashion that rejection would imply fascistic tendencies (Nos. 12, 20, and 28: 1, Table 1 (VII), pp. 226–227). Two of them discriminated negatively (Nos. 12 and 20) and ranked 37th and 38th in rank discriminatory power in the item analysis (1, Table 3 (VII), p. 245). These two items were believed to be poor because they were "unclear or ambiguous" (1, p. 247) and were dropped from further revisions of the F scale. The third reversal (No. 28) had poor discriminatory power and was not included in subsequent revisions of the F scale. It does emerge worded in the *opposite* direction, i.e., in conformity with the rest of the F-scale items, in Form 60 A of the F scale.

The difficulties in constructing satisfactory item reversals of the F scale that are hinted at in this initial attempt are highlighted by four recent studies in which F-scale items were reversed. Correlations between the scales composed of reversed items and the original F scale (or an abridgment) indicate little success in constructing adequate reversed items. If scales composed of these reversed items measured "authoritarianism" defined as the rejection of democratically worded items it would be expected that the correlation between them and the original F scale, which was based upon agreement with authoritarian or nondemocratic statements, would approach +1.00—if subjects are ideologically consistent and the reversals are adequate. This is clearly not the case in these four studies. Bass found a correlation of but +.20 (2), Chapman and Campbell ones of +.17 and −.01 in two samples (7), Jackson, Messick, and Solley one of −.35 (14), and Leavitt,

Hax, and Roche ones varying from —.66 to +.42 in five small samples (17).[1]

Four independent studies leading to findings of negligible if not negative correlations between F scale and scales composed of reversals of its items must be taken seriously. The lack of high positive correlations was attributed to the influence of response set by all four groups of investigators. Bass even went so far as to assign three-fourths of the "reliable" variance and 59 per cent of the total variance to response set (2, p. 622). This conclusion has been challenged by Messick and Jackson who pointed out that Bass misidentified his factors when they were reflected and that a factor analysis was not justified given the nature of Bass' data (20). Although Bass acknowledged the validity of this criticism he still argued that acquiescent response set is an important component in results obtained with the F scale (4), as did his two critics.

Such an evaluation is at least partially consistent with other data. Cohn (6) was one of the first to consider seriously the possibility that the F scale was in part a measure of acquiescent tendencies. He found a correlation of +.41 between a "plus" scale of diverse items from the MMPI and an unspecified version of the F scale. Bass mentions finding only positive correlations among 13 scales of 20 aphorisms each although the content areas covered by the scales varied (2, p. 617). Items from these scales appear to be used in a scale of "social acquiescence" which is reported to correlate

+.49, +.48, and +.16 respectively with the F scale in three samples (3, p. 297). Chapman and Campbell report obtaining a "rather pure" measure of response set by scoring 74 questionnaire items that were balanced in positively and negatively worded direction for a general tendency to agree. This measure was correlated with the F scale to the extent of +.43 (7, p. 131). Leavitt, Hax, and Roche cite an unpublished study by Mullery in which correlations between the F scale and acceptance of contradictory maxims of +.46, +.41, and +.38 respectively were found in three small samples (17, p. 215). A subsequent study by Carey, Rogow, and Farrell (5) on the relationship between agreement with positive and negative aphorisms and the F scale indicated that in three of four samples, agreement with both sets of aphorisms was significantly correlated with F-scale scores (positive aphorisms were defined as affirming Christian, humanist, or democratic values; negative aphorisms were those judged to deny these ideals). Webster found that a measure of response set correlated +.26 with the F scale (26, p. 31) among Vassar students.

These findings are congruent with those of Newcomb (21) in the Bennington study. He had heard Thorndike speak of the "tendency to agree" and although he was not familiar with any studies analyzing what Cronbach was later to call response set he analyzed the P.E.P. (political-economic progressivism) scale in terms of this "tendency to agree" and found that the split-half reliability on the P.E.P. scale among seniors in the class of 1939 was +.68 when scored by subtracting the number of disagreements from the number of agreements (21, p. 194). The correlation between tendency to agree as Freshmen and Seniors was

[1] The sign of the correlations in these studies has been standardized in this discussion so that a positive correlation indicates consistency of content and a negative one a lack of relationship between the F scale and a reversal scale scored so that rejection of the items is scored as authoritarian.

+.33 (21, p. 195). These and other findings reported by Newcomb are of particular interest in the present context since the P.E.P. scale was a modification of Stagner's pioneering scale of fascist attitudes (21, p. 20).

Thorndike had actually conducted research on the tendency to agree during the 1930's. This material has not been published but an abstract of a paper given by Lorge on the topic at a regional psychological convention exists (18). Cronbach also summarizes additional material on reliabilities of scales in these studies (11). Briefly, split-half reliabilities for given response categories were high (.88 and .95), and an unspecified positive correlation was found between the number of "yes" responses on the Bernreuter and the number of statements checked on a Thurstone scale.

The preceding studies are similar in that the measure of response set is based upon statements that may vary in the extent to which they are ambiguous to respondents. In other words, the presence of response set is confounded to a certain degree with the item content.

Gage, Leavitt, and Stone have used a different technique to measure response set. They used true-false information items in a test pitched at such a level of difficulty that their respondents could not achieve better than a chance score. The split-half reliability of an acquiescent set, i.e., the number of "true" responses, was +.68. (This is identical with that found by Newcomb on the P.E.P. scale and suggests hypotheses about the nature of the political and economic attitudes of his Bennington sample.) A similar scale constructed by Gage et al. had items at a 75 per cent level of difficulty and the reliability was but +.09, a result indicating that ". . . difficult and ambiguous items are re-quired to elicit the acquiescent set. . . ." (12, p. 98, italics added).

Gage et al. also administered, among other measures, Cohn's "plus" scale and the F scale. The latter correlated +.44, a finding similar to Cohn's. The correlation between their Information-True (items at chance level) test and the F scale was +.35. This strikes us as the most clearcut indication of the relationship between the F scale and a response set measure that is free from variance attributable to the attitudinal content of the items. Roughly an eighth of the variance in response to the F scale would then be attributable to response set—at least among studies conducted on the usual samples of American college students (the lower correlation obtained by Webster is believed to be attributable to the fact that his sample was probably more intellectually sophisticated than members of the other samples reviewed).

Although the weight of evidence indicates that responses to the F scale are affected by response set, it does not support the notion that response set is the primary determinant. The lack of consistent positive correlations between the F scale and reversed F scales in the four studies cited therefore cannot be attributed primarily to a tendency to acquiesce.

There are other reasons for questioning an attempt to equate responses to the F scale and acquiescent response set (2, 4). The F scale correlates highly with many measures which are free from this artifact, e.g., the analysis of incomplete sentences reported in The Authoritorian Personality. (One of the oversights connected with much of the justifiable methodological criticism of that research is that the methodologically more sophisticated work such as this has been largely ignored.) Another qualification should be apparent to anyone who has ever scored the F scale and observed how remarkably inconsistent many people can be in their responses—can a response set underlie such variability? Finally, most of us who have ventured outside the ivied halls have known individuals who emphatically endorse statements such as those embodied in the F scale. Yet they are not only reluctant to acquiesce to statements reflecting approval of any liberal political activity of the past quarter century but emphatically affirm that anyone making such statements is a fool if not a traitor. Among those who represent the quintessence of the F syndrome, placid agreement to explicit liberal statements is rare in our experience.

The preceding considerations indicate that acquiescent response set is one component of scores on the F scale but that its importance has been over-emphasized in the four studies using reversed items. A scrutiny of the data suggests two possible reasons. One is that the reversed items which were used have deficiencies as meaningful psychological opposites to original F-scale items. A second reason appears to lie in the distributions of F-scale scores in the samples studied; these are not congruent with the supposition that the high scoring subjects are acquiescent. These points are worthy of further elaboration.

PROBLEMS IN REVERSING
F-SCALE ITEMS

The following considerations seem important to us in the construction of item reversals which should be accepted by those who reject F-scale items and rejected by those who accept them:

(1) *Logical opposition to the original items.* This point is by far the simplest and the studies under consideration are not subject to criticism on this basis. We do not, however, consider logical opposition

in itself a sufficient condition for meaningful reversals. This point may be illustrated by one of the few items which was reversed in all four studies—"familiarity breeds contempt." The reversals of this laconic aphorism were:

Familiarity does not breed contempt. [2]
Familiarity breeds respect more often than it does contempt. [7]
We are bound to admire and respect a person if we get to know him well. [13]
The more you get to know people the more you get to like them. [17]

These statements are all *logically* incompatible with the original item. Yet they differ in wording and, we would argue, in their *psychological* incompatibility with the original statement and one another.

(2) *Avoidance of extremity of wording.* The statements in the F scale are frequently couched in all or none terms: "everybody," "the most important," "never do anything," "no sane, normal, decent person," "no weakness or difficulty," etc. Since this form itself has been hypothesized as appealing to those high on the F scale and who are presumed to be intolerant of ambiguity it would appear appropriate to couch reversals in probabilistic form by using such qualifications as "some," "many," "one of the most important," etc.

In varying degrees, items used in the four studies failed to meet this criterion, e.g.:

No people are born with an urge to jump from high places. [2]
It is *completely absurd* to believe that some people may be born with an urge to jump from high places. [7]
It is *known with complete certainty* that the urge to jump from high places is learned, not inborn. [13]
All the mysteries surrounding our lives will sooner or later be cleared up through the progress of science. [17] [2]

---

[2] Leavitt, Hax, and Roche did not reverse the "urge to jump" item. The italics are ours.

The theory underlying the F scale suggests that a truly nonauthoritarian individual would be taken aback by the unqualified wording of such statements. Agreement with the underlying premise that suicidal tendencies are most plausibly explained by the vicissitudes of an individual's life circumstances rather than heredity might be masked by a nonauthoritarian disinclination to agree with a dogmatic statement.

(3) *Psychological opposition to original items.* Many of the reversals in these studies may be nondiscriminating because they are irrelevant to the *psychological* significance of the originals. In some instances we would predict that the reversals would be accepted by *both* high and low scorers on the F scale; in other cases that the reversals would not be acceptable to either group. Our judgments in these cases are largely subjective since they are based upon our interpretation of the theory underlying *The Authoritarian Personality* and familiarity with subsequent studies. Since it is difficult to formulate general rules in such a situation, we shall cite a few of the many statements that are relevant.

Consider two reversals of the statement: "Nowadays when so many kinds of people move around and mix together so much a person has to protect himself especially carefully against catching infection or disease from them":

Nowadays, since democracy demands that people of widely different backgrounds and station mix together, a person should not be finicky about catching disease from any of them. [13]

You need to get out and rub elbows with all kinds of people to get new ideas and broaden your understanding of life. [17]

The first reversal should presumably be accepted by low scorers since they, theoretically at least, should not be overanxious about "contamination" by others. High scorers might also be expected to accept the reversal since it is loaded in the direction of a conforming response; rejection of the statement implies rejection of democracy, and, despite their implicitly anti-democratic ideology, their need for conformity is usually associated with the acceptance of the *symbols* of the sanctioned democratic ethos.

The second reversal, it is suggested, misses the psychological point of the original statement which was intended to arouse anxiety about catching diseases from unwashed outgroups. Instead, a folksy democratic statement was used. The basic concept is unlikely to be rejected by low scorers although they might wonder about the "need." Rejection of the item by high scorers would imply that they were intraceptive, which runs counter to theory. For these reasons, the item should theoretically be accepted by both high and low scorers and thus be nondiscriminating.

These considerations suggest that one of the reasons why the scales composed of reversed items fail to correlate with the F scale lies in the nature of many of the items of which they are composed. Many strike us as being subject to rejection by low scorers because of their extremity of wording, irrationality, or lack of compatibility with the psychological significance with items in the F scale. Other reversed items are believed to be nondiscriminating because they might reasonably be expected to be accepted by both high and low scorers. There are enough items subject to these strictures in the studies under review to afford a plausible explanation for the findings reported without the necessity of invoking response set as *the* crucial variable. These considerations are believed to be especially crucial for the studies of Bass, who explicitly attempted to construct *logical* rather *psychological* reversals, and of Jackson and Messick whose reversals were in the *style* of the original items.

ACQUIESCENT RESPONSE SET AND SAMPLING

Three of the four samples under review used college samples, apparently largely composed of students at the beginning of their college training. The majority of respondents in the fourth (17) appear to have been highly educated. This point is of methodological interest because college samples do not tend to make *absolutely* high scores on the F scale. More precisely, if the range of item mean scores is defined as ranging from 1.0 (strong rejection of every item in the scale) to 7.0 (strong acceptance of every item), it is found that most college samples reported in the literature have a mean score below the theoretical neutral point of 4.0.

This distribution of scores is important in evaluating the purported relevance of response set to the F scale. Those in the lowest quarter of the typical distribution usually have an item mean score of well below 3.0 which indicates that they must fairly consistently disagree "slightly" or "somewhat" with the items with an occasional agreement or "strong" disagreement. Those who score in the highest quarter typically have mean scores in the 4.0 or 5.0 range with a few scoring slightly higher.

The importance of such distributions for the equation of high scores on the F scale with acquiescence is due to the fact that "neutral" responses are not customarily allowed. Any scores between 3.0 and 5.0 therefore have to be obtained by balancing off agreement and disagreement with specific items. The typical college student "high" authori-

tarian *cannot,* by virtue of the scale format and scoring, *be consistently accepting items.* This fact suggests that if these studies are based upon typical college samples, the lack of positive correlations reported cannot be attributable to acquiescence response set on the part of the high scorers in these samples since the latter are inconsistent in their responses. (It is hypothetically possible that some of the reported correlations are due to "negativism" on the part of low scorers who reject both the original F-scale items *and* the reversals!)

It is impossible to delineate fully the possible effects of the range of responses on the F scale in the samples used in these four studies. Bass (2) reports an item mean of 2.83 which is equivalent to one of 3.83 in the conventional scoring of the F scale (a constant of three rather than four was added to raw scores). He reports an *SD* of 2.00 (2, Table 2, p. 620). This means, if correctly reported, that his sample was necessarily uniquely bimodal on the F scale since it would be impossible to have a normal distribution on a scale with a six-point range and a standard deviation of a full two points. In view of this and other errors in these data, no reliable estimates can be made about the characteristics of the sample.

Chapman and Campbell do not report the mean or distribution of F scale responses for their two samples. They used a five-point response scale with an undecided category so that the preceding comments about the lack of a neutral category do not apply to their data. An item mean computed from unpublished data indicates that the item mean for their second sample was 2.90, just below the theoretical neutral point of 3.00. Since these data were in the form of responses to items, it was not possible to compute an *SD* based upon *S*s. It is therefore impossible to determine the extent to which high scoring *S*s were consistent in their acceptance of F-scale items.[3]

Jackson, Messick, and Solley report an item mean of 3.10 with an *SD* of .67 on 42 *S*s. Their scoring procedure differed slightly from the conventional one and yields a mean equivalent to 3.77. If their distribution of scores was normal, approximately one or two *S*s would have scored above 5.0. Leavitt, Hax, and Roche studied two small samples of foremen, (*n*'s = 6 and 13), two of executives (*n*'s = 34 and 52), and one of Unitarians (*n* = 28). A composite plot of their data (17, Fig. 1, p. 219) indicates that low scoring *S*s greatly outnumbered high scoring ones. As nearly as we can determine by inspection, eight *S*s had an item mean agreement varying between "slight" and "somewhat" and a single *S* had an item mean above 6.0. The relatively high scorers in these samples thus fell largely within or slightly above the neutral range.

---

[3] The item mean is higher than generally found in schools of Northwestern's caliber. Since Chapman and Campbell did not randomly sample F-scale items and used but 16 of them, the possibility of bias with the items was considered. The 14 items taken from the Form 40 of the F scale had an item mean (our computations) identical with the other items in this form in the original samples (based upon 1, Table 9 (VII), p. 260). Their other two items were taken from the Form 60 and had an item mean of 4.46 in contrast to that of 3.71 on the whole scale (1, Table 6 (VII), p. 253). Since there is reason to believe that the relative "pull" of F-scale items is fairly consistent in college samples, a slight contribution to the unexpectedly high item mean in this sample may be attributed to the popularity of these two items. The effect of allowing a "neutral" option upon item mean scores is unknown.

ADDITIONAL COMMENTS

It should be emphasized that the preceding comments about these studies are based upon an advantage that the original authors did not have, i.e., the opportunity to be familiar with one another's work. The seemingly paradoxical finding in independent studies that F-scale reversals did not correlate appropriately with the F scale raised questions which led to analysis of possible reasons. Chapman and Campbell have an insightful discussion of the problems of reversing items and because of the difficulties did not try to reverse more than ten items in their initial attempt (7, p. 129). Since they were the only investigators to report an item analysis, a study of their items which did successfully reverse gave us clues as to the possible failures of their other items and those of the other investigators. Further hunches were suggested by Bass' analysis of reversed items as to the degree of judged logical difference from the originals, the strikingly negative correlation found by Jackson *et al.* with reversals that were stylistically similar to F-scale items, and the different correlations among samples reported by Leavitt *et al.*

An Exploratory Investigation of Reversed F-Scale Items

The present study was undertaken to explore the implications of our examination of earlier studies. Clarification of the problem of the role of response set in the F scale required, we believed: (*a*) reversed items which were constructed according to the criteria previously specified and (*b*) the testing of these items on samples believed to contain a wide range of scorers on the F scale.

THE ITEM POOL

It was decided that the larger the number of reversals attempted, the greater the probability of empirically finding ones which were correlated with the F scale. In two studies (7, 17), the researchers did not test reversals of all the items in the F scale. In three of the studies (2, 13, 17), F-scale items were reversed although they had been explicitly mentioned in *The Authoritarian Personality* as being poor discriminators (1, Nos. 22 and 44, pp. 254–257). We attempted to reverse every F-scale item which was acceptable in its original form.

The final version of the F scale described in *The Authoritarian Personality* contained 29 items. We attempted to reverse the 27 which were found to be discriminating. One, "wars and social troubles may someday be ended by an earthquake or flood that will destroy the whole world," baffled us in our attempts to construct a meaningful reversal. Three items which were in the subsequent Form 60 A were added to the pool. A fourth additional item, taken from the earlier Form 60, was also added. It had discriminated between high and low scorers (1, Table 6, (VII), item 41, p. 258) but, for unstated reasons, was not included in subsequent revisions of the F scale.

THE ITEM REVERSALS

After discussion of the problems of item reversal along the lines indicated above, the authors individually attempted to write one or more reversals of each item in the pool. These reversals were then discussed and one of them, or more often a modification of one, was accepted for provisional inclusion in the reversed scale. The reversals were then circulated among colleagues familiar with the F scale; their critical comments were solicited and, in most cases, accepted.

THE SUBSCALES

Two questionnaires (Forms A and B) were prepared. Each was composed of 15 of the 30 original F-scale items and reversals of the other 15 since it was believed that the presence of the original and reversed form of the same item in the same questionnaire would lead to possible artifacts in response. The assignment of items to the two forms was based upon the use of a table of random numbers and the serial numbering of the items within the questionnaire was also random. There was no a priori reason for assigning items since earlier research had indicated that individual items in the F scale fell into different empirical clusters in different samples (8). Each scale was a mirror image of the other, i.e., if a given item appeared in its original wording on Form A its reversal was in the same serial position on Form B. The item reversals used, their allocation to Form A or B, their position within the subscales, and the source of the original item are given in Table 1.

SCORING

The customary procedure in scoring the F scale was followed, respondents being given an option of agreeing strongly, somewhat, or slightly or disagreeing slightly, somewhat, or strongly. No neutral or undecided option was allowed, but omission of an answer was scored as neutral. Both scales were scored so that high scores reflected "authoritarianism" as indicated in Table 2.

THE SAMPLES

We were interested in obtaining samples which included Ss who would show great variability of scores on the F scale

TABLE 1. REVERSALS OF F-SCALE ITEMS

Orig. No.[a]	Form	No.	Reversed Statement
31	B	1.	There are times when it is necessary to probe into even the most personal and private matters.
37	A	2.	It would be a good thing if people spent more time thinking and talking about ideas just for the fun of it.
21	A	3.	If it weren't for the rebellious ideas of youth there would be less progress in the world.
9	B	4.	When a person has a problem or worry, it is best to face it and try to think it through, even if it is so upsetting that it keeps him from concentrating on other things.
19	B	5.	Insults to our honor are not always important enough to bother about.
2	B	6.	There are many difficulties a person cannot overcome no matter how much will power he has.
39	B	7.	It's nobody's business if someone is a homosexual as long as he doesn't harm other people.
8	A	8.	It's all right for people to raise questions about even the most sacred matters.
29	B	9.	It is highly unlikely that astrology will ever be able to explain anything.
13	A	10.	In the long run it is better for our country if young people are allowed a great deal of personal freedom and are not strictly disciplined.
18	B	11.	Even though people of all sorts mix together nowadays, you don't have to worry very much about catching an infection or disease.
34	B	12.	Even if there were no immoral, crooked, or feeble-minded people there would still be many serious social problems.
16	A	13.	An urge to jump from high places is probably the result of unhappy personal experiences rather than something inborn.
26	A	14.	It doesn't make much sense to divide people into groups like the weak and the strong; too many people are strong in some ways and weak in others.
4	A	15.	The findings of science may some day show that many of our most cherished beliefs are wrong.
41	A	16.	People ought to pay more attention to new ideas, even if they seem to go against the American way of life.
43	B	17.	You may dislike a person very much, but the chances are that if you get to know him well you'll have more respect for him.
1	A	18.	One of the most important things children should learn is when to disobey authorities.
59	A	19.	Most people can be trusted.
53	B	20.	You'll do better work in the long run if you do things your own way rather than by following tried and true procedures.
23	B	21.	It is more important for this country to have a just legal and political system than a series of trustworthy leaders, however courageous, tireless, and devoted they might be.
25	A	22.	Sex crimes, such as rape and attacks on children, are signs of mental illness; such people belong in hospitals rather than in prison.

TABLE 1. (*Continued*)

Orig. No.[a]	Form	No.	Reversed Statement
38	A	23.	Many people have too great a fear of plots hatched in secret by politicians.
42	A	24.	It's only natural for people to sometimes have thoughts about hurting a close friend or relative.
41	B	25.	The artist and professor are probably more important to society than the businessman or manufacturer.
27	A	26.	Most honest people admit to themselves that they have sometimes hated their parents.
6	B	27.	Human nature doesn't make war inevitable; man may some day establish a peaceful world.
35	B	28.	In spite of what you read about the wild sex life of people in important places, the real story is about the same in any group of people.
12	A	29.	People should be willing to overlook failures in the manners and unpleasant personal habits in other people.
58	B	30.	Books and movies ought to give a more realistic picture of life even if they show that evil sometimes triumphs over good.

[a] All items are taken from 1, Table 7 (VII), pp. 255–257 except for No. 16 which was found in Table 4 (VII), p. 250 and Nos. 19, 20, and 30, the originals of which are in 8, Table 3, p. 464.

and were especially interested in finding high scorers. Like other investigators, we were hampered by the difficulty of obtaining noncollege samples. Through the cooperation of friends, the scales were administered to their classes at two colleges that were believed to contain a higher proportion of high scorers than would be found in most colleges with which we were familiar. One of these was a private university in the Southwest, the other, a Northeastern public university. The scales were administered during the 1956 summer session when the student bodies were more heterogeneous than usual since they also contained many elementary and high school teachers who were attending summer school.

Ss in each of the two college samples were divided in half by administering odd (Form A) and even (Form B) scales to adjacent Ss. Results on four samples will be discussed: SW-even ($n = 75$), SW-odd ($n = 75$), NE-even ($n = 39$), and NE-odd ($n = 40$). Item mean scores and SDs on the 15-item F subscales were respectively: 3.81, .97; 3.39, .93; 3.26, .99; 3.35, .93. We are unable to explain why the SW-odd sample

TABLE 2. SCORING OF STRAIGHT AND REVERSED F-SCALE ITEMS

Response	Score	
	Straight F	Reversed F
Agree Strongly	7	1
Somewhat	6	2
A Little	5	3
No Answer	4	4
Disagree a Little	3	5
Somewhat	2	6
Strongly	1	7

scored so surprisingly much lower than the SW-even sample since the alternate forms were distributed to adjacent students and the two SW samples do not differ significantly in proportion of males (roughly two-thirds), age, or major in college. Roughly half of the NE samples were male. Fourteen per cent of both samples were psychology majors, 25 per cent were education majors, and 19 per cent were business administration majors. The bulk of the remainder of the NE samples was composed of nursing students, that of the SW samples of students in engineering and liberal arts. Respondents ranged from freshmen to graduate students in all samples.

Results

ITEM ANALYSIS

In analyzing the reversals, scores made by the Ss on the appropriate F subscale were divided into quarters. Two comparisons were then made of the scores on individual reversed items—the magnitude and direction of the individual item mean differences of those in the upper and lower quarters on the F subscales and the pattern of differences in all four quarters.

Of the 30 reversals, 22 discriminated in the appropriate direction between high and low quarters on the F scale in both samples responding to them, four in one sample but not the other (Nos. 7, 11, 14, and 17), and four discriminated negatively in both samples responding to them (Nos. 1, 20, 21, and 23). This differs from chance expectancy at better than the .01 level as tested by chi square. The attempt to find workable reversals is thus viewed as moderately successful.

Individual F-scale items were similarly analyzed against extreme quarters on the

total scale. All discriminated in the appropriate direction but there was great variability in discriminatory power and mean level of acceptance.

AN EXAMINATION OF RESPONSE SET

Although these findings indicate that F scale items are, at least within limits, reversible, they do not clarify the more basic problem as to how response set is linked with the F scale. Given the facts that the F scale has been found to be correlated with a host of measures that do not involve response set, that its construct validity is tenuous, and that response set plays some role—although not the dominant one in the acceptance or rejection of its items—how best to proceed?

Since we had selected our reversed items against the criterion of scores on F subscales we decided to examine further the most successful five in each form. This procedure eliminated the negatively discriminating items and those of marginal discrimination and left only those found to be systematically related to response to the F scale.

We also pared down the number of F-scale items for more intensive scrutiny to five in each subscale. These were the ones with the highest discriminatory power in the item analysis. So doing tended to get rid of not only those items which were poor discriminators but those which were widely rejected or accepted. For example, the item mean on the statement, "People can be divided into two distinct classes: the weak and the strong," was but 1.77 in the SW-even sample and even those scoring in the high quarter tended to reject this "authoritarian" item, their item mean score being but 2.0 (disagree "somewhat"). On the other hand, the SW-odd sample tended to accept the statement, "The wild sex life of the old Greeks and Romans was tame compared to some of the goings-on in this country, even in places where people might least expect it," the item mean being 5.15. Slightly greater acceptance than rejection of this statement on the part of low scorers was found (item mean of 4.20). The ten reversed items (five from each form) used in this analysis were Nos. 3, 5, 13, 15, 16, 18, 25, 28, and 30 in Table 1. The F-scale items were the originals of Nos. 1, 6, 8, 9, 15, 18, 20, 22, 24, and 30.

surprising that the magnitude of the correlations is similar. It is clear, however, that the correlations fall far from what would be expected if the reversals were adequate and response set did not play some role.

Scores of the 299 Ss in the four samples were grouped and ordered in terms of their item mean response on the F scale. The 58 Ss making scores of 5.0 and over were considered to be high scorers and their responses to the reversed items were examined. Sixteen of these individuals had item mean scores of 6.0 or higher on the short F scale.

TABLE 3. CORRELATIONS BETWEEN LONG AND SHORT FORMS OF STRAIGHT AND REVERSED F-SCALE ITEMS

	Scales Being Correlated		
Sample	15 Item F+ and F−	15 Item F+ and 5 Item F−	5 Item F+ and 5 Item F−
SW-Odd	.35	.42	.45
SW-Even	.14	.27	.23
NE-Odd	.34	.27	.37
NE-Even	.45	.66	.44

These short five-item scales had a mean part-whole correlation of .82 with the longer 15-item forms and thus may be viewed as tapping the essence of the F scale. They are also useful since they are presumably the most susceptible to response set if response set is part and parcel of the "authoritarian" syndrome. After all, items that are universally accepted or rejected cannot yield much information about differential response set among individuals.

The correlations between these abbreviated scales and the original 15-item scales is given in Table 3. Since the items in the short scales were selected against the longer F subscales, it is not

Despite this high degree of "acquiescence" with "authoritarian" items, it did not generalize to the reversed items. Their scores here all fell in the neutral range (3.2 to 4.8) with the exception of one slightly deviant case with a score of 5.0 (disagree slightly). There are many ways of balancing off responses to attain a "neutral" score and these Ss displayed a most consistent inconsistency in doing so. They used the extreme categories in answering the reversed items; 84 per cent of their total responses were in terms of "somewhat" or "strong" acceptance or rejection. No one accepted or rejected more than three or less than two of the reversed items. Further, there was no observable difference in the acceptance or rejection of specific items. These individuals who whole-heartedly and consistently endorsed the most discriminating F-scale items displayed an enthusiastically random pattern of response to the reversed items. Our interpretation is that they have a tendency to make extreme responses and are ideologically somewhat confused.

Those scoring from 5.0 to 5.8 ("slight" to almost "somewhat" agreement) on the short F scale differ in showing extreme variability on the reversals, the item mean range varying from 1.8 to 5.6. Those at the extremes of this continuum display quite different behavior.

Five of these individuals had item mean scores of over 5.0 on both the F and reversed F subscales, a higher score on the reversed scale, incidentally, than any of 16 individuals with scores of 6.0 or over on the F subscales considered earlier. These are clearly ideologically consistent individuals and are moderately fascistically oriented. Their modal response pattern is that of accepting four out of five items on the F subscales and rejecting four out of five on the reversed F subscales. The small *n* does not suffice for an evaluation of the intensity of response although there is a lack of use of extreme categories (there was not a single "strong" approval of a reversed item). This fraction of the Ss shows no evidence of response set.

Acquiescent response set is definitely manifested in a group of 13 Ss with F subscale scores above 5.0 and reversed subscale scores of 3.0 or below. The modal pattern was acceptance of four of five items on *both* the F and reversed F subscales. The "authoritarianism" manifested by these individuals on the F scale appears nonideological in nature

and a reflection of a tendency to agree with incompatible items.

The remaining 24 Ss in this range of scorers show a mixed pattern of responses, the mean on the reversed F subscales falling between 3.2 and 4.8. Although tendencies in the response set direction may be present among some of them, it is equally plausible that they tended toward a consistency which was masked by the analysis of a relatively small number of items.

A similar analysis was made of those scoring low on the F subscale. There were 21 Ss who disagreed "somewhat" or greater (scores of 2.0 or below). Thirteen of these had a general pattern of acceptance on the reversed items and may be considered consistent lows. Eight, however, had mean reversed scores in the neutral range and thus resemble mirror images of our extreme high scorers. They differ from the latter, however, in not predominantly utilizing extreme responses to items: 38, 40, and 23 per cent of their responses fell in the "slight," "somewhat," and "strong" agree and disagree categories. There is thus no evidence of response set among these respondents.

The moderately low scoring Ss who scored from 2.2 to 3.0 on the F subscales can be identified as ideologically consistent or as subject to response set just as those with moderately high scores. A total of three Ss displayed a consistent *negative* response, i.e., they tended to disagree with items on *both* subscales. Eighteen Ss were identified as consistently low since they accepted the reversed items while rejecting the original ones. The remaining 20 Ss in this range had scores in the neutral range on the reversed scales and are considered a mixed group.

Within these samples, at least, three

general findings emerge: (*a*) there is a much higher proportion of ideological consistency among low than high scorers, (*b*) response set is more prevalent among those who moderately agree than those who agree extremely and although slightly present among those who moderately disagree is not found among extreme disagreers, and (*c*) there is a higher proportion of ideological inconsistency on the reversed items among extreme high scorers than among other groupings.

The consistency of the low scorers is congruent with the findings of Leavitt *et al.* They combined their groups and correlated the original F-scale items used and their reversed scale and found a positive correlation in the bottom third of the combined samples of $+.45$ (the high third on the F scale had a correlation on the two scales in the *negative* direction: $-.32$). Although we have not replicated their analysis, an inspection of our data indicates (as can be easily guessed from the earlier discussion of response patterns) that the low scorers are responsible for the overall positive correlations; the correlation between original and reversed items among the high scorers in these samples would not differ appreciably from zero.

The greater presence of response set among those with moderate rather than extreme attitudes is not at all surprising. This is precisely what would be expected according to Cronbach's formulation of the conditions under which response set is most likely to be found. A person sophisticated enough to reject most of the F-scale items out of hand has a well enough formulated ideology to know where he stands and is unlikely to find reversed items vague or unfamiliar. An extreme high scorer is of different persuasion but his devotion to the irrational

does not indicate bland acceptance of contrary statements, at least in light of current theory and knowledge. Although the preceding point seems exceedingly obvious, it has not been prominent in recent discussions of response set. One possible value of the present findings, limited as they may be, may be the reiteration of basic considerations about the relationship between extremity and intensity of attitudes. These, in conjunction with Cronbach's observations, suggest that it is precisely those persons who do not have strong attitudes pro or con who should be most apt to display response set.

The one unexpected finding was the complete abandon with which the extreme high scorers rejected or accepted the reversed items. There is considerable discussion in *The Authoritarian Personality* about the irrationality of such individuals but no indication that it would take such a remarkable form.

Further Studies

Although the preceding findings appeared plausible, they were descriptive and left several matters in doubt. First, how stable were they? Our procedure of concurrently analyzing items from separate samples is similar but not identical to doing an item analysis on an original sample and cross-validating on a new one. Further, our results were obtained on samples of summer school students who can be viewed as representative of neither the more usual college samples nor of the general population. Replication of the findings in other samples therefore appeared called for.

The second matter of concern was the unanticipated behavior of the extreme high scorers on the reversed items. Some confusion would not have been surprising but the failure to find a single high scorer who would firmly reject reversed items was most puzzling. Since these individuals were key members of our samples whose responses served as the basis for the item analysis, it was not clear whether this might be due to an artifact arising from the method of item selection, whether it reflected the possibly aberrant nature of our samples, or whether it was indeed a characteristic of high scorers on the F scale.

Data have therefore been collected on eight additional samples. These, in all candidness, were "targets of opportunity," i.e., they were not systematically selected to test specific hypotheses about the relationship between the straight and reversed forms of the F scale. They are samples made available informally through the kindness of friends in testing their classes or in permitting the inclusion of the scales in ongoing studies directed toward other ends.

THE SCALES

The reversed F scale was composed of Items 3, 9, 13, 15, 16, 18, 25, 26, 28, and 30 in Table 1. With the exception of Item 26, these are identical to those used in the subscale analysis in the exploratory study.

The F-scale items were the originals of Nos. 1, 6, 8, 10, 12, 20, 22, 23, 24, and 27 in Table 1. They differ from those used in the subscale analysis in that the originals of Items 9, 15, 18, and 30 were deleted and substitutions were made to prevent the presence of a reversal and its original in the same questionnaire.

Ordering of the items was random. The customary response options were provided. All samples received the same 20-item scale under conditions noted in the description of each.

THE SAMPLES

(1) Undergraduate students in a Northeastern public university were given the 20-item scale during the first week of a course in introductory psychology. It was administered by the instructor (male) in charge of the classes with assurances about the preservation of anonymity and the use of the results for research. The respondents were young (median age of 18.7 years), 72 per cent were male, and they were predominantly lower middle-class in background. Sixty-two per cent were freshmen and 30 per cent were sophomores.

(2) Students in a graduate seminar in social psychology at a major Eastern university filled out the 20-item scale and also were required as part of the course to administer it to friends and acquaintances. Protocols of individuals familiar with the F scale were discarded. The sample as a whole did not respond to the questionnaire under standardized conditions. It is unusually high in years of formal education.

(3) Students in a summer school course in remedial reading at a prominent Eastern teachers college filled out the 20-item scale at the end of a class period. It was administered by a female introduced by the instructor as carrying out research. Most of the respondents were female school teachers from a broad geographic area and had a median of roughly 15 years of teaching experience. Most of them had done their undergraduate work in teachers colleges and were taking the course to maintain teaching credentials.

(4) A nonrandom but fairly representative sample of registered Washington lobbyists was given three separate questionnaires to be filled out and returned after each had been interviewed about his role as a lobbyist. One of the questionnaires contained six F-scale items and four reversals. These were interspersed with 25 other items constructed by the senior author which were largely taken from the writings of Machiavelli. A five-point response scale which included a neutral or undecided

category was used. The majority of this sample held law degrees and most had previously held elective or appointive political office.[4]

(5–8) These samples consisted of senior medical school students (with one junior class) in three top-ranking medical schools. Students in two which were located in the East had predominantly received their undergraduate training at the more prestigeful Eastern liberal arts colleges. Those in a Midwestern school were largely from the better Midwestern colleges.

Items from the 20-item scale were randomly distributed among 20 Machiavellian items (half of which were worded in the reversed direction) in an "opinion inventory." These and other psychological measures were part of a lengthy questionnaire devoted to experiences in medical school. In some instances the questionnaire was answered in a class setting, in other cases individuals filled it out at home.[5]

RESULTS

The data summarized in Table 4 indicate the consistency with which positive correlations between the F and reversed F scale were found. The samples varied in education from beginning college students to those with eight years of undergraduate and professional experience in the finest of our educational institutions, from predominantly female elementary and high school teachers to lobbyists with a bad case of "Potomac Fever," some answered the questionnaires anonymously in class while others filled them out in

[4] This study of the role and personality attributes of lobbyists was carried out under the auspices of the Brookings Institution under the supervision of Lester Milbrath.
[5] The samples were studied as part of ongoing research on the Sociology of Medical Education by the Bureau of Applied Social Research at Columbia University under a grant from the Commonwealth Fund.

conjunction with personal interviews, the items were sometimes presented as an individual scale and were sometimes mixed with other items and in five samples were given along with a large number of unrelated questions, and in general the customary seven-point scoring system was used, but in one case five-point response categories with a neutral option were used.

Despite all these variations that might possibly affect the nature of the responses positive correlations were found in all eight samples. When these are combined with the findings in the exploratory study it is found that in twelve of twelve samples using various combinations of these items the results are such as to indicate that response set is not important enough to produce negative correlations.

The other problem that intrigued us —that of the behavior of the extreme highs on reversed items—is partially clarified by a closer inspection of these data. The distribution of responses on the F scale was leptokurtic in the undergraduate sample, there being but eleven individuals with a mean score of 3.0 or below and five with scores of 6.0 or above. The heavy concentration of respondents in the neutral and slightly accepting range casts some light on the very low correlation between the scales in this sample since the generalizations made earlier about the relationship between mean acceptance of F-scale items and acquiescence were confirmed. However, of the five high scorers, two displayed acquiescent tendencies, two behaved similarly to the extreme highs discussed earlier, and one was consistent.

Further evidence that the extreme high was not necessarily inconsistent came most strongly from the lobbyist sample where there was very little evidence of acquiescence. Indeed, we found one "perfect" high scorer (within the limits of the items used) who strongly accepted all six F-scale items and strongly rejected all four reversals. Unfortunately, there were not enough extreme high scorers among these samples to serve as a sound basis for generalizations.

nine samples totaling some 2,000 Ss tested to date. This finding parallels their results on the F scale. Similarly, Sample 5, composed of a particularly aberrant (statistically speaking) group of medical students, showed inconsistency similar to that on the F scale when responding to Machiavellian items but

TABLE 4. SUMMARY RESULTS ON F AND REVERSED F IN EIGHT SAMPLES

Sample	N	F Scale			Reversed F Scale			Correlation between F and Reversed F Scales [a]
		M	SD	Rel.	M	SD	Rel.	
1. Northeastern Undergraduates	152	4.54	.84	.52	3.73	.78	.43	.10
2. Graduate Students	57	2.74	.95	.78	2.72	.93	.57	.58
3. Lobbyists	86	3.05 [b]	.59	.54 [c]	3.03 [b]	.81	.41 [d]	.55
4. Remedial Reading Teachers	61	3.43	1.05	.68	3.20	.94	.60	.29
5. Midwestern Medical Students (Seniors)	72	3.50	.69	.34	3.35	.55	.18	.45
6. Midwestern Medical Students (Juniors)	80	3.55	.88	.66	3.47	.70	.26	.23
7. Eastern Medical Students [1] (Seniors)	73	3.38	.92	.75	3.35	.91	.72	.38
8. Eastern Medical Students [2] (Seniors)	121	3.76	.86	.58	3.17	.68	.42	.48

[a] All correlations were corrected for attenuation.
[b] A five point scale was used in this sample. These figures are comparable to slightly over 4.0 in other samples.
[c] Based on only six items.
[d] Based on only four items.

The wide range of reliabilities on both the original and reversed F scales and the varying correlations between them posed problems in interpretation. It should be added that where data from other attitude scales were available, they indicated that the amount of ideological consistency present was not unique to the F scale. The Washington lobbyists, for example, had the highest internal consistency on the Machiavelli scale of

were very consistent on a measure of manifest anxiety. Such findings suggest that samples vary widely in the amount of acquiescence that they will display in response to items of an ideological nature.

The investigation of differences from sample to sample demands a more refined technique of measuring response set than that used in the preceding examples. Before pursuing the substantive problem, it is necessary to indicate the method used.

A Method of Measuring Acquiescence

The diagnosis of acquiescence used with the four exploratory samples was crude and obscured the interaction of content and response style. The correla-

cided that it was simplest to use the number of statements agreed to on the F and reversed F scales as the basic data. This convention permitted the use of the binomial expansion and the ascertainment of the probability of a given pattern of response.

Although the technique is basically simple, we are unfamiliar with examples

F - SCALE ITEMS

NO. OF AGREES →	0	1	2	3	4	5	
SCORE →	0	1	2	3	4	5	
PROB →	1	5	10	10	5	1	

REVERSED F-SCALE ITEMS

(AGREES / SCORE / PROB)	col 0	col 1	col 2	col 3	col 4	col 5	Σ
0 / 5 / 1	1 (0, 5)	5 (+1, 6)	10 (+2, 7)	10 (+3, 8)	5 (+4, 9)	1 (+5, 10)	1
1 / 4 / 5	5 (-1, 4)	25 (0, 5)	50 (+1, 6)	50 (+2, 7)	25 (+3, 8)	5 (+4, 9)	10
2 / 3 / 10	10 (-2, 3)	50 (-1, 4)	100 (0, 5)	100 (+1, 6)	50 (+2, 7)	10 (+3, 8)	45
3 / 2 / 10	10 (-3, 2)	50 (-2, 3)	100 (-1, 4)	100 (0, 5)	50 (+1, 6)	10 (+2, 7)	120
4 / 1 / 5	5 (-4, 1)	25 (-3, 2)	50 (-2, 3)	50 (-1, 4)	25 (0, 5)	5 (+1, 6)	210
5 / 0 / 1	1 (-5, 0)	5 (-4, 1)	10 (-3, 2)	10 (-2, 3)	5 (-1, 4)	1 (0, 5)	
Σ	1	10	45	120	210		252

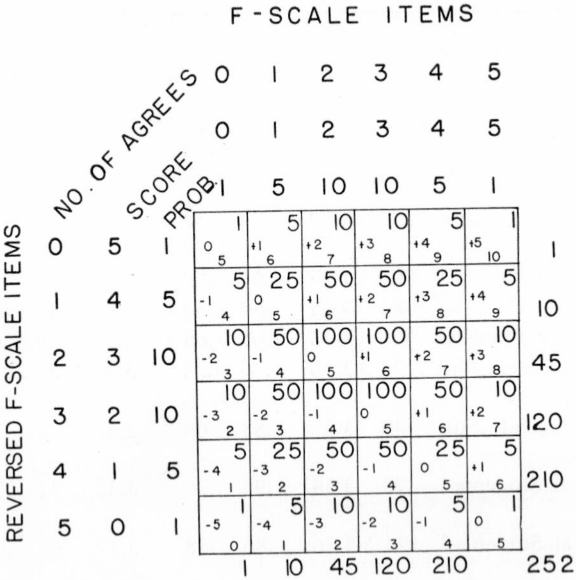

FIG. 1. Matrix for determining the probability of a given pattern of response on 5 items F and reversed F Scale. The number in the upper right hand corner of each cell indicates the chance expectancy in 1024 times of a given pattern. The upper small number indicates the discrepancy score; the lower one the total F score on the combined scales. The numbers at the right and bottom are the summed frequencies for the cells with identical discrepancy scores along the diagonals of the matrix.

tions and reliabilities indicated in Table 4 suggest widely varying probabilities of response set in different samples. These respondents were subjected to different numbers of items and in some cases different choices of response categories. In considering the problem of comparability from sample to sample, it was de-

of its application and are illustrating its use with two five-item scales.

There are six possible degrees of agreement for each five-item scale. Cross-multiplication of the binomial frequency for each response category on each scale indicates the chance probability in 1024 times of the frequency of a given cell in the matrix, e.g., the probability of a given individual agreeing with all five items in each scale is one in 1024. The expected frequency of any given pattern of response is indicated in Fig. 1.

The second information in the matrix is the discrepancy scores between the two scales. If the two scales are measuring essentially the same thing—and the means on two sophisticated samples (graduate students and lobbyists) as indicated in Table 4 suggest that this is approximated—then an individual who agrees with all five F-scale items should tend to disagree with all five reversed items. A simple way to check for consistency is to reverse the number of agreements on the reversed scale so that agreement with all five is scored 0 and disagreement with all is scored 5. Subtraction of the reversed scale score from the F-scale score gives a measure of content consistency. A perfectly consistent individual should have identical scores on both scales. A person who is indiscriminately accepting will have a discrepancy score of $+5$. If he is recalcitrantly negativistic he will have a discrepancy score of -5.

The next step is to determine the probability of occurrence of a given discrepancy score. Summing along the diagonals composed of cells with the same discrepancy scores gives the appropriate frequencies. It will be noted that this distribution is the binomial expansion of 2^{10}. The probability of occurrence of a discrepancy score of $+3$ or greater is .055 ($[1 + 10 + 45]/1024$). This is as close to the more customary .05 level as can be obtained and is sufficient for present purposes. Since the matrix is symmetric, discrepancy scores of -3 or greater indicate a tendency to disagree significant at the same level.

A combination of scores on both scales can also be used to obtain a measure of overall F by scoring along the orthogonal diagonal. An individual who rejects all five of the original items and accepts all five reversals is clearly low on the dimension and is given a score of 0 as indicated in Fig. 1. His opposite number obtains a score of 10. Scores of 2 or less and 8 or more differ significantly from chance expectancy.

ACQUIESCENCE IN THE COLLEGE TRAINED POPULATION

A clearer picture of the operation of acquiescence response set may be had by introducing data collected on one further sample. This is a subsample of the 1956 post election survey conducted by the Survey Research Center of the University of Michigan. Adult respondents selected in a nationwide probability sample were asked their education and 103 reported having at least some college training. In the course of an interview they responded to five F-scale items and five reversed items.[6] The preceding method of analysis was employed and it was found that five per cent were significantly acquiescent, 28 per cent slightly so, 23 per cent were completely consistent, 33 per cent showed slight negative tendencies, and 11 per cent had a significant negative response pattern. It is of considerable interest, in light of current

---

[6] The relationship between education and response set in the entire sample is currently being analyzed and will be reported in a separate publication. The items were slightly modified from the wording indicated in Table 1 for use with respondents of varying verbal sophistication. Details of the sampling procedures and the analysis of the interview material will be found in the forthcoming book on the 1956 presidential election by Angus Campbell and Warren Miller. This study was carried out by the Survey Research Center with a grant from the Rockefeller Foundation.

equation of acquiescence with response set, that this sample displayed slightly more negativism than acceptance in responding to items. The amount of observed response set does not, however, differ from chance expectancy.

This finding takes on possible significance since graduate students and Washington lobbyists also displayed a negligible amount of response set. These are samples which are presumably the least confused ideologically. The sample which is most distinctive is that composed of Northeastern undergraduates. A technique similar to that indicated in Fig. 1 was employed for the two ten-item scales they answered. The probability of having a discrepancy score of ± 4 or greater is .059.

Thirty-five or 23 per cent of these students showed a significant amount of acquiescence and five (three per cent) showed significant negative tendencies. Although the definition of significance level is slightly different for these undergraduates and the nationwide sample, the difference is quite striking. Why should undergraduates be so much more acquiescent than a nationwide sample of adults exposed to college (only two-fifths of whom were graduates)? A precise answer would require a detailed investigation of factors influencing changes over time. It should be noted, however, that such a finding is congruent with a variety of data on attitude changes in the first years of college. Jacob has summarized a number of studies dealing with changes on the F scale and other measures such as favorableness toward civil liberties and other attitudes indicative of liberalism (16). The general finding is that students are most conservative when they enter college. Exposure to the more liberal norms of college usually leads to high scorers dropping out of

school, changing in a more liberal direction, or adamantly holding to their original beliefs (Newcomb has furnished graphic illustrations of the last two reactions [21]). The weight of the evidence indicates that this conflict of values is most severe during the initial year or so of college.

Our tentative interpretation is that many among these undergraduates—who were in the very early days of college—were in a stage of value transition and possibly conflict. They still tended to accept F-scale items which are more widely accepted in noncollege circles such as those from which they had just come. At the same time, the reversed items were presumably more in keeping with the value climate of the university to which they were adjusting. Many of the students tended to accept both sets of items. This "acquiescent response set" does not strike us as a mere mechanical way of responding; it probably reflects another facet of Cronbach's discussion of the ambiguity of an item. In this case, items reflecting contradictory views of the world are accepted because the student has not yet decided for himself which is *the* right response; both are supported by different reference groups.

Discussion

Although the preceding digression is slightly speculative, it has important implications if valid. An initial question about some of the studies emphasizing response set focused upon the actual scale scores of the Ss and the fact that "high" scorers appeared to be only relatively high and were in actuality inconsistent in their responses. Upon the basis of these later considerations, based, it is true, upon a limited sampling of undergraduates, it would appear that the majority of these studies have used subjects who were most liable to display response set of any populations with exposure to higher education, i.e., undergraduates at an early stage of training.

There is another obvious implication of the relatively high number of acquiescent respondents in the undergraduate sample. Most of the studies involving Ss high and low on the F scale use samples drawn from undergraduate populations and most usually those in the first two years of college. This means, quite bluntly, that the high scorers are quite likely a mixed group. Some are genuine high scorers with a consistent set of authoritarian attitudes that involve rejection of reversals as well as acceptance of the F-scale items. Others may be simply agreeing to statements of this sort and the fact that some of them are "authoritarian" and others are not is a reflection of their value confusion and not necessarily indicative of potentially fascist inclinations at the personality level.

The possible confusion that might result from treating all individuals with high F-scale scores as equivalent in a study relating the F scale to a measure of intolerance of ambiguity, for example, should be obvious. Those who are high scorers by virtue of being acquiescent are by definition tolerating a considerable amount of ambiguity since they are agreeing to psychologically incompatible statements! That undue reliance on the F scale alone as a measure of authoritarianism might be misleading can be indicated by examining the pattern of responses of those undergraduates in the Northeastern sample who accepted eight or more of the ten F-scale items. Twenty of the 37 turn out on inspection to be significantly acquiescent but not significantly high on the overall measure of F, eleven are significantly authoritarian but

not acquiescent, and seven are not significantly high on either measure (one individual with a score of 15 on F and a + 4 discrepancy score was both significantly authoritarian and significantly acquiescent). A virtue of the suggested method of scoring is that it gives two scores to an individual—one a measure of authoritarianism in which response set is balanced out and one a measure of response set. With a large enough number of items, it is possible to have overlap on the two measures, e.g., two Ss among the 72 per cent of the graduate student sample who were significantly low on the overall measure of authoritarianism were also significantly acquiescent and another two low scorers were significantly negativistic.

It is not news, of course, to point out that the F scale is not unidimensional. The present argument suggests, however, that there are possibly greater differences among high scorers than low scorers in the customary undergraduate samples. When relatively high and low scorers are compared differences will be found when the low scoring Ss are different from all other groups. This may account for many of the correlations found with other attitude scales when the generally more sophisticated low scorers differ from both the consistent high scorers and the confused acquiescent high scorers. The generally murky picture that prevails, however, as to the relationship between the F scale and measures of such behavioral tendencies as intolerance of ambiguity and rigidity might arise from the fact that the low scorers are similar to consistent high scorers in having an organized *Weltanschauung* but are more similar to acquiescent high scorers in being able to tolerate certain kinds of ambiguity.

These are speculations and their validity can be determined only by empirical studies using techniques that clarify the meaning of the F-scale scores of a given S. It must be emphasized that the majority of the samples reported on in this discussion were accidentally and not randomly drawn so the only generalization about the distribution of response set which is justified is to the nationwide population of adults with some college training where no significant amount of acquiescence was found. The presence of some acquiescence among college undergraduates raises questions about the meaning of some of the results found with other samples of undergraduates but does not necessarily imply that they too are laden with acquiescent individuals.

It should also be noted that the possibility of response set in samples studied by means of the F scale does not necessarily indicate the relevance of response set to studies where the E scale was used as the independent variable. A study on response set by Shelley yielded a correlation of $+.27$ ($p = .05$) between the anti-Semitism subscale and the use of "like much" responses to 60 pictures on the Perceptual Reaction Test of Berg and Hunt (25). This is a lower correlation than the majority of those cited earlier between the F scale and various measures of response set. Prentice found 16 favorably worded items toward Jews and Negroes correlated less highly ($+.78$) than did 16 unfavorable statements which correlated $+1.00$ with the E scale. Although we are in basic agreement with Prentice's conclusion that the use of positive or negative items is of little relevance in the measure of ethnic prejudice, we note as do Gage et al. that it does make some difference, a conclusion in agreement with the earlier research of Campbell and McCandless

(23). Actually, this slight difference is somewhat surprising since some of the items used by Prentice violate standards we have suggested earlier, e.g., "*No* Jews are especially loud, noisy and overbearing" (23, Footnote 3, p. 420, italics added).

Our interpretation is that in these two studies, slight evidence of response set was found but, given the difficulties of comparing studies using different techniques and samples, that the amount of response set is even less than that found in studies using the F scale. This result is consistent with the general thesis that response set is greatest in ambiguous situations; the use of a minority group as a referent in an attitudinal statement is presumably less vague for most respondents than people in general or the sex life of the ancient Greeks and Romans.

In concluding, the data indicate that acquiescence is not identical with authoritarianism. This interpretation is at variance with the earlier studies reviewed, a discrepancy here attributed at least partially to the fact that many of the reversed items used in them were irrelevant to a meaningful measure of authoritarianism. It also appears that the nature of the samples used was a contributing factor since the high scoring subjects in many of these studies were inconsistent in their responses partly because they were drawn from populations containing a relatively large proportion of individuals who were, although probably but temporarily, ideologically confused.

Summary

Four recent studies which have found a lack of positive correlations between the F scale and scales of reversed items were examined. It was argued that the attempts at reversals were often characterized by items that were not psychologically opposed to the original items. It also appeared that calling upon the operation of an acquiescent response set as an explanation of the results was questionable since many of the "high" scorers in these samples were inconsistent in their responses and were not generally agreeing with F-scale items.

A new set of items designed to overcome some of our objections was developed. An item analysis indicated that the majority of the reversed items discriminated positively between individuals high and low on the F scale in two pairs of subsamples. An examination of the response patterns on the most discriminating items indicated that a minority of the respondents showed response set and that they were among the individuals who showed slight agreement with the F-scale items.

Further results were obtained on eight additional samples. All correlations were positive although there was great variability. A method for determining the significance of response set was developed and data from an additional representative nation-wide sample of adults with a college background indicated no significant degree of acquiescence. This was also true of our most sophisticated samples but appreciable amounts of acquiescence were found in an undergraduate sample. Possible implications of this finding for research using the F scale on undergraduate samples were noted. It is concluded that the data do not support the identification of acquiescence with authoritarianism.

References

1. ADORNO, T. W., FRENKEL-BRUNSWIK, ELSE, LEVINSON, D. J., & SANFORD, R. N. *The Authoritarian Personality,* New York: Harper, 1950.

2. BASS, B. M. Authoritarianism or acquiescence? *J. abnorm. soc. Psychol.,* 1955, **51,** 616–623.

3. ———. Development and evaluation of a scale for measuring social acquiescence. *J. abnorm. soc. Psychol.,* 1956, **53,** 296–299.

4. ———. Reply to Messick and Jackson's comments on authoritarianism or acquiescence. *J. abnorm. soc. Psychol.,* 1957, **54,** 426–427.

5. CAREY, GLORIA, ROGOW, A. A., & FARRELL, CALISTA. The relationship between the F scale and aphorism usage and agreement. *J. Psychol.,* 1957, **43,** 163–167.

6. CAMPBELL, D. T., & McCANDLESS, B. R. Ethnocentrism, xenophobia, and personality. *Human Relat.,* 1951, **4,** 185–192.

7. CHAPMAN, L. J., & CAMPBELL, D. T. Response set in the F scale. *J. abnorm. soc. Psychol.,* 1957, **54,** 129–132.

8. CHRISTIE, R., & GARCIA, J. Subcultural variation in authoritarian personality. *J. abnorm. soc. Psychol.,* 1951, **46,** 457–469.

9. COHN, T. S. The relation of the F scale to a response set to answer positively. *Amer. Psychologist,* 1953, **8,** 335. (Abstract)

10. CRONBACH, L. J. Response sets and test validity. *Educ. psychol. Measmt.,* 1946, **6,** 475–494.

11. ———. Further evidence on response sets and test design. *Educ. psychol. Measmt.,* 1950, **10,** 3–31.

12. GAGE, N. L., LEAVITT, G. S., & STONE, G. C. The psychological meaning of acquiescent set for authoritarianism. *J. abnorm. soc. Psychol.,* 1957, **55,** 98–103.

13. JACKSON, D. N., & MESSICK, S. J. A note on 'ethnocentrism' and acquiescent response sets. *J. abnorm. soc. Psychol.,* 1957, **54,** 132–134.

14. JACKSON, D. N., MESSICK, S. J., & SOLLEY, C. M. How 'rigid' is the 'authoritarian'? *J. abnorm. soc. Psychol.,* 1957, **54,** 137–140.

15. JONES, M. B. Authoritarianism and intolerance of fluctuation. *J. abnorm. soc. Psychol.,* 1955, **50,** 125–126.

16. JACOB, P. E. *Changing values in college.* New Haven: Hazen Foundation, 1956.

17. LEAVITT, H. J., HAX, H., & ROCHE, J. H. Authoritarianism and agreement with things authoritative. *J. Psychol.,* 1955, **40,** 215–221.

18. LORGE, I. Gen-like: halo or reality. *Psychol. Bull.,* 1937, **34,** 545–546. (Abstract)

19. MEER, S. J. Authoritarian attitudes and dreams. *J. abnorm. soc. Psychol.,* 1955, **51,** 74–78.

20. MESSICK, S. J., & JACKSON, D. N. Authoritarianism or acquiescence in Bass's data. *J. abnorm. soc. Psychol.,* 1957, **54,** 424–425.

21. NEWCOMB, T. M. *Personality and social change.* New York: Dryden, 1943.

22. PERLMUTTER, H. J. Some characteristics of the xenophilic personality. *J. Psychol.,* 1954, **38,** 291–300.

23. PRENTICE, N. M. The comparability of positive and negative items in scales of ethnic prejudice. *J. abnorm. soc. Psychol.,* 1956, **52,** 420–421.

24. PROTHRO, E. T., &. MELIKIAN, L. H. The California public opinion scales in an authoritarian culture. *Publ. Opin. Quart.,* 1953, **17,** 353–362.

25. SHELLEY, H. P. Response set and the California attitude scales. *Educ. psychol. Measmt,* 1956, **16,** 63–67.

26. WEBSTER, H. Some quantitative results. *J. soc. Issues,* 1956, **12,** (4), 29–43.

YEASAYERS AND NAYSAYERS: AGREEING RESPONSE SET AS A PERSONALITY VARIABLE

Arthur Couch and Kenneth Keniston

Psychologists have realized for a number of years that various response sets have considerable influence on most objective psychological test scores (Lorge, 1937). But only in the past few years, inspired by Cronbach's two articles (1946, 1950), has there been any systematic study of this biasing effect of response set and its implications for questionnaire validity.

Many of these investigations, recently

Reprinted by permission of the American Psychological Association and the authors from *The Journal of Abnormal and Social Psychology,* Vol. 60, 1960.

summarized by Jackson and Messick (1958), have dealt with *agreeing* response set, defined as a tendency to agree (or disagree) with items regardless of their content. Psychological tests are frequently based on Likert-type scales with response alternatives ranging from Strongly Agree to Strongly Disagree. The agreeing tendency is of crucial importance with response scales of this type, since it is intrinsically involved in the method of measurement itself. In recent years, there has been a growing concern about the degree to which this agreeing set permeates the objective measures of many well known personality variables. Many studies have investigated the influence of agreement tendency on the "Authoritarian" F scale (Bass, 1955; Christie, Havel, & Seidenberg, 1958); on the variables on the MMPI (Fricke, 1956; Barnes, 1956), and on vocational interests (Roulon, 1931; Berdie, 1943; Holland, 1958).

A review of the literature reveals two general approaches to agreeing response set. From one viewpoint, response set is seen as primarily a statistical nuisance that must be controlled or suppressed by appropriate mathematical techniques. The agreement tendency is considered a rather superficial and ephemeral set, chiefly important as a mathematical factor that is compounded in scale measurements. While the statistical properties and consequences of the response set are given prominent attention, little interest is focused on the psychological determinants of the agreeing set in the individuals taking the tests. Cronbach, despite qualifications in other publications (1949, p. 51), summarizes this position in a recent discussion of accuracy of person perception: "In other instruments, the elevation score—the average response on all items—represents a trivial response set, such as the tendency to say 'yes' to both favorable and unfavorable questions. In that case, the dimension should probably be removed from the data" (1958, p. 366).

A second approach is represented by several researchers interested in agreeing response set as a manifestation of the responders' personality, interests, or personal "style" (Berdie, 1943; Jackson & Messick, 1958). Many of these investigators, though they view response set as a reflection of personality, postulate that agreement tendency is merely what it "appears" to be—a general "acquies-

cence" tendency that results in agreement with the rather general and authoritative statements of most questionnaires. Bass (1955) suggests that the response set is an indication of "social acquiescence"; while Leavitt, Hax, and Roche (1955) believe that the set is an "agreement with things authoritative." This view of response set as general acquiescence has led to the conclusion that many well-studied variables such as "authoritarianism" can be primarily explained in terms of the agreement phenomenon.

A somewhat different position is taken in the present study. Although response set is indeed a mathematical factor having major repercussions on objective test scores, exclusive concern with these statistical consequences may distract from the equally significant problem of the psychological determinants of response set. The basic hypothesis of this study is that response set is a manifestation of a deep-seated personality syndrome—whose underlying determinants serve to explain the phenotypical phenomenon of "acquiescence" or "agreement."

This study attempts to analyze agreeing response set as a personality variable —using both objective test measurements and a program of clinical assessment. The first part of this report outlines the development of a reliable and valid measure of agreeing response set as it manifests itself in questionnaire items. We then show that this measure has the stability and generality which would characterize it as an index of an underlying personality dimension. This agreement measure was correlated against a series of objective test scales and items. The pattern of results suggested a set of hypotheses concerning the personality differences between individuals who tend to agree (yeasayers) and those who disagree (naysayers). The second part of this report presents a set of hypotheses about the personality dynamics behind the agreement tendency and attempts to validate these formulations by a clinical study of subjects with marked tendencies to "agree" and "disagree." Results of a structured interview and sentence-completion test given to these "yeasayers" and "naysayers" enabled us to verify and conceptualize more clearly the inner dynamics behind this "agreeing" personality syndrome. A general interpretation and discussion of the results obtained in both parts of the study is presented in the concluding section.

Part I: Questionnaire Studies

The initial problem was to obtain a valid measure of response set, which we have defined as a general "tendency to agree or disagree with questionnaire items, regardless of their content." It is obviously important that the measure of response set not be "contaminated" by the undue presence of any specific cluster of content variables, as would certainly happen if the amount of agreement on any one or two standard psychological test scales were considered an adequate indicator of this general response tendency.

In order to create an appropriate measure of agreement tendency that was not affected by "content" variables, we decided that the questionnaire items included in it would have to fulfill three criteria: (a) the items should measure heterogeneous content variables from widely different psychological areas; (b) these content variables should be selected so that the total set is psychologically "balanced" to insure an over-all diffuseness of content; and (c) the total number of individual items in the over-all response measure should be very large

(at least 300) so that the general response tendency has sufficient opportunity to manifest itself by permeating the answer pattern in a consistent way. With these purposes in mind, we began our study.

DEVELOPMENT OF THE OVER-ALL AGREEMENT SCORE (OAS)

Subjects. As part of the assessment procedure in the selection of Ss for a clinical research project, a large battery of objective personality tests was administered to 61 paid volunteer students from Harvard College. These Ss had been selected on formal criteria (male, sophomore, satisfactory grades) from 200 volunteers enrolled in an undergraduate course in the social sciences.

Procedure. Most of the objective test items were answered in a series of three weekly sessions in the fall; a final group of tests was given later in the spring. The Ss gave responses to 681 items, using a scale of the Likert type. The response categories were given values from 1 to 7, and were worded as follows:

(1)	(2)	(3)	(4)
Strongly Disagree	Disagree	Slightly Disagree	No Answer

(5)	(6)	(7)
Slightly Agree	Agree	Strongly Agree

The items included many from previously developed tests, such as Davids' Affect Questionnaire (1955), the factorial scales from Couch and Bales' Value Profile (1955), the Authoritarianism F Scale (Adorno, Frenkel-Brunswik, Levinson, & Sanford, 1950), Thurstone's Temperament Schedule (1949), Cattell's 16 P.F. Personality Inventory (Cattell, Saunders, & Stice, 1957), Rokeach's

Dogmatism Scales (1956), and Bass' Social Acquiescence Scale (1956). In addition to these tests, well over 200 new items were included in an attempt to develop factor scales for a variety of psychological concepts in the areas of orality, anality, introspectiveness, psychological inertia, depression, elation, superego integration, insightfulness, self-concept, and attitudes towards American culture.

To control the effect of content variables in our measure of agreeing response set, we based it entirely on 360 selected items out of the total of 681 items of the Likert-scale type. In an attempt to fulfill our criteria for a response measure unaffected by specific content, we chose items from a large number (30) of heterogeneous scales that had "psychological" opposites, such as Trust-Distrust, Dependency-Self-sufficiency, Rationalism-Religiousness, Optimism-Pessimism, etc. By including an equal number of items on "opposite" ends of each of the dimensions measured, we hoped to "cancel out" the effect of any content variable on the Over-all Agreement Score. This diversity and "psychological balancing" of content reduced the possibility that the measure of agreeing tendency would be unduly influenced by some extraneous pattern of personality variables—a total score over all items makes no psychological sense. To the extent that this "content cancelling" has been achieved, the sum score of all 360 item responses is a pure measure of agreeing response set, that is, of the *S*'s tendency to agree (or disagree) with items *regardless* of content. This approach should also reduce the possibility that correlations between the agreement measure and other scales or items are produced by content variables unwittingly built into the measure itself.

An Over-all Agreement Score (OAS)

was computed for each *S* by taking the mean of their responses to the 360 items. The range of scores was from 3.1 to 4.5, with a mean value of 3.9 and a standard deviation of 0.3. The first sign of the importance of this measure was indicated by the high (+.85) Spearman-Brown split-half (even-odd) reliability of the entire 360 item scale. The OAS thus provides a reliable measure of agreeing response set as defined in this study.

GENERALITY OF THE OAS

Having established the statistical reliability of the OAS, it is necessary to demonstrate that this measure has empirical characteristics which support our contention that it measures a generalized agreement tendency. Since the OAS was based on an arbitrary selection of items, we considered that it was necessary to test its generality by correlating it with the grand sum of all 681 items of the Likert type in our questionnaire battery. This "grand sum" correlated +.94 with the OAS, a high value even considering the 53% overlap of items. Although the larger number of items also appears to serve the function of guaranteeing heterogeneity and content "elimination," in this study we have used the OAS as the scale that most fully meets our criteria for a valid measure of response set.

To test the extent that response set varied from one testing session to the next, we computed the correlations between the sum of "content-cancelled" items (120) from the first two weeks of testing and the sum of "content-cancelled" items (240) from the third week of testing. The correlation coefficient was +.73, indicating that agreeing and disagreeing response set operates fairly consistently over time, and is not merely the product of the *S*'s momentary mood.

The OAS as a mean score indicates

the average point along the Likert scale around which the *S* tends to center his responses. However, this mean score does not tell us what actual response category preferences are associated with high and low OAS scores. To investigate these relationships, we computed the percentage frequency with which the *S*s choose each of the six Likert response categories and then correlated these figures with the OAS scores. The mean and standard deviation of these percentage frequencies are presented along with the correlation coefficients in Table 1.

TABLE 1. CORRELATIONS OF RESPONSE CATEGORIES WITH OAS

Likert Response Categories	Per-centage (Mean)	Fre-quency (*SD*)	Correla-tions with OAS (*N* = 61)
Strongly Agree	4.8	3.3	+.41
Agree	17.1	4.6	+.55
Slightly Agree	25.5	5.4	+.23
No Answer	0.2	0.6	−.10
Slightly Disagree	22.8	6.0	−.23
Disagree	21.8	4.9	−.54
Strongly Disagree	7.9	4.0	−.38

These results demonstrate that the OAS is most highly related to a response preference for the categories of Agree (in a positive way) and Disagree (in a negative way). These correlations are affected by the relative contribution to the OAS of each response category—as reflected in the Mean Percentage Frequency. This "part-whole" effect may explain the lower correlations for Strongly Agree and Strongly Disagree, but since other response categories have about the same mean frequency, the uniquely high

correlation of the Agree and Disagree categories point to a real relationship of response preference and the agreement tendency. The preference for definite "agreement" responses supports our interpretation of the OAS measure. It should also be noted that the frequency of using *disagreement* categories is an equally prominent indicator of the agreement tendency—only the direction of scoring is reversed. Thus, to label the response tendency *agreement* is only an arbitrary preference on our part; the opposite *disagreeing response tendency* would be an equally appropriate conceptualization.

Yeasaying and true-saying. If this tendency to agree or disagree is a manifestation of a general response set, this set should also permeate objective tests that do not employ Likert-scale items but use response categories that are similar in psychological meaning to agreement and disagreement. In order to test the generality of response set, we investigated the relationship of the OAS with the agreement equivalent (marking true) on the MMPI (Minnesota Multiphasic Personality Inventory). About six months after the initial testing sessions, the *S*s filled out the entire 566-item MMPI. As a measure of a "true-saying" response tendency, we computed a Sum True score for each *S* by counting the total number of True responses on all items. This score, though perhaps also reflecting dispositions other than response set, had a correlation of +.64 with the OAS. A correlation of this magnitude indicates that response set influences answers both to Agree-Disagree Likert items and to True-False answer patterns.

Yeasaying and yes-saying. To test further the generality of agreeing response set in the objective test domain, we examined the characteristic response pattern of our *S*s on another standard personality inventory—Cattell's 16 P.F. Test. This test consists of Forms A and B, with a grand total of 374 items, of which 217 (about 60%) have an answer pattern which offers the choices: Yes, In Between, No. We counted the total number of times each *S* had marked Yes on those 217 items where that response was possible. This Sum Yes score was then correlated with the OAS, giving a correlation of +.56. This finding adds support to our hypothesis that agreeing response set is a disposition of considerable influence and stability, and indicates again that the OAS functions as a reliable and valid measure of this general agreeing tendency.

CORRELATES OF THE OAS

The results obtained in developing the Over-all Agreement Score, namely the high reliability, stability over time, and generality of agreeing response set, support the view that this set is the manifestation of a personality syndrome. We therefore proceeded to treat the OAS as a criterion measure of this agreeing response set, and correlated the score with a series of objective test domains. This step-wise search for the correlates of the agreement response set gradually built up a consistent and meaningful pattern which characterized the personality of individuals who tend to "agree" (or conversely "disagree") on questionnaires regardless of item content.

Relationship to the MMPI. There are intrinsic difficulties in the task of relating a measure of agreeing response tendency to any series of objectively measured personality variables; for the response tendency itself is an *integral part of the measurement technique* involved in assessing the personality variable. This is especially true when the variable measured uses items scored mainly in one direction, when, for example, some variable X is scored by counting all items marked Agree, True, or Yes.

On the MMPI we have already noted that the tendency to mark True is highly related to the general agreeing response set. For each of the 32 MMPI scales [1] that were computed for each *S*, a tabulation was made of the percentage of items in the scale which count towards a high score on that scale when marked True. All scales were then correlated with the OAS. These correlations and the Percentage True counts are presented in Table 2.

The analysis presented in Table 2 illustrates the very close relationship between the amount of agreement response component inherent in the scale as measured by the Percentage True count and the correlation of that scale with our measure of agreement tendency. Scales that rely primarily on True responses for a high score tend to have positive correlations with the OAS, while scales relying on False responses for a high score tend to have negative correlations. In fact, over the 32 standard scales, these two measurements have a rank order correlation of +.86, indicating that scales with an unusually high (or low) percentage of items scored True are significantly influenced by the agreeing response set.

Because of this possible source of "contamination," an interpretation of the psychological implications of the correlations between the MMPI scales and the OAS measure requires caution. The pattern of scales having significant positive and negative correlations with the OAS

---

[1] Fuller descriptions of each scale and appropriate reference are available in the article by Kasselbaum, Couch, and Slater (1959).

TABLE 2. CORRELATIONS OF THE MMPI SCALES WITH THE OVER-ALL
AGREEMENT SCORE (OAS)

Scales		Per-centage "True"	Correlation with OAS (N = 61)	Scales		Per-centage "True"	Correlation with OAS (N = 61)
ST	Sum True	100	+.64 **	St	Social Status	44	−.07
Pr	Prejudice	88	+.51 **	Hy	Hysteria	22	−.08
A	Anxiety	97	+.50 **	Oi	Originality	16	−.26 *
Dp	Dependency	86	+.48 **	Ie	Intellectual Effi-	38	−.28 *
X2	Impulsivity	90	+.46 **		ciency		
Pt	Psychasthenia	81	+.45 **	Lp	Leadership	28	−.31 *
Ma	Mania	76	+.41 **	R	Repression De-	0	−.34 **
Sc	Schizophrenia	74	+.38 **		nial		
Fm	Feminine Mas-	66	+.33 *	Es	Ego Strength	37	−.35 **
	ochism			Ac	Achievement via	22	−.35 **
Hs	Hypochondriasis	33	+.29 *		Conformance		
D	Depression	35	+.22	K	Suppressor Scale	3	−.38 **
F	Validity Scale	69	+.20	Rp	Role-playing	41	−.40 **
Do	Dominance	25	+.15		Ability		
Pd	Psychopathic	48	+.15	L	Lie Scale	0	−.42 **
Si	Social Introver-	49	+.07	Ai	Achievement via	19	−.44 **
	sion				Independence		
Pa	Paranoia	63	+.06	Re	Social Responsi-	28	−.48 **
Sp	Social Ability	68	+.03		bility		
Mf	Feminine Inter-	47	+.01	To	Tolerance	10	−.52 **
	ests						
X1	Social Presence	25	−.06				

   * .05 level of significance $(r = .26)$.
   ** .01 level of significance $(r = .33)$.

clearly suggests pervasive psychological differences between yeasayers and naysayers. However, in so far as these correlations are related to the Percentage True counts of the scales, the importance of the interpreted "content" of these MMPI variables may seem to be decreased. With the exception of the few scales with approximately 50% True counts—such as (Ie) Intellectual Efficiency, (Es) Ego-strength, and (Rp) Role-playing Ability—none of the variables with significant correlations are free of the "contaminating" effect of response set on their level of relationship with the OAS—thus presenting difficulties in us-

ing the correlations to identify the "psychological" characteristics of the agreement response tendency.

Nonetheless, it should be remembered that most MMPI scales were developed by the use of "criterion" groups, and therefore the "psychological" nature of agreement response set would have contributed to the empirical pattern of item responses that differentiated individuals high vs. low on the variable of the scale. We can probably infer that the original populations of Ss high and low on Prejudice, Psychasthenia, Mania, Achievement via Independence, and the other concepts of the empirical scales had personality differences related to an "agreement" or "disagreement" response tendency. In other words, the Percentage True of the empirical scale reflects personality differences in the criterion groups that are related to the response tendency. To the extent that this inference is valid, the correlational results can be helpful in identifying the personality correlates of response set, despite the apparent "contamination" of the scale scores with response set.

Table 2 shows a number of significant correlations of MMPI scales with the OAS. The positive correlations of (X2) Impulsivity, (Dp) Dependency, and (Ma) Mania with the OAS suggest that individuals high on the agreeing tendency show signs of an extrovertive impulsivity. The centrality of this general dimension seems borne out by the cluster of high negative correlations with the variables: (R) Repression-suppression, (Re) Responsibility, (Ai) Achievement via Independence, and (Ac) Academic Achievement via Conformance. All these scales point to introvertive intellectual interests, inhibitions, and a control of impulsivity. Another dimension which seems indicated is that of ego strength. Yeasayers are high on such scales as (A) Anxiety and (Pt) Psychasthenia, while naysayers obtain high scores on the scales of (Es) Ego strength and the (K) Supressor scale. In terms of a recent factor analytic study of the MMPI (Kasselbaum, Couch, & Slater, 1959) this pattern of results places the agreeing response tendency along the axis of a fusion factor conceived as Impulsivity vs. Intellectual Control. The fact that the (Pr) Prejudice scale has the highest correlation (+.51) with the OAS and (To) Tolerance scale the lowest correlation (−.52) may be primarily explained by this main factorial dimension.

TABLE 3. CORRELATIONS OF THE CATTELL 16 P.F. SCALES WITH THE OAS SCORE

Scale	Correlation with OAS (N = 61)
A —Warm, Sociable vs. Aloof, Cold	+.27 *
B —Intelligent vs. Dull	+.07
C —Mature, Calm vs. Emotional, Unstable	−.35 **
E —Dominant, Aggressive vs. Submissive	+.22
F —Enthusiastic, Talkative vs. Silent	+.23
G —Conscientious vs. Undependable	+.15
H —Adventurous vs. Timid	+.02
I —Sensitive vs. Tough	+.02
L —Suspecting, Jealous vs. Trustful	+.39 **
M —Eccentric vs. Conventional	+.10
N —Sophisticated vs. Simple	+.19
O —Insecure, Anxious vs. Unshakable	+.38 **
Q1—Critical vs. Conservative, Accepting	−.02
Q2—Self-sufficient vs. Dependent	−.17
Q3—Controlled, Exact vs. Lax, Unsure	−.35 **
Q4—Tense, Excitable vs. Phlegmatic, Poised	+.38 **

* Significant at the .05 level.
** Significant at the .01 level.

Further implications of these findings are best discussed after more of the correlates of the OAS are considered.

Relationship to the Cattell and Thurstone personality tests. In Tables 3 and 4, we have presented the correlations of the OAS with each of the 16 standard scales (Forms A and B combined) in the Cattell 16 P.F. Test and with the seven factor scales of Thurstone's Temperament Schedule. The percentage of Yes responses is presented for the Thurstone scales. These figures are not appropriate for the Cattell test which uses a large number of (a) vs. (b) alternative choices as item responses.

TABLE 4. CORRELATIONS OF THURSTONE'S
TEMPERAMENT SCALES WITH THE
OAS SCORE

Scale (Factor)	Percentage Scored "Yes"	Correlation with OAS (N = 61)
	%	
A—Active	65	+.13
V—Vigorous	100	+.01
I —Impulsive	90	+.19
D—Dominant	70	+.14
E—Stable	35	−.38 *
S —Sociable	80	+.10
R—Reflective	95	+.16

* Significant at the .01 level.

In this battery of tests, the highest positive correlations with the OAS are with Cattell's scales (L) Suspecting, Jealous vs. Trustful, (O) Insecure, Anxious vs. Unshakable, and (Q4) Tense, Excitable vs. Phlegmatic, Poised. The highest negative relationships are with Cattell's (C) Mature, Calm vs. Emotional, Unstable, (Q3) Controlled, Exact vs. Lax, Unsure. In the Thurstone test, there is a significant negative correlation with the (E) Stable temperament scale —which also has the lowest percentage of Yes responses involved in its score. We note again the theme of emotional control vs. impulsivity. The naysayers present a picture of calm, controlled stability; while yeasayers seem more emotionally determined, openly admitting anxiety and distrustfulness. The highest correlation (+.39) is with the Suspecting, Jealous vs. Trustful Scale, indicating that a *lack* of trust is associated with the OAS. This datum reminds us that one should not too quickly generalize from the apparent "acquiescence" of the yeasayer.

It is interesting to note the lack of relationship of the OAS to intelligence as measured by the (B) Intelligent vs. Dull scale (+.07). This pattern was verified by nonsignificant correlations of the OAS with SAT (Verbal Aptitude Subtest) (−.04) and MAT (Mathematical Aptitude Subtest) (.00) of the College Entrance Examination Board scores. In our population, it appears that intelligence is not an important aspect of agreeing response set.

Relationship to basic disposition scales. As part of other research at the Harvard Psychological Clinic Annex, we had developed a set of factorial scales to measure basic dispositions in the areas of Orality, Anality, Alienation, and Psychological Inertia. In a series of unreported studies large domains of test items in each of these four areas were factor analyzed. Several reliable factor scales were developed, each possessing the statistical characteristics of factorial purity and domain orthogonality. For some variables, both Positive and Balanced scale measures are available. These latter scales are "balanced" in the sense that an equal number of items are scored "positively" and "negatively." Thus, Balanced scales should serve to cancel out any contamination due to agreeing response set. The Positive factor scales, reported below, consist of items scored only in one direction. Table 5 presents the correlations of the OAS with these Basic Disposition Factor Scales, sub-

TABLE 5. CORRELATIONS OF THE BASIC DISPOSITION FACTOR SCALES
WITH THE OAS

Basic Disposition Factors	Correlations with OAS (N = 61)	Basic Disposition Factors	Correlations with OAS (N = 61)
Positive Scales:		Quick Reactions	+.33 *
		Perseveration	+.17
Conventional Anxiety	+.57 **	Slow Reactions	−.02
Conscious Hostility	+.46 **	High Psychological Inertia	−.20
Alienation	+.44 **		
Distrust	+.32 *	Balanced Scales:	
Pessimism	+.18		
Optimism	+.17	Distrust vs. Trust	+.20
Trust	−.07	Optimism vs. Pessimism	+.01
		Oral Dependency vs. Coun-	+.25
Oral Aggression	+.43 **	terdependency	
Oral Dependency	+.40 **	Anal Orderliness vs. Messi-	+.07
Oral Involvement	+.14	iness	
Oral Rejectiveness	+.03	Emotional Inertia: High vs.	−.43 **
Oral Counterdependency	−.03	Low	
Anality Total Scale	+.75 **	Equilibrium Inertia: Emo-	−.33 *
Anal Preoccupation	+.75 **	tional Stability vs. Varia-	
Anal Submission	+.67 **	bility	
Anal Rebellion	+.61 **	Secondary Process Inertia—	−.30 *
Anal Concern with Power	+.55 **	Impulse Control vs. Ex-	
Anal Orderliness	+.25	citability	
Anal Messiness	+.20	Quick Reactions vs. Slow	+.20
		Reactions	
Secondary Process Inertia—	+.57 **	Inconstancy vs. Persevera-	+.10
Excitability		tion	
Low Emotional Inertia	+.56 **		
Equilibrium Inertia—Emo-	+.48 **		
tional Variability			
Inconstancy	+.37 **		

* Significant at the .05 level.
** Significant at the .01 level.

divided into Balanced and Positive scales.

This table permits us to compare the correlations of Balanced and Positive scales designed to measure the same concept. In every case where the comparison is possible, the correlations of Balanced scales with the OAS are *less* positive than that of their Positive scale counterparts, the average drop being .18. This difference is of course statistically determined by the fact that the agreeing response set is actually built into all Positive scales and systematically cancelled from Balanced scales. The comparison again points out the important contribution that agreeing response tendency makes to the variance of Positive scales, and demonstrates that "balancing-out" response set reduces the response set component in the scale score.

With this effect of response set on the variables kept in mind, the pattern of correlational results in Table 5 brings out new facets of the agreeing response tendency. Several of the recently developed Basic Disposition Factor scales have significantly positive correlations with the OAS. Many of these scales were derived from our factor analysis of the Anality domain. Since these scales are not yet described in the literature, we have included here a characteristic item for the scales mentioned. It can be seen that the highest positive correlations are for the dispositional scales of Anal Preoccupation ("I enjoy exploring slums and alleys, dirty though they are"); Anal Rebellion ("I could really shock people if I said all of the dirty things I think"); and Anal Submissiveness ("People need someone strong to lean on"). These results suggest that the previously noted relationships of the OAS to impulsivity and rejection of emotional control may be part of a more basic dispositional complex centered around anality. We also note a positive relationship to the scales measuring Alienation ("The idea of adjusting to society as now constituted fills me with horror"); and Conventional Anxiety ("There are few more miserable experiences than going to bed night after night knowing you are so upset that worry will not let you sleep"). These variables seem related to the general maladjustment and distrustfulness noted in the MMPI scales and in the Cattell factors.

On the opposite end of the agreeing tendency, a group of Balanced scales in the area of *psychological inertia* is found to characterize the naysayers. The factor scales with the highest negative correlations with the OAS are: Secondary Process Inertia ("I have to think things through thoroughly before I act"); Equilibrium Inertia ("Uncontrolled impulsiveness is not part of my make-up"); and Emotional Inertia ("Whatever emotional mood I have is likely to stay with me for a long time"). This pattern of general retention of impulses and the

reluctance to respond quickly to situational demands may very well represent the opposing reaction to the anal expressive syndrome pointed out by the cluster of positively correlated scales, and contribute a new meaning to the general emotional stability indicated by the previously reported correlational results. It may be that standard measures of ego strength, adjustment, and maturity, when used on populations of normals, are related primarily to this kind of pervasive control of impulses by dominant secondary processes.

Relationship to authoritarianism. Much of the previous research on agreeing response set has focused on its relationship with authoritarianism. It has been argued that scores on the F scale are in large part a function of this agreeing tendency, with the implication that the original formulations concerning the authoritarian personality may be invalidated by this fact. To investigate this question, we made an especially intensive study of the relationship between the F scale and the OAS.

The literature on authoritarianism and "acquiescence" often concentrates on the question of what percentage of F scale variance can be attributed to the agreeing response tendency. With the OAS, a fairly direct measure of this percentage can be obtained from the correlation of the OAS with the F scale. But many objective measures of authoritarianism suffer from a lack of knowledge of their dimensional purity. In an effort to avoid these difficulties, we used as measures of authoritarianism two scales that had been developed by Couch and Bales (1955) in their factor analysis of the Value Profile. These scales are factorially pure measures of authoritarianism, both having very high saturation on the first factor of their analysis which uniquely defines a 30-item F score with a loading of $+.90$. One scale, called the Positive F scale, consists of 10 items all scored in the positive direction: for example, "Obedience and respect for authority are the most important virtues children should learn." The other scale, the Balanced F scale, consists of 5 items scored positively and 5 items scored negatively. The factorial purity of this scale is achieved by a balancing out of other factor components. Thus, negative items that are not pure "reversed" authoritarianism can be used when properly compensated for by complementary factorially "impure" positive items. With

TABLE 6. CORRELATIONS OF AUTHORITARIANISM MEASURES WITH THE OAS

Factor Scales	Correlations with OAS ($N = 61$)
Positive F scale	$+.37$ *
Balanced F scale	$+.09$ **

* Significant at the .01 level.
** Significantly different from the above $r = +.37$ at the .01 level.

this Balanced F scale, agreeing response set is effectively cancelled out; thus, the correlation with the OAS should reflect the lack of this "contaminating" influence. The results of correlating these two factorially "equal" measures of authoritarianism with the OAS are presented in Table 6.

As Table 6 indicates, the Positive F scale correlates significantly with the OAS, supporting the view that the F scale, if measured by positive items, is influenced to some extent by agreeing response set. But the percentage of variance attributed to this agreement effect is only 14%, if we assume that the correlation with the OAS is an appropriate

measure of this influence. More substantial evidence that "pure" authoritarianism is actually uneffected by agreement tendency comes from the nearly zero ($+.09$) correlation between the Balanced F scale and the OAS. Since both F scales are highly loaded on the authoritarianism factor and are significantly intercorrelated ($+.56$), these results suggest that the agreeing response tendency is not related to "pure" authoritarianism when its measurement is not inherently contaminated by response set. In another section, we return to this issue in a more substantive context where a factor analysis supports the same conclusion.

Relationship to social acquiescence and dogmatism. We turn to the areas of social acquiescence and dogmatism where previous research had suggested certain relationships to response set. Bass (1956) developed a Social Acquiescence Scale in a manner somewhat similar to the method we used in obtaining our Over-all Agreement Score, although only aphorisms were involved in his scale. One-half of Bass' scale (28 odd-numbered items) was included in our original test battery. In addition to these items, we gave Rokeach's (1956) Dogmatism Scales, which consist of 40 items measuring different aspects of ideological and functional dogmatism. Table 7 presents the correlations of these scales with the OAS.

The Social Acquiescence Scale correlates significantly ($+.30$) with the OAS, but at a lower level than would be expected if "acquiescence" were actually a central variable in the agreeing response tendency. This rather low correlation is especially indicative, since all items are scored in the direction of agreement. Given the general pattern of positive correlations between other Positive scales and the OAS, this result suggests that the Social Acquiescence Scale is not distinctively related to agreeing response set.

TABLE 7. CORRELATIONS OF SOCIAL ACQUI-
ESCENCE AND DOGMATISM WITH THE OAS

Scales	Correlations with OAS (N = 61)
Bass' Social Acquiescence Scale	+.30 *
Rokeach's Dogmatism Scales	
Structure Scale	+.26 *
Content Scale	+.29 *
Function Scale	+.42 **
Total Scale	+.40 **

* Significant at the .05 level.
** Significant at the .01 level.

With the Dogmatism Scales, we found the highest correlation between the Function Scale and the OAS (+.42). The items here are of the type: "I would like it if I could find someone who would tell me how to solve my personal problems." This scale attempts to measure the underlying function of dogmatism in the individual's personality, especially in controlling the fear of aloneness and apprehension about the future. The relationship between the Dogmatism Scale and the OAS appears to reflect the diffuse anxiety of the yeasayer, and to suggest that he seeks dependency on external figures for support.

DEVELOPMENT OF THE AGREEMENT RESPONSE SCALE

As the next stage of our research we correlated the OAS to each of the 681 items in our questionnaire battery. The item-to-OAS correlations ranged from

—.21 to +.54; the mean correlation for all items was +.17. The high mean correlation demonstrates again the extent to which response set has influenced all item responses. This trend was also apparent from the fact that 88% of all items correlated positively with the OAS. Well over 100 items had correlations

TABLE 8. CORRELATIONS OF INDIVIDUAL
ITEMS WITH THE OAS SCORE

Correlation with OAS (N = 61)	Mean	SD	Items [a]
+.54	4.9	1.4	Novelty has a great appeal to me.
.54	4.5	1.7	I crave excitement.
.51	3.5	1.6	It's a wonderful feeling to sit surrounded by your possessions.
.48	3.3	1.6	There are few things more satisfying than really to splurge on something— books, clothes, furniture, etc.
.47	4.2	1.7	Only the desire to achieve great things will bring a man's mind into full activity.
.46	3.6	1.6	Nothing is worse than an offensive odor.
.45	3.6	1.3	In most conversations, I tend to bounce from topic to topic.
.44	2.9	1.6	I really envy the man who can

Correlation with OAS (N = 61)	Mean	SD	Item [a]
			walk up to anybody and tell him off to his face.
.44	4.1	1.8	I could really shock people if I said all of the dirty things I think.
.42	4.3	1.7	There are few more miserable experiences than going to bed night after night knowing you are so upset that worry will not let you sleep.
.42	3.8	1.6	I tend to make decisions on the spur of the moment.
.41	3.8	1.8	Little things upset me.
.41	3.0	1.3	Drop reminders of yourself wherever you go and your life's trail will be well remembered.
.40	2.1	1.3	I like nothing better than having breakfast in bed.
.40	4.2	1.6	My mood is easily influenced by the people around me.

[a] The 15 items listed here we now consider the best short scale measure of the agreeing response tendency.

with the OAS greater than +.30. Table 8 lists a sample of items with the highest positive relationship to the response tendency, along with the item means, standard deviations, and correlations with the OAS.

These items with the highest positive correlations serve to identify the agreement response tendency on the most specific level of separate statements. Since the average of these 15 item means (3.7) and of item standard deviations (1.6) is almost identical to the average mean for all 681 items (3.8) and their average standard deviation (1.5), no purely statistical factors are determining the correlational results. The items reflect to a great extent the same array of variables that we have already noted—impulsivity, anality, and instability. A more detailed analysis of these implications is presented in the final stages of the scale development.

A selection of 20 items with the highest correlations to the OAS constituted our first approximation to an Agreement Response Scale (ARS). The split-half reliability of this scale was very satisfactory (+.86). With all items being scored in a positive direction, the response set is, of course, working in our favor—as is uniquely desired in this case. This 20-item scale (ARS) correlates +.79 with the OAS, thus giving it considerable criterion validity.

However, it is obvious that all of the statistical uniqueness of our single sample is contributing to this pattern of results for the ARS. We felt it necessary to test the internal consistency of the tentative scale by administering it to an independent population. A 120-item questionnaire was developed which included this ARS scale, as well as an array of items that we hoped would bring out new facets of the agreeing tendency.

We also included a number of standard F scale items and several new ones written to measure "low" authoritarian attitudes.

The questionnaire was given to 54 students in an upper-level psychology course. For this new sample, the split-half reliability of the ARS remained quite high ($+.72$), indicating that our measure had the characteristics of internal consistency. As a next step in scale development, we did a factor analysis of the 120 items. These items were intercorrelated and the resulting matrix factor analyzed by the Thurstone complete centroid method. Four factors were extracted, which altogether accounted for 28% of the item domain variance. By Thomson's (1939) Pooling Square technique, we computed the factor loadings of the total 20-item Agreement Response Scale, and then made orthogonal rotations so as to define the ARS by the first factor.

With the assumption that the ARS remained a valid measure of agreeing response set, the first factor of this new analysis may be considered a dimensional representation of our central variable. In Table 9 we have listed those items with the highest positive and negative loadings on Factor I, which might best be labelled the "Agreement Response Scale" dimension.

A difference in emotional responsiveness seems to be the central concept of the agreement dimension. Items with high positive loadings on this Agreement Response Scale factor tend to emphasize an impulsive acceptance of immediate internal stimuli ("I'm apt to really blow up, but it doesn't last long") and the desire for external stimuli in the form of emotional sensations and thrill-seeking ("Novelty has a great appeal to me"). This pattern might be summarized by the

TABLE 9. FACTOR LOADINGS OF ITEMS ON AGREEMENT RESPONSE SCALE DIMENSION

Loading Factor I	Item
$+.66$	Let us eat, drink, and be merry, for tomorrow we die.
$+.63$	I tend to make decisions on the spur of the moment.
$+.61$	There are few things more satisfying than really to splurge on something—books, clothes, furniture, etc.
$+.57$	Here today, gone tomorrow—that's my motto!
$+.50$	Novelty has a great appeal to me.
$+.49$	My feelings about others fluctuate a good deal.
$+.48$	Conscience is another name for fear.
$+.46$	Movement, travel, change, excitement—that's the life for me!
$+.45$	I'm apt to really blow up, but it doesn't last long.
$+.42$	It's great fun just to mess around.
$+.41$	There's nothing so satisfying as really to tell someone off.
$+.40$	I really enjoy plenty of excitement.
$-.61$	One should not give free rein to the passions, but rather control and weigh them before expressing them.
$-.51$	I seldom if ever lose my temper.
$-.49$	Uncontrolled impulsiveness is not part of my makeup.
$-.37$	It's hard to get me upset.
$-.34$	My speech is quite slow and deliberate.
$-.33$	I feel uncomfortable when people get too emotional.
$-.33$	I almost never respond impulsively to people or events.
$+.86$	Agreement Response Scale

term "stimulus acceptance," indicating a tendency to enjoy and yield to immediate, situational, short-term forces of both an internal and external nature. The items with high negative loadings stress just the opposite, namely, rejection of these same emotional and environmental pressures. The central theme of the naysaying position is the effort to control and minimize internal and external forces seeking expression. Naysayers emphasize ego control of libidinal impulses ("One should not give free rein to the passions, but rather control and weigh them before expressing them") as well as delay and inhibition of responses to provocative press in the environment ("I am not easily provoked").

Importance of item tone. An examination of items with high loadings on the agreement factor suggested the importance of item tone in the distinction between yeasaying and naysaying characteristics. The positive items indicated that the yeasayers' impulsiveness was revealed most clearly in statements whose *item tone* was extreme and enthusiastic. Exclamatory phrases and colloquial slang seemed to have intrinsic appeal to the personality of the yeasayer: for example, "Here today, gone tomorrow—that's my motto!" and "It's great fun just to mess around!" On the opposite end of the agreeing response dimension, we noted that items with negative loadings were phrased in guarded, qualified, and cautious language. Items such as "I seldom if ever lose my temper," and "I almost never respond impulsively to people or events," point out the degree that "careful," "realistic," and intellectually qualified phrasing are inherent in the item tone of naysaying items. We feel that this aspect of item phraseology is highly related to the agreement response tendency on questionnaires. If the item has an en-

thusiastic, colloquial tone, it will serve to attract the yeasayer and to repel the naysayer. On the other hand, a qualified and hesitant statement will appear reasonable and bring forth agreement from the generally disagreeing naysayer, while provoking the generally effusive yeasayer to one of his infrequent disagreements. Although the psychological content of "expression" vs. "control" of emotional impulses certainly influences the language of the statements used for measurement, the characteristic phraseology of items high on this factor suggests that *item tone* itself contributes to eliciting special agreement from yeasayers and disagreement from naysayers.

The factor analysis serves to support the conclusions we had arrived at from the previous investigation of the empirical correlates of the Over-all Agreement Score in the realm of objective personality scales. The factor dimension of the Agreement Response Scale shows a conceptual similarity to the pattern of variables that were highly correlated to the OAS.

Factorial relationship of Agreement Response Scale to authoritarianism. A number of items in the area of authoritarianism were included in this factorial study in order to clarify further the relationship of agreeing response tendency to this variable. In addition to the regular "positive" F scale items, we added several new items designed to measure "low" authoritarianism in an agreement direction. The second factor was rotated through the F scale measures. This two-dimensional factor pattern of Agreement and Authoritarianism is presented in Fig. 1.

The factor plot of item loadings on Factors I and II shows that the dimension of the Agreement Response Scale was orthogonal to the dimension of authoritarianism. The Positive F scale items were scattered around the plus end of Factor II, while our new Negative F scale items defined the opposite pole. Several items were loaded on both main factors and these served to define the "fusion" locations of the factor space. The ARS items were split into two types by the authoritarianism dimension; those expressing a Desire for External Stimulation were associated with high au-

trated in Fig. 1 supports our earlier finding that "pure" authoritarianism is independent of the agreeing response set. The measure of the agreement tendency, the Agreement Response Scale, uniquely defines the first dimension that is orthogonal to the second dimension of "authoritarianism." Although some of the agreement items had a component of *desiring stimulation,* while others reflected *expressing unacceptable impulses,*

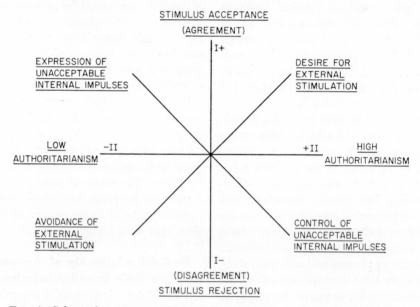

Fig. 1. Schematic representation of "agreement" and "authoritarianism" factors.

thorianism, while items favoring an Expression of Unacceptable Internal Impulses were associated with low authoritarianism. On the opposite end of Factor I, items measuring the Disagreement tendency were also divided into two different types. High authoritarianism was reflected in items favoring a Control of Unacceptable Internal Impulses; while low authoritarianism was reflected in items favoring an Avoidance of External Stimulation.

The factor pattern of loadings illus-

these items taken together balanced out the second factor and left the ARS a "pure" measure of response set. The very fact that the ARS contains these two complementary external and internal components supports our previous interpretation that Stimulus Acceptance vs. Stimulus Rejection represents the more abstract central concept involved in agreement response set.

Development of "Low" F scale. Our research on the agreement response tendency suggested a new approach for the construction of a "reversed" or "low" F scale. It is clear that if items on opposite ends of the authoritarian dimension all contain a substantial component of the response set variable, then these "opposing" scales will tend toward a positive relationship regardless of the reversal of authoritarian content which would tend to cause a negative relationship. Other researchers (Bass, 1955; Jackson & Messick, 1958) have tried this type of "content reversal" with only limited success in obtaining negatively related scales. Our research has pointed out the importance of "item tone" in the agreement response tendency. Since the phraseology of an item contributes to the amount of agreement or disagreement which it attracts, we hypothesized that by manipulating the item tone of low authoritarian items so as to attract naysayers and repel yeasayers, we could increase the negative relationship between the "high" and "low" authoritarian scales. Several "nonauthoritarian" statements were therefore phrased in a "naysaying manner" that emphasized qualification and a lack of exclamatory enthusiasm. The five items of this kind with the highest negative loadings in the previous factor analysis formed a new "Low F scale." These "naysaying" type items are listed below.

"Naysaying" Low F scale

1. People tend to place too much emphasis on respect for authority.

2. It may well be that children who talk back to their parents actually respect them more in the long run.

3. I seldom have any enthusiasm for respect and obedience for authority.

4. It would be preferable if there were less enthusiasm about strict discipline, rugged determination, and the will to work and fight for family and country.

5. I would not myself consider patriotism and loyalty to be the first requirements of a good citizen.

We combined this 5-item "naysaying" Low F scale with five items of the Positive F scale to form a new 10-item Balanced F scale. Thus, for this second population we had three different measures of authoritarianism: (a) the previously used (10-item) Positive F scale, (b) a new (10-item) Balanced F scale, and (c) a new (5-item) Low F scale. The correlational results indicated that we had been quite successful in constructing a "better" reversed F scale than has previously been reported. Our Naysaying Low F scale correlated highly negatively (−.70) with the Positive F scale. These "low" items also improved the Balanced F scale, as evident from its extremely high correlation (+.93) with the Positive F scale.

The correlations of these three F scales with the Agreement Response Scale are presented in Table 10.

None of the correlations of the F scales indicate any significant relationships to the ARS—further supporting our view that these dimensions are unrelated. We were puzzled that in this new sample the Positive F scale had no positive correlation to our new response tendency measure. Population differences may be involved, but other evidence, such as the slight positive relationships of "low" F scale items to the Agreement Response Scale, suggested that the new response scale was slightly "rotated" from the position expected from our original OAS criterion. But the ARS still seems quite adequate [2] as a

---

[2] Additional validation of the Agreement Response Scale is provided by the correlation of +.61 with the sum of all 120 items in the second questionnaire battery.

"short" substitute measure; the general pattern of results reflects all the previous findings with the OAS measure.

Considering the correlations between response measures and authoritarian scales in our two samples, and also considering the orthogonality of the variables in the factor analysis of items, the best conclusion is that "pure" authori-

TABLE 10. CORRELATON OF VARIOUS F SCALES WITH AGREEMENT RESPONSE SCALE

Scales	Correlation with ARS (N = 54)
Positive F Scale	+.00
Balanced F Scale (new)	−.04
Low F Scale (new)	+.16

tarianism has little or no relationship to the agreeing response tendency.

Preliminary Formulation of Personality Determinants from Questionnaire Results

From our investigation of the agreeing response tendency in the questionnaire realm, we have arrived at a fairly consistent picture of the variables that differentiate yeasayers from naysayers. Yeasayers seem to be "id-dominated" personalities, with little concern about or positive evaluation of an integrated control of their impulses. They say they express themselves freely and quickly. Their "psychological inertia" is very low, that is, very few secondary processes intervene as a screen between underlying wish and overt behavioral response. The yeasayers desire and actively search for emotional excitement in their environment. Novelty, movement, change, adventure—these provide the

external stimuli for their emotionalism. They see the world as a stage where the main theme is an "acting out" of libidinal desires. In the same way, they seek and respond quickly to internal stimuli: their inner impulses are allowed ready expression. They have little tolerance for a delay of gratification: immediate reduction is sought for any tension that may have arisen. Thus, to both external and internal stimuli, the yeasayers' general attitude is one of *stimulus acceptance*, by which we mean a pervasive readiness to respond affirmatively or yield willingly to both inner and outer forces demanding expression.

The "disagreeing" naysayers have the opposite orientation. For them, impulses are seen as forces requiring control and perhaps, in some sense, as threats to general personal stability. The naysayer wants to maintain inner equilibrium; his secondary processes are extremely strong in this ego maintenance of the balance between emotionally impulsive and value-maintaining forces. We might describe this as a state of high psychological inertia—impulses undergo a series of delays, censorships, and transformations before they are permitted expression. Both internal and external stimuli that demand response are carefully scrutinized and evaluated: these forces appear as unwelcome intruders into a subjective world of "classical" balance. Thus, as opposed to the yeasayers, the naysayers' general attitude is one of *stimulus rejection*—a pervasive unwillingness to respond to impulsive or environmental forces.

This formulation of the dynamics of the response tendency was developed from an analysis of the empirical correlates of the Over-all Agreement Score. As such, the formulation suffers from all the limitations of psychological interpretation based on objective paper-and-pencil tests. Since the response tendency itself influences the objective test measurements by which we initially identified its nature, there were in this case additional reasons for further investigation. We felt that our study of the personality dynamics and determinants of agreeing response set would benefit from a clinical analysis of extreme yeasayers and naysayers. Therefore, a clinical study was designed to validate these theoretical formulations about the personality syndrome determining this general response set.

Part II: Clinical Study of Yeasayers and Naysayers

The research in Part I led us to the formulation that a personality syndrome may help to explain the psychological dynamics of agreeing response tendency. It seemed evident that for many persons the tendency to agree or disagree was actually a significant and functional part of their personality structure. The pattern of variables correlated with our two measures of the agreement tendency (OAS and ARS) suggested a set of hypotheses concerning the deeper dynamics and determinants of this pervasive response set. A clinical assessment of Ss on the extreme ends of the dimension would allow us to test the main theoretical tenets of this "personality syndrome" view of the agreement response tendency.

HYPOTHESES ABOUT PERSONALITY DIFFERENCES

Specific predictions were made about differences between yeasayers and naysayers in seven major areas: (A) External vs. Internal Orientation; (B) Id-ego-superego Integration; (C) Impulse Control; (D) Hostility and Distrust; (E) Intellectual Orientation; (F) Secondary Process; and (G) Conflict Manifestations. These hypotheses were tested by a research design employing a sentence completion test and clinical interviews to be described below.

(A) *External vs. Internal Orientation.* The yeasayer is externally oriented with strong tendencies towards extraception and extraversion; the naysayer is internally oriented, intraceptive, and introverted.

A–1 Yeasayers have superficial, conventional identifications; naysayers' identifications are deeper, less conventional, and defined more by internal values.

A–2 Yeasayers are anti- or nonintraceptive; naysayers are intraceptive and psychologically minded.

A–3 Yeasayers are oriented outward, towards the group values; naysayers are oriented inward, towards their own values.

A–4 The self-concept of yeasayers is behaviorally defined and evaluated by conventional standards; that of the naysayers is subjectively defined and evaluated by personal standards.

A–5 Yeasayers have little concern with values and ideals, which if held at all are conventionally realistic and superficial; naysayers are continuously influenced by values which are felt as an integral part of themselves.

(B) *Id-ego-superego Integration.* The personality structure of yeasayers has a high degree of compartmentalization of id-ego-superego; naysayers have a more integrated personality with much stronger ego control.

B–1 The behavior of yeasayers is determined more by external factors in the immediate situation; naysayers are determined more by internal control and response to inner subjective reflections.

B–2 Yeasayers tend to externalize the

source of their problems; naysayers tend to feel that they themselves are to blame for their problems.

B–3 Ego strength is low in yeasayers; high in naysayers.

B–4 Yeasayers tend to have weak, externalized superegos; naysayers are more guilt prone, having strong, internalized superegos.

B–5 Yeasayers show a low perseveration of mood and emotional cathexes; naysayers have a high perseveration of their feelings and attachments.

(C) *Impulse Control.* Yeasayers are able to express their emotions and impulses freely and openly without inhibition; naysayers tend to suppress, repress, and control their impulses by strong ego domination.

C–1 Yeasayers express aggression and hostility immediately and openly; naysayers express hostility mostly in a covert way, while open aggression is extremely controlled.

C–2 Yeasayers express affection, sex, tenderness more directly and easily than naysayers who are more constricted, inhibited, and repressed in the expression of libidinal impulses.

C–3 Yeasayers have anal expulsive characteristics and respond to "anally colored" situations with typical expressive reactions; naysayers have anal retentive characteristics and show typical controlled reactions.

C–4 Yeasayers were socialized by punitive, physical methods; naysayers were socialized by deprivation of love and rational persuasion.

C–5 Yeasayers tend to have emotionally intense, "Dionysian" expressive behavior; naysayers stress an avoidance of strong feelings and favor a balanced, "Apollonian" form of expression.

(D) *Competition and Distrust.* The yeasayer tends to admit a distrust of others' altruism and to accept competition as a "realistic" part of life; naysayers have a

"reactive" trust of others and try to minimize competition and conflict.

(E) *Intellectual Outlook.* The intellectual orientation of the yeasayers tends to be loose and emotional; naysayers are more consistently intellectual and have a high regard for rationality.

(F) *Secondary Process.* The yeasayer tends to have a minimum degree of secondary processes intervening between inner "stimulus" and manifest "response"; the naysayer has long secondary processes causing considerable delay in emotional responsiveness.

(G) *Conflict Manifestations.* Yeasayers show more evidence of conflict, ambivalence, and disparity between values and behavior than naysayers.

METHOD IN CLINICAL STUDY

Subjects. From our original population of 61 *S*s, the 10 with the highest scores on the Over-all Agreement Score (yeasayers) and the 11 with the lowest scores (naysayers) were selected for the clinical study. The mean OAS score of the extreme yeasayers was 4.3 (range 4.2 to 4.5); the naysayers' mean was 3.6 (range 3.1 to 3.7).

Procedure. The yeasayers and naysayers were divided into two groups which were interviewed by one or another of the two *E*s. The OAS score of every *S* was carefully concealed from the *E*s. The interviews were oriented around a 55-item sentence completion test [3] which had been designed to test the major hypotheses outlined above. Several sentence "stems" in each hypothesis

---

[3] The Sentence Completion Test used in this study has been deposited with the American Documentation Institute. Order Document No. 6134 from ADI Auxiliary Publications Project, Photoduplication Service, Library of Congress, Washington, D.C., remitting in advance $1.25 for microfilm or $1.25 for photocopies. Make checks payable to Chief, Photoduplication Service, Library of Congress.

area were constructed to elicit responses that would differentiate yeasayers and naysayers along the lines of our theoretical formulations.

At the beginning of each individual interview, each *S* took the sentence completion test. The *E* then discussed the meaning of the *S*'s responses with him and tried to obtain information concerning the major areas of the authors' hypotheses. These interviews lasted from 2 to 4 hr. The *S*s were free to amplify, illustrate, or qualify their responses, and were frequently encouraged to digress when interesting themes appeared. The *E*s took extensive notes on the amplification of each response and also wrote short clinical evaluations of the *S*s in the different personality areas under study.

After all interviews were completed, both *E*s made independent ratings of sentence completion responses. Each *E* made 4 ratings of each of the 55 responses of the 21 *S*s on the basis of the following criteria:

(1) Verbal content of response: Using *only* the written response, each item was rated on a 5-point scale (+2, +1, 0, −1, −2) which indicated the degree that the response corresponded to a "theoretical" yeasaying (+) or naysaying (−) orientation.

(2) Degree of secondary process: On the basis of the written response alone, *E*s used the 5-point scale to rate the degree that each response was impulsive and immediate (+) showing a direct and uncensored reaction to the item; as contrasted with reflective responses (−) showing hesitation, qualification, rationalization, or other evidences of secondary processes.

(3) Degree of conflict: Using both written responses and additional elaboration from the focused interview, each item was rated on a scale from 0 to +2 for the degree of conflict, ambivalence, and disparity between values and behavior.

(4) Clinical assessment: Taking into account the elaboration and clinical material concerning each item, a clinical rating was made using the 5-point scale that assessed the degree of correspondence to a "typical" yeasaying or naysaying response.

A number of precautions were taken to reduce the possibility of interviewer bias in these ratings. After discussing the theoretical basis of the rating scheme, the *E*s did not discuss their ratings with each other. All identification was removed from the data. *E*s' ratings for each item were made separately; that is, all responses to an item were rated for all 21 *S*s before proceeding to another item. Thus, the *E*s did not know whom they were rating or what ratings the *S*'s other responses had been given.

As a first step in the analysis of the data, the Spearman-Brown reliability of the ratings was studied. Table 11 presents the reliability coefficients for the sum of *E*s' clinical ratings for the variables in each of the major hypothesis areas.

For the sums of subareas and for individual items, reliability coefficients were somewhat lower; the average for subareas was +.69, for individual items +.61. On the whole interrater reliability seemed very satisfactory; therefore, ratings of the two *E*s were pooled to provide the basic data for the authors' subsequent analysis.

RESULTS OF THE CLINICAL ANALYSIS

The main analysis of the data was a series of *t* tests on the difference of means between the groups of extreme yeasayers and naysayers. The tests were performed for each of the major hypothesis areas, and for the subareas that were stated in the previous section. In Table 12, the results of the *t* tests are given. Each hypothesis area is stated in a yeasaying form, so that a positive t value indicates that extreme yeasayers have a higher mean than extreme naysayers. After each hypothesis, we have indicated in parentheses the number of sentence completion items included by design in testing that particular hypothesis. The results for ratings using only the verbal content of the sentence completions, and for ratings that include clinical assessment are tabulated separately.

TABLE 11. RELIABILITY COEFFICIENTS FOR INTERVIEW RATINGS

Major Hypothesis Area	Verbal Content Ratings ($N = 21$)	Clinical Assessment Ratings ($N = 21$)
A—External-Internal Orientation	.57	.68
B—Id-ego-superego Integration	.80	.86
C—Impulse Control	.95	.89
D—Competition and Distrust	.47	.60
E—Intellectual Outlook	.56	.83
F—Secondary Process (sum for all items)	.76	—
G—Conflict Manifestations (sum for all items)	—	.65

In the five major areas of personality —(A) External-Internal Orientation, (B) Id-ego-superego Integration, (C) Impulse Control, (D) Competition and Distrust, and (E) Intellectual Outlook —for which we had formulated systematic hypotheses, all results for the clinical assessment ratings were signifi-

cant at the .01 level or greater. The analysis of the verbal content ratings shows the same pattern at somewhat lower levels of significance. For the sub-area hypotheses, 9 out of 15 tests on the clinical ratings were significant at the .05 level or greater, with particularly high t values for Anal Expulsive Expression. These results indicate that ratings that take into account the additional material from the interview (Clinical ratings) differentiate the extreme groups better than the ratings based only on the written answers to the sentence completion items (Verbal Content ratings).

The hypothesis that yeasayers would show less evidence of Secondary Processes than naysayers was supported at only the .10 level of significance ($t = +1.62$). However, additional evidence from the data supports the hypothesis: of the 55 items involved in these ratings, 45 are in the predicted direction, giving a highly significant chi square of 21.9.

Despite the positive nature of most results, some hypotheses were not confirmed. The supposition that Conflict Manifestations would be greater for yeasayers was not at all supported ($t = -0.65$). The expected Conventional Identification of yeasayers was not indicated by either the Verbal Content ratings ($t = +0.40$) nor by the Clinical ratings ($t = +0.94$). In the same way, the hypothesized Externalization of Problems, Weak Superego, and Punitive Physical Socialization, as characteristics of yeasayers, were not significantly supported by the data.

DISCUSSION OF CLINICAL FINDINGS

The clinical study clearly supports the main lines of the hypothesized personality syndrome behind the agreeing response tendency. The analysis of interview ratings showed that yeasayers and naysayers were significantly differentiated in the areas of External-Internal Orientation, Id-ego-superego Integra-

manifestations supports our contention that response set is based on an underlying dynamic syndrome. The nature of the syndrome makes it possible to ex-

TABLE 12. THE *t* TESTS OF DIFFERENCES BETWEEN EXTREME YEASAYERS AND NAYSAYERS

Hypothesis Area	Verbal Content Ratings	Clinical Ratings
A—External Orientation (10)	+1.89 *	+3.89 **
A–1 Conventional Identification (2)	+0.40	+0.94
A–2 Anti-introception (2)	+1.86 *	+2.33 *
A–3 Outward Group Orientation (2)	+1.67	+4.21 **
A–4 Conventional Self-concept (2)	−0.10	+1.96 *
A–5 Superficial Values and Ideals (2)	+3.19 **	+2.94 **
B—Lack of Id-ego-superego Integration (10)	+1.48	+2.52 **
B–1 Situational Determinism of Behavior (2)	+1.10	+2.27 *
B–2 Externalization of Problems (2)	−0.14	+1.28
B–3 Low Ego Strength (2)	+1.77 *	+1.55
B–4 Weak Superego (2)	−0.19	+0.61
B–5 Rapid Changes in Emotions (2)	+1.31	+1.70
C—Impulse Expression (25)	+2.35 *	+3.03 **
C–1 Overt Expression of Hostility (5)	+2.36 *	+3.27 **
C–2 Overt Expression of Affection (5)	+1.74 *	+2.27 *
C–3 Anal Expulsive Expression (5)	+2.69 **	+3.28 **
C–4 Punitive Physical Socialization (5)	+0.57	+1.09
C–5 Intense "Dionysian" Expressiveness (5)	+1.02	+2.47 **
D—Acceptance of Competition and Distrust (5)	+3.01 **	+3.30 **
E—Lack of Intellectual Outlook (5)	+1.74 *	+3.22 **
F—Low Secondary Processes (55) (verbal content alone)	+1.62	—
G—Conflict Manifestations (55) (clinical rating alone)	—	−0.65

* Pooled *t* tests were used for testing the significance of the differences in means between ratings for (10) yeasayers and (11) naysayers. For 19 *df* the .05 level of significance for a one-tailed test is 1.73.

** The .01 level of significance is 2.43.

tion, Impulse Control, Competition and Distrust, Intellectual Outlook, and Secondary Processes. These personality differences appear in many diverse areas of functioning. The generality of the

plain a marked response set to the "stimuli" of questionnaire items as a functional consequence of inner forces in the responding individual. Questionnaire items are another kind of stimuli demanding response. As such they bring forth typical reactions of immediate acceptance from yeasayers and of inhibited resistance from naysayers.

External orientation. Many facets of the difference in External Orientation between yeasayers and naysayers were made evident by observation of their general manner and behavior during the interview situation. It was apparent from our clinical reports that yeasayers were much more extraverted in their social orientations. They were usually more voluble, spoke more easily about themselves (though often with little depth), took suggestions readily, reacted in more obvious and overt ways to their moods, appeared less complex psychologically, tended to wander from the subject at hand, and made themselves thoroughly at ease with the interviewer. Naysayers, on the other hand, were characteristically more introverted. They were often shy and always reserved about themselves. Throughout the interview, they required more questioning and prodding; they felt easily criticized, weighed and considered each answer, and tended to express themselves in indirect and complicated ways—perhaps a consequence of the fact that for many of them introspection and self-analysis seemed virtually a full time occupation. By their introverted behavior and general lack of social spontaneity, the naysayers tended to create a task oriented atmosphere and usually initiated and maintained an intellectual relationship with the interviewers.

Impulse control. Our hypotheses concerning Impulse Control, which had been fully supported by the empirical analysis of Clinical ratings, were verified more indirectly by our observations during the interview. In discussing impulsivity and the expression of feeling, yeasayers and naysayers were especially different. Yea-

sayers talked with enthusiasm about their impulsivity and their love of emotionally exciting and novel situations. Sexuality and aggressive feelings were discussed quite openly, often with exhibitionistic exaggeration. Yeasayers sometimes expressed the fear that they were excessively uncontrolled and attributed their interpersonal difficulties to impulsiveness, hastiness, or unthinking rashness. Naysayers, on the other hand, were often defensive and embarrassed about emotional impulsivity and their manner of expressing inner feelings. They were frequently worried about their shyness and lack of social poise. They seemed concerned about their excessive emotional constraint and lack of spontaneity. Yet beneath this surface of emotional constriction, there appeared to be a depth of strong feelings which could only come out in close personal relationships.

Intellectual Orientation. A striking difference in the Intellectual Orientation of naysayers and yeasayers was apparent throughout the interview. Naysayers had a pervasively rational and intellectual approach to whatever topic was discussed, while yeasayers were typically less conceptual, viewing the world in terms of emotional reactions and concrete instances. In exploring this area, we asked the subjects about their attitude towards questionnaires. Yeasayers and naysayers described how they approached the task of answering Likert scale items in consistently different ways. The yeasayer responded to the "surface" of the items' meaning, did not reflect on their possible full implications, and thus gave impulsive, immediate answers. This pattern is consistent with the yeasayer's preference for blunt, straightforward, and extreme opinions, which reflect his emotional feelings at the moment. In quite an opposite manner, the naysayer analyzes and dissects each item, considering it from several points of view and attempting to be "logical" in his responses to the highly "interpreted" statements of the questionnaires. As was noted in our discussion of item tone, there seems to be an affinity of the yeasayer and naysayer for items phrased in his characteristic style of thought. Yeasayers are themselves enthusiastic, colloquial, and given to extreme opinions. Naysayers are guarded, qualified, and somewhat negative in their intellectual orientation. When the phraseology of a questionnaire item approaches one of these patterns, it presents a differential attraction to these two types of individuals. These differences in verbal style and intellectual approach contribute to the opposing patterns of the extraverted, fun loving, emotional yeasayer and the introverted, serious-minded, and rational naysayer.

Personality Integration and Conflict. In the area of Id-ego-superego Integration our hypotheses were supported on an over-all basis, but some of the sub-hypotheses were below normal significance levels, in particular, Externalization of Problems and Weak Superego. A similar error had been made in our hypothesis about personality conflict. The ratings of Conflict Manifestations had failed to show the evidence of ambivalence, denial, and dissociation that we had expected to differentiate yeasayers and naysayers. In attempting to explain these negative findings, we noted that all of these hypotheses had been derived from the questionnaire results that portrayed yeasayers as anxious, psychasthenic, schizoid, unstable, and generally maladjusted. Our clinical study indicates that the implications of these scale correlations must be re-evaluated. From the interview, it was apparent that yeasayers were more *able and willing to*

admit their "unacceptable" impulsive feelings; whereas naysayers were unusually susceptible to denial mechanisms and a general inhibition or repression of libidinal and aggressive desires. In discussing competitive situations and aggression, the naysayers were often unaware of hostilities which seemed obvious to the interviewers. Their "reactive" trust had, at times, the characteristics of repressed hostility and resentment. On the other hand, the yeasayers were in much closer contact with their unacceptable impulses and had fewer inhibitions about revealing them than the naysayers.

It is thus probable that the yeasayers' higher scores on "maladjustment" scales, which had suggested our hypothesis of dissociation and conflict, are chiefly attributable to their greater frankness and willingness to admit impulsive feelings and ambivalences. Clinical results also suggest that the naysayers may be presenting a "mature" picture colored by strong denial mechanisms. Two of our naysaying Ss later in the year developed rather severe neurotic disturbances requiring therapeutic treatment; the questionnaire results gave woefully inadequate indications of these trends. We would now reformulate our hypotheses about these aspects of dissociative tendencies to predict the type, but not the degree of conflict or maladjustment. The agreeing and disagreeing dimension seems indicative only of the central area where psychogenic deviation may occur: yeasayers' problems center around inadequate controls, while naysayers' are focused on excessive inhibition. To the extent that yeasayers lack personality integration, they deviate in the direction of "id domination" associated with an externalized superego and ineffectual controls. On the other hand, the naysayer who becomes maladjusted should tend towards "superego domination," frequently maintained by emotional dissociation and repressive controls.

Conventionality. In the area of superego strength and conventional values, another set of hypotheses was not fully supported. Besides the Weak Superego hypothesis already mentioned, two others, Conventional Identification and Punitive Physical Socialization, indicated an error in prediction, based in part on the premise of dissociation discussed above, but also on the assumption of greater "conventionality" for the yeasayer. This latter assumption seems to be in error. Contrary to prediction, many naysayers had conventional religious ideologies that were strongly internalized; naysayers were also more conventional in many areas of social behavior and attitude than the more "liberated" and exhibitionistic yeasayers. Interview material also indicated that the type of identification with the socializer was more relevant to the response set dimension than the particular method of socialization. The parents remain external figures to the yeasayer; whereas the naysayer identifies more completely with them. Yeasayers seemed freer to express their impulses with little concern for interpersonal consequences. Yet these same yeasayers had "strong" but rigid superegos which had little influence on their everyday behavior, except in the sense that this "control" had to be opposed and subverted. They experienced guilt as something external to their central selves. Naysayers, on the other hand, had superegos firmly integrated into their ego ideals. In our original formulations, we had erred in stressing superego strength, instead of the degree of value internalization. It is the degree of internalization and not the degree of conventionality that determines the differentiating influence of values on the behavior of yeasayers and naysayers.

Awareness of response set. Toward the end of each interview, the topic of response set was brought up explicitly. The Ss were reminded of the questionnaires they had taken earlier in the year, and were asked whether they had, in general, agreed or disagreed more with the items. More than three-fourths of the Ss characterized their response set accurately; one was inaccurate and the rest had no recollection. Most Ss reported some awareness of response bias as they filled out questionnaires. Several commented that they had consciously compensated for their tendency to mark predominantly in one direction or the other, but as is evident from the basis of their selection as extreme yeasayers and naysayers, in all cases the original response set had prevailed.

General Interpretation and Conclusion

STATISTICAL IMPLICATIONS OF RESPONSE SET

Our research originated with a realization that agreeing response set was of far-reaching importance in the realm of objective questionnaire tests. The usual assumption of psychological test construction is that agreement or disagreement with a scale of items measures primarily the variable for which the test was designed. But many of the statistical techniques used in scale development result in a contamination of the final scale with an unwanted component of response set. No matter how a scale is developed, it is virtually impossible to eliminate the effect of agreement bias in an S's answer pattern. As a consequence questionnaire items seem almost "possessed" by a tendency to correlate positively with one another regardless of content. The *S* is, in part, responding to the "meaning" of the item, but also, in part, to the answer scale associated with the item. Although this answer scale is a necessary part of the measurement technique,[4] it also evokes the agreement response tendency that subsequently becomes inextricably interwoven into the item score. It is quite possible that many factor analyses of item domains have revealed a first centroid factor which might best be explained as a manifestation of response set.

This same phenomenon is evident with multi-item Positive scales which tend to have suspiciously high positive intercorrelations with one another. The diagnosis is again "response set," operating all the more powerfully when several items are summed in the same scoring direction to measure an intended variable. These scale scores also measure in varying and unknown degrees a component of the agreement response tendency. It is this "common factor" of response bias which often causes the "operational" measurements of variables to correlate positively, regardless of the degree of psychological "opposition" of the measured concepts. The sum of any group of Likert scale items scored positively will always be a somewhat valid, though perhaps unintended, scale for response set. These Positive scales will show the effects of this additional component, partly by being prone to positive interrelationships with other Positive

scales, and partly by reflecting in their pattern of highest correlations some of the psychological aspects of the agreement personality dimension. Since all intercorrelations with scales of this type are pushed in a positive direction, correlational results must be interpreted with this response variable in mind. It also follows that significant negative correlations will appear only when there are extremely strong factors operating against the positive influence of response set. An indication of this bias was apparent in the questionnaire battery where nearly 90% of all items correlated positively with our measure of agreement tendency.

Balanced scales. In our attempt to study the response tendency in the questionnaire realm, we remained acutely aware of these difficulties. In trying to identify the properties of the response variable, we had occasion to make use of "balanced" scales, containing an equal number of items scored positively and negatively. This type of scale is a useful method of cancelling out at its source the contaminating influence of agreement response set on sum scores, and thus provides at least a statistical solution to some of the difficulties raised by this biasing tendency.

RESPONSE SET AS A PERSONALITY VARIABLE

Our primary interest in this study has been in the fundamental psychological determinants of agreeing response set within the responders themselves. Basing our approach on the conviction that response set is a reflection of personality dynamics, we set out to explore its correlates in the realm of objective personality tests. An analysis of these relationships suggested that the best single characterization of the traits associated with

---

[4] Some measurement techniques such as Thurstone's Paired-Comparison Method, Guttman Scale checking, forced choice alternative responses may avoid some of the intrinsic effects of the agreement tendency. But even here the response bias may appear in subtle ways, such as a tendency to check every item or the most extreme item.

agreeing response set is *Stimulus Accept-ance* vs. *Stimulus Rejection*. The yea-sayer accepts stimuli both by admitting them to consciousness without censor-ship, alteration, or assimilation and by agreeing with, acting out, and otherwise yielding to the pressures of stimuli ex-erted on him. The naysayer tends to re-ject these same stimuli, which may be either internal (impulses, needs, whims, sudden moods) or external (suggestions, provocations, coercions, excitement, novelty). The most obvious manifesta-tion of the general acceptance of stimuli takes the form of "agreeing" with, mark-ing Yes, or checking True to a wide variety of otherwise unrelated items and statements.

Our interview study brought to light many facets of inner dynamics which permit us to go beyond a simple trait explanation of the agreeing and disagree-ing response tendencies. In terms of per-sonality structure, the most salient differ-ence between yeasayers and naysayers is in their mode of *ego functioning*. Our results suggest that yeasayers have rela-tively "passive" (releasing) egos, as con-trasted with the more "active" (con-trolling) egos of the naysayers. This difference appeared most clearly in the contrasting strength of secondary proc-esses in their personality structure. For naysayers, the secondary processes of de-laying, censoring, rationalizing, subli-mating, and integrating were far more prominent than in the less active egos of yeasayers who portrayed themselves as unreflective, quick to act, easily in-fluenced, and unable to tolerate delays in gratification.

These differences in ego functioning might best be characterized in terms of the *psychological inertia* of secondary processes. High inertia characterizes the active egos of naysayers who have a high

resistance to movement and change, a slowness in their responses, a strong tendency toward equilibrium in their inner world, and an ego domination that frequently appears in excessive control and inhibition. On the other hand, yea-sayers are low in psychological inertia, reacting quickly and overtly to emo-tional pressures without the "dampen-ing" effect of inhibiting and delaying mechanisms.

THEORY OF DEVELOPMENTAL DYNAMICS OF RESPONSE SET

To achieve a deeper understanding of this pattern of personality factors, it seems necessary to formulate the devel-opmental dynamics of agreeing response set. The data in both parts of the study suggest that the contrasting personality patterns of yeasayers and naysayers have their developmental origins in the differ-ential reactions to what are often called anal socialization problems. Such an in-terpretation, while not directly tested by this analysis, nonetheless helps to inte-grate the results of our study.

Psychoanalytic theory (Freud, 1908, 1916) emphasizes that the resolution of early problems centering around the con-trol of elimination underlies later pat-terns of impulse control. The child's par-ents exert pressure on him to control his own evacuation (and other antisocial, value-violating impulses) with the hope that he will internalize their commands and enable them to relax their vigilance. One type of reaction to such parental pressure is *not to internalize* the parental edicts, but to retain the need for external control and guidance, especially in the area of impulse control. This "solution" involves the child in a continual conflict between his desires and those of the re-straining authorities, but at the same time allows him (both as child and adult) the pleasure of expressing impulses which are supposed to be suppressed. The pleasure is often a double one; partly a narcissistic gratification and partly the attention-getting satisfaction of annoying external authorities. This reaction could be called the *anal expressive* or expulsive resolution of early socialization pressures, and is associated with ineffectual control of impulses. The second type of resolution involves *a complete internalization* of parental control functions, perhaps related to an unusually strong identification with the parents. In addition to the supergo development stemming from this internalization, the ego of the child gains autonomy and power. In a sense, he becomes his own parent by transferring to his own personality the previously external power of the parents to control and reward, thereby gaining self-control and active mastery of his instinctual demands (Erikson, 1950, pp. 76–81). He thus gains his freedom from external restraint, but at the price of severe internal control. When acting like the controlling parent, the child is rewarded from within for suppressing his own "childish" impulses. With these developments comes the desire and ability to delay gratification, the main component of active ego functioning. Since the parent-like ego of the child now has the ability to "retain" or suppress impulse expression, this resolution of control problems may be termed anal retentive or *anal suppressive*.

Our results suggest that yeasaying and naysaying are closely related to these two opposite reactions to parental pressure for control of antisocial behavior. Yeasayers show many manifestations of the anal "expressive" type of resolution that involves the lack of internalization of impulse control. Their original uncon-

trolled expressiveness is only slightly transmuted into a conscious preoccupation with "anally tinged" gratifications and expressive exhibitionism. Not having strong inner controls, they express their impulsive desires with little or no guilt. Evidences of these anal concerns among yeasayers are especially prominent in our questionnaire studies. The Anal Preoccupation factorial scale, which correlated $+.75$ with the OAS, contains items expressed in implicitly anal metaphors, such as: "really splurging on something," "sitting surrounded by your possessions," "sitting in the seats of the mighty," "smelling offensive odors," "saying dirty things," "spending money freely," and "exploring dirty slums and alleys." The Anal Submission factorial scale, which correlated $+.67$ with the OAS, contains a set of items expressing a general need for external control: "The college student needs advice and guidance from someone wiser than himself," "I often wish that someone could make my decisions for me," etc. In these items, we see the anal pattern in all of its manifestations; on the one hand, the craving for excitement and the continual search for and indulgence in the pleasures of impulse expression that remains unrestrained by the ego, and on the other hand, the need for external control and guidance, closely coupled with resentment of this same control.

The naysayers' retentive or suppressive resolution of anal problems shows many manifestations of their internalization of parental demands for control and of their subsequent aversion for "anally expressive" impulses. On questionnaire items of the "anal" variety discussed above, the naysayer consistently disagrees. He is emphatically *not* interested in "splurging," "messing around," or "blowing up"—he has learned his early lessons well, and these impulses have ceased consciously to trouble him. His identification (sometimes overidentification) with the antianal concerns of his parents is also shown by his rigidly maintained "suppressive" control of emotional responsiveness.

The focused clinical study considerably expanded this formulation of the role of anality in the personality dynamics of naysayers. Their identification with the socializing pressures of their parents appears not only in their dislike of anal concerns but also in their avoidance of "childish" expressions of impulses. Having taken upon themselves the full burden of what was once external control, they no longer feel any need for external advice, guidance, or counsel. The necessity of friction and aggressiveness in competitive situations is strongly denied, and replaced consciously by reactive trust and tolerance for others. In interviews, naysayers are extremely reluctant to admit to any hostility toward their close friends, and overt aggressiveness is avoided at all costs. They avoid all other situations that provoke emotional expressiveness or an abandonment of ego controls. Much energy is expended in the effort to maintain a calm equilibrium. Lacking the youthful exuberance or carefree spontaneity of the yeasayer, the naysayer stresses sublimated satisfactions, stability, and self-control, damping down potentially disruptive emotions and avoiding situations which might disturb his balance. With little visible affect and great surface calm, he turns his attention toward introspection and his complex inner life. But, in extreme form, this overcontrolled personality pattern suggests that something may be amiss beneath the defiantly calm surface. Avenues toward libidinal gratification are blocked and the transmutation of aggression into reactive trust and tolerance may, in some cases, cause extensive parataxis and constriction of interpersonal relationships.

In conclusion, we have tried to integrate the findings of our study of response set by presenting a theory of the developmental dynamics of "yeasaying" and "naysaying." This theory is speculative, but the consistent evidence from both the questionnaire data and clinical results supports our contention that agreement response tendency is ultimately related to a meaningful personality syndrome which is consistent with psychoanalytic accounts of the resolution of problems of impulse control.

Summary

This study began with a realization of the importance of the agreeing response set in the field of personality measurements. It was evident that an agreeing-disagreeing tendency was permeating the answer patterns of our subjects to a series of questionnaire items. Our first step was to develop an appropriate measure of this response set which would be essentially independent of any specific content. By increasing the number and heterogeneity of items, and by "cancelling out" positive and negative statements of each variable, we obtained a 360-item Over-all Agreement Score (OAS) that met this criterion.

This measure of response bias showed considerable internal reliability, consistency over time, and generality over tests. The agreeing tendency was highly related to "true-saying" and "yes-saying" on other standard tests. We then investigated the correlates of the OAS to the variables of several objective test domains. A cluster of scales characterized the positive end of the agreeing tendency: Impulsivity, Dependency, Anxiety,

Mania, Anal Preoccupation, and Anal Resentment. The opposite end, the "disagreeing tendency," was defined by such scales as: Ego strength, Stability, Responsibility, Tolerance, and Impulse Control. When a factor analysis of individual items was performed, a major dimension of Stimulus Acceptance vs. Stimulus Rejection emerged as central to the agreeing-disagreeing response set. Personality test results also indicated pervasive differences in ego functioning, particularly as regards the high vs. low psychological inertia of secondary processes.

In the course of our study with objective questionnaires, we explored the technique of constructing Balanced scales and noted their effectiveness in eliminating the influence of the agreement response set on scale scores. By using an equal number of positively and negatively scored items, the agreeing response set can be balanced out at its source. In this manner, we could demonstrate the lack of any strong relationship of authoritarianism to agreement response set. The independence of response set and authoritarianism was supported by a factor analytic study where these variables emerged as orthogonal dimensions. In our further research with questionnaire items, we noted that "item tone" was a significant influence in attracting or repelling agreement. By using this knowledge, we constructed a "Naysaying" Low F scale that showed the expected characteristics of a nonauthoritarian measure.

Having discovered a fairly definite psychological pattern of objective scales that were empirically related to the Overall Agreement Score, we proceeded to a clinical analysis of extreme Ss at opposite ends of this agreeing response tendency. A series of hypotheses were formulated about the personality differences between "yeasayers" and "naysayers." Using a clinical interview structured around a sentence completion test, we confirmed the main aspects of our personality formulation of the agreement response tendency. Yeasayers were shown to be individuals with weak ego controls, who accept impulses without reservation, and who "agree" and easily respond to stimuli exerted on them. The naysayer inhibits and suppresses his impulses, in many ways rejecting all emotional stimuli impinging on him.

The clinical study suggested a possible developmental explanation of the deeper determinants of the yeasayer's and naysayer's personality structure. During their early socialization period, they tend towards opposite resolutions of the "anal" problems around control of impulses. The passive and receptive egos of yeasayers seem to be an outgrowth of their lack of internalization of parental control. While maintaining the need for external control, yeasayers can freely indulge in impulse gratification. On the other extreme, the active, guiding egos of the naysayers apparently result from an internalization of the controlling functions of the parental figures they had strongly identified with during childhood. The egos of naysayers take over the controlling functions of the parents, and the suppression of impulses is subsequently self-maintained and self-rewarded.

In conclusion, we feel that this integrated study, though limited by the size and nature of our population, has demonstrated both the far-reaching importance of response set in the area of psychological tests and the major proposition that the agreeing response tendency is based on a central personality syndrome.

References

ADORNO, T. W., FRENKEL-BRUNSWIK, ELSE, LEVINSON, D. J., & SANFORD, R. N. *The authoritarian personality.* New York: Harper, 1950.

BARNES, E. H. Response bias in the MMPI. *J. consult. Psychol.,* 1956, **20,** 371–374.

BASS, B. M. Authoritarianism or acquiescence? *J. abnorm. soc. Psychol.,* 1955, **51,** 616–623.

——— Development and evaluation of a scale for measuring social acquiescence. *J. abnorm. soc. Psychol.,* 1956, **53,** 296–299.

BERDIE, R. F. Likes, dislikes, and vocational interests. *J. appl. Psychol.,* 1943, **27,** 180–189.

CATTELL, R. B., SAUNDERS, D. R., & STICE, G. E. *The 16 P. F. questionnaire.* (rev. ed.) Champaign, Ill.: Inst. Pers. and Ability Testing, 1957.

CHRISTIE, R., HAVEL, J., & SEIDENBERG, B. Is the F scale irreversible? *J. abnorm. soc. Psychol.,* 1958, **56,** 143–159.

COUCH, A. S., & BALES, R. F. *Factor analysis of value profile.* 1955. (Mimeo.)

CRONBACH, L. J. Response sets and test validity. *Educ. psychol. Measmt.,* 1946, **6,** 616–623.

——— *Essentials of psychological testing.* New York: Harper, 1949.

——— Further evidence on response sets and test design. *Educ. psychol. Measmt.,* 1950, **10,** 3–31.

——— Proposals leading to analytic treatment of social perception scores. In R. Tagiuri & T. Petrullo (Eds.), *Person perception and interpersonal behavior.* Stanford: Stanford Univer. Press, 1958.

DAVIDS, A. Alienation, social apperception, and ego structure. *J. consult. Psychol.,* 1955, **19,** 21–27.

ERIKSON, E. H. *Childhood and society.* New York: Norton, 1950.

FREUD, S. Character and anal eroticism (1908). In *Collected papers.* Vol. II. London: Hogarth Press, 1946.

——— On the transformation of instincts with special reference to anal eroticism (1916). *Collected papers.* Vol. II. London: Hogarth Press, 1946.

FRICKE, B. G. Response set as a suppressor variable in the OAIS and MMPI. *J. consult. Psychol.,* 1956, **20,** 161–169.

HOLLAND, J. L. A personality inventory employing occupational titles. *J. appl. Psychol.,* 1958, **42,** 336–342.

JACKSON, D. N., & Messick, S. J. Content and style in personality assessment. *Psychol. Bull.,* 1958, **55,** 243–252.

KASSEBAUM, G. G., COUCH, A. S., & SLATER, P. E. The factorial dimensions of the MMPI. *J. consult. Psychol.,* 1959, **23,** 226–236.

LEAVITT, H. J., HAX, H., & ROCHE, J. H. "Authoritarianism" and agreement with things authoritative. *J. Psychol.,* 1955, **40,** 215–221.

LORGE, I. Gen-like: Halo or reality. *Psychol. Bull.,* 1937, **34,** 545–546. (Abstract)

ROKEACH, M. Political and religious dogmatism: An alternative to the authoritarian personality. *Psychol. Monogr.,* 1956, **70,** (18, Whole No. 425).

ROULON, P. J. *A statistical study of the Strong Vocational Interest Blank.* Unpublished doctoral dissertation, Univer. of Minnesota, 1931.

THOMSON, G. H. *The factorial analysis of human ability.* London: Univer. London Press, 1939.

THURSTONE, L. L. *Thurstone temperamental schedule.* Chicago: Science Research Associates, 1949.

Field Dependence–Field Independence as a Personality Type

DEPENDENCE ON EXTERNAL INFLUENCE: CORRELATES IN PERCEPTION, ATTITUDES, AND JUDGMENT

Harriet B. Linton

Although it is reasonable to assume that people who are highly responsive to external influence in one situation also are likely to be so in other situations, attempts to demonstrate such a relationship have often been unsuccessful (1, 2, 3, 11, 12, 15). Allport (1) and Murphy, Murphy, and Newcomb (12) conclude, therefore, that "suggestibility" is rarely a consistent personal trait, but is rather a function of the specific situation.

The recent work of Witkin, et al. (16, 18) on individual differences in the effect of the perceptual field on response to selected elements within the field has, however, yielded consistent correlations among tasks. Some Ss tend to be strongly affected by the perceptual field in a number of situations. Such Ss tend also to be dependent and to have low self-esteem. Other Ss tend to resist the influence of the field in a number of situations. These Ss are more likely to be analytic, self-aware, and self-sufficient (18).

The personality correlates found in the Witkin study are ones that seem likely to play a part in suggestibility. The

present study tests the validity of this impression by relating performance in several of Witkin's situations to behavior in three situations that have often been used to study suggestibility. The following rather general hypothesis is tested in the present study:

The tendency for behavior to be modified by an external stimulus, regardless of whether the external stimulus is personal or impersonal in nature, is a function of enduring attributes of the person; consequently, Ss whose performance in perceptual tasks is highly affected by the perceptual field will be those whose behavior in other situations is most likely to be modified so as to conform to an external standard.

The experimental situations used are described below; the hypothesis leads to the prediction of positive correlations among all measures.

Method

SUBJECTS

The subjects (Ss) were 53 male students in their first semester at Brooklyn College. None had taken any courses in psychology and all were volunteers.

Reprinted by permission of the American Psychological Association and the author from *The Journal of Abnormal and Social Psychology,* Vol. 51, 1955.

PERCEPTUAL TESTS [1]

Tilting-room-tilting-chair (TRTC). The apparatus and procedure are those used by Witkin (18). The S is placed in a chair which can be tilted; the chair is within a room which can be tilted independently. The visual field and the effect of gravity on the body can thereby be varied independently so as to lead to conflicting impressions of the true vertical. It is then possible to measure the relative extent to which each S relies on each type of cue in his perception of the upright.

There are four subtests: TRTC 1a (four trials): room and chair initially tilted to the same side (room at 56°, chair at 22°); S must make the room upright. TRTC 1b (four trials): room and chair initially tilted to opposite sides (room at 56°, chair at 22°); S must make the room upright. TRTC 2a (three trials): room and chair initially tilted to same side (room at 35°, chair at 22°); S must make the chair upright. TRTC 2b (three trials): room and chair initially tilted to opposite sides (room at 35°, chair at 22°); S must make the chair upright.

The score for each series is the sum of the deviations from the true upright on all trials of that series, expressed in degrees. A high score reflects greater reliance on the external (visual) field and less reliance on bodily sensations, while a low score reflects the reverse. Since the experimental conditions lead to skewed distributions of scores, the data for each subtest are normalized.

Embedded-figures test (EFT). In 24 different trials the S is required to find a simple figure hidden in a more complex figure; the figures are those adapted from Gottschaldt by Witkin (17). The simple figure is seen alone and is removed when the complex figure is presented. The time taken to find each figure is recorded to the nearest second and the times for all trials are added to give a single score. A high score indicates difficulty in overcoming the influence of the surrounding field. Scores are normalized; the normalized distribution is very similar to that obtained by a logarithmic transformation.

CONFORMITY TESTS [2]

The conformity tests used are typical of those used in previous studies of suggestibility. They were selected to provide variety in the source of influence, the nature and difficulty of the task, and the S's awareness of influence.

Autokinetic situation. The autokinetic situation follows the general procedure used in many previous experiments (e.g., 5, 13). Potential influence was exerted by a confederate presented as a fellow S; he was identified (correctly) as a senior psychology major in order to endow him potentially with some degree of prestige. There were 20 trials in which Ss wrote in booklets their estimate of the amount of movement, in inches, following which the E computed each S's initial norm (average of Trials 11–20) and conveyed this norm, to the nearest integer, to the confederate. There were then 40 trials in which judgments were made aloud after the confederate, by prearrangement, had given us first on each trial; the confederate's "judgments" in each case were made to average 5 inches above the S's initial norm. For each S, the difference between his mean

[1] More complete descriptions of apparatus, materials, and experimental procedure are available elsewhere (7).

[2] The writer wishes to thank Arthur Shaw for his skillful performance in the role of confederate.

for the oral series and his initial norm was obtained, and the t ratio of this difference computed.

After the autokinetic experiment, each S was interviewed about his reactions to the situation and the interview material was coded.

Syllogisms test. This test attempts to measure the extent to which reasoning is modified by the S's attitudes toward the issues involved. The syllogisms are of the sort used by Morgan and Morton (10), Janis and Frick (4) and others

TABLE 1. INTERCORRELATIONS AMONG PERCEPTUAL MEASURES

Sub-tests	TRTC 1b	TRTC 2a	TRTC 2b	EFT
TRTC 1a	.20 †	.33 **	.27 *	.39 **
TRTC 1b		.02	.04	−.07
TRTC 2a			.31 *	.38 **
TRTC 2b				.35 **

* Significant at the .05 level.
** Significant at the .01 level.
† Significant at the .10 level.
Note.—The r's for the EFT are based on 52 cases; all others are based on 53 cases. Product-moment r is used and, since predictions were made, significance levels are based on one tail of the probability distribution.

(6, 14) to measure the "atmosphere effect": some of the items are neutral since there is no conflict between the S's personal attitudes and the logically correct answer, while in others the correct response conflicts with the S's attitudes.

The Ss were given 42 syllogisms and asked to judge whether each was valid solely in terms of the logical operations involved. After that, they were given a questionnaire to ascertain their attitudes on the issues dealt with in the syllogisms; it was thus possible to determine in each case whether a syllogism conflicted with

the attitudes of a particular S. Two measures were obtained: $E_N\%$, the percentage of errors on neutral items, and the A index, which is the extent to which errors on conflict items exceed the amount that would have been predicted (by a regression formula) solely from the S's $E_N\%$. The A index is taken to represent the S's tendency to make wish-fulfilling errors.

Attitude change test. This test gives an opportunity for the S's attitudes on issues of relatively low personal significance to be influenced through written material. The issues were (a) the future number of movie theaters, (b) the practicality of an atomic-power submarine, and (c) the selling of antihistamines without prescription. Agreement or disagreement with a stated position on each issue was ascertained both before and after reading articles [3] about the issues attributed to authoritative sources; certainty of opinion was rated on a four-point scale. Criteria were established for scoring an S as having changed or not changed his opinion on each issue in the direction favored by the articles; scoring was not possible in all instances.

Results

PERCEPTUAL TESTS

All Ss were scored on the four TRTC subtests, and all but one on the EFT. The means and sigmas of raw scores for the five perceptual measures did not differ significantly from those found by Witkin (18); split-half reliabilities ranged from .80 to .93.

Table 1 shows that TRTC 2a, TRTC 2b and the EFT seem to cluster, and

[3] The writer wishes to thank Irving L. Janis for providing the articles and for his helpful suggestions about their use.

TRTC 1b is unrelated to these three tests. TRTC 1a is the only measure that shows any tendency to relate to TRTC 1b; it is significantly related to the other three tests.[4]

CONFORMITY TESTS

In the autokinetic situation, two Ss saw no movement, so that $N = 51$. The sample as a whole showed an increase in judgments significant at the .001 level.

Behavior occurring before the introduction of the confederate's "judgments" was characterized as *adequate coping* if the S was not unduly disturbed by the situation and made active efforts to work out a solution for himself (29 Ss); otherwise it was rated as *inadequate* (22 Ss). A rating of *responsive* was given to 20 Ss who reported that after the confederate was introduced they felt he was more likely to be correct than they; the re-

TABLE 2. INTERCORRELATIONS AMONG CONFORMITY MEASURES

	Autokinetic Situation				Syllogisms	
	Inadequate Coping	Responsive-ness	Negativism (lack of)	Attitude Change	A Index	$E_N\%$
Autokinetic Change	.88 **	.85 **	.67 **	.36	−.18	−.10
Inadequate Coping		.54 **	.20	.17	.02	−.07
Responsiveness			.32 †	−.29	−.31	.11
Negativism (lack)				.37	−.07	.10
Attitude Change					.15	−.12
A Index						.00

** Significant at .01 level.
† Significant at .10 level.

Note.—The N on which r's are based varies from 44 to 52. Scores on the syllogisms test are continuous; all other scores are dichotomized. As a result, the table includes both tetrachoric and biserial r's. Since predictions were made, significance levels are based on one tail of the probability distribution.

The t ratio of the difference between the initial norm and the mean of the oral series was used as a criterion, and the sample dichotomized (for reasons for dichotomizing, cf. 8) into 17 *changers*, who were considered to have been markedly influenced by the confederate, and 34 *nonchangers*. The interview formed the basis for three additional measures that seem to reflect predispositional tendencies of the person to be influenced by the confederate or to resist influence.

maining 31 were classified as *unresponsive*. Twelve Ss who reported deliberate attempts to avoid being influenced were rated as *negativistic,* and the remaining 39 as *not negativistic.*[5]

[5] The interviews were scored by a second judge, using written criteria. All scorings agreed with those of the E except for two Ss on *coping*, one S on *responsiveness,* and three Ss on *negativism.* For each measure, discrepancies were all in one direction, so that differences between judges amounted to a change of cutoff point. Disagreements were submitted to a third judge, whose decision was accepted. The writer wishes to thank Ruth Belov and David Linton for their help.

[4] When the data are not normalized (cf. 7), the r's are similar to those found by Witkin (18), who did not normalize the measures.

In the syllogisms test, when items are selected for equal difficulty, the group of Ss as a whole made more errors on conflict than on neutral items ($p < .01$); this indicates that an atmosphere effect was elicited by the test. The odd-even r (corrected for attenuation) for $E_N\%$ was .76 and for the A index it was .73; it should be noted that the r between the two measures is zero by definition. This test was scored for 52 Ss.

In the attitude change test, an S was scored as having been influenced if he was rated as changing on two or three

are among the four autokinetic measures; this supports the notion that adequacy of coping, responsiveness, and negativism represent different variables that help to determine whether or not an S's actual judgments will be influenced. There are no significant correlations among the three different basic conformity measures (italicized r's).

PERCEPTUAL-CONFORMITY INTERRELATIONS

Table 3 includes, in addition to the correlations between perceptual and con-

TABLE 3. CORRELATIONS BETWEEN PERCEPTUAL AND CONFORMITY MEASURES

Conformity Measures	Perceptual Measures						
	TRTC 1a	TRTC 1b	TRTC 2a	TRTC 2b	EFT	Multiple R	Perceptual Index
Autokinetic Change	.42 *	.34 *	.33 *	.26 †	.43 **	.60 **	.54 **
Inadequate Coping	.36 *	.04	.20	.28 †	.61 **	.63 **	.46 **
Responsiveness	.25 †	.12	.25 †	−.02	.21	.37 *	.21
Negativism (lack)	.49 **	.11	.51 **	.29 †	.62 **	.72 **	.65 **
Attitude Change	.53 **	.49 *	.19	.36 *	.32 †	.70 **	.66 **
Syllogisms: A Index	.01	−.24	.23 *	.24 *	−.01	.42 **	.15
$E_N\%$	.03	−.38	.11	.36 **	.16	.53 **	−.02

* Significant at .05 level.
** Significant at .01 level.
† Significant at .10 level.
Note.—Since predictions were made, significance levels are based on one tail of the probability distribution.

out of a scorable two or three items. Not all items were scorable, since there were instances where an S's original opinion was in the direction in which influence was exerted. As a result only 46 Ss were retained in the final scoring, 8 rated as *influenced* and 38 as *not influenced*.

Table 2 shows the interrelationships among the measures obtained from the conformity tests. The only significant r's

formity measures, the multiple R of each conformity measure with the five perceptual tests as well as the r of the conformity measures with a Perceptual Index. The Perceptual Index is obtained by adding each S's normalized scores for the five perceptual tests and normalizing the resulting distribution; it is, consequently, a measure of over-all field dependence in the perceptual battery. All measures are oriented so that a positive *r* supports the predictions. Correlations involving attitude change are based on an *N* of 46; the other *r*'s are based on *N*'s of from 50 to 52. The four autokinetic measures and attitude change are dichotomized, while the syllogisms scores and all perceptual measures are continuous, so that Table 3 contains both biserial and product-moment *r*'s.

TABLE 4. RELATIONSHIP BETWEEN PERCEPTUAL INDEX AND AMOUNT OF CONFORMITY

	PERPETUAL INDEX		
Amount of Conformity	Highest Quartile	Middle Quartiles	Lowest Quartile
Number of situations in Which *S* Conforms			
None	—	13	9
One	6	14	4
Two	6	—	—
Three	1	—	—
Percentage of Situations in Which Conformity Occurs	57%	19%	11%

Note.—Not all *S*s participated in all three situations; the total number of situations in which the 53 *S*s participated was 149.

Table 3 shows that the conformity measures correlate with the perceptual measures, on the whole, to at least the same extent that the perceptual measures correlate with each other. The conformity measures differ from each other, however, in both the extent and the pattern of their relationships to the perceptual tests.

The strength of the relationship between over-all perceptual field dependence and over-all level of conformity is shown in Table 4.[6] When the sample is dichotomized into those who conform in at least one situation and those who conform in none, the r_{bis} of conformity with the Perceptual Index is .60 ($p < .001$). The relationship is not linear, however, since *S*s in the lower three quartiles on the Perceptual Index conform less than chance (=26%), while only the high group conforms more.

Discussion

When the perceptual and conformity situations are considered separately, the results support previous studies: the perceptual tests correlate with each other, as Witkin has found, and the conformity tests do not correlate with each other, as many previous studies have found. The most noteworthy finding is that the perceptual and conformity measures correlate with each other appreciably.

The *r*'s between perceptual and conformity measures are far from uniform. While the implications of that fact cannot be explored here, it can be noted that a factor analysis of the data [7] indicates that there are several factors operating. Two of them correspond to the classification of the perceptual tests by Witkin (18) into (*a*) situations where

[6] Criteria for conformity in the autokinetic and attitude change tests have been described above; in the syllogisms test, all *S*s with a positive A Index of 15% or more are classified as conforming.

[7] This discussion is based on a factor analysis of the data (cf. 7; based on somewhat different *r*'s, since perceptual tests were not there normalized). The small sample makes the reliability of the obtained factors questionable, but they suggest interpretations that could be tested further.

acceptance of the field is facilitated (TRTC 1a and 1b), and (*b*) situations where the field must be resisted to deal effectively with an item within that field (TRTC 2a and 2b, EFT). The present data yield at least one other meaningful factor; that factor seems to distinguish between impersonal tasks and those involving another person as the source of influence. While the obtained factors are distinct from each other, they are not independent.

Differences in their loadings on the various factors lead the conformity measures to have differing patterns of correlation with the perceptual measures. Change of judgments in the autokinetic situation correlates most consistently with the perceptual battery, while each of the three supplementary autokinetic measures has its own pattern of r's with the five perceptual tests (for the different personality test patterns associated with each measure, cf. 9). Attitude change also correlates highly with the perceptual battery, particularly the TRTC room-adjustment tests. The A index has the lowest relationship to perception, and not always in the predicted direction (the r with TRTC 1b would have $p < .10$ if direction were not predicted). The same is true of $E_N\%$, not intended as a conformity measure (its r with TRTC 1b would have $p < .01$ if direction were not predicted). The significant multiple R's of these measures indicate that they are related to perception, but in a more complex manner than was anticipated; they cannot be said to be related to "field dependency," per se. It may be noted that this is the only task in which the source of influence is not external.

The results indicate that there is a common basis for behavior in the perceptual and conformity situations. The common element, whatever it may be, is apparently more uniformly expressed in the perceptual situations since they are significantly intercorrelated, on the whole, while the conformity situations are not. It may be that the perceptual tasks tap a deeper, more enduring layer of the person than do the cognitive or social situations. As an expression of the person's characteristic ways of responding to stimuli, perception is primary, since it must precede any cognitive or social behavior. It is also less subject to conscious control. In the TRTC, for example, responses are typically given as direct perceptions and not as considered judgments, and the S is given no cues for his accuracy.

In the conformity situations, however, more conscious control can be exerted, as in the autokinetic situation, where some Ss made deliberate efforts to resist influence. These situations also depend on specific experiences that are peripheral to personality: the confederate may resemble someone he likes or dislikes, he may have personal knowledge of the attitude change issues, etc. Factors of this sort, that play less part in the perceptual tests, would reduce r's among conformity measures, leading to the impression that they have little or nothing in common with each other.

It is understandable, then, that Ss with similar perceptual scores will not necessarily conform in the same situations, although they may conform to approximately the same extent if enough situations are sampled. As Table 4 shows, over-all perceptual performance permits a prediction of over-all resistance to external pressures; it does not, however, allow as strong a prediction of behavior in any one situation. The attributes reflected in the perceptual tests seem, then, to represent rather deep-seated personal tendencies that reflect a generalized predisposition to conform or to resist pressure, with more peripheral factors determining just when these tendencies will be expressed in overt behavior.

One of the important personality factors that play a part is expressed in the Rorschach records produced by these Ss. The degree of assertiveness in human movement responses was scored. Predominantly assertive M's were given by none in the highest quartile on the Perceptual Index, and by 18%, 50%, and 92% of Ss in successive quartiles; predominantly assertive M's were given by none who conformed more than once, by 48% of those conforming once, and by 90% of those who did not conform at all. Other personality test correlates of the experimental measures are available elsewhere (7, Appendix; 9; 18), and this would seem to be a profitable technique in searching for the basis of experimental behavior.

In conclusion, the results support the initial hypothesis that there is a common basis for response to external influence in both perceptual and conformity situations. Two suggestions may be advanced to explain the pattern of relationships found as well as the lack of relationship found in other studies. It is probable that consistent personal modes of reaction are best observed when behavior is studied not only in standard tests of suggestibility per se, but also in situations that are less easily affected by conscious control or peripheral factors, such as the perceptual tasks or projective tests. The data also indicate that there is a group of separable but related tendencies that contributes to conforming behavior, rather than a unitary "trait of suggestibility."

Summary

The hypothesis that people have a generalized tendency to accept or reject external influence was tested in perceptual and conformity situations, using 53 male college freshmen as Ss. Perceptual tests were (a) a four-part test of ability to determine the upright in space when gravitational and visual cues are put in conflict, and (b) the Gottschaldt-Witkin embedded-figures test. Conformity tests were (a) effect of planted judgments of estimates of autokinetic movement, (b) attitude change after reading authoritative articles, and (c) the effect of personal feelings on logic.

Results: (a) Ss who were highly influenced by the field in one perceptual test performed similarly in other perceptual tests, (b) conformity measures were not significantly interrelated, and (c) field-dependent perceptual behavior was associated with high conformity in the other tests, particularly the autokinetic and attitude change measures.

The correlational patterns suggest that several variables determine conforming behavior, rather than a single "trait of suggestibility." It is suggested that perceptual performance reflects central tendencies of the person that may or may not emerge in a specific test of conformity, while behavior in any one conformity situation is subject to greater fluctuation as a result of more peripheral factors.

References

1. ALLPORT, G. W. *Personality, a psychological interpretation.* New York: Holt, 1937.

2. BAUMGARTNER, M. The correlation of direct suggestibility with certain character traits. *J. appl. Psychol.*, 1931, **15**, 1–15.

3. ESTABROOKS, G. H. Experimental studies in suggestion. *J. genet. Psychol.*, 1929, **36**, 120–139.

4. JANIS, I. L., & FRICK, F. The relationship between attitudes toward conclusions and errors in judging the logical validity of syllogisms. *J. exp. Psychol.*, 1943, **33**, 73–77.

5. KELMAN, H. Effects of success and failure on "suggestibility" in the autokinetic situation. *J. abnorm. soc. Psychol.*, 1950, **45**, 267–285.

6. LEFFORD, A. The influence of emotional subject matter on logical reasoning. *J. gen. Psychol.*, 1946, **34**, 127–151.

7. LINTON, HARRIET B. Relations between mode of perception and the tendency to conform. Unpublished doctor's dissertation, Yale Univer., 1952.

8. ——— Autokinetic judgments as a measure of influence. *J. abnorm. soc. Psychol.*, 1954, **49**, 464–466.

9. ——— Rorschach correlates of response to suggestion. *J. abnorm. soc. Psychol.*, 1954, **49**, 75–83.

10. MORGAN, J. J. B., & MORTON, J. T. The distortion of syllogistic reasoning produced by personal conviction. *J. soc. Psychol.*, 1944, **20**, 39–59.

11. MURPHY, G. *Personality, a biosocial approach to origins and structure.* New York: Harper, 1947.

12. MURPHY, G., MURPHY, LOIS, & NEWCOMB, T. M. *Experimental social psychology.* New York: Harper, 1937.

13. SHERIF, M. A study of some social factors in perception. *Arch. Psychol.*, 1935, No. 187.

14. THISTLETHWAITE, D. Attitude and structure as factors in the distortion of reasoning. *J. abnorm. soc. Psychol.*, 1950, **45**, 442–458.

15. WILLIAMS, G. W. Suggestibility in the normal and hypnotic states. *Arch. Psychol.*, 1930, No. 122.

16. WITKIN, H. A. The nature and importance of individual differences in perception. *J. Pers.*, 1949, **18**, 145–170.

17. ——— Individual differences in ease of perception of embedded figures, *J. Pers.*, 1950, **19**, 1–15.

18. WITKIN, H. A., LEWIS, HELEN B., HERTZMAN, M., MACHOVER, KAREN, MEISSNER, PEARL B., & WAPNER, S. *Perception through personality.* New York: Harper, 1954.

The Creative Personality

THE DISPOSITION TOWARD ORIGINALITY   Frank Barron

There has been a marked tendency in psychological research on originality to focus attention upon the single original act in itself, rather than upon the total personality of the originator. This is understandable, for the birth and development of the original idea is usually more immediately interesting and dramatically vivid than the birth and history of the man who had the idea. Newton's apple and Archimedes' tub and the well of Eratosthenes are thus naturally the circumstances with which we associate the remarkable insights of these original geniuses; we do not often ask ourselves whether these men were for the most part disposed to express or to suppress erotic impulses, or whether their emotions were fluent or turgid, or how subject to intense anxiety they were, or how much given to violent action. We tend to disembody the creative act and the creative process by limiting our inquiry to the creator's mental content at the moment of insight, forgetting that it is a highly organized system of responding that lies behind the particular original response which, because of its validity, becomes an historical event.

Reprinted by permission of the American Psychological Association and the author from *The Journal of Abnormal and Social Psychology*, Vol. 51, 1955.

There is good reason for believing, however, that originality is almost habitual with persons who produce a really singular insight. The biography of the inventive genius commonly records a lifetime of original thinking, though only a few ideas survive and are remembered to fame. Voluminous productivity is the rule and not the exception among individuals who have made some noteworthy contribution. Original responses, it would seem, recur regularly in some persons, while there are other individuals who do not ever depart from the stereotyped and the conventional in their thinking.

If, then, some persons are regularly original, while others are regularly unoriginal, it must be the case that certain patterns of relatively enduring traits either facilitate or impede the production of original acts. Rather than focusing on the immediate conditions which have triggered the original response, the present study was concerned with the underlying disposition toward originality which it may be presumed exists in those persons who are regularly original. The research was directed first of all toward identifying individuals who performed consistently in a relatively more or relatively less original way; when this had been done, the more original were compared with the less original in terms of personality organization. Independent evidence concerning the personalities of the Ss was obtained both through the use of standardized paper-and-pencil tests and through employment of the living-in assessment method, with its emphasis upon observation of the Ss through several days of informal social interaction, situational tests, group discussions, psychodrama, and the like. The observers were of course kept in ignorance of the scores earned by the Ss on tests of originality.

The Relativity of Originality

It is a basic assumption of this study that acts are original only in relation to some specified commonality. The original must be defined relative to the usual, and the degree of originality must be specified statistically in terms of incidence of occurrence. Thus the first criterion of an original response is that it should have a certain stated uncommonness in the particular group being studied. A familiar example of this in psychological practice is the definition of an original response to the Rorschach inkblots, the requirement there being that the response should, in the examiner's experience, occur no more often than once in 100 examinations.

In the present study, we propose to deal with a relatively low order of originality, its limits being set by the nature of the sampling of Ss. The Ss are 100 captains in the United States Air Force, and originality as discerned here is originality in relation to the usual responses of only 100 persons. Furthermore, these 100 persons are not themselves especially selected for originality in relation to the population in general. Nevertheless, as we shall show later, some of the 100 captains are regularly original in com-

parison with the remainder, while others are regularly unoriginal in relation to the entire group. Apart from their military status, the sample may be described as a group of normal, healthy young men, of average intelligence, socioeconomically of the lower middle class in their pre-army background, and similar to young men in general in terms of the usualness and the unusualness of their responses to the tests of originality employed in this experiment.

A second criterion that must be met if a response is to be called original is that it must be to some extent adaptive to reality. The intent of this requirement is to exclude uncommon responses which are merely random, or which proceed from ignorance or delusion. An example of the application of this second criterion may be taken from the scoring of one of the measures of originality used in this experiment: the measure is a count of the number of uncommon *and correct* anagram solutions to the test word "generation." Many Ss did not hesitate to offer solutions that were incorrect, and that were usually unique. In such instances, the application of the second criterion of originality was straightforward and decisive. Not all of the tests called for such purely cognitive responses with unambiguous denotative meaning, however: in the case of inkblot tests, e.g., we come closer to the problems involved in evaluating fantasy or works of art, and verification cannot be had by recourse to a dictionary. Instead, when E himself cannot "see" the form pointed to by S, he must have recourse to other psychologists who have given many Rorschachs and who can be considered fairly open to suggestions as to what the blots might reasonably look like. Consensual verification is thus sought for such imaginings. Poor forms, or uncommon responses that did not sufficiently respect the inkblot reality, were not credited as original in this study.

The Measurement of Originality

Eight test measures were accepted here as indicative of originality. They are described below. The first three of these measures are taken from the creativity battery developed by Guilford and his associates (5, 6) in the Project on Aptitudes of High-Level Personnel at the University of Southern California. These three tests had significant loadings on the Originality factor in the Guilford researches.[1] Of the remaining five measures, two are derived from commonly used projective techniques, the Rorschach Psychodiagnostic (10) and the Thematic Apperception Test (9); another is a commonly used anagram test, and the remaining two tests were devised by the writer.

(1) *Unusual Uses*. This test calls upon the subject to list six uses to which each of several common objects can be put. It is scored for infrequency, in the sample under study, of the uses proposed. Odd-even reliability in this sample is .77.

(2) *Consequences B*. In this test, S is asked to write down what would happen if certain changes were suddenly to take place. The task for him is to list as many consequences or results of these changes as he can. The responses are scored according to how obvious the imagined consequences are, the less obvious responses receiving the higher scores. Interrater agreement is .71.

(3) *Plot Titles B*. Two story plots are presented, and S is asked to write as many

titles as he can think of for each plot. The titles are rated on a scale of cleverness from 0 to 5. The number of titles rated 2, 3, 4, or 5 constitutes the cleverness score. Interrater agreement in this study was .43.

(4) *Rorschach O +*. This is a count of the number of original responses given by S to the 10 Rorschach blots and adjudged by two scorers, working separately, to be good rather than poor forms. Standard Rorschach administrative procedure was followed. Interrater agreement was .72, and only those responses scored by both scorers as 0+ were credited.

(5) *Thematic Apperception Test: Originality rating*. Two raters, working independently of one another, rated the TAT protocols of the 100 Ss on a 9-point scale, using approximate normal curve frequencies for each point along the scale. Interrater agreement was .70. The S's score was the average of the two ratings.

(6) *Anagrams*. The test word "generation" was used, and the anagram solutions were scored for infrequency of occurrence in the sample under study. If S offered a solution that was correct and that was offered by no more than two other Ss, he received one point for originality. Total score is therefore the number of such uncommon but correct solutions.

(7) *Word Rearrangement Test: Originality rating*. In this test, S is given 50 words which were selected at random from a list of common nouns, adjectives, and adverbs. He is told to make up a story which will enable him to use as many as possible of the listed words. His composition is rated for originality on a 9-point scale, just as the TAT was. Interrater agreement in this instance was .67.

(8) *Achromatic Inkblots*. This is a set of 10 achromatic inkblots constructed locally. The S is asked to give only one response to each blot. Responses were weighted according to their frequency of occurrence in the sample under study, the more infrequent responses receiving the higher weights. Score is the sum of the

---

[1] The present writer is indebted to Dr. Guilford and the personnel of the Project not only for permission to use the tests, but also for the actual scoring of the protocols.

weights assigned to S's responses on all 10 blots. Odd-even reliability was .43.

It is worth noting that all eight of these tests are free-response tests; the respondent is not presented with alternatives devised by the test maker, but must instead summon from within himself his own way of solving problems, seeing the blots, interpreting the pictures, putting together the words or letters, and so on. There is considerable latitude allowed for self-expression and for idiosyncratic interpretation.

we should expect the intercorrelations of these measures to be positive and to be statistically significant; we should not, however, expect the coefficients to be very high, for it is reasonable that the dimension of originality would have its variance apportioned to several media of expression. Even regularly original persons can be expected to be outstandingly original in only one or two ways. The extent to which these expectations are confirmed in the present study may be seen from Table 1, in which the Pearsonian correlation coefficients of all eight

TABLE 1. INTERRELATIONS OF EIGHT ORIGINALITY MEASURES

Test Measures	1.	2.	3.	4.	5.	6.	7.	8.
1. Unusual Uses	—	.42	.37	.08	.17	.29	.06	.17
2. Consequences B	.42	—	.46	−.02	.21	.21	.16	.09
3. Plot Titles B	.37	.46	—	.17	.26	.17	.16	.07
4. Rorschach O+	.08	−.02	.17	—	.21	.03	−.05	.17
5. TAT: Originality	.17	.21	.26	.21	—	.36	.41	.02
6. Anagrams	.29	.21	.17	.03	.36	—	.33	.38
7. Word Synthesis Orig.	.06	.16	.16	−.05	.41	.33	—	.09
8. Inkblot Originality	.17	.09	.07	.17	.02	.38	.09	—

Furthermore, diverse media are presented for the respondent to express himself through. The two inkblot tests allow for original visualization, or original perceptual organization of visual forms. The TAT and the Word Rearrangement Test permit originality of verbal composition to show itself. Consequences and Unusual Uses call for bright ideas in more or less discrete form. Plot Titles evokes epigrammatic or sloganistic originality, while Anagrams requires a combination of word fluency and ease of perceptual reorganization.

If originality is indeed a dimension, and if some persons are regularly original while others are regularly unoriginal,

test measures with one another are given. (With an N of 100, a Pearsonian r is significant at the .05 level if it is .20 or greater; an r of .26 is significant at the .01 level.)

As Table 1 shows, the correlations of the eight measures with one another tend to be positive and to be significantly different from zero. The inkblot tests alone appear to bear little relationship to the other measures; indeed, they do not even correlate significantly with one another. If the two inkblot tests are excluded, however, two-thirds of the intercorrelations of the remaining six measures are significant at the .05 level, and all are positive. Table 1 thus provides satisfactory evidence of the expected coherence or regularity of the manifestations of originality, with considerable reservations, however, concerning the relevance of inkblot originality to the dimension here being measured.

Since it is quite possible that originality is simply a multifactorial dimension in which certain factors bear little relationship to other factors but yet are positively related to the underlying dimension

TABLE 2. RELATIONSHIP OF EIGHT TEST MEASURES TO RATED ORIGINALITY AND TO COMPOSITE TEST ORIGINALITY

Test Measures	9	10
1. Unusual Uses	.30	.60
2. Consequences B	.36	.59
3. Plot Titles B	.32	.62
4. Rorschach O+	.18	.38
5. TAT: Originality	.45	.59
6. Anagrams	.22	.62
7. Word Synthesis Originality	.45	.51
8. Inkblot Originality	.07	.46
9. Staff Rating: Originality	—	.55
10. Composite Test Originality	.55	—

as a whole, it would probably be premature to exclude the inkblot measures from this battery of tests of originality. Considerable doubt must be entertained concerning their validity, however, and there is another piece of evidence which reinforces the doubt. The staff psychologists who conducted the three-day living-in assessments were particularly interested in two theoretically central variables which they sought to rate on the basis of their observations: one of these variables was Originality (the other was Personal Stability). The correlations between this final over-all rating on Originality and the eight test measures of originality are shown in Table 2. Also

given in Table 2 are the correlations of the eight measures individually with a variable which is the sum of the standard scores earned by each S on each of the eight tests; in other words, each test measure is correlated with a composite of which it is itself a part. The correlations thus show the relative contributions of each test to the total score on the battery of tests.

Table 2 provides evidence that the test battery is in substantial agreement with the staff psychologists who gave ratings on Originality without knowledge of the test scores. The correlation of .55 between the test composite and the observers' ratings is encouraging evidence that inexpensive, objective, and efficient measurement of originality is possible.

Again, however, the inkblot measures have relatively little relationship to these composite variables. The staff rating of Originality correlates significantly with six of the eight measures (well beyond the .01 level of significance with five of them); but neither Rorschach Originality nor Inkblot Originality is significantly related to the staff rating. As would be expected, these measures also have the least contribution to make to the test composite.

In spite of this situation, both inkblot measures were retained in the battery for purposes of identifying regularly original and regularly unoriginal Ss. The reasoning was as follows: On the face of it, uncommon responses to inkblots are original acts within the definition of originality being employed here. Tendencies toward uncommon visual perceptions are of course not readily recognized in ordinary social situations, since they have to be verbalized to be socially visible. Hence the failure of inkblot tests to correlate with the staff rating of Originality, based on observations of social behavior alone, should be discounted. The lack of a verbal component in perceptual originality, and its conspicuous presence in the other originality tests, may also account for the relative independence of the inkblot tests in the test composite. Finally, if the inkblot measures contribute only error variance to the composite, their retention will result in failure of some true relationships to appear, but this will be an error on the conservative side; and if they do in fact contribute true variance not contributed by any other test, they may add appreciable validity to the picture of the personality correlates of originality. They were therefore retained for the purpose of identifying regularly original and regularly unoriginal subjects.

A dual criterion was now established for calling a given subject regularly original: (*a*) he had to be at least one standard deviation above the mean on the test composite; (*b*) he had to be at least two standard deviations above the mean on at least one of the eight measures. Fifteen regularly original *S*s were thus identified; more than half of them were at least two standard deviations above the mean on two or more of the eight tests.

For comparison purposes, the 15 lowest scorers on the final distribution of summed standard scores were selected; all of these *S*s also met the criterion of being at least two standard deviations below the mean on at least one of the eight measures. They will be referred to as the regularly unoriginal subjects.

Some Hypotheses Suggested by Previous Work

The existence of a very general attitude toward experience, of a sort which disposes toward complexity of outlook, independence of judgment, and originality, has been suggested by the results of studies reported earlier by the present writer. It was found, e.g., that individuals who refused to yield to strong pressure from their peers to concur in a false group opinion described themselves, on an adjective check list, as "original" and "artistic" much more frequently than did subjects who yielded to such group pressure (1). In addition, the independent (nonyielding) *S*s showed a marked preference for complex and asymmetrical line drawings, as opposed to simple and symmetrical drawings. This preference for the complex and asymmetrical had been shown previously to be highly correlated both with the choice of art as a vocation (3) and with rated artistic ability among art students. Furthermore, in a sample of Ph.D. candidates in the sciences, preference for the complex and asymmetrical figure proved to be significantly related to rated originality in graduate work (2). This same relationship was found among graduating medical school seniors who were rated for originality by the medical school faculty. Other evidence indicated that the opposed preferences, for complexity or for simplicity, were related to a generalized experiential disposition: the preference for complexity is associated with a perceptual attitude which seeks to allow into the perceptual system the greatest possible richness of experience, even though discord and disorder result, while the preference for simplicity is associated with a perceptual attitude which allows into the system only as much as can be integrated without great discomfort and disorder, even though this means excluding some aspects of reality.

From all of these considerations, certain hypotheses as to the characteristics of original persons were derived and put to the test in the present study. The hypotheses, and the ways in which they were tested, or partially tested, are described below.

HYPOTHESIS 1.

That original persons prefer complexity and some degree of apparent imbalance in phenomena.

Test 1a. The Barron-Welsh Art Scale of the Figure Preference Test. Preference for complex-asymmetrical figures earns the subject a high score.

HYPOTHESIS 2.

That original persons are more complex psychodynamically and have greater personal scope.

Test 2a. Psychiatric interviewer rating on "Complexity and Scope as a Person." The *S*s receiving high ratings are those who were diagnosed by a psychiatric interviewer, on the basis of a two-hour interview, as having a "more complex personality structure and greater potential for complex ego-synthesis." Ratings were on a 9-point scale with approximate normal curve frequencies being assigned to each point along the scale.

HYPOTHESIS 3.

That original persons are more independent in their judgments.

Test 3a. The Independence of Judgment Scale. On this inventory scale, which was developed against the criterion of actual behavior in the Asch group pressure experiment in previous studies, high scores indicate similarity to persons who manifest independence.

Test 3b. A modification of the Asch group pressure experiment.[2] This is a situational test in which *S*s are put under pressure from their peers to agree to certain apparent group judgments. High scores indicate yielding to such pressures; regularly original persons should therefore have lower scores.

HYPOTHESIS 4.

That original persons are more self-assertive and dominant.

Test 4a. Dominance-submission ratings in a psychodramatic situation especially designed to elicit such tendencies in the subjects. Ratings were on a 9-point scale.

Test 4b. The Social Dominance scale of the California Psychological Inventory (4). This is a thoroughly studied and validated scale for the measurement of dominance in real-life social situations.

Test 4c. Staff rating on Dominance, based on three days of observation of social behavior. Dominance was defined for the raters as follows: "Self-assurance, ascendance, and self-confidence in dealing with others; forceful, authoritative, resolute, not easily intimidated." A 5-point rating scale was used.

Test 4d. The Self-assertiveness scale of the California Psychological Inventory.

Test 4e. The Phallicism scale of the Personal Preference Scale (8). This scale is intended as a measure of the derivatives and residuals in the adult personality of propensities which were highly cathected in the phallic stage of psychosexual development. High scores indicate an emphasis on personal power and desire for recognition.

---

[2] This version of the group pressure experiment retains the prototypical psychological situation used by Asch, but introduces novel methods of experimental control and greatly expands the kinds of judgments on which group pressure is brought to bear. The new technique was devised by Richard S. Crutchfield, who has reported its details in his presidential address, "Conformity and Character," before the Division of Personality and Social Psychology, American Psychological Association, New York City, September 4, 1954. (*Amer. Psychologist*, 1955, 10, 191–198.)

HYPOTHESIS 5.

That original persons reject suppression as a mechanism for the control of impulse. This would imply that they forbid themselves fewer thoughts, that they dislike to police themselves or others, that they are disposed to entertain impulses and ideas that are commonly taboo, and in general that they express in their persons the sort of indiscipline which psychoanalytic theory would ascribe to a libidinal organization in which derivatives of the early anal

TABLE 3. TESTS OF HYPOTHESES

Hypotheses	Originals (N = 15)		Unoriginals (N = 15)			
	M	SD	M	SD	t	P
1. Preference for Complexity						
Test 1a. Barron-Welsh Art Scale	19.40	12.28	12.67	10.69	2.16	.02
2. Complexity as a Person						
Test 2a. Psychiatric Rating: "Complexity as a Person"	6.40	1.82	4.00	1.67	3.58	.001
3. Independence of Judgment						
Test 3a. Independence of Judgment Scale	9.60	1.67	8.00	2.94	1.74	.05
Test 3b. Group Pressure Situation *	5.00	1.87	8.60	1.80	3.93	.001
4. Self-assertion and Dominance						
Test 4a. Psychodrama: Dominance Rating	41.13	11.70	38.40	7.78	0.72	.23
Test 4b. CPI: Social Dominance Scale	36.60	3.74	28.87	4.75	4.74	.001
Test 4c. Staff rating: Dominance	34.40	7.10	25.40	4.06	4.05	.001
Test 4d. SCPI: Self-Assertiveness Scale	15.73	1.44	15.07	2.74	0.78	.22
Test 4e. PPS: Phallicism Scale (VIK)	13.20	2.37	9.13	4.27	3.08	.01
5. Rejection of Suppression; Tendency towards Expression of Impulse						
Test 5a. MMPI: (L + Hy + K) − (Pd + Ma)	43.47	26.24	58.87	12.30	1.78	.045
Test 5b. SVIB: Policeman Interest Scale	44.67	9.87	55.00	10.81	−2.61	.01
Test 5c. PPS: Early Anal Scale (IVB)	20.33	4.57	17.87	2.90	1.66	.06
Late Anal Scale (VB)	23.53	4.59	26.80	4.85	−1.81	.05
Test 5d. CPI: Impulsivity Scale	23.13	7.86	16.60	6.08	1.98	.03
Test 5e. Staff Rating: Impulsivity	32.27	6.41	27.80	5.42	4.74	.001

* For the test of this hypothesis, only eight Ss in each group (eight Originals and eight Unoriginals) were available. This occurred because half of the subjects in the study were used as controls in the Crutchfield experiment, and hence made the judgments without being under pressure to conform to group opinion.

rather than of the late anal stage in psychosexual development predominate.

Test 5a. An index of suppression-expression on the Minnesota Multiphasic Personality Inventory (7) is obtained by adding the T scores on the Lie, Hysteria, and K scales and subtracting from that sum the sum of T scores on Psychopathic Deviation and Hypomania. On this index, regularly original Ss should obtain lower scores.

Test 5b. The Policeman Interest scale of the Strong Vocational Interest Blank (11). While this is bound to be a somewhat derivative measure of the personality tendency toward suppression of outlawed impulse, it does at least reflect the similarity of the subject's interests to those of persons who are regularly employed at maintaining law, order, and civil discipline—who, in short, seem vocationally suited to policing. Regularly original Ss should earn low scores.

Test 5c. The Early Anal and the Late Anal scales of the Personal Preference Scale (Grygier revision).[3] If the scales are valid and the hypothesis is correct, regularly original Ss should score higher on Early Anal and lower on Late Anal than do regularly unoriginal Ss.

Test 5d. The Impulsivity Scale of the California Psychological Inventory. Since high scorers are those who express impulse readily, the regularly original Ss should earn higher scores than the regularly unoriginal Ss.

Test 5e. Staff rating: Impulsivity. Again, regularly original Ss should receive higher ratings.

The group comparisons specified in these predictions are presented in detail

in Table 3. As that table shows, 12 of the 15 predictions proved correct. A fairly conservative criterion of confirmation was adopted: significance at the .05 level when the two-tailed test was applied. The theoretical formulation suggested by the previous work on complexity-simplicity and on independence of judgment is substantially confirmed by these results.

Discussion

The five major hypotheses in this study have been stated in terms derived directly from previous observations. There is another way of looking at them, however, which permits the results to be considered in somewhat other terms, and in a broader context. Since the hypotheses had already been stated and to some extent justified, it may be appropriate in discussing these results to venture somewhat beyond the literal meaning of the findings to date.

We have spoken here of the disposition toward originality, with originality being so measured as to be equivalent to the capacity for producing adaptive responses which are unusual. But unusualness of response may be considered a function as well of the objective freedom of an organism, where this is defined as the range of possible adaptive responses available in all situations. As the response repertoire of any given organism increases, the number of statistically infrequent responses, considered relative to the population of like organisms, will also increase. Thus the ability to respond in an unusual or original manner will be greatest when freedom is greatest.

Now freedom is related in a very special manner to degree and kind of organization. In general, organization, in company with complexity, generates freedom; the more complex the level of

---

[3] The form of the Personal Preference Scale used in this study is a revision made by Tadeusz Grygier. The revision consisted chiefly of the addition of items to certain scales, including the Early and Late Anal scales.

integration, the greater is the repertoire of adaptive responses. The tendency toward organization may, however, operate in such a fashion as to maintain a maladaptive simplicity. We are familiar in the political sphere with totalitarian states which depend upon suppression to achieve unity; such states are psychodynamically similar to the neurotic individual who suppresses his own impulses and emotions in order to maintain a semblance of stability. There are at hand enough case histories of both such organizations, political and private, to make it clear that the sort of unity and balance that depends upon total suppression of the claims of minority affects and opinions is maladaptive in the long run.

Suppression is a common way of achieving unity, however, because in the short run it often seems to work. Increasing complexity puts a strain upon an organism's ability to integrate phenomena; one solution of the difficulty is to inhibit the development of the greater level of complexity, and thus to avoid the temporary disintegration that would otherwise have resulted.

Originality, then, flourishes where suppression is at a minimum and where some measure of disintegration is tolerable in the interests of a final higher level of integration.

If we consider the case of a human being who develops strongly the disposition toward originality, we must posit certain personal characteristics and personal history which facilitated the development of such a disposition. In our hypotheses, the term "dominance" was used to describe one trait of the regularly original individual. This may be translated as a strong need for personal mastery, not merely over other persons, but over all experience. It initially involves self-centeredness, which in its socialized form may come to be known as self-realization. One aspect of it is the insistence on self-regulation, and a rejection of regulation by others.

For such a person, the most crucial developmental crisis in relation to control of impulse comes at the anal stage of socialization. What our hypotheses have suggested is that there is a positive rebellion against the prohibition of unregulated anal production, and a carrying of the derivatives of anal indiscipline into adult life. The original person, in adulthood, thus often likes things messy, at least at first; the tendency is toward a final order, but the necessary preliminary is as big a mess as possible. Viewed developmentally, the rejection of externally imposed control at the anal stage is later generalized to all external control of impulse, with the tendency toward socially unlicensed phallic activity, or phallic exhibitionism in its more derivative forms, being simply another expression of the general rejection of regulation of impulse by others, in favor of regulation of impulse by oneself.

The disposition toward originality may thus be seen as a highly organized mode of responding to experience, including other persons, society, and oneself. The socially disrated traits which may go along with it include rebelliousness, disorderliness, and exhibitionism, while the socially valued traits which accompany it include independence of judgment, freedom of expression, and novelty of construction and insight.

Summary

This research was directed first of all toward identifying individuals who performed consistently in a relatively more or relatively less original way. The *S*s were 100 captains in the United States Air Force, who took part in three days of living-in assessment at the house of the Institute of Personality Assessment and Research. Originality was defined in terms of uncommonness of response to eight tests which could be scored objectively or rated reliably. To be called original, a response had to be uncommon in the sample under study, and at the same time be adequate to the realistic demands of the problem situations. For the most part, the eight tests proved to be significantly correlated with one another and with an over-all staff rating of Originality based on observation of the Ss through three days of social interaction.

Two groups of Ss, the regularly original and the regularly unoriginal, were then defined, and were used to test a set of five major hypotheses which generated 15 predictions concerning originality and which were suggested by previous findings from studies of independence of judgment and of the preference for complexity as opposed to simplicity. Twelve of the predictions were confirmed. Originality was found to be related to independence of judgment, to personal complexity, and to the preference for complexity in phenomena, to self-assertion and dominance, and finally to the rejection of suppression as a mechanism for the control of impulse.

References

1. BARRON, F. Some personality correlates of independence of judgment. *J. Pers.,* 1953, **21,** 287–297.

2. ——— Complexity-simplicity as a personality dimension. *J. abornm. soc. Psychol.,* 1953, **48,** 163–172.

3. BARRON, F., & WELSH, G. S. Artistic perception as a factor in personality style: its measurement by a figure-preference test. *J. Psychol.,* 1952, **33,** 199–203.

4. GOUGH, H. G. *A preliminary guide for the use and interpretation of the California Psychological Inventory.* Berkeley: Research Bull. Institute of Personality Assessment & Research, 1954.

5. GUILFORD, J. P., WILSON, R. C., CHRISTENSEN, P. R., & LEWIS, D. J. *A factor-analytic study of creative thinking: I. Hypotheses and description of tests.* Los Angeles: University of Southern California, 1951, Psychol. Lab., No. 3.

6. GUILFORD, J. P., WILSON, R. C., & CHRISTENSEN, P. R. *A factor-analytic study of creative thinking: II. Administration of tests and analysis of results.* Los Angeles: University of Southern California, 1952, Psychol. Lab., No. 8.

7. HATHAWAY, S. R., & McKINLEY, J. C. *Manual for the Minnesota Multiphasic Personality Inventory.* Minneapolis: Univer. of Minnesota Press, 1943.

8. KROUT, M. H., & TABIN, J. K. Measuring personality in developmental terms. *Genetic Psychol. Mongr.,* in press.

9. MURRAY, H. A. *Thematic Apperception Test Manual.* Cambridge, Mass., Harvard Univer. Printing Office, 1943.

10. RORSCHACH, H. *Psychodiagnostics.* Bern: Huber, New York: (Grune and Stratton, Distributors), 1942.

11. STRONG, E. K., JR. *Vocational Interest Blank for Men.* Palo Alto: Stanford Univer. Press, 1938.

THEMATIC DRIVE CONTENT AND CREATIVITY   Fred Pine

The processes involved in the creation of artistic and scientific productions, as well as the personal characteristics of the creator, are subjects of increasing scientific interest. The present study deals with variations in the ways in which drive-related content is used in the imaginative literary and scientific productions of a group of college students. The findings are suggestive regarding some of the differing personal characteristics of individuals who create high, rather than low, quality productions, and permit inferences to some of the processes involved in creative activity. The study also concerns the degree to which individual tendencies to give high or low quality productions are generalized over a variety of tasks.

Psychoanalytic theorists have long emphasized the role of primary process modes of thinking in creative activity. Primary process is characterized by non-logical forms of thought (notably condensation, displacement, and symbolization) and by drive direction and drive organization of thinking (Freud, 1900). In the act of creation, the creator temporarily gives up rational thinking and makes use of primary process; Kris (1952) termed this phenomenon "regression in the service of the ego." Although drive-directed thinking may thus characterize a phase of some creative processes it by no means follows that drive content necessarily appears in the final products of creative activity. The aim of the present study is to examine the modes of expression of drive content in completed productions and to study the relation of such expression to the quality of the production.

In a recent study (Barron, 1955) it was found that "original" people were characterized by expression rather than suppression of drives to a greater degree than were unoriginal people.[1] In the present study, Ss producing stories of higher literary quality were expected to express drive content more readily in them. Drive content appearing in a creative production is not per se a manifestation of primary process. In such productions, drive material is ordinarily subordinated to the requirements of esthetic value or scientific sense; in primary process, by contrast, drive expressions tend to dominate the cognitive activity. In a finished creative product drives appear in a secondary-process (logical, goal-directed) way. Their expression in creative productions implies that the individual maintains some degree of control over them. It is the ego control over drive expression in the creative process (Kris, 1952) which differentiates a socially valued creative production from a drive-laden and bizarrely original psychotic production.

Control over drive expression in a literary production could be reflected in the degree to which drive material is integrated into the product and in the degree to which it is altered from more primitive and blatant aggressive and sexual forms. These two forms of control were investigated. It was expected

---

[1] A similar finding was reported by J. Adelson in his paper on "Creativity and the dream" (Paper read at the Amer. Psychol. Ass., N. Y., Sept., 1957).

Reprinted by permission of the journal and author from the *Journal of Personality,* Vol. 27, 1957.

that Ss producing better stories would tend to integrate drive content more fully into their stories than Ss producing lower quality stories. The view that creative people were characterized both by drive expression and by drive control led to the further expectation that Ss producing better stories would express drive material more directly (undisguisedly) than other Ss, though still not in totally unsocialized ways. The relationship of drive expression and of these two forms of drive control to the quality of scientific productions in the present sample was also investigated.

The term "drive" is used throughout this paper in the psychoanalytic sense to refer to instinctual drives and their derivatives. This includes aggressive and libidinal drives and partial drives (oral, anal, phallic, genital, exhibitionistic, voyeuristic, sadistic, masochistic, homosexual, narcissistic). The terms "drive content" and "drive material" refer to observable ideational derivatives of the inferred aggressive and libidinal drives. These derivatives appear in the content of the specific responses that Ss gave to the various tests in the present study.

Method

Subjects. Ss were 13 male and 14 female undergraduates at a large urban university. They were a group of volunteers who were intensively studied through clinical and systematic research techniques by numerous investigators for about one year. Ss had been selected for a large research project on the basis of gross indications on the MMPI of emotional stability and average or better intelligence as measured by the Ohio State Psychological Examination. They had no particular excellence in creative arts or science nor, with two exceptions, did they have any professional commit-

ment to these areas. The present study focuses on six tests administered to all Ss:

Thematic Apperception Test. The Thematic Apperception Test (TAT) was used in investigating literary productions and drive content. Nine stories were considered here, those given to cards 1, 4, 11, 13MF, 16, 2, 18GF, 19, and 18BM (males) or 15 (females). The test was administered individually. Standard instructions were given and Ss were told to take about five minutes per story and, on card 11, to tell a fairytale such as one might tell a child. Stories were recorded verbatim, half of them tape-recorded and half of them written out by S. All stories were rated for literary quality, and all but the stories to TAT card 11 were rated for drive content (these were excluded because the special "fairytale" instruction set them apart somewhat from the other stories). Ratings for literary quality and for drive content are described in detail below.

The Science Test. The Science Test consisted of two problems, each posing a scientific dilemma which S was asked to resolve. One item (#2) was drive-related while the other was more drive-neutral. Ss were required to write out three different theories to account for each problem. Instructions were to make the theories complete and realistic (i.e., probable) and to use imagination in a down-to-earth scientific manner. There was no time limit. The Science Test called for skill in imaginative hypothesis formation; analysis and synthesis of information were only minimally required and testing of hypotheses was not required at all. The problems were as follows:

(1) A general idea of the way that coal forms is first that trees fall and decay;

then owing to certain upheavals of the earth, land gets on top of them and over time the pressure of the earth turns the original material into coal. Now, there are no trees in Antarctica. Yet, I want you to assume that coal has been found there. How could this be accounted for?

(2) It is known that the differentiation of male and female sexes came about fairly early in animal evolution. That is, even in the lower animals male and female sex organs are in different individuals—there are separate male and female sexes. Now, I want you to assume that recently a very advanced animal species, almost like the human species, has been found in which all individuals have both male and female sex organs. How could this be accounted for?

Responses were rated for the quality of the given theory and for drive content; ratings are described in detail below. Both the Science Test and the TAT were used to investigate relationships between the quality of imaginational production and the expression and control of drive material.

Additional tests. Four additional tests were administered to all Ss. Each permitted derivation of a score for imaginational excellence. In conjunction with the TAT and the Science Test, these were used to study cross-test consistencies in level of imaginational excellence.

The Humor Test consisted of 15 cartoons for which Ss invented captions. It was administered individually with no time limit. Ss were asked to write out responses and to make the captions as funny as possible.

The Consequences Test (Guilford, 1957) consists of four items, each describing some hypothetical event. S's task was to list possible consequences of the event.

The Brick Uses Test (Guilford, 1957) required Ss to list as many uses as possible for an ordinary brick.

The Animal Drawing required S to draw a "fantastic animal," making it as unusual as possible.

Results

LITERARY QUALITY AND DRIVE CONTENT

Ratings of literary quality. The TAT protocols were rated on 12 different aspects of the stories which were expected on a priori grounds to provide a fair sampling of the components of the over-all literary quality of a story. The twelve were: length, figures of speech, vocabulary, variety in sentence structure, naming characters, use of direct speech, characterization, time perspective, unity and continuity, genuineness, originality, and specification. Each was rated by one rater; five raters were used in all. Although it was necessary to use each rater for more than one rating, only ratings which were unlikely to be confused with one another (e.g., variety in sentence structure and characterization) were assigned to one rater. Ss were ranked on all 12 ratings. Over-all ranks were derived by summing the twelve ranks for each S and reranking the totals. These final scores were used for the data analysis throughout this paper and are considered the literary quality scores.[2]

[2] Initial evaluations of the TAT protocols had been made with global judgments of literary quality of stories. Four raters each rated the nine stories from each S; reliability of the average rating by the intraclass correlation technique was .94. Because of the possibility that these raters were influenced by S's handling of drive material in the stories, thus contaminating the literary quality and the drive ratings, the more specific analysis of story quality was undertaken. The ranking based upon the global judgments correlated (rho) .87 with the ranking based on the more detailed analysis. Furthermore, findings re-

Reliability of the final scores was determined by the intraclass correlation technique (Ebel, 1951) applied to the twelve discrete ratings; reliability is .82.

A manual was developed which outlined specific criteria for all ratings. Brief details of the twelve ratings are as follows. (*a*) *Length*. Average number of lines per story (counting until first inquiry question). (*b*) *Figures of speech*. Number of figures of speech (words or phrases used with nonliteral intention) per line of story. (*c*) *Vocabulary*. Average rating of "best" words in each story. One "best" word was selected for every five lines of story. Ratings of these words were on a three point scale from "excellent" to "ordinary." (*d*) *Variety in sentence structure*. Proportion of sentences which were structurally different from preceding sentence. A change from a simple to a complex sentence or from a declarative to an interrogative sentence would be counted, for example. (This was scored only for the four stories written out by *S:* TAT cards 2, 18GF, 19, and 18BM for males or 15 for females.) (*e*) *Naming characters*. Number of stories in which any characters were given names. (*f*) *Direct speech*. Number of stories in which direct speech (by characters in story) was used. (*g*) *Characterization*. Average number of characterizing statements about the main character in each story. Characterizing statements included traits (enduring qualities), characteristic (repeated) behavior, and statements about personality development. Transient moods, affects, and motives were excluded. (*h*) *Time perspective*. Average rating (on a four point scale) of time span of stories. Criteria were specified in detail. Ratings

garding correlations with drive material were substantially the same using the scores from either the global or the specific ratings.

ran from 4 for stories taking place in the immediate present (less than one hour) to a rating of 1 for stories with full development of at least two different time periods (of past, present, and future). (*i*) *Unity and continuity*. Average rating for all stories. Ratings ran from 4 for stories which were extremely disjointed or which had major elements missing to 1 for stories told in connected narrative fashion and which had some over-all integrating theme. (*j*) *Genuineness*. Average rating for all stories. Ratings ran from 4 for stories with major elements of "façade" to 1 where façade elements were absent and where *S* seemed truly task-involved. Façade elements included ostentatious use of language or special knowledge, facetious avoidance through silliness or bizarreness in the stories, and "pollyannaism" (superficial avoidance of sincere feelings, sticky-sweet sentiments, and the like). (*k*) *Originality*. Average rating for all stories. This rating was based on a normative definition of originality, using the "frequent plots" list in Henry's *Analysis of Fantasy* (1956) as a criterion. Ratings ran from 4 for stories which added nothing new to the frequent plots to 1 for stories with almost entirely unique content. (*l*) *Specification*. Average rating for all stories. Ratings ran from 4 for stories where vagueness and evasion were so dominant that the story never got going to 1 for stories which were specific throughout.

Ratings of drive content. Three kinds of ratings of drive content in the TAT were made: (*a*) presence or absence of drive, (*b*) level of directness-socialization of drive expression, (*c*) degree of integration of drive content.

The rating manual for (*a*) and (*b*) draws heavily upon one developed by Holt (1956) for rating drive content in the Rorschach test. As noted earlier, psychoanalytic theory provided the framework for rating drive material; aggressive and libidinal drive derivatives were rated. (*a*) *Presence:* Drive material was rated if it appeared at any point in *S*'s response to a TAT card except in response to a direct inquiry question. More than one rating could be given for each story. Drive content which was too far removed from aggressive or libidinal connections was not rated (gazing at scenery, friendship, achievement motivation), but more direct expressions were rated even if of minor importance in a story. (*b*) *Level:* Three levels of drive expression were distinguished. Level I included direct and unsocialized drive expression (murder, rape, alcoholism); level II included direct and socialized expression (love, anger, eating); level III included indirect or disguised expressions of relatively strong drive (accidental death, explosions). Context was always considered in rating drive level. (*c*) *Integration:* Again three degrees were distinguished. The TAT task is to tell a story about a picture. Drive material given other than in meeting this requirement was rated *nonappropriate* (unintegrated into the story); this category included drive-tinged slips and misperceptions, side comments and exclamations, and descriptive comments that were not included in the story. Appropriate drive material, that which is given as part of the story, was rated in one of two categories. *Thematic* integration was rated when the drive content was part of the main theme of the story. *Incidental* integration was rated when drive material was part of the story but irrelevant to its main theme. The rating manual defined and illustrated all rating categories.

The investigator and one other rater (both unaware of the literary quality scores) rated all stories. The proportions of interrater agreement on presence of drive material were 68 per cent and 70 per cent for males and females respectively. Agreement on level of expression and degree of integration was computed only when there was agreement on the presence of drive material. The proportion of agreement was 82 per cent for both males and females on level of expression and 91 per cent for males and 96 per cent for females on degree of integration. Disagreements were resolved by discussion between raters. *S*s were each given seven scores: total number of drive presence ratings, number of level I, level II, level III, thematic, incidental, and nonappropriate.

Results. Rank correlations were computed between literary quality on the one hand and each of the seven drive content scores listed above on the other. Kendall's tau (Siegel, 1956) was used in correlating quality with drive presence. Since this correlation was significant and since drive level and integration scores are obviously dependent upon total amount of drive present, total drive presence was held constant in all correlations between the quality score on the one hand and drive level and integration scores on the other. Kendall's partial tau (Siegel, 1956) was used. There is unfortunately no significance test for partial rank correlation but an approximation can be made from the nonpartial significance level using N minus 1 *df*. A partial correlation of .27 approximates the 5 per cent level of significance (two tail) and can be used for evaluating the correlations to be reported. Since statistical significance can only be approximated, it should also be noted for evaluating the findings that tau correlations are generally lower in absolute amount than Spearman's rho. All correlations are corrected for tied ranks. Results for males and females were similar and the reported results are based on the combined total sample of 27. Correlations are presented in Table 1.

TABLE 1. RANK CORRELATIONS BETWEEN LITERARY QUALITY AND THE HANDLING OF DRIVE MATERIAL IN THE STORIES

Drive	Correlations with Quality
1. Amount Present	.51
2. Level I Expression	−.10
3. Level II Expression	.01
4. Level III Expression ...	.36
5. Thematic Use of Drive .	.36
6. Incidental Use of Drive .	−.08
7. Nonappropriate Use of Drive	−.25

As indicated in row 1, literary quality and total drive presence were positively correlated ($p < .01$); higher quality stories tended to include more drive material.

Correlations between quality and level of drive expression are given in rows 2 to 4 of Table 1. The hypothesis that the direct expression of drive material with some control (level II, socialized drive expression) would be correlated with the quality scores is not confirmed. Only the correlation between quality and level III (indirect and disguised drive expression) is of substantial size (tau = .36; $p < .05$). This does not mean that Ss producing better stories did not express drive material directly; in fact all Ss tended to use level II drive expression primarily, level III somewhat less, and level I least. However, only level III expression varied with the literary quality scores. Ss producing better stories used

level II expression predominantly but in this they were no different from Ss giving poorer stories.

Correlations between quality and the degree of integration of drive material into the stories are presented in rows 5 to 7 of Table 1. Incidental use of drive material (part of story but incidental to main theme) is unrelated to the quality scores. However, literary quality is positively related to thematic use of drive material (part of the main theme of the story) and negatively related to nonappropriate use of drive material (extraneous to the story). Both correlations approximate the 5 per cent level of significance or better.[3] It is striking, furthermore, that Ss producing high quality stories used less nonappropriate drive material even though they introduced more drive material in total; the correlation between quality and nonappropriate use of drive material was −.19 even before partialling out total drive presence. These findings do not mean that Ss producing poorer stories used nonappropriate drive material instead of thematic drive material; only 11 of the 113 instances of use of drive content were nonappropriate in the one-third of the sample with poorest quality stories. Thus,

---

[3] The question arose whether these results were a function of a particular correlation between the drive integration scores and two components of the literary quality scores: (i) unity and continuity and (1) specification. These two bear on the "integrated" quality of the stories themselves and might contribute to contamination between the variables. The data were analyzed to examine this point. While there *was* a significant correlation between the drive integration scores and each of these components of literary quality taken alone, removing the two from the over-all literary quality score and reanalyzing the data for the remaining ten components of literary quality produced no change in the pattern or level of correlations reported in Table 1.

nonappropriate use of drive material was relatively rare for all Ss. Ss who told poorer stories used less drive content in total and a relatively greater proportion of nonappropriate drive content (10 per cent in the low one-third of the sample and only 2 per cent in the high one-third). Ss telling better stories, in contrast, used more drive content in total, and a higher proportion of well integrated drive content (91 per cent in the high one-third and 84 per cent in the low one-third).

At a theoretical level, Hartmann's (1955) concept of "neutralization" of drive energies is useful in making sense of the correlation between literary quality and drive presence. Ss who produced higher quality productions were able to divert drive energies into the constructive ego activity involved in creating a story rather than discharging all such drive energies in the direct pursuit of libidinal and aggressive goals. A comparable finding has recently been reported by Eiduson.[4] The relationship between quality and the integration of drive material in appropriate ways bears some similarity to "regression in the service of the ego," the concept which Kris (1952) used to describe the controlled use of drive involved in creativity. Present findings differ from Kris's formulation in that they concern controlled expressions of drive material in a relatively finished product while Kris's concept refers to early stages in the intrapsychic processes of creativity. If the Ss' productions here be viewed as projections of personality, however, it is possible to infer from these productions to an intrapsychic availability of drive material

which can be expressed with some control in appropriate (here creative) contexts. There may thus be a similarity in the processes involved in creative activity in the present group of college students and in the more creative persons whom Kris discussed.

One variant pattern in the relation of quality of production to drive integration is of interest. Some Ss who utilized a fair amount of drive material and who rather consistently used it with adequate control were nonetheless ranked low in literary quality. This, as well as the modest size of the obtained correlations, emphasizes that the manner in which drive material is handled is certainly not the only determinant of story quality or of creative activity. Such factors as intellectual capacity, sensory sensitivity, social receptivity, and family culture also play a part. A negative constellation of such factors, as well as particular kinds of drive dynamics, may underlie the incapacity of uncreative individuals to use creative expression as a controlled outlet for drive material.

DRIVE CONTENT AND THE
SCIENCE TEST

Ratings of quality of theory. Evaluations of the quality of responses to the Science Test took account of general modes of scientific thinking reflected in the response and also of the specific hypotheses advanced by Ss. Parsimony of hypotheses, use of known facts, a questioning attitude, specification as opposed to vagueness of ideas, and the use of rational rather than magical explanatory concepts were all considered.

A manual describing and illustrating a four point rating scale was devised; the four possible ratings were that the given theory was (a) adequate, (b) adequate with some weaknesses, (c) inade-

---

[4] Eiduson, Bernice T. Artist and research scientist: A comparative study. Paper read at Amer. Psychol. Ass., Washington, D. C., Sept., 1958.

quate but with saving graces, and (*d*) inadequate. The investigator and one other rater rated all responses. Since the responses of some Ss had been used in developing the manual, interrater reliability was computed for only the remaining Ss (eight males and ten females). Spearman rho between scores derived from each rater's ratings was .89 for males and .62 for females. Disagreements were resolved and final scores derived by discussion between the two raters. This evaluation of the quality of scientific hypothesis formation, based on only two items, is somewhat unreliable; findings are regarded as suggestive only. The internal consistency of the test (inter-item rho on the quality scores is —.18) is nil, and findings are presented for each item separately.

Ratings of drive content. A manual for rating drive content in the Science Test, similar to the one for the TAT, was developed. Drive presence and level of expression ratings were based on principles identical with those described for the TAT. Ratings of degree of integration paralleled those for the TAT but had to be adapted for the Science Test. The task was to give three different realistic theories to resolve the scientific problem. Drive material given other than in meeting these requirements was rated nonappropriate; this included drive-tinged slips, drive content repeated in identical theories (not "different"), and drive material appearing in intentionally unrealistic theories (fantasy, humor). Appropriate drive material was again rated either thematic (essential to the theory) or incidental (distant background, secondary consequences, alternative hypotheses). Raters, reliability procedures, and final score derivations were identical with those described above

for the TAT; because the manual was based on examination of some protocols, reliability was computed for a sample of eight males and ten females. Proportions of interrater agreement, computed separately by sex, item, and kind of rating, ranged from 66 per cent to 100 per cent and averaged 84 per cent.

Results. Rank correlations were computed between the quality scores and the drive content scores. Correlations be-

TABLE 2. RANK CORRELATIONS BETWEEN ADEQUACY OF THEORIES AND THE HANDLING OF DRIVE MATERIAL IN THE SCIENCE TEST

	CORRELATIONS WITH QUALITY IN:	
DRIVE	Item II (drive)	Item I (neutral)
Amount Present ...	.34	.08
Level II Expression .	—.02	...
Level III Expression .	...	.11
Thematic Use of Drive	.43	.04

tween the quality scores and total drive presence were again carried out with Kendall's tau; drive presence was partialled out on all other correlations between quality and the drive content scores. Because there was relatively little drive content in responses to the single items of the Science Test (as compared to the nine TAT stories), there was very little score variation on some of the drive content scores; level I expression and nonappropriate use of drive content, for example, were rated too rarely to permit statistical analysis. All correlations which could be computed are reported in Table 2.

There is a strong correspondence between the results with science item II which is drive related (bisexual animal) and results with the TAT. Total drive content is positively associated with adequacy of the theories ($p < .02$). In addition, the tendency to use drive material with maximal (thematic) appropriateness by incorporating it into the core of the theory is also positively associated with adequacy of the given theories ($p < .01$). As in the TAT, the relationship between level II drive expression and the quality score on the Science Test was negligible; almost all Ss tended to use mainly level II expression (direct-socialized) for this problem.

The results with the neutral science item (item I, coal formation) are quite different. Here, all correlations between drive content and adequacy of theories are negligible.

These results suggest that the handling of drive material is involved in scientific thinking in areas where drive content and the content of scientific thought are closely related. It may be, for example, that the scientist dealing with sexual topics in biology or psychology would find his thinking disrupted by anxiety or limited by constricting defenses unless he had adequate access to and control over those of his own impulses that are related to his work. On the other hand, the present results with the more drive-neutral item show no clearcut relationships between quality of a scientific production and the use of drive material where drives are not specifically implicated in the problem. In a normal sample, where impulses are under at least fair control, the external demand for the expression of drive material was thus a critical factor in determining whether either intrusive or adaptive drive expressions emerged in a reality-oriented task.

CONSISTENCIES IN QUALITY OF IMAGINATIONAL PRODUCTIONS

The degree of crosstest consistency in the quality of imaginational productions was investigated. In addition to the scores for the TAT and the Science Test, quality scores were derived for the remaining four tests.

The quality scores on the Humor Test were defined in terms of humorousness of response, rated on an eight point scale. Five raters rated all captions given by the female Ss, and seven raters rated those of the male group. Each rater's fifteen ratings for each S were summed to give a final score. Interrater agreement by the intra-class correlation technique was .86 for the males and .87 for the females.

Ratings of the Consequences Test were based on Guilford's (1957) manual which gives a score having high loading on his originality factor. The proportion of agreement between two raters was 86 per cent (based on a sample of 19 Ss).

For the Brick Uses Test, Guilford's (1957) scoring manual permits derivation of a score having high loading on his spontaneous flexibility factor. The proportion of interrater agreement was 89 per cent.

Two judges ranked the Animal Drawings for originality. Agreement was low (rho .29 for males and .42 for females). Disagreements were discussed until a final ranking was achieved.

Spearman rank correlations were computed between all pairs of tests on the quality scores (literary and scientific quality, humorousness, originality, flexibility). Correlations were corrected for tied ranks when indicated. Results are presented in Table 3.

It can be seen that, while the stronger correlations between pairs of quality scores were all positive, there are several negative correlations. There is some, though slight, individual consistency in quality of performance on the several tests; different aspects of imaginational productivity appear to be tapped by the various tests. Differences in kinds of low-quality output were apparent in the contrast between Ss whose productions were generally of poor quality and those who did poorly only when drive material was demanded by the task (as in TAT card

ented forms of scientific thinking, are likely to be more like the imaginative literary productions of the TAT than productive scientific thinking would ordinarily be. For item II, a further similarity is that drive material enters in strongly, as it does in storytelling.

Discussion

The present study gives empirical evidence of relationships between drive dynamics and quality of literary productivity. Particular ways of handling drive material in created products were found

TABLE 3. RANK CORRELATIONS BETWEEN QUALITY SCORES IN PAIRS OF TESTS

Test	Science II (drive)	Science I (neutral)	Humor	Animal	Brick	Consequences
TAT	.61 *	.05	.37 *	.45 *	−.03	.16
Science II	...	−.18	.23	.12	.06	.10
Science I		.....	−.24	.13	.16	−.02
Humor			.....	.36 *	.03	.25
Animal				...	.35 *	.07
Brick					.....	.59 *

* Significant at 10 per cent level or better (two-tailed test).

13MF or the bisexual animal problem). Some Ss, on the other hand, improved when drive material was demanded; a freeing as opposed to a constricting influence of drives on the imaginational process is suggested here. A further contrast was between Ss who did well on all tests and those whose high-quality performance was circumscribed in one area; breadth of imaginational excellence is a significant dimension of individual difference.

The large correlation between the TAT and Science item II points up that the two have some things in common. Responses to the Science Test, involving imaginative hypothesis formation rather than more analytic and empirically ori-

to be related to quality of production in the literary task under consideration. There was more drive material in productions rated as of high quality and it was more consistently controlled than was true of productions low in quality. Control may be of more than one kind. In the highly rated productions, control over drive material took the form of successful integration of drive material into the production. Controls involving the modulation of drive material were also related to the quality dimension. These relationships between quality and drives tended to hold up in a test of scientific hypothesis formation only when the scientific problem involved drive-related content. Individuals were only moderately consistent in the quality of their productions across several areas of imagination.

The relation between creativity and drives warrants further comment. The creative person in either literature or science may be described as one with a heightened receptivity to thought contents which can be molded into a creative production. Jones (1956) described the skepticism and credulousness of scientific geniuses and related the latter to the "receptive nature of genius." He suggests a parallel between receptiveness to external stimuli and "openmindedness towards the ideals pressing forward from the preconscious and ultimately from the id" (Jones, 1956, p. 30). The greater use of drive material by Ss in the present study who produced higher quality stories suggests greater receptivity to drive derivatives. The availability of appropriately controlled drive content has significance for much literary productivity; for example, for the writer to draw upon in describing the motivations of his characters. Availability of well controlled drive material also has significance for scientific creativity when the external problem demands that drive-related concepts and hypotheses be generated by the individual from his own thought contents. Receptivity to external stimuli, which is of great significance for scientific creativity, is also likely to be important in literary creativity.

The genetic roots of a receptivity–creativity relationship may lie in individual structural differences in sensory, motor, and memory apparatuses producing differential capacities to "receive" experiences (from within or without) and thereafter to put them to creative use (cf. Rapaport, 1954). One may speculate, further, that an early developed need to defend against drive content in thought may spread to a generalized tendency to limit thinking; dynamically, anxiety over an encounter with drive material when thought is given free rein may underlie unreceptivity to experience from within or without.

These theoretical suggestions are limited here to literary and some aspects of scientific productions. Both of these tasks as given to the present Ss were similar in requiring a somewhat extended ideational production. Heightened receptivity to drive content may be of particular relevance to this kind of production. On the other hand, the processes involved in each of these two kinds of production are not likely to be identical. There may, for example, be a difference in the conditions of drive arousal; the arousal of drive material may be more often triggered off by an external problem in science and by internal dynamics in literary creativity; although this difference is unlikely to be absolute, some of the findings point in this direction. An essential similarity between the two areas was in the kind of integrating controls over drive material which was expressed.

Summary

The present paper described a study of relationships between the creative quality of imaginative productions on the one hand and the ways in which drive content appeared in these productions on the other. Ss were 27 male and female undergraduates. The principal sources of data were Ss' responses to two problems involving scientific hypothesis formation and stories told to nine TAT cards.

A central finding was that higher quality literary productions included more drive content than did lower quality productions; a similar result was found in scientific productions where drive content was evoked by the given problem. Furthermore, a positive correlation between controlled drive expression and quality of production was also found; controls involved modulation of the directness of drive expression and integration of drive content into the created product. Poorer quality story productions included a greater proportion of nonappropriate (unintegrated) drive content. Individual consistencies in quality of created products tended to be positive, though not consistently so, in the several areas tested.

Inferences were made regarding some of the personal characteristics of more creative individuals, and findings were discussed in terms of the processes involved in creative activity.

References

BARRON, F. The disposition toward originality. *J. abnorm. soc. Psychol.,* 1955, **51,** 478–485.

EBEL, R. L. Estimation of the reliability of ratings. *Psychometrika,* 1951, **16,** 407–424.

FREUD, S. *The interpretation of dreams.* New York: Basic Books, 1955. (Original German edition, 1900.)

GUILFORD, J. P., *et al.* A factor-analytic study of flexibility in thinking. *Rep. psychol. Lab.,* Univer. Sth. Calif., 1957, No. 18.

HARTMANN, H. Comments on the psychoanalytic theory of the ego. In Ruth Eissler *et al.* (Eds.), *The psychoanalytic study of the child.* Vol. 5. New York: International Univer. Press, 1955.

HENRY, W. E. *The analysis of fantasy.* New York: Wiley, 1956.

HOLT, R. R. Gauging primary and secondary processes in Rorschach responses. *J. proj. Tech.,* 1956, **20,** 14–25.

JONES, E. The nature of genius. In *Four centenary addresses.* New York: Basic Books, 1956.

KRIS, E. *Psychoanalytic explorations in art.* New York: International Univer. Press, 1952.

RAPAPORT, D. The autonomy of the ego. In R. P. Knight and C. R. Friedman (Eds.), *Psychoanalytic psychiatry and psychology.* New York: International Univer. Press, 1954.

SIEGEL, S. *Nonparametric statistics.* New York: McGraw-Hill, 1956.

CREATIVE ABILITIES IN THE ARTS   J. P. Guilford

In 1950, the writer set forth some hypotheses concerning the component abilities that were believed to be needed to account for creativity (1). These hypotheses were developed by way of preparation for systematic studies of this

Reprinted by permission of the American Psychological Association and the author from the *Psychological Review,* Vol. 64, 1957.

phenomenon by a combination of experimental and factor-analytic approaches. In order to complete the setting of these studies, which is important in preparation for some of the things to follow, something must be said about the scope of the studies of creativity.

The aptitudes project has not been confined to the study of creativity, but has investigated all types of thinking abilities, including also those traditionally known as reasoning abilities, and those we chose to include under the headings of planning and evaluation. This inclusiveness was fortunate, for we find that the whole area of thinking abilities or functions is rich with interrelations and parallels. The understanding of some parts of this total area is very helpful in understanding others.

On the other hand, the studies of creativity proper, up to the present, have been more limited than they might have been. In setting up hypotheses concerning the component abilities in creativity, we were guided mostly by the kinds of creative activity recognized as such in scientists, engineers, inventors, and in supervisory and administrative personnel; in other words, types of personnel that are of concern in the military setting. We did tolerate the general hypothesis that the abilities that make these kinds of personnel creative might be the same as those that make the painter, the composer, the writer, and others creative, but we did not reject the contrary hypothesis, for we had no basis for doing so. To be sure, it would be a simpler outcome to find that the same qualities of fluency, flexibility, and originality, for example, account for performances of artists and scientists alike. But in our research we have never been very strongly influenced by the goal of simplicity. We have seen that all too often the compulsion of this goal has been unfortunately restricting of the investigator's outlook.

We did favor the notion that creativity, whatever its range of application, is by no means a unity but is rather a collection of different component abilities or other traits. Our results have definitely supported this general point of view. They also suggest the hypothesis

that in the areas of the performances of the graphic artist and the composer, at least, we shall find new factors; factors that are distinct from those that are important in creativity of scientists, technologists, and managers, yet that are parallel to them. It is from the information concerning abilities that we have already investigated that we can deduce something about creative abilities that we should find to be important in the arts. The artistic, creative abilities that I shall mention are thus mainly hypothetical, but I should say that there are better precedents for these hypotheses than for those presented in 1950. We have made a beginning toward relating some of the known factors to the art of writing. It is hoped that the presentation of the hypotheses in this article will stimulate other investigators to test them in connection with other arts as well.

In general, the support for the expected factors thought to be important in the arts lies in the systematic nature of the whole collection of thinking factors, also the memory factors. Enough of the thinking and memory factors are known for us to see the lines of a system. A conception of the entire collection of intellectual factors has been presented in a recent issue of the *Psychological Bulletin* (2). It will pay us to review briefly the features of that system that are relevant in support of factors that are predicted to be important in the arts.

The System of Intellectual Factors

One of the significant principles of the system is that the factors fall into three parallel groups, depending upon the kind of material involved in the activity. Let us think of them as being in three parallel columns. Psychologists have had a long-standing recognition that different abilities are involved in verbal tests on the one hand and nonverbal tests on the other. In nonverbal tests the psychological material dealt with by the examinee is in the form of figures, letters, numbers, or other symbols. Our project results show that we must make a further distinction within the nonverbal area. The consequence is that the intellectual factors tend to come in groups of three parallel abilities or traits. For example, there are three abilities for seeing relationships between things. One of them applies to relations between perceived figures. A second has to do with relations between meanings or concepts. There is a third relations-seeing factor that has to do with the ability to see relationships between such materials as letters, numbers, or other simple symbols. In the latter case, it is neither their figural nor their meaning properties that determine the relationships; it is some other property. We have called this category of factors the "structural" group. In everyday life, the structural type of thinking is perhaps most evident in mathematics. It does not appear that the structural factors have much significance for the arts, as such, and that we shall have to look for the significant artistic abilities among the figural and conceptual factors.

One or two additional comments will help to show just where the artistic-creative factors fit into the general scheme of intellect. The thinking factors seem to fall into three general groups of another kind, in a cross classification. This grouping is based upon the kind of *action* performed. There is a group of *cognition* factors, a group of *production* factors, and a group of *evaluation* factors. We become aware of the things with which we are confronted; we produce something of our own in response to that awareness, or something that it

calls for; and we evaluate our products of thought. A total creative act involves all three aspects—cognition, production, and evaluation. A schematic view of all the classes of intellectual factors is shown in Figure 1.

In view of the active nature of creative performances, the production aspects or steps are most conspicuous and probably most crucial. Among the productive-thinking abilities another logical distinction appears. With some productive-thinking factors, and the tests that measure them, thinking must at some time converge toward one right answer;

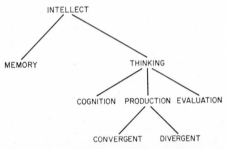

Fig. 1. Diagram of the major categories of intellectual factors and their logical relationships.

the significant type of thinking involved has been called "convergent" thinking. With other productive-thinking factors and their tests, thinking need not come out with a unique answer; in fact, going off in different directions contributes to a better score in such tests. This type of thinking and these factors come under the heading of "divergent" thinking. It is in divergent thinking that we find the most obvious indications of creativity.

This does not mean that convergent thinking and divergent thinking never occur together. They frequently do, in a total act of problem solving. Creative steps are necessary in solving new problems. Actually, we can hardly say there is a problem unless the situation presents the necessity for new production of some kind. Factors are abstractions of components from total activities. Some of the components are recognized as being more creative than others, for example, qualities of fluency, flexibility, and originality. These come under the category of the divergent-thinking aspect. While they may contribute toward reaching one right answer where that is demanded, they are more obvious in activities where this is not the case. In the arts there is usually *no* one right answer. Some answers are regarded as merely better than others. There is a matter of evaluation.

Let us consider the fluency factors first. Two of them, *word fluency* and *associational fluency,* have to do with the production of single words. Tests of *word fluency* are best characterized by the fact that the words produced must meet specified structural requirements, such as listing words beginning with a certain letter or words ending in a certain suffix. Meanings or concepts are of no importance. The *word-fluency* factor thus falls in the structural column. Parallel to it, the *associational-fluency* factor is measured by tests that involve listing words having some meaningful require-

TABLE 1. A TABLE OF THE PRODUCTIVE-THINKING FACTORS OF THE DIVERGENT-THINKING TYPE

Type of Result Produced	Type of Content		
	Figural	Structural	Conceptual
Words		*Word Fluency*	*Associational Fluency*
Ideas			*Ideational Fluency*
Expression			*Expressional Fluency*
Shifts	*Flexibility of Closure*	*Adaptive Flexibility*	*Spontaneous Flexibility*
Novel responses			*Originality*
Details	*Elaboration* *		*Elaboration* *

* At present regarded as the same factor, but future results may indicate two separate factors.

Fluency Factors

Let us consider first the potential factors in the more obvious creative areas of fluency, flexibility, and originality. Our project results thus far have clearly indicated four fluency factors, two flexibility factors, and one originality factor. For the most part, our tests of these factors fall into the conceptual column. Table 1 is given to show the whole matrix of productive-thinking factors and their interrelationships.

ment, such as listing synonyms or opposites for a stimulus word. To complete this triad of factors, there should be one involving the production of letter combinations that satisfy certain *figural* requirements, such as the activity of producing monograms or other artistic effects with words.

The factor of *ideational fluency* stands alone at present in another incomplete triad. It is the ability to produce rapidly a succession of ideas meeting certain meaningful requirements. The number of words produced in each response may be one or several. For example, tests of this factor may call for the listing of things round, of ideas about a man going up a ladder, of titles for a story plot, or of predictions of consequences of events. Quantity is important but quality is not.

A parallel factor in the figural column would be an ability to produce a variety of artistic ideas in limited time. Rough ideas for themes, rough sketches, and the like would be sufficient output so far as this ability is concerned. At this point we must face a question that has general significance, beyond the *ideational-fluency* areas. This is the question whether ability to produce numerous ideas in the graphic arts is the same as the ability to do so in music.

There is a precedent at one place in the system of intellectual factors for a distinction between visual and auditory functions. This occurs among the memory factors. We have an apparent triad of memory factors in all of which the learning and retention of associative connections between contents is the important thing, and a second triad in which memory for the contents themselves is essential. In the latter triad, there is an ability to remember the substance of meaningful verbal material. Parallel to it are two factors, rather than one, having to do with remembering substance in figural form. There is a factor of *visual* memory, and this is separate from a factor of *auditory memory*. The latter involves memory for such things as melodies and rhythms. We may regard melodies and rhythms as auditory figures.

The separation of two figural-memory factors, visual and auditory, suggests that a similar distinction may be found elsewhere in the system, and hence possibly

in the area of the production of figural ideas. This would mean that the ability to produce ideas in the graphic arts is distinct from the ability to produce ideas in music. With this separation of factors, we should have four ideational-fluency factors, not forgetting the one in the structural column, rather than the one factor already known. There could even be a fifth ideational-fluency factor connected with the kinesthetic sense, also in the figural column. This ability would presumably be of importance to the successful choreographer or creative acrobat.

The fourth known fluency factor is called *expressional fluency*. Thus far confined to verbal tests, this factor is recognized as an ability to put ideas into words. Tests requiring the putting of words together in appropriate, connected discourse are best measures of the factor. The distinction of this factor from *ideational fluency* is support for the common observation that it is one thing to have an idea and it is something else to be able to put it into words.

Three of the known fluency factors should go a long way to account for talent for writing. *Ideational fluency* should give the writer something to write about; *expressional fluency* should enable him to put it into appropriate words; and *associational fluency* should help to find words with the right shadings of meanings without the help of word-finding aids.

Is it likely that there are factors to complete a triad of expressional factors? The concept of expression is surely not foreign to the arts. Having a graphic or a musical idea is short of the total creative production. Putting the idea into appropriate organizations of figural material would be necessary to complete the process. And possibly, again, we shall find that expression in graphic form depends upon a different ability than expression in musical form, just as both differ from expression in verbal form.

A general conception of creativity that calls for so many distinctions and separations of function may be somewhat surprising to readers. Why, after all, should there not be much in common between having ideas in the graphic arts, in music, and in writing? Why should there not be much in common in expressing ideas in the different media?

Notice that I have referred to such abilities as being distinct; not necessarily as being independent or uncorrelated. I suspect that there *is* something in common among parallel factors. This should not preclude their statistical and experimental separation, provided that performances of these different kinds or with different materials are not perfectly correlated when correction is made for unreliability. I suggest that we proceed to find out whether the factors are statistically separable and, if so, whether they separate along the line hypothesized or along some other lines. Then we can more appropriately raise the question about their interrelationships.

There is some evidence from everyday observation to lend support to the separateness of the expressive abilities. For example, the production of a popular song often involves the collaboration of a composer and a lyricist. To be sure, some individuals do both successfully. Actually, the correlation could be zero between these two performances, and yet there would be by chance *some* individuals who show high status in both respects. The production of a motion picture, in which musical, graphic, and conceptual ideas are commonly expressed in blended combination, is a synthetic task of specialists, just as, more and

more, even single cinema characters represent synthetic blends of talents of different performers.

Flexibility Factors

The two flexibility factors that we have found differ in more than one respect. One difference is that one factor is found in verbal tests and the other mostly in nonverbal tests. One therefore belongs in the conceptual column and the other in the structural column, or possibly it cuts across structural and figural columns; we are not sure. The other difference is in the role that each factor plays or the degree of compulsion vs. freedom involved.

The conceptual-flexibility factor is called *spontaneous flexibility* because the examinee shows flexibility on his own initiative; the test items do not necessarily require it. It is possible that this quality is a temperamental trait or a motivational trait rather than an ability; a disposition to avoid repeating oneself, or an urge to vary one's behavior. If this is true, the trait might be accounted for under the Hullian concept of "reactive inhibition," or under the concept of a general psychological refractory phase, or under the concept of satiation. Being quite general in its determination of behavior, such a trait might serve as the basis for very fanciful, creative imagination wherever it is found, for example, in artist and scientist alike.

The other factor in this area we have called *adaptive flexibility,* because it is important in the solution of problems—particularly those that require the discarding of familiar or habitual methods and striking out in new and unusual directions. We have more recently expected to find three factors of this kind, but thus far have not found them, probably because our test variations have been inadequate to effect their separation. To the extent that there are problems involved in the arts, this kind of ability or trait would seem to play a significant role. It remains to be seen whether an adaptive-flexibility factor that is unique to figural material is required.

Originality

The one factor of *originality* seems to be rather general, in one sense at least. That is; it is indicated by varied tests; tests that require unusual or uncommon responses, remote associations or connections, or clever responses. The use of an unusual variety of tests has provided much opportunity for a separation into two or more originality factors along the lines of such differences. All the tests have been verbal, or have involved verbal meanings in some way. We have as yet provided no opportunity for finding a triad of originality factors, distinguished along the lines of the materials involved.

There is a possibility that the factor of *originality* will prove to be fundamentally a temperamental or motivational variable. For example, it might be a general set to be unconventional or to avoid repeating what other individuals do. A single trait of this kind could be expected to cut across material categories. There would then be one originality factor; not a triad. Some of our future research will be directed along these lines with regard to originality as well as with regard to flexibility.

We have already made a beginning toward relating fluency, flexibility, and originality factors to temperamental and motivational variables. At present, it does not appear that any of them can be accounted for on the basis of such non-aptitude variables as we are exploring

in this connection. This leaves the way clear for testing the hypothesis that there are complete triads of factors in these three areas.

Other Factors Related to Creativity

In 1950, in addition to factors of fluency, flexibility, and originality, it was hypothesized that there would be an ability to see problems, an ability to analyze, an ability to synthesize, and an ability to redefine or reorganize objects of thought. The hypotheses concerning analyzing ability and synthesizing ability were rather decisively discredited by the results. In spite of the opportunities for such unitary abilities to make themselves known, they failed to appear. This does not mean that, in thinking, no such activities as analyzing and synthesizing take place, for too many activities can be described as such. The unitary abilities that individuals have in common and that have a bearing upon success, however, are better described otherwise. This kind of conclusion is not unique. No one would deny that we indulge in activities that are properly called thinking, and yet there is no generalized unitary ability to think. There are many thinking abilities, as previous discussion has demonstrated. An all-too-common error in psychology has been to assume that because a range of phenomena can be subsumed under a single name there is therefore a unitary function. Every such assumption must be tested by empirical procedures.

A factor was found that could be defined as the ability to see problems. It is a cognition factor rather than a production factor. It proved to be much less general than was originally expected, being confined to seeing defects and deficiencies in such practical matters as everyday gadgets and implements and in social institutions and practices. The tests that measure the factor have been exclusively verbal. Will the use of comparable nonverbal tests give us completion of a triad of problem-seeing factors? This hypothesis should be tested. To the extent that the artist has problems, we may suppose that there are individual differences in ability to recognize them. The problem might be in the form of the need for a theme or a particular kind of theme, or in the form of expression or treatment, or in the use of techniques and implements. Among these would be problems involving figural properties of things. The triad hypothesis would lead us to expect little correlation between the ability to detect *such* problems and the ability to detect the kind represented in verbal tests.

The factor of redefinition involves the ability to desert one interpretation or conception of use of an object, or part of an object, and to adapt it to some new function or use. For example, the cover glass of a watch can be removed and used as a condensing lens to start a fire. How readily can the individual arrive at such a transformation? How good is he at improvising in similar situations in general? This variable is a divergent-thinking factor that involves the production of a shift of meaning of an object. Are there parallel factors involved anywhere in the arts?

Actually, there is a factor of *visualization,* which seems to be to the figural column what *redefinition* is to the conceptual column. The factor of *visualization* is the ability to think of changes or transformations of a figural kind in visually perceived objects, or in objects visually thought of. The relation of such an ability to work in the visual arts can be readily imagined. There might even be such a factor in the auditory field, enabling a composer or arranger to produce variations on a theme with changes in use of phrases so radical that they take on new values or functions.

A factor of evaluative ability was hypothesized, not as a contributor to the production of creative results but as a means of determining whether such results are good, suitable, correct, or adequate. In our investigation of this area of thinking, we gave ample opportunity for more than one evaluative-ability factor to emerge. There are different bases or criteria by which a product is judged. One is its logical consistency with known facts. Another is its less-than-logical consistency with other experiences. There are also different kinds of products to be judged, depending upon the kind of materials involved. We included tests with both figural and verbal material. At the time of the study of evaluative abilities, the third category of structural materials had not yet been recognized.

We found three general evaluation factors. *Logical evaluation* is an ability to judge products on the basis of their logical consistency with given facts. A factor called *experiential evaluation* seemed to fit the picture of an ability to judge products in terms of consistency with past experiences. In the interpretation of this factor, if the emphasis is placed upon ability to make use of past experiences in the act of judging, it could be a rather general ability. If, however, emphasis is placed upon the past experiences, we face the real possibility of many common factors of this kind, depending upon the more or less coherent bodies of information that people acquire, for example, mechanical, mathematical, and so on. As for the rest, the use of experience would be a rather specific matter.

A third factor, which was called *perceptual evaluation,* is of uncertain generality. It can readily be hypothesized that there are as many perceptual-evaluation factors as there are coherent areas of perceptual functioning. The variety of psychophysical judgments is, of course, almost unlimited. The tests that defined our *perceptual-evaluation* factor emphasized comparisons of lengths of lines and total sizes of figures. The factor we found may therefore have been the more limited *length-estimation* factor that was previously known.

The whole area of evaluative abilities is still largely unexplored. I have hinted that we may expect to find a very large number of rather narrow evaluative-ability factors. As for evaluation in the arts, presumably the *logical-evaluation* factor would not apply. Experiential-evaluation abilities might account for aesthetic tastes in terms of aesthetic values. Perceptual-evaluation abilities would have much bearing on the acceptability of art forms, visual, auditory, or kinesthetic. They would perhaps be numerous and also generally of narrow scope.

The factors mentioned thus far are those we originally regarded as belonging in the creative category. Recognizing that some aspects of planning are also creative, certain newly obtained factors in that area could also be regarded as creative. But as the system of the intellectual factors developed, cutting across our original categories of reasoning, creativity, and planning, these category concepts have shrunk in importance. Furthermore, it became more apparent that, in the creative activity of everyday life, other abilities than those regarded as primarily creative also play roles to some degree. For example, is it not likely that a large vocabulary is desirable for

the creative writer? Should not the developer of ideas in descriptive geometry be able to think readily in terms of visual-spatial arrangements? These two examples imply the usefulness of the factors known as *verbal comprehension* and *spatial orientation,* respectively. Norman C. Meier has also emphasized the finding that individuals with recognized artistic talents are unusually able to observe and to remember clearly things they perceive (3). This implies a high degree of the factor known as *visual memory,* an ability to remember visual content. The factor of *auditory memory* may play a similar role for the composer.

Thus, a great number of primary mental abilities that would not be regarded as creative abilities nevertheless play their roles at times in creative work. We might say that minimal levels of such abilities are desirable, if not necessary, for success in various artistic activities. We might say that to that extent these are necessary but not sufficient conditions for creative production. The factors of fluency, flexibility, and originality, and the like, are not only necessary but, when possessed in adequate amounts, are sufficient. All of this, of course, assumes adequate motivating conditions, also. In the process of surveying the resources of creative artists of any kind, therefore, whether this is for the sake of better understanding of talent or for the practical purposes of prediction and guidance, it would be well to ask whether any of the intellectual factors may play a significant role, and where and how, if so.

Summary

(1) It is hypothesized that creative artistic talent is not a unitary or uniform commodity but is to be accounted for in terms of a large number of factors or

primary mental abilities. From what is already known, we should expect that the creative abilities of artists will be found to involve some factors other than those among creative abilities in fields such as science and management.

(2) Of the known factors, certain ones, of fluency, flexibility, and originality, are the most obviously creative abilities. All of them come under a general class of factors known as productive-thinking abilities and in a subclass of divergent-thinking abilities.

(3) A developing system of all the intellectual factors indicates the relationships of the more creative factors to one another and to other factors. From certain relationships and parallels, unknown factors that are probably important in the arts can be hypothesized with some confidence.

(4) A full account of complete creative-artistic performance involves evaluative abilities and abilities that are not primarily creative, many of which are already known.

References

1. GUILFORD, J. P. Creativity. *Amer. Psychologist,* 1950, **5,** 444–454.
2. ——— The structure of intellect. *Psychol. Bull.,* 1956, **53,** 267–293.
3. MEIER, N. C. Factors in artistic aptitude: final summary of a ten-year study of a special ability. *Psychol. Monogr.,* 1939, **51,** 140–158.

THE ASSOCIATIVE BASIS OF THE CREATIVE PROCESS

Sarnoff A. Mednick

The intent of this paper is the presentation of an associative interpretation of the process of creative thinking. The explanation is not directed to any specific field of application such as art or science but attempts to delineate processes that underlie all creative thought.

The discussion will take the following form. (*a*) First, we will define creative thinking in associative terms and indicate three ways in which creative solutions may be achieved—serendipity, similarity, and mediation. (*b*) This definition will allow us to deduce those individual difference variables which will facilitate creative performance. (*c*) Consideration of the definition of the creative process has suggested an operational statement of the definition in the form of a test. The test will be briefly described along with some preliminary research results. (*d*) The paper will conclude with a discussion of predictions regarding the influence of certain experimentally manipulable variables upon the creative process.

Creative individuals and the processes by which they manifest their creativity have excited a good deal of interest and curiosity. There are extended analyses of novels and novelists, poems and poets, mathematics and mathematicians, both biographical and autobiographical. Perusal of the introspections of manifestly creative individuals uncovers a surprising vein of similarity in the processes they describe (Ghiselin, 1952). Thus we find Albert Einstein's self-searching to suggest that "The psychical entities which seem to serve as elements in thought are certain signs and more or less clear images which can be combined

. . . This combinatory play seems to be the essential feature in productive thought." Samuel Taylor Coleridge is described as having developed his ideas in the following manner: "Facts which sank at intervals out of conscious recollection drew together beneath the surface through the almost chemical affinities of common elements." In the field of art, we find André Brèton referring to a collage by Ernst as being distinguished by a "marvelous capacity to grasp two mutually distant realities without going beyond the field of our experience and to draw a spark from the juxtaposition." Most explicit, however, is the oft-quoted statement by the mathematician, Poincaré, who talks about an evening when "ideas rose in crowds; I felt them collide until pairs interlocked so to speak, making a stable combination. By next morning I had established the existence of a class of Fuchsian functions." From these experiences, Poincaré felt that he could state that "to create consists of making new combinations of associative elements which are useful. The mathematical facts worthy of being studied . . . are those which reveal to us unsuspected kinships between other facts well known but wrongly believed to be strangers to one another. Among chosen combinations the most fertile will often be those formed of elements drawn from domains which are far apart." An exceptionally compelling illustration of a useful combination of elements "drawn from domains which are far apart" occurs in a line from the poem, "The Monkey Puzzle" by Marianne Moore (1951), "The lion's ferocious chrysanthemum head."

We will state our basic hypothesis regarding the nature of creative thinking in the form of a definition. With these introspective statements serving as background, we may proceed to define the creative thinking process as the forming of associative elements into new combinations which either meet specified requirements or are in some way useful. The more mutually remote the elements of the new combination, the more creative the process or solution. An additional criterion of the level of creativeness of a product is described below.

Creative thinking as defined here is distinguished from original thinking by the imposition of requirements on originality. Thus, 7,363,474 is quite an original answer to the problem "How much is $12 + 12$?" However, it is only when conditions are such that this answer is useful that we can also call it creative. There are many original ideas expressed in institutions for the mentally ill and mentally retarded; few of these are likely to be creative. There are many fields of creative endeavor in which the usefulness of products would be difficult to measure reliably. While these difficulties must eventually be faced, for the present our research efforts have been concentrated on laboratory situations in which criteria for usefulness can be arbitrarily experimenter-defined and unequivocally explained to the subject. The originality of a response is simply inversely related to its probability in a given population.

It should be pointed out that this definition of creativity is quite similar to basic notions advanced by British associationists from Locke (1690) to Bain (1855), and by those psychologists whose work is based in large measure on their speculations. Freud (1938), Hollingsworth (1928), and Binet (1899) may serve as examples.

Ways of Achieving a Creative Solution

In terms of associative theory, we may point to three ways of achieving a creative solution. Generally, any condition or state of the organism which will tend to bring the requisite associative elements into ideational contiguity will increase the probability and speed of a creative solution. Therefore, the following three ways of attaining creative solutions are all methods of bringing the requisite associative elements together.

Serendipity. The requisite associative elements may be evoked contiguously by the contiguous environmental appearance (usually an accidental contiguity) of stimuli which elicit these associative elements. This sort of creative solution is often dubbed serendipitous. This is the manner of discovery to which is popularly attributed such inventions as the X-ray and such discoveries as penicillin. One physicist has described how he has reduced serendipity to a method by placing in a fishbowl large numbers of slips of paper, each inscribed with a physical fact. He regularly devotes some time to randomly drawing pairs of these facts from the fishbowl, looking for new and useful combinations. His procedure represents the operational embodiment of this method of achieving creative solutions.

Similarity. The requisite associative elements may be evoked in contiguity as a result of the similarity of the associative elements or the similarity of the stimuli eliciting these associative elements. This mode of creative solution may be encountered in creative writing which exploits homonymity, rhyme, and similarities in the structure and rhythm of words or similarities in the objects which they designate. The contiguous ideational occurrence of such items as alliterative and rhyming associates may be dependent on a factor such as primary stimulus generalization. It seems possible that this means of bringing

about contiguity of associational elements may be of considerable importance in those domains of creative effort which are less directly dependent on the manipulation of symbols. Here we might include certain approaches to painting, sculpture, musical composition, and poetry.

Mediation. The requisite associative elements may be evoked in contiguity through the mediation of common elements. This means of bringing the associative elements into contiguity with each other is of great importance in those areas of endeavor where the use of symbols (verbal, mathematical, chemical, etc. . . . .) is mandatory. For example, in psychology, the idea of relating reactive inhibition and cortical satiation may have been mediated by the common associates "tiredness" or "fatigue" (Köhler & Fishback, 1950).

Individual Differences

From the definition given above, the factors that will make for individual differences in the probability of achieving creative solutions may be deduced. Any ability or tendency which serves to bring otherwise mutually remote ideas into contiguity will facilitate a creative solution; any ability or tendency which serves to keep remote ideas from contiguous evocation will inhibit the creative solution.

Listed below are several illustrative predictions concerning individual differences that one may make from this theoretical orientation.

NEED FOR ASSOCIATIVE ELEMENTS

It should be clear that an individual without the requisite elements in his response repertoire will not be able to combine them so as to arrive at a creative solution. An architect who does not know of the existence of a new material can hardly be expected to use it creatively.

ASSOCIATIVE HIERARCHY

The organization of an individual's associations will influence the probability and speed of attainment of a creative solution. There is a whole family of predictions that one may draw from this concept of the associative hierarchy. As an initial example, let us take the question of the manner in which the associative strength around ideas is distributed. If we present an individual with the word "table," what sort of associative responses does he make? The individual who tends to be restricted to the stereotyped responses, such as "chair," may be characterized as having an associative hierarchy with a steep slope (see Figure 1). That is, when you get past the first one or two conventional responses to the stimulus, the individual's associative strengths to other words or ideas (lower in the hierarchy) drops rapidly. We can also conceive of a second sort of individual whose associative hierarchy is characterized by a rather flat slope. This is an individual who perhaps also has as his strongest response the conventional chair. But for him this response is not overly dominant and so it is more likely that he will be able to get to the less probable, more remote kinds of associations to table. It is among these more remote responses that the requisite elements and mediating terms for a creative solution will be lurking. This slope factor may be related to the mathematical analysis of associative production developed by Bousfield, Sedgewick, and Cohen (1954). It probably is closely approximated by their constant, *m,* measuring rate of depletion of the as-

sociative reservoir. They found a high negative correlation between rate of association and total number of associations. It would be predicted from Figure 1 that the high creative subject (flat hierarchy) would respond relatively slowly and steadily and emit many responses while the low creative subject (steep hierarchy) would respond at a higher rate but emit fewer responses.

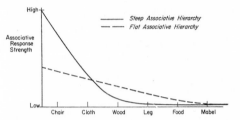

FIG. 1. Associative hierarchies around the word "table."

It would be predicted that the greater the concentration of associative strength in a small number of stereotyped associative responses (steep hierarchy) the less probable it is that the individual will attain the creative solution. Thus, the word association behavior of the high creative individual should be characterized by less stereotypy and commonality. This last prediction is supported by a study by Mednick, Gough, and Woodworth (Mednick, 1958). Research scientists rated for creativity were divided into relatively high ($N = 15$) and relatively low ($N = 15$) groups. The low creatives gave more stereotyped responses on 80% of a group of 36 test words from the Kent-Rosanoff list. (These test words were chosen for their tendency to elicit stereotyped responses. Stereotypy was defined by the Minnesota Kent-Rosanoff Word Association Norms, Russell & Jenkins, 1954). It should be pointed out that these results lend themselves to another possible interpretation. The highly creative individual may also have a steep hierarchy but a deviant one. That is, his most dominant associative response may be quite strong but quite different from the popular, dominant associative response. There are different predictions that can be made for the flat-associative-hierarchy creative and the steep-deviant associative-hierarchy creative. The latter is more likely to be the one-shot producer (a not uncommon phenomenon among novelists). If he does create further products, they will tend to resemble closely the first product. The former is more likely to be a multiproducer; he is more likely to produce in a variety of avenues of creative expression.

The prediction suggesting an expectation of less creativity from an individual with a high concentration of associative strength in a few responses leads to another prediction. The greater the number of instances in which an individual has solved problems with given materials in a certain manner, the less is the likelihood of his attaining a creative solution using these materials. Such an individual will "know the meaning" of the elements of the subject matter. That is, he will have a steep associative hierarchy around these elements. An example of the operation of this principle recently occurred to the writer while teaching an honors freshman introductory course in psychology at the University of Michigan. I was giving a well known interpretation of a well known experiment in stimulus generalization when interrupted by a student who calmly stated that the interpretation was in error. After a few minutes of blustering I asked him to explain. His explanation proved him to be correct. I had been dealing with this material for years and

"knew" the "correct" interpretation; for him this material was new, he had a low, flat associative hierarchy. Thus, if a newcomer to a field has the requisite information, he is more likely to achieve a creative solution than a long-time worker in the field. This may be the reason that theoretical physicists and master chess players are often said to have passed their prime by the age of 25.

NUMBER OF ASSOCIATIONS

The greater the number of associations that an individual has to the requisite elements of a problem, the greater the probability of his reaching a creative solution. This variable is not independent of the preceding one since an individual with a high concentration of associative strength in few associative responses is not likely to have a proliferation of associations. The more associates which are evoked by a requisite element of a problem, the more likely it is that an associate will exist which will serve as a mediating bridge to another requisite element, facilitating combination. It seems likely that this variable will not be related to speed of creative solution since it may take a good deal of time to get to the mediating links.

COGNITIVE OR PERSONALITY STYLES

Previously learned or innately predisposed methods of approaching problems will influence the probability of a creative solution. If the requisite associational elements of a new and useful combination are probable associates of the concrete representations of relevant aspects of the problem, an individual with a predominately "perceptual" approach will be more likely to reach a creative solution. If, however, the requisite associational elements are not elicited as responses to these concrete representations or if there is no concrete representation then an individual with a "conceptual" approach will be more likely to reach a creative solution.

Another cognitive style of importance may lie along the "visualizer-verbalizer" dimension. The visualizer is one who tends to call up relatively complete memorial sensory representations of the relevant concrete aspects of problems. If the problem deals with horses, he tends to picture a horse in terms of its sensory qualities. On the other hand, the verbalizer explores the problem by associating with words around the word "horse." If the requisite elements are high in his verbal associative hierarchy to the word horse, the verbalizer will be more likely to attain a creative solution; the visualizer may be thrown off or at least delayed by many false leads. On the other hand, if a requisite verbal associative response to the word horse is very low, or not present in the verbalizer's hierarchy, then the visualizer will be more likely to attain the creative solution. It is therefore clear that some types of problems will be solved more easily by the visualizer and some by the verbalizer.

Factors such as these (admittedly very poorly defined) may be partly responsible for differential aptitudes for creative work in differing fields.

SELECTION OF THE CREATIVE COMBINATION

The creative combination of elements is only one among the many which may present themselves to the subject. How or why is the creative combination selected? Some speculations regarding this problem follow. The explanation of the process of selection may be related to the nature of the problem. Problems either entail a specific and relatively objective set of testable criteria (Paint a realistic portrait of this individual. Design a refrigerator so that it will be automatically free of frost.) or they do not (The chemist mixes two liquids out of curiosity. The painter dabs hopefully at a fresh canvas waiting for an idea. The psychologist tosses a new test into a correlation matrix). When specific criteria are provided, they form an important part of the stimulus set which is determining which associative elements are being elicited and thus becoming eligible for entering into combination with other elements. Important sets of associations to each of these combinations are the consequents of the combinations. The set of consequents for each combination (If I put x, y, and z together, a and b will happen) is continually compared with the set of requirements of the problem. When the set of consequents of a new combination achieves a close fit with the set of problem requirements, this combination is selected. When there is complete overlap of sets, "search behavior" is terminated. As with the other requisite elements of the problem, individual differences in this case will vary with (among other things) the structure of the associational hierarchies around the requirements of the problem. When the refrigerator-defroster problem was presented to an undergraduate class almost all of the proferred solutions were based on the principle of ridding the refrigerator of already heavily accumulated frost. A couple of individuals (possibly familiar with the defroster principles presently in use) suggested methods which disposed of the frost before it built up to an overly annoying level. In addition to these there were two unique responses, i.e., a "new" method of preventing moisture from condensing in the freezer compartment, and a method of allowing frost to accumulate but limiting the location of accumulation to a small box which could be regularly and conveniently removed and emptied. Thus it may be seen that an individual's associations to the requirements may be characterized as to their stereotypy; the imposed requirements of the problem may be viewed as part of the requisite elements in the situation. The earlier theoretical statements concerning these elements may be seen as being relevant here. The foregoing suggests an explanation of the selection process for the case where the subject must hunt for a combination of elements which will satisfy given criteria. In the case where no criteria are specified, the subject is typically producing random combinations of elements; the task of selection in this case consists in finding relevant criteria for the given partial products.

If we may continue along a bit further with this example of the defroster, we may begin to see some glimmerings of a solution to the most serious problem in research on creative thinking—how may we determine to what degree behavior is creative? We have suggested one criterion in our hypothesis. In the following an additional criterion is developed. To begin with let us examine the requirements as originally stated—"Design a refrigerator so that it is automatically free of frost." The first thing that strikes us is that while some requirements have been stated, there are even more that are strongly implied and essential, many that are desirable, and a number that we would only become aware of after some method of satisfying them had been suggested.

Let us examine some possible solutions:

(1) Simply refraining from opening the refrigerator door would solve the problem as stated since this would prevent moisture from entering and condensing as frost. This solution meets many of the implied requirements. It is cheap, convenient, effective, does not require special training, etc. . . . However, it is not an optimal solution since it violates one essential, implied requirement—the usefulness of the refrigerator must not be impaired. (This is the cutting-off-your-nose-to-spite-your-face solution.)

(2) A primitive solution is the hammer-and-screwdriver method. This is tried and true and meets many of the essential requirements. It falls down in that it is inconvenient, messy, uneconomical (when caked with frost, the refrigerator unit is very inefficient), endangers the mechanism, and is hardly automatic.

(3) In a refrigerator we once owned another solution was used. The opening and closing of the refrigerator door operated a counter. At a certain count the refrigerator unit was automatically heated and the melted water evaporated outside the refrigerator. The superiority of this solution is immediately apparent. The source of this superiority lies in the number of requirements which it meets. It is economical, automatic, convenient, peculiarly appropriate (the operation of the heating element is contingent upon the number of door openings. The amount of frost accumulated is also in part dependent on the number of door openings.), does not interfere with the normal use of the refrigerator, and does not require special training. Note that the principle behind this highly creative solution (not allowing massive build-ups of frost) was infrequently suggested in the classroom group. However, this solution is not wholly successful at meeting some criteria. The frequent heating and cooling may injure frozen food stored near the heating element. Secondly, since the heating process must be brief and mild, it is inevitable that not all frost is removed. While this solution does effectively curtail the number of defrostings, it does

not eliminate them completely. It is clear that a method which would encompass all of the advantages of the "counter" method, but which would, in addition, eliminate defrosting altogether would be even more creative. What is suggested by this discussion is that the creativeness of a product is some function of the number of requirements that the product meets. The most ready application of this definition will be in laboratory research in which tasks, solutions, and requirements may be arbitrarily constructed and varied.

A Test of Creativity

The definition of the creative process has suggested a way of testing for individual differences in creativity. The test items are intended to require the testee to perform creatively. That is, he is asked to form associative elements into new combinations by providing mediating connective links. Since the test situation is contrived, the combination must meet specified criteria that are experimenter imposed.

The definition dictates the structure of the test. We must provide stimulus items from two mutually distant realities and ask the subject to "draw a spark from their juxtaposition." To state it more usefully, we must provide stimulus elements from mutually remote associative clusters and have the subject find a criteria-meeting mediating link which combines them. A first problem concerns the type of material of which the stimulus item should be composed. If the test is to be appropriate for all fields of creative endeavor, the material must either be nonsensical so as to avoid bias favoring any specific means of creative expression, or it must be so common in society that familiarity could be assumed to be high across fields of interest. The problems involved in constructing the nonsense materials so as to

avoid favoring any interest groups soon proved to be apparently insurmountable. This left us searching for materials with which most individuals in the culture could claim acquaintance; this, in turn, brought us to verbal materials.

While it may be true that certain occupational groups have extensive experience in dealing with words, there are some verbal associative habits that could reasonably be assumed to be familiar to almost all individuals that have been brought up in this (USA) culture. Among such habits are the associative bonds between words like "ham and eggs," "bed-bug," "pool-hall," "hound-dog," "whole-wheat," "chorus-girl," "kill-joy," and "red-hot." These became the materials for the test.

Having decided on the materials, the test almost constructed itself in accordance with the definition. Several words from mutually distant associative clusters must be presented to the subject; his task must be to provide mediating links between them. Further, (a factor of extreme importance), the mediating link must be strictly associative rather than being of a sort that follows elaborate rules of logic, concept formation, or problem solving. In their final (or at least present) form, the test items consist of sets of three words drawn from mutally remote associative cluster. One example might be:

Example 1:   rat   blue   cottage

The subject is required to find a fourth word which could serve as a specific kind of associative connective link between these disparate words. The answer to Example 1 is "cheese." "Cheese" is a word which is present in the word pairs "rat-cheese," "blue-cheese," and "cottage-cheese." The subject is presented with several examples so that he has an adequate opportunity to achieve the specific set necessary for the task.

Example 2:	railroad	girl	class
Example 3:	surprise	line	birthday
Example 4:	wheel	electric	high
Example 5:	out	dog	cat [1]

(None of these examples is a test item from any form of the actual test.) The two college level forms of the test (one coauthored by Sharon Halpern and the other by Martha T. Mednick) have 30 items each; the subject is allowed 40 minutes; his score is the number right.

The test, called the Remote Associates Test (RAT), has some interesting correlations with other measures.

Comparisons with criteria. A study was conducted at the College of Architecture, University of California, Berkeley, by the writer and Sharon Halpern. Ratings of creativity by faculty members of the College who taught the Design courses were correlated with RAT scores. These ratings form an unusually excellent criterion of creative performance since the raters had been advising and evaluating the students in the creation of new designs and models of structures. They had been working with these students for at least a year and in many cases two or more. The ratings and RAT scores correlated significantly ($r = .70$, $df = 19$, $p < .01$). In this study an early form of the RAT was used.

The RAT was administered to a group of first year psychology graduate students at the University of Michigan whose native language was American English ($N = 35$). Faculty research supervisors (who had been directing the independent research efforts of the students), rated the eight highest and eight lowest RAT scorers either "high" or "low" in research creativity (no middle category allowed). Research creativity was defined as being demonstrated if the student developed new research methods and/or pulled together disparate theory or research areas in useful and original ways. Of the 16 research supervisors, one felt that he had not had enough contact with his student to make the judgment. His student was a low RAT scorer. Of the eight high RAT scorers, six were rated high on research creativity and two were rated low; of the seven low RAT scorers, only one was rated high, the other six being rated low. By Fisher's exact test the probability of these events occurring by chance is less than .05. Miller Analogies Test (MAT) scores were available for these students. Of the seven high MAT scorers, three were rated high on research creativity; of the eight low MAT scorers, four were rated high in research creativity.

Reliability. The Spearman-Brown reliability of the RAT was .92 in one sample (289 women, almost all the students at an Eastern women's college, tested as part of a project under the direction of Theodore Newcomb) and .91 in another (215 men tested at the University of Michigan as part of a project under the direction of Warren T. Norman).

Correlation with grades. One of the present forms of the RAT correlated negatively with the first-two-year grade point averages of a group of undergraduates at a large Eastern technology college. ($r = -.27$, $N = 74$, $p < .05$). This same correlation was obtained with the summer grades of a smaller group, $N = 34$, of summer students at a large Eastern liberal arts college (not statisti-

---

[1] Answers to sample RAT items: 2. working; 3. party; 4. chair or wire; 5. house.

cally significant in this case). In a study by Miller (1960) it was found that high RAT scorers tended to get higher grades from teachers rated as flexible than from teachers rated as dogmatic. Low RAT scorers received higher grades from teachers rated dogmatic than from teachers rated as flexible.

Correlation with social attitudes and occupational interests. It is clear that creative individuals must have access to improbable associative responses. Kowalski (1960) hypothesized that this is a general tendency which also manifests itself in their attitudes and interests. She tested and interviewed 15 high RAT scoring and 15 low RAT scoring undergraduate women. The two groups had radically differing views on sexual morality and women's rights. The views of the high creatives were more atypical and "liberal" ($U = 37$, $p < .001$). On the Strong Vocational Interest Blank, Mens' Form (SVIB), the high creative group showed "significantly higher interest on the artist ($p < .05$), psychologist ($p < .005$), physician ($p < .025$), mathematician ($p < .025$), and author-journalist ($p < .05$) keys. The low creative group showed higher interest on the farmer ($p < .05$), math-physical science high school teacher ($p < .05$), office man ($p < .05$), and pharmacist ($p < .01$) keys" (p. 19). (These are the probability values of obtained chi squares.) The only one of these keys related to ACE scores was that of physician. "The commonality of these interest patterns was evaluated by noting the per cent overlap of the specific key with the general population of interest expression. For example, the Farmer key overlaps 45% with the general population, while the Artist key overlaps 20%" (p. 20). The significant keys of the

higher creatives had significantly less commonality than the significant keys of the low creatives. These differences were independent of the influence of intelligence as measured by the ACE.

Associative behavior. In the discussion of illustrative predictions it was suggested that highly creative individuals would be characterized by a flat associative hierarchy rather than a steep associative hierarchy. Further, it was proposed that the greater the number of associations that an individual has to the requisite elements of a problem, the greater the probability of his reaching a creative solution. From these two independent statements it may be deduced that when required to display his reservoir of associations to single stimulus words, the highly creative individual will have greater access to less probable associates and therefore produce a greater number of associates. A study by Craig and Manis (1960 unpublished [2]) supports this deduction. Thirty-eight college students had the RAT and an associative task administered to them. In the associative task they were given 1 minute to write as many associates as they could to each of 20 words. The correlation of the number of such associates with RAT scores was .38 ($p < .01$).

In two related studies, Karp (1960) and Kowalski (1960) found RAT scores to be directly related to the originality and quantity of anagrams constructed using the test word "Generation." In the Karp study 40 undergraduates were given 5 minutes to produce as many four letter anagrams from the test word

---

[2] Craig, M., & Manis, M. Prediction of scores on the Remote Associates Test by size of response repertoire. Unpublished manuscript, 1960.

as they could. The productions were scored for quantity (number of acceptable answers) and originality (a weighted score for each response was developed from the frequency with which the response was given by the 40 subjects). The correlation of the RAT with the quantity scores was .44 ($p < .01$); the correlation of the RAT with the originality score was .37 ($p < .05$). Kowalski presented the anagrams task to 15 high RAT scorers and to 15 low RAT scorers, giving them 5 minutes to produce words of any length from the test word "Generation." In this study originality was measured by computing the percentage of responses given by an individual which had not been given by any other of the 30 subjects. The difference on this measure between high and low RAT scorers was significant ($U = 68, p < .04$). "Only four subjects in the low creative group gave *any* original responses at all while eleven subjects in the high creative group did" (p. 19).

At the Institute of Personality Assessment and Research, University of California, Berkeley, the RAT was included as part of the assessment battery administered to a group of 40 highly eminent architects. The RAT correlated .31 with the Originality (O-I) Scale of the IPAR Questionnaire Scale and −.31 with the total Conformity Score obtained in the Crutchfield Conformity Experiment (Crutchfield, 1955). Interviewers rated high scorers as significantly higher in "graceful and well-coordinated in movement" and "reticent and taciturn in speech." The college grade point average which the subjects reported correlated −.34 with RAT score, a result which tends to confirm findings reported above.

Experimentally Manipulable Variables

While only one experimental study (described below) which makes use of this general framework has been completed in this laboratory, it may be useful to indicate briefly the kinds of experimental investigation it suggests.

Massed vs. distributed work sessions. Total time of work being equal, massed sessions of creative work should be more successful than distributed sessions. There are two reasons why this would be so. The first is that the individual making use of the massed session technique is more likely to achieve temporal contiguity of the requisite associative elements within a single intensive work period than is an individual who has distributed his work in shorter periods over several days. Secondly, it may take some time for an individual to work on a problem enough to go beyond its obvious aspects. In the first hour of work, he may get through only the conventional and stereotyped associations to the elements of the problem, while it is perhaps in the later stages of intensive work on a problem that one can begin to entertain the more remote associations that are evoked by elements of the problem. It is, of course, among these remote associations that the key to the creative solution will lie.

Warmup. In creative work a warmup session should serve to arouse the more remote associations to the requisite elements of the problem. While their work has gone considerably beyond the problem of warmup, Maltzman, Bogartz, and Breger (1958) have demonstrated that the repeated elicitation of different word associations to the same stimulus words does indeed tend to produce remote associations to these stimulus words. Further, this induced originality tends to transfer to other relatively unrelated tasks presented after this associative warmup. Associative warmup of this type should become more effective as the warmup stimuli are more similar to the task materials. It may be that the effects of warmup will prove to be a further advantage that massed sessions have over distributed sessions for creative productivity.

Stereotyping associative responses. As stated above, if an individual's associative response to a stimulus element of a creative problem is of excessive strength, this will tend to reduce the likelihood of occurrence of more remote associative responses. This will reduce the probability and speed of creative solution. It would therefore be predicted that extensive training of a specific response other than a requisite one to a stimulus element of a problem requiring a creative solution should retard later attempts at solution of the problem. This prediction is related to the concept of "functional fixedness" introduced by Duncker (1945). Birch and Rabinowitz (1951) and Adamson and Taylor (1954) completed experiments which are related to this prediction. Their test situation was the two string problem. The subjects are asked to tie together two strings suspended from the ceiling. When the subject grasps one string he finds that the other string is hanging out of his reach. The solution to the problem requires the subject to attach a weight to one of the strings, get the weight swinging and catch it while holding the other string. Various objects can be used as a weight. The subjects that had been pretrained by having them use a switch in its usual manner of functioning tended to be unlikely to use it as a weight. They had developed strong response strength for the association "switch-close circuit" which had reduced the probability of the remote association "switch-weight."

Another feasible experimental approach would make use of the RAT item as a creative task and test the influence upon it of certain variables. For example, the words of which an item is composed may be presented at varying rates to test the massed trials hypothesis. In addition, various pretraining conditions may be evaluated in terms of their effectiveness in increasing or decreasing RAT performance.

Another possible experimental approach would entail separating out high and low RAT scorers and observing the differential effect of certain variables upon their behavior. In an experiment just completed Houston and Mednick (in press) postulated that an important motive impelling the behavior of the creative individual was a need for improbable associative stimulation. It was reasoned that if such stimulation were supplied, it would tend to satisfy this need and be reinforcing. Further, if such stimulation regularly followed a given response the high creative individual should tend to learn that response. Thirty high and 30 low RAT scorers were asked to read aloud only one of two typed words on a 3×5 card. Excepting buffer items and including 40 pairs aimed at gauging the free operant level of noun-choice, there were 160 pairs of words, each pair consisting of a noun and a nonnoun (verb, adjective, adverb, etc.). If a subject in the experimental group (15 high RAT subjects, 15 low RAT subjects) responded with the noun member of a pair, the experimenter responded with an improbable association; if the subject chose the nonnoun, the experimenter responded with the most probable association. In the control group (15 high RAT, 15 low RAT) both the nouns and the nonnouns were invariably followed by their most probable associate. Associative probabilities were obtained from the Russell and Jenkins (1954) and Deese (1960) norms. If the improbable response was satisfying a need, the probability of noun-choice should increase over the 160 trials. It did significantly in the high RAT experimental group; the low RAT experimental group showed a decrease. The high and low RAT control groups showed no reliable change.

Some of the positions which have been taken in this paper are assumptions and not deductions. As more data are gathered some of these assumptions will assume the status of facts, some will be revised. For example, the opening paragraph suggests that the paper is not meant to apply only to one field of creative endeavor but attempts to delineate processes that underlie all creative thought. This may require modification.

The explanation may fit the process of scientific discovery and not be appropriate to discussions of painting or music. For the present (paradoxically enough), the more encompassing assumptions seem more parsimonious. It may eventually turn out (as is hinted at in the body of the paper) that the differences between the fields are more determined by differences in suitability of the three means of achieving contiguity, i.e., serendipity, similarity, and mediation.

Summary

An associative theory of creative thinking has been outlined. Differences between high creatives and low creatives have been predicted along specified dimensions. Predictions have been made regarding the effect on the creative process of some experimentally manipulable variables.

The associative definition of the creative process has taken the operational form of a test. Some preliminary research with this test is described.

References

ADAMSON, R. E., & TAYLOR, D. W. Functional fixedness as related to elapsed time and to set. *J. exp. Psychol.*, 1954, **47**, 122–126.

BAIN, A. *The senses and the intellect.* 1855.

BINET, A. *The psychology of reasoning.* Chicago: Open Court, 1899.

BIRCH, H. G., & RABINOWITZ, H. S. The negative effect of previous experience on productive thinking. *J. exp. Psychol.*, 1951, **41**, 121–125.

BOUSFIELD, W. A., SEDGEWICK, C. H. W., & COHEN, B. H. Certain temporal characteristics of the recall of verbal associates. *Amer. J. Psychol.*, 1954, **57**, 111–118.

CRUTCHFIELD, R. Conformity and character. *Amer. Psychologist,* 1955, **10**, 191–198.

DEESE, J. Word association norms. Author, 1960. (Ditto)

DUNCKER, K. On problem-solving. *Psychol. Monogr.* 1945, **58** (5, Whole No. 270).

FREUD, S. Wit and its relation to the unconscious. In, *The basic writings of Sigmund Freud.* New York: Modern Library, 1938.

GHISELIN, B. *The creative process.* Berkeley: Univer. California Press, 1952.

HOLLINGSWORTH, H. L. *Psychology: Its facts and principles.* New York: Appleton, 1928.

HOUSTON, J. P., & MEDNICK, S. A. Creativity and the need for novelty. *J. abnorm. soc. Psychol.,* in press.

KARP, S. A validity study of a measure of creativity. Senior honors thesis, University of Michigan, 1960.

KÖHLER, W., & FISHBACK, J. The destruction of the Müller-Lyer illusion in repeated trials: II. Satiation patterns and memory traces. *J. exp. Psychol.*, 1950, **40**, 398–410.

KOWALSKI, J. Attitudes and occupational interests of creative individuals. Senior honors thesis, University of Michigan, 1960.

LOCKE, J. *Essay concerning the human understanding.* 1690.

MALTZMAN, I., BOGARTZ, W., & BREGER, L. A procedure for increasing word association originality and its transfer effects. *J. exp. Psychol.*, 1958, **56**, 392–398.

MEDNICK, S. A. An orientation to research in creativity. (Res. Memo. No. 2) Berkeley, Calif.: University of California, Institute of Personality Assessment and Research, 1958.

MILLER, B. A study of creativity in college students and teaching method types. Senior honors thesis, University of Michigan, 1960.

MOORE, MARIANNE. The monkey puzzle. In, *Collected Poems of Marianne Moore.* New York: Macmillan, 1951.

RUSSELL, W. A., & JENKINS, J. J. The complete Minnesota norms for responses to 100 words from the Kent-Rosanoff Word Association Test. Technical Report No. 11, 1954, University of Minnesota, Contract N8 onr 66216.

UNDERWOOD, B. J. An orientation to research on thinking. *Psychol. Rev.*, 1952, **59**, 209–220.

CHAPTER 7

Examples of the Cross-Cultural and Case-History Methods

A CROSS-CULTURAL SURVEY OF SOME SEX DIFFERENCES IN SOCIALIZATION

Herbert Barry III, Margaret K. Bacon, and Irvin L. Child

In our society, certain differences may be observed between the typical personality characteristics of the two sexes. These sex differences in personality are generally believed to result in part from differences in the way boys and girls are reared. To the extent that personality differences between the sexes are thus of cultural rather than biological origin, they seem potentially susceptible to change. But how readily susceptible to change? In the differential rearing of the sexes does our society make an arbitrary imposition on an infinitely plastic biological base, or is this cultural imposition found uniformly in all societies as an adjustment to the real biological differences between the sexes? This paper reports one attempt to deal with this problem.

Data and Procedures

The data used were ethnographic reports, available in the anthropological literature, about socialization practices of various cultures. One hundred and ten cultures, mostly nonliterate, were studied. They were selected primarily in terms of the existence of adequate ethnographic reports of socialization practices and secondarily so as to obtain a wide and reasonably balanced geographical

Reprinted by permission of the American Psychological Association and the authors from *The Journal of Abnormal and Social Psychology*, Vol. 55, 1957.

distribution. Various aspects of socialization of infants and children were rated on a 7-point scale by two judges (Mrs. Bacon and Mr. Barry). Where the ethnographic reports permitted, separate ratings were made for the socialization of boys and girls. Each rating was indicated as either confident or doubtful; with still greater uncertainty, or with complete lack of evidence, the particular rating was of course not made at all. We shall restrict the report of sex difference ratings to cases in which both judges made a confident rating. Also omitted is the one instance where the two judges reported a sex difference in opposite directions, as it demonstrates only unreliability of judgment. The number of cultures that meet these criteria is much smaller than the total of 110; for the several variables to be considered, the number varies from 31 to 84.

The aspects of socialization on which ratings were made included:

(1) Several criteria of attention and indulgence toward infants.
(2) Strength of socialization from age 4 or 5 years until shortly before puberty, with respect to five systems of behavior; strength of socialization was defined as the combination of positive pressure (rewards for the behavior) plus negative pressure (punishments for lack of the behavior). The variables were:

(*a*) Responsibility or dutifulness training. (The data were such that training in the performance of chores in the productive or domestic economy was necessarily the principal source of information here; however, training in the performance of other duties was also taken into account when information was available.)

(b) Nurturance training, i.e., training the child to be nurturant or helpful toward younger siblings and other dependent people.

(c) Obedience training.

(d) Self-reliance training.

(e) Achievement training, i.e., training the child to orient his behavior toward standards of excellence in performance, and to seek to achieve as excellent a performance as possible.

nographer not reporting separately about boys and girls.

Sex Differences in Socialization

On the various aspects of attention and indulgence toward infants, the judges almost always agreed in finding no sex difference. Out of 96 cultures for which the ratings included the infancy period, 88 (92%) were rated with no sex difference by either judge for any of those variables. This result is consistent with the point sometimes made by anthropologists that "baby" generally is a single status undifferentiated by sex, even

TABLE 1. RATINGS OF CULTURES FOR SEX DIFFERENCES ON FIVE VARIABLES OF CHILDHOOD SOCIALIZATION PRESSURE

Variable	Number of Cultures	Both Judges Agree in Rating the Variable Higher In		One Judge Rates No Difference, One Rates the Variable Higher In		Percentage of Cultures with Evidence of Sex Difference in Direction Of		
		Girls	Boys	Girls	Boys	Girls	Boys	Neither
Nurturance	33	17	0	10	0	82%	0%	18%
Obedience	69	6	0	18	2	35%	3%	62%
Responsibility	84	25	2	26	7	61%	11%	28%
Achievement	31	0	17	1	10	3%	87%	10%
Self-reliance	82	0	64	0	6	0%	85%	15%

Where the term "no sex difference" is used here, it may mean any of three things: (a) the judge found separate evidence about the training of boys and girls on this particular variable, and judged it to be identical; (b) the judge found a difference between the training of boys and girls, but not great enough for the sexes to be rated a whole point apart on a 7-point scale; (c) the judge found evidence only about the training of "children" on this variable, the eth-

though "boy" and "girl" are distinct statuses.

On the variables of childhood socialization, on the other hand, a rating of no sex difference by both judges was much less common. This finding of no sex difference varied in frequency from 10% of the cultures for the achievement variable up to 62% of the cultures for the obedience variable, as shown in the last column of Table 1. Where a sex difference is reported, by either one or both judges, the difference tends strongly to be in a particular direction, as shown in the earlier columns of the same table. Pressure toward nurturance, obedience, and responsibility is most often stronger for girls, whereas pressure toward achievement and self-reliance is most often stronger for boys.

For nurturance and for self-reliance, all the sex differences are in the same direction. For achievement there is only one exception to the usual direction of difference, and for obedience only two; but for responsibility there are nine. What do these exceptions mean? We have reexamined all these cases. In most of them, only one judge had rated the sexes as differently treated (sometimes one judge, sometimes the other), and in the majority of these cases both judges were now inclined to agree that there was no convincing evidence of a real difference. There were exceptions, however, especially in cases where a more formal or systematic training of boys seemed to imply greater pressure on them toward responsibility. The most convincing cases were the Masai and Swazi, where both judges had originally agreed in rating responsibility pressures greater in boys than in girls. In comparing the five aspects of socialization we may conclude that responsibility shows by far the strongest evidence of real variation in the direction of sex difference, and obedience much the most frequently shows evidence of no sex difference at all.

In subsequent discussion we shall be assuming that the obtained sex differences in the socialization ratings reflect true sex differences in the cultural practices. We should consider here two other possible sources of these rated differences.

(1) The ethnographers could have been biased in favor of seeing the same pattern of sex differences as in our culture. However, most anthropologists readily perceive and eagerly report novel and startling cultural features, so we may expect them to have reported unusual sex differences where they existed. The distinction between matrilineal and patrilineal, and between matrilocal and patrilocal cultures, given prominence in many ethnographic reports, shows an awareness of possible variations in the significance of sex differences from culture to culture.

(2) The two judges could have expected to find in other cultures the sex roles which are familiar in our culture and inferred them from the material on the cultures. However, we have reported only confident ratings, and such a bias seems less likely here than for doubtful ratings. It might be argued, moreover, that bias has more opportunity in the cases ambiguous enough so that only one judge reported a sex difference, and less opportunity in the cases where the evidence is so clear that both judges agree. Yet in general, as may be seen in Table 1, the deviant cases are somewhat more frequent among the cultures where only one judge reported a sex difference.

The observed differences in the socialization of boys and girls are consistent with certain universal tendencies in the differentiation of adult sex role. In the economic sphere, men are more frequently allotted tasks that involve leaving home and engaging in activities where a high level of skill yields important returns; hunting is a prime example. Emphasis on training in self-reliance and achievement for boys would function as preparation for such an economic role. Women, on the other hand, are more frequently allotted tasks at or near home that minister most immediately to the needs of others (such as cooking and water carrying); these activities have a nurturant character, and in their pursuit a responsible carrying out of established routines is likely to be more important than the development of an especially high order of skill. Thus training in nurturance, responsibility, and, less clearly, obedience, may contribute to preparation for this economic role. These consistencies with adult role go beyond the economic sphere, of course. Participation in warfare, as a male prerogative, calls for self-reliance and a high order of skill where survival or death is the immediate issue. The childbearing which is biologically assigned to women, and the child care which is socially assigned primarily to them, lead to nurturant behavior and often call for a more continuous responsibility than do the tasks carried out by men. Most of these distinctions in adult role are not inevitable, but the biological differences between the sexes strongly predispose the distinction of role, if made, to be in a uniform direction.[1]

The relevant biological sex differences are conspicuous in adulthood but generally not in childhood. If each generation were left entirely to its own devices, therefore, without even an older generation to copy, sex differences in role would presumably be almost absent in childhood and would have to be developed after puberty at the expense of considerable relearning on the part of one or both sexes. Hence, a pattern of child training which foreshadows adult differences can serve the useful function of minimizing what Benedict termed "discontinuities in cultural conditioning" (1).

The differences in socialization be-

---

[1] For data and interpretations supporting various arguments of this paragraph, see Mead (2), Murdock (3), and Scheinfeld (6).

tween the sexes in our society, then, are no arbitrary custom of our society, but a very widespread adaptation of culture to the biological substratum of human life.

Variations in Degree of Sex Differentiation

While demonstrating near-universal tendencies in direction of difference between the socialization of boys and girls, our data do not show perfect uniformity. A study of the variations in our data may allow us to see some of the conditions which are associated with, and perhaps give rise to, a greater or smaller degree of this difference. For this purpose, we classified cultures as having relatively large or small sex difference by two different methods, one more inclusive and the other more selective. In both methods the ratings were at first considered separately for each of the five variables. A sex difference rating was made only if both judges made a rating on this variable and at least one judge's rating was confident.

In the more inclusive method the ratings were dichotomized, separately for each variable, as close as possible to the median into those showing a large and those showing a small sex difference. Thus, for each society a large or a small sex difference was recorded for each of the five variables on which a sex difference rating was available. A society was given an over-all classification of large or small sex difference if it had a sex difference rating on at least three variables and if a majority of these ratings agreed in being large, or agreed in being small. This method permitted classification of a large number of cultures, but the grounds for classification were capricious in many cases, as a difference of only one point in the rating of a single variable might change the over-all classification of sex difference for a culture from large to small.

In the more selective method, we again began by dichotomizing each variable as close as possible to the median; but a society was now classified as having a large or small sex difference on the variable only if it was at least one step away from the scores immediately adja-

the customs of most of these societies [2] and which seemed of possible significance for sex differentiation. The aspects of culture covered include type of economy, residence pattern, marriage and incest rules, political integration, and social organization. For each aspect of culture, we grouped Murdock's categories to make a dichotomous contrast (sometimes omitting certain categories

TABLE 2. CULTURE VARIABLES CORRELATED WITH LARGE SEX DIFFERENCE IN SOCIALIZATION, SEPARATELY FOR TWO TYPES OF SAMPLE

Variable	More Selective Sample		More Inclusive Sample	
	ϕ	N	ϕ	N
Large Animals Are Hunted	.48 *	(34)	.28 *	(72)
Grain Rather Than Root Crops Are Grown	.82 **	(20)	.62 **	(43)
Large or Milking Animals Rather Than Small Animals Are Kept	.65 *	(19)	.43 *	(35)
Fishing Unimportant or Absent	.42 *	(31)	.19	(69)
Nomadic Rather Than Sedentary Residence	.61 **	(34)	.15	(71)
Polygyny Rather Than Monogamy	.51 *	(28)	.38 **	(64)

* $p < .05$.
** $p < .01$.
Note.—The variables have been so phrased that all correlations are positive. The phi coefficient is shown, and in parentheses, the number of cases on which the comparison was based. Significance level was determined by χ^2, or Fisher's exact test where applicable, using in all cases a two-tailed test.

cent to the median. Thus only the more decisive ratings of sex difference were used. A culture was classified as having an over-all large or small sex difference only if it was given a sex difference rating which met this criterion on at least two variables, and only if all such ratings agreed in being large, or agreed in being small.

We then tested the relation of each of these dichotomies to 24 aspects of culture on which Murdock has categorized

as irrelevant to the contrast). In the case of some aspects of culture, two or more separate contrasts were made (e.g., under form of marriage we contrasted monogamy with polygyny, and also contrasted sororal with nonsororal polygyny). For each of 40 comparisons thus formed, we prepared a 2 x 2 frequency table to determine relation to each of our

[2] These data were supplied to us directly by Professor Murdock.

sex-difference dichotomies. A significant relation was found for six of these 40 aspects of culture with the more selective dichotomization of over-all sex difference. In four of these comparisons, the relation to the more inclusive dichotomization was also significant. These relationships are all given in Table 2, in the form of phi coefficients, along with the outcome of testing significance by the use of χ^2 or Fisher's exact test. In trying to interpret these findings, we have also considered the nonsignificant correlations with other variables, looking for consistency and inconsistency with the general implications of the significant findings. We have arrived at the following formulation of results:

(1) Large sex difference in socialization is associated with an economy that places a high premium on the superior strength, and superior development of motor skills requiring strength, which characterize the male. Four of the correlations reported in Table 2 clearly point to this generalization: the correlations of large sex difference with the hunting of large animals, with grain rather than root crops, with the keeping of large rather than small domestic animals, and with nomadic rather than sedentary residence. The correlation with the unimportance of fishing may also be consistent with this generalization, but the argument is not clear.[3] Other correlations consistent

with the generalization, though not statistically significant, are with large game hunting rather than gathering, with the hunting of large game rather than small game, and with the general importance of all hunting and gathering.

(2) Large sex difference in socialization appears to be correlated with customs that make for a large family group with high cooperative interaction. The only statistically significant correlation relevant here is that with polygyny rather than monogamy. This generalization is, however, supported by several substantial correlations that fall only a little short of being statistically significant. One of these is a correlation with sororal rather than nonsororal polygyny; Murdock and Whiting (4) have presented indirect evidence that co-wives generally show smoother cooperative interaction if they are sisters. Correlations are also found with the presence of either an extended or a polygynous family rather than the nuclear family only; with the presence of an extended family; and with the extreme contrast between maximal extension and no extension of the family. The generalization is also to some extent supported by small correlations with wide extension of incest taboos, if we may presume that an incest taboo makes for effective unthreatening cooperation within the extended family. The only possible exception to this generalization, among substantial correlations, is a near-significant correlation with an extended or polygynous

---

[3] Looking (with the more inclusive sample) into the possibility that this correlation might result from the correlation between fishing and sedentary residence, a complicated interaction between these variables was found. The correlation of sex differentiation with absence of fishing is found only in nomadic societies, where fishing is likely to involve cooperative activity of the two sexes, and its absence is likely to mean dependence upon the male for large game hunting or herding large animals (whereas in sedentary societies the alternatives to fishing do not so uniformly require special emphasis on male strength).

The correlation of sex differentiation with nomadism is found only in nonfishing societies; here nomadism is likely to imply large game hunting or herding large animals, whereas in fishing societies nomadism evidently implies no such special dependence upon male strength. Maximum sex differentiation is found in nomadic nonfishing societies (15 with large difference and only 2 with small) and minimum sex differentiation in nomadic fishing societies (2 with large difference and 7 with small difference). These findings further strengthen the argument for a conspicuous influence of the economy upon sex differentiation.

family's occupying a cluster of dwellings rather than a single dwelling.[4]

In seeking to understand this second generalization, we feel that the degree of social isolation of the nuclear family may perhaps be the crucial underlying variable. To the extent that the nuclear family must stand alone, the man must be prepared to take the woman's role when she is absent or incapacitated, and vice versa. Thus the sex differentiation cannot afford to be too great. But to the extent that the nuclear family is steadily interdependent with other nuclear families, the female role in the household economy can be temporarily taken over by another woman, or the male role by another man, so that sharp differentiation of sex role is no handicap.

The first generalization, which concerns the economy, cannot be viewed as dealing with material completely independent of the ratings of socialization. The training of children in their economic role was often an important part of the data used in rating socialization variables, and would naturally vary according to the general economy of the society. We would stress, however, that

[4] We think the reverse of this correlation would be more consistent with our generalization here. But perhaps it may reasonably be argued that the various nuclear families composing an extended or polygynous family are less likely to develop antagonisms which hinder cooperation if they are able to maintain some physical separation. On the other hand, this variable may be more relevant to the first generalization than to the second. Occupation of a cluster of dwellings is highly correlated with presence of herding and with herding of large rather than small animals, and these economic variables in turn are correlated with large sex difference in socialization. Occupation of a cluster of dwellings is also correlated with polygyny rather than monogamy and shows no correlation with sororal vs. non-sororal polygyny.

we were by no means using the identical data on the two sides of our comparison; we were on the one hand judging data on the socialization of children and on the other hand using Murdock's judgments on the economy of the adult culture. In the case of the second generalization, it seems to us that there was little opportunity for information on family and social structure to have influenced the judges in making the socialization ratings.

Both of these generalizations contribute to understanding the social background of the relatively small difference in socialization of boys and girls which we believe characterizes our society at the present time. Our mechanized economy is perhaps less dependent than any previous economy upon the superior average strength of the male. The nuclear family in our society is often so isolated that husband and wife must each be prepared at times to take over or help in the household tasks normally assigned to the other. It is also significant that the conditions favoring low sex differentiation appear to be more characteristic of the upper segments of our society, in socioeconomic and educational status, than of lower segments. This observation may be relevant to the tendency toward smaller sex differences in personality in higher status groups (cf. Terman and Miles, 8).

The increase in our society of conditions favoring small sex difference has led some people to advocate a virtual elimination of sex differences in socialization. This course seems likely to be dysfunctional even in our society. Parsons, Bales, et al. (5) argue that a differentiation of role similar to the universal pattern of sex difference is an important and perhaps inevitable development in any social group, such as the nuclear family. If we add to their argument the point that biological differences between the sexes make most appropriate the usual division of those roles between the sexes, we have compelling reasons to expect that the decrease in differentiation of adult sex role will not continue to the vanishing point. In our training of children, there may now be less differentiation in sex role than characterizes adult life—so little, indeed, as to provide inadequate preparation for adulthood. This state of affairs is likely to be especially true of formal education, which is more subject to conscious influence by an ideology than is informal socialization at home. With child training being more oriented toward the male than the female role in adulthood, many of the adjustment problems of women in our society today may be partly traced to conflicts growing out of inadequate childhood preparation for their adult role. This argument is nicely supported in extreme form by Spiro's analysis of sex roles in an Israeli kibbutz (7). The ideology of the founders of the kibbutz included the objective of greatly reducing differences in sex role. But the economy of the kibbutz is a largely nonmechanized one in which the superior average strength of men is badly needed in many jobs. The result is that, despite the ideology and many attempts to implement it, women continue to be assigned primarily to traditional "women's work," and the incompatibility between upbringing or ideology and adult role is an important source of conflict for women.

Note on regional distribution. There is marked variation among regions of the world in typical size of sex difference in socialization. In our sample, societies in North America and Africa tend to have large sex difference, and societies in Oceania to have small sex difference.

Less confidently, because of the smaller number of cases, we can report a tendency toward small sex differences in Asia and South America as well. Since most of the variables with which we find the sex difference to be significantly correlated have a similar regional distribution, the question arises whether the correlations might better be ascribed to some quite different source having to do with large regional similarities, rather than to the functional dependence we have suggested. As a partial check, we have tried to determine whether the correlations we report in Table 2 tend also to be found strictly within regions. For each of the three regions for which we have sizable samples (North America, Africa, and Oceania) we have separately plotted 2 x 2 tables corresponding to each of the 6 relationships reported in Table 2. (We did this only for the more inclusive sample, since for the more selective sample the number of cases within a region would have been extremely small.) Out of the 18 correlations thus determined, 11 are positive and only 3 are negative (the other 4 being exactly zero). This result clearly suggests a general tendency for these correlations to hold true within regions as well as between regions, and may lend further support to our functional interpretation.

Summary

A survey of certain aspects of socialization in 110 cultures shows that differentiation of the sexes is unimportant in infancy, but that in childhood there is, as in our society, a widespread pattern of greater pressure toward nurturance, obedience, and responsibility in girls, and toward self-reliance and achievement striving in boys. There are a few reversals of sex difference, and many instances of no detectable sex difference; these facts tend to confirm the cultural rather than directly biological nature of the differences. Cultures vary in the degree to which these differentiations are made; correlational analysis suggests some of the social conditions influencing these variations, and helps in understanding why our society has relatively small sex differentiation.

References

1. BENEDICT, RUTH. Continuities and discontinuities in cultural conditioning. *Psychiatry,* 1938, **1,** 161–167.

2. MEAD, MARGARET. *Male and female.* New York: Morrow, 1949.

3. MURDOCK, G. P. Comparative data on the division of labor by sex. *Social Forces,* 1937, **15,** 551–553.

4. MURDOCK, G. P., & WHITING, J. W. M. Cultural determination of parental attitudes: The relationship between the social structure, particularly family structure and parental behavior. In M. J. E. Senn (Ed.), *Problems of infancy and childhood: Transactions of the Fourth Conference,* March 6–7, 1950. New York: Josiah Macy, Jr. Foundation, 1951. Pp. 13–34.

5. PARSONS, T., BALES, R. F., *et al. Family, socialization and interaction process.* Glencoe, Ill.: Free Press, 1955.

6. SCHEINFELD, A. *Women and men.* New York: Harcourt, Brace, 1944.

7. SPIRO, M. E. *Kibbutz: Venture in Utopia.* Cambridge: Harvard Univer. Press, 1956.

8. TERMAN, L. M., & MILES, CATHERINE C. *Sex and personality.* New York: McGraw-Hill, 1936.

OLEG: A MEMBER OF THE SOVIET "GOLDEN YOUTH"

Helen Beier and Raymond A. Bauer

Studies of "national psychology" or "national character" [1] ordinarily concern themselves predominantly with uniformities in the psychological traits of the members of national communities. For understanding the functioning of

Reprinted by permission of the American Psychological Association and the authors from *The Journal of Abnormal and Social Psychology,* Vol. 51, 1955.

[1] We use the term "national character" with the greatest reluctance, and with full acknowledgement of the extreme oversimplification and abuses that have been committed in its name. Our sole premise in discussing "national character" is that it is reasonable to assume that groups of people raised under

such societies, however, it is frequently of equal importance to focus on the variations within the group; particularly, to study such subtypes in the context of the specific institutional framework within which they live. For this purpose, the individual case history has the advantage of illustrating, in a concrete fashion, the

rather homogeneous conditions, or exposed historically to a relatively common culture and life conditions, will tend to develop certain modal psychological characteristics which will distinguish them statistically from other populations. We make no assertion that such traits characterize all members of the society; as a matter of fact, the present article is an explicit challenge to this notion.

pattern of psychological and sociological forces which are at work within subgroups of the population. While the individual case seldom "proves" any of the propositions which it illustrates, it is, nevertheless, a fruitful source of insight and hypotheses to be checked against other data, and an indication of certain problems which may face the society in the future. This is one in a series of such case studies which are being made as a part of a larger project aimed at understanding the crucial psychological and sociological dimensions of Soviet society.[2]

An Introduction to Oleg

This young man, whom we shall call Oleg, is one of several hundred former Soviet citizens who were interviewed by the Harvard Refugee Interview Project in Germany in the fall of 1950 and the spring of 1951.[3] Oleg was interviewed by four persons, including the two present authors. He discussed his life history and answered a battery of questions concerning his attitudes and values. In addition, he took a series of psychological tests including the TAT, Rorschach, a sentence completion test, and a battery of projective questions and episodes. This procedure consumed more than a week. We were in day-to-day contact for several months and our knowledge and understanding of him were enhanced by informal contacts.

Oleg's position in the Soviet subculture. Oleg P. is the product of a very

restricted subculture in Soviet society, the artistic intelligentsia. To a great extent this subculture has much in common with those of the artists of other societies. Its members have the same general values, and an interest in a common body of literature and art. Oleg's orientation is considerably more western than that of the ordinary Soviet citizen. He is one of the "homeless cosmopolitans" berated by the Soviet press in recent years. Even he refers to his "damned westernism" as one of the factors alienating him from the regime. The Soviet regime, particularly since the war, has brought strong pressure on the intelligentsia as a group to neutralize the influence of western culture on the allegiance of these people. The extent to which the regime succeeds in this goal will lessen one of the factors alienating this group from the regime, but it will alter neither certain characteristics of the life experience of the artistic intelligentsia nor their basic character structure.

The artistic intelligentsia share with a few other privileged groups a sheltered life existence, isolated to a large extent from the realities of Soviet life. Unless their parents indoctrinate them successfully with anti-Soviet attitudes, children growing up in such an environment usually develop an initial enthusiasm for the Soviet regime. This enthusiasm is challenged when they have the opportunity to contrast Soviet reality with what they are taught in school and the Communist youth organizations.

Oleg and the "New Soviet Man." Oleg is a particular variant of what is generally considered to be the modal personality of Russian males. This traditional "national character," particularly as it refers to the intelligentsia, is ordinarily depicted as marked by underly-

---

[2] One of the present authors (H. Beier) is preparing, together with Eugenia Hanfmann, a book-length study based on clinical interviews with 57 Soviet refugees.

[3] Done under contract AF No. 33(038)-12909. The over-all project now bears the title, The Harvard Project on the Soviet Social System.

ing passivity, by a lack of discipline, and by the projection of grandiose, impractical plans which are never followed up. This stereotype of traditional Russian character has been tacitly accepted by the Soviet regime and is reflected in attempts at character training, The New Soviet Man, the ideal image of the Soviet citizen as depicted in Soviet literature, has an iron will and is marked both by concentration of energy and interests and a great deal of self-discipline. Other cases studied from among our sample suggest that these latter traits are achieved only by the imposition of a shell of external controls over an underlying personality which is relatively passive and undisciplined. An example of such a person is "Kamen," previously described by Bauer (1). Whereas many other members of the new Soviet elite seem to represent a reaction formation again the traditional passivity of the Russian male, Oleg exhibits this passivity directly, without the overlay of strong external defenses. The more overtly disciplined members of the elite generally seem to have developed the veneer of toughness, either as a compensation for difficult environmental conditions or through the interiorization of the values of some particular subgroup (such as those of the military caste). The humanistic values of Oleg's family, the protectiveness and permissiveness of his home environment, and the relatively sheltered early years of his life produced in him a "softer" personality.

Oleg's Family and Cultural Background

Oleg was born in a large Russian city in 1925, the second son of a writer and of a Czarist official's daughter. His mother had attended engineering courses and had worked both as draftsman and, for a short while, in an office of a factory. After her children were born she stayed at home. The family was unusual in several respects. They had suffered none of the deprivations of the rank-and-file Soviet citizen. Oleg's family provided him with an excellent cultural background, in addition to good material conditions. Furthermore, whereas most children were left to shift by themselves during the day while both parents worked, he had the attention of both his mother, who did not work, and his father, who had considerable daytime leisure.

Regime versus family. Oleg's parents were opposed to the regime but, like many other Soviet parents, they made no explicit mention of this fact until he was fairly well grown up. In the meantime, under the influence of the school and his brother, he became an enthusiastic supporter of the regime.

Since I was a younger brother, the beginnings of Communist education which my brother received in school were transmitted to me. He brought from school elementary Communist slogans, for example, that "religion is the opiate of the people."

He tells how he and his brother arranged an "antireligious demonstration" by placing a portrait of Stalin in front of the ikon of a very religious aunt. His mother punished them and impressed on them the fact that such an act was more than a joke. In general, however, parental efforts to wean him from the regime were indirect. His parents tried to divert him from reading the regime's propaganda by providing him with classical literature and "other instructive and interesting books." In a quite natural fashion, however, he joined the Pioneers while still at school. Although his parents never made their own political attitude explicit, he believes that he sensed it by implication because, "I tried to propagandize them and show them they didn't understand."

The extent of his devotion to the regime at this period is illustrated in his reaction to the public trials of opposition leaders in the late thirties:

At the age of ten years I admired Stalin extremely, and when he conducted the trials against older Communists, Bukharin, and so on, I was happy about it, and I even did the following: I had an album with portraits of Communist leaders. As soon as one leader was tried and shot, I took the photo out of the album, nailed it on the door, and shot the photo.

Later ambivalence and dichotomization. The next five years in his life were years of progressive exposure to Soviet life, and to the opinions of his parents. But even while the change was taking place he sought for reaffirmation of his faith in the regime:

[What happened in these five years?] What happened? I acquired a more serious attitude toward life. Then there were things people said. Also, I came in contact with people, especially the talks and conversation of my parents. As I got older they talked more freely to me, told me about life in Czarist Russia. I also acquired a deeper knowledge of literature, both classical Russian and western. This made me understand that life in the west is not so terrible as it is painted by Soviet propaganda. It is true that even at the age of fifteen when I did not believe in Soviet propaganda, I still wanted to believe in it. . . .

This is an interesting psychological process. The process of disbelief developed unconsciously. Externally I remained a loyal Pioneer, but inwardly I felt differently. I continued to argue and tried to convince other people. I was looking for external

support. I think that this process, this split state of mind, is characteristic of the vast majority of people of that age in the Soviet Union.

.   .   .   .   .

At the age of fifteen, when there was a rumor that Stalin was assassinated, I was happy about it. In these five years, I had gradually shifted from these earlier ideas.

While a person lives in the family he may not believe rumors that somewhere there are hunger and executions. This is all far away and does not touch you . . . Then I went to work. There I really learned what the life and conditions of the workers are. This gave me further material for thought.

The effect of the war. Major doubts about the Soviet order developed at the start of the war. The rapid advance of the Germans weakened his belief in the truth of Soviet propaganda. During the war he took a job as a common worker, in order to get increased rations. This brought him in direct contact with "Soviet reality" and seems finally to have crystallized his disaffection.

Because of his disillusionment he decided, toward the end of the war, to enter a school for creative writing and to retreat from Soviet life.

After having seen Soviet reality in all its beauty, or rather in all its ugliness, a young person wants to get away from it and choose a profession where he can forget all this.

Selection of a Career

But with the defeat of the Germans there was an upsurge of patriotic enthusiasm. Furthermore, he began to realize that it was not going to be easy to become a distinguished artist. This combination of circumstances lessened his resistance toward participation in the system. "You think, Communism may not be so good as a system, but you have to work with it."

Oleg as an intelligence officer trainee. At the age of eighteen he entered an institute which trained young officers for foreign intelligence work. Oleg emphasizes that he was not seeking "military fame," but that he was interested in "journalistic work" as a means of being sent to the west. The chances for a Soviet journalist to leave the country, however, were much slimmer than those for an intelligence agent. The position of the latter was, also, more privileged than that of an ordinary officer, although not as privileged as the work of the intelligence staff of the MGB (the Soviet security police). Oleg was ambitious, he "thought much about a career," and was determined to see the western countries. Once a member of the institute, he had no choice and had to accept whatever the government decided he should do. "My parents were upset and worried, they asked me to be careful, but I could not refuse. I would have been sent to Siberia, and my desire was to go abroad."

The result of this decision further complicated his attitude toward the regime. He learned more about western life, and became more fundamentally disaffected from the Soviet regime. At the same time, he realized that by entering this institute he had committed himself to overt support of the Soviet regime. This forced him into an elaborate rationale, that he was making these compromises only to fight eventually against Bolshevism. With his characteristic insight, he comments: "This at any rate brings some equilibrium to your conscience." He claims that in either 1946 or 1947 he finally decided that if he went abroad he would not return. In this sense he was growing even farther away from the regime.

Relationship of party to career. In another sense, however, he was growing closer to the regime. His entire story of the process whereby a young man, opposed to the regime in principle, gets "sucked into it," is too long and detailed to quote in full, but selected excerpts give the essentials of the picture.

In the institute you advance little by little into the Party machine. I still had at that time an aversion against this, but once they proposed a task to me I didn't refuse. I explained to myself that I had to do it in order to grow. . . .

Furthermore, the decision was by no means exclusively in his own hands. It is vital for the security of the system that persons such as he be drawn into the Party, where they can be better controlled.

First of all the institute prepares specialists, that is people who will occupy higher positions, and, therefore, it is important to have them in the Komsomol or in the Party. Secondly, it is easier to draw a student into the Party than a worker, because a student is an ambitious person, he want to get high, and thus the Party can promise him more than it can the average worker.

During his first few months at the institute, he fended off suggestions that he join the Komsomol. Then, after a half year of study, he received the top grade, "five," in all his subjects. Pressure to join the Komsomol grew. He pocketed the application that he was forced to accept, and stalled the secretary of the Komsomol for another half year.

Finally the higher organs became interested in me. I was called to the political deputy, the Zampolit, and I had a serious talk with him. The talk was about as follows. He asked me: "Why have you not joined the

Komsomol yet?" You know that I had always said, "I am too young, I am inexperienced, I am unprepared for such a high honor." This I said again. Then he said to me: "I know better than you whether or not you are prepared. You have been studying well, you have shown good discipline, you follow political events, so what else do you want?" Then he played up the topic that everything in life would be open to me if I joined the Komsomol, later became a Party candidate, and finally a Party member. After that he proposed that I fill out an application right on the spot. Well, I threw up my hands and said, "What the hell," and was accepted as a member of the Komsomol meeting a week later.

Polarization of sentiments and break with the regime. Although this first step was taken reluctantly, successive steps were made more readily.

If you give them a finger, they take the whole hand. A year later I became a Party candidate, and by the time I graduated from the institute I was already a Party member. Thus, I was a completely loyal person, externally that means. . . .

All this process of promotion of a man played very skillfully on the careerist aspirations of a young person. At that time I was already an accomplished double thinker. (He pronounces this phrase in English.) I made a deal with my conscience for careerist purposes, and then this process of promotion satisfies a man's ambition. . . .

This is the process by which they suck you in. It is true that I had an antidote against it. I thought that I would go along with them only until a given moment, but other people are sucked in for good. . . .

Thus, ironically he grew simultaneously closer to and farther from the regime, with an ever increasing disparity between his behavior and ambitions and his inner feelings and values. Under these conditions he was sent abroad. Several months later he deserted the Red Army and fled into the American zone.

He has given us a very complete account of the circumstances leading to his departure and, on one level, an adequate "explanation." A more detailed exploration of the sort of person he is will give us a better understanding of his defection and his behavior within the system before defecting.

Oleg's personality. He is an extremely gifted person, of superior intelligence, and of striking artistic abilities. He came from a protected home which satisfied his needs and put comparatively little restraint on him. He always received understanding support and encouragement from his parents, and they fostered his intellectual talents and ambitions. Other aspects of his development found less emphasis. There was little in the family atmosphere that nourished a capacity to work in a disciplined fashion. Oleg grew up with high expectations for himself— expecting gratifications to come as his natural due, not as a result of his efforts. The mother was considerably the stronger of the two parents and had much more influence on his development. Both parents seem to have been quite indulgent; the father particularly was very permissive and he let Oleg have his own way in both small and large matters. Oleg had a strong affection for his father in childhood. In later life, as he found his father lacking in strength of personality, his feeling toward him became more ambivalent. Characteristically, he admires capable, educated people who, at the same time, are energetic and effective. However, he put himself repeatedly outside of this group. In many instances he still appears as a rebellious adolescent, exclusively concerned with himself, disregarding others, and fundamentally quite contemptuous of them. He views others first of all as admirers of his abilities, as mirrors of his superiority; he feels that he is above them and delights in this feeling. (On the Sentence Completion Test he says: "When he was advised to follow the example of others—he was offended, seeing in it an unjustly low evaluation of his labors.") During the days of his boyhood and early adolescence, he experienced bursts of enjoyment when he felt that he was creating something outstanding, and was sure that he was destined to become great. At the time of the interviews, when Oleg was only 24 years old, he looked back at these ecstatic moments with nostalgia. He remembered even more poignantly his disappointment when, looking at what he tried to create after the enthusiasm had worn itself out, he became convinced that his efforts had been entirely worthless. In one of the TAT stories, in which he described such an experience, he says: "And as he looks back on those moments he finds that the most valuable part of the experience was not the writing itself but the creative impulse." Disappointment was not followed by constructive effort, but mostly by an attempt to seek success in another area. His real talents are crippled by his tremendous ambition and the fundamental passivity that he never succeeded in overcoming. He manifested a disinclination and disability to maintain a disciplined work effort over a long period of time.[4] He

hoped that success would come semi-magically, or at least without plodding efforts. Untoughened by the rigors of life, he is reminiscent of the passive, dreaming Russian of nineteenth century literature, rather than the tough, militant activist extolled in Soviet literature, often found in the younger Soviet generation. To say that he was fundamentally passive, however, is not to imply that passivity dominates all his actions, since he was frequently moved to bursts of activity in an effort to overcome this underlying passivity. What is pertinent is the fact that he was not able to sustain this activity in a disciplined manner.

His general attitude that success should come without excessive effort is exemplified in several stories on the Thematic Apperception Test. To the first card, which shows a young boy sitting and looking at a violin, he says:

This is a picture of a boy after his first violin lesson. Maybe his father had just bought him the violin and hired the teacher, the first lesson came. The boy took it with enthusiasm, thinking that wonderful sounds would begin pouring out from under his bow. Then he heard only miserable screeches coming from the violin. He doesn't even know how to hold it. Well, the lesson came to an end. The teacher leaves. The boy sits down on the chair in front of the violin. There is a letdown in his enthusiasm. He is in a depressed mood. He meditates: what shall he do now? Before him is the prospect of dull scraping on the violin, of scales and exercises.

---

[4] His ambition permeates all the projective material. His completion of the sentence, "Most of his acquaintances . . ." is merely illustrative. He answers, ". . . found in his character traits which made him akin to the famous political leader . . ." Or, "Alexander considered himself . . . a great expert on the human soul."

In the Rorschach test this ambition is exhibited in the fact that he gave 12 W's on 13 responses. But the $W:M$ ratio is 12:4, indicative of the inability to make effective use of his creative ability, as his life story reveals. The Rorschach reflects also his deficiency in control. There are only three additional FC's, whereas there are two main CF's.

This is essentially the attitude he took toward his own career as a writer. "I found out that I am not a great writer . . . a quick sketch came out all right, but I had no perseverance. I did not want to be a mediocre writer, and a mediocre teacher."

The disparity between his extreme ambition and his rather considerable ability gave rise to his decision to forsake writing and enter the institute. With less ambition, he would have been content to be an ordinary writer. With greater perseverance, he might have become a successful writer. In either case he would have succeeded in his intention to withdraw from the most highly politicized areas of Soviet life. The combination of ambition and lack of perseverance made him an easy prey to lures of advancement through political channels, where membership in the Party could insure a career.

Superficially he is probably capable of establishing fairly effective social relationships, but he can sustain them only if he experiences his position in accordance with his idea of himself. On a deeper level, he shows that he does not know the meaning of adult ties to other people. He is still in the grip of a more primitive experience with an unresolved relation to his mother, enhanced now by his guilt for having left her. The mother-son relationship is the predominant theme in his TAT stories. The picture of an older, strong, and supporting woman, who provides for his needs and holds him back from dissolute and degrading ways of living permeates the projective responses. The father faded more and more into the background as Oleg grew up. It was as if he became lost behind an actor's mask and his son sees only masks and cannot approach the real people.

The men in his Rorschach responses are seen as "masks," "a dwarf," and as "a Mongol" whose face is not visible. At the same time, knowing that he must leave his mother, he left her in a manner that simultaneously cut off any possibility of his return to her and endangered her own safety. He remembers his mother's grief when his older brother was killed at Stalingrad and constantly thinks about what losing him must have meant to her. He tries to minimize the actual harm that his desertion might have brought to his parents and tries to justify his action by attributing it to ideological motives.

His Defection—Cause and Effect

His defection from the Soviet regime reflects, to a great extent, his adolescent and self-centered attitude. While intellectually, and to some extent emotionally, opposed to the regime, this rejection was not sufficiently deep to cause him to struggle against the system. Everything that he now says about his reasons for defection only partly reflects the true story of his motivation. One is never quite convinced that fighting Bolshevism was his primary and only goal. The ease with which Oleg changed from the school of creative writing, which would have given him the chance of retreating to a great extent from political life, to the intelligence institute, thereby identifying himself more closely with the regime, does not bespeak a resolute opposition to Bolshevism. After failing to achieve magical success in one area, he was able to switch over to a fundamentally different one when there were no pressing external reasons to choose this career. He repeated this pattern when he left Austria and joined the Americans. Again, no external pressure necessitated such a step. His dislike of the Soviet regime and his intellectual background certainly were related to his desertion, as presumably was his fear of becoming alcoholic in the occupation army. But mainly, his flight from the Soviet regime seems to have represented an adventure in an unknown world in which—precisely because it was unknown—it was possible still to dream of magical success.

Conclusions

Oleg is no less well-integrated or flexible as a person than most of those whom we interviewed. He is simply less overtly disciplined and driving. As such, he does not have the requisite traits for an effective, aggressive executive such as is needed for the functioning of the Soviet state and economic apparatus. Furthermore, his lack of strong external defenses makes him a more ready immediate prey to his own moral conflicts. His sole defense against his conflict over supporting a regime he opposed attitudinally was a feeble rationalization that his compromises would be offset by some later action against the Bolshevik regime. The modal response of young male refugees of his age and status when faced with such a problem is expressed in the recurrent phrase: "I pushed my doubts into the background." That is to say, repression or suppression of conflict is more characteristic than Oleg's pattern of rationalization.[5] In these respects he is atypical. He is typical of the young Soviet generation in the extent to which his own self-interest—rather than his

___

[5] This statement holds, of course, only with appropriate qualification for the level and type of conflict involved. Even the more rigidly defensive among our Ss, of course, use the mechanism of rationalization rather often. We are speaking here only of relative importance of the two types of defense.

idealism—is the strongest motive which keeps him functioning effectively within the system. But his "softness," combined with the extent to which he remained consciously aware of his moral conflicts in compromising with the regime, make him a less effective and desirable person from the regime's point of view.

Oleg and "other" Soviet youths. Oleg is not among the majority of Soviet youth, judging either from the evidence of our own respondents or inferentially from Soviet literature and official statements. The modal Soviet type of the middle and upper classes seems to be a youth of considerable ambition, relatively unscrupulous, fairly hard-driving, and described in official and unofficial commentaries as a "careerist." Granting all the overstatement and exaggeration involved in descriptions of "national character," it appears that the dimension of activity-passivity is probably a central dilemma in the personality development of Great Russian males. Soviet official literature and life histories of our respondents suggest that a large proportion of responsible posts in Soviet society have gone to persons who advance upward by virtue of a reaction formation against the underlying passivity that seems to plague Russian males (1). Furthermore, the present generation of Soviet "successful men" appears to be successful also in passing many of their values on to their sons.

Soviet "Golden Youth." While Oleg is in a minority among the Soviet youth, he may represent a mode which will be of increasing importance in future generations. It is true that the number of the pre-Revolutionary intelligentsia, such as Oleg's parents, are decreasing rapidly. But new privileged groups are developing, and children of the upper class enjoy preferential access to education and to posts of responsibility (2), and a privileged and sheltered life in their youth. Even the Soviet press affords occasional glimpses into the overprivileged lives of upper-class children. It was Oleg who identified himself as a member of the Soviet "Golden Youth," and told us that this term was used colloquially in recent years to refer to a sizable proportion of the urban younger generation. To some extent the new Soviet upper classes are acquiring the style of life of the class they dispossessed. With his characteristic capacity for social analysis, Oleg commented on this transformation among the students with whom he associated.

The people who were just becoming members of the intelligentsia did not have much interest [in literature], for example our students who came from the peasantry and the working class . . . [Q. Did you notice whether or not the workers and peasants in your class got more interested in western literature as the courses progressed?] Oh,

yes. It was easy to notice. You know at first they just wanted to get diplomas, but in the course of their studies they became very interested in the subject matter.

Future trends. If present trends continue, the future Soviet upper classes will become increasingly stable and will consist less and less of persons who have risen from the ranks. Should this actually occur, we may also anticipate the possibility that the upper classes will consist of an increasingly smaller proportion of men who have the traits of personality characteristic of the "careerist," and that more of them will approximate Oleg. This would mean that the men assuming posts of responsibility would not be adapted to the hard-driving pace that the present rulers favor so strongly. The crucial question, of course, is whether the Soviet leadership, faced with such a prospect, will be able to offset the process of social ossification sufficiently to permit a flow of recruits from the lower classes who are not dominated by the passivity that was observed in Oleg.

References

1. BAUER, R. A. The psychology of the Soviet middle elite. In C. Kluckhohn, H. A. Murray, & D. M. Schneider (Eds.), *Personality in nature, society, and culture.* (2nd Ed.) New York: Knopf, 1953. Pp. 633–650.

2. FELDMESSER, R. A. The persistence of status advantages in Soviet Russia. *Amer. J. Sociol.,* 1953, **59,** 19–27.

Index to Contributors and Authorities Cited

Subject Index